THE MYTHIC PAST

Biblical Archaeology and the Myth of Israel

The Mythic Past

*Biblical Archaeology
and the Myth of Israel*

Thomas L. Thompson

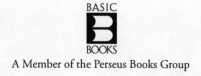

BASIC
BOOKS
A Member of the Perseus Books Group

First published in Great Britain in 1999 by
Jonathan Cape
Random House, 20 Vauxhall Bridge Road,
London SW1V 2SA

Copyright © 1999 by Thomas L. Thompson.

Published by Basic Books,
A Member of the Perseus Books Group

$^1/_{00}$

FIRST U.S. EDITION

A CIP catalog record for this book
is available from the Library of Congress

ISBN 0-465-00622-1

99 00 01 02 /RRD 10 9 8 7 6 5 4 3 2 1

V

To all my children

Christina
Samir
Hilary
Jacob
Andreas

and to their beautiful mothers

Contents

PART TWO
HOW HISTORIANS CREATE A PAST

PART THREE
THE BIBLE'S PLACE IN HISTORY

Preface: the academic debate

At the moment of writing this preface, I am preparing to go to Lausanne for a meeting of the 'European Seminar on Historical Methodology of the History of Israel', and reading the papers to be discussed at the seminar. The topic is 'the exile' as a subject of history. The issues centre on how we are to correlate the many Assyrian, Babylonian and Persian texts relating to war, the destruction of cities and the deportation of peoples throughout their empires, the growing archaeological evidence from Palestine, and the wide variety of biblical traditions that deal with themes of destruction, exile and return, but rarely of a period of exile itself. Half of the papers produced for the seminar share much the perspective of this book. Each of them, in its own way, points out difficulties in reading the biblical narratives about deportation and return as if they were historical. They point to the lack of a story in the Bible which tells us of an Israel or a Judah in exile. While they express few doubts that an exile must have occurred, they question whether a history of this exile can be written. The other half of the papers disagree strongly and argue that a history of 'the exile' is at least possible. No one, however, proposes that the Bible's traditions provide us with adequate evidence for that history. As I read through these papers, I cannot help thinking about the changes in our approach to the Bible and its relationship to archaeology that have come about over the past twenty-five years. Long past is the assumption that ancient history can be written by merely paraphrasing or correcting the stories of the Bible. It has rather become quite difficult to understand these stories as recounting events from their authors' past.

It would be ingenuous of me to pretend that this book on the subject is uncontroversial. For me, the debate began as early as in the late 1960s and was first voiced in a doctoral thesis started in 1967 at the University of Tübingen and completed in 1971. My original thesis stemmed from the idea that, if some of the narratives about the Hebrew patriarchs could in fact be dated historically to the second millennium BCE, as nearly all

archaeologists and historians then believed, I should be able to distinguish
the earliest of the biblical stories from a later expanded tradition.

When I first began this work, I had been so convinced of the historicity
of the tales about the patriarchs in Genesis that I unquestioningly accepted
parallels that had been claimed with the Late Bronze Age family contracts
found in the excavations of the ancient town of Nuzi in northern
Mesopotamia. It was therefore all the more upsetting when, in 1969, after
more than two years' work, it became clear that the family customs and
property laws of ancient Nuzi were neither unique in ancient Near Eastern
law nor implied by the Genesis stories. Many of these contracts had been
misread and misinterpreted. At least one contract had been mistranslated
with the purpose of creating a parallel with the Bible. The entire claim of
Nuzi parallels to the patriarchal customs had been a thinly veiled
fabrication, a product of wish-fulfilment. An entire social world had been
created which had never existed.

This led to a discussion of the larger question of history and the
patriarchs generally. I went on to review the central arguments that had
been used to create and support the patriarchal period. The single most
important argument had been a very complex 'Amorite hypothesis',
asserting a nomadic migration of West Semites out of the Arabian desert,
which disrupted the established agricultural civilizations of the fertile
crescent late in the third millennium BCE and developed new settlements
from Southern Mesopotamia to the Egyptian Delta. This related nearly
every important text find from the third and second millennium to the
Bible and to Palestine: whether from Ur, Babylon, Mari, Amarna, Ugarit,
Egypt, Phoenicia, or from Palestine itself. These arguments for Amorite
migrations and for the existence of a patriarchal period in the history of the
ancient Near East also collapsed. They were often arbitrary and wilful.
Scholars had taken for granted what they set out to prove. What was
presented as the assured results of decades of science and scholarship
amounted to careless assertions.

The dissertation was finished in late 1971. Reactions to it were strong. I
found it impossible to get my PhD in Europe or to publish my book in the
United States. As things worked out, the book was eventually published in
Germany in 1974 and I was able to receive my degree from Temple
University in Philadelphia in 1976.

The arguments against the historicity of the patriarchal narratives were
strongly confirmed by the independent publication in 1975 of the Canadian
scholar John Van Seters' *Abraham in History and Tradition*. Van Seters'
book took the argument even further by showing that the biblical stories
themselves could not be seen as early, but must be dated sometime in the
sixth century BCE or later. In 1977, John Hayes and J. Maxwell Miller
published *Israelite and Judaean History,* a large volume of essays written by
a number of younger scholars, in which current historical research on each

successive biblical period was reviewed. It was now clear that the previous confidence in the view that the Bible was an historical document was collapsing. Widespread doubt was expressed about the historicity not only of the patriarchs of Genesis, but of the stories about Moses, Joshua and the Judges as well. These historians first felt confident in speaking of history when dealing with the period of Saul, David and Solomon.

While Van Seters' late dating of the Pentateuch received strong support in Germany and his work led to radical changes in our understanding of these early books of the Bible, the mid-Seventies also saw the publication of a number of new and innovative journals that have changed the direction of research across the entire field of biblical studies. The *Dielheimer Blätter* published from Heidelberg was certainly the most radical and original. The Sheffield *Journal for the Study of the Old Testament*, however – publishing in English and providing an early forum for debate on a wide spectrum of controversial topics – was by far the most influential. The launching of *Semeia* by the Society of Biblical Literature supported the growing interest in the United States in reading the Bible with techniques developed in literary criticism. Research on the Old Testament entered a generation-long period of transition marked by rapid change and innovation.

Up through 1975, I continued my research on Bronze Age agriculture and the settlement history of both the Sinai and Palestine. In two books and a series of maps for the *Tübingen Atlas of the Near East*, I related archaeological to geological and ecological data in an effort to develop histories of the settlement and use of Palestine's many regions. I employed a history of agriculture and technology, settlement patterns and change in climatic conditions as a basis for understanding long-term change in each region. This work was based largely on archaeological surveys that had been carried out by such Israeli scholars as Benno Rothenberg, Yohanan Aharoni and Moshe Kochavi, supplemented by the archives of the Israeli and Jordanian Departments of Antiquities. While my research on this atlas project was one of the earliest attempts to develop a regional history of agriculture for Palestine, it lacked the consistency of systematically collected data that has been developed by the Survey of Israel and by most archaeological surveys carried out since the early Seventies.

In 1975, I left Germany and returned to the States. The controversies over my book on the patriarchs shut me out of university teaching. I became a full-time house-painter and handyman. My weekends and evenings were given to the study of Old Testament narrative and the Pentateuch. After nearly a decade of such isolation, my exclusion from the field reached an unexpected end. I was appointed by the Catholic Biblical Association as annual professor to the École Biblique in Jerusalem for 1985. The climate of biblical scholarship had shifted. Sociology and anthropology had grown strong in historical studies. Palestinian archaeologists had become increasingly frustrated with the biblical framework for their work. The literary nature of the Bible had become the central focus of biblical studies, and the history of religions had come to compete with theology as a dominant context for the study of the Bible. My understanding of the patriarchal narratives was no longer controversial. It had become part of the mainstream of the field.

My trip to Jerusalem was to last nearly a year, during which I finished the first volume of my study of the Pentateuch and did some preliminary work with one of my colleagues at the École in historical geography. We eventually published this as a project proposal on regional histories with the title, *Toponomie Palestinienne*. After returning for a brief period to house-painting, I was awarded a National Endowment fellowship for 1987, which allowed me to begin a project on the history of Israel's origins. This return to full-time research led to teaching appointments at Lawrence and Marquette universities in Wisconsin.

Much had changed in both history and archaeology by the late 1980s. In the development of my own re-education, two books were overwhelmingly important: the social-anthropological study from 1985, *Early Israel*, by a Danish scholar who was to become my colleague and close collaborator, Niels Peter Lemche, and the comprehensive synthesis of archaeological surveys of the Palestinian highlands from 1988 by the Israeli archaeologist Israel Finkelstein, *The Archaeology of the Israelite Settlement*. Both Lemche's and Finkelstein's research confirmed the basic analysis of settlement patterns and interpretation of social structures which had been central to my earlier studies of the Bronze Age. These two works convinced me that a history of this region was possible, though it would have to be a very different history than we had grown used to. Rather than attempting to write paraphrases of biblical narratives of unknown historical value, we had the chance to develop an independent historical perspective of the past. In 1987, I began work on the question of Israel's origins in an effort to show that such a history was possible. In doing so, I retraced a line of argument I had originally set out in an article in 1978, under the title, 'The Background of the Patriarchs' (now republished in a book edited by John Rogerson). This article had located the origins of an historical Israel in the growth of centralization of the highlands north of Jerusalem during the ninth century BCE. This implicitly excluded any trans-regional political unity embracing most of Palestine. That is, there could not have been a 'United Monarchy' with a Saul, David or Solomon in Jerusalem during the tenth century BCE. I published my completed study in 1992 under the title *The Early History of the Israelite People*.

Reactions to this book were stronger even than those to my book on the patriarchs had been. Although the historical nature of the David stories had been doubted since the 1970s by literary scholars, and even though the

Italian Semitist Giovanni Garbini had already questioned the historicity of the 'United Monarchy' in 1986, my finding no place for David or his empire in my history of Israel created a scandal. A review of my book appeared on the front page of the London newspaper, *The Independent on Sunday*. I was coming up for tenure at Marquette University, where officials were already very unhappy over my research. Publicity stirred up conservative theological dogma, and my work was found 'incompatible with the Catholic mission of the university'. While this breach of academic freedom could have led to personal disaster, it proved to be an unequivocal blessing. I was called to take up a chair in Old Testament at the University of Copenhagen, where I have been now since 1993.

Since 1992, and fuelled by the publication of Philip Davies' *In Search of Ancient Israel*, a broad debate has raged on the history of Israel and Palestine. The debate has been heated, but it has also been open, and the field as a whole is engaged in it, as the coming meeting in Lausanne witnesses. The long preoccupation of biblical studies with the question of origins has led to many distortions in our understanding of the tradition. Today we no longer have a history of Israel. Not only have Adam and Eve and the flood story passed over to mythology, but we can no longer talk about a time of the patriarchs. There never was a 'United Monarchy' in history and it is meaningless to speak of pre-exilic prophets and their writings. The history of Iron Age Palestine today knows of Israel only as a small highland patronate lying north of Jerusalem and south of the Jezreel Valley. Nor has Yahweh, the deity dominant in the cult of that Israel's people, much to do with the Bible's understanding of God. Any history we write of this people will hardly resemble the Israel we thought we knew so much about only a few years ago. And even that little will hardly open to us the Bible's origins in history. Our history of biblical tradition has come topsy-turvy. It is only a Hellenistic Bible that we know: namely the one that we first begin to read in the texts found among the Dead Sea scrolls near Qumran. I have argued that the quest for origins is not an historical quest but a theological and literary question, a question about meaning. To give it an historical form is to attribute to it our own search for meaning. Biblical scholarship used to believe that we might understand the Bible if we could only get back to its origins. The question about origins, however, is not an answerable one. Not only is the Bible's 'Israel' a literary fiction, but the Bible begins as a tradition already established: a stream of stories, song and philosophical reflection: collected, discussed and debated. Our sources do not begin. They lie already *in medias res*.

We can say now with considerable confidence that the Bible is not a history of anyone's past. The story of the chosen and rejected Israel that it presents is a philosophical metaphor of a mankind that has lost its way. The tradition itself is a discourse about recognizing that way. In our historicizing of this tradition, we have lost sight of the Bible's intellectual centre, as well as of our own. The question of origins which has dominated modern research into the Bible belongs to theology rather than to history. It asks after the meaning of the Bible in its beginnings. In this, it shares the same Hellenistic quest that was also the Bible's: to trace our traditions of ourselves and God back to the creation.

Ever since the opening of the controversies over my *Early History* book, I have been encouraged to present my work on the Bible in its relationship to historical research in a comprehensive way. In particular, the support and ever-generous help from the archaeological journalist, David Keyes, my literary agent, William Hamilton, and my editor at Jonathan Cape, Jörg Hensgen, have been indispensable. This encouragement led me to write this present work in the way that I have. Part One discusses the literary qualities of biblical stories and tradition, and takes up the implicit argument that the Bible hardly intends to be read as if it were a history book. Part Two is based on my 1992 book and takes up many of the themes of my earlier work on the patriarchs and my studies in historical geography. Since I moved to Copenhagen, I have become more involved in the theological and intellectual significance of biblical texts. This, together with an interest in literary studies, gives the historical work a context it otherwise would lack. Part Three attempts to structure this context through a historical discussion of the social, literary and theological worlds that the Bible's authors were part of.

The first half of the research that I had published in 1992 presents my view of the history of scholarship on ancient Israel. There is no need to repeat any of that here. There are a number of works, however, which, like those of Van Seters, Lemche and Finkelstein, have influenced me a great deal. There are also many which I believe might be helpful to any who would wish to read further. The following list of works is offered with the hope of encouraging such reading.

Thomas L. Thompson, Copenhagen, 25 July, 1997

Recommended Reading

G.W. Ahlström, *The History of Ancient Palestine* (Sheffield Academic Press, 1993).

R. Albertz, *Religionsgeschichte Israels*, 2 vols (Neukirchen, 1992).

B. Albrektson, *History and the Gods* (Lund, 1967).

*W.F. Albright, *From the Stone Age to Christianity* (Garden City, 1946).

*A. Alt, *Kleine Schriften*, 3 vols (Munich, 1953).

H. Barstad, *The Myth of the Empty Land* (Oslo, 1996).

Bob Becking, *The Conquest of Samaria*, SHANE 2 (Brill, Leiden, 1992).

T. Binger, *Asherah: Goddesses in Ugarit, Israel and the Old Testament*, Copenhagen International Seminar 2 (Sheffield, 1997).

E. Blum, *Studien zur Komposition des Pentateuch*, BZAW 189 (Berlin, de Gruyter, 1990).

T. Bolin, *Freedom Beyond Forgiveness: The Book of Jonah Re-examined*, Copenhagen International Seminar 3 (Sheffield, 1997).

*J. Bright, *A History of Israel* (Philadelphia, third edition, 1981).

J. and T. Bynon, *Hamito-Semitica* (The Hague, 1975).

R. Carroll, *The Wolf in the Sheepfold* (London, 1991).

R.B. Coote and K.W. Whitelam, *The Emergence of Early Israel in Historical Perspective*, SWABAS 5 (Sheffield, 1987).

F. Cryer, *Divination in Ancient Israel and its Near Eastern Environment* (Sheffield, 1995).

P.R. Davies, *In Search of Ancient Israel* (Sheffield, second edition, 1997).

—— and V. Fritz (eds), *The Origins of the Ancient Israelite States* (Sheffield, 1996).

D. Edelman, *The Fabric of History: Text, Artifacts and Israel's Past* (Sheffield, 1991).

——, *The Triumph of Elohim: From Yahwisms to Judaisms* (Pharos, Kampen, 1995).

I. Finkelstein, *The Archaeology of the Israelite Settlement* (Jerusalem, 1988).

L.P. Fokkelman, *Narrative Art in Genesis* (Assen, 1975).

W. Frey and H.P. Urpmann, *Beiträge zur Umweltgeschichte des vorderen Orients* (Wiesbaden, 1981).

H. Friis, *Die Bedingungen für die Errichtung des davidischen Reiches in Israel und seiner Umwelt*, DBAT 6 (Heidelberg, 1986).

* Important works of traditional scholarship dominant in biblical studies through the 1970s.

G. Garbini, *History and Ideology in Ancient Israel* (translated from the 1986 Italian version: London, 1988).

N. Gottwald, *The Tribes of Yahweh* (Maryknoll, 1979).

L. Grabbe, *Judaism from Cyrus to Hadrian*, 2 vols. (Minneapolis, 1992).

——, *Can a History of Israel be Written?* (Sheffield, 1997).

——, *The Exile in History and Tradition* (Sheffield, 1998).

A.F. Harding, *Climatic Change in Later Pre-History* (Edinburgh, 1982).

J.H. Hayes and J.M. Miller, *Israelite and Judaean History* (Westminster, Philadelphia, 1977).

I. Hjelm, *Samaritans and Early Judaism: A Literary Analysis, Copenhagen International Seminar* (Sheffield, forthcoming).

A. Horowitz, *The Quaternary of Israel* (New York, 1979).

E. Jamieson-Drake, *Scribes and Schools in Monarchic Judah* (Sheffield, 1991).

E.A. Knauf, *Ismael* (Wiesbaden, second edition, 1989).

——, *Die Umwelt des alten Testaments* (Stuttgart, 1994).

N.P. Lemche, *Early Israel* (Brill, Leiden, 1985).

——, *Ancient Israel* (Sheffield, 1988).

——, *The Canaanites and Their Land* (Sheffield, 1991).

——, *Die Vorgeschichte Israels* (Kohlhammer, Stuttgart, 1996).

——, *The Israelites in History and Tradition* (Westminster, Louisville, 1998).

*J. Neusner, *From Politics to Piety* (New York, 1979).

H. Niehr, *Der Höchste Gott*, BZAW 190 (Berlin, de Gruyter, 1990).

F.A.J. Nielsen, *The Tragedy in History, Copenhagen International Seminar* 4 (Sheffield, 1997).

E. Nodet, *A Search for the Origins of Judaism: From Joshua to the Mishnah*, *JSOTS* 248 (Sheffield, 1997).

*M. Noth, *The History of Israel* (Westminster, Philadelphia, 1950).

B. Oded, *Mass Deportation and Deportees in the Neo-Assyrian Empire* (Wiesbaden, 1979).

G.W. Ramsey, *The Quest for the Historical Israel* (Atlanta, 1981).

D.B. Redford, *Egypt, Canaan and Israel in Ancient Times* (Princeton U. Press, Princeton, 1992).

R. Rendtorff, *Das Überlieferungsgeschichtliche Problem des Pentateuch*, BZAW 147 (Berlin, 1977).

J. Rogerson (ed.), *The Pentateuch: A Sheffield Reader, The Biblical Seminar* 39 (Sheffield, 1996).

H.H. Schmid, *Der sogenannte Jahvist* (Zurich, 1976).

J. Van Seters, *The Hyksos* (New Haven, 1966).

——, *Abraham in History and Tradition* (New Haven, 1975).

——, *In Search of History* (New Haven, 1983).

Th.L. Thompson, *The Historicity of the Patriarchal Narratives*, BZAW 133 (Berlin, de Gruyter, 1974).

——, *The Settlement of Sinai and the Negev in the Bronze Age* (Wiesbaden, 1975).

——, *The Settlement of Palestine in the Bronze Age* (Wiesbaden, 1979).

——, *The Origin Tradition of Ancient Israel* (Sheffield, 1987).

—— (with F.J. Gonçalves and J.M. van Cangh), *Toponomie Palestinienne* (Louvaine la Neuve, 1988).

——, *The Early History of the Israelite People* (Brill, Leiden, 1992).

—— (ed.), *Changing Perspectives: Collected Essays of F.C. Cryer, N.P. Lemche and Th.L. Thompson*, 3 vols (Sheffield, forthcoming).

E. Tov, *Textual Criticism of the Hebrew Bible* (Fortress, Minneapolis, 1992).

H. Weippert, *Palästina in vorhellenistischer Zeit, Handbuch der Archäologie* (Munich, 1988).

*M. Weippert, *Die Landnahme der israelitischen Stämme* (Göttingen, 1967); Eng. trans.: *The Settlement of the Israelite Tribes in Palestine* (London, 1971).

*Julius Wellhausen, *Prolegomena zur Geschichte Israels* (Berlin, 1876); Eng. trans. *Prolegomena for the History of Israel* (London, 1883).

K.W. Whitelam, *The Invention of Ancient Israel* (London, 1996).

PART ONE

HOW STORIES TALK ABOUT
THE PAST

Introduction to Part One[1]

Saul's election and rise to power over Israel; his fall from grace; mad king Saul whose depressions are soothed by David the inspired musician of the psalms; the great warrior Saul, scourge of the Philistines, crazed with murderous jealousy of the faithful and constant young lieutenant who surpasses him in all his exploits; the idyll of David's love for Jonathan in the midst of court intrigue and violence; the young shepherd boy in his pious simplicity and innocence overcoming in personal combat the warrior giant and heroic champion, Goliath of the Philistines; David's succession to the throne and the greatness of his empire; his Homeric-modelled sneak attack on Jerusalem; David the lecher who has his faithful follower killed out of lust for the man's wife; David the helpless old man who in his dotage needs a young girl's body to keep him warm in bed; Solomon's succession to the throne – a classic rendition of the success of the unpromising and inheritance of the youngest; the Croesus-like Solomon whose wealth rivals the legends of Assyrian kings plastering their walls with gold; Solomon the great builder and exploiter of international trade, the consort of a princess of Egypt, the equal in wisdom to the fabulous Queen of Sheba, a philosopher-king in the mould of Alexander, his wisdom protecting the simple virtues of family and guiding an empire; the building of the temple dedicated to the one true God as the crown of Solomon's piety – a temple whose desecration serves as Solomon's own undoing; Solomon lured away from pristine faith by foreign wives, the syncretistic corruption of empire and of the great world of government and wealth; the tragic Solomon whose hubris and apostasy were responsible for the breakup of his kingdom, again like the struggles that followed the death

[1] Unless stated otherwise, all translations of biblical texts are my own. They are based on the Hebrew and Greek Bibles. The numbered citation of chapter and verse, however, follows the *Revised Standard Version*. Quotations of other ancient Near Eastern texts are taken from J.B. Pritchard (ed.), *Ancient Near Eastern Texts Relating to the Old Testament* (Princeton, 1969).

of Alexander the Great between the true south and the faithless north; an epic narrative creates the mythic period of the United Monarchy in Israel and delivers it as the 'golden age' of the Davidic dynasty's forty kings, and as the product of Hellenistic literature.

The lack of a reliable historical context for the Bible has been a great hindrance to modern biblical studies. The lack of sound historical methods, however, has condemned to failure the search for the Bible's place in history from the very start. Ancient texts are very hard to read unless we know something about the world they are written in and for. A century ago, Bible scholars made up their own world, their own context for their texts. They drew it from the Bible itself, and it amounted to little more than a paraphrase of selected biblical accounts. Because no other ancient world of Palestine was known, it seemed better to present this traditional world as history than to have no history at all. However, the historical context that emerged was an uncritical assumption that guaranteed only that the Bible was misread. In the past century, ancient Near Eastern studies and the growing dominance of archaeology in writing the history of Palestine has transformed ancient history. The mainstream of biblical scholarship has resisted change vigorously, preferring whenever possible to defend a paraphrase of the biblical tale as 'the Bible's view of the past'. Many in the field of biblical archaeology have gone so far as to argue that this traditional history should be maintained as valid except where it has been proven to be historically impossible. Only in very recent years has archaeology begun to develop a history of Palestine independent of such theological prejudice.

As a result of the archaeological interests awakened by the conquest of the Middle East by Napoleon's armies, the nineteenth century had given historical scholarship the exciting goal of reconstructing the Bible's place within the history of the ancient Near East. Although biblical scholarship has roots in this critical historical work of the nineteenth century, the twentieth century has seen critical advances eroded by the growth in an understanding of the Bible that might best be described as a form of 'naive realism'.

The Bible's own story of the past, centred on the rise and fall of old Israel, still dominates historical reconstructions within biblical studies, yet, the art and delight of these stories is little appreciated. They are seen only in their transformations as accounts of events: they have become history. The study of all the texts from the ancient Near East and of all the excavations in Israel and Palestine has been infected by a rather singular aspiration of biblical scholarship: to understand the Bible as an account of the historical past. The stories that we read from Genesis to the end of II Kings have come to serve as an historical context for all the rest of the Bible's literature, including its poetry and its philosophical writings.

Such thinking, posing as an historical and critical scholarly discipline, has been a great embarrassment to modern research. Rather than being historical, it broke the first rule of history by failing to distinguish it from myth. Rather than being critical, it used a logic entirely circular. Rather than being a self-correcting, self-critical science, it took for granted its own assumptions and contented itself merely to 'correcting' the Bible where plausibility required it. The miracles, it seems, had to go, but the rest could remain as unchanged as possible. While such a need to read our sacred texts as history begs explanation, biblical archaeology has resolutely failed to provide the Bible with an historical context in which it might reasonably be understood.

While many have pointed to the transcendent theological value of these unexamined traditions to justify the lack of academic integrity in research, few have asked why our theology should be willing to pay so high a price to protect its vision of our world. Why is an understanding of the Bible as fictive considered to undermine its truth and integrity? How does historicizing this literature give it greater legitimacy? Why, in fact, does a literary work as influential as the Bible need further legitimation? There is no virtue in confusing the Bible's meaning with what we used to think it meant, and still less in defending a narrow theology by calling it the Bible's view. To learn that what we once believed is not what we should have believed, is the ordinary intellectual process by which understanding grows.

It is awkward to speak so bluntly about one's own academic field. Biblical scholarship's rationale for such uncritical thinking has been a feckless excuse: 'Everyone has been doing it.' That is true enough. For now more than three generations, most of ancient history has attempted little more than to paraphrase old stories and legends. Historians who write of ancient Greece have their Herodotus; Egyptologists their Manetho; Assyriologists their Berossus, and the students of Phoenicia their Philo of Byblos. Even Judaic studies has its Josephus! If such interesting 'histories' work, and we somehow need them, why listen to critics who would undermine them? Why can't biblical studies have its Deuteronomist and its Jahwist as Israel's own first historians worthy of paraphrase? Why can't we allow the tradition to reify its own self-understanding? Why not make the Bible's tradition our history?

The present book is a response to such questions. It is an attempt to look at the Bible's view of the past on its own terms. Throughout Part One, I will try to explain how it is that the Bible has been misunderstood as history. Traditions such as the Bible's, which provided ancient society with a common past, are very different from the critical histories that play a central role in contemporary intellectual life. The differences between two perspectives, ancient and modern, reflect different perceptions of reality. I will try to make this clear in the opening discussion of chapter 1. Particularly central is the discussion I epitomize with a quotation from the philosopher king of the Book of Ecclesiastes: 'There is nothing new under the sun.' This ahistorical axiom of ancient Hellenistic thought gives voice to the structures of the traditions about the past which were created in the ancient world. It puts these traditions at odds with the goals of modern historical methods which are rather centred in defining events of the past as unique.

In Part Two I wish to present a clear and accurate idea of the kind of historical knowledge we have about ancient Palestine. I compare this perspective with the very different view of the Bible and of ancient Israel that biblical archaeologists have given us. In drawing this contrast, I will give a lot of space to how the writers of the Bible understood the divine, and I will compare this with the ancient West Semitic deity, Yahweh, as he is known from ancient Near Eastern inscriptions, and especially from personal names. The god Yahweh plays a central role in the story of Moses and Israel's beginnings, though it is a far different role than he ever played in the history of Palestine's religion. In fact, one could describe the story of the Books of Exodus and Numbers as being about a god who was without either a home or a people. He chose a people who similarly were without either a home or a god. The troubled interplay of this lonely god and this homeless people lies at the heart of the biblical story's plot. This is what I call the story of old Israel.

Part Three takes up an issue that any critical understanding of the Bible has to address: the historical contexts in which the text was written and in which the tradition was formed. These are the contexts – intellectual, literary and social – which have given the Bible its particular structure and language. They will help us recognize both the unique and the common contributions of this ancient tradition, which has so profoundly affected our own intellectual life.

How the Bible is related to history has been badly misunderstood. As we have been reading the Bible within a context that is certainly wrong, and as we have misunderstood the Bible because of this, we need to seek a context more appropriate. As a result, we will begin to read the Bible in a new way. These questions are questions about ancient history, but they are also our questions. They bring us close to some of the earliest streams of the tradition of our language and thought. They affect our intellectual self-understanding. Controversies surround these questions, not so much because the ideas of the past generation have become false, though that has happened. Far more important have been the changes that have come in our own generation. As that world has changed, so has our perception of the past. Our history has changed.

The sheer accumulation of data useful to historians from finds and texts in archaeological excavations has grown beyond summary. The growth in knowledge and use of such disciplines as sociology, anthropology, economics, geography, historical linguistics and comparative literature has been such that the ancient Near East, in both its history and its literature, requires major revisions of all branches of our historical understanding. Even works written as recently as the mid-1980s hardly reflect the changes in our understanding of the history of Israel and Palestine that are now taken for granted by most scholars. The conclusions of those who educated the current generation and formed the foundation for almost all currently written books on archaeology and the Bible are no longer accepted or acceptable. Their effort to integrate the results of Palestinian archaeology, biblical research and ancient Near Eastern studies in a comprehensive synthesis has been refuted in both principle and detail. This has left the field with shifting foundations that have created major faults in all related fields of research. Revision and change in all of our methods is required.

The success of historical methods worked out in the mid-1980s has had profound effects on the way we write the history of ancient Palestine today. Moreover, it has substantially altered our understanding of the Bible's place in history. The Bible's narratives are much like other ancient writings that collected the story traditions of the ancient world: of Egypt, Mesopotamia and Phoenicia. Whether we are talking about the sixth-century BCE Greek writer Herodotus, thought of by many as the Western world's first historian, the Jewish writer Josephus more than six centuries later, or the writers of the biblical narratives from Genesis to II Kings, Chronicles to Ezra and Nehemiah, or I-II Maccabees, these collections of old stories and legends do not provide us with evidence for history, as biblical archaeology has so long believed and hoped to prove. If today we have no viable history for what we used to call 'ancient Israel', there are good reasons for not having one. History-writing tries to explain the evidence of the past that has survived, and sets out to give clarity and coherence to what we know about the past. However, if our knowledge is fragmentary, uncertain or nonexistent, our history must take such ignorance into account.

CHAPTER I

History and origins: the changing past

1 When texts are confirmed by texts

The issue of Israel's origins has dominated approaches both to the Bible and to the history of Palestine. The resulting dilemma is one that all historical 'origin' questions face because of their implicit anachronism, and it seriously affects the way we integrate whatever biblical or extra-biblical evidence we have about Israel's earliest history. While any historical reality we can identify with biblical Israel is necessarily a product of the 'origins' question, and must be understood to post-date it, the fact remains that historical evidence for origins must be sought earlier than Israel, in a time when there was no such place or concept. But then, how is such evidence to be recognized specifically as belonging to Israel's origins? Given the fragmented nature of all evidence for ancient history, a question of origins is structured by hindsight. It is entirely dependent on the understanding we have of Israel as it comes to us from biblical tradition, whether or not that ideologically oriented self-understanding has any historical warrant whatever.

Another dilemma is that of the evidence itself. What is well understood as primary evidence comes from data that is contemporary with Israel's emergence. This is largely evidence that derives from archaeological research and exploration, and is commonly sought among the fragmented remains of the Bronze and early Iron Ages of ancient Palestine. It is our secondary evidence, namely the Bible and extra-biblical traditional literature, that purports to identify what this Israel is, whose origins we are trying to identify. It is also these secondary sources that provide what we assume is the appropriate time-frame for our primary quest for archaeological evidence. However, these assumptions relating to both identity and chronology are taken from texts known to us first from the Hellenistic period – that is, in the earliest biblical texts that have been found among the Dead Sea scrolls.

The obvious dilemma should make any historian uncomfortable. As long as the primary and secondary sources for our history of Israel's origins remain separated by as much as a thousand years, there can be little hope of establishing possible links between the Bible and early archaeological materials. We are looking for the origins of Israel as we know it from the Bible, yet we are unable to confirm any biblical narrative as historical until we first have a separate, independent history with which we might compare the Bible's account. If, moreover, we are trying to create a history capable of providing the context in which biblical narrative developed, this history can hardly be identical with that story of the Bible. Without an independently established history of Palestine and ancient Israel, the question of historicity – whether or not the Bible describes events that occurred in the past – remains a riddle.

These issues have grave consequences when we try to write history for very early periods. Our primary sources, which come to us mostly through archaeology, are very fruitful, but they tell us mostly about the structures that ancient societies had – how people lived, how their economies developed, the variety of relationships traceable by studying the remains of the physical culture that excavations have given us access to. With the largely unwritten materials that archaeology brings us, our history tends to become a description of societies with their long-range developments and changes, rather than a history of persons and events. Inscriptions add much to this. They tell us about language, political boundaries and structures, religious beliefs, social and legal customs, trade and business organization. When we are very lucky we get an insight into the way ancient people thought. We learn about their prejudices, fears and beliefs, their sense of humour and beauty, as well as about their loyalties and values. Palestine, however, is very poor in texts from periods earlier than the Hellenistic period, and we have nothing of the wealth or complexity of Egypt and Mesopotamia. This is especially true for the period of the Iron Age in which the early states of Israel and Judah existed. Moreover – as we shall see – Palestine never developed a political power of any great international significance. It was always so divided by its many small regions that it never developed a common history except when it was controlled by some power from outside, such as Egypt, Assyria and Babylonia. High culture, as expressed in art, architecture, literature and pageant, hardly existed. Most of what has survived is either foreign in origin or derivative from Phoenicia on the Syrian coast. Both culturally and intellectually speaking, Palestine ever remained Syria's southern fringe.

There is a particularly strong contrast between this poverty of primary historical sources for Palestine's Bronze and Iron ages, and the rich secondary literature available to us in texts and traditions from the Persian, Hellenistic and Greco-Roman periods. This literature recounts traditions about the past. In fact, preoccupation with the past and with its role in understanding and defining the present is a striking characteristic of the literature of these later periods. This literature includes not only the Bible's texts, but a large body of non-biblical literature, including traditional historiographies centred in questions of origin. They give us detailed accounts of what writers represented as the past. Much of this literature is well known, and historians have long used it in an effort to reconstruct Palestine's earlier history.

These texts, however, are not very easy to use. Not only are they filled with all kinds of legends and stories, but their authors did not much care to distinguish between stories which were interesting, humorous or entertaining, and stories which actually related something that had occurred in the past. They did not hesitate to change their sources and reconstruct the past whenever there were gaps in their knowledge, or indeed in any manner that they saw fit. As we have grown more aware of such typical characteristics of traditional historiographies about Palestine's past, the way that scholarship once used them for reconstructing the history of Israel has grown less and less acceptable. Historical scholarship's indolent habit of offering paraphrases of ancient historians and correcting them only when evidence proves them wrong will no longer do. Nor will it do any longer to view such traditional historians as in some degree 'dependable'. What they conceived as 'historiography' were historical fictions about the past, using whatever materials came to hand. What we learn when we read them is not data about any earlier period of the past, but rather an account of what they thought, and what they understood to belong to the genre of literature they were writing. These texts are historically useful for what they imply about the author's present, and about the knowledge available to him and his contemporaries, not for their author's claim about any projected past. One of the most striking and wonderful things about an 'historian' like Josephus is that he knows almost nothing about 'the past' that we ourselves do not already know from other sources. When an account he gives of a supposed event of two centuries earlier 'confirms' something we can read in other works, it is only because he has copied or paraphrased it. Josephus has been well described as a person one wouldn't buy a used car from.

We do get an accumulating body of stories from such works as Josephus writes and from the traditional historiographies given in the Bible, but it is a mistake to suppose that we can use one text to confirm what another says about the past. The most important historical information we can learn from such ancient historiography has very little to do with the quality of their history, and almost nothing to do with what they say about the past. Ancient inscriptions have often been found, which refer to one or other character or narrative which we otherwise know only from the Bible. Yet, even here, a confirmation of the biblical narrative, which would allow us to read it as if it were history, is still elusive. The reason that these ancient texts always seem to fail to give us the evidence we need is that our way of understanding the past is not shared by the authors of these or of any other ancient texts. This, I hope, will become clearer with the help of two examples of biblical stories which have been emphatically confirmed by extra-biblical inscriptions.

The first example comes from an excavation at Tell Deir Alla in the Jordan valley. The text found dates to the late eighth century BCE. It presents a story centred on the visions of a seer of the gods, Balaam, son of Beor, who is known to us from Numbers 22–24. The Bible's tale is the well-known story of the prophet and his talking ass. In the Deir Alla inscription, Balaam is a seer of ancient Moab, while the biblical story describes him as a prophet living in Syria, on the Upper Euphrates. Both are figures who speak with the voice of God, which determines the fate and destiny of nations. In the Bible's story, Balaam is a prophet of Yahweh. In the Deir Alla text, he is associated with a god with the name *Shgr*, as well as with what are called *Shadday* gods and goddesses – much like the god *El Shadday* of Genesis 17: 1 and Exodus 6: 3 – and with the goddess Ashtar. The biblical story is presented within the context of the narratives about Israel's wanderings in the wilderness with Moses. The inscription, however, is centuries younger than any period associated with Moses. In spite of these differences, both narratives are obviously stories centred on the same ancient literary figure. What is established by this remarkable parallel is not the existence of an historical Balaam, but an ancient way of telling stories about prophets or holy men who bless and curse nations and their kings. It is precisely the *story* character of the prophet Balaam that the Deir Alla inscription gives evidence for. The extra-biblical evidence shows that the biblical role of prophets from Balaam to Samuel and from Amos to Jeremiah belongs to a long-established literary tradition of ancient Palestine. Balaam is Palestine's earliest known example of this tale type.

My second example of a biblical narrative confirmed by ancient texts relates to another early Moabite monumental inscription of about the same date or slightly earlier than the Tell Deir Alla text. It has long been claimed that Omri, who in the biblical narrative built the city of Samaria and founded the ruling dynasty of the northern kingdom of Israel, is the earliest king in the Bible whose reign has been confirmed by extra-biblical evidence. In fact, Omri's historicity has been thought doubly strong, as it has been confirmed by inscriptions from both Assyria and Moab. Assyrian records refer to the state of Israel with its capital in Samaria by a dynastic name, *Bit Humri* ('House of Omri'). We find similar names for small states in other Assyrian inscriptions, such as *Bit Illani* and *Bit Agusi*. Omri is also mentioned on the Mesha stele, an inscription found in 1868. The inscription on this monument was thought to have been commissioned by a near contemporary of Omri and his son Ahab: Mesha, the king of Moab. The biblical narrative of II Kings 3: 4–8, which has much in common with this inscription from Transjordan, has been thought to refer to the same political conflicts between Israel and Moab that the inscription does. On the basis of the reference to Omri (and 'his son') and the correspondence of the events with the Bible's story, the inscription and the reign of Mesha has been dated by historians to some time between 849 and 820 BCE. The part of this text that clearly describes Omri as king of Israel reads as follows (ll. 4–8):

> As for Omri, king of Israel, he humbled Moab many days, for Chemosh was angry at his land. And his son followed him and he also said, 'I will humble Moab.' In my time he spoke (thus) but I have triumphed over him and over his house, while Israel has perished forever! (Now) Omri has occupied the land of Madeba and had dwelt there in his time and half of the time of his son: forty years; but Chemosh dwelt there in my time.

The monument on which this inscription was written was originally erected at a sanctuary. Its purpose was to give honour to Chemosh, the god of Moab. Chemosh is a god much like Yahweh in the Book of Kings. He was angry at Moab and so allowed Omri to conquer it. The contrast drawn between the images of first Omri and then Chemosh 'dwelling in Moab', expresses the difference between the land as conquered by Israel and then as once again set free. Together with the motif of Omri's hubris, this literary and highly metaphorical language belongs to the world of story. It is the same kind of language we find in tales in the Bible, where Yahweh controls Israel and Judah's fate and where he sends enemies against them when he is angry.

Rather than an historical text, the inscription, in fact belongs to a substantial literary tradition of stories of kings of the past. We find a similar story (told, autobiographically, in the first person), which dates back at least to the thirteenth century BCE. It is about the king of Alalakh, Idrimi, who in fact had reigned over this city some two centuries earlier. Like Idrimi's tale, the Mesha story is written in the first person and presented in the voice of the king himself. The monument presents us with an epitome of the king's reign: his enemies defeated, his campaigns completed, like Idrimi's, so too Mesha's kingdom is established in peace and prosperity, ready to be handed on to his successor. His work was done. Both inscriptions are tributes to a great king of the past, epitomizing his reign.

The same monumental style of writing introduces us to the birth story of the ancient king of Akkad, Sargon the Great, which lived on to become a standard piece of Neo-Assyrian and Babylonian legend. It offers one of the finest renditions of the stock birth-of-a-saviour episode, found throughout ancient literature, and most famously in the story of King Oedipus and in the Bible's story of Moses' birth in Exodus 2. The inscription on the monument to Sargon begins much like the inscriptions on those to Idrimi and Mesha, as a first-person, epitomizing biography: 'I am Sargon, the mighty king, king of Agade . . . my mother, the high priestess, conceived me; in secret she bore me. She set me in a basket of rushes; with bitumen, she sealed my lid. She cast me into the river, which rose not over me . . .'

By far the most famous of monuments from the ancient Near East which epitomizes a great king of the past by using the common formulae and metaphors of the king as faithful servant of God and using a pseudo-autobiographical first person address is the stele of Hammurapi which created the Hammurapi 'Code'. While the original of this monument possibly goes back to Old Babylonian times, it remained a staple of Mesopotamian literature for centuries later.

As with the Hammurapi, Sargon and Idrimi monuments, it is more than style and form that establish the fictive qualities of Mesha's inscription. Literary metaphor also lies behind the use of the name Omri itself. Omri 'dwelling in Moab' is not a person doing anything in Transjordan, but an eponym, a literary personification of Israel's political power and presence. It is clear that the reference to Omri in the Mesha stele is literary, not historical. This forces us to look more closely at the Assyrian geographical and political name for Israel: the 'House of Omri'. From this early historical name for ancient Israel's ruling house, the Bible's story of one Omri as builder of Samaria and founder of its dynasty might grow. The language of patronage supports the folklore that behind a political name such as *Bit Humri* lies hidden the founder of the state. Literary elaborations and play on geographic and ethnic names belong to a well-known pattern of story-telling, built on eponymous ancestors. This type of tale is closely associated with genealogies and dynastic lists, and is especially common in both biblical and early Greek stories.

Similarly, the use of family metaphors, as in Omri's 'son' and 'house', is drawn from the metaphorical language of patronage, the political system dominant throughout the history of ancient Palestine and Syria. The use of rounded numbers, such as thirty and forty years, for reigns, which we find shared both by Idrimi's and the Bible's tales; the motif of a god becoming drunk on the blood of his enemies, known from the Late Bronze Age poems from Ugarit in Syria and from the creation mythology of Egypt. These are all classical tale motifs. The literary nature of the Mesha stele needs to be taken seriously. It is quite doubtful that it refers to an historical person when it refers to Israel's king. 'Omri, king of Israel', eponym of the highland patronate, *Bit Humri*, belongs to the world of stories. In a description of a battle against Israel for the town of Nebo, the Mesha stele presents the enemy as dedicated to total destruction as a sacred offering to the God Chemosh in a manner that is very familiar to us from the books of Joshua and I Samuel: '. . . slaying all, seven thousand men, boys and women, for I had devoted them for destruction for Ashtar-Chemosh'.

Finally, in the biblical variant of the Moabite story in II Kings 3: 4–8, the two kings of Israel that are involved are not Omri and his son (namely Ahab), but rather Ahab and *his* son Jehoram. The motif of a king of Israel and his son attacking Moab remains constant; only the names of the characters vary. This is a pattern of variation that occurs often in stories, but in history only by mistake. It would be an error to pit the Bible against the Mesha stele in a contest of historicity. It is also wrong to date the stele by using the biblical tradition as if it were an account of an event. Nor do the roles the characters play in either version of the story allow us to understand the narratives as reflecting historical events or persons. The similarity of the Mesha narrative to the posthumous tale of Idrimi forces us to see the inscription as a monument celebrating Mesha's completed reign, and to date it somewhat later or at the very close of this historical king's reign. What we have in the Mesha stele is an early variant of the same tale that we find in the Bible. As with the Balaam story of Numbers, the Mesha inscription gives us evidence that the Bible collects and re-uses very old tales from Palestine's past.

Even evidence from extra-biblical texts which proves that some of the biblical narratives do derive from very early sources does not confirm the historicity of these stories. Quite the contrary, it confirms the Bible's own presentation of them as fictive tales of the past. In a similar way, the discovery of very close variants of passages of Leviticus used in early Palestinian *tephilim* dating to the seventh century BCE gives no evidence for the historicity of the story of Moses in the wilderness. The wilderness story offers us the Bible's aetiology, a story fictively establishing the foundation of this ancient ritual tradition of wearing sacred texts on one's person. Just so, the story of Exodus 12: 14–20 presents an origin story for the feast of Passover. What the archaeological evidence does confirm is the antiquity of the use of *tephilim* in Palestine, as well as the function of biblical narrative as both a collection and an interpretation of past traditions.

The theme of 'exile', which dominates so much of the Bible's narrative, needs a discussion of its own, and must wait for another chapter. Extra-biblical evidence for the exile of Israel and Judah by the Assyrian and Babylonian armies is overwhelming. Even the Mesha stele, which we have just discussed, reflecting the military ambitions of what was but a very small state, refers to this ancient war crime of forced population transference. With the example of the exile, we are confronted with how ancient Near Eastern texts mark the Bible's stories as part of a world of story and interpretation. While it is a hard-won principle of biblical archaeology that the historicity of ancient biblical narratives about old Israel cannot be affirmed unless we have extra-biblical evidence, it is just as important to be aware that even when we do have such extra-biblical confirmation, it is more likely to confirm the Bible's literary and metaphorical tropes than to establish it as historical record-keeping.

Of course, the existence of kings such as Ahab and Jehu in history has long been confirmed. Assyrian records leave us in no doubt. The biblical stories must be understood as using the names of historical kings of Israel. These extra-biblical confirmations also support the approximate dates the Bible gives for these kings, within a modest range of error. Nevertheless, we cannot conclude that the Bible's use of such real names of kings of the past was based on hypothetical but otherwise unknown dynastic lists, which might give us the hope of using the other, unconfirmed names as if they were historical. Our historical knowledge comes, rather, not from the Bible's references but, independently, from their occurrence in Assyrian texts. The evidence suggests that the Bible, like Shakespeare, often invokes fictional kings in confecting its stories. This is the very nature of literature. Though I reside within the community of Elsinore in Denmark, and can see Hamlet's castle every time I go to the seashore, I cannot hope to find in the patterns of Shakespeare's poetry any evidence that this storied king might have been historical.

2 There is nothing new under the sun

When we ask whether the events of biblical narrative have actually happened, we raise a question that can hardly be satisfactorily answered. The question itself guarantees that the Bible will be misunderstood. One of the central contrasts that divide the understanding of the past that we find implied in biblical texts from a modern understanding of history lies in the way we think about reality. This difference is so fundamental to our understanding of ancient texts that we need to address it directly.

Just like our own, the ancient understanding of what is real was based on experience. Both Plato and Aristotle repeatedly appeal to experience to express their philosophical arguments and conclusions. This is also a constant of the collections of proverbs and poetic couplets that we find in the wisdom literature of the Bible, such as the books of Proverbs, Ecclesiastes or Job. Principle is the product of observation and experience. So we read in Proverbs 17: 1: 'Far better is a dry crust eaten in peace than a great feast in conflict.' Even the most profound of philosophical principles are couched in the language of what is known. This philosophy is not pollyannish. It often displays an edge of hardness, aware of harsher realities: 'A man that is born from a woman has a few days, full of trouble; he blossoms like a flower; then withers' (Job 14: 1f.). So too in Ecclesiastes 11: 7–8: 'Light is sweet, and it is pleasant for the eyes to see the sun. If a man lives many years, he should enjoy them all; yet remember all the same that the days of darkness are many.' Biblical authors delight in drawing ironic conclusions about the quality of our ignorance on the basis of the limitations of our experience. So Solomon reflects on the surprising contrast that observation can bring to the expected: 'One man gives freely, yet grows the richer for it; another keeps what he should give, and still does not have enough.' (Proverbs 11: 24). The awareness of human ignorance is almost always drawn in analogies from experience. In Ecclesiastes 11: 5 the philosopher, with implicit reference to the 'quickening' motif in the 'birth of a son of God' tale-type, draws the sweeping indictment of human knowledge: 'Just as you do not know how the (divine) spirit becomes bones in the womb (of a woman), so you can hardly know God's work, and he has made everything!' This basis in experience gives ancient philosophy a sharp, critical directness which more abstract and theoretical arguments often lack. Nowhere is this more emphatically realized than in the Book of Job's devastating critique of traditional knowledge about God. Job confronts Yahweh addressing him from the whirlwind: 'I had only heard of you as one hears with the ear, but now my eyes see you' (Job 42: 5). Again and again, the intellectual voice implicit in our texts confronts the tradition with its knowledge of experience. Ancient philosophical thought, no more systematic than it is abstract, is held together in this way by recurrent *ad hoc* references to experience: either the author's own or his audience's collective experience. The way things are is always the proving ground of truth in argument.

Nevertheless, the abstraction from particular experiences to a larger sense of the real and the unreal follows a different logical path in the Bible than does our own. In the ancient world, individual experiences are filtered through perceptions of a greater reality, an implicitly greater experience. The immediacy of events in time can be deceiving and the world is not always as it appears. The particulars of everyday experience are perceived as transient, changeable expressions of what is more stable, lasting and real. Such change and transience is a constant characteristic of our material human experience. Even a great river, as stable as it may seem, is in constant flux. Nothing that we know lasts. All living die. Life itself, like the life-creating spirit of Solomon's proverb above, is not our own, but evades our grasp. What is spirit, however, free from the change of the world of matter, lasting and therefore real as it may be, is beyond our experience. Like Job's knowledge of Yahweh, we know of it only from hearing. Form and matter, the spiritual and the physical, reality and appearance develop a cosmic irony, frustrating the human ideals of understanding.

In ancient thought, the abstract understanding of reality became closely tied to the sense of the lasting and the permanent: the eternal. The concrete world of our experience suffers change and transformation, is observably transient, and therefore comes to be identified with the unreal. Logically, the very reality of such change is to be denied. The truly real, the eternal, unchanging spirit, is also the unknown. Man has only the thought – and a transient thought to boot – of the eternal, not its grasp. This inescapable pessimism and frustration, which was seen as fundamental to being human, undermined any sense of history as we think of it: an account of the changes and development of a society over time. Events, far from being real or important for themselves, were but the surface of a reality that underlay change and transformation. They were not so important in themselves, but were important for the hints they give of unchanging, transcendent and eternal reality to those who reflect on the past with understanding.

As such an understanding of reality comes to inform a tradition of discussion of the past, what we clumsily call ancient historiography, but might better think of as discussions about origins (including the account of creation itself) takes on the central role in the genre. One is understood by one's origins in ancient thought, because everything exists already at the creation. Fate and the destiny of humanity are central concepts that see the essence of all reality and events as the outcome of the divine work done at the creation. What we understand as the historical world of change and events is for the biblical authors a peripheral unfolding of what has always been. The transience of historical events needs interpretation so that the reality they mirror may be perceived.

Chronology in this kind of history is not used as a measure of change. It links events and persons, makes associations, establishes continuity. It expresses an unbroken chain from the past to the present. This is not a linear as much as it is a coherent sense of time. It functions so as to identify and legitimize what is otherwise ephemeral and transient. Time marks a reiteration of reality through its many forms. Nor is ancient chronology based on a sense of circular time, in the sense of a return to an original reality. The first instance of an event is there only to mark the pattern of reiteration. It is irrelevant whether a given event is earlier or later than another. Both exist as mirrored expressions of a transcendent reality. Closely linked with this ancient perception of time is the philosophical idea we find captured in the Book of Ecclesiastes (1: 9–11):

> There is nothing new under the sun. If we can say of anything: that it is new, it has been seen already long since. This event of the past is not remembered. Nor will the future events, which will happen again be remembered by those who follow us.

When God created the world, he created the heavens and the earth and everything in them. All of history is already included in the creation. This is also what lies behind the idea of 'fate', which, as a classic premiss of Greek tragedy, reflects the human struggle against destiny. The only appropriate response is acceptance and understanding.

The central structure of the sense of reality within this world-view is not complicated. It is a central argument already in Genesis' opening chapter, in the great poem celebrating the creation of the world within the context of great acts of creation on each of the days of the week, ending with the creation of the Sabbath day on which both the world and its creator rest. Each day of the creation is marked with a reiteration of the summarizing statement: 'And God saw that it was good' (Gen. 1: 4). This reiteration closes on the sixth day of creation with the observation that 'God saw everything he had made, that it was very good' (Gen. 1: 31). This reiterated declaration that all that God made was good does two things. It opens the classical discourse on theodicy: how can God be good and still have created the world we live in? The problem is the existence of evil in a world created by God. The author enters the discussion emphatically on the side of God. Each act of creation was good, and the whole was very good. But the story also does a second thing, silently and implicitly. Drawing on a fundamental motif of patronage, the creator is sketched as absolute benefactor. He establishes all that is good in this world. Good is what he sees as good. In fact, it is good *because* he sees it that way. In all biblical narrative, God is perceived as the only one who is truly autonomous, one 'who does what in his own eyes is good'. We know that the world at creation was good, because God saw it so. The divine is the absolute standard. What he sees as good is good – by that fact.

And just as this is said, the author deftly undermines the gushing optimism of the picture he has created. The tension implicit in this picture of an all-good-seeing God looking at the world we know outdoes the Polyanna stories in its irony. On the sixth day of creation, which closes with God's satisfying view of the world as 'very good', God makes a mistake! He makes humanity in his own image! What had been planned as the creation's epitome, is the flaw in God's otherwise perfect tapestry. Mankind too – in God's own image – will do precisely what it sees to be good. And so, evil enters the world. It could hardly be a surprise to any ancient that, given such a creation in God's image and likeness, the woman in the very next story – this 'mother of all living' – sees the fruit of the forbidden tree 'good' (Gen. 3: 6). Being like God, and obedience hardly a divine virtue, nothing less could be expected. The intellectual perspective of these two narratives is clear. The unbridgeable difference between what God sees and what humans see as good is present already at the creation. The whole of biblical history is sketched in terms of human fate implicit in the way we are. There is nothing new under the sun, and the long narrative which sets out from Genesis is but an ever-expanding illustration of this eternal conflict of will, as the divine Father struggles with his children; even his first-born Israel.

This sense of history as an illustration of creation, this view of humanity living out a fate determined by its nature, dominates the biblical view of history as a reiteration of what always has been. It can best be seen through the many stories that present the recurrent theme of new creation, new beginnings and new hope. All play out their contrast to stories of human wilfulness. In the creation of such reiterative story chains, one finds recurrent echoes of characters who perform the same or a similar function. Within a biblical perspective, all reflect a single transcendent reality. Three examples of such echoing clusters of stories should make this clear.

1) There are two great stories in the Bible in which old Israel is led through water to begin a new life. In Exodus 14–15, Moses leads the people through the sea on dry land. The waters stack up like Jello on each side. Those who had been helpless slaves in Egypt become a victorious people led to victory by their God. The same motif of crossing the waters from defeat to victory finds its place in Joshua. The divine presence leads the people dry-shod across the Jordan River, whose waters 'stand in one heap' (Josh. 3: 7–17). It is a new Israel, coming out of the wilderness that enters the land. A minor echo of this motif can also be seen when the patriarch Jacob crosses the Jabbok in Genesis 32: 22. In this crossing, he becomes Israel. The transcendent reality that each of these stories reiterates is the original division of the waters of chaos at the creation, when God caused the waters 'to be gathered in one place, letting the dry land appear' (Gen. 1: 9).

2) The great collection of poems that prophesies Babylon's destruction at the hands of 'Yahweh of the Armies', in the Book of Jeremiah (chapters 50 and 51) rings with obvious echoes of Genesis 11's story of the tower of Babylon. That story, however, also reiterates the paired and nearly indistinguishable stories of the destructions of Samaria and Jerusalem we find in II Kings 17 and 25. All of the prophecies of destruction against Israel's enemies (Jer. 46–49) are mere variations of a single theme. As commentary on human events, such poems and stories about God's wrath against cities and nations reiterate the transcendent reality of Yahweh's war against the godless. The fundamental mythology that structures this war and destruction metaphor is seen much more clearly in the obviously cosmic allusions in the stories of the great flood (Gen. 6–9) and of Sodom and Gomorrah (Gen. 19). Noah and Lot both fill the exilic role of Israel's surviving remnant. They find 'favour in Yahweh's eyes' (Gen. 6: 8). Yet another mythic variation of this leitmotif recurs throughout the Book of Psalms, where the transcendent struggle between the way of righteousness and the way of evil is captured in the metaphor of the cosmic war that Yahweh and his Messiah wage against the nations, as in Psalms 2, 8, 89 and 110. All are expressive of the divine dominance over reality. Offering a template for comparable recreations of this theme in the Books of Daniel and Revelations, Yahweh says to his Messiah (as well as to the poet's implicit audience, revealing for a moment this metaphor's importance in the language of piety): 'Pray, and I will give the nations into your possession, and you will own the ends of the earth. You will crush them

with an iron mace, break them into pieces like the shards of a pot' (Psalms 2: 8–9).

3) My third example of a cluster of metaphors reiterating transcendent reality throughout the Bible's narrative of the past is a central part of the structure of what has been thought Israel's historical past. The theme of crossing the wilderness forms an initial setting for the expansive collections of law and wisdom we find throughout the rest of the Pentateuch. Israel sets out across the desert after the crossing of the sea and is prepared as early as Exodus 23 to enter into the promised land. Moses accumulates his ever-growing *torah* as he climbs Mount Sinai at least eight different times. 'Murmuring' and 'backsliding' are used to delay the plot throughout their wilderness trek. Finally, at the end of Numbers, Yahweh in his anger declares that this generation will never enter the land of promise. The desert becomes a place of exile for 'those who refuse to walk in Yahweh's path'. The story line waits the full generation of forty years for its new Israel to enter the land with Joshua. The transformation from the motif of wilderness-crossing to one of being held captive in a desert of exile is a shift that allows the entire final portion of the Pentateuch to be the subject of an exile's reflection with Moses on Mount Nebo in the Book of Deuteronomy. Israel progresses through the themes of punishment, understanding and acceptance, allowing the Pentateuch's narrative to close in mirrored step with the similarly meditative closure of II Kings in the city of Babylon.

No less striking are the few traditions we have that give us a glimpse of Jerusalem from alternative traditions to that which, with Jeremiah, repeatedly sees all of Jerusalem taken into exile. In the opening chapters of the Book of Nehemiah, Jerusalem is deserted; the city lies in ruins; its gates are burned. Nehemiah, an official of the Persian court, sets about its restoration. While this picture has come to dominate our imagination of the past, the Book of Lamentations uses the metaphor of Jerusalem as a metaphysical desert. Its wilderness is the absence of God from the city. It offers a picture of Jerusalem filled with lawlessness and violence – a moral wasteland. In the Bible, the metaphors of wilderness and exile belong to a common cluster of motifs. They echo each other. Both prepare the life of a 'new Israel'. The mythical and theological overtones of this literature are emphatically stressed in Jeremiah 4: 23–28. Citing the same language of primordial 'formless emptiness' with which Genesis 1 had opened, Jeremiah describes Jerusalem as just such an empty nothingness as before the creation. Even the heavens are without light. Jerusalem's mountains have been removed from their pillars of wisdom. Jeremiah sounds echoing images of the opening of the garden story (Gen. 2: 6). The poet looks at Jerusalem (the Song of Songs' garden of Yahweh) and 'there was no humanity'; even the birds of the sky had fled; there was no rain; a fruitful land had become desert.

Far from offering structures to any history of the past, this kind of desert emptiness and exile is akin to the wilderness traditions of the monastery and the desert fathers. It is the mystic's 'dark night of the soul', expressing the experience of pietism and seeking conversion through prayer and fasting. What has been consistently neglected in all of our naive readings of the Bible as history is the voice of our texts. How should we read them? What is the reality to which the text implicitly refers? These questions should create a leitmotif for our discussion.

I would like to close this description of reiterative history with a final example. The Bible does not present us with narratives and then leave us to interpret them as best we can. If it did, we might well think it possible to read one story or poem as echoing contemporary piety, while another might better be understood as referring to events of history. The historian might then best confine himself to those aspects of the tradition that appeared to preserve referents of an historical nature. However, the Bible also interprets what it collects. That is, it tells us how to read and how to understand the tradition. This ubiquitous commentary, reflecting an ancient discourse about the tradition's meaning, is fundamental; it is the voice of the tradition. This too we will return to again and again in the continuing thread of our own discussion. At present, I wish only to introduce this issue with an example. In the Book of Psalms, we often find brief headings, giving various songs story settings and commenting on them. Some of these headings link the songs to David and tell the reader how to understand the psalm. In doing this, the scribe implicitly informs us how he understands David, through the choice of songs that David is given to sing. David is always running from his enemies, in desperate trouble; or, as the psalmist might have seen it, 'seeking refuge with Yahweh'. He sings of his own sorrow and fears, and gives voice to his hope that God will save him. The first-person voice allows the audience to identify their own, private, problems vicariously. They too sing the song with David; and, in doing this, evoke an understanding of a transcendent David. These passages tell us how the psalms' collectors thought about the David of the tradition.

The techniques of this discourse are similar to the way the gospel stories at times present Jesus in the classic philosopher's role of the man of piety and discernment, a role we find played throughout the literature of the ancient world, and not only by the Jobs and Solomons of the biblical world, but in all ancient philosophical literature from the schoolroom textbooks of Bronze Age Egypt to the peripatetic cynic philosophers of Hellenistic literature. I can think of no clearer example than two paired stories of David and of Jesus. In each, the central hero of the narration goes to the mountain to pray.

In II Samuel 15, David, hunted by the army of his son Absalom, abandoned by all his friends and despairing of all hope, reaches the top of the Mount of Olives, overlooking the seat of his kingdom, Jerusalem, where Absalom holds power. It is important that this scene is set at the top of the Mount of Olives, because as the text tells us, it is 'there that men are wont to go to pray' (I Sam. 15: 32). It is time for David, the man of action, to give himself to prayer. The story implicitly responds to and illustrates the divine exhortation of Psalms 2: 8: 'Pray, and I will make the world your inheritance.' The story becomes a parable on the power of prayer. David has nothing left, and it is with a mood of despair that he climbs this mountain as to a last refuge. David weeps as he climbs the mountain. He is barefoot, his head bowed, and all his companions hold their heads bowed, weeping. For David, Absalom is already king. It is in David's speech to Zadok that the story clarifies its theme. Zadok's name, 'righteousness, discernment', cues the reader. It is as an illustration of piety's way of righteousness that the story takes its place in tradition. It is travelling this theological path with righteousness that David climbs, not merely the geographical and historical slope outside Jerusalem, but the mountain which tests his life to the core: 'If I find grace in Yahweh's eye, he will let me see once again his ark and his dwelling' (namely, Jerusalem). And then comes pietism's key, with which the entire tale is unlocked. 'But if he says that he no longer cares for me, so may he do to me as he sees is good!' David walks up the mountain as the man of piety, emptied of all self-will. He is the apogee of the ideal king, every pious man's representative as 'servant of Yahweh'. In his humility's success, David crosses over the mountain. Absalom is dead. Though Yahweh's Messiah, he has died ignominiously, hanging from a tree. Returning as its king, David rides a donkey down to Jerusalem; he is Yahweh's anointed, entering his kingdom!

It is as an everyman's tale of piety that the gospels have Jesus reiterate David's story as in Mark 14: 32–42, an illustration of Psalm 2: 8's exhortation to prayer. In the closure of his story, Mark transforms Absalom's role in his version of Yahweh's messiah on Golgotha. Foreshadowing the closure of the story, Jesus had been received into his kingdom, riding on his donkey in the story of his first entrance to Jerusalem. On the night before he dies, he fills David's role as pietism's everyman on the Mount of Olives. He climbs the mountain to Gethsemane's garden, returning us to Yahweh's garden and to the tree of life. Like David, Jesus is abandoned by his followers. He suffers despair, and is without hope. He goes to his mountain to pray, paraphrasing David's words in the voice of tradition: 'not my will but yours be done.' What does the text mean by its reiteration of this event? Both David and Jesus play the pious philosopher of reflection and discernment for one who wishes to walk in the path of righteousness with the story. Both pray where one is wont to pray, seeking his inheritance. The reader implied is the one who recognizes that it is not by the will of man but by the will of God that one enters his kingdom. This is reiterated history, a philosophical discourse of a tradition's meaning.

3 Stories of conflict

The central questions regarding the Bible and history do not in fact concern issues of history so much as how texts work. When we are dealing with the hypothetical lists of kings for the states of Israel and of Judah which presumably were used in writing the Book of II Kings, the interests are issues of legitimacy and continuity, epitomizing balance. If there were gaps in the writer's sources, they were filled by fantasy, even by echoes of names which were already contained in the lists themselves. What harm an extra Jeroboam? The lists are drawn to parallel each other, to confirm and reiterate the other. It is the balance and coherence that convinces. 'During Ahaz, king of Judah's twelfth year, Hosea, Elah's son, became king over Samaria. He ruled nine years; he did what was evil in the eyes of Yahweh, but not like the kings of Israel before him' (II Kings 17: 1–2).

Polarity and contrast is the other central functional construct of biblical narrative, especially of the extended chain of stories about old Israel that we find from Genesis to the end of II Kings. It is a structural element of the narrative, and every bit as important as reiteration in creating an account of Israel's past. The polarization of characters explores variations on two themes: echoing and competition. Many stories interweave the two.

The stories about the patriarchs in Genesis, for example, are ordered on the basis of a reiteration of central themes through three successive heroic pairs: Abraham and Lot, Isaac and Ishmael, Jacob and Esau. They all develop roles as founding ancestors of the ancient peoples of Palestine. Each participates in the re-echoing plot motif that constructs the plot of peoples whose lands have been promised them by their deity since earliest times. The theme is a universalist variant of Exodus' more particularist story of Israel in the wilderness, which centred on the theme of a God without a people finding a people without a God. All nations have such a divinely created destiny. This dominating plot-line is used now to open the greater story of the extended narrative from Genesis to the end of II Kings, creating a self-identifying leitmotif of the 'children of Israel' as quintessentially human. They are wanderers through life. In the patriarchal stories, this motif is linked to one of tenacious destiny. The land is theirs not so much by divine gift and promise as by fiat. This theme of being bound to the land by destiny can best be glimpsed in the song-variant of these stories about Yahweh's originating links with 'his people'. The 'Song of Moses' of Deuteronomy 32 functions as a theological commentary on the narratives that precede it. It epitomizes and closes the five books of the Pentateuch, the long narrative of origins which Genesis opens. Moses' song reminds the reader of the cosmic and eternal significance of the narratives of Israel as humanity's representative and Yahweh's first-born. The opening of the song calls the listener to remember the accounts of ancient wisdom and its tales of the earth's beginnings:

> Think of the days of yore; attend to generations past. Ask your father; let him tell you. Let the old one recount to you how El Elyon divided the nations; how he separated humanity from each other and how he established the boundaries of peoples according to the number of his messengers. Yahweh's lot became his people: Jacob was his inheritance (Deut. 32: 7–9).

This story of the supreme God, *El Elyon*, distributing the nations of the world among his sons or 'messengers' is also a close variant of the more geographical 'table of nations' (Genesis 10) that follows the flood story. That list of descendants follows lines of succession according to Noah's three sons. Each represents the three continents of the ancient world: Shem (Asia), Ham (Africa) and Japheth (Europe). All the children listed are represented by geographical names in these regions. Each patriarch is portrayed as the father of his own particular city, region or people. Moses' song of Deuteronomy 32 represents the heavenly side of this myth and is cast in the form of a paraphrase of old legends about the father of the gods surrounded by his children. They are his messengers. They represent him for all the nations. He is present through his sons, each of whom is given a land of his own. Yahweh received Jacob for his inheritance; *El Elyon* has made Yahweh God for Israel. This song interprets stories for us such as the one in Genesis 32: 13–32, when Jacob crosses the Jabbok to begin his new life as Israel. Jacob wrestles with a night demon on the bank of a river. In this self-identifying struggle, Jacob is renamed 'Israel' because he has 'struggled with *El*'. The story closes with yet another naming pun as Jacob names the place *Peniel*, because there he saw the 'face of *El*'. Deuteronomy 32 interprets all of the stories of Yahweh and the gods of the patriarchs as stories through which *El Elyon*, or 'God the Most High' might be glimpsed. The tradition does not merely collect stories; it interprets them theologically.

It is in the exilic theme of wandering, of obediently following wherever God might lead that we find the dominant motif of the larger chain-narrative of Genesis to II Kings. This has drawn its plot from Israel's journeys, beginning already with the stories of Adam, of Cain and of the tower of Babel, in which the whole of mankind comes from the mythical land of Qedem (literally, 'the East') from which human life as we know it first begins. The Tower of Babel story of Genesis 11 bears implicit echoes of the tales of destruction and exile reiterated in the narratives to come, of divine wrath against the implicitly mirrored cities of Sodom, Samaria and

Jerusalem. The people in building the tower did 'as they saw fit' and built a tower up to the sky 'to make a name for themselves'. To stop them from becoming like gods ('in that nothing they wanted to do would be impossible to them'), Yahweh confused their languages. This story is not only an origin story for all the world's languages, it epitomizes the recurrent story of humanity seeking its own will. This narrative thread had first begun with the paired stories of Adam and Eve in the garden and of Cain's murder of his brother Abel. In response to the hubris of each of these stories, Yahweh sends them out from Qedem, the place of creation, into the real world. The leitmotifs of such stories are wandering and rootlessness. It is the plot-line of the story of Israel's exile, which opens here, not to close until the destruction of that second Babylon of Jerusalem and its temple. Jerusalem too had been built not by God, but 'by men's hands'. The story of the Babylonian deportation brings the narrative to its ironic closure in II Kings.

This mainstream story of human ambition, beginning with Babylon and coming back to Babylon, which now dominates the biblical tradition, is one focused on the competing wills of God and men. The great contrasting structural theme of the choosing of Israel, followed by Yahweh regretting his choice, rejecting and destroying Israel, is played off against Israel's acceptance of the pact with Yahweh that defined them as his people, followed by the betrayal and rejection of their God. This created a destiny defined by divine anger. The dominant story is one of hubris and destiny, strife and struggle. It is more than a story of promise delayed. This chain-narrative which characterizes the story of Israel's origins from Abraham onward is intrinsically marked as a story of supersession. The past is a scene of failure, ever to be overcome by a 'new Israel' that will finally follow God's will for them. It is a story, not of biblical faith, but of human apostasy. Such a story demands a rejection of the past and a reorientation to a new future. It is this future orientation of the idealistic concept of 'new Israel' that marks the self-identity of the bearers of the tradition.

The narrative that epitomizes this theme, and offers us a prototype of it, implicitly interpreting the narrative chain it introduces, is the story of the flood, that biting, ironic tale of Noah as the man whose story finally brought mankind 'relief' and 'reconciliation' (*nah*). In Noah, humanity finds an end to its alienation from the ground from which it was made (Gen. 5: 29). Just as Abraham's progeny was to be Yahweh's first-born and inheritance, to become a great people and to number as the stars of the sky and the sands of the sea, the creation story introduces a mankind created by the divine as his own child, in his image and likeness. God had blessed humanity that it might be fertile and fill the earth. The flood story opens just as 'the children of mankind had begun to multiply over the surface of the earth' (Gen. 6: 1). In contrast to the divine creator who sees all creation good, 'humanity's heart is such that he thinks only evil' (Gen. 6: 5). The story introduces a remarkable and disturbing motif that will echo ominously throughout all the stories to come. 'Yahweh regretted that he had ever created mankind, and he repented of it in his heart' (Gen. 6: 6). This theme of regret, and of the divine questioning the value of his creation, is a universal one tied to the philosophical dilemma of freedom: the intrinsic struggle between mankind and its destiny.

The story of Israel's origins that develops in the patriarchal narratives continues and reiterates the same themes. This creation too, Yahweh comes to regret. The Babel story is not about Babylon alone. Israel and all humanity was in the valley of Shinar. The story offers illustration of the nations scattered over the face of the earth. This account of Israel's origins that begins with the tower of Babel story is not a particularistic or a national epic. It is a universalist's narrative. Israel is the Bible's primary example of the 'way of all flesh'. It stands in contrast to the 'way of righteousness'. Old Israel's story is an etiological paradigm for all the world's humanity, whose hubris recurrently leads it 'to walk in the way of the godless' rather than in 'the path of the torah'.

The successive patriarchs are set in contrasting opposition to competitors: Abraham and Lot, Isaac and Ishmael, Jacob and Esau. The first chain of stories displays mere polar opposition. There is no conflict as such. The struggle is literarily ironic and controlled. Abraham is superior to Lot in generosity and in patronage. By his own choice, Lot moves to the fated land of the Dead Sea valley (Gen. 13). Through no choice of his own, he becomes the ancestor of the nations of the Transjordan, Ammon and Moab (Gen. 19). Abram is left the Cisjordan and is renamed Abraham, which Genesis 17: 5 interprets as a cue name. He will be 'the father of many nations'. It is this theme of Palestinian folklore that is used in the Abraham stories to introduce the dominant *topos* of the rejection of the first-born, as successively Palestine's Isaac is chosen over Arabia's Ishmael, Israel's Jacob over the Edomite Esau, and finally, in the Joseph story, Samaria's Ephraim is chosen to dominate the highlands of Manasseh. The story-line, however, is hardly triumphalist, but ironic and supersessionist: Israel's origin lies in being chosen against all expectation to be Yahweh's first-born and to receive the divine inheritance as interpreted in Genesis 49 and Deuteronomy 32. The predictive clouds of the flood story become darker against the coming twilight of the stories of Samaria's and Jerusalem's monarchies. God will come to repent once again his creation as we rediscover the reiterative warning against his first-born, that is implicit already in the flood story's closure. It is only as surviving remnant that Israel will inherit that promise, while Yahweh's first-born goes 'the way of all flesh'. So, Genesis 9: 14: 'When the clouds gather over the earth, and my bow is seen in them, I will remember my covenant . . . the waters will not destroy all that is flesh.' This is the God evoked in Jeremiah's great poem about Israel's restoration: 'With weeping they will come; pleading they will return. I will make them walk along streams of (life-giving) water; in the right path and they will not stumble in it; for I will be Israel's father and Ephraim (will be) my first-born' (Jer. 31: 9)!

A motif of family struggle between the parents of Isaac and Ishmael structures the patriarchal narratives. In both the stories of Isaac and Jacob, the mother favours the younger child and stands against the father. The motif is first introduced as Isaac's mother, Sarah, beats her Egyptian slave girl, Hagar, the mother of Ishmael, and forces her to flee (Gen. 16) to the desert's harshness. Sarah's violence against Hagar is replete with competitive contrasts to Exodus' well-known story of Pharaoh's harsh treatment of Isaac's descendants. In a doublet of the Hagar story, she is banished once again to the desert of her son's descendants (Gen. 21: 8–21). Ishmael's destiny is the historical Ishmaelites, early Arabs who lived in the desert lands to the south and east of Palestine.

The story of Isaac succeeds that of Abraham. It is, however, the third story of this series that bears the weight of the growing chain-narrative. It gains emphasis, confirms and closes the plots of the preceding segments of the chain. The Jacob and Esau theme of conflict takes over the centre of Genesis' stage. Even before they are born, the brothers fight within Rebecca's womb for their future (Gen. 25: 21–23). Their future destiny as hostile nations is the story of their birth. Esau, with his ruddy and hairy skin, marks Edom's red hills and the steppeland of Se'ir's goats. He is born first. Every nuance of Jacob's story bears upon the contortions of his struggle. Like Abraham before him, he is renamed, and both names, the old and the new, Jacob and Israel, function as 'cue names', representing old and new Israel. Their meanings are reflected in the story role their character plays, developing themes of both destiny and identity. In a series of puns, Jacob 'struggles' to 'supplant' Esau, and is born 'gripping' his brother's 'heel'. Jacob's name in Hebrew can mean 'deceive' and 'supplant' or 'grasp', and sounds like the word for 'heel'. So Jacob in his birth, grasping Esau's heel, is born to deceive and finally to supplant Esau as first-born. Similarly, the story will play with the name Israel, not only as the ancestor of the people Israel, but also as a pun on the Hebrew words 'struggle' (*sharit*) and 'to be straight' (*yashar*), including the sense 'to be right' or 'correct'. In the closing scene of Jacob's career as trickster, Jacob struggles with a night demon on the banks of the river Jabbok (Gen. 32: 24–32). Fighting him to a draw, Jacob forces the deity to give him a blessing before freeing him from the threatening dawn. God, accordingly, changes Jacob's name to Israel, 'because you have struggled with both God and men'. While this powerful naming story has the task of identifying Israel's essence and establishing its destiny as a new nation of righteousness through struggle 'with both God and men', it also plays a role within the Jacob and Esau story. With this wrestling scene, Jacob's relationship to Esau has been transformed. Prior to the visit of the night demon, Jacob dreaded meeting his brother and was in fear of his life. Now, however, they meet in peace and mutual recognition. It is no longer the scheming Jacob but now a 'just' Israel who meets his brother across the Jabbok. Esau is at peace in his Edom as Israel is in Shechem, a town near Mount Gerizim, through which Israel's religious future is identified as that of the 'children of Israel'; namely, the Samaritans who had their temple here.

The transformation motif of this tale's climax is revisited in the interpretive song of Deuteronomy 33, which Moses sings just before he dies. This commentary links the story of Israel's wilderness wandering with the conflict story of Jacob and Esau, and marks that story too as a story of supersession: the new surpasses the old. Israel's struggle with God in the wilderness is also over. Moses can now say farewell. Like the later exiles from Samaria's and Jerusalem's destructions, the whole of the wilderness generation has been rejected by God. The song prepares a new Israel to enter the land of promise. In the opening verses, Moses identifies Yahweh as a god from the lands of Sinai and Se'ir, a god from Edom's mountains. Moses identifies him as the transcendent, philosopher-king of the gods:

> Yahweh comes from Sinai; he rises up from Se'ir; he shines from Paran's mountain. 'You are from the army of gods.' In his right hand is his strength, yet he loves all peoples. The holy ones are in his power. 'They sit at your feet; they listen to your command.' The law which Moses gave us belongs to the gathering of Jacob, that there be a king (namely, Yahweh) in Yeshurun to gather the leaders of the people, the assembly of the tribes of Israel (Deut. 33: 2–5).

This god, Yahweh, here identified with Deuteronomy 32's *El Elyon*, holding the power of all the gods in his hands, gives not only Israel but the gods themselves his *torah*. This, of course, is the very law of Moses, which Deuteronomy paraphrases. It is this tradition, the 'law of Moses', which is now Jacob's property, the inheritance of all of Israel's tribes. In this last song of the Pentateuch, stories of ancestors and origins are interpreted in the form of teaching and instruction. The poet doesn't hesitate to transform the long chain of prose narrative his song closes with this interpretive revision. The tribes assemble on the borders of the promised land, ready to leave the wilderness and cross the Jordan with Joshua. Like Jacob before them, they are on their journey to Shechem. They set out to meet once again in Joshua 24. Shechem, the forerunner of Samaria with its temple on Mount Gerizim, is where Yahweh is Israel's king, where his law and *torah* is to be its wealth. In Deuteronomy's interpretation, the story of Jacob supplanting Esau leaves the realm of ethnographic commentary and becomes religious story. Those strugglers with God, surviving the wilderness, now enter their inheritance. Moses' song interprets and transposes the metaphor of promised land into law and *torah*. Even the gods must sit at Yahweh's feet and study *torah*.

When Joshua enters Canaan, Israel's enemies are the Canaanites, the eponymous aborigines of the 'land of Canaan'. Obedience to Yahweh's *torah* leads Israel victoriously to Shechem. It is there that they pledge their allegiance to Yahweh and reject the gods of their ancestors. They have peace while Joshua is alive. In the following stories of the judges and of Saul and David's kingdom, the role of enemies is taken over by 'Philistines' of Palestine's coastal region. It is the acceptance of Yahweh, the extent to which he is recognized as king and patron, that confirms Israel's fate. In I Samuel 15, because Saul does what he himself sees as right, Yahweh rejects him and chooses David to take his place. In these stories, both the Canaanites and the Philistines, like the Egyptians of the Exodus story, are mere puppets of Yahweh's will. The real struggle is a religious one. It is the struggle for the recognition of Yahweh as Israel's king and patron. The Book of Kings offers a variant on this theme in the Solomon stories. Intermarriage with foreigners and worship of foreign gods becomes the competing path of darkness in Israel's struggle for true religion. Similarly, just as Solomon's wealth marks him as a great king, the rival of emperors, his wealth also corrupts. His final apostasy causes his kingdom to be divided between north and south. Israel and Samaria follow the 'path of evil', while Judah and Jerusalem follow haltingly the 'path of Yahweh'. The Book of II Kings leads us through the stories of Jeroboam and of 'those who follow in the path of Jeroboam', such as Ahab and Jezebel. The story is drawn in black and white and pits evil against good. The role of the good is finally highlighted with the massacre in which Elijah brutally and ruthlessly murders all of the Ba'al prophets of the north.

What takes the pattern of an alternating cycle of good and evil culminates in a reiterated closure of punishment and destruction: first of Samaria and then Jerusalem. On this 'day of wrath', Israel's God visits his people with the armies which are described as armies of Yahweh's servants; namely, the kings of Assyria and Babylonia. It is in this double closure of total destruction that the narrative's fundamental polarity returns with clarity. That contrasting conflict is no more between Jerusalem and Samaria than it is between Jacob and Esau. It certainly never lay between Israel and the Canaanites or the Philistines. 'Israel' has rather played a role within a morality story. The role it has played is for all humanity. Israel struggled with God: a destiny defined already in the stories of Genesis 1–11 as one which is everyman's fate. To struggle with God is to be human, the fate of all. One might argue that Israel is presented as a nation that has lost its inheritance. One might, however, better say – more in line with the tradition – that it is neither the land nor the kingdom, neither Samaria nor Jerusalem, but God's *torah* which is the true inheritance. The bearers and collectors of this tradition understand themselves as survivors, as remnants returning, and as belonging to a 'new Israel'. This is not merely a history as tradition accumulated. It is an interpreted tradition. This story of old Israel defines for the bearers of the tradition the truth of being human.

These stories of polarity and conflict in the biblical origin traditions about old Israel are not stories that reflect the regional and ethnic conflicts of the past. Those are merely illustrations of what is for the tradition a transcendent conflict between good and evil. The ultimate conflict, reiterated through all of the struggles of this traditional past, involves the divine search for a people, for those who reject the 'way of men' and, unlike old Israel, unlike Samaria and the Jerusalem of the past, commit themselves to the values of a true Israel of the *torah*. The Bible's story of conflict and war, from Moses to Joshua and to Jerusalem's destructions, are reiterative occurrences of the eternal struggle between God's will and the hubris of mankind.

The story does not come to rest. It ends problematically. We do not have an origin tradition that closes with a sense of belonging. The story closes in rejection on the day of wrath. With Samaria's and Jerusalem's fall from grace, reiterating the fall of Sodom and Gomorrah, Israel re-enters with Lot the wilderness cave of exile to wait for a new creation. The bearers of this tradition are not the Israel whom Yahweh had set out to create in Genesis with his promises to Abraham. Nor are they the Israel who were people chosen to be Yahweh's first-born in Exodus, the Israel who had received the *torah*, obedience to which would make them an eternal people of God. That Israel never came to be. We have an origin tradition in the Pentateuch, and a story of Israel becoming a great nation in Joshua, Judges and the Books of Samuel, only to discover that our 'people' is the generation that was lost for forty years in the wilderness. Hardly a people of God, they are the apostates of Samaria and the backsliders of Judah. They are an Israel that had been worthy of destruction at the hands of Yahweh's servant Nebuchadnezzar. Recipients as they are of Yahweh's eternal promise to his servant David, it is a promise that Yahweh repents having made. The story hardly ends in mercy or grace. 'Yahweh did not turn from his great wrath, which burned against Judah. Rather, he decreed: "I will rid myself of Judah as well just as I took away Israel. I will reject this city, Jerusalem, that I had chosen: this house, in which I once said that my name would live" ' (II Kings 23: 26f.). The curtain falls on David's eternal dynasty with the scene of his humiliated successor receiving his daily ration of food in Babylon . . . 'every day, all the days of his life' (II Kings 25: 30).

4 The Bible as survival literature

To involve ourselves in this question of the history of biblical Israel's origins, we first need to identify the historical context of these origins. From what perspective is the question of origins being asked? It is important to recognize that such a context cannot be found within a *history of events* in Palestine. Origins belong to the intellectual and literary worlds, not to the world of events, either political or social. Such constructs are aspects of *intellectual history*. The historical question of biblical Israel's origins begins within the intellectual concepts that formed the central core of Israel's tradition as a whole. Israel's origins are to be sought in that complex composite of legal, cultic and folk tradition, whose preservation was central to the formation of a self-understanding linked quite specifically to the 'new Israel' that the tradition both creates and gives an identity to.

The Bible might well be described as a survival literature, if you will. Certainly, it is a literature that offers an understanding of themselves as survivors to those who identify with it as their own tradition. These bearers of the tradition understand themselves as the ubiquitous 'children of Israel'. Certainly the early *shomronim,* or Samaritans, of the Hellenistic period understood themselves as these same 'children of Israel'. Their descendants still do today. They also understood themselves as the 'new Israel', much in the manner we find in II Chronicles. This often sectarian concept also occurs in some of the Dead Sea scrolls, in the New Testament and elsewhere among other early Jewish texts. Whatever actual term of self-identification is used, the voice implied in the tradition is one that understands itself either in terms of a surviving remnant from old Israel, or as a resurrected or reborn Israel. Through its process of collecting traditions, some of which can, as we have seen, be traced back to the Iron Age, the tradition represents itself as truly from the past. It is composed of fragments of memory: written and oral, chains of narrative and more complex literary works, administrative records, songs, prophetic sayings, the words of philosophers, lists, and stories. All are understood as meaningful within a cumulative whole, a discriminatingly assembled and organized *torah* and commentary on the origins of the *torah*. These writings are all interpreted in the tradition as a past now shattered.

The 'exile' – that event of the past in which Israel was carried off from its homeland first by the Assyrians and then by the Babylonians – plays a central role in the formation of the Bible's tradition. However, the importance of the exile in the Bible is hardly that of the historical events that overwhelmed the populations of ancient Samaria or Jerusalem during the Iron Age. Rather it is a metaphor for the psychological events from which new beginnings are launched. 'Exile' is the means by which those who identify themselves with the tradition can understand themselves as saved. The radical trauma of exile is used as a literary paradigm by which the collectors of the tradition identify both themselves and the tradition as belonging to 'the way of the *torah*'. In the many forms of what we might call early Judaism, the individual came to identify with Israel as one of the 'children of Israel', the surviving remnant of lost Israel. Identification with the stories of exile made this possible, whether or not one's ancestors had ever actually come from Babylon, from Nineveh, or from Egypt, or whether they had always, or had never, been in Palestine. To identify with the true Israel was to find one's roots in the reflected glory of a Davidic empire lost, in the failed conquests of Joshua, and in the wilderness with Moses' lost generation.

This central core of biblical tradition, this *torah* of instruction, was centred on the belief in a universal and transcendent God. This belief is more philosophical than religious; in fact, it was a way of understanding traditional religions that had ceased to be entirely acceptable within the Persian and Hellenistic periods. As the ancient world had became increasingly integrated by the political and economic controls of empire – already at work in the Assyrian period – ideas about the gods began to change accordingly. Polytheism, which had its roots in the complexity of life as well as in the many different groups interacting within any single society, began to give way to an increasingly integrated sense of divine power that was transcendent, beyond human understanding, and apart from people as well as peoples. Such distant power, mirroring also the increasingly distant and centralized seat of political power, was often expressed by the concept of a 'God of gods' and especially 'the God of heaven'. The roots of monotheism are planted deeply within polytheism itself. Polytheism and monotheism were hardly originally antagonistic forms of thought. In the ancient world, we already find both a universal and an inclusive monotheism in Syria of the Assyrian period. *Ba'al Shamem* is understood as God and comprised all that was meant by the divine. This 'Lord of Heaven' is comparable to the Neo-Babylonian concept of a spiritual, heavenly supreme deity, such as the god named Sin we find in the ancient city of Harran. He is the universal God of heaven and creator of all. Such a god is known to the Persians as Ahura Mazda and shows up in the Bible as *El Elyon* and *Elohei Shamayim* ('God most high' and 'the God of heaven'). The world-view that this kind of understanding implies, coming as it does out of the growing perception of imperial power as both universal and transcendent of any particular people's politics, is comparable to the philosophy of the Greek writer Plato. Transcendent reality and the divine is one, true, good and beautiful. It is beyond human perception, which deals only with particular images and mere reflections of the ideal. So too, the God of heaven is beyond human ability to understand. The divine as people experience it – through the diverse regional and particular gods and their cults – is a limited reflection of that transcendent reality. The Bible is a literary work that has its roots in this intellectual transformation of antiquity.

CHAPTER 2

Confusing stories with historical evidence

1 Confusing naive realism with historical method

However much archaeologists might need a story world to flesh out the bones of their history, or however much they might wish that the Bible's nations were scattered among their potsherds, the wish for the Bible to be history has only confused the discussion about how the Bible relates to the past. The Bible's world does not belong to the discipline of archaeologists. It has never been found in any tell: not even Jericho or Megiddo. The question is not really the simple one of historicity: whether the Bible's tales in fact happened, or might be dramatically illustrated with the help of biblical archaeology's naive realism. Of course, there was an Israel! The name itself is used already at the close of the Late Bronze Age on an Egyptian monument to refer to the people of Canaan that Pharaoh Merenptah's military campaign into Palestine fought against. But it is not this Israel that the Bible deals with. Our question involves more complicated issues of literary historicality and reference, of metaphor and literary postures, evocation and conviction. The Bible doesn't deal with what happened in the past. It deals with what was thought, written and transmitted within an interacting intellectual tradition.

It may perhaps appear strange that so much of the Bible deals with the origin traditions of a people that never existed as such. This metaphorical nation's land and language; this imagined people's history, moreover, is an origin tradition that belongs to the 'new Israel', not the old. The Bible does not give us Israel's story about its past – or any origin story confirming Israel's self-identity or national self-understanding. The tradition gave not Israel but Judaism an identity, not as a 'nation' among the *goyim*, but as a people of God: an Israel *redivivus* in the life of piety. Naively realistic questions about historicity have always been most out of place when it has come to Israel's origins – if only for the fact that the genre of origin stories that fills so much of the Bible relates hardly at all to historical events, to anything that might have happened. It rather reflects constitutional questions of identity. In the history of the scholarship – both Jewish and Christian – that has been interested in historicizing these origin stories, central questions have too often turned on uncritical and arbitrary choices: Which of the Bible's many stories of origin are to be read as if they were narratives about *events* of the past, and which are to be discarded as *mere* story? Each choice made involved the elimination of alternative stories. Each affirmation of the historicity or historical rootedness of one tradition bore with it implicit denials of the historicity of an alternative tradition. Each positivistic assertion that this or that aspect of tradition was 'rooted in history' bore with it a covert denial of other traditions. Hidden in the choice of the patriarchs and the conquest as epitomizing biblical archaeology's 'assured results', had been the denial of historicity to other hardly less viable alternative origin stories. But, even so, scholars never asserted the historicity of the narratives of Genesis as we have them, nor of the patriarchs as persons as the Bible presents them. They did not try to claim that the stories of Genesis and Joshua happened just so. After all, these scholars were archaeologists. They were interested in Jericho's walls, not Joshua's trumpets. Ever loyal to their wider interests in constructing the history of the whole of the ancient Near East, they were inclined to find the stories of the Pentateuch distantly reflecting early West Semitic or 'Amorite' migrations from Ur, from Mesopotamia, from Egypt and from the Sinai. Many chose Joshua and his invasion stories in preference to the stories that open the Book of Judges, but they never understood them as very specific. They thought of them as long-fictionalized 'memories' of a real historical conquest by semi-nomads. Such a conquest also served the important archaeological function of explaining what was thought to be an historical-cultural transition from the Late Bronze period to the Iron Age.

Others focused on different stories for their historical reconstructions, and therefore found it necessary to dismiss the tales of Genesis and Joshua 6–12 as fiction. Some preferred the legend of Joshua 24, and the less bellicose stories of Judges 1–3. While arguing effectively against accepting the stories of Joshua as historical memory, they passed in silence the conquest stories of Judah and Simeon in Judges 1. They did not try to explain the Bible. They raided it for whatever they found illustrative or useful for their own historical interests. As the archaeological excavation of the tell of Jericho led to an affirmation of Jericho's conquest for some, others preoccupied with anthropological questions supported the preference of a more peaceful process of transition and change. For them, not armies of conquest, but transhumance shepherds moved into the region, took control of unoccupied grazing areas, and gradually evolved into a small village culture of farmers, which they could imagine to be early Israel. In this way, they created a transition from a Palestine dominated by Canaanite city-states in the lowlands during the Late Bronze Age to an early Iron Age controlled by sedentarizing Israelites developing regional and national states in the highlands. Their goal was neither to interpret nor to understand the Bible, but to use it as illustration for their archaeological research.

Debate and disagreement about how the Bible was to be used for history hardened the process of such selective affirmation and increased conviction that the theological meaning of a biblical tradition hung on an understanding of the stories as reports. Questions about the accuracy of what had become the imaginary equivalents of war correspondents, created burning issues for historical scholarship over two generations. The historical scenarios involved in the debate took on a life of their own. The nature and validity of the Bible was being defended in these debates, but the texts themselves were hardly seriously consulted. 'Plain readings' were preferred. The presence or absence of collapsed fortifications and the nature of nomadism and its relationship to the villages of the South Levant were matched to harmonized readings of the Bible.

In German scholarship of the 1930s to the 1950s, historical explanations of Israel's origins were based on a specific analogy from classical antiquity of ancient cultic assemblies of twelve tribes. This ancient Greek 'amphictyony' was seen as confirming the Bible's stories about the twelve tribes of Israel. Joshua 24 was identified as an origin story of just such a cultic union. This historicized tribal union was linked to the story in Joshua 4 of Israel's crossing of the Jordan, and to the collection of narratives about God speaking to Moses from Mount Sinai in Exodus 19–29. Like Moses' victory 'song of the sea' in Exodus 15, the story of God speaking to Moses from the burning bush in Exodus 3–6 and Moses' farewell speeches in Deuteronomy, Joshua 24's story of a tribal pact with Yahweh was recognized as an historical event that had created Israel as a nation. In spite of other well-known origin stories, scholars chose to argue that this story in Joshua reflected historical realities of the past rather than an intellectual or literary understanding. The competing historiographical constructs of this common theological agenda hid the fundamental irrationality of the scholarly project as a whole. One could be either for a conquest or for a peaceful settlement, as if there were not dozens of equally unverifiable alternatives among the Bible's near-endless stream of origin stories. Why did the Americans and the Israelis not concentrate on *Jerusalem*'s conquest? This city offered a threefold wealth of stories of its conquest by early Israel. Why did they choose to use Jericho, Ai and Hazor for their arguments? From the Bible's perspective, all variants were equally plausible. Was the decision meretriciously decided because Jericho, Ai and Hazor were being dug? Have the competing sides of the biblical-archaeological debates been determined by who had dug what? It is hardly accidental that when Germany lost power and influence in the Middle East after World War One and, as a result, German archaeologists found it increasingly difficult to excavate in British Mandate Palestine, German theologians a generation later ceased to be interested in interpreting the Bible with the help of destruction levels of great tells. The interests of British and American scholarship in such efforts increased, however, while interests in surface explorations and settlement theories, based as they were on methods demanding only a modest level of direct involvement in archaeology, grew among German scholars throughout the early post-war period. Such strategies were determined by the financial realities of archaeological field work, not by questions posed by biblical studies. Was a reading of the Bible ever seriously engaged in the theories of biblical archaeology, or were such theories, which in fact interpreted the Bible, more involved in how archaeology was developing? The European excavations at Shechem, Shiloh and Jericho were set against those of the American and Israeli excavations at Tell Beit Mirsim, Hazor and Et-Tell in nearly a half-century of debate. This was of great benefit to both the standards and the quantity of field archaeology carried out in Palestine. However, to what extent has twentieth-century historical work in Palestine been determined by the lack of a theological focus among the biblical scholars who participated? I can think of no better argument against theologians and biblical scholars continuing to dominate archaeological and historical research than that it has kept them from reading the texts that should be the centre of their research.

Today, theories of tribal federations no longer fit the world of Palestine's early history, and few take an early Israelite conquest of Canaan as historically plausible. Yet, although the original arguments and the evidence accumulated on their behalf have long left the debate, both the conclusions and the methods that created them still remain, spectral as they may be. Most scholars still look to Iron I settlements for the origins of a people called Israel, and they still look to a David or a Solomon and to a 'united monarchy' in the archaeology of the tenth century BCE as a key for solving the uncertainties of archaeology's chronological and interpretive frameworks. Why? And more specifically, why this harmony and not another? Is it harmonious? Is it plausible? Are benefits gained by using such biblical frameworks worth the problems they create in an academically responsible archaeology? While the financial benefits of tying the Bible to archaeology have increased, historical and intellectual benefits have just as rapidly diminished.

Finding an archaeological Jerusalem fit for a David, for example, is proving just as difficult and more embarrassing than it was to find an archaeologically suitable Ai or Jericho for a Joshua three generations ago. Archaeology has need for a sound historical perspective of ancient Palestine as a background and canvas on which to work. Biblical studies is no less interested in an historically sound context for its texts. These quite different functions and goals are certain to ensure continued differences as long as both Palestinian archaeology and biblical studies play out their roles of divorced parents of a history over which they share custodial interests. In the past, biblical scholars had been reluctant to give up their influence and control over archaeology's role in the writing of history. Today, biblical archaeology must give up its historicized Bible as the intellectual centre of its historiography.

It hasn't helped that those who are interested in the development of historical research in this region have avoided the implications of the mythical and literary overtones that are a constant of all of the Bible's stories. They have chosen rather a rhetoric that supports the assumption of historicity. For example, even when speaking of stories filled with literary fantasy, they speak of a 'biblical record' and of the Bible's 'account of the past'. This rhetoric of archaeology avoids the useful scepticism that historians usually have ready at hand whenever iron is reported to float on water.

Certainly the favourite choice in the history of scholarship for an archaeological argument for biblical historicity – the story of Jericho's walls – demonstrates that lack of plausibility or verisimilitude in a story hardly ever hinders the historicizing imagination. The Bible's story in Joshua 2 and 5: 13–6: 27 begins with Joshua sending two spies into Jericho. They come to 'Rahab the prostitute's' house, built into the city wall. Rahab later hides the Israelite spies when a search is made for them. In reward for her help, she is instructed to tie a scarlet thread to her window, so that she and her house may be spared the city's destruction. The motif is a close variation on the episode in Exodus 12: 22 where Moses instructs all the Israelites to paint the blood of the passover lamb on their doorways, so that, seeing the blood, the messenger of death will 'pass over' their houses and they will be spared. When Joshua lays siege to Jericho, his army is led by another angel of death: the heavenly 'commander of Yahweh's army'. He tells Joshua to march around the city. This he is to do each day for six days, while seven priests blow trumpets. Joshua obeys. On the seventh day, they march around the city seven times. When the Israelites hear the sound of the trumpet, they shout and the walls fall down. Except for the house of Rahab and her family, the entire city is destroyed and burnt.

How can such a story have anything to do with archaeology, or with an archaeologically supported reconstruction of an historical past? What does one look for in an excavation that would ever confirm the history of such a story? How do you recognize a prostitute's house in a dig? Would you look for the scarlet thread, or would a house within a wall which had not collapsed be enough? Would you look for walls that have collapsed without observable cause? Or is one left to a treasure hunt for the trumpets? As it is, they never found the walls at all. This has resulted in the archaeological discussion deteriorating into a quarrel about chronology in an effort to save the story for history!

One of the Bible's most delightful and most implausible stories is that of the spies in Numbers 13–14. Its account is of a magic valley of giants, the grandeur and fantastic fertility of which is expressed by the motif of a land whose rivers flow with milk and honey. Certainly, this is the stuff of Homer's Odyssey. Most, I think, would agree that this tale is an implausible candidate for historicity. Far preferable would be our story's demythologized variant, which we can find when we turn to the first chapter in the Book of Deuteronomy. Yet, for all of Deuteronomy's greater realism, few exegetes would give this version preference over the preposterous tale in the Book of Numbers. Not only is Numbers' story more interesting as adventure tale, but it is linked, as we shall see when we return once again to this story, with Genesis 6: 4's mysterious Nephilim: the children resulting from sons of God marrying beautiful women. It is ironic that it is the Book of Numbers' unbelievable, mythological variant of the tale, and not the more 'realistic' version in Deuteronomy that has provided biblical archaeological scholarship with a basis for calculating its 'historical' chronology for the exodus from Egypt as having been forty years earlier than Israel's entry into Palestine. It is the story of Numbers that closes with the divine punishment of Israel for its lack of trust in Yahweh's leadership. This serves to explain why Israel was sent back into the desert to wander for forty years. Biblical archaeology does not hesitate to use the chronology, although it rejects the historicity of the story that gives that chronology its foundation. The acceptance of just such calculations is typical of biblical archaeology's extraordinary confidence in the accuracy of the Bible's chronology.

As a whole, we historians have not done very well in using biblical stories to write our history with. If one feels bound to understand the history of Israel as a revision of the Bible's traditions, one must admit the near total lack of warrant that these stories have for being accepted as historical. Nevertheless, to begin with archaeological evidence apart from any particular Bible stories is not of much help either. This has been apparent ever since archaeologists first recognized the indigenous character of the South Levant's material culture. If an Israel once entered Palestine from outside, we have no evidence for this in the archaeological record. But, of course, if such a people had always been part of the population of this region, we equally lack evidence.

We need to ask, moreover, why we have always assumed that biblical Israel was inautochthonous, that is, a people who came from outside Palestine. Even this nearly unanimously assumed understanding of the biblical story does not have clear warrant in the Bible itself. The primary plot-line of Genesis 11 describes the spread of mankind after the building of Babylon's tower is abandoned. This 'spread' accomplishes much the same result as the table of nations of Genesis 10. It distinguishes an originally united humanity of one family and language, according to known peoples, regions and languages. The geographical names represented by the 'children' of Noah offer a genealogical origin story or 'aetiology' of the three great continents of the ancient world. In Genesis 11 we are given a list of *Shem*'s descendants, which describes the spread of *the Semites* throughout Asia. We come to Terah, to his Aramaean sons and eventually to the stories of Abraham. These narratives offer legendary origins of nations as Abraham fathers them according to their lands and languages. Such genealogies and stories are not history writing, but folk aetiologies. Through such tales, Abraham is brought to the land that is to be his destiny. Implicit is an understanding that Abraham and his descendants, including the biblical Israel, are indigenous to Palestine. He is the ancestor of Palestine's population. Just like all the other cities and peoples in this geographic picture of the ancient world, the nations of Abraham spread each to their own land. Genesis 11: 26–12: 4, which tells the story of Terah leaving Ur and of Abraham's call from Harran, does not present ancient Israel as having been foreign to Palestine, however much competing origin stories may. This story expresses Hellenism's belief in the common origin and universal quality of humanity, in spite of its obvious diversity. Israel becomes an alien people first when the family of Jacob enters Egypt at the end of Genesis. From Egypt it returns to the land of its fathers. Such implications of an indigenous Israel are neither unique nor accidental.

Deuteronomy 32 similarly recalls the ancient knowledge of the gods' division of the world according to its many peoples, each people with its own god. The origin story implied in this song sits comfortably together with Exodus 3–6, a central story in the long chain of narrative that takes us from the creation in Genesis to the destruction of Jerusalem in II Kings. As Abraham separates from Lot, the story world gives an explanation of how the real world's Ammonites and Moabites are both related to and distinct from the other ancient peoples of Palestine. When Isaac separates from Ishmael and Jacob from Esau, Arabs, Edomites and Israelites each find their destinies as peoples of the region. This organization of stories of patriarchs and their genealogical lists has its roots in the origin tales of ancient geography, well known to us also in traditions from both ancient Greece and pre-Islamic Arabia.

There is also another and quite different structure, which runs throughout the biblical narratives and casts the story of old Israel in a reiterated pattern of conflicts and opposition. When Joshua enters Palestine, Israel finds its opponents in the legendary Midianites, Canaanites, Amorites and Jebusites. The mythic quality of these enemies is often described, like the traditional twelve enemies in texts about Assyrian military campaigns, by a recurrent often-shifting grouping of six legendary enemies of old Israel: the Amorites and the Hittites, the Perizites and the Canaanites, the Hivites and the Jebusites (Exodus 23: 23). In Judges and in the stories of Saul and David, Israel's enemies are called 'the Philistines'. They are described as a single people, established in a Hellenistic grouping of five cities, a *pentapolis* on Palestine's southern coast. The name of this legendary people, in fact, dates back at least a thousand years to Late Bronze Age Egyptian references to Aegean immigrants who settled in the Egyptian delta and along the southern coast of Palestine. They were the *Peleset*. This name from Egyptian texts is echoed in the Iron Age name for the region of southern Syria as a whole, *Palashtu* or *Palæstina*, which we find in both Assyrian texts and in the writings of the Greek writer Herodotus, and which is later adopted by the Romans.

In II Kings, the biblical dichotomy between old Israel and its enemies is recast. Judah and Jerusalem take over the primary roles of nations opposed in conflict and hatred, as Jacob and Esau had been in Genesis. This literary motif, mirroring as it does the breakup of Alexander's empire between a Seleucid north and a Ptolemaic south, is later picked up by the Roman period writer Josephus as a religiously implicated conflict between true 'Jews' and schismatic 'Samaritans'. The biblical polarity of north and south does not have its roots in politics and wars of Palestine's past. It is, rather, a sectarian way of thinking that reflects an understanding of the world as it appears to the writers of our texts. The variations of such conflicts are endless. Again and again, the polarity surfaces in our narratives, as long as we have stories to reference. It is a moral world of black and white, of good and evil locked in eternal conflict. The reader is offered a radical choice. One walks either in the 'path of righteousness', in the 'way of the torah', in 'God's way', or one 'walks in the way of sinners' and 'seeks the counsel of the godless'. There is no middle way and no alternative to this choice. This sectarian mode of seeing reality is behind the varying contrasts so constantly reiterated in the biblical narrative of old Israel as rejected, standing against a new Israel of promise. The story of Israel's origins as a people is the story of Exodus: an old Israel of slavery in Egypt leads through a wilderness crossing to a new life, a return to a land that Yahweh has prepared. The story of testing and purification in the desert crossing with Moses has not only created a metaphorical paradigm for countless stories answering to the human longing for hope and salvation from oppression, it already reflects an established biblical metaphor and tale-type that is reiterated throughout the Bible.

The story of Israel's exodus has three very close variants. The first we find in the song of Moses' vision in Deuteronomy 32. This sings of the desert from which Yahweh carried Israel 'on eagle's wings', an image echoed in Psalm 91: 11–12's voice of piety: 'He will give his angels instruction to protect you in your every path; they will carry you in their hands that you not stub your foot on a stone . . .' Psalm 34: 7 establishes this pious metaphor on a basis of theological principle: 'The angel of Yahweh camps around those who fear Him, and he will rescue them.' This motif is echoed and expanded with interpretive overtones of a saint surviving the suffering of spiritual purification in the story of Elijah at

Horeb, in I Kings 19: 1–18 when the great prophet, despairing of his life, goes out into the desert to discover the truth of Yahweh's silent voice. He returns from the desert – himself living out the role of the lost generation – to preach a new life of the remnant of Israel saved.

It is in Jeremiah's description of the desert's nothingness that we come once again to the root of the metaphor. This spiritual nothingness of the wilderness in Jeremiah is Jerusalem's destruction in Jeremiah 4. It is from this that a new beginning and a new Israel springs. Speaking as the prophet with Yahweh's voice, Jeremiah complains, offering echoes of Genesis' garden story: 'My people are fools; they do not know me. They are stupid children, without understanding, skilled in doing evil, but do not know how to do good' (Jer. 4: 22). Yahweh had been described as a hot wind from the desert threatening Jerusalem (Jer. 4: 11–17). Now Jeremiah has a vision of Jerusalem's destruction for playing the fool of the garden story: 'I looked on the earth and it was shapeless and empty . . . I looked, the fruitful land was a desert' (Jer. 4: 23–26). Such metaphor, seeing Jerusalem's destruction as a desert that Israel must enter, is couched in the terms of the origin story of the world, created from nothingness. It is not just a national story about Jerusalem or Israel. Jerusalem is a motif which mirrors all humanity, which has its creative centre in the story of the origins of the world that we find in Genesis 1. As we have seen already, the creation story uses the same metaphor as Jeremiah's *tohu wa-bohu*, an 'empty and shapeless' desert, from which a new Israel must be born. One must enter the desert to find the new creation. This is a world that stands opposed to Genesis 11's caricature of *Jerusalem* in the story of the primordial Babel, with its city and tower built by men's hands.

When we now turn to answer the question about the audience for such reiterative echoes of the metaphors of the desert, purification and new beginnings, which we hear whenever we open the Bible, there is little need to guess. The literature itself has created clear expectations. When we ask for whom the Bible was written, it is hardly a particular historical event that confronts us. It is the historical context of an intellectual world of piety and philosophy that sees itself in terms of a very emphatic construct. I would describe this as a learned world of discourse and commentary, centred in a philosophical discussion about tradition. The world-view is sectarian in its structure. It is created by those who understand themselves as seekers after truth. It is critical thought: distinguishing the opinion of fools from sound reflection, understanding and wisdom. One could well cite Plato's Socrates as expressing the central ideology of the Bible's composition: to know oneself is the beginning of wisdom.

The Bible's compilers, however, speak more metaphorically, with a touch of religious piety, but hardly less critically. The beginning of wisdom is 'the fear of God'. That is 'righteousness'; that is philosophy. However, the 'fear of God', that appears in so much of the Bible's philosophical writing, is not quite the same as the 'terror of God' one can find it dressing up as in a story world – not even poor Job's nightmare Yahweh, roaring from his whirlwind (Job 38–41). 'Fear of God' and 'righteousness' begins, Plato-like, in the self-understanding of human ignorance. It is nothing other than the respect understood as due the unknown and unfathomable, the transcendent God of Heaven. Wisdom begins in the recognition of our ignorance. God is known to us – to paraphrase Job – only as we have heard about him (Job 42: 5). Even Yahweh, that formidable God of ancient Israel, is God as Israel has known him: a human God: a God for us. This world of philosophical discourse, which I would identify with the authorial voice implied throughout biblical narrative, addresses the reader most directly and immediately in the wisdom literature of Proverbs and especially Ecclesiastes, and most emphatically in the Book of Psalms. This voice speaks clearly and forcefully to us in the confident cadences of Psalm 1 and 2's joint introduction to the Psalter:

> Blessed is he who does not follow the counsel of the ungodly, who does not walk in the path of sinners, who does not sit among those who scorn, but who has his joy in Yahweh's torah and bases his life in his law, day and night. He is like a tree who is planted on the banks of a canal. It will bear fruit at the right time and its leaves never fall. Everything he does survives . . . Happy is everyone who seeks refuge in Him.

The way of thinking, the emphatically sectarian world-view, implicit in such a song is a reflection of the historical reality that gave rise to our literary traditions. The ungodly, like the lost generation, remain marooned in an empty wasteland – a desert of the spirit. This is the motif that is reiterated throughout the tradition of the stories of Israel murmuring against Moses, in Jeremiah's vision of Jerusalem's destruction as a return to the nothingness before creation, and, as we shall see, in I Samuel's great story of Saul's fall from grace. All of these stories and songs exist to celebrate the believer's ultimate victory over the ungodly. Such pietism has historical roots not in a distant past, but in the philosophical preoccupations of the implied audience.

Associations between a lost and faithless generation in the wandering stories and the story of Samaria and Jerusalem and their 'destruction' are particularly marked. Many narratives reiterate this common theme. They do not reflect events of the past, but interpret narrative traditions about the past, reflecting the historical piety of the collectors of the traditions. An origin story is not so much a story that relates the origins of a people, as a narrative within a genre of literature. It gives expression to what is understood as essential to a group's self-identity. Its historical context lies within the structure of a given society's concept of reality. The didactic theme 'happy are those who seek refuge in Yahweh' is the dominant theme of the Psalter and of its 'theology of the way'. It is within such a discourse about tradition and the past that the Bible has its historical roots.

2 The Bible's many views of the past

When one begins to describe historical developments within the regions of South Syria on the basis of archaeological data, one finds a very different picture of Palestine's past than in many books of biblical archaeology. The sketch of ancient Israel that comes from a harmonizing of archaeology with the biblical story is not congruent with the Bible's view. Even if one were to adopt the most conservative of methods urged by scholars today, and try to accept a 'biblical view of the past' wherever this has not been proven false, one faces nearly insurmountable difficulties. Removing the unbelievable and the impossible, correcting what is clearly wrong and tendentious, and reconstructing what remains in a more or less coherent account is hardly adequate and fails to deal with the Bible's unhistorical qualities. Removing miracles or God from the story does not help an historian, it only destroys narratives. One can never arrive at a viable history with such an approach.

For example, consider the question of how the Israelites of the Bible come to occupy Jerusalem. In Joshua 10, Jerusalem's king, Adonizedek, the leader of five Amorite kings, was defeated by Joshua and his army in a running battle. Yahweh killed more enemies than Joshua did by throwing huge stones down on them from heaven. The kings were captured hiding in a cave and executed by Joshua. To endorse this story, the author tells us that five of these large stones are laid at the entrance of the cave 'to this day'.

The humour of this closing ought not be missed. The author is very aware of the audience's critical sensibilities. Just as Yahweh is hurling the large stones down from heaven, killing the enemy, the dead are described as having been killed by 'hailstones'. After all, everyone knows – even the minimalist – that God sends hailstones. And this is where the author traps his listeners! The memorial set up at the cave, five of Yahweh's stones, is an obvious argument for the story's historicity. Such an argument is a common folktale motif, quite like the closure of Hans Christian Andersen's story of 'the princess and the pea' with its historicizing details that the pea is still in the museum . . . 'that is, if someone hasn't stolen it'.

Similarly, in allowing Yahweh's stones to be hailstones, the biblical author intentionally subverts his monument to the tale's historical authenticity! Such deconstructive humour highlights some of the difficulties that occur when such a story is taken for history by readers of any time. We simply cannot escape the discomfort of this glimpse of the author laughing at us. The laughter won't be resolved if one tries to remove the big stones, the melted hailstones or God from the story.

While Joshua 10 tells this tale about the defeat of Jerusalem's king, Joshua 18 tells of Jerusalem being given as spoils of war to the tribe of Benjamin. This narrative obviously confirms the assumption of the story of chapter 10 that the city of Jerusalem was one of the cities of Joshua's conquest, part of what one might call Joshua's 'view of the past'.

Judges 1, on the other hand, sets its tale of Jerusalem's conquest to a time after Joshua had died. Jerusalem is not Amorite in this story, but Canaanite. Even more surprising, it is Jacob's sons, the founders and patriarchs of the tribes themselves, Judah and Simeon, who defeat the Canaanites in Jerusalem, kill the inhabitants and burn the city to the ground. Accordingly, in I Samuel 17: 54, Jerusalem is already part of Israel, when the young David brings Goliath's head there as a trophy!

Yet a third story of Jerusalem's conquest is offered to us. It comes in two variations: one in II Samuel 5: 6–10, and the other in I Chronicles 11: 4–9. Both offer aetiologies of Jerusalem as 'City of David' and 'Fortress of Zion'. The capture of Jerusalem in this tale is set during David's reign as king in Hebron. Jerusalem is neither Amorite nor Canaanite; it is a Jebusite city, as in the story of Judges 19: 10–12. Drawing on motifs well-known from Homer's sack of Troy, Jerusalem's fortifications are presented as so strong that it could not be successfully stormed. What cannot be taken by storm needs to be taken by wit and courage. Joab enters the city by stealth, crawling up the water tunnel whose construction II Kings 20: 20 has described as one of the great deeds of Hezekiah. Ignoring both the story's tradition in epics of war and its anachronism, this most famous of Jerusalem conquest stories has become an essential part of biblical archaeology's view of the past. That three different books of the Bible have at least three different stories about how Israel came to possess Jerusalem is hardly to be wondered at. Jerusalem is a city at the very centre of the tradition, and would naturally attract many such stories.

3 The stories of Yahweh as patron and his messiah

It is a fundamental error of method to ask first after an historical David or Solomon, as biblical archaeologists and historians often have done. We need first to attend to the David and Solomon we know: the protagonists of Bible story and legend. The Bible does not hesitate to tell these stories as tall tales.

In the beginning of the first tale in which David has Saul's life in his hands (I Sam. 24), language is used which is as much theological as it is political. Saul had been made king by Yahweh's prophet and priest, Samuel. However, Saul, good king and general that he was, did what he himself saw to be good, while Yahweh, his patron, had wanted obedience to God's view of the good. For this reason, Saul lost favour with Yahweh, who decided to replace him with David. Rejected by Yahweh, Saul goes mad, sees David as a potential usurper and becomes jealous of David's growing reputation as a killer of Philistines. Saul hunts David with an army of 3,000 hoping to kill him, when our scene first opens in I Samuel 24. Unexpectedly, David has an opportunity to kill Saul thrust on him as Saul enters a dark cave where David is hiding. Instead he cuts off the edge of Saul's robe – not only evidence to the reader that Saul had been in his complete power, but also a euphemistic allusion to the prophecy of Samuel (I Sam. 15: 27–28) that David will lift Saul's house from him, which is interpreted as Saul's power and potency. The story plays with the Hebrew word *kanaf*, which can be used in different contexts for both the 'edge' or 'skirt' of a robe, and for the male sexual organ, as in Deuteronomy 23: 1, where it is used for a man's testicles. This well-worn pun is used euphemistically in the Book of Ruth to allow the heroine to ask Boaz to 'cover her with his *kanaf*', and take her in marriage (Ruth 3: 9). In I Samuel, David becomes deeply repentant, and scolds his men for having encouraged him in emasculating Saul: 'God forbid that I do this to my lord . . . seeing that he is Yahweh's messiah' (I Sam. 24: 6). Yahweh's messiah is the one through whom Yahweh's will is carried out on earth. It is how God is present in history.

David will have nothing to do with the killing of the messiah. He ceases to be Saul's competitor, and subordinates his own regime to Saul's. Recognizing that it is through Saul that Yahweh acts, he pledges his allegiance to Saul, calling him 'father'. Similarly, Saul accepts his role as David's patron and responds with the language of patronage: 'Is this your voice, my son David?' This pledge of mutual recognition of 'father' and 'son' closes the story with Saul's declaration of David's destiny as future king of Israel. This story deals with the plot-sensitive question of succession. It is not a dynastic issue, but one of patronage. Both Saul and David are servants of the ultimate patron Yahweh, who is Israel's true king in the Bible's story. Saul, as 'king', is the head of a great 'family', control of which David is to take over. The fictional familial language of the patronage system transfers Saul's 'father's house' to his 'son' David.

With David's pledge, the story – and the ironic humour of I Samuel shows itself once again – has Saul return to his 'house', while David goes to his 'fortress'. This introduces the David-Nabal story, which centres on the question of whether David is his own man and in possession of his own 'house'. Who is this David?

We meet – folktale fashion – Nabal and his wife Abigail: 'Now Nabal was a great man, but ugly and evil, while his wife, Abigail, was clever and very beautiful' (I Sam. 25: 3). The story proper opens with a scene that is best described as a 'shakedown'. David sends ten of his 'retainers', to explain to Nabal that he has long been giving Nabal's shepherds needed protection. David now demands a favour in return. The language of the story makes it very clear that David seeks to put the house of Nabal under his own patronage. Nabal refuses to recognize David as patron and rejects his extortion with the question: 'Who is David? Who is the son of Jesse? There are many servants today who are breaking away from their masters.' Through the mouth of Nabal – who is described as a great man with his own house – the question is asked that is so central to the stories of chapters 24 and 26. Is David just another Hebrew, as it were, a *pezzonovante?* Is he just another young renegade who has broken allegiance with his patron? Or is David, himself, a great man in possession of his own house? Nabal's refusal of David's 'protection' leads David to commit to a *razzia* against Nabal, bringing four hundred of his 'soldiers' to the attack.

However, the story pauses briefly. We must remember that Abigail is both beautiful and wise. One of David's soldiers offers David's protection to Abigail. This invitation to treachery against her husband is done within the hardly veiled threat: 'For evil has captured him (David) and all his house.' The wise Abigail, faced with an offer she cannot refuse, hurries to present David with her tribute to ward off the threatened vendetta. In this dramatic, eleventh-hour meeting, the story echoes a scene from Genesis 33, where Jacob faces Esau, who has brought *his* four hundred retainers to punish Jacob. That variant story closed with the 'client' Jacob, like Abigail, being invited to join the patron's house. Unlike Jacob, however, who wrestles with God, Abigail, the beautiful woman, submits herself entirely to David's machismo. She explains her husband's intrinsic stupidity. She excuses herself in that she had not seen 'my lord's retainers'. Abigail swears a curse against David's enemies: that they become like Nabal! To be like Nabal is to be assassinated by David's patron. Yahweh's responsibility for this necessary killing is important for Abigail's allegiance. For only so can David avoid blood-guilt, which Abigail herself would be obliged to avenge. The killing of Nabal is carried out only after the allegiance of Nabal's house has already passed to David. Abigail's speech uses the client-and-patron language of 'servant' and 'Lord', so familiar to us from the portrayal of Homer's hero Odysseus. The heroine of II Samuel's story expresses her allegiance to David by taking on a prophetic role which defines for us David's destiny. In this ironic passage, Abigail plays the philosophical role of the author's alter ego. She answers her husband's question, about who this David is, in an interesting rendition of the classical motif of hubris provoking a great fall. Nabal's house now plays out its role as 'servant' to David as 'Lord'. More: David is interpreted by Abigail. Her *pesher*, her commentary, marks him as the servant standing under his Lord, Yahweh's, protection. The complex irony of the story plot is reiterated as David grants Abigail's house his patronage, the role of 'service' requested of him.

When we come to I Samuel chapter 26's variant to chapter 24's story in the cave, we are no longer within the context of an established peace between David and his 'father' Saul. We are entering the context of David's destiny, which had been prophesied by Abigail, a destiny which lies outside the world of the tale, in the philosophical dimension of the story's meaning and of the implied reader's piety:

> When men arise to threaten you and pursue your life, the life of my lord will be bound in life's bundle which is in the care of Yahweh your God, while your enemy's lives will be shot out as from a sling's cup (I Sam. 25: 29).

The theological overtones of Abigail's speech mark David as the reader's messianic representative. It echoes the Psalter's understanding that one lives under God's protection. We have the voice of one explaining the meaning that David has for the tradition. It is the same voice that sounds at the very end of the narrative about David in the Books of Samuel, just before David sings the song of his 'last word' in II Samuel 23. In chapter 22, the collector of the David stories has David sing Psalm 18. He has him thank Yahweh for having saved him from all his enemies. It is a song that marks David as the messiah, piety's 'everyman', struggling against life's enemies, a figure we see recurrently in the headings to the psalms of the Psalter. Psalm 18 expands on the speech of Abigail, epitomizing the story's pedagogical goal. One who puts himself in Yahweh's care will be saved in life's conflicts. Yahweh is the singer's God, his fortress, the rock on which he stands, against which no threat can last. David's life takes its meaning here at the centre of the Bible's reception, at the heart of life's piety and belief in divine care and providence.

The prophecy of Abigail in I Samuel 25 underlines the point of the story that is now played out in chapter 26 in what becomes a reiteration of Saul and David's meeting. Saul is used to illustrate Abigail's interpretation of David's role in the tradition. Saul plays the enemy to the path of righteousness, as he hunts David once again with his 3,000 crack troops.

Although this version of the story does not have David either repenting a wish to kill Saul or rebuking his own men, it does have him argue against Abishai to the same purpose. David points out that since Saul is 'Yahweh's messiah', he cannot be touched without guilt. Not David but Yahweh himself must be the one that takes Saul's life. The spear standing in the ground at Saul's head should be taken instead. This variant of the euphemistic cutting the fringe of Saul's robe, hiding the Hebrew poet's pun-threatening castration in chapter 24, is also a demonstration of power and will: a proof that David had Saul's life in his hands. The spear gives violent evidence for David's claim of having done no evil. Saul overhears David talking to Abner, and interrupts him. 'Is this your voice, David, my son?' In response to Saul's 'my son', David addresses and recognizes Saul as 'my Lord, my King'. David here speaks of himself as Saul's 'servant' so that he may make the complaint that although 'servant of the king' and guiltless, he has been pursued by a murderous Saul.

It is interesting that David offers in this closing argument two possible reasons for Saul having tried to kill him. The first is that Saul is acting on behalf of his patron Yahweh. If this be the case, David offers the bargaining suggestion that he give a sacrifice in compensation. It is quite clear that the story-teller, in presenting David as piety's representative, cannot help showing off David's knowledge of the law by implicitly citing Leviticus 5: 15. The other exonerating possibility David suggests is that if humans have influenced Saul to act against David (notice that David avoids accusing Saul directly), they should be charged before Yahweh, Saul and David's common patron, because their actions have resulted in separating David from the 'patronage of Yahweh', leaving David no choice but to become a 'client' of other gods.

Quite unequivocally, this speech of David bears the implication that in this story world, ultimate sovereignty is divided, as in the opening of the song of Moses in Deuteronomy 32, among the different 'houses' of the gods. That 'house' to which both David and Saul's allegiance is due is Yahweh's. David's complaint against Saul is that Saul, who is Yahweh's messiah and representative – his *consigliere* – does not accept and acknowledge his role as 'Father' and 'Lord' to David. In this neglect, he has forced David out of Yahweh's patronage, which is his rightful inheritance. David's complaint is very important if the story is to be understood. We are in a story world of theological ideas, where the role of king is not Saul's to play. Yahweh is king, Saul but his messiah and representative. Saul is not the true king and ultimate patron here. That is Yahweh. Saul listens to David because he knows his patron demands it, and therefore he recognizes David's allegiance: 'my son'.

David, whose path is the path of righteousness, shall succeed in all that he does, while Saul, the enemy of David's path, shall fail. This interpretive core of the narrative refers directly to the literary and theological context in which the narratives were collected and valued. This is the context of intertextual echoes of the Aristotelian principle of wisdom that beauty lies in the eye of the beholder, which we find placed so centrally in the contrasting stories of Saul and David's faithfulness to Yahweh in I Samuel 15 and II Samuel 15. In such echoes, we recognize that Saul's rejection by Yahweh – for doing what was good in his own eyes – stands in an intense structural parallel to David on the top of the Mount of Olives, prayerfully accepting whatever Abraham-like destiny might be found to be good in the eyes of Yahweh. David submits as the true servant of Yahweh. Not his own, but Yahweh's will be done. This is the same context as that implied by Psalm 18's theological interpretation of the whole of David's life which closes the Bible's story of David in II Samuel 22. Just as the first of our three tales of I Samuel 24–26 had closed in a final reference to the thematic contrast of Saul's house and David's fortress, and just as the second story was epitomized in Abigail's story-interpreting blessing, our third story marks the narrative as a dramatization of one of the basic truths of Old Testament wisdom: that which is good is one, and – like beauty and truth – to be found in the eye of the divine beholder, Yahweh.

4 Forgetting Saul's head on the battlefield

The pivotal story of Saul's death marks yet another group of tale variants that expose for us how biblical stories work. The variations of this episode, all coming within the same story, make particularly clear the fact that the composition of the biblical books of I–II Samuel pays little heed to events as such. The concern is literary and theological rather than historical. Three central texts are involved in collecting the stories and story-fragments about Saul's death. They are found at the very end of the Book of I Samuel in chapter 31, in the first chapter of II Samuel, and in chapter 10 of the Book of I Chronicles. The problem is relatively simple to pose. The narrative does not follow a plot-line. Saul's death stops the plot entirely. Instead of a story, we are treated to a series of plot segments and variants, which are collected successively. All the time – to the horror of any story-interested reader – Saul's body and armour hang in the temple, and his head rolls forgotten somewhere across the battlefield.

Instead of a narrative account dealing with the transition of Saul's kingdom to David – as the historically oriented scholarly world would have us expect – we find bits and pieces of story echoed and reiterated, all of them dominated by a single motif that first entered the narrative in chapter 24, when David had the chance to kill Saul. This ruling motif is the fear of killing Saul because he is Yahweh's messiah, the same fear that first induced David to be faithful to his role as Saul's son and as Yahweh's servant. The story has interpreted David's faithfulness as of one 'walking in the path of righteousness'. It interprets this fear of killing Saul as the 'fear of God', the central virtue associated with the Book of Psalms, which I will discuss below along with the metaphors of the 'theology of the way'. In the Book of Job, such 'fear of God' is the philosophical understanding that is the beginning of wisdom (Job 28: 28). Rather than either history or story, the collector of the traditions of Saul's death is intent on the finer points of theology!

At the close of Saul's life, the 'fear of God' gets in the way of everyone who steps on to the scene. The narration of the text recites successively a chain of tale variants regarding Saul's death. Entirely apart from the double variant of the godfather story in I Samuel 24 and 26, we find at least three and possibly five different and independent fragments of tradition concerning the 'event' of Saul's death. In I Samuel 31, we see Saul and his armour-bearer both commit suicide at the end of a losing battle. Immediately following this, in II Samuel 1, the role of armour-bearer is played by an Amalekite who happens by, finds Saul's body, and reports his death to David. When David asks this Amalekite how he knows that Saul is indeed dead, the man offers David what is yet a third variant of this story. After identifying himself – redundantly for the present audience's sake – as an Amalekite, he tells David that he has killed Saul, having been requested to do so by the king himself.

These three variant scenes are similar in that each of them places Saul dead on the battlefield. The differences become significant and, as a story account, unbearable, when we notice what happened to Saul's body, his armour and his head. In chapter 31: 8, before Saul's armour-bearer has become the Amalekite, the Philistines find 'Saul's body and that of his three sons'. As with the Amalekite's discovery of Saul's body, nothing is said about Saul's armour-bearer, who is neither sought after nor found. The scene of the Philistines finding Saul's body harmonizes two quite different episodes at the beginning of the chapter, one dealing with the death of Saul's sons and the other with Saul's own death. When they find the bodies, Saul's head is cut off and his armour stripped from his body. Once this is done, the story as story turns difficult once again. The Philistines announce the news back home to their gods and people. They place Saul's armour in the temple of the divine Ashtarot and they tie his body to the walls of the town of Beth Shan. When the townspeople of an Israelite settlement hear of this, their 'brave soldiers' go and take Saul's body and the bodies of his three sons from the walls of Beth Shan and return home to cremate them and bury the bones. The story closes, leaving one to puzzle over Saul's head, apparently rolling unnoticed across the battlefield. Such a rendering is very difficult to read as history when it is presented in such fragmented scenes.

This becomes quite clear when we look to the account of Saul's death in the variant biblical story found in I Chronicles 10. As in the story of I–II Samuel, Saul's sons are killed in the battle. Saul has been wounded by Philistine archers and commits suicide 'by his own hand' because his armour-bearer is too afraid to kill him. The armour-bearer also commits suicide, which must encourage us to ask why he has earlier refused Saul's request out of fear. The next day, when the Philistines discover the bodies of Saul and his sons, the armour-bearer goes unmentioned. However, after cutting off Saul's head and stripping the armour from his body, they put his armour in the temple of 'their gods', and fasten his head to Beyt Dagon. The awkward redundancy of one temple for their gods and another for Dagon leaves us uncertain about translating what could be a place name as 'the temple of Dagon', as is frequently done in modern bibles. This difficulty, however, appears relatively minor as soon as we notice that the

Philistines this time have forgotten not the head, but the bodies on the battlefield. This allows the 'brave soldiers' of the Israelite village to recover them (apparently from the battlefield) without having to run the risk or display the 'bravery' required in approaching the walls of Beth Shan. Moreover, in I Chronicles 10: 10 another story variation is glimpsed. We are told that the Philistines had nailed Saul's head to *Beyt Dagon*, which is perhaps best understood as a place associated with a temple named Beyt Dagon located in Philistian Ashdod in I Samuel 5: 2. The Philistine god Dagon is also mentioned as associated with the town of Gaza in Judges 16: 23, and a Beyt Dagon also occurs as a place name in Joshua 19: 27, up near the northern coast in the tribal territory of Asher. No Beyt Dagon or Temple of Dagon, however, is known in or anywhere near Beth Shan. While exposing this even richer expanse of tale variation, the Chronicles text does rather well in resolving the problem of fear of God killing Yahweh's messiah by saying that Yahweh himself killed Saul.

It should be stressed here that the difficulties of these texts do not lie in our understanding of them. The texts are abundantly clear about what they are doing: they are clearly built from shattered shards of stories, and are largely uninterested in events. The episodes have been collected, organized and ordered specifically as broken and lost tradition. They hardly have the coherence we associate with what we call literature. Nor do they render an account of an event. They are traditions collected to give echo to and to call up a past forgotten or lost. Before we try to make history of them, we must ask ourselves whether there are any grounds at all for assuming that the actual texts we have ever possessed concrete political, historical referents. Do these broken narratives as such, that is, as tradition blocks, have what we might seriously identify as an originating context implied in them?

5 How the Bible's collectors understood David

I would like to add to the arguments already put forward a discussion that relates to how the biblical tradition was first received, collected and formed as a valued view of the past. Certainly the way in which the Bible understood David while the Bible was still being written and put together is relevant to our discussion. This argument involves an effort to understand what David meant to the people who told stories about him. The argument is relatively simple, and proceeds primarily from a study of headings that have been added to thirteen psalms of the Hebrew Psalter sometime before the collective work was completed. Each of these headings comments on its psalm by evoking it as a song once sung by David when he was in one or other crisis among the many that occur in the stories about him. These added comments give evidence that the psalm transmission at this point in the Bible's development looks back on David and his story – whether historical or literary – as part of tradition past. It should be stressed that this is demonstrably an early perspective on the David tradition, at least relative to the tradition of the collected stories about him as they are known from the completed text of I–II Samuel.

Not only does each of the thirteen headings refer to a narrative about David, they imply a narrative that is not identical in detail with the one that we now have in the Bible. Rather, the headings know a variant of the stories we have. One heading refers to a tale we no longer have. We might infer from this that the headings derive from a time before the present I–II Samuel became normative. It is difficult not to date these commentaries to some time before the completion of the Books of Samuel. This is not a particularly adventurous assertion as a close variant of one of the psalms glossed by these headings – Psalm 18 – is used, replete with title, in the current Bible's version of the David stories in I Samuel 22.

The inclusion of this psalm seems to be tied to the effort to create the extensive narrative chain from Genesis to II Kings – from the creation of the world to Jerusalem's destruction – as a literary whole. Psalm 18 and its interpretive heading closes the story of David's life. This is done much in the way that the songs found in Deuteronomy's chapters 32 and 33 are used to close the story of Moses' life, and the song of Jacob in Genesis 49 is used to close the story of his life in the final form of the text of Genesis. In the process of this larger editorial work, the song is set within the narrative we have with the purpose of interpreting the function of the David story for the tradition's greater audience. In recognizing this, it becomes clear that when the story of I–II Samuel, the most extensive narrative that speaks of David and his empire, took its current shape, that story was already being understood, interpreted and read by Psalm 18 in the same manner that the psalms associated with David's adventures in the Psalter do.

The interpretive function of these headings is two-directional. On one hand they fulfil a dramatizing need of the psalms by giving them a narrative context within the adventures of David. They interpret the psalm as one of the songs sung by the character David who had been both Saul's personal musician and the author of the Psalter's psalms of David. This is done in the same manner that I Chronicles 16 gives the role of official psalmist for the temple to Asaph, who is credited with writing some of the psalms of the Bible. The headings allow the psalms to be easily understood by psychological transference: a method of interpretation that is found among such Hellenistic Jewish commentators as Philo. The implied message is that as David seeks help and salvation, so do I, who identify with the voice of his song. I also share in David's already secured, past victories. On the other hand, just as this heading spells out the context of the psalms' 'origins' in terms of David's life, the psalm itself and its field of communication interpret David for its audience. In all of our psalms this interpretation is consistently theological and mythical in significance. David as the first-person voice of the psalms becomes everyman, theologically representing before God both the psalmist and his listener in their prayer in a time of need. The psalms are also messianic: both implied and explicit. This role is found in a functional clustering of wisdom motifs that adhere to the metaphors of the son of God and messiah, as in Psalms 2, 8, 89 and 110. Through such historicizing headings, David is interpreted as the messiah struggling against the *goyim*. He is the representative of the righteous in a cosmic struggle of Yahweh against the nations and against God's enemies. Finally, and associated with this same cluster of motifs highlighted in Psalms 1 and 2, David represents the philosopher struggling to remain on the path of righteousness. In his song, David epitomizes the singer of Psalm 2's closure, who – much like the Jesus Ben Sirach of the Greek Bible's Ecclesiasticus and like the Solomon of the Psalms of Solomon – seeks refuge in Yahweh.

It is quite clear, from these titles that interpret David by giving him these particular psalms to sing, that David's significance is seen, not in terms of any historical role he may have played in the past, but rather, in his meaning within the lived pietism of the implied author and within the cosmic struggle between Yahweh and the evil nations. Some of these psalms, like Psalm 18, used to interpret the whole of the David story, explicitly speak of David as a cosmic and messianic presence. All use a cluster of motifs that comment on David within the larger literary context of the cosmic messiah. Psalm 18 twice makes particular reference to the war against the nations that is described in Psalm 8. It also ties Jerusalem's temple to the heavenly throne. The song calls up an earthquake and evokes the creation's contrast between light and darkness in the manner of Genesis 1 and the prologue of John's gospel. The true historical context of this war in Psalm 18 is the personal struggle that belongs at the heart of early Jewish pietism's religiously conceived self-understanding, described in the metaphors of the 'theology of the way'. In verses 20–24, for example, the song addresses this explicitly: 'Yahweh rewarded me because of my right understanding; according to the purity of my hands he repaid me; *for I have remained along Yahweh's path* . . .' David is not significant in this psalm as a figure of history, as one living in a distant past. He is the saviour of all who hold to the *torah*. Psalm 18's David is like Psalm 8's messiah: the implicit voice of the psalm, the pious man's representative, saved by Yahweh in his struggle against his moral enemies. It is this 'I' who Yahweh makes cosmic emperor over the nations.

II Samuel's use of a variant of Psalm 18 to close the stories about David suggests that not even the biblical version's edition of the David story – our primary source about David – has an historiographic ideology as its primary focus. It represents, rather, a tradition for quite other purposes of theological and philosophical discourse.

6 Commenting on II Kings: Isaiah, Jonah and Elijah

The thesis that biblical narrative is not historiographical can be supported when we consider the developing tradition's understanding of a work like II Kings. This narrative is certainly the backbone of all naively realistic readings of the Bible. II Kings' narratives have long been recognized as having played a central role in the prophetic books of Isaiah, Jeremiah and Jonah. The ideology of II Kings' traditions is so close to that of Jeremiah that few Old Testament scholars have avoided linking these two books. The Isaiah text is often assumed to be citing directly from II Kings.

Isaiah's composition can be discussed as a product of three different kinds of material: first, a paraphrastic heading that opens chapter 1, as well as the narrative section of chapters 36–39, which offer a context for the songs in the life of Isaiah much as presented in II Kings; second, an original 'proto-Isaiah', which is found among the poems of chapters 1–36, especially the visions and prophecies of doom about old Israel; and third, various expansions of songs with an anonymous voice that are set at the time of Israel's imminent return from exile. Expansive variants of this interpretive perspective have long been interpreted as suggesting the existence of originally independent texts of a deutero- or 'Second Isaiah' and even of a trito- or 'Third Isaiah'. Chapters 36–39 of the book of Isaiah share a story about the prophet and King Hezekiah with chapters 18–20 of II Kings, replete with some prophecies (see II Kings 19: 21–34). The historicizing function of the paraphrastic summary in the opening verse of Isaiah, likewise drawn from the tradition of II Kings, creates an historicizing context for 'proto-Isaiah'. Most scholars accept this summary as reflecting the historical context for what they assume was an historical Isaiah.

The association between Isaiah and II Kings is quite comparable to Psalm 18's relationship to the Book of II Samuel. Isaiah's poems are related to tradition past, and particularly to the tradition about Yahweh's rejection of old Israel. They expand and fill out the intimate and ambivalent role of Yahweh's presence in human affairs. At the same time, the prophet's introduction of Yahweh's interpretive voice at the close of the citation from II Kings brings the Assyrian threat against Jerusalem into Isaiah's world of theology and myth. The Assyrians are placed in the same role as the builders of Babylon's tower. They mock Yahweh when they lift their eyes and ambitions to heaven. In trying to bring destruction to Egypt, they oppose Yahweh, Egypt's creator.

This interpretive voice, this *pesher* or commentary of the prophet, belongs to a scholarly discourse that we also find in the introductory heading of Isaiah 1: 'The vision of Isaiah the son of Amoz, which he saw concerning Judah and Jerusalem in the days of Uzziah, Jotham, Ahaz and Hezekiah, kings of Jerusalem.' The editor is addressing his composition from the perspective of his entire book, including the sections that refer to the return of Israel from Babylon in the time of the Persians. However, this context referring to the prophet of II Kings belongs to the collections of songs and poems we find in Isaiah 1–36. It offers a commentary to the life story of the Isaiah we find in II Kings.

Right from the opening song of his collection, the editor reads the Isaiah tradition mythologically and theologically. It is a history known only from the perspective of salvation determined by the merciful God. The book's heading, which first connects us to the traditions of II Kings, is already understood by the Book of Isaiah's audience. The author understands the 'history' he refers to as a story about 'old Israel', lost Israel, an Israel that neither knows nor understands: 'Israel does not know me, my people understands nothing' (Isa. 1: 3).

The collection of poetry following chapter 39 to the end of the book is sung with a voice from within the same 'new Israel' context of the editorial commentary. Throughout these 'Isaiah' songs condemning Israel, one hears echoes of the implicit saving voice of chapter 40: 1–2: 'Comfort, comfort my people, says your God. Speak tenderly to Jerusalem and cry to her that her warfare is ended, her iniquity is pardoned.' Implicit in all the songs of wrath is this song of hope. It is in the return, in the understanding of the 'new Israel', that the story of old Israel's destruction first makes sense. The meaning of the book's prophecies of doom is interpreted in chapter 40: 3–5.

> A voice cries, make ready Yahweh's way in the wilderness; in the desert, make straight the path to your God. Every valley will be lifted; every mountain and peak will be levelled; the cliffs will be levelled and the hills be made into the plain. Yahweh's glory will be revealed and all humanity will see it. Yahweh himself has spoken.

It is in exile, in the suffering in the wilderness, that the theology of the way is finally made right.

The metaphors here in Isaiah 40 echo Jeremiah 4: 23's and the creation story's formless wilderness from which creation and new life spring. It is from suffering that one creates the way of life. The prophecies of doom offer us a doublet or variant of the story of Exodus 24: 16–18. All the people of Israel, having come through the purifying sufferings of the wilderness, finally see the glory of Yahweh revealed on Mount Sinai. It is not an account of the past that we are dealing with, but an interpretation of a past lost.

Two other prophets of II Kings, Jonah and Elijah, tell us much about the reception of this tradition within the world of Old Testament texts. Words such as irony and caricature are hardly foreign to discussion of the Book of Jonah, with its prophet playing the role of anti-prophet. He is the only one of all of the Bible's prophets – beginning already with Moses and the murmuring traditions of Exodus – whose prophecies were listened to! This observation, given the central role that the concept of prophecy has played in modern scholarship's creation of ancient Israel, should lead to healthy self-criticism among scholars, if not deconstructive laughter.

In fact, this ironic understanding of prophecy is central to the tradition's view of prophecy. Rather than playing the role of messengers of God's word in Israel's history, prophets have functioned as catalysts for old Israel's faithlessness and betrayal. Prophets harden hearts. They provoke stories of Israel's disobedience. They create rejection of the way of God's torah. As Isaiah has already stressed, the prophets present the proof that Israel neither knows nor understands anything. This is the role that the Book of Jonah unfolds in its well-known spoof on II Kings' prophet Jonah.

The Jonah of II Kings is the prophet who, as the servant of Yahweh, had instructed the king in Samaria, Jeroboam ben Joash, to save Israel by destroying its enemies. Following Jonah's instruction, Jeroboam brings Israel to greatness, expanding its boundaries to the Dead Sea and southward. Such a Jonah – this saviour of Israel – is the kind of prophet that the prophet in Jonah's book implicitly imagines himself to be. He wants to bring down destruction on all of God's and Israel's enemies. He wants to save Israel in its great need. This is a prophet unlike others. He is not disloyal and unpatriotic like Jeremiah, nor does he oppose the great king Jeroboam, nor anyone who 'walks in the way of Jeroboam'. He stands with, not against Israel. However, the irony of his fate is that he cannot be the Jonah of Kings. Hardly! This poor Jonah is ordered to bring Yahweh's word to Israel's enemies.

When this prophet receives the divine call to go to Nineveh to preach repentance, he runs; he wants none of it. 'Knowing that Yahweh was a gracious and merciful God, slow to anger and, overflowing with faithful love, and that he would repent of the evil' (Jonah 4: 2) that he intended against Nineveh, Jonah ran. Jonah at heart was a prophet like Elijah of the stories of I Kings 17–19. Jonah would be a prophet of doom and wrath. He wants destruction and disaster on all of Yahweh's enemies: especially over great Nineveh. However, when Jonah is caught in the belly of the great fish, he can no longer resist God's importunities and submits to the divine will. This, after all, the story insists, is Yahweh, *'elohei shamayim*, 'the God of Heaven', the 'creator of both heaven and earth'. Jonah preaches to Nineveh.

Just as Jonah had predicted, Nineveh to his horror listens to Jonah's preaching, and Yahweh repents the evil he had planned. Even the animals, fasting and covered in sackcloth and ashes, cry out to God. As for Jonah, he is angry, and in his anger the author presents us with a discourse on the great Elijah: a prophet's prophet. It is strikingly instructive, however, that the text turns specifically to Elijah's words of I Kings 19: 4: 'he prays to God that he might die.' Unlike Yahweh – slow to anger – Jonah is quick. Frustrated by Nineveh's acceptance of Yahweh, which he himself had been forced to preach, Jonah wishes to die. Yahweh responds by asking Jonah, as he asks Cain in Genesis 4, if 'he did well to be angry' (Jonah 4: 4): a motif that points to the story's central theme.

Jonah's implicit discussion with the story in I Kings is an interesting one. I Kings 19 finds Elijah hunted by his enemies after the slaughter of Ba'al's prophets and running for his life. The scene unexpectedly turns comic. Once again we hear the rough humour of II Kings' implicit author, the same who had Elisha call on bears to eat the children who had called him 'baldy' (II Kings 2: 23–24). In I Kings 19, the humour is deconstructive, turned against Elijah as prophet of doom. The aim is to mock the 'man of God' the author himself created. Even the tale's setting is made wry fun of. Elijah takes a day's journey out into the desert, only to sit under a tree. Again a joke: in fear for his life he prays to die. The humour is laconic. The story closes when Elijah falls asleep and, like Jesus in his turn, is saved by angels who minister to him in the desert.

The Jonah story takes up the comic line which I Kings had opened. Jonah too wishes to die, but he wishes to die because his preaching was successful. Jonah builds a shelter beyond the city (Elijah's desert) and waits to see what will happen. The humour of I Kings leaks into our Jonah story. Although Jonah is already sheltered from the heat of the sun, Yahweh causes a plant to grow up overnight to shade his head. Jonah is quite pleased by this. The next day, God causes a worm to kill the plant. He then increases the heat and the swelter to the point that Jonah wishes again for death: now, because of the heat. Yahweh repeats his question for Jonah's Cain: 'Do you do well to be angry (4: 9)?' The narrator didactically ties the shade tree parable to that other cause of anger, Nineveh's impending salvation. The story centres attention on this reiterated echo of Genesis 4: 6's question. In the context of wisdom's discourse, the story develops through its questions. Whether one is dealing, like Cain, with sacrifices offered to God, or, like Jonah, with trees one doesn't need, growing one day and dying the next, or indeed, with the life and death of a single man or a great city, one is always dealing with the will of God. All that happens are events to be accepted. Good is not as men see it, but rather, only that is good which God sees as good. That is the central message, while Jonah's story formally concludes on a moral note on the virtue of pity.

The central theme of the Jonah story is the same as in the scene of Cain's sacrifice. This theme is also given a dominating role in the Book of

Job. The will of God is not what men will have it. It is a variation of the structural paradigm of the Psalter's theology of the way. The way of the godless and the torah's path, the will of men and the will of God, are the fundamental alternatives in life. One lives with choices and these are voiced without compromise. Decisions are the radical questions of either/ or. This theme is also a variant of that taken up with such force in I Samuel's stories of Saul and David. As in the creation story, the good is what Yahweh sees to be good.

The deconstructive theme that God and his action in history are not what we expect is taken up explicitly in a close variant of the same Elijah narrative in I Kings 18 that Jonah quoted from. In a dramatic reversal of Cain and Abel's competitive sacrifices offered to be accepted and refused by God in Genesis 4: 3–5, Elijah challenges the Ba'al prophets to a life-and-death contest of divine reality. The prophets of Ba'al have called upon their god: 'O Ba'al answer us!' Ba'al doesn't answer. Yahweh, however, does respond, and consumes Elijah's offering with fire from heaven (I Kings 18: 38). Ba'al's prophets lose the challenge, and they are all slaughtered by Elijah. As a result, life becomes dangerous for Elijah – like Cain, and by chapter 19 he is hiding in a cave in fear for his life. A 'word of Yahweh' asks him what he is doing there. Elijah answers – and this surely is the same Elijah that Jonah had admired – that he has been 'filled with zealotry for Yahweh the God of armies', destroying altars and killing prophets. Only he is left. The reference to the divine epithet of 'Yahweh, the God of armies', which is a particularly frequent favourite of the prophets of doom, is hardly accidental. It emphasizes the bloody qualities of Elijah as a prophet and acts as a preface to the parable that follows.

Yahweh's word tells Elijah to stand on top of God's mountain (Mount Horeb) before Yahweh. Yahweh passes by! However, first comes a great storm-wind that breaks rocks in pieces, but Yahweh is not in the wind. After the wind an earthquake, but Yahweh is not in the earthquake. After the earthquake a fire passes by, but Yahweh is not in the fire. And then after the fire 'a voice of soft silence . . .' The critique is a critique of the tradition. All the expectations of the divine that Elijah and the prophets of doom and violent war embody are deconstructed in this little tale tucked away in the heart of a history that is so strongly marked by the acts of Yahweh, the true God of *heaven*'s armies. It is, I think, the thematic centre of the Book of II Kings.

The use of such narratives in prophetic works, especially in Isaiah but also in Jeremiah, clearly indicates a purpose other than historical. It tells us much about how II Kings was understood, and undermines totally any claim that the author of Isaiah had understood it as historical.

In dealing with the strongly interpretive narratives of Jonah and Elijah in II Kings, even a mere surface attribution of history to the book must be given up. It is not only that stories from II Kings are thrown into the role of ironic caricature by the book of Jonah, but the same kind of discourse within II Kings itself indicates that we are dealing with a didactic function, stories told for the purpose of teaching. That this is the primary reason the stories have been collected undermines scholarly assumptions about II Kings as history. This didactic function cannot be dismissed as extraneous to the goals of Kings simply because of such fairy-tale motifs as Elijah's child-eating bears. In fact, we should concentrate on just such didactic and philosophical motifs. It is these motifs, belonging to fairy tales even as they do, that are central to the purpose of the book.

I think the conclusion is inescapable. The Book of Kings does not involve us in an historicist's presentation of past events. Whatever historical roots this tale tradition might preserve, are but accidental remnants of the narrative's unknown sources such as implied in the synchronic listing of royal successions of the houses of Omri and David, which provides the chronological framework that has been chosen by the narrator. In reading II Kings, we – like the commentators within II Kings – are engaged in a discourse about the philosophical principles and truths of which the stories about old Israel are dramatic illustrations.

To restate the central issue more theologically: the historicizing prose of Isaiah 1: 1 and chapters 36–39 gives the poems of this book a context. To place these poems in the mouth of II Kings' prophet Isaiah interprets the poems and gives them a transcendent reference. This technique is very similar to the one used in Exodus in which Yahweh's torah is presented to Moses on Mount Sinai. For Isaiah to sing these songs makes them the words of God through his prophet, much as II Samuel's placing of Psalm 18 in David's mouth transforms the David of I–II Samuel into Yahweh's messiah, and offers the reader the transcendent perspective of myth.

A central goal in creating the Book of Isaiah was to unite the songs of doom and divine anger with the songs of mercy and comfort that the collection, opening with Isaiah 40, presents. Past destruction is interpreted as dramatic preparation for the mercy and comfort that Isaiah's audience hears. The mythological task of the composition is well captured in the song of Isaiah 11: 1–9, which discusses the central messianic virtue: Ecclesiastes' beginning of wisdom. It instructs the audience on the 'fear of Yahweh' that transforms the world. This 'fear of Yahweh' is not Job's human wisdom, which can judge only on the basis of what we hear. Isaiah rather points to the true discernment and understanding that judges the weak and the helpless of his audience. The poem begins with a warlike Yahweh who kills the unrighteous and it ends with the famous evocation of peace: 'The wolf will lie down with the lamb . . . the lion will eat straw like the ox.'

This is the same mythological interpretation that transforms the bloody stories of Elijah! Yahweh is not a storm God who cracks mountains; he is to be found in the stillness of the silent voice. The entire discourse is explicit in Jonah. Jonah's Elijah-like fantasies of destruction and wrath are contrasted to Nineveh's barnyards dressed out in sackcloth and ashes. This discourse raises a very specific challenge to II Kings' readers in its transformation of the flood story's God: Jonah's variation of the 'fear of Yahweh' as the beginning of wisdom is the grace and mercy of a God, who is 'slow to anger, abiding in steadfast love and repenting his wrath'![1]

---

[1] Jonah 4: 2; see also Genesis 6: 5 and 8: 21, and contrast Exodus 34: 6.

CHAPTER 3

How the Bible talks about the past

1 Stories and their references to an historical world

In the last chapter, a number of biblical narratives were discussed that were obviously not accounts of an historical past, though they were central stories in books that scholars often speak of as historical. These tales were both written and passed on as tradition for quite other reasons. Even as the collectors of biblical tradition were putting together a tradition of origins, establishing a self-understanding as the 'new Israel', interest lay more in transcendent meaning than in developing either a real or an imagined past. Our questions about this tradition cannot be limited to whether it is an 'accurate' or an 'exaggerated' account of the past. What the narratives and the tradition are talking about has to be our point of departure.

Asking whether biblical narratives have other motives and purpose than historical ones is useful, but it only takes us so far, and only helps us with those narratives that are most clearly fictive. The issue is more complicated than asking questions about whether the story's iron floats on water. Not all of the Bible's stories are obviously fictional. This can best be seen by comparing two variants of a single story. It is a story about the Nephilim, who appear as a race of giants in a tale recounted in Numbers 13, and as more normal human beings in a paraphrasing reference to the same tale in Deuteronomy 1.

The first time that the Nephilim appear in the Bible is in a brief episode in Genesis 6: 1–4, just before the flood story. Although short, the episode has an important theological role to play in Genesis, which we will discuss later. Here, we need to limit ourselves to the legend of the Nephilim. Gods, or 'sons of God', Genesis tells us, came down to earth, where they learned that women are beautiful. They marry those they want. The children of these marriages the writer identifies as Nephilim. In closing this scene, we read an added gloss, seemingly of a passing scholar: 'These were the heroes of old: men of renown.'

Stories about children born of gods and humans are also found outside the Bible. The great early Mesopotamian epic is of Gilgamesh, a man whose mother is a goddess. He is described as two-thirds god and one-third man. He is a giant of a man, a great warrior and brawler: a 'Superman', without a childhood in Nebraska to teach him humility. Like the Bible's Samson, Gilgamesh is heroic: perfect for an adventure story except for a fatal flaw, creating tragedy. The central plot takes up the theme that arises from Gilgamesh's relationship to the divine world: Gilgamesh's mortality. The same plot element is encountered by Homer's half-god/half-man hero, Achilles, who was immortal except for the vulnerability of his heel. It is not merely that these heroes were part gods. Ironically, that defined the heroic qualities of their 'manliness'. They were men of great violence. They did heroic deeds. They had unsurpassable strength. That is what the stories that created them are most interested in. Such 'big bow-wow' motifs have formed a tradition of entertaining tales that is now more than 4,000 years in the telling and still growing. In the Bible – perhaps in tribute to their story competitors of Greek literature – the tales of the wars against the Philistines centre on three such figures: Samson, with the tragic story of his love for Delilah, Saul, who has killed his thousands and whose life struggles with fate, and David, who has killed tens of thousands – not a giant himself, but a giant-killer – who, in competition with Saul, plays out the messianic role of obedient 'servant of Yahweh'.

The brief reference to the Nephilim in Genesis 6 hardly gives us a story. It is little more than an explanatory clarification and comment: an aetiology for the heroes and giants of old. It explains where these extraordinary figures of folklore originally came from: how the Nephilim and heroes of the past first had their beginning. While heroes in the Bible are individuals, the Nephilim are a quite specific people or race of giants, whose story is found in Numbers. This story is excellent, with rich possibilities of wonder and fantasy.

In Numbers 13, Moses has brought the Israelites through the wilderness to the edge of the 'land of Canaan'. Following Yahweh's instructions, he sends a leader from each of the twelve tribes of Israel to spy out the land and to report back to him. The spies go out as ordered. They are stunned by what they find. The account they bring back strikes horror in the hearts of the Israelites. 'The land we passed through and spied out is a land that would eat its own people. Everyone we saw there was huge. We saw the Nephilim . . . We felt like grasshoppers. In fact, we *looked* like grasshoppers to them' (Num. 13: 32–33). Both the land and the people were giants. The first, variant account the spies bring of the Neshtol Valley (the 'Valley of the Cluster') makes this abundantly clear. Having been instructed to bring back samples of the fruit in the land, the spies cut a *cluster* of grapes in the valley and return to camp with it, a scene one can still see today in the logo of the Israel Department of Tourism. It takes two soldiers to carry the cluster of grapes. So too, the cows and bees must have been giants; for the rivers of the valley flowed with milk and honey (Num. 13: 23–24)!

The giant motif dominates the story to introduce the leitmotif of Yahweh's power to do whatever he wishes. Yahweh brags to Moses: 'I can make you into a people greater and mightier than this' (Num. 14: 12). However, the people are terrified of the giants. Suffering Yahweh's anger and scorn at their cowardice, all of Israel except Joshua and Caleb refuse to enter the land. The story has a double function. On one hand, it illustrates the recurrent moral of the wilderness chain of stories: that Israel must do God's will, not merely what is humanly reasonable. On the other hand, it helps structure the larger chain of tradition from Genesis to II Kings around the thematic cluster of faithlessness, punishment and exile. Yahweh punishes Israel for its disobedience. The whole generation will die in the desert. They are the lost generation, laying the foundations for stories of deportations yet to come. Joshua and Caleb are spared to serve as 'the remnant' who lead a 'new Israel' into the promised land.

When Moses offers us a paraphrase of this story in Deuteronomy 1, both the refusal to follow Yahweh and the lost generation motif are maintained. The whole of the story's fantastic picture of a land of giants, however, has been translated and transformed into something quite prosaic. The people of the valley are large and numerous, their cities are huge. Fruit was gathered, but nothing is either extraordinary or interesting about it. Giants and 'sons of God', the fear-inspiring description of a 'land that would devour its own people', all are invisible in Deuteronomy's demythologizing version of the story. In Deuteronomy's account, we have commentary. We do not have story, but a description of Israel in its betrayal, and we have divine judgement. What has been lost is the adventure, that insight into transcendent reality. Deuteronomy's interpretation is not so very far from many modern readings: moralistic rather than theological. It portrays a righteous God and a feckless Israel, but nothing of the fateful centre of the tale.

Yet Deuteronomy's own story hardly survives the implicit commentary of the text. We momentarily lose sight of Moses and his farewell speech to the Israelites, who are poised to begin their journey into the promised land. The moralist's voice that we hear speaks in a different time than Moses', and has a different audience than ancient Israel. The original story of Numbers was intended to strike vicarious terror. How else evoke a responsive and courageous 'Nevertheless!' or 'Even so!' from this adventure's audience? How else, in fact, convince them that only God can save them in their history? The ethical demand of such a story is not bravery of any ordinary sort, such as that demanded of soldiers to fight against superior forces. That belongs to Deuteronomy's realism. Rather, God's command in the Numbers story is absolute: to do his will and not their own. He will have Israel fight against giants! Deuteronomy's rationalistic paraphrase replaces the tale's passionate demands with the reasonable one of the moralist. The implicit disagreement in such competitive interpretations of the tradition is characteristic of the discourse that recurs throughout the Bible. It reaches its most dramatic height in the great debates of the Book of Job, which pit the Hellenistic revolt of Job's rationalism against the traditional pietism of his friends. Like the collection of sermons in Deuteronomy, the great opera of Job's book uses a story of the past to create a stage for moral discourse.

2 Don't go back to Egypt for horses

Similar to Deuteronomy's revision of the story of the giants in Numbers is the discussion in Deuteronomy 17: 16 of Solomon's horses. Here in the reiteration of Deuteronomy's Moses and II Kings' Solomon, the difference between a past created and a present referenced becomes clear. Moses' speech in Deuteronomy takes its setting as part of his second farewell speech to the Israelites from on top of Mount Nebo, as the Israelites are preparing to enter the promised land, having crossed the wilderness. Moses summarizes the larger narrative's attitude towards Kings, commenting pointedly on the coming story of I Samuel 8, where Israel's elders ask Samuel to give them a king 'just like all the other nations' (I Sam. 8: 5). In Deuteronomy, Moses tells the people that they can have such a king, but adds to this a threefold warning which is on its surface most baffling:

> Only he [the king] must not multiply horses for himself, or cause the people to return to Egypt in order to multiply horses, since Yahweh has said to you, 'You shall never return that way again.' And he shall not multiply wives for himself, lest his heart turn away; nor shall he greatly multiply for himself silver and gold. (Deut. 17: 16–17)

The narrator does not remain inside the role of Moses of the farewell speeches. Nor does he address anything that is meaningful to Moses' audience on Mount Nebo. The author addresses his own audience and refers implicitly to a narrative his readers know. He is commenting on and interpreting a story yet in the future. The reference is to the narrative of I Kings 10–11, the story of Solomon and his legendary wealth. The whole earth sought the king's presence and brought him gifts of silver and gold. Solomon made silver as common as Jerusalem's stones. He brought horses from Egypt, having in all 1,400 chariots and 12,000 horse: fabulous numbers for an ancient army. Solomon's wealth is also measured in women, 700 in number from foreign nations, who the story's sectarian and xenophobic voice tells us 'turned his heart away' from his God.

Yet the narrator's Moses-voice of Deuteronomy is not interpreting the story he refers to in Kings after all. Solomon's betrayal of his God, which causes his ultimate rejection by Yahweh, is already quite explicit in that story. Deuteronomy merely recalls it to his audience's attention. Why he does so, becomes clear in the close of Moses' second sermon on the mount at the end of Deuteronomy 28: 66. Here, Moses is referring to the time in the future when Israel will lose the land and be scattered 'from one end of the world to another'. He marks his rhetoric starkly, with threats of degradation and humiliation: 'Yahweh will bring you back in ships to Egypt, *a journey which I promised that you should never make*; and there you shall offer yourselves for sale to your enemies as male and female slaves, *but no man will buy you.*' The closing phrase is important to mark well, as it strikes a note of scornful sarcasm. This is not a reference to an enslavement in Egypt from which Yahweh had once saved Israel – the motif with which Moses' second sermon begins (Deut. 5: 6) – but to far worse. The scorn and ironic diatribe lift this closure of Moses' sermon out of its narrative context. Departing from the specific literary references of old Israel and tradition, the text engages a subtext of political commentary involving the real world of the author. Who are these people who go back to Egypt by ship? Are they, like Solomon before them, buying horses, marrying foreign women and preferring to gain wealth at the expense of their religion? Are they known to the narrator's implied audience? Do we here have a thinly veiled, Taliban-like polemic against the substantial number of diaspora Jews living in Egypt at the time that Deuteronomy was written? There is abundant evidence of Jews living in Egypt. In his *Antiquities*, the first-century author Josephus refers to many Jews who moved 'back' to Egypt, and especially to Alexandria, during the course of the third century BCE. Does the story talk about a present, which is projected into the past it creates?

3 *A story's access to reality*

One of the issues we need to address in order to distinguish the different voices and ideologies that are implicit in the Bible's texts is the reality to which some of the early stories refer. What kind of reality did they grow out of? Scholars have had different opinions about this. Some have argued that the stories began in folktales. Over time, they gradually became more and more historical. Such arguments are used to explain what is described as a baffling mixture of legend and history. Others have argued the opposite: that first there were events, and the accounts of these events became increasingly fictionalized. This explanation is often used to justify the nearly universal tendency in biblical archaeology to ignore elements of a story that are obviously fictional in a search for a story's 'roots' in historical events.

The well-known nineteenth-century critical dictum that a biblical narrative reflects the historical context of its writing rather than the more distant past of its referent is one that has hardly been answered by the archaeological research of the past century. The essential thrust of this axiom continues to haunt our reading. Even when we are dealing with texts that do refer to an historical past, the reference is always to a knowledge that is part of the world and understanding of the composition. It reflects an understanding of the past. Our interpretation and reconstruction must begin with this later period of the text, and not with any earlier period, which we might prefer to think of as a story's reference.

To understand how stories talk about any possible real world of history, we have to look at their context and at whatever the text might refer to. We also have to recognize that most of our Bible stories are neither whole nor original compositions. They were not put together as narrative accounts of the past, but as collections of fragmented traditions that survived the past. Recognizing their presentation as collections of stories, songs, poems, lists, records and wisdom sayings means that we need to distinguish between the collectors and what they collected. We should pay attention to how and why the traditions were collected and recognize the heuristic function of collection as a literary form. We need to speak of both the traditions and the literary 'baskets' that have held them and have allowed them to be transmitted as a coherent tradition about ancient Israel. In fact, we can hardly speak about an ancient biblical Israel as existing apart from the stories and literary constructs that first gave expression to such a people. In creating a tradition through which they could find their religious self-identity as the new generation, children and remnant of Israel, the writers of these texts presented the torah and the tradition as the religious centre of the people of God, in which all peoples – both in Palestine and the diaspora – attained a synthetic identity. The literature reflects what Israel came to mean as a result of this tradition's accumulation, rather than anything about the political state that existed during Palestine's earlier Iron Age. The relationship between these two historical realities, the social and political reality of the distant past and the later reality of literary traditions, is not obvious. We need to examine it further. That the traditions collected were used as paradigms for a philosophical discussion of morality cautions us that we are not always dealing with simple historical questions about whether something happened or could have happened.

When we start with Israel as we understand the term, the Israel we know from the Bible, we need to recognize that our understanding of Israel as a people and as a nation is unrelated to any known historical Israel. The Israel we know was created by this literature: any examination of its origins is forced to move in lock step with an examination of the development of the Bible's tradition. Nor is this Israel open to independent historical research and judgement. The Bible is our starting-point. Within the context of the Persian or Hellenistic renaissance, the authors of the tradition created the understanding of the population of Palestine as Israel. They created this 'Israel', not as it once existed in an earlier period, but in a way that was meaningful for themselves.

History is by definition anachronistic. It is not objective – something that exists in the past, waiting to be uncovered – for the past is in ruins and exists no longer. If, when we write our history of ancient Israel, we write a history that is reasonable and makes sense, it is a history that makes sense to *ourselves*. This is also true of those who originally put together traditions from the past. They 'understood' their sources and presented them as traditions of 'old Israel'. The coherence and meaning that they gave to these traditions did not reflect the past, that is, the actual relations of events among groups and individuals of the early Iron Age. It reflected and answered rather the needs of the writers and their audiences, who, centuries later, developed a world-view in which commitments to a moral and philosophical life dominated. In this view, old Israel and its traditions of the past represented human failure. It was an example of error and sin. The tradition was important as warning, and it defined the listeners' hopes in the commitment to a 'new Israel' of their own lives and of their own future. That is how the tradition made sense for them.

In talking about the anachronisms of biblical stories, I am dealing with how the narratives made sense to those who told and wrote them, and especially to those who understood them as their own traditions. It might be useful to consider how typical scenes or events are reiterated in biblical narrative, much in the way we saw the theme of the crossing of the waters reiterated in the stories of Jacob, Moses and Joshua. All shared the common metaphorical goal of leaving the past behind and creating a new beginning. It is this anachronistic core of our narratives, reflecting the values and interests of the much later society of early Judaism, that creates 'history' for us. It is built not on the basis of linear time, but of reiterated flashbacks. It recasts metaphorical memories of the present as images of the past, defining them as origin story. An interesting integration of this motif with 'historical' events, meaningful to the audience's contemporary audience, is the variant to the crossing of the waters motif which is found in Josephus' *History of the Jews*. Josephus refers to a story about the Macedonian conqueror of Persia, Alexander the Great, who crossed through the sea, dry-shod to carry out God's work by marching his army against the Persians. Josephus uses this tale to mark what he viewed as the new beginnings of Hellenism. The crossing stories in the Bible are variants of Josephus' Alexander story. But even in Josephus the reference is made merely to give context to a fictive claim of historicity. The audience knows the 'event' and recognizes its reference to the transcendent 'baptism' metaphor, of crossing over the waters to salvation.

The exodus miracle of crossing through the sea is not dependent on the story in Joshua – or vice-versa – any more than the episode of Aaron and the golden calf of the wilderness story-chain is drawn from the story of Jeroboam's golden calves that were set up at shrines in Bethel and Dan. Both hold story metaphors in common about a false understanding of religion based on sacrifice rather than obedience. They are both variants of the much more explicit tale of Saul's fall from grace in I Samuel 15. The philosophical theme is addressed directly: 'Does Yahweh prefer burnt offerings and sacrifice to obedience to his voice? No, obedience is better than sacrifice; listening is preferable to a ram's fat' (I Sam. 15: 22)!

Such a theme, so central to the intellectual currents of Hellenism, is echoed repeatedly in the pages of the Bible. Yahweh complains centuries later through the prophet Isaiah that he is 'tired of the burnt offering of rams and with the fat of calves. What is he to do with all these sacrifices?' (Isa. 1: 11) More philosophically, Yahweh presents us with a teacher's view of this critique of temple cult in Hosea 6: 6: 'I want loyalty, not sacrifices; the knowledge of God, not burnt offerings.' He refuses to accept such sacrifices at all in Amos 5: 22, and the prophet Micah lends summary finality to the discussion: 'Man [that is, *Adam*], you know well what is good, what Yahweh demands of you. Deal with understanding. Show steadfast love. Keep awake and walk with your God' (Micah 6: 8). Hardly departing from this discussion, the gospels draw on Micah's metaphor of this Adam's knowledge, as Matthew has Jesus echo Micah's philosophy: 'Had you understood what it means: "I will have mercy and not sacrifice," you wouldn't have condemned the innocent. The son of man is master of the Sabbath' (Matt. 12 :7–8). Such histories as we find in I–II Samuel, reiterating the moral and philosophical discussions of tradition as they do, do not reflect events, but beliefs that were current when the collections were made.

Yet another example of story-writing by creating echoes through history is the practice of interpretive retelling of a story. This is a quite common technique in writing the stories of Jesus. One well-known story echo is in Acts 7. The story of the death by stoning of Stephen has but a thin veil separating it from Luke's story of Jesus' crucifixion. Stephen's last words before he dies (Acts 7: 59–60), 'Lord Jesus, receive my spirit,' and 'Do not charge them with this sin,' evoke Jesus' own 'Father forgive them, for they do not understand what they do' (Luke 23: 34), and 'Father, into your hands I entrust my spirit' (Luke 23: 46). Such techniques support and are supported by a reiterative understanding of history. Stephen plays the same role in his story as Jesus did in his, just as Jesus plays story roles comparable to the roles of David, Moses or Elijah. The technique can also be used to make very specific theological statements. Following a motif established in Exodus 7: 1, where Moses plays the role of God for Pharaoh and Aaron takes up the role of his prophet, the story in Acts presents Jesus in the role of God for Stephen, while Stephen is his prophet. The implied commentary of this rather bold, but none the less orthodox, reiteration of the Moses tradition is very similar to Matthew 1: 23's echo of the Moses story of Exodus 3: 12's interpretation of the name of Yahweh as the God who 'is with Israel', by citing Isaiah 7–8's Immanuel story. The story of the naming of Jesus for Matthew, as with the story of Yahweh's name reflects how God is present in the world.

One of the most striking examples of historical echoing is in the structuring of Matthew's story of Jesus on the Mount of Olives the night he is arrested (Matt. 26: 30–46). While Jesus is walking to the Mount of Olives he talks to his friends of their coming betrayal and rejection of him. When they arrive, he asks Peter and John to pray with him, but they fall asleep. He is full of anxiety, abandoned by his friends, and prays that he might avoid his coming fate. Yet, in the end, he submits to the divine will: 'Not as I will, but as you will.' The story is told in a threefold repetition of this prayer, alternating with the motif of his disciples' carefree slumber. When the scene closes, Jesus announces that the 'son of man is betrayed into the hands of sinners'.

Our model for Matthew's account is found in the story of David in II Samuel 15: 13–37. In that story, David's son Absalom has just been declared king in Hebron, causing civil war. The people go over to Absalom and David is isolated and has to flee Jerusalem. Only Ittai and the Gittites remain faithful to him, as David crosses the Kidron and goes out into the wilderness in preparation for new beginnings. David then goes to the Mount of Olives, crying the whole way, and everyone who goes with him bows their head and weeps, 'the whole country and all the people' (II Sam. 15: 23). It is here that we find the wellspring of the gospel story's pathos, in this first story of the Messiah's rejection. In mortal danger, David decides to entrust himself to what God wants and accepts his fate: 'so shall God do with me as he sees fit' (I Sam. 15: 26). David then goes up to the top of the Mount of Olives, 'where it is the custom to pray to God'. Luke's gospel picks this motif up in the line that opens his story: 'So he rose and went out to the Mount of Olives, as was the custom' (Luke 22: 39).

Although both Matthew's and Luke's gospels centre their scenes on Jesus' prayer and build them on David's commitment, confided to Zadok, whose cue-name marks the 'righteousness' of David's prayer that he will follow God's will rather than his own, the David story does not present this as David's prayer. In fact, though David goes up the mountain to pray, the prayer itself is not given. This is provided by the interpretive setting given in the title of Psalm 3: 'This is the psalm that David sang when he fled from his son Absalom.' The song is remarkably appropriate to its dramatic task: 'My enemies are many; many rise against me; many say: "God will not save him" ' (Psalm 3: 2–3). The psalmist's David commits himself totally to Yahweh, who 'answers him from his holy mountain' (Psalm 3: 4). David prays to be saved from his enemies and Yahweh answers him from his holy mountain. With Yahweh's support, David will not fear, for he knows that Yahweh destroys his enemies and crushes the ungodly. All salvation and all blessing come from Yahweh.

The interpretive technique that Matthew uses shares the perspective of the Psalter. Matthew 26: 30 introduces the story of Jesus' prayer in the garden of Gethsemane: 'After they had sung a psalm, they went out to the Mount of Olives.' The reference to singing a psalm at first appears inconsequential, until one realizes that Matthew knows his Psalter well. Not only does he use the David story of II Samuel 15 for Jesus' prayer, but he introduces his reiteration of this story with a cryptic reference to the singing of Psalm 3, the very same song that the titles in the Book of Psalms had placed in David's mouth. Psalm 3: 6–7 makes this argument certain. 'I lay down to sleep; I awake because the Lord has supported me.' Matthew reiterates this verse as his audience's voice of a new Israel, in a subtle contrast to the threefold episode of the faithless disciples who sleep but do not wake (Matt. 26: 38–46).

In II Samuel 16: 1–2, David passes the summit of the Mount of Olives and is given an ass to ride as a symbol of his royalty. He is given food and wine for his return from the wilderness. This scene finds its echo in Matthew 21, when Jesus first goes from the Mount of Olives to be hailed by the people as king, like David. The scene offers a humble foreshadowing of the celebration of Jesus entering his kingdom on that other mountain Golgotha at the gospel's close (Matt. 28). The theme of the David story stresses David's acceptance of the fate that God wills him: 'perhaps, God willing, Yahweh will hear his plea and give him happiness instead of this curse' (II Sam. 16: 12). The Mount of Olives scene closes, but the story continues until chapter 18: 9 when the threat to David and to his kingdom is finally resolved. David's son Absalom, who has also been anointed as king and God's messiah, is killed, 'hung fast on a tree', a scene that will be echoed in the story of Jesus' crucifixion. When David hears of Absalom's fate, pierced through the heart by Joab with three arrows (II Sam. 18: 14), the king weeps over his son's death, and in chapter 19 David is brought home to Jerusalem to rule his kingdom. The shared interpretation of the David story by both Psalm 3 and Matthew's story is glimpsed once again in the personal emotion both the Jesus story and the original David story captures. The use of Psalm 3's first-person voice supports an identification between the reader and each text's messiah (David or Jesus). This transference has pedagogical purpose. So, too, should the reader accept his fate. The story has positive implications. God brings all things to good. Even despair, betrayal and loneliness presage salvation. It becomes quite clear that the characters who play such roles have their primary purpose in dramatically illustrating virtue.

These narratives, in their mythic reiteration of transcendent realities, not only present themselves as collecting a tradition that belonged to the past, they collect and represent old traditions. Implicit, and often explicit, comments and interpretations give abundant evidence of this. Many of the traditions have survived successive dislocations in different literary contexts primarily because they found echo and meaning in the lives of the people that preserved them. These collectors of the biblical tradition were those who used books for education, leisure and reflection. They formed the Bible as we know it: some few teachers, philosophers and scholarly bibliophiles.

That the individual stories, songs and poems collected in the Bible were 'from the past' and were about the past was among the primary reasons they were included in the tradition. How past they were is another question that needs to be taken up with each different tradition in the collection. What we can know in answer to such questions is restricted to our understanding of the world, and of the traditions, that existed at the time our texts were written. Even as more ancient sources are claimed by the text, our judgement regarding the accuracy of such claims is limited by what we understand to have been the knowledge of the past that was available to the original writer. Traditional stories reflect both real and literary worlds. Without a detailed and independent understanding of the historical contexts in which a story once had its relevance, our ability to distinguish historical writing from fiction is fragile at best. Nowhere do the narratives directly reflect the world of old Israel that they tried to revive and preserve. The biblical traditions reflect but incoherent, part fictive, remnants of a past that those who came to see themselves as the survivors of the destruction were able to put together and give meaning to in the radically new worlds in which they lived. It was these stories' meaningful expressions of the old order – expressions that gave hope and direction to the new – that affected their preservation. Dependability in reflecting the past had nothing to do with the selection. It is the meaning that the stories could bear that brought about their preservation and transmission. One rarely finds original stories in the Bible. What are found are stories that are interpreted. And it is most often the interpretation, not the story, that matters to the writer of our text.

A very simple example of such stories that have been preserved for the sake of interpretation occurs in chapter 6 of John's gospel. Jesus is up on a mountain in Galilee. The story pivots on the need to feed a great crowd of people. However, there are only five barley loaves and two fish. John, like Matthew 15 before him, reiterates the old Elisha story of II Kings, where the prophet plays the role of a holy man feeding large crowds with just a few pieces of bread and some fish. How wonderful it was. There were even leftovers! Furthermore, John's five loaves of barley bread which become twelve baskets of crumbs add a riddle to the story: the five loaves of the torah's five books are more than enough to feed the twelve tribes of Israel. It is the cryptic message that underlies the story that is responsible for John's interest. John sets up a contrast. On one hand, there are 'those men' (John 6:

14) who interpret the miracle as a sign that Jesus is 'the prophet that should come'. This is seen as a threat to Jesus, who, like Moses before him, goes back up the mountain alone. In a paired scene on the next day, John, echoing the author of Psalm 78: 12–31, presents his interpretation of this basic story of Moses and Elisha in order to illustrate a fundamental principle of early Jewish piety and to offer a polemic against 'those men's' interest in signs and wonders: 'God, himself has set *his seal* on the son of man, who gives food for eternal life, not food that perishes' (John 6: 27). John goes on to refer to the 'bread of heaven', which Moses gave old Israel to eat, when they were in the desert. Exodus 16's manna of the wilderness story John now interprets as a foreshadowing of the 'true bread which gives life to the world' (John 6: 31ff). This is the bread of true teaching; namely the torah. People live not through magic, but by doing what God wants. This is exactly the kind of interpretation to which the Pentateuch's other variant of the story directs the miracle of the manna and the quails (Num. 11)! Moses' Israelites, like Jesus' crowds, are the opponents, misunderstanding a teaching about the spiritual values of loyalty and truth. John's story is nothing other than a faithful transmission of the tradition before him.

4 Techniques in writing Genesis

Genesis is a very good text to use when talking about how biblical narratives construct their pictures of the past. For example, three kinds of technical structures can be observed here. These three interrelated techniques are used to create coherence and unity in Genesis' 'history', in fact they offer the essence of Genesis' role as an account of the past. All are very important for the larger discussion. A naive or excessively realistic reading of Genesis can easily cause confusion about what is understood as historical by the tradition.

a) *Chronologies* The chronology that we find used in the book of Genesis in the Hebrew Bible is based on a very simple system, yet it has little to do with what we would normally understand as either chronology or history, and much more to do with highlighting and emphasizing the importance of events. The system is a construction based on a chronological scheme using the Hellenistic motif of a 'great year' of 4,000 years' duration. The history consists of a chain of traditions reaching back into the past, to a central event that is celebrated as the focus of the tradition's chronology. The projected completion of a 'great year' in the tradition's future allows the whole to be read as an implied prophecy. The identification of the great year's closure provides the hidden key to interpretation. The Hebrew Bible's great year finds its focal point in the year 2666 BCE, the date of the Exodus and of the creation of old Israel. The great year of this tradition's future, the equivalent of the year 4,000, which marks the goal of this tradition, is timed to fall in 164 BCE, the year in which the temple of Jerusalem was rededicated to Yahweh in the course of the Maccabean revolt. This is the year of the birth of the new Israel that gives meaning to the tradition. The key to this chronological revision of the stories is found in the implicit warning for the new departures that the temple's rededication inaugurates. The pivotal events on which the dating system is based, counting back from the Hellenistic period's Maccabean rededication of the temple, are: the edict of the Persian king Cyrus, who ordered the building of the second temple; the destruction of the first temple and the beginning of exile; the original construction of the temple by Solomon; the exodus of the Israelites from Egypt under Moses (marked with special emphasis); Yahweh's call of Abraham; and finally Abraham's birth. The whole begins with the creation of Adam in *anno mundi* (AM) 1. The known historical information on the basis of which the system begins – that is from the viewpoint of the system's creators – was knowledge of the temple's rededication under the Maccabees (164 BCE) and the length of time between that event and the date of the legendary edict of Cyrus (538 BCE). This was 374 years, the exact length of time necessary to complete the needed total of a 'great year' of 4,000 years' duration since the beginning of the world. The pivotal date of the structure is the dating of the Exodus to the year 2666 AM, representing both two-thirds of a 'great year' and $26 \frac{2}{3}$ of the Bible's forty generations, an average of 100 years' duration since the time of Adam. It is for this reason that the antediluvian patriarchs are given such great ages, up to Methuselah's 969 years. We find only a remnant of what appears to be a 100-year generation scheme in Genesis 15: 12–16, where the period of enslavement in Egypt is measured both as 400 years and as four generations long. A similar calculation is found in the frequent forty-year generation scheme in both the wilderness story, the Book of Judges and in the lives of some of Genesis' heroes. For example, Abraham lives for 100 years in Canaan. Isaac is born when Abraham is 100 years old. Isaac marries at the age of forty, and, at the age of sixty, has his first-born son Esau, who in his turn marries at the age of forty when Isaac is 100 years old. From the birth of Abraham in 1946 AM to Solomon's temple in 3146 AM, we have twelve generations totalling 1,200 years. Similarly we also have twelve generations, but of forty years each, totalling 480 years, from the Exodus to the building of the temple. From that time to the exile we have 430 years + 50 years for the exile itself, to find once again a paired time-span of 480 years. The 430-year period, from the building of the temple to its destruction, occurs again as the length of time from the entrance into Egypt to the exodus. The systemic quality of such calculations is assured when we note that the total length of the time of the patriarchs is exactly half of this total; i.e., 215 years long.

Adam..	1 AM
Birth of Abraham...	1946 AM
Call of Abraham	2021 AM
Entrance into Egypt...	2236 AM
Exodus from Egypt...	2666 AM
Solomon's temple..	3146 AM
Exile to Babylon	3576 AM
Edict of Cyrus	3626 AM = 538 BCE
Rededication of temple	4000 AM = 164 BCE

All the data dependent on the 480–430–215 year scheme, as well as the date of the Exodus in the year 2666 and Abraham's birth in 1946, are explained within this Hellenistic ontology of time.

b) *Toledoth* Unlike the close variant of Genesis found in the book of Jubilees, and also unlike the rather loose accumulation of genealogies that can be found in the First Book of Chronicles, Genesis' narrative forms a continuous and quite complicated chain from the creation of the world to the origin of Israel as a people. The chain used is genealogical: a list of ancestors, following a pattern of father and son, without gap or break. I would describe this as the *toledoth* or 'genealogy' framework – see figure 1 on p.76

The system is a relatively simple one. It has its starting-point in the original title of Genesis, found in Genesis 5:1: 'This is the Book of the *Toledoth* of Adam'. Genesis is the *Book of Adam*'s *Tradition*: what comes after and from his existence. It is 'the story of humanity'. The *toledoth* structure binds together the distinct parts of Genesis into a continuous narrative. So we find the phrase: 'this is the *toledoth* of the sky and the earth' used to link the creation story of Genesis 1 with the quite different doublet-story of the garden of Eden in Genesis 2–3 and of Cain and Abel in Genesis 4. First the world is created. The text then presents what follows from that creation; that is *toledoth*. These narratives are used as an introduction to the book, which begins with the genealogy of Adam in Genesis 5 and leads up to the flood story of Genesis 11. The flood story is followed by four major movements, structured consecutively: the three-fold list of Noah's sons down to Terah, Abraham's father, is used to introduce the Abraham and Isaac stories. These lead us to the tales of Jacob and his sons, which, in turn, are used to open the Joseph story. Each of these long chain-narratives is introduced by a genealogical preface. Just as the genealogy of Genesis 5 leads to the *toledoth* of Noah, so Genesis 11's *toledoth* of Shem introduces Terah. Similarly, the genealogy of Ishmael introduces the story of Isaac, and those of Esau lead us to the stories of Jacob and his sons. The *toledoth* does not introduce the character named, but the history that follows him. For example, Jacob's *toledoth* does not begin the story of Jacob but that of his sons. It even includes Genesis 38's tale of Judah, which is unrelated to the tale of Joseph and his brothers that closes Genesis.

Figure 1

The toledoth structure in Genesis

Gen. 1: 1–2.3 (used as a preface to the *toledoth* of the sky and the earth)

Gen. 2: 4 – *toledoth* of the sky and the earth (sectional title for Gen. 2: 4–4: 26)

Gen. 5: 1 – *toledoth* of Adam (title of book, Genesis 1–50; Gen. 5: 3–32 is used as a preface to the *toledoth* of Noah)

Gen. 6: 9 – *toledoth* of Noah (sectional title for Gen. 5: 32–9: 29)

Gen. 10: 1 – *toledoth* of the sons of Noah (expansion of the Noah *toledoth*, Gen. 10: 1–11: 9)

Gen. 11: 10 – *toledoth* of Shem (Gen. 11: 10–26 is used as a preface to the *toledoth* of Terah)

Gen. 11: 27 – *toledoth* of Terah (sectional title for Gen. 11: 27b–25: 11)

Gen. 25: 12 – *toledoth* of Ishmael (Gen. 25: 12–18 is used as a preface to the *toledoth* of Isaac)

Gen. 25: 19 – *toledoth* of Isaac (sectional title for Gen. 25: 19–35: 29)

Gen. 36: 1 – *toledoth* of Esau (Genesis 36 is used as a preface to the *toledoth* of Jacob)

Gen. 37: 2 – *toledoth* of Jacob (sectional title for Gen. 37: 2–50: 26)

c) *Eponymy*   The third technique used in creating Genesis' history writing is the fiction of eponymy. Eponyms are forms of 'cue-names', names in stories that tell the audience something about the role the character plays in the narrative. The most frequent forms of eponym in Genesis reflect geographical and political toponomy. Quite commonly, these names appear listed in the genealogies. They are often interpreted as ancestors of the groups represented by their names. Sometimes small stories and legends are attached to such names. The use of eponymous ancestors in tradition creation is also well known in early Arabic, Greek and Latin literature. These eponymous characters often travel, and become associated with origin stories of peoples and nations. Such characters can also have story lives simply as heroes, quite apart from the nations or historical realities they represent.

The most elaborate use of this fictive technique is in classical sources. A good parallel to Israel and his twelve sons, representing the nation and its tribes, is mentioned by Diodorus Siculus. The hero Aeolus had twelve sons who were the ancestral founders of the twelve legendary towns of earliest Aeolia. In Pindar, we have a story about a man Opus who, having been adopted by Lokrus, went on to found the city of Opus in the region of Lokris. Travel in these stories usually has a purely fictional function, with no known association with historical events. Aetolus fled the Peloponnesus because of a murder. He then settled on the northern shore of the Gulf of Corinth, a region that was called Aetolia, which had two major towns: the names of Aetolus' two sons, Pleuron and Kalydon. Sometimes the heroes have adventures. Such is the story of Danaos and his son Aegyptos. Aegyptos (ancestor of the Egyptians) had fifty sons who wanted to marry the fifty daughters of Danaos, the father of the Danoi, an ancient people of the Aegean. To prevent this, Danaos sent his daughters on a ship with fifty oars bound for Argos. The sons followed and all but one were murdered. He is not only named Argos, but became the king of Argos.

A variation on the eponymous ancestor was that of a founding father. In the Latin traditions, the wandering of Aeneas, like the wandering of Abraham, was well suited to the building of genealogies and the creating of small geographical legends. Like Abraham, the father of many nations, yet not himself an eponym of any, Aeneas was the legendary founder of settlements in Thrace, Delos, Arcadia, the islands of Kythera and Zakynthus, areas in southern Italy, Sicily, Carthage, Misenum and Latium. The motive of most of these genealogies and wandering stories was to account for the origin of the various groups referred to. The persons connected by the genealogies are personified districts, nations, towns, patronages, lineages, trades, guilds, mountains, springs, lakes and rivers. This type of fictive ancestor is quite at home within lineage and patronage systems, because of their frequent use of family metaphors to describe themselves. This might well explain the abundance of such material in the Bible, as the patronage system was established throughout Palestine and throughout the Mediterranean world. The names are connected as fathers, mothers, sons or daughters. Stories and legends filled out the genealogy. Certainly, the vast majority of the names in Genesis follow one or other type of this pattern, from the great table of nations, Ham, Shem and Japheth representing the geography of Africa, Asia and Europe, in Genesis 10 to each of the central characters of most of the book's collected tales.

5 The biblical Israel as fiction

Biblical Israel, as an element of tradition and story, such as the Israel of the murmuring stories in the wilderness, or the people of the stories of II Kings who are faithless as their kings are faithless, or the lost Israel, which is the object of prophetic diatribe in Isaiah and Amos, is a theological and literary creation. This Israel is what I have called 'old Israel'. It is presented as the polar opposite of an equally theological and literary 'new Israel', which is the implicit voice, for example, of II Chronicles, the Book of Psalms, the Damascus Covenant and the gospels.

The discussion about the fictional quality of biblical narratives, and especially this chapter's discussion about how such stories refer to an historical world is central to the issue of the Bible and its relationship to the past. We can best understand this if we consider briefly the fictional qualities of Israel in the Bible. This Israel stands in sharp contrast to the Israel that we know from ancient texts and from archaeological field work. Of course, the Israel of the Jacob story who wrestled with God and who was the father of twelve children, all of whom became in their turn fathers of Israel's twelve tribes, is a character of fiction, based on the assumed existence of Israel in its twelve tribes. Few biblical scholars would doubt this today. Such 'eponymous' figures of story have a life of their own, quite apart from any real or assumed past. Odysseus' struggle with the Cyclops need not have anything to do with a known past and hardly gives us cause to believe in historical Cyclopses in the Aegean's past. Similarly, Israel's tribes need not have been either twelve or tribes in reality. More than that, names in both history and tradition have a very long life. They change over time and can have a variety of real references. This section's title, emphasizing the fictive quality of the Bible's Israel, refers not merely to the Bible's use of eponymy but to the way the Bible created an entire past for its 'old Israel'. It built this fiction out of traditions, stories and legendary lore from Palestine's past. Some of the sources for such 'knowledge' are very old, and it is useful to take a look at how such knowledge changes over time.

The name 'Israel' goes back in history to at least the thirteenth century BCE. It was once the name of the people of Canaan (western Palestine) who are said to have been destroyed by the Egyptian army under Pharaoh Merenptah. However, the reference to an 'Israel' as the spouse of Canaan in an early Egyptian inscription is hardly the same as evidence for the historical existence of the Israel of the Bible. This text renders only the earliest known usage of a name. It does not refer to the 'Israel' we know from the Assyrian period and which is mentioned in both Assyrian and Palestinian texts. That Israel was a small regional state that controlled the highlands north of Jerusalem, and which first developed some centuries after Merenptah. Apart from the obvious difficulty that the Egyptian stele reports that 'Israel's seed' had been destroyed and 'was no more', it does not correspond with the highland Israel or any biblical Israel. If the Merenptah stele expresses any 'real' history, we know nothing of that from the Bible. When the Israelites leave Egypt in the Exodus story, they are a great nation threatening Egypt itself. This is hardly the Israel whose children Merenptah has 'annihilated'. In Joshua this people is opposed to Canaanites and conquer the entire 'land of Canaan', and in the stories of Judges and I Samuel, they come to dominate the coastal plain's Philistines. In the Books of II Samuel and I Kings, biblical Israel controls the whole of the South Levant between Egypt and the Euphrates, a region that, with the help of Judah, Israel holds until the story of its destruction in II Kings 17. Outside of this narrative in Genesis–II Kings and the related books named after prophets, the name Israel is a constant of biblical literature especially in the form the 'children of Israel', with reference either to the patronage states of Jerusalem and Samaria, or to later groups of Jews, Samaritans, Galileans, Idumeans, Christians and still other religious groups who understood themselves with the theological metaphor of a 'new Israel'.

That it is hard to identify any of these biblical and biblically related Israels with specific historical peoples or nations should not be surprising. There are a number of names of 'peoples' that first appear in texts of the Bronze Age. These names also take a variety of meanings over the course of centuries. For example, although the name 'Hebrew', used for the language of the Bible, belongs to the period of the Bible's formation, the name 'Hebrew' used as a gentilic – that is, as a term referring to a people – goes much further back to refer to a class or a type of person. Related terms show up in Sumerian, Assyro-Babylonian and Egyptian texts in the forms *SA.GAZ*, *Hapiru* and *'Apiru*. These terms refer to individuals and groups who were not accepted within the accepted political structures of patronage alliances and loyalties that governed society. These 'Hebrews' were both literally and figuratively 'outlaws', not terribly unlike such legendary characters in story as the David of I–II Samuel or the Abraham of Genesis 12 and 14, where they are called 'Hebrews'.

The word 'Amorite' first appears in cuneiform texts in the form *amurru*. Already in the late Early Bronze Age, it is used to signify geographic direction, as in the *amurru*, that is, 'western', regions. As a name, it refers rather generically to the people of and from this region. By the Late Bronze Age, it appears as the name of a region of Syria. A similar-sounding but unrelated name, '*Amw* – a word originally referring to the 'boomerang' throwing-stick used as a weapon by these people – is used in early Egyptian texts to refer generally to the people of Asia, and especially to Semites and culturally related groups who inhabited the desert regions and the Egyptian Delta. In the Bible, the name 'Amorite' is used as a variant of the term 'Canaanite', as a name used for the indigenous population of Palestine.

The term 'Philistine' has had perhaps the richest variety of usage: now over more than 3,000 years. It first appears in the form *peleset* in thirteenth-century BCE Egyptian texts, where it is used as a gentilic, and refers to one of several groups of immigrants from the Aegean, or perhaps from coastal Anatolia, who have settled along the southern coast of Palestine and who attack the Delta. They are finally settled and accommodated within Egyptian territories, including Palestine's coast. By the Assyrian period, the name, in the form *Palashtu*, occurs in cuneiform texts. It refers to a geographic region covering most of southern Palestine. In the writings of the sixth-century BCE Greek author, Herodotus, 'Palestine' is a geographic name for the whole of Southern Syria.

This also seems to have been the sense in which the Romans used it centuries later. The term Palestine was used by European scholars since at least the sixteenth century much in the Roman manner. After the First World War, it was used by the British mandate government, as well as by Jews, Muslims and Christians living in the region. Increasingly, it has come to refer to the territory to the west of the Jordan River. Since 1948, and especially since the war of 1967, the term Palestine has been used for the territories that were not part of the state of Israel. Historical and biblical scholarship, however, has generally continued the use of the term as in the period of the British mandate, to refer to the entire region south of the Litani River and the Lebanese mountains to Gaza and the Sinai in the south and from the Mediterranean to the Transjordanian opening to the Arabian desert in the east. The gentilic, 'Palestinian', has come into use increasingly to refer to the indigenous, non-Jewish population of this greater area, and is beginning to take on exclusively ethnic connotations. According to biblical lore, the Philistines were the pre-Abraham inhabitants of the southern coast and the Shefelah – where they appear frequently in stories from Genesis to II Samuel. They are said originally to have come from Caphtor (Crete), and to have built cities and kingdoms at such places as Gerar, Gaza, Ashqelon and Ekron.

The term 'Canaanite' is badly used by most everyone in archaeology and ancient Near Eastern studies today, thanks to the Israeli archaeological practice of identifying the Bronze Age as a 'Canaanite period'. Biblical archaeologists use it as if it referred to an ethnic and culturally coherent fact. Unfortunately, this does not correspond with any known historical reality. Not only is the term 'Canaan' originally a geographic name, without a specific, historically defined identification; it is unknown as a name of a people at this early date. It has more to do with coastal Syria and Phoenicia than Palestine's lowlands, and does not correspond with the larger towns of Palestine even in the Bible. The sharp boundaries that the use of the terms 'Canaanite' and 'Israelite' makes possible are wholly unwarranted. 'Canaan' appears on the Merenptah stele and has been shown to be paired with 'Israel' as his spouse. They are the metaphorical parents of three towns destroyed by the Egyptian army. The only historical group known to refer to themselves as Canaanites were Jewish merchants of North Africa in the fourth century CE. It has also been well argued that the name 'Canaanite' is used in the Bible as a literary and fictive term to contrast with the biblical Israel. It is a negative term for those who worship foreign gods, and especially Ba'al. In the stories of Genesis to Joshua, Canaanites play much the role that Philistines play in Judges and I–II Samuel, and the role that Israel itself often plays in II Kings; namely as a universal term for the enemies of Yahweh.

The development of the biblical tradition reflects the formative process by which names such as 'Israel' and its counterparts in the Bible's stories were created out of the fragments of Palestinian folk traditions and literature that had survived the political and historical disruptions of the Assyrian and Neo-Babylonian periods. The formation of biblical narrative was a process that created the Israel we know. It had its earliest roots in the period of Assyria's domination of Palestine, but the understanding of Israel we know from the tradition first arose during the late Persian or early Hellenistic period, and was not fully developed before the time of the Maccabees. Long after the destructions of Samaria and Jerusalem, in the course of the gradual restructuring of Persia's conquered territories by both the Persians and their Hellenistic successors, the Israel of tradition presented itself to history, like the phoenix, specifically in the form of an *Israel redivivus*. The true essence and significance of Israel – and implicitly its future glory – was traced in the tales of the patriarchs, the stories of the wilderness and of the judges, and the great legends about the golden age of the united monarchy. Idealistic sentiments of futuristic incipient messianism ring throughout this tradition with the recurrent affirmation of one people and one God. It is this God, the only true king of a finally new Israel, who is projected to some day come to rule his chosen remnant from his throne in Jerusalem's temple. This idyllic reality of piety is the Israel of tradition.

CHAPTER 4

Myths of origins

1 The origin stories of humanity

Although the creation story in the first chapter of Genesis may appear to us as very naive, it still honestly reflects the world that people experience. Light, earth, air and water, the four basic elements of the creation story, answer to the expectations of traditional elements in Hellenistic philosophy, namely, earth, air, fire and water. They also answer to experience. There is a great light that controls the day and a small one for the night. These lights and the stars are the basis for our calendars. They tell us when to have our holidays. Earth, air and water are three basic aspects of the world we experience. They are separate from each other, and each might well be described as having its own life-forms: animals, fish and birds. And the earth lets plants and trees of all kinds grow including those that give us food and some that are beautiful. Who but a literalist would deny that the earth gives birth to animals as the sea does to its creatures? The images of the sky as a barrier that holds back water high above us, and of the land surrounded by and floating on the sea, are metaphors that have grown from the observation of rain and storms on the one hand and of wells, springs and rivers on the other.

When it comes to people, the poet who wrote the creation story of Genesis was hardly the first person who had imagined people to be unique and with some special value. Few humans avoid this conceit. Nor was the teller of the garden story the first to present the case in a different way. What were people like? They were like gods, made, as in Genesis 5: 1, in the divine image. It is not for nothing that ancient critics described humans ironically as 'gods with clay feet'. They were male and female, like the gods and goddesses of all the world's temples. They looked just like the gods in temples do. That the poet might have smiled when he uttered this metaphor, and could hardly have avoided thinking of Jeremiah's cynical comment that the best one could say of such gods was that they were made by clever men, is not grounds for dismissing either the perception or the humour of the metaphor. No more should we dismiss the garden story's contrasting proposal that animals and people alike came from the ground, and that it was life that was divine – and wisdom – and definitely not people. Neither life nor wisdom was possessed wholly by humans. Neither remained with them. Life stayed with men for only a short time, as it were a visitor, and it has always been hard to hold to the belief that men truly possessed wisdom. If, by chance, it is found here and there, we still call it 'inspiration'. It has been most unbecoming for theologians to bicker so long about whether it was a man or a woman who was made first, and which brought sin into the world. Both theses distort Genesis' story, which includes us all in each of the garden's couple: in Adam as the 'earthly' source of our 'humanity' (*adamah/adam*), and in Eve as the 'mother of all living' (*hevah*). The story sketches vividly the alienations that are so fundamental to our being human: women from the men they love and all of us from the earth we were born from. Nor can we hope to deny the ironic contradictions that both stories shame us with. We must think of this perspective on people with the full impact of Genesis 1:26's tragic irony. God would have the world good as he saw it. Then he made people just like him.

Does the garden story talk about the first historical human beings? Does it state that such early humanoids lived in a garden paradise at the beginning of time? Is the whole of the cosmos evolved in the space of six days, replete with geological stratification and fossils to test our faith? Or do we have to create scenarios of how seven days might somehow be God-speak for seven eras of millions of years? Is this crisp, striking story really threatened by any modern desire to read geology and anthropology with intelligence? Are we condemned in each generation to argue anew that our knowledge of the great antiquity of the world and of the process of life's development in the past does or does not contradict the Bible? Surely not.

The authors of biblical texts knew precious little about the immediate past and next to nothing about the distant past. They had neither magic glasses nor any special knowledge. But they were good poets and skilful story-tellers. Their theology was adventurous and at times courageous, though their philosophy was unexceptional. With their own human limitations, their stories take us, not back to the beginning of time, but to an imaginary time, a mythical time, before the world was the way it is. Such a time is enclosed within the transcendent space of a Narnia-like, legendary land of Qedem in which our world comes into contact with the transcendent. It is here that our world was born in story, and from Qedem that the narrative begins.

The garden story doesn't begin with the first man, 'Adam'. It begins with *humanity*, which is personified as an individual. That's what the Hebrew word *adam* means: not male, not female – they come later in this story. What does it mean to be a human being? Well, this is an old story. It comes from a time when most people were farmers, and all – like today – lived because of farmers. Farmers of course live from the ground. And so our story tells us that this humanity ('*adam*) was made out of a piece of ground ('*adamah* in Hebrew). This pun on '*adam* and '*adamah* runs the story. We begin with the soil from which we were made, just as we return to the soil when we die. This speaks to the essence of being human within a world of metaphor. The reason God's Yahweh first made the human being was to be his gardener; the garden had need of him. Later in the story, when the human is transformed into Adam and Eve, Adam becomes the farmer, fighting his losing battle with the ground for life, alienated from what made him what he was. This frustration – as we all know – doesn't end. One doesn't have to attend too many funerals in order to understand humanity's final transition to that peaceful reconciliation with its essence. Emotionally, the story is perceptive.

The garden story is no less sparing in its humour when it discusses what it means to be a woman. Debates about women's equality and descriptions of the oppression that is created by their subordination to men of power and wealth didn't begin with the suffragettes. Certainly this story-teller needs to be recognized as one of the first of such voices. The tale's politics of sexual alienation begins with a simple truth that we have all experienced as one of the most painful aspects of being human: 'It is not good for people to be lonely.' The deity, having been the first of us to notice, decides to make a second living creature to be 'mates' with his human. He hopes with this to overcome the problem of loneliness. The task the story assigns Yahweh is to make a creature just like the first one. Now, there are two simple ways of doing this, which most every ancient villager would know. The first is the way of the potter. The task seems easy: use the same materials and do it the same way. And so God's Yahweh takes more soil and forms another creature. He brings it to the human. In this episode, the deity of the story becomes the victim of the narrator's sense of humour, and he is forced to play the dumbling until the end of the scene. Something's wrong! It doesn't work. Over and over, the creator forms one creature after another. Each time he brings it to the person he had originally made. Each time, the person is dissatisfied. What the deity brings is not quite right: not quite his mate. We might imagine hearing his complaints to the ever-helpful Yahweh: 'No, that's a horse. That's a cow. That's a cat!' None of them is quite like the person; none is quite the creature to overcome loneliness. This is how all the animals of the earth and all the birds of the air were created, yet now the creator was at a loss.

God's Yahweh then tries a second way, the way of the gardener, and performs the world's first clone. If you really want a second plant in every way comparable to the first, the best way is to use part of the one you have. It works the same with humans: like from like! Aiming at closing the scene with an old well-known rhyming ditty about families and patronage, the story moves quickly. The deity puts the human to sleep, takes one of its ribs and forms it into a woman. He brings her to what the story now calls 'the man'. Immediately, and without the least effort to hide his exasperation with the deity, the man sings out: 'Now, finally! Bone of my bone; flesh of my flesh.' The further citation of an obscure proverb about marriage rounds off the story.

Having changed the person into male and female, with the woman a recognized equal, a true mate to her husband, the story does not end. That isn't at all the way the real world is. We all know that. It is, after all, rather a very harsh world in which we and the story's audience live. The garden story is an aetiology. It is a fictional tale that evokes a perspective of reality that helps us understand the truth of things, and here, the truth about being human. The garden story isn't a story about a romantic place of paradise where no one is hungry, no one suffers and no one dies. Quite the contrary, its story's goal is the real world we live in, where hunger, pain and death are commonplace, and where each, unfortunately, does a thorough job of defining us as human. The story does not talk about history. It talks about the realities of human life, and how we are defined through our hunger, our pain and our deaths.

This story is a very ambitious one. Although the garden or 'paradise' story is often explained as a story of 'original sin' and a contest between evil and good, Satan and God, in fact it is not about these things at all. It is both more subtle and more fragile. Yahweh and the talking snake do not represent good and evil, God and the devil. Yahweh and the snake are characters in a story: they are what they say and do there. Yahweh does reflect the world of the divine, but the snake is not evil, he is merely a friendly talking snake who knows what is really going on in the story. He helps people get what little knowledge is ours. Whatever that knowledge is worth, the snake is punished for his efforts. He is alienated forever – as real snakes are – from those he would befriend.

The story is painted with quick strokes and in bold colours. To be human is first and foremost to be nothing in oneself. Only the divine has lasting value. To be alive is to share in the divine. God takes this worthless piece of clay and breathes into it, and so it becomes a living creature. To die is to return to one's essence. People are not gods, and the story-teller and his audience know that. One can use poetry about God's spirit and his breath, but it does not stay. People do not succeed. They do not last. Human beings die. A doubling of this metaphor is explored in the motif of wisdom. People are not naturally intelligent. Our story understands this well. People need to learn to know. The wisest learn to know that they do not know. The couple of the garden story – having eaten the fruit to achieve wisdom – only know that they are naked.

It begins in a scene, comic and ironic. The deity tells the person that the whole garden is at its disposal. Yet one small demand is made: do not eat any of the fruit from the 'tree of knowledge of good and evil, because it will kill you!' It is important to remember that the people in this story are not yet very bright. They still do not know they are naked. So they don't recognize this strange idea – this tool of oppression – that knowledge is dangerous and can kill the one possessing it. One can, however, be sure that no audience will miss such an emphatic echo of reality's world. It is only when the friendly talking snake enters the story that humanity's ignorant bliss is shattered. Unlike people, the snake understands. In fact, the snake is wiser than any other of God's creatures. When the woman tells him of the danger of the Tree of Wisdom, he takes what she tells him quite literally. He tells her that God knows this isn't true. The snake explains to her that in fact if she eats this fruit, she won't be killed. Her eyes, in fact, will be opened and she will become like God, having wisdom herself. A Tree of Wisdom is, after all, a tree of wisdom! And so the woman looks at the tree and sees it once again. She doesn't see the dangerous tree of the divine patron's warnings. It appears to her now as attractive. She sees it as good to eat in order to gain knowledge.

In this scene in which the woman and her husband take their fate in their own hands, the story stresses an implicit contrast and alienation between human understanding and divine wisdom, a perspective similar to Genesis 1. With the woman playing the everyman's role in the garden story, she takes the world as it seems good to her, from her own perspective. The garden story explores this human perspective as the woman sees eating the forbidden fruit as good, because it will make her wise. When she reaches for the fruit to eat it, the story presents her as the philosopher seeking wisdom. She takes on the cloak of the philosopher king. She is Solomon of the Book of Ecclesiastes. He too gave his life to seek wisdom, only to find that he had been chasing the wind. Only in the Book of Ecclesiastes does a philosopher offer such self-criticism as our narrator of Genesis' tale does.

The literalist predictions of the snake now come true. The eyes of the woman and her husband are opened. They now possess wisdom and understanding. But what is that wisdom they now have? What is human knowledge and understanding? In answer, the story-teller offers us heavy-handed mockery. His summation of human wisdom is that great divine quality that distinguishes us from other animals – that, in the language of the Bible, makes us a little less than angels. What is the wisdom? Nothing less than knowing we are naked! The irony doesn't stop there. As soon as they find out that they are naked, they busy themselves making skirts of fig leaves to hide all that they have learned! As it does to us, knowledge makes the couple afraid: they become afraid of their nakedness and hide when Yahweh walks through the garden.

The second prediction was that they will become like gods. This too comes true in its own way, as God himself tells us at the close of the story.

Even so, this fruit turns to ashes in their mouths. In the next scene, the couple hear God coming for a walk in the garden 'in the spirit of the day'. The language here, with its echoes of the classical world's *carpe diem*, exposes ironic implications of creative opportunities lost through the couple's, implicitly contrasting, lack of a true 'fear of God'. They rather trust in their own understanding of what is good. With their so human knowledge, they now hide, while the spirit moves them to 'fear God' and to the beginning of wisdom. Adam explains that when he heard God's Yahweh coming, he hid in fear. This motif grows out of the joke on the anxieties of nakedness. Having failed to understand the 'fear of God' (namely, discernment and understanding), they live out the added irony of fearing the knowledge of their nakedness; that is – from a philosopher's perspective – the knowledge of their own ignorance. This is the essence of the biblical wisdom tradition's 'fear of God'!

The motifs of comic irony in the scene about the nakedness of human wisdom prepare the audience for the scene of questioning that now opens. Yahweh's response does not address the issue that the man has been startled. He rather asks: 'Who told you that you were naked?' Quite clearly this God realizes that they didn't have the intelligence to notice this themselves. He takes only this short time to ask and to draw his rhetorical conclusion: 'Did you eat the fruit that I forbade you to eat?' The implications of this guess at once resolve the story's tension. Yahweh well understood – as the talking snake had explained to everyone already. This fruit did give knowledge.

There follows a brief comic scene, in which the man and the woman both try to pass the blame along the poet's chiasm: from the woman to the snake, and from the man to God, with the exquisite sexism of the line: 'The woman, whom *you* gave me . . .' Now the deity turns to establish the destinies of the three conspirators with his curses. As in the tower of Babel story, he alienates those who once cooperated with each other: there, alienation is the fate of our languages; here, it lies in our hatred, our sex and our humanity. The woman is condemned to love one who would rather dominate her. She is to be alienated from her own passion, and it will bring her only pain and labour. With blunt humour, the man has his sexism thrown back at him: 'Because you listened to your wife . . .' Adam's curse is the all-paraphrasing curse of everyman. The author plays once again with the pun of Adam and adamah: with the humanity and earth of our essence. Our alienation is such that it is even echoed in our longing for the reconciliation that is to be our deaths. This is the world of the story's referent.

But we still have a problem with the story's plot. Did eating the fruit of the tree of wisdom bring death? Adam and Eve live on in the story, and in other stories to come. Theirs is not a story about mortality. Humanity's mortality, its substance of clay, is already implicitly marked from the story's opening scene. The motif of death is directly associated with wisdom. The metaphor is rather a commentary on the impoverishment of human knowledge and understanding compared to divine wisdom. The issue of mortality still remains unresolved after the curses. It is the theme of the story's closing soliloquy. Here God's Yahweh asks himself what is to be done now that people have become 'like gods, having understanding'. What might happen if they now get to the tree of life and, eating that fruit, live forever? It is to prevent people from becoming gods that the divine Yahweh puts them out of the garden. He guards 'the way to the tree of life' with the monstrous cherubim. Return is impossible; we can not re-enter Qedem. The path to the tree of life is closed, as the monsters are armed with a magic, flaming sword: one that cuts in all directions at once and can not be parried. The closure of the story extends the threefold alienation of human destiny. This is the death that humanity's independence has wrought: that impulse to do what is seen as good in one's own eyes, to be like God, to choose for oneself, to have knowledge oneself both of what is good and evil. That, the story tells us, excludes us from the garden of Yahweh, from the path of life, where we might be his servants, and live.

Life as the life of piety, of submission: this is the way of life that the ideology of this story illustrates. The narrative voice of this story is aware of tradition's Yahweh. His use of irony and humour, moreover, suggest the divine incompatibility with human self-worth. The narrative is not uncritical of the piety it illustrates. In fact, it is this sense of critical observation, which marks so much of biblical narrative, that distinguishes it so markedly from religious propaganda. God and humanity are not compatible. The whole of the Bible that follows develops within the tension of this discourse.

While there are few stories in the Bible that match the *tour de force* of our garden story, many lesser stories use the same techniques of punning declarations of destiny to explain how our world got to be the way it is. These stories talk about the present, not the past. They talk about the real world of the story's narrator. Like the garden story and the creation story before it, they do not tell us about what God once did, but rather about how the implied authors and their audience saw and viewed their world. Puns and 'cue-names' abound. As the Hebrew meaning of Adam's name expresses our humanity, and Eve's echoes the word for 'life' (Gen. 3: 20), Abel's name (from *hebel*, 'dew': Gen. 4: 2) reflects the fragility of his life, and Enosh's name (Gen. 4: 26) is the same word for the 'mankind' that descends from him. Noah's cue-name echoes his story in an ironic joke. Humanity finally 'finds rest' (*nah*) from its alienation from the ground. Babylon (*babel*) reflects the babble (*balal*) of voices that once occurred within its walls, as well as the everyday experience of the alienating potential of human communication.

The stories collected in the Bible's first book open with a poem describing the beginning of the world. In this poem, the divine spirit touches chaos, and, separating and distinguishing what had been undifferentiated matter, brings form and order from barren darkness. It creates a world that the poem presents as the work of God, a world that is understood by the divine craftsman as good. However, the following stories, from the garden story of Adam and Eve to the tale of the building of the city of Babylon and its tower, complicate the plot, long before the world comes to be anything that any of us might recognize as historical. These stories tell us of the human desire for wisdom and of the dangers of a little knowledge. The stories are humorous and ironic. They are presented in a stream of wordplay and puns. They end with a sceptical story about humans working in harmony and peace, building something for themselves. It will be a great city with a tower as high as the sky! The author, with his Babylonian mirror of Jerusalem, and with his tower hardly veiling David's Zion of legendary fame, offers us a world in conflict with God, where people do their own will, and make a world that *they* see as good. It is a pious narrative, yet it is one that hardly expects much good to come of a creation that increasingly resembles the world we live in. The moral of this whole story from Genesis 1–11 is about conflict and alienation. It is intentionally unsettling.

2 Of nations and heroes

In the book of Genesis, we find lists of names attached to, introducing and expanding into many kinds of stories. The lists themselves hardly make thrilling reading. Many today skip past them when reading the Bible. Many put up with them for the sake of the stories that surround them. Nevertheless, these lists lie at the heart of the central story-line. While the stories of Moses in the wilderness that are collected in the next four books of the Pentateuch deal with Israel as an example, Genesis starts from the perspective of the unity of mankind. Its perspective ever remains broader than that of Israel alone.

The 'table of nations' of Genesis 10 and the tower of Babel story of Genesis 11 are variant parallel stories. Conceptually independent, they cannot be read as if Genesis 11 happens after Genesis 10. They evoke the same aetiological reality. Both begin in an imaginary world of human unity. The one takes its departure from the flood, with Noah's family. The other begins as a single people with a single language, who come out of the mythical land of Qedem to the valley of Shinar. Both give an account of how the earth's many peoples developed, each with its own land and language. Genesis 10 does this with a genealogical tree that portrays a single family of mankind. This genealogical list presents the eponymous 'fathers' of countries, cities and peoples of the ancient world: Canaan and the Semites, Tarsis and Rhodes, Cush, Egypt and Sheba, Babel and Akkad, Sidon and Gaza and many, many other nations and places of history and story. It organizes them geographically according to the three great continents known to the ancient Near East. Shem, Ham and Japhet reflect in turn Asia, Africa and Europe. Geographical names play the roles of characters of story. This kind of list lends itself readily to expansive and creative story collection. Notes of commentary, explaining the origin of the coastal peoples, tracing the Philistines to Caphtor, or adding an historical note on when the Canaanites had spread into their land, give us insight into how ancient geography was taught. Other similar lists of names in Genesis, such as Genesis 4, present us with origin stories and aetiologies for trades and occupations. Jabal is the father of shepherds and tent-dwellers, while his brother Jubal was the ancestor for everyone who plays the lyre and flute. The composite Tubal-Cain is given the role of patron for desert-dwelling metal-workers. Other lists, like the Ishmael genealogy of Genesis 25, trace and speculate on political alliances. Still others, like Esau's in Genesis 36 about Edom, present dynastic lists of Iron Age states.

The tale of the tower of Babel gives us a different view from Genesis 10's: an aetiology of the origins of nations, as well as of the quarrelling disunity of a single mankind. The story has little interest in any specific nation. It is a story that explains how it is that people are scattered, why they speak different languages and, like today, are incapable of getting along together. The story also ironically plays the tragic theme of the hubris of all human efforts to make one's name great.

The end of Genesis 11, following the tower of Babel story, continues the theme of this story's closure. By using the long genealogy of Shem, the narrator sketches another geographical picture, this time giving us a list of Semitic-speaking towns of northern Mesopotamia, which closes with Abraham's immediate family. The ancient Assyrian cities of Til-sha-Turachi (Terach), Til-Nachiri (Nachor) and the great North Mesopotamian trading centre of Harran are given story roles here as Abraham's brothers. The name of Abraham itself is not an eponym, but a 'cue-name'. In Genesis 17: 5, Abraham is called *aber-hamon*, 'the father of many nations'. Abraham as the father of Palestine is the central plot motif in the stories collected in Genesis 12–36. It tells us how all the many peoples of Palestine came into their lands and developed their languages and nations. Lot was the ancestor of Ammon and Moab of the Transjordan. Isaac's wife Rebecca and her father Bethuel, Jacob's wives Leah and Rachel with their brother Laban, all link Abraham closely to the Aramaeans of the Northern Transjordan and Syria. Jacob's brother Esau is presented as the father of Edom and Seir. He links Abraham to the south and southeast. Isaac's brother Ishmael ties him to many of the Arab tribes of the desert fringe. Abraham through his concubine Keturah becomes the ancestor of yet other Arab groups of the steppe. Jacob, in his quarrels with everyone, including God, epitomizes ancient Israel. He is presented as the father of twelve sons, the legendary twelve tribes of Israel. Joseph is the father of the Palestinian highlands of Ephraim and Manasseh, while Judah plays the role of the southern highlands' eponym and David's ancestor. It is not historical realities that create the genealogies. The links within the lists create a self-understanding regarding closeness and distance among different groups.

Similar fantasies creating self-identity grow with stories as well as genealogies. Many of these are positive stories, but they need not be. Judges 19 and Genesis 34, with their tales of rapes leading to the massacres of the tribe of Benjamin and the town of Shechem, are profound examples of the dark side of self-understanding. The stories of Isaac at Gerar (Genesis 26) on the other hand, as well as the conflict story chain of Jacob–Laban (Genesis 31), Rachel–Leah (Genesis 32) and Jacob–Esau (Genesis 33), are good stories of conflicts resolved. The Philistines of Gerar are presented as honest, trustworthy and peace-loving people with whom both Abraham and Isaac (Genesis 20 and 26) created the closest of alliances. The Hittites of Hebron were those from whom the patriarch's burial grounds were purchased (Genesis 23). The king of Salem blessed Abram and his brothers-in-arms from the towns around the Dead Sea (Genesis 14). Even the Egyptians were good neighbours to the patriarchs (Genesis 12 and especially the Joseph story of Genesis 37–50). Eliezer of Damascus was Abraham's heir (Genesis 15). Such references to the larger world of Palestine continue to be used in the books of Exodus, Joshua, Judges, Samuel and Chronicles and extend these geographical commentaries on associations and alliances to the Amalekites, the Kenites, Jebusites, Gibeonites and others. The Philistines, and especially the Canaanites, on the other hand, play roles of implacable hostility and come to represent false religious belief.

In most of the Bible's narratives, the conflict is not one of ethnic hatred, though it is too often understood this way. The polarity, epitomized by Israel and Canaan – both essentially fictive realities – is determined by a theological structure of sectarianism from Exodus through II Kings. As Israel follows the will of Yahweh, who brings them out of Egypt and leads them to the promised land, and there governs them as their king, they 'find refuge in him'. He defeats their enemies and saves them with inspired saviours and messianic kings. In the theological language of piety, Israel 'walks in the way of Yahweh', in the 'path of righteousness'. Within this paradigm, Amorites, Canaanites and Philistines are all illustrations of 'the godless'. They 'walk in the way of evil'. The opposition is black and white: implicitly sectarian. Who is not with us, is against us. In II Kings, 'foreign wives' corrupt first Solomon and then, in Ezra's reiteration, Israel as a whole. The northern kingdom, with its evil king Jeroboam, draws Yahweh's people into 'the way of the godless', the 'way of Jeroboam'. They are destroyed as the Canaanites and Amorites had been before them. The reforms of the pious kings of Jerusalem, Hezekiah and Josiah, delay the coming 'day of wrath' for Judah. Judah too, however, must stand condemned for its hubris, for abandoning the way of its God. II Kings closes with Yahweh rejecting the people he himself created. He destroys Jerusalem where his name had its home. The story is a tragedy, not a piece of national propaganda.

3 Of God's people

When Exodus 19 states that Israel was Yahweh's people and Yahweh Israel's God, it reflects a way of looking at the world that was very common in antiquity. A similar theme is expressed in the song of Moses in Deuteronomy 32, which views the world as divided among gods and nations. This song presents Israel as Yahweh's inheritance. When the world was created there were different peoples. Each had its own language and each its own form of religious expression. The relationship that was described between gods and lands was a rational reflection on international politics. The story structures of religious thought understood the world of the divine and the world of peoples as mirror reflections of each other. The god of a nation protects it, provides for its people and determines the destiny of its political life. The fate of a God in such a world of story was inextricably linked to the fate of his people. Through obedience to the law given by God, to one's king understood as a servant of God, and to one's traditions understood as established by God, a person fulfils conditions of piety. If gods acted in the world, provided and cared for their peoples and assured their survival and destiny, one required a divine world that was just as complex as the political world. The metaphors of a people chosen by their God, and of a people as being the possession of their God, existed long before the Bible. Long before they were taken up in the stories about old Israel, such metaphors were common throughout the entire ancient Near East. These motifs about gods were central in the development of the divine as personal and as caring. An understanding of one's God as personal is the very essence of belief as a commitment. Faith in the divine was expressed as in the role of a client to his patron, namely, with love and loyalty. Within the West Semitic world of Syria and Palestine such an understanding was gradually integrated, beginning first in the Assyrian period, with the growing dominance of a more inclusive understanding of the divine as universal spirit.

Those who collected and wrote the Bible, wrote about being human. They wrote their philosophy in competing stories, in the form of divine laws, and in songs and moral poems sung by the old kings, priests and prophets of history and legend. Like the knowledge condensed in old folk sayings, placed in the mouth of the wise king and teacher of the distant past, origin stories used the concept of past on the principle that one is what one has been. To describe what one has been is to express one's self-understanding. The story told is instruction.

While giving expression to the complex and often conflict-ridden relationship between humanity and their idea of God, the Bible's compilers also created a past: a history. The Bible's creation stories, for example, centre themselves in the flood story. Foreshadowing the story of his own people, Israel, God is angry and regrets that he has made humanity. It was a mistake. He now sees them simply as evil, without any redeeming quality. He sends rain and floods to kill them all . . . except Noah whom he likes, just as arbitrarily! After Noah and his sons make a new beginning, the story-line continues through a series of tales linked through the next five books. They form a chain of fathers and sons, from Noah, the survivor of the flood, to the wandering ancestors of Israel: Abraham, Isaac and Jacob. The story reaches Egypt with Jacob and his family at the end of Genesis. In Egypt, Jacob's family becomes the people Israel. The collective thread of the next few books follow a very simple story of God searching for his people.

Again, as in the garden story, the people are nothing: slaves. Yahweh chooses an entirely unpromising fellow to be their leader. This odd choice of Moses is not quite as arbitrary as had been his choice of Noah. Moses is chosen with irony in mind: because he is unheroic. Not a single line of the narrator's pen sketches a heroic man. Moses has none of the stuff of greatness or leadership in him. His inabilities make it very clear to the audience that God is the one in charge here. This god wants to be treated like God; that is, the ultimate patron of his people. He wants to decide things, and he wants his people above all to follow and obey *him*. He demands very little of this nation . . . only that they follow him wherever he should take them, and that they obey him. But they don't. They complain whenever anything goes wrong, and they do what they want whenever they get the chance. Finally, Yahweh decides they are hopeless. He gets rid of a whole generation of complainers by making them wander in the desert for forty years (a story-teller's full generation). A new generation can become his new people in their new land. This echo of the flood story marks the plot-line of the Pentateuch. It not only points back to that first destruction, but it also points ahead to destructions and new beginnings to come. The story is a story of loss, written about old Israel and its failure. It is also a survival story, written from the perspective of the new Israel. The Pentateuch is only the first movement of this theme. It pauses rather than closes in the testimony of Moses that comprises the three farewell speeches he delivers from Mount Nebo in Deuteronomy. These addresses offer a three-fold recap of the Pentateuch as a parable.

Moses looks ahead to Israel's entry into the land and warns them of the disaster to come.

The story chain continues. There follows a series of warlike heroes who take the role of Moses' successor. First there is Joshua. He is instructed by the deity to conquer the land. A loose collection of tales of conquest and settlement follow, grouped around figures of warrior saviours. Although arbitrarily linked to each other, they tell a story of inspired leaders, each hero possessed by God's spirit in turn. Each defeats Israel's enemies, against all expectation. The reiterated plot develops: God will save them when they turn to him in their need. This plays out in story form a central theme of the Psalter: 'Happy are they who seek refuge in him.' The tempo of this group of tales is set with the help of contrasting motifs: the saving deity and his backsliding people. The deity helps his people conquer all their enemies – whenever they let him. As soon as they turn to their own interests, their enemies gain strength and suppress them once again.

This chain of saviour stories does not close. The last is the magnificent story of Samson and Delilah. The last chapters of Judges are bridge narratives, offering a prelude to the stories of the kingdom. They mark the time of the Judges as a dark and evil time. It was a time when 'everyone did what was right in their own eyes', a lawless time, a time of chaos. 'There was no king in Israel.' There was no servant of Yahweh, no one to carry out his will. Such, the story-line tells us, is a recipe for disaster.

Drawing direct attention to this leitmotif of the Bible's narrative, the plot turns to the theme of God as Israel's king. A new beginning is created with the birth of Samuel. His mother, miraculously impregnated by the divine spirit, dedicates him wholly and entirely to God. He is God's servant: priest and prophet alike. In his guidance of Israel, Israel knows exactly what God wants. Israel has peace and prosperity. The dramatic focus shifts away from the people to the leader. While Samuel is with them, all is well, because Yahweh rules his people through him. Samuel, however, grows old, and his sons are worthless. The people want a king like other people. The greater story's plot defines itself. How can they be like other nations and be Yahweh's people too? The story goes to great pains to point out that they are not like other people. Only God can be Israel's king. The request is treasonous; it 'tempts Yahweh'. The implicit and relentless cynicism of the narrative voice leads the reader to expect disaster, even as Yahweh accepts a king whom he alone will choose, anoint as his own, and guide.

Saul is Yahweh's chosen messiah. He is a hero's hero: a head taller than all other men. He becomes the scourge of the Philistines, who now play the Canaanites' role as archetype of Israel's enemies. The picture of the early Saul is an attractive one. It is the story of good king Saul, who does what he believes a good king should do. Good King Saul, however, is shaped from a template of classical tragedy. It lies at the very heart of the narrative's description of its likeable hero that the narrator, in I Samuel 15, insists that Yahweh must reject the hero, this good king and good general. His tragedy and fault are none other than his being a man. This is the reason he is rejected. The God of this story does not want a king who does what he thinks is right. He wants a king who will do what *he, Yahweh, the true king*, sees as good. Goodness is not what lies intrinsic in actions. Good is what God sees to be right. What is astonishing in this presentation is not merely the personal, arbitrary, cruel or controlling personality of the deity. It is rather that *the author is aware* of Yahweh's action as despotic. In this way, he drives home the uncompromising nature of the religious demand of obedience.

The story of Saul offers a reverse reflection of the story of Abraham, whose faith was praised in Genesis 22 because he had been willing to sacrifice his son Isaac. However, we need to read our text carefully; we might easily grossly misread a simple, delicate story, constructed from horrific motifs. Yahweh is not a God who likes killing children, or demanding that fathers do it for him! No more does the Yahweh of the Saul story reflect a God who likes decapitating enemy kings in order to give lessons in obedience. Both the gore and the terror, however, do belong to the Saul story. Nevertheless, they are disastrously misunderstood if historicized. So too, the picture of Yahweh as uncompromising godfather. Saul's story, like Abraham's, is a morality tale. They are both variations on the theme of piety's commitment to the divine will. They shock to draw their theme. They preach to their audiences: 'Walk in God's will.' Abraham passes his test, demonstrating unshakable confidence that 'God will provide.' Saul fails his for lack of that quality. In any real world, Saul would be a great man: we do not have enough soldiers like him. And Abraham would be ostracized. In the world of story, however, Saul fails and Abraham succeeds! Saul fails the only test he was ever given: to be Yahweh's servant. The plot draws on stories of battles and kings, stories of bravery, honour and personal integrity. It is, however, cast in the spirit of early tragedy, at the heart of which is a rather unworldly piety that calls for allowing the gods to rule one's life. Saul's story is a variant of the story of old Israel.

The tale of the mad King Saul stands in stark relief to the heroic David, that Cinderella whom Samuel had found in Bethlehem. Saul, who had first tried to kill David, ends, humiliatingly, recognizing David as his heir and son. David's is a cue-name, the divine epithet 'beloved' (Hebrew: *dwd*), which marks the role he plays in the story. As Yahweh's 'beloved', he is the eponymous founder of the dynasty, through whom Yahweh is to be eternally king, the one whose son will build the once homeless Yahweh a house in Jerusalem. It is there that Yahweh will live and rule over Israel forever. At least that was the plan. The story offers the reader an invitation to reflect on God's plans, to remember his regret and the destruction of all that he had made in the flood, to recall Israel, his 'first-born's', fate in the wilderness and to think once again on the tragedy of Yahweh's chosen one, good king Saul. Israel's new king is his 'beloved'. Yahweh believes he has found a home and a people to rule.

No one, however, reflecting on the tragic leitmotif of this tradition is likely to forget the uncomfortably threatening story-line, suggesting as it does, that having a king for Israel had been an unwelcome human idea to Yahweh! Rather than relaxing and closing in peace and serenity after David's submission to God's will on the Mount of Olives in II Samuel 15, the story takes a relentless turn. David, Yahweh's faithful servant, goes on to arrange the murder of his own faithful servant. David, the once 'beloved' of Yahweh, is now rejected. His son Solomon is chosen to be God's beloved in his stead, to rule over Israel as Yahweh's messiah. With David's fate, the story-teller is entirely pitiless. After Yahweh brings a plague against his people as punishment for his crime, David is left to die an old man, humiliated, cold and impotent. He needs to be nursed like a child, with a young girl to warm his bed.

Solomon's story, the third of this series, repeats the pattern. The dominant theme is played out fully. God gives Solomon divine wisdom and understanding. Like Alexander, he plays the role of philosopher-king, ruler of a great kingdom. The tale presents him as world-renowned, fabulously rich, the lover of women. He builds Yahweh a home and the whole kingdom is at peace. This time it is forever.

However fabulous the story is, it is not a simple one. Just as the narrative describes Solomon as a saint who, *like his father before him*, followed God in everything, and just as the narrative reiterates the promise that God will live in his house in Jerusalem forever, so these promises of expectation also recur with a warning. The warning reiterates the one given to Moses in Exodus 23: 21, when the lost generation first set out on its wilderness trek: 'Do not disobey [my messenger]; for he will not forgive your sin. My name is in him.' This warning was reiterated when the people turned to the golden calf (Exodus 32: 34 and 33: 2), and again it was in fulfilment of this threat that Yahweh first abandoned his people in the wilderness story (Num. 14: 27–30). The promise to David and Solomon, however eternal it may have been, is conditional. It is an eternal promise – as to Eli and his sons in the opening chapters of I Samuel. However, if the king does not obey, or if his successors do not and take other gods for their own, then Israel will be removed from the land. The eternal temple will lie in ruins. The promise to David does not bind Yahweh. Its permanence depends wholly on the arbitrary and, yes, despotic will of David's patron: 'Everyone will see the ruins and hiss scornfully, talking about the shame that brought on such evil.' Here is a statement obviously written from the perspective of just such humiliation, shame and loss (I Kings 9, especially verses 8–9).

This is a difficult theology. Its author stands among the scornful gossips. The story is never sad; nor does it allow pity. It is similar to classical tragedy. The human being – so terribly promising: the very image of God – cannot escape his clay feet. They are his destiny. From the height of Solomon's glory, when God was truly with Israel, the story moves inexorably towards its closure. Although the scenes need yet to be played, Israel's and Jerusalem's fate are both sealed by their common humanity. After Solomon's death, the narrative reconstructs the fragments of two dynastic lists, containing names and perhaps some of the regnal years of kings who had once ruled over the states of Israel and of Judah. It portrays these two kingdoms as siblings and rivals in a civil war, which the story presents as having broken out following Solomon's death. The pattern for this story is the break-up of the Hellenistic empire, which had separated into two integral parts: the southern Ptolemies of Egypt ruling from Alexandria, and the Seleucids of the north ruling from Antioch and Babylon. Seleucid Syria and the hated religious syncretism of Antiochus IV is reflected in II Kings' descriptions of Samaria, whose king goes to war with Solomon's successor. Samaria plays the metaphorical role of Hosea's faithless prostitute who abandons Yahweh her true husband (Hebrew: *ba'al*) and turns to the God Ba'al. Variously, Samaria's king Jeroboam replays the wilderness story of the golden calf. He makes two calves of gold and sets them up as statues of Yahweh in the towns of Bethel and Dan. Samaria's kings thereafter follow 'in the way of Jeroboam'; that is, in the way of the ungodly, a pattern which seals an inevitable fate. The unfaithfulness of Samaria's kings brings disaster after disaster, until finally God has enough and chooses the Assyrian king Shalmaneser and his army to rid himself of this people.

Only Judah and Jerusalem are left. Jerusalem's king, Hezekiah, is a reformer, a good king who brought Judah back to its religion. The country prospers, and when the Assyrians, now under Sennacherib's rule, come to lay siege to Jerusalem and threaten to destroy it completely, Jerusalem's God sends a plague against the Assyrian army as an act of grace to Israel. The king is forced to abandon the siege. The relief, however, is but temporary as the plot turns inexorably towards Jerusalem's final destruction. Yahweh promises Hezekiah that there will be 'peace in his time'. He also warns that the end is coming; the storm-clouds are heavy over Jerusalem.

As soon as Hezekiah dies, the new kings, each in succession, do more evil than any before them. One king brings temporary relief. Good King Josiah, like Hezekiah, reforms the country. In an ironic caricature of his Maccabean variant John Hyrcanus, he even attempts to force conversions with his soldiers. This has strikingly little effect on Judah's predetermined fate. Yahweh regrets having chosen Israel as his son and Judah as his first-born. He remains resolved to rid himself of this people and to destroy

Jerusalem and its temple. The audience fidgets impatiently for Josiah's successors to do evil and for the Babylonians to carry out God's will. In three successive variants, they punish Jerusalem. First they attack the city with a series of armed bands. Then, the city is besieged and all but the poorest deported. Finally, the temple is burnt, the walls of the city torn down, and the rest of the population carried off. The story closes with a scene of exquisite banality. The last of David's dynasty is a guest at the king of Babylon's table . . . 'for as long as he lived'. The story closes here. Old Israel is dead, and Judah too. The closure is unequivocal and complete. The heartless and humiliating image of Jerusalem's last king, living off an allowance granted him by his conqueror, brings down the curtain.

This is a past and a lesson learned, a history that only a new Israel can bear. It is the story of the old Israel, whom God loved and lost. What is a human, that God should think about it? A little less than the angels; almost a god; a fallen angel. The buildings that humans build are Babylon's tower, Jerusalem's walls. What began as a story of the whole of humanity, centres itself on the story of lost Israel. In its closure, it becomes again a story-paradigm for everyman. It affects the self-understanding of every reader: all the women and all the men who stand within the tradition and identify with it as their own.

4 A collapsing paradigm: the Bible as history

It is here that modern understandings of the Bible have come to grief. The voice of the tradition, only implicit in our text, has been lost to us in our efforts to make it our own. It is this voice that the present book hopes to recapture – an interesting, powerful voice. It animates the stories and songs of the past. It plays the narrator, transcending millennia, and it assumes the role of God for old Israel. Yet – and this the reader is never allowed to forget – this old Israel is lost. This voice of memory remembers a shattered past and a God forgotten. That alone makes it interesting. The voice we listen to as we read the Bible, and especially the voice that animates those first twelve books that define the origin and destiny of Israel's twelve tribes, opening with the creation of humanity in the image and likeness of God, and ending with the destruction of a God-forsaken Israel – this is not a voice that belongs to the past of any people. The Bible does not present us with a national literature or the book of a people. Genesis begins and remains 'the book of the development of humanity' (Gen. 5: 1). Abraham is a father of many nations. The story never abandons that universalist perspective. Beginning with a God that created a world that was good . . . as he saw it to be good, Genesis closes with this same understanding. This is the God of Joseph. What Joseph's brothers saw and did was evil, at least evil in so far as men can understand such things. 'God meant it, however, as good, to bring it about that many should have life, as they do this day (Gen. 49: 20).' The way of Joseph's brothers is the way of the world. It sees what is good or evil only from within its own, human, perspective. Good and evil, however, are as God sees them. Such a deity is not merely Israel's God, but the universal God of heaven. As the story continues into Exodus, and into the long story of Israel lost, its voice does not change. The story that recreates the past of old Israel is ever a paradigm of the way of mankind. It is the tower of Babel story in greater detail. Its voice holds to the universalist perspective, with an edge of self-identifying criticism. They were gods with clay feet, fallen angels.

We have in the Bible some of the most beautiful poetry: pious, lyrical and erotic, and also some of the angriest. We have narratives of epic proportions, aetiologies and folktales that are at times stunningly profound and evocative, romances and adventure stories, some of them are ideologically tendentious or moralistic. There is patent racism and sexism, and some of the world's earliest condemnations of each. One of the things the Bible almost never is, however, is intentionally historical: that is an interest of ours that it rarely shares. Here and there, the Bible uses data gleaned from ancient texts or records. It often refers to great figures and events of the past . . . at least as they are known to popular tradition. But it cites such 'historical facts' only where they may serve as grist for one of its various literary mills. The Bible knows nothing or nearly nothing of most of the great, transforming events of Palestine's history. Of historical causes, it knows only one: Palestine's ancient deity Yahweh. It knows nearly nothing of the great droughts that changed the course of Palestine's world for centuries, and it is equally ignorant of the region's great historical battles at Megiddo, Kadesh and Lachish. The Bible tells us nothing directly of four hundred years of Egyptian presence. Nor can it take on the role of teaching us anything about the wasteful competition for the Jezreel in the early Iron Age, or about the forced sedentarization of nomads along Palestine's southern flank.

The reason for this is simple. The Bible's language is not an historical language. It is a language of high literature, of story, of sermon and of song. It is a tool of philosophy and moral instruction. To argue that the Bible has it wrong is like alleging that Herman Melville has got his whale wrong! Literarily, one might quibble about whether Jonah has it right with his big fish, but not because the story could or could not have happened. On the story's own terms, the rescue of Jonah is but a journeyman's device as far as plot resolutions go. But no false note is sounded in Jonah's fig tree, in Yahweh's speech from the whirlwind in the Book of Job, or in Isaiah 40's song of comfort.

PART TWO

HOW HISTORIANS CREATE
A PAST

Introduction to Part Two

Part Two of this book offers examples of how historians describe the early roots of the peoples of Palestine, whose later traditions, songs and stories make up the bulk of our Bible. This history begins on the Neolithic farms of North Africa before the creation of the Sahara. It has as its central core the causes and aetiology of the development of Semitic languages, which had their roots in Africa, and which came to dominate the fertile crescent of Southwest Asia over at least the last 5,000 years. People who migrated from North Africa and became integrated with the populations of Palestine played a critical role in creating the Semitic languages. The early history of Palestine is a story of farmers and shepherds; of villages and markets. It is about local patrons and their clients and all the early ways of life that have lasted so long in this corner of the Mediterranean. The history of a richly varied people over an extended period of time cannot be complete in the small space that we offer here, but although we cannot write a full history here, we will try to describe a past. What I sketch centres on beginnings. It asks what we know about the different peoples who lived in Palestine, how we know anything at all about them, and what they may have to do with the Israel we know from the Bible. Our study of the roots and beginnings of historical developments also focuses on the people who wrote the Bible. How are Palestine's historical peoples related to those who created literary Israel? This is not an idle question. The new history of Palestine's peoples and their distant beginnings stems almost entirely from archaeological and linguistic research undertaken over the past fifty years. It presents a picture so radically unfamiliar, and so very different from a biblical view as to be hardly recognizable to the writers of the Bible, so thoroughly has our understanding of the past been forced to change.

There is no Adam or Eve in this story, nor a Noah, Abraham and Sarah. And there is no place for them. Not even Moses and Joshua have roles in this history about the people who formed the Bible and its world. One good reason for leaving them out is that modern history is very limited in its ability to speak about the past. We can only write what we have evidence for. If we have no evidence, if we do not know anything about a period, we cannot write history about it. As a result, ancient history has many blank pages. There is another important limitation. When the writers of the Bible wrote about the Israel of their traditions, where it came from, and what it was that God had created, they were doing something different than talking about the past or writing history. When present-day archaeologists and critical historians piece together the civilizations in which the biblical writers arose, they describe a world in which the authors of the Bible lived, but the best of them do so without using the Bible's own story. This is not because they disagree with it, but rather because they are doing something that the writers of the Bible never meant to do.

The problem is not that the Bible is exaggerated or unrealistic, and it is certainly not that the Bible is false. The writers of the Bible are surprisingly realistic and truthful. In their own terms – which are not the terms of critical historical scholarship – they express themselves well about the world they knew. They are talking about a real world, and they write about it in ways we can often understand quite well. They write however with ideas, thoughts and images, metaphors and motifs, perspectives and goals, that are quite at a tangent to those of the present day. For the most part, it could be said that what modern historians and archaeologists are normally interested in has little to do with the Bible. The conflict surrounding the Bible and history – one that has played a considerable role in Western thought since Napoleon occupied Egypt at the end of the eighteenth century – is essentially a false controversy. It has occurred only because our commitment to myths of origin as part of an historically based modern world has caused us to interpret the biblical perspective as historical, until faced with definitive proof to the contrary. We should not be trying to salvage our origin myths as history. That hides their meaning from us, and ignores the strong anti-intellectual strain of fundamentalism that underlies so many of the historical interests invested in biblical archaeology.

CHAPTER 5

Beginnings

1 Genesis: c. 1,400,000–6000 BCE

The earliest known remnants of humans in Southwest Asia, fossils of *Homo erectus*, have been found in Palestine at Ubediya on the southern shore of the Sea of Galilee. These skeletal remains have been dated to about 1.4 million years old. Today a small handful of sites have been found here, along the Mediterranean shore and in the Orontes valley in Syria, where remains of *Homo erectus* from at least a million years ago have been found. The sites we know from both the Early and Middle Acheulian (until about 250,000 years ago) were open to heavy periods of erosion. As a result, many sites are likely buried deep in thick layers of sediment. There are very few of them that we can know. The few we have clearly show considerable spread of settlement during these early periods. Palestinian tools from the Middle Acheulian period developed independently from their African variants.

Finds are abundant from the Late Acheulian period. They extend over many different types of habitats, in areas ranging from good agricultural lands to what is now desert, and are associated with dwellings in caves, drainage valleys and along the tops of plateaus. 'Archaic *Homo sapiens*' developed during this period. A much wider variation, complexity and refinement in the tools has been developed. The locations of some sites are associated with annual spring migrations of herd animals, from the valley of the Wadi Araba, south of the Dead Sea, to the high Jordanian plateau.

From early in the Middle Palaeolithic period, some 100,000 years ago, the climate began to change from a dominant regime of favourable weather to increasingly arid conditions whose effect was to accelerate evolution and cultural adaptation. From about 40,000 to 30,000 years ago, these changes were so severe that the number of people supported by the region during what is called the 'Upper Palaeolithic' period was smaller than earlier. The continuing severity of the climate led to an increase in the variety of subsistence strategies from region to region. Evolution was hardly a gentle process. Necessity and hunger drove people to learn new ways of surviving. By the Natufian period (10,000–8500 BCE) people began to use mortars and pestles for grinding wild nuts and grains. Both the abundance of such food and the ease of gathering and storing it created new ways of life. The enduring aridity drove early humans to change their migrating patterns from the mobile strategy of hunters and gatherers to a more sedentary life in hamlets and villages situated close to permanent sources of water and stands of wild grains. Food storage and permanent dwellings in villages, with perhaps a hundred or more persons, required corresponding changes in political life, and also brought the beginnings of social stratification. Individual burial patterns and art work in stone, bone, shells and horn demonstrate a rich development of art and symbol. The quality of this art reflects a developed sense of the person by the Natufian period. Jewelry is found everywhere.

After about 8500 BCE, cultural development – especially food production – changed life in Palestine. It was during this 'Neolithic' period that domestication of both plants and animals occurred. Grains, particularly wheat, barley and oats, were the first to be planted and harvested. Lentils and peas were added by the end of the eighth millennium. Meat and milk production were revolutionized by the domestication of the goat. This quickly surpassed hunting as a meat source. By 6000 BCE sheep, pigs and beef cattle were added to the agricultural economy. Hundreds of villages supported on average some 500 or more people, and some quite substantial towns of several thousands developed in most regions of the Levant. Among the best-known settlements in Palestine were the oasis town of Jericho, the town of Beidha not far from Petra, Ain Ghazal near Amman and Byblos on Lebanon's coast.

Goods which had been brought by long-distance trade, such as from the Red Sea and Anatolia, are found at sites of this period. Jewelry and a variety of art work are also common, and ritual – particularly associated with burials – is developed. By 6500 BCE, distinct regional cultures had developed. The sites of the South Levant distinguish themselves from those further north in Syria and Anatolia. One unique characteristic in the art of Palestine is the development of plaster statues in the round in human shapes. Statuary in the form of human heads was also created by plastering over human skulls.

The landscape of this period was different from today's. The water-table was much higher, and the Sea of Galilee ('Lake Beisan') not only extended northwards within the Jordan rift to fill the Hula Basin, it also stretched southward, filling parts of both the Jordan and Beth Shan valleys. Much of the Jezreel and large areas of the central coastal plain were marshland. These supported fishing and fowling, but little agriculture or stock-breeding could be developed. The rainfall pattern, with its epicentre in the Mediterranean northeast of Cyprus, was similar to today's.

Abundant rain fell in the mountains of Lebanon and Syria and in the high hills of the Galilee. Adequate rain for dry forms of agriculture fell in the highlands of the south. Farming was also possible all along the rivers and wadis, in oases and wherever springs were found. However, the much higher water-table of this period, combined with at least initially deep fertile topsoil, allowed Neolithic villages to develop in grasslands of areas that are now desert or very marginal steppeland. The Wadi Araba, the northern Negev and central Negev highlands and the Transjordanian plateau all supported settlements.

Recurrently throughout the seventh millennium BCE, disaster struck. Settlements faced overpopulation, which limited their ability to respond constructively to stress. Some towns covered 20–30 acres or more. Most of these have been found in what are today Mediterranean climatic areas of the region. Some few sites, but of only modest size, were built in what is now the steppe zone. Although sites in Syria continued to thrive, large numbers of settlements in more arid Palestine, especially in areas that now mark a border between arable lands and the steppe, were abandoned. By 6000 BCE, the vast majority of Palestinian sites had been abandoned. Although evidence is not yet conclusive, three causes for this collapse seem interrelated: a) Ocean levels and the water-table began to fall around the middle of the Neolithic period. This factor made it particularly difficult for settlements in more arid regions to recover from their ever-recurrent drought years. b) Periods of long droughts increased. Syrian sites were relatively immune to the drought. In dry years, when rainfall can be reduced by 20 per cent or more, regions of plentiful rain, as in most valleys of Syria, are only moderately affected. In marginal areas, however – and this would include Palestine south of Amman and Jerusalem – a drought year reduction of less than 20 per cent, bringing water available to plants below the threshold for viable farming, can cause a nearly total loss of crops. When drought is extended over several consecutive years, a collapse of agriculture in entire ecological enclaves is threatened. This forces abandonment of settlements and, in the worst of times, widespread emigrations from regions. c) Finally, human miscalculations and misuse of lands recurrently raised agricultural collapse to epidemic proportions. Given the stress of drought and the loss of springs and water resources due to the falling water-table, overgrazing of the diminishing grasslands can be predicted – especially prior to the outbreak of starvation and emigration. Similarly, reduced crop production typically leads to overcropping, the abandonment of normal fallow systems and a reduction in the fertility of soils, erosion and the widening of areas of immature desert soils and steppeland. This is perhaps the best-known cause of desert creation.

The changes in the foundation of the Neolithic subsistence economy induced by the dry years around 6000 BCE also introduced a shifting pattern of land exploitation that over time became a recurrent feature of the region's economy. In the face of relentless drought and the increasing loss of agricultural lands, corresponding with the drift of the border of aridity northwards, dispossessed village farmers began to spread themselves out in small transient groups over an increasingly larger area. Dependence on herding – particularly on the sturdy breeds of drought-resilient goats – increased. Agriculture abandoned intensive cultivation and adopted patterns of shifting patch cultivation, especially in the lower valleys and along the drainage channels of the steppe. Migratory patterns of nomadism, with shepherds shifting their flocks between seasonal grazing lands, became the norm in the steppe regions of the Levant during the third millennium BCE. This developed cultural and language differences between people living on the steppe and those settled more permanently in villages within agricultural zones. This process seems to have begun during the disaster of the early Neolithic. The collapse of sedentary life and intensive agriculture lasted nearly a millennium throughout most of the southern fringe of Syria.

2 An African Eden: c. 7000–6000 BCE

The explanation that we use today to explain the development of Semitic languages is a theory. It is a best explanation for many different kinds of information we have about the common features that North African languages have with early Egyptian, and linguistic similarities between Egyptian and the Semitic languages of Asia. The theory also integrates archaeology data from North Africa with ecological and climatic history relating to the spread of the Sahara. It is a far cry from the old romantic fantasy of the origin of the Semites from dashing desert Bedouin tribes of Arabia, which captured Western imaginations about the Orient during the nineteenth century. The idea that the desert of Arabia had given birth to successive waves of migrations to the lands of the Fertile Crescent that border it had been supported by the long-held belief that the Arabic language had preserved old verbal forms. Because of this, what scholars could reconstruct of the earliest form of the Semitic languages seemed a lot closer to Arabic than it did to the oldest Semitic texts that we have: whether the Old Accadian and Babylonian texts of ancient Mesopotamia or the Ugaritic texts of Syria. The idea that these languages all took their origins from Arabia encouraged scholars to think of Semites as if they were a single people, who had conquered and settled the territories of the Fertile Crescent from the Arabian Sea to Suez in successive vast tribal migrations from the third to the end of the second millennium BCE. The development of different Semitic languages was explained as a development of a single language family. Differences among the languages in this family were marked by the period in which they had left the desert. The Accadians and

Babylonians had been the earliest, meeting and eventually displacing the ancient Sumerians of southern Mesopotamia.

They had been followed, it was thought, by 'Amorites', who had supposedly migrated into the Fertile Crescent in successive raids from late in the third millennium until around 2000 BCE. These 'Amorites' were described as having established ruling dynasties in Babylon and Mari and as having conquered most of Syria. Their migration into Palestine was credited with destroying the Early Bronze civilization and creating a period in which Palestine fell under the control of nomads.

Scholars used this image of marauding Amorites as plundering Bedouin so as to make sense of the then unexplained political disruptions in Egypt during the First Intermediate (*c.* 2150–1990 BCE). Migrations of Amorites were credited with the development of the earliest Semitic languages of Syria and Palestine and the ancestors of Canaanite and Hebrew. This migration scenario was also used to explain the differences between Aramaic and Hebrew. New emigrations from Arabia were suggested, now in the second half of the second millennium BCE. This was used to explain the appearance of Aramaic: first in North Mesopotamia and then in the newly formed states of Aram, Ammon, Moab and Edom in eastern Palestine from about 1200 BCE.

If this theory now appears exaggerated, and – given its vast scope – even silly, the function it served was necessary in its time. The theory's coherence enabled scholars to relate the origins of many different groups over a vast geographical range and enormous time-span. Writing ancient history has been a far more creative pursuit than we usually understand history to be. Before the end of the Second World War there was little specialization in ancient Near Eastern studies. Everyone did everything. Yet there was an increasingly vast number of texts, and archaeological data have poured into the field from excavations ever since the close of the First World War. This material needed to be integrated before it could be understood. We had only bare outlines of ancient history to work with, yet needed to interrelate data, texts and other information from sources widely scattered in time and space. The migrations-from-Arabia theory was not simply a blind reflex of the Western imagination about the noble savage, supported by a romantic picture of the desert blossoming as a metaphor of nature's fertility, though it was both of these. With the help of the scholarly myth of an eternal struggle between the desert and the sown – that is, between shepherds and farmers – these fantasies made it possible for a relatively small number of scholars to create a history where we had none. While myth-making and treasure-hunting were characteristic of work in biblical archaeology before the Second World War, it was only the specialization and prosperity of ancient Near Eastern studies during the 1950s and 1960s that allowed and required historians to use more careful and more critical methods.

The Hebrew language, in which much of the Bible was written, has had a history in Palestine that reaches back to at least the sixth or fifth millennium BCE. The earliest texts relating to Palestine were written in Egypt around 1800 BCE. These were small clay bowls and figurines in human form on which an Egyptian scribe had written long lists of towns and their leaders. Three different groups of these texts were found. The names of both the towns and people clearly show that the language of the South Levant was an early western form of Semitic, the large language family of Western Asia in which Hebrew eventually developed. The time of our earliest texts is already several thousand years from its origins and earliest development in the South Levant. For origins we need to go far back to the North African ancestors of the speakers of Semitic languages. They lived in the 'Green Sahara' until late in the seventh millennium BCE, when a long and relentless drought – responsible for the creation of the desert of the 'Great Sahara' that we know today – forced the farmers and herdsmen of North Africa to leave their homes and villages and emigrate to the Berber lands of the west, to Chad and areas to the south, to the Nile valley in the east, and finally, crossing the Nile, to Palestine by way of the Sinai.

As early as 1950, German scholars had begun to recognize close similarities between verbs in the Akkadian language and in some of the languages of North Africa. This was apparent in the Berber language of the northwest, but also in Libyan. The similarities in both made it very difficult to see the Semitic languages as entirely independent of these. Scholars also connected the two languages in North Africa that were separated from each other by more than a thousand miles of desert. Further study of language families by the 1960s made it clear that the earliest characteristics of Semitic languages were closely related to a number of African languages, not only Berber and Libyan, but also ancient Egyptian and the later Coptic language spoken in Egypt. These languages were also closely allied with Cushite of the modern Sudan and with Chad south of the Sahara. Borrowing the language of the Bible's geographical story of Noah's sons: Shem, Ham and Japheth, to represent the ancestors of the peoples of Asia, Africa and Europe, scholars began to speak of a single Semito-Hamitic language family. Such a family of languages must lie at the historical roots of most of the languages of the ancient Near East and Central and North Africa. Metaphorically speaking, linguistic scholars have rewritten the history of Noah's family. This linguistic argument is very strong. By the late 1960s, linguistic historians looked to North Africa rather than Arabia for the changes that had led to the development of Semitic languages first among the sedentary agriculturalists of Syria-Palestine and then in the Mesopotamian heartland. The one thing that stood in the way was the great impassable expanse of the Sahara desert, which separated Berber from Libyan, Libyan from both Chad and ancient Egyptian, and all from the Semitic world.

That was the argument from the point of view of language classification. Closely tied to this theory was a revision of our understanding of the Semitic languages themselves. While Arabic seemed earlier because so much of its grammar had preserved antique forms, Akkadian – known from inscriptions dating to as early as the third millennium BCE – had in fact been the earliest Semitic language we had direct evidence of. Although the western branch of the Semitic languages, which represented languages spoken in Syria and Palestine, had been unknown before the second millennium BCE, texts from ancient Ebla in Syria were discovered in the 1970s. These showed that West Semitic had been the language spoken in the regions of Syria and Palestine in the third millennium BCE. Arabic, Akkadian and the West Semitic languages have a common vocabulary for words related to agriculture, horticulture, and sheep – and goat-herding. Such a vocabulary must have come from a period *before* Semitic divided among its many regionally distinct languages and dialects. The earliest speakers of that original Semitic language could hardly have been Arabia's Bedouin. They must have been both a sedentary and an agricultural people. As Mesopotamia had only a very short period of pre-Bronze Age settlement, Syria and Palestine became the most promising area for the earliest development of the Semitic language.

The close association of archaeology with linguistics brought strength to this direction of research by bringing a clear historical dimension to what had always been primarily a linguistic theory without a chronology. Semito-Hamitic (also known as Afro-Asiatic), and proto-Semitic were no longer merely theoretical models. they began to look like actual historical languages. Though we had no texts written in this language, we knew when it existed! Proto-Semitic was to be dated to the period before Akkadian went its own way and took on its own character as a language. We know when that happened: when Semitic speakers first entered the Tigris and Euphrates valleys and joined with the Sumerians of South Mesopotamia in the course of the third millennium BCE. This merger of peoples created the first of the great 'Akkadian' cultures.

The different historical and archaeological understandings about the development of Semitic languages were satisfactorily brought together in the early 1980s. The history of these developments is still schematic. Between 9000 and 7000 BCE, global sea levels were considerably higher than they are today. This supported an extended period of Neolithic prosperity in the South Levant, A warmer and wetter climate existed throughout the Mediterranean region. Winters were longer and summer monsoon rains, rather than the summer droughts we have today, were typical. In Palestine, the area put under agriculture was greater than ever. It extended in the east at least to the watershed of the Transjordanian plateau. In the south, it included the great plain of the Beersheva Basin and the northwestern slopes of the central Negev and North Sinai highlands.

In North Africa, the Sahara was not yet closed. The favourable climate supported agriculture and steppeland grazing across this now very inhospitable area. The Kordofan-Darfur region of the Sudan supported wide-ranging groups of transient goat-herders. Some have suggested this as the birthplace of the earliest speakers of Afro-Asiatic. If this is correct, the development must have come sometime before 6000 BCE. The Berber language, which today is found both south and north of the Sahara, must have entered the area of the Sahara before desert isolated North Africa from the Sudan. Alternatively, Afro-Asiatic may have developed within agricultural zones in the area of the Sahara itself, at some time before the spread of the desert had closed the Berber regions from Libya, and Libya from Chad.

Nine thousand years ago, the Great Sahara of North Africa did not exist. The region rather supported a village culture of farmers and shepherds. They left remains of their art, religion and culture from the mouth of the Nile in the east to Gibraltar in the west. It was from such Neolithic villages that there emerged the ancestors of the people whose changes in language developed the first Semitic speakers of Asia. Before North Africa became the great closed desert that it is today, Neolithic farmers were settled in small villages along the many valleys of this immense coastal region. They lived primarily from croppings of wheat and barley, supplemented by hunting and herding of pigs and beef cattle, sheep and goats. One must also assume that, as in Asia, groups of pastoralists lived in the steppelands that bordered the better-watered, agricultural zones of the 'green Sahara'.

3 Paradise lost: c. 6500–4500 BCE

A radical change in climate took hold of the entire Mediterranean Basin by the end of the seventh millennium BCE. Sea levels fell steadily, as did the water-table in most regions. Higher temperatures and longer dry summers dominated the climate, especially to the east and south of the Mediterranean. Rainfall diminished sporadically. An increasing frequency of drought years brought famine, overgrazing and the gradual abandoning of agricultural lands. North Africa entered a long transition from a Mediterranean climate to steppelands. These changes continued in an extended and intensifying series of droughts that lasted for well over a thousand years. What started out as agricultural collapse and famine in marginal zones became a region-wide disaster. People were forced to abandon completely what had been rich agricultural lands. The Sahara relentlessly encroached on every front, eventually leaving only small pockets of farmers and herders near oases fed by the few and distant springs that survived the drastic lowering of the water-table. As the Green Sahara collapsed and forever disappeared, leaving only a few traces in the drawings and tools of the farmers from this once prosperous region, the great Sahara of today, with its shifting dunes of sand, nearly impassable expanses of empty wilderness and wholly unforgiving climate, took its relentless hold across the entire northern rim of the continent of Africa.

The desiccation of the Sahara did not only affect the farmers of the Green Sahara, it also impinged on their close neighbours of the steppe zones. The expansion of the Sahara sand-dunes was particularly unfavourable to the steppe-dwelling herders of sheep and goats. These were denied not only the stands of wild grasslands of their homelands, but also the support of the patch agriculture that normally formed such a staple of pastoral nomadism. As a result, such groups were driven to the fringes and highlands bordering the expanding desert.

Many of the refugees from the drought were driven westward and southwestward. They settled down in what became the Berber lands in the extreme northwest corner of Africa. Still others moved southward into North-central Africa. They settled in the area of Chad and in the Darfur region. Many more moved eastward to the central Nile Valley and laid the foundations of the Egyptian language. The migrants became geographically and physically isolated from each other as the expanding Sahara cut off further contact. The greater the isolation, the more distinctive were the languages that developed. As the migration spread over larger and ever more complicated regions, whole families of languages were created over time. The expansion of the Libyan dunes separated the people of the Berber lands from Egypt, and both from North-central Africa. These separations led to the historically distinct but related languages that we know in North Africa.

Most major areas of the ancient Near East were altered by this great change in the climate. In addition to North Africa, the Sinai Peninsula that separates Africa from Asia shifted from what was dominantly a steppeland to a desert, comparable to what we find today. Arabia, apart from the region of Arabia Felix in the southern corner of the peninsula, changed like the Sahara into a vast expanse of desert where occupation was limited to its few scattered oases. However, while this extended period of drought destroyed agriculture over areas of both Africa and Arabia, turning the survivors of starvation, famine and disease into refugees, the falling water-table and more arid climate also dried up many great swamps and marshes. This opened new areas to farming and sedentary occupation for the first time. The Delta marshlands at the mouth of the Tigris and Euphrates valleys drained off and exposed one of the ancient world's richest expanses of agricultural lands. This was to become the heartland of ancient Sumer: the earliest of the great ancient Near Eastern civilizations.

In Egypt, agriculture moved on to the Nile floodplain, characterized by recurrent and relatively predictable annual flooding, for the first time. Dense settlement occupied stretches of the banks of the Nile from Asyut in the south to the Delta in the north. The draining of the Delta, where annual floods were gradually confined by a patchwork of interlocking streams, created a richly mixed landscape of marshlands, agriculturally viable floodplain, and a steppe with rich grasslands. The settlement of this region opened up a migration route to the east and to Asia. Refugees from the many recurrent droughts gained access to the Sinai, to Palestine and beyond. Sometime before 4500 to 4000 BCE, the expanding desert of North Africa closed the Sahara. Egypt was isolated from the west. This ended the eastward migrations. Similarly, the desiccation of the Sinai effectively closed the migration route of pastoralists moving through the Delta from the Nile valley to the Fertile Crescent of Southwest Asia. By 4000 BCE, as refugees from the Sahara established themselves in various subregions of Palestine and Syria, the process of developing the Semitic family of languages and cultures had begun.

With the drought, the shores of Lake Beisan in central Palestine retreated to what became the Sea of Galilee and Lake Hula. The reduction of swampland in the central lowland valleys of Palestine and Syria offered farmlands to the Sahara's refugees. Palestine was particularly inviting to the economy of pastoralism and patch agriculture that supported the gradual migration northwards. Not the empty desert of Arabia but the grasslands of the expansive steppe of Sinai and Syria provided the fertile womb for Asia's Semites. This homeland formed the coastal plain of Palestine, the intersecting Jezreel valley, the Jordan rift and – further to the east – the Transjordanian plateau bordering the Arabian desert. It broadens as one moves northwards into the vast expanse of the Syrian steppe. This provided a broad cultural and linguistic continuum. Once the creation of the Sinai desert brought the migrations to a close, the integration of the newcomers with indigenous populations supported the development of distinct Semitic languages.

Over a period of nearly two millennia, refugees from the Sahara crossed the Nile with their flocks and moved northwards into the Sinai, and on into greater Palestine, Arabia and Syria, where they gradually merged with this region's indigenous farmers and shepherds. By the early third millennium, immigrants had followed the Euphrates southward into Mesopotamia. As they moved southward to the Persian Gulf, they met and merged with the ancient Sumerians. They adapted to the intensive irrigated forms of Sumerian agriculture and the more complicated social structures of their cities. Once integrated, Mesopotamia developed the East Semitic languages of the Accadian, Old Babylonian and Old Assyrian civilizations. Still other migrating groups moved along the fringe of the desert from Transjordan and entered southwestern Arabia. Here too they merged with the indigenous population and formed the cultural basis of what was to become Old South Arabic in the agricultural lands of Arabia Felix.

The earliest newcomers to Palestine and Syria had followed a pastoral and nomadic way of life throughout most of the period of the drought. They lived off herding and patch agriculture, and occupied regions that were confined to the broad plains and steppe. Only gradually did they enter some of the more fertile areas of Palestine and Syria. They met and, over time, were assimilated by the indigenous population of the early Neolithic villages that had survived the economic disasters of the late seventh and sixth millennia. This period, during which the immigrants, developing early forms of the Semitic language, joined and adjusted their lives to the culture and customs of the indigenous population was a very long one. In the course of what may have been nearly a thousand years, both natives and newcomers survived the drought. Together they formed a new population and a new culture. Settling down in villages, in the very many different and often isolated agriculturally viable regions of Palestine and Syria, they created the distinctive languages and dialects that form West Semitic. As the transient, but never truly nomadic, pastoralists and patch farmers of the plains began to settle into permanent villages, they became separated from other comparable groups. They developed their own histories, and along with such common histories, each one of dozens of closely integrated but specific dialects and languages took on its distinctive character. Each separate region of Palestine and Syria developed its own unique way of life.

4 *A Mediterranean economy: c. 6000–4000* BCE

The indigenous Neolithic population of fifth-millennium Palestine had roots that went back to the eighth- and seventh-millennium cultures that we know from the excavations of such towns as Jericho and Beidha. These towns were based on a widely developed and integrated economy of intensive agriculture, sheep- and goat-herding, hunting and fishing. Most of the population lived a sedentary existence in villages and shared a surprisingly integrated culture.

With the spread of the drought in North Africa, refugees first entered the region of Syria and Palestine as pastoral nomads. Some settled in the inhabited regions side by side with the indigenous population, affecting their cultures, languages, religions and arts, while others settled previously uninhabitable regions. By the fifth millennium BCE, these new immigrants into Palestine joined already established populations in the northern coastal regions of Phoenicia and the Carmel range, in the southern Jordan valley, in the northern Transjordan and all along the central and southern coastal plains. They discovered and began to exploit the now agriculturally viable former swampland of the Jezreel valley. They settled intensively in the abundantly watered and rich topsoil of the deep lowland area earlier submerged by the great Lake Beisan.

The impact of the drought on the geography and ecology of Palestine varied considerably in different regions. Prior to the onset of the drought, much of the hill country had been heavily wooded. The lowlands of the coastal plain and the Jezreel valley had been filled with watery and malarial marshlands, and the central and northern part of the Jordan rift was former Lake Beisan. As the drought took hold and persisted over centuries, most of the woodlands of the southern Negev hills were lost to drought and erosion. The southern coastal plain and the Beersheva Basin were transformed into steppe. The desert conquered the Judaean hills east of the watershed as well as the whole of the eastern slopes of the Jordan rift from Beth Shan southward. In the north, however, the falling water-table was beneficial, drying up many swamps. Many areas rich with fertile soils and water became open to agriculture and settlement.

While the climate from the end of the seventh millennium BCE, until the end of the fifth had featured a prolonged succession of intense droughts, this dry period was followed by what is called a 'sub-pluvial' period: a period in which average rainfalls surpassed today's norm by some 20 per cent. Temperatures were cooler and the summer often featured monsoon rains instead of the drought so common today. The border of aridity, separating farming lands from steppe, receded. This allowed farming and herding in many places of the northern Negev and Syrian steppelands where it is no longer possible today. By the end of the fourth millennium BCE, farming and related activities had become a permanent feature of Palestine's landscape.

This early sub-pluvial period added immensely to the economic potential of all of the surviving populations in the ancient Near East. It radically altered the basis for agriculture in Palestine and created a major shift in the region's settlement patterns. The bulk of the population centred upon regionally dominant towns, whose surrounding fields had good soils and major springs. Towns such as Megiddo and Beth Shan, Acco, Ashqelon and Gaza in the lowlands, and Hazor, Shechem, Jerusalem, Lachish and Gezer in the highlands, were developed. They formed the backbone of the Palestinian population for centuries to come.

Once the great drought that had closed the Sahara gave way to this wetter, cooler climate, the newly integrating population throughout Palestine and Syria began to build an economy that took on an extraordinary stability. It developed common features that can be found throughout the Levant: from the rich valleys of Syria in the north to the edge of the steppelands in the south. This economy was balanced between three very different kinds of farming, each typically carried out in its own region, and whose unique integration came to be known as a *Mediterranean economy*. The same basic structure has prevailed in Palestine and Syria for more than 5,000 years, and is still important today. It combines selective regional commitments to grain agriculture in plains and valleys, horticulture and viniculture centred in the production of olives and wines in highland areas, and sheep- and goat-herding in the grassy steppelands. Such an economy required close regional cooperation and was dependent on an active trade network, both within the specialized and distinct economic zones of Palestine, and beyond.

The stabilizing core of this Mediterranean economy centred on the dry farming of grain cereals: especially wheat, barley and oats. This was the key pattern throughout the broad coastal plain, the inland valleys from the Yarmuk to the Jezreel, the broad, flat Transjordanian highland plateaus, the steppeland basins of Arad, Beersheva and Damascus, as well as the smaller intermontane valleys that are so characteristic of Mediterranean regions. The fields were planted shortly after the first rains of autumn, and were harvested during the late spring and early summer dry season.

While beef cattle and pigs were raised by the farmers of the north and in many areas of the south where water was readily available, recurrent drought favoured the development of the hardier small livestock: especially the goat. The somewhat less resilient sheep soon matched and even surpassed the goat in popularity because of its greater value in wool. Both sheep- and goat-herding – like the herding of pigs and beef cattle – were an aspect of farming. Sheep's wool (for clothing), goats' hair (for coarser textiles), milk and cheese were the principal products. Young males and older animals were periodically culled for meat. The hides were used for clothing and some of the bones for tools.

Meanwhile, small groups of herders settled the steppe, probably in response to the periodic destabilizing of village life by drought. Growth in the overall population may also have intensified demands on herding. Shepherds developed a more transient form of life, centred in regionally based summer and winter grazing lands. Their economy was supplemented by the patch agriculture of grains in the drainage valleys of the steppe. Permanent dwellings in the villages and hamlets typical of the agricultural heartland gave way to a wide variety of shelters of less sedentary forms: subterranean, cave, circular huts built of stone and hide, and goatskin tents. By the end of the fourth millennium BCE, migrant herders were a significant part of the population of the South Levant. They provided meat, wool and cheese to the permanent villages and towns of the heartland. In summer they entered the agricultural regions to graze their flocks and to fertilize the farmers' harvested fields.

Horticulture, producing olives, fruits and nuts, and viniculture required both an adequate and regular supply of water, and good drainage. Their spread in the South Levant, eventually becoming an equal partner with grain agriculture and animal husbandry, was closely associated with the development of drainage channels, irrigation and terracing. The earliest forms of terracing, developed in the course of the fourth millennium, had two functions: the channelling and control of flood waters and the reduction of erosion on the slopes of hills. Rows of stones built across the breadth of wadi beds and run-off channels broke the downward flow of water and preserved topsoil by catching eroded silt in a series of descending plateaus. The plateaus, in turn, formed the basis for orchards and vineyards. Much later, in the second half of the second millennium and especially early in the first millennium BCE, such soil-preservation techniques were used to create new regions for planting trees and vines. Terraces were built near springs in the higher hills and all along the steepest slopes, once forests had been cleared. New regions of the highlands opened to settlement for the first time. The basic technology for this development was introduced very early and formed a necessary part of farming in the highlands, throughout the lower foothills, and along the many drainage channels of the rolling steppelands.

There were other economic specializations in the South Levant that were regionally determined and of considerable importance. Dates were produced in desert oases. Metal-working was carried out in the Araba, the Negev and the Sinai. Fishing is found in the Sea of Galilee. Salt was produced along the Phoenician coast, bitumen tar was farmed from the Dead Sea, and timber was cut in the highlands. Villages and small towns of the South Levant developed their own skilled crafts. Among the most common were pottery, bee-keeping, leather-working, dying, weaving, olive-oil production and wood-working. Palestine's economy was anything but a subsistence economy founded on small independent units of the population. It was rather an interactive population, centred on a cooperative network of trade. Forms of barter between families and closely related peers (for example, village shepherds and bee-keepers) were engaged within individual economic regions. Larger-scale forms of trade in essential goods, and symbiotic relationships between representatives of different groups (for example, shepherds and farmers), developed in neighbouring, but economically distinct, regions. Large-scale inter-regional and international trade in cash crops and luxury goods thrived by sea and by land, over great distances. Trade was typically undertaken by a professional merchant industry, which involved a variety of political controls. Banking formed the foundation for such trade, and great political powers controlled access to the trade and the profits from it.

Trade formed the backbone of the economy. Few people could live entirely off their own labour. Even fewer did. Even the simplest forms of farming and shepherding involved specialization and barter. Given the regional location of distinct forms of production, such trade involved constant interaction between different groups and the development of complex networks of political relationships between the producers and their representatives from different economies. The interdependence of all aspects of the greater economy, compelled by the lack of a basic subsistence economy and coupled with the extensive geographical fragmentation of the South Levant generally, prevented the consolidation of political or economic power within any single region or around any single population centre. Even the relatively dense population of the Beth Shan or northern Jordan valleys found the population fragmented among a number of small economically autonomous towns and moderately sized villages. Each competed with the other in an economy that discouraged the monopolization of resources. While there were shifting coalitions among neighbouring villages, and while many of the relatively coherent regions developed centralized pyramids of economic patronage, no great powers of any significance ever developed in Palestine. This part of the Levant was ever the southern fringe of Syria. It was a buffer region between the great agricultural regions and cities of Syria, the Euphrates and Egypt, one that lacked its own unity or coherence, and sat ever in closest contact to the steppelands that bordered the deserts of Arabia and the Sinai. While its political fate vacillated between fragmented autonomy and domination by outside powers, it never possessed a culture or a politics of its own.

This unique form of agriculture, the Mediterranean economy, was to determine the basic structure of Palestine's economy and much of its history for more than 5,000 years. Palestinian agriculture pioneered the development of a type of farming that has become the hallmark of the Mediterranean world. Its centre is trade. Rather than a subsistence agriculture, which involves trade only as a result of a tentative and slow development of surpluses, or through an oppressive exploitation by more powerful neighbours, Palestine's economy was oriented from its beginning towards the barter and exchange of basic trade goods. Its agriculture was rooted in cash crops: grains, olive oil, fruits and nuts, wine; sheep and goats and their products; timber, salt, copper and turquoise. These were not surpluses but the fundamentals of the economy.

While the agriculture of Palestine was regionally differentiated, with one area growing wheat, another investing in olives or grapes, and yet another committed to livestock and grazing, this did not encourage regional isolation. Rather, survival depended on the communications of one village with another, and on the interchange of goods within and between regions. Since no part of the economy could survive without the other, communication and tolerance became dominant currencies. This form of economy, dependent as it was on the flow of goods inter-regionally, also opened Palestine to the outside, and brought it under the influence and domination of more powerful neighbours.

5 A heartland of villages: c. 3500–2400 BCE[1]

Because of Palestine's close association with the Bible as the setting of stories and events that have long engaged the imagination and education of the Western world, a tendency has developed to describe the history and culture of this region with the help of idealistic and romantic metaphors. This has been the case especially when the earliest-known complex forms of ancient Palestine's economic and political structures have been discussed. In their pristine form, Palestine's economy and politics were assumed to be simple. This was not because they were known to be so, but because scholars favoured an evolutionary development from the simple to the more complex. Economic and political development, including the experience of history itself, brought with them not merely a greater complexity, but corruption. With the origins of the state and kingship came a fall from grace. Such romantic idealism, glorifying the simple virtues of the frontier, are unwitting reflections of the biblical narratives themselves, from the Garden of Eden story to the long complex tale about the origins of kingship in I–II Samuel.

In histories of Palestine from the 1960s and 1970s, this romantic tradition was extended to many descriptions of the origins of the Semitic languages and their civilizations in the ancient Near East. These were described as the result of an evolutionary development from free, wild, desert-dwelling shepherds, through the independent and self-sufficient homesteading of village farmers, to the corruption and oppression of an urban underclass by the power and wealth of an elite. Kings were ever 'despotic' and 'oppressive', and cities were drawn in the image of Sodom and Gomorrah.

Such imaginary pictures of the past have little to do with any historical reality of the ancient world, or with any evidence that we have from either archaeology or ancient texts. The real historical picture is both more complicated and more interesting. The population of Palestine has not only progressively expanded over centuries, it has also developed a dense network of farms, villages and towns. Severe economic depression and collapse is endemic to the region, but such disasters did not come about because of any myth-like struggle between types of people. Towns and villages, and the political power that developed from them, did not depend on monopolies of surplus wealth, nor on the exploitation of any underclass by any oppressive elite. Rather, the development of commerce, markets and political structures in ancient Palestine developed from the relationships between very many specific groups of people, who lived in very different environments and geographic settings. Moreover, responses to

[1] The changes in culture from the Neolithic to this period of the Early Bronze has a very uncertain chronology. A transition period usually called the Chalcolithic – or 'copper-stone age' – is commonly dated from c. 5000–3500 BCE.

the demands of these different regions and to each other were even more varied than the settings themselves.

There were few common denominators that affected all people throughout the whole of Palestine, let alone throughout the many regions and periods of the ancient Near East. Nevertheless, historical change was hardly arbitrary. Major common factors, and frequently a direct cause of historical change were alterations in climate and the availability of natural resources, especially as they affected the efficiency of agriculture and herding. In terms of large-scale historical changes, affecting centuries of development or decay in Palestine's past, the stability of rainfall and access to water resources can well serve us as a bell-wether for other changes and developments across the society.

It is a mistake to think globally about the development of agriculture and society in the ancient world of the Near East. We rather must think regionally. In Egypt's great and immensely fertile Nile valley, a form of farming was developed based on floodplain drainage and an irrigation network. This involved a market system that was both centralized, efficient and unified across a large region. Egypt's economy developed both a dense and an homogenous population, as well as a great-state form of political structure that engaged hundreds of thousands of people along the central Nile. At the same time, the narrow geographical confinement of arable lands to the Nile's floodplains, with their rich and densely populated farmland abutting wasteland and desert, encouraged a coherent and unified political and social structure: the large and centralized regional state was at home here.

In contrast, the Nile Delta, with its diverse landscape in lakes, swamps, floodplain and steppe regions, resisted political consolidation. With a mixed population of Egyptians and West Semites, the region formed a buffer zone: between central Egypt and the Mediterranean, and between the Egyptian world of the Nile valley and the Semitic world of the eastern desert and Asia. Only during times when Egypt wished to extend its power into the world beyond did its interests centre on the Delta. Otherwise this economically difficult and marginal region, was – like the South Levant – given over to small villages of farmers and pastoral shepherds.

In contrast to the coherent and comparatively predictable world of the Nile valley, with its floodplain agriculture, southern Mesopotamia, with its low-lying delta and swampland, required extensive drainage and flood control for agriculture to be viable at all. The agricultural requirements of large-scale irrigation and canal systems in Mesopotamia, required central-ized and regionally oriented political organization for permanent settle-ments to develop in cities, in towns and villages. Distinct societies centred in structurally independent and competitive cities developed here at a very early period. They created the political and intellectual potential of the competitive city-state.

Syria's cities were centred in agricultural valleys. These supported regionally oriented political structures of patronage, with each city holding numbers of nearby villages and towns in pyramids of subordination. With the rise in the importance of international trade along the Mediterranean coast, the Syrian seaside towns, lying astride the Phoenician coast's many natural harbours, developed commercial empires such as Byblos in the south and Ugarit in the north.

In Palestine's fragmented geographical context, different forms of society developed which displayed little common ground. During the cooler and wetter climate of the late fourth and third millennia, the different peoples of Palestine, while developing the first and perhaps best-understood example of the 'Mediterranean economy', created as many different ways of earning a living in Palestine as its regions varied. The agriculture, fishing and hunting associated with swampland and floodplain supported a different life than that found among the grain fields of the lowland valleys and coastal plain. Separate and distinct political structures and histories developed as well. Even greater differences existed on spring-fed hillsides and rocky terraces, in isolated intramontane valleys, on the grasslands of the steppe and in the oases of the desert. Like most humans, the early people of Palestine both cooperated and competed with each other. They fought, and – like people elsewhere – they had reasons for doing so.

The water-rich Early Bronze period in Palestine hosted a number of agricultural settlements. These ranged in size from a single family or a few dozen people to towns of a few thousand. This period set a pattern for the society and for the political structures of Palestine that has dominated the region throughout history. Over nearly a thousand years, people lived in settlements, in village clusters of homes. These were most densely situated in the larger, agriculturally rich valleys and plains. Remains of them have also been found on the gentler and more fertile slopes of Palestine's central mountain range, on the tops of hills, plateaus and on terraces. One could well say that wherever sufficient water was available to support its population through the arid summers, and wherever sufficiently rich soil was available, a village was formed. In all of these, one notices a direct proportion between the size of a village's population and a specific region's potential for farming. Palestine was a land of small farmers; a heartland of villages.

In the marshlands of the Beth Shan and Jezreel valleys, small systems of canals were used to drain marshlands. These supported local and small-scale efforts at water control. Simple ditch-irrigation networks were also dug throughout the floodplains and near this region's largest springs, creating zones of intensive agriculture. Through neglect, these areas occasionally reverted to malarial swamps. Already by the third millennium BCE, this region had become the most densely populated in all Palestine.

Along the coastal plain, north of Acco, in the Jezreel valley, in the drainage area of the Wadi Gaza in the northern Negev, and in many areas throughout Palestine, where the water-table comes close to the surface, wells were dug. In the hill country and throughout most of Palestine's Mediterranean zone, dry-farming techniques and methods for storing supplemental water for human and animal consumption were necessary. This limited both farming and the development of permanent settlements to those areas where the average annual rainfall rose above 250–350mm per year. Some villages have been found along dry wadi beds where additional run-off water was available for grain agriculture. The fissured character of the limestone stratum underlying many areas of the central highlands made the building of cisterns very difficult and prevented the exploitation of these areas. Certainly, availability of water was the single most important item that determined the existence of both farming and village life in ancient Palestine. This is to be expected in a region that is bordered both to the east and the south by steppe and desert.

Palestine's social system was structured in the form of extended families that were village-based with personal networks centred in ownership of houses, fields and orchards, exchange of goods and produce, and a limited range of intermarriage, which supported the development of lineage systems and clans. Wealth was accumulated through long-term investments, such as the clearing and cutting of timber, the development of water resources and irrigation systems, the building of protective terraces along moderate slopes and in wadis, the cultivation of vineyards and orchards, the improvement of herds and the creation of stable markets and systems of credit. Prosperity took years to develop and was dependent on both political and social stability. The economy was driven by the production of export goods. The olive – a staple of the ancient diet and the primary source of oil for lamps – was paramount. In favourable regions, villages of the Early Bronze period grew quite large and supported as many as a few thousand inhabitants. Many of these were defended with high stone fortification walls. Some of the towns that have been excavated reflect town planning, and a few had public buildings, palaces and temples.

The vast bulk of the population – commonly estimated at about 90 per cent – was engaged as farmers and shepherds. The very small and regionally limited political structures connected the town centres with a few small dependent villages and hamlets. Only a relatively small number of people were engaged by caravans and trading ships. Transhumant movements of pastoralists were usually confined to specific grazing lands and regions. Finally, the sedentary nature of most occupations had the effect of fragmenting Palestine's population into numerous small groupings, each of them confined to its own unique region, with its own specific occupation. The more mobile steppe pastoralists, as well as many of the mountain men (woodsmen and hunters), metal-workers and traders, certainly began to develop identifiable clans and societies of their own. These were related to but distinct from the sedentary villagers and townspeople with whom they traded.

Geographically, Palestine's regions are diverse. Many are physically isolated from each other. The largest population centres are small market towns rather than cities. In those regions where the population is most dense, as in the Jezreel and Beth Shan valleys, no single town had the size or the political power to dominate even their own region, let alone centralize large areas of Palestine. This diverse situation fostered the development of politically independent towns, which were led by local hereditary patrons or groups of elders. A small elite organized commerce and defence. The patronage system in Palestine, in which the patron provided support and protection in exchange for loyalty and obedience, was based on personal commitments of individuals. Regional and inter-regional political developments were created by pyramiding coalitions. These were modelled on the economic interdependence of autonomous villages and towns that is characteristic of a 'Mediterranean economy'.

Rather than a bureaucratic state form of governance, such as was characteristic in Egypt and in the city-states of Mesopotamia, the patron-client political structures of Palestine, with its small population centres and fragmented geographical diversity, prevented the development of trans-regional statehood until the very end of the Hellenistic period. Defence measures in Palestine were locally organized. While fortification walls were created to such an extent that Early Bronze settlements resembled fortress towns or burghs, armies as such did not exist, either for conquest or defence.

There were no great powers that originated in Palestine during the Bronze Age. The diversity of the area and the absence of paramount population centres prevented any of the early neighbouring states from dominating it imperially, prior to the Egyptian takeover during the fifteenth century BCE. Palestine's heartland was ever a conglomerate of villages, independent and cooperative.

6 On towns and trade

The world of Bronze Age Palestine that was created by the Mediterranean economy functioned well in spite of being so diverse. This was largely due to the ubiquitous trading that drove the economy and its specialized production. Small holdings and autonomy, but especially interdependence, were the hallmarks of Palestine's economy. The shepherd traded with the farmer, and the farmer exchanged his products with the orchard, wine and olive growers, as well as with the merchants and craftsmen of the towns. This interdependence, which brought together many different kinds of people, linked one region of Palestine with another: the hills with the lowlands and the farmlands with the steppe.

The Bronze Age villager produced 'cash crops'. Wool, flax, meat and cheese, fish, grains (especially barley, wheat and millet), nuts and fruit, olive oil, wine, timber, pottery, salt, leather and cloth, flint tools, copper and turquoise were among the leading products in the market place. These were all produced by people working their own lands and herds, or by specialists working in cottage industries. Palestine had neither slave gangs nor a distinctly stratified society. There were no great kings here. A family living within an autonomous village or small town was the norm. Slavery did exist, but the slave belonged to and was part of the family. Poverty existed, but poverty was part of the landscape of Palestine, not its social structure. Quintessentially, the poor were those who fell outside of the social structure: strangers, debtors, widows and orphans.

Palestine's cash crops linked it with Egypt to the south and with Phoenicia, Syria and the Euphrates to the north and the northeast. Overland international trade was minimal throughout most of the Early and Middle Bronze Ages. Trade between Egypt and Syria went primarily by sea. Trade with Mesopotamia was funnelled through border towns such as Hazor, which (like nearby Tel Dan) was more Syrian than Palestinian. Most other overland trade was inter-regional. There were good reasons for this. Throughout most of these nearly 1,500 years, Palestine had no true cities and only very few true towns.

Political power within Palestine – and the military capabilities that went with it – was centred in the sphere of a wealthy landowner: a single man or family whose patronage legitimated the rights and authority of lesser men. It was a power based on character, influence and personal allegiance, and rarely outran the environs of very limited subregions. No single force, military or political, for example, controlled the Jezreel or the Beth Shan valleys. Dozens of towns competed for influence in the fertile regions of the coastal plain as well. Palestine featured fortifications even at some of its most modest villages. These burghs give clear evidence of autonomous and competing bosses, or 'great men'. Few towns and few political structures controlled more than a few thousand people, and most only a few hundreds. Small fortified villages, each one supported and defended by its patron, competed and cooperated with each other for trade and influence. In times of stress and conflict, coalitions were struck. Battles and even wars could be fought, but there were none among the many petty princes or their towns, capable of controlling any large portion of this complex region over time.

Although historians of early Palestine commonly refer to the towns of early Palestine as 'city-states' and to their rulers as 'kings', both of these terms are misleading. In Hebrew, the word for city has almost as wide a range as the word 'place' or 'settlement'. It can refer to a homestead or hamlet, to a village or town, or even to a few scattered tents. Our modern word misleads more than it translates. It is used to refer to Babylon or Nineveh, which were truly great cities of a quarter of a million people or more. It can also refer to the smallest village of a dozen or more people in the highlands of Galilee. Similarly, the word commonly translated as 'king' can refer to both Egypt's pharaoh, the dynastic monarch of several million people, and to most any autonomous village headman. Some scholars have recommended using the word chieftain, but even this word is too ambitious and should be used only for some of the most powerful of Palestine's rulers.

The villages of Palestine were for the most part independent of each other. They were strongly fortified and ruled by autonomous patrons, each with his own group of clients and sub-families. The power of a patron extended as far as his personal influence and protection. Both protection and allegiance were given through personal commitments and were maintained by mutual obligations. These involved paternalism on the one hand and absolute obedience on the other. The breaking of agreements was understood personally: in terms of betrayal.

Each town had its own patron, or 'godfather'. The impressive, but quickly and easily built, fortifications with which Palestine bristled until the close of the Middle Bronze Age were the hallmark of a 'family's' protection. Because of such extensive local autonomy, larger political alliances that would bind together larger regions were fragile and limited to situations of special need and stress.

State power did not exist in any indigenous form in Palestine. While local bosses could support and protect local and even inter-regional trade, commerce over great distances was beyond them. What long-distance trade existed was wholly dependent on the great powers and states of the Fertile Crescent: those of Egypt, Syria and Mesopotamia. Egypt extended its influence to create international trade along the Mediterranean coast and throughout Palestine's lowlands, by sea with Phoenicia and overland with Palestine's southern coast. The cities of inland Syria: Ebla, Hama, Aleppo, Mari, Damascus and Hazor, periodically extended their trade to the lowlands, to the Jezreel and the Jordan. The great international trade routes, however, linking the Nile valley with Syria, Anatolia and the Euphrates valley overland, came to use Palestine and the Sinai as a land bridge. During the Late Bronze Age, such overland international trade was the result of the cooperation and competition between the Egyptian and Hittite empires. That competition came to determine much of Palestine's political future.

By the fifteenth century BCE three major routes crossed Palestine.

1) *The Way of Horus*. This primary north–south route moved from the Nile's Delta across the eastern desert to Suez. It traced the North Sinai coastal ridge eastward to Gaza, where it turned northwards to travel up

Palestine's coastal plain to Ashqelon, Ashdod and Jaffa. Branch roads along the Wadi Gaza linked the highway to settlements scattered across the northern Negev, centred at Arad. Further to the north, wadi beds draining the southern hill country towards the sea linked the highway to the towns of Lachish and Gezer of the Shephelah. The Ayyalon valley linked Jerusalem and Beth Shemesh to the coast. The coastal route turned northeastward, crossing the Iron hills by way of the Megiddo pass, to enter the Jezreel and bring Egyptian trade within reach of both its towns and the villages of the Lower Galilee further to the north. From the western edge of the Jezreel valley, the route forked. One branch moved westward along the Nahal Qishon to Tell Abu Hawan, Tell Kisan, the town of Acco and the lucrative Phoenician ports that were vital links in East Mediterranean shipping. From here, connections could be made to Egypt, Cyprus, Syria, Anatolia and the Aegean.

The main road, however, continued eastward, along the southern rim of the Jezreel, from Megiddo and Taanach and from there to Beth Shan and the Jordan valley. Moving northwards, along the east side of the Sea of Galilee, the route quickly reaches the northern Jordan rift. It links such large Bronze Age settlements as Beth Yerah and Tel Kinnereth with Hazor and Dan. It continues into the central Biqa valley of Lebanon to the Syrian cities of Hama and Aleppo. A secondary route, after leaving Beth Shan, crossed the Jordan near Pella and moved northeastward up the Wadi Zarqa and across the Jaulan to Damascus. There, circling the northern rim of the Jebel Bishri highlands, the highway crossed the Great Syrian Steppe, finally reaching the Euphrates and Haran.

2) *The Desert Crossing.* The second major trunk route, linking the regions of Palestine to international trade, entered the Sinai from the eastern Delta just north of the Bitter Lakes. It crossed the Sinai along the northwestern slopes of the North Sinai and Central Negev deserts to the springs of Kadesh Barnea. After joining a branch road to Arad this route descended to the Jordan rift just south of the Dead Sea before moving northwards along the western shore to the springs of En Gedi and on to Jericho. It then moved north along the Jordan to Beth Shan and the north.

3) *The Kings' Highway.* This third overland highway left the Nile valley by way of the Wadi Tumilat. It crossed the Sinai just north of the Sinai massif by way of Wadi Firan and the springs near the present-day monastery of St Catherine. A major function of this route linked the mining regions of Serabit al-Kadim, Timna and the Wadi Araba, as well as the seaports of the Gulf near modern Elat and Aqaba. This route turned northwards from Aqaba. It travelled just west of the watershed along the Transjordanian plateau, and followed the very narrow belt of steppe and grazing lands that form the western perimeter of the Arabian desert. Avoiding the impassably deep gorges of the Transjordanian drainage system, this 'King's Highway' linked the commerce and trade of the

shepherds and farmers of the regions of Edom, Moab, Ammon, Gilead and the Jaulan on its way to Damascus.

The large villages and towns that were linked to this complex trade network in the Late Bronze period were already among the most stable and important of Palestine's regional market centres. The international trade brought prosperity to the economies. It encouraged expansion and further specialization. Crafts and related activities developed that were oriented to servicing the trade routes. Important among these were the breeding of draft animals, tanning and related industries. Populous towns quickly developed as regional centres. They monopolized their region's access to outside markets. Depending on the regional industries and the demands of their trading partners, many of these centres found prosperity and expansion through the spread of single-product dominance, such as in herding, timber, vineyards and olive-growing, oil and wine presses, dyeing, weaving, pottery and the like. This development not only brought prosperity but an increase in dependence and vulnerability to the fortunes of international trade, and eventually to the Egyptian empire that controlled it.

Palestinian links to the Egyptian–Phoenician sea routes lay with the port towns of the northwest. In the bay area of modern Haifa and along the northern Mediterranean coast, Phoenicia's trade created vital links with the whole of the Mediterranean world. As a result, a string of prosperous port cities and towns stretched from Tell Abu Hawam below the Carmel and included Tell Keisan, Acco, Achziv, Tyre, Sarepta, Sidon, Beirut, Byblos, Arvad and Ugarit. The technical demands of ship-building and navigation created these Phoenician towns as asparagus beds of the trades and crafts. The cosmopolitan and multi-lingual character of these towns marked them quickly as the only true urban centres of which Palestine could boast. Their economies and eclectic traditions marked Phoenicia as the centre of Palestine's culture. Literarily, Phoenicia was the *only* source of high culture in Palestine. It was from these port centres that the civilization of the greater world gradually reached Palestine's farming regions and steppelands.

Although Palestine continued throughout the Bronze Age as an illiterate backwater, this was not true of Phoenicia. Its towns resembled the great cities of Syria. A literate artistic culture of considerable merit developed at Ugarit in the fourteenth and thirteenth centuries, and scribes communicated regularly between the major towns of Palestine: from Byblos, Shechem and Jerusalem and the Egyptian court. Writing had long been established in Syria, at the market town of Ebla, from as early as the twenty-fourth century BCE, and a few examples of literary texts have been found from Alalakh to Megiddo.

Most writing was done for commercial reasons. This took the form of accounts and contracts, and for political and military communications.

Most forms of writing were complicated, using combinations of cuneiform symbols and signs. Writing and reading required skill and years of training. It was confined to professionals, employed by commercial interests and the courts of imperial states.

Phoenicia led the way to a wider literacy through the development of the alphabet. At Ugarit we find a fully developed alphabet written with cuneiform signs as early as the Late Bronze Age. Similar systems were in place elsewhere in Syria and Palestine. The invention of the linear alphabet, which formed the basis not only of Hebrew and Aramaic but also – by way of the Phoenicians – of the Greek and Latin systems, is still obscure, but seems to be developed from cursive forms of Egyptian writing. During the Bronze Age, literacy was an aspect either of the Egyptian empire or of Phoenician commerce and the literary activities they supported. The population of Palestine did not gain much from these developments before Assyria began to use Aramaic as a lingua franca for its empire. They developed a system of scribes and schools in the course of the eighth and seventh centuries.

CHAPTER 6

A Mediterranean economy

1 Farmers and shepherds: a shifting economy: c. 2400–1750 BCE

While the discussion of the early use of Semitic languages in Asia and their relationship to the speakers of Afro-Asiatic in the Neolithic settlements of North Africa is essential for understanding both the indigenous nature of the people of Palestine and the development of Hebrew and related languages, the historical development of a people involves much more than their language. The origins of the authors of biblical tradition are also rooted in the lands in which they lived and in the forms of economic and social life to which they were born. In this respect, our authors' roots lay equally deep in the soil of Palestine, drawing from the same Early West Semitic culture as their neighbours in Syria.

Until the mid-1970s, biblical and archaeological scholarship understood the transition between the Early Bronze and Middle Bronze periods in terms of the old theory of a migration of Semitic nomads from Arabia. Many linked this theory to cuneiform and Egyptian texts that referred to *Amurru* and *Amu*. Historians had created a history of Amorite migrations and invasions that overwhelmed the Fertile Crescent from the Persian Gulf to the Egyptian Delta. These nomadic tribes were thought to have destroyed the Early Bronze cultures of both Mesopotamia and Palestine, to have created Egypt's First Intermediate and, after several centuries, to have led to the development of an Amorite dominance among the Mesopotamian states in Syria and Palestine. Biblical archaeology had linked this 'Amorite movement' to the tales of the biblical patriarchs, especially to the stories of Abraham and Jacob. They read behind the stories a history of movements of peoples.

In doing this, they created a double history of origins for early Israel: one as nomads from North Mesopotamia in the early second millennium and the other as semi-nomadic pastoralists at the end of the Bronze Age, around 1200 BCE. This 'history' depended on carefully selected biblical stories for its coherence. Abraham moved from Ur of southern Mesopotamia to Harran in the north. From there, he entered 'Canaan' with his family. Yet later, Jacob and his family went down to Egypt, there to become Israel and return to Palestine under Joshua. This story was thought to reflect a second invasion of Palestine by Israelites, who shared in a wider 'Aramaean' migration that created the peoples of the Transjordan.

This was neither really an historical synthesis nor an historical reconstruction on the basis of argument. It was an assertion of harmony and identity between selected biblical stories and archaeological data. It was the Bible's story, however, not the archaeological data that gave this history coherence and continuity. The collapse of this synthesis, which had placed an impossible demand on our evidence, was both sudden and definitive. With the acceptance of Afro-Asiatic as the ancestor of the Semitic languages, not only had the romantic picture of Arabian origins to be given up, but the successive migrations of 'Amorites' and 'Aramaeans' from Arabia's fertile womb evaporated. Old ideas of invasions had made it possible for historians to use hordes of nomads to wipe away earlier cultures and to start over with a new culture. In this way, they shifted from Early to Middle Bronze, and from the world of Late Bronze Canaanites to a new world of Iron Age Israelites. Without the Amorite and Aramaean invasions to explain these transitions, the continuities of culture became clearer. What differences there were – and they were not so great as the history books of the 1960s and 1970s led us to believe – they were far better explained as internal changes and developments of the economy.

The spectrum of sedentarization from farmers living in towns to shepherds living in forms of seasonal nomadism is related to different ways of making a living. In Palestine, such differences are created by recurring efforts to adapt to changes in the climate and the environment. The dominance of one form over another is due to the effects of trade, on which the whole of Palestine's Mediterranean economy was dependent. The population as a whole was stable only to the extent that it was flexible. It used many forms of both nomadism and settlement, depending on the needs of the region in which they are found and on the temporary changes in weather and economy.

The prosperity that the favourable climate of the third millennium brought to the South Levant was extraordinary. This prosperity lasted some 500 years. By around 2400 BCE, the economy of southern Palestine was bolstered by a thriving trade with the high civilization of Old Kingdom Egypt which had built the pyramids. The north was closely tied to Syria.

With greater rainfall during the Early Bronze Age, the Sinai and the central and southern Negev – normally desert terrain with some patches of steppe – was able to develop considerable ranges of grassland, within a steppe that included much of West and South Arabia. Continuous grazing land connected these regions with the Great Syrian Steppe to the north. A population of transhumance pastoralists developed over a vast region that stretched along the whole of the Levant's eastern and southern flanks. Wheat and barley were grown on the lower slopes of the hills and in the gullies and valleys that drained them. Turquoise, copper, natron and bitumen industries along the shores of the Dead Sea, the southern Araba and the central Sinai massive provided supplementary occupations for these farmer-shepherds in the off-season. They created and guaranteed the necessary links with the trade routes on which the survival of these populations depended.

During the twenty-fourth century BCE this prosperity collapsed. The entire region of the eastern Mediterranean entered a long period of devastating drought that threatened the survival of a population whose previous prosperity and expansive growth could be said to have itself been partly responsible for this collapse. South Palestine's prosperity had increased the inability of its population to respond to the drought's depressive impact on the economy.

A good example of this might be found in the Early Bronze town of Arad. This had been a large and prosperous settlement on Palestine's southern fringe. The stretch of steppelands that separates the agricultural heartland from the great expanse of desert from the Sinai to Arabia had already developed its own pattern of farming and settlement. The semi-arid zone stretched across grassland from the coastal plain of Ashqelon to Gaza and eastwards through the Beersheva and Arad basins. Because of the aridity and especially the irregularity of the rainfall, permanent settlement over the course of the Bronze Age was at best unstable. The area's villages and towns are almost all found in the northernmost regions, close to the major drainage wadis. These villages also seem to have had an economy balanced between drought-resistant sheep- and goat-herding and grain agricultural. As a result, areas developed by villages in this region were proportionately much larger, and the population density much less, than in the farming regions of the north.

The larger towns, like Arad, also served as border towns, markets for the much larger population of nomadic groups from the steppelands, oases and hills of the Negev and the Sinai, who lived from sheep- and goat-herding and supplemented their income with patch agriculture in the wadi beds of the uplands. The overwhelming evidence from excavations and patterns of settlement over this large area is that the onset of the drought brought catastrophic change. While many scholars of the late 1960s and early 1970s had hoped to explain this disaster with a scenario of nomadic Amorite pastoralists invading the region from the Syrian steppe and from North Mesopotamia, there was no evidence for this. Worse, this theory hardly explained the near-total collapse of the region's best grasslands.

The roots of the disaster that overtook the Early Bronze period in southern Palestine lay within Palestine itself: in its prosperity, its largest towns, and its rapidly increasing population. The prosperity of Arad in the second quarter of the third millennium stands not merely in stark contrast to the poverty and emptiness of the Arad Basin during this millennium's fourth quarter; it is its cause. At the height of the Early Bronze's prosperity, Palestine witnessed an unprecedented expansion of population. Towns of more than five acres, with several thousand people in them, have been found in many of the more fertile regions of Palestine. Small villages and hamlets scattered themselves throughout the regions where good soils and abundant water were to be found. Settlement expanded up into the more difficult highlands, with the building of enclosures and terraces along the more gently sloping drainage valleys. The population of the Early Bronze period also expanded beyond such favourable regions. Settlements were created in the more marginal regions. They are found in steppe zones, which could support only a very limited population, and agriculture, only in the best of times.

The one near-constant of history, population growth, made these settlements increasingly precarious. With growth, the settlements of the marginal lands became dependent on favourable weather and soil conditions. Also with growth, grazing and cropping intensified. Longer fallows gave way to shorter, and the land was given ever less time to recover its fertility. To compensate, more marginal lands with poorer soils were put under production. In the primary agricultural areas, pressure for emigration mounted as the maximum population density was approached. This migration moved into newer areas of the highlands and steppe, but also into the towns and increasingly into non-agricultural areas of the economy. This increased the pressure on the agricultural sector. At the same time, this sector was becoming less capable of meeting the rising demands made on it. The growth of towns brought inflation and collapse of over-stressed economies became commonplace as the drought intensified. In the more marginal regions the eventual catastrophe may have been inevitable. In such areas, where agriculture is nearly entirely dependent on dry farming, even normal climate variations from year to year bring with them recurrent periods of crop failure from short-term drought. Moreover, these areas, where rainfall is already only marginal at best, a 15 or 20 per cent diminution of rainfall can be catastrophic. It can result in the loss of much of the harvest. In areas of adequate rainfall such fluctuation creates only a more moderate stress on production.

Overuse of marginal lands and a rising demand for water, combined with recurrent and lengthening dry spells, also directly affected the water-table, whose lowering resulted directly in the loss of shallow springs and wells. In coastal areas, it led to increasing salinization of the groundwater. With ever larger areas being opened up, the already poor lands must fail to produce consistently high yields. In turn, this encouraged farmers to shorten and even abandon fallow systems on their good land in order to compensate for their losses. With the abandonment of fallow systems, salinization increased and production declined. In overpopulated marginal areas such as the Arad Basin, the onset of drought at the end of the Early Bronze period not only contributed to agricultural failure, it led to widespread overgrazing by the nomadic part of the population associated to the town. Overgrazing brought erosion and soil denudation.

The water-table of the Arad Basin did drop, and with it collapsed the once great town of Arad's chances of survival. Once serious food shortages began to occur, the danger of widespread famine caused towns, the primary sources of food storage, to grow even more. The towns were needed, politically. Their ability to stabilize, police and regulate limited resources became issues of survival. Even short-term famines, spread over a very large region, could threaten the stores of the towns with depletion, creating political conflict and war. A prolonged period of such instability, such as occurred at this time, so disrupts normal life as to cause an internal collapse of the local economy and can eventually lead to the abandonment of whole areas. Before the end of the third millennium, many regions of Palestine had collapsed. The steppe zones, which were ecologically the most fragile, were likely the first areas abandoned. The effect of the lengthening drought was eventually to transform the whole of Palestine.

The southern fringe of Syria entered yet another period of great drought that was severe enough to disrupt its agricultural economy. The drought caused civil unrest and political conflict in regions from Egypt to the city-states of southern Mesopotamia. The densely occupied agricultural regions of Palestine were devastated. The expanding steppelands forced the region's farmers into more nomadic forms of livelihood. Patch agriculture and herding of sheep and goats increased – especially in the more agriculturally uncertain highlands and the more arid south. The border of aridity, which separated lands capable of being farmed without irrigation from the steppe, moved inexorably northwards. Full agriculture survived only in the richest and best-watered regions. A much-reduced number of the village farmers of the northern Jordan, the Beth Shan and the Jezreel valleys were able to survive the drought as sedentary farmers. Others were forced out. Even the richest-watered of Palestine's valleys were able to support only small villages.

The lowered water-table, salinization and denudation of soils prevented easy recovery in marginal lands. The population of Palestine as a whole was diminished through starvation, warfare and emigration. It concentrated itself in the richest and largest agricultural zones, especially where continued fertility was supported by irrigation. Yet the economy was frugal, village-oriented and isolated from the world beyond Palestine. The lack of significant defence structures around 2000 BCE suggests a modest return to stability and a withdrawal of the population pressures that had led to the collapse.

In response to the increasing aridity and starvation that had accompanied a succession of disastrous years, the population was forced to expand its investment in herds, which were less vulnerable to the immediate impact of drought. As a result, the population spread in smaller groups over an ever larger region. Because of this drought in the last quarter of the third millennium BCE, pastoral nomadism and patch agriculture became permanent and distinctive ways of life throughout the steppe regions of greater Palestine. Displaced persons from the towns and villages of the heartland were forced into the marginalized fringes of the Mediterranean zone in order to survive. Refugees created hundreds of small hamlets across the central Negev highlands, in a region that had previously never supported a sedentary population, and which had known small settlements of shepherds only during the rainy periods of the Early Bronze sub-pluvial. Many families were forced out of greater Palestine altogether during this drought that closed the Early Bronze period. They emigrated northeastward into the highlands of Jebel Bishri of the Great Syrian Steppe. Yet others emigrated into the oases of the Arabian desert, destined to return to the fringes of Palestine a thousand years later as Arabs.

Such cycles of economic depression and destabilization of the agriculture of the region are recurrent in Palestine's history. They find their counterpoint in peaks of prosperity and dense sedentarization. The Early Bronze II, Middle Bronze II, perhaps the Late Bronze II and the Iron II periods are all marked by relative affluence, population growth and political concentration. These prosperous periods might well illustrate Palestine's optimal economic potential. Each successive period – Early Bronze IV, Middle Bronze II/Late Bronze I, Iron I, and the early 'Persian' period – finds its fate in economic collapse and a dramatic Malthusian culling of the population. It is these periods that most require historical explanation, for these depressions are departures from the expected.

Some limited forms of nomadism existed in the Sinai already from the fourth millennium. Nomads there lived off metal-working, some sheep- and goat-herding, hunting, limited patch agriculture and farming in occasional oases. They were supported by the very favourable rainfall regime of that sub-pluvial period. We find such desert-dwelling groups in the Sinai in even larger numbers during the second quarter of the third millennium. Although they were active in trade with towns in Egypt's Delta region and in southern Palestine (such as Arad), they seem to have formed their own distinct society.

These nomadic groups are economically quite different from the kinds of steppe pastoralism that develops later in the grazing areas of Palestine's southern and eastern steppeland, which then formed an extension of the Great Syrian Steppe. Although this geographically very large steppe can seasonally support a considerable population, the forms of pastoralism were of a 'transhumance' type. That is, they involved seasonal migration between at least two different climate areas. For example, the shepherds of this area typically graze their herds in the steppes throughout the winter. But when the hot summers come and the steppe grasses fail, they move into the agricultural heartland, feeding off the stubble of harvested fields and fertilizing them in turn. The relationship between the farmer and the shepherd is 'symbiotic'. It involved a mutual dependence. In this context, the shepherd's is a specialized trade. It forms part of the agricultural society. Whether nomadic shepherds also formed separate societies depended on the specific historical experiences of each group. However, the great range of the steppe, in contrast to the intensive settlement of the agricultural heartland, makes the development of transhumant societies likely over time. By the beginning of the second millennium, we have written evidence of such developments. The economic depression at the end of the Early Bronze Age shifted the normal economy of the region towards pastoralism and towards a grain agriculture of more drought-resistant types. The spread of the population that resulted in hundreds of small hamlets, dotting the steppelands of the northern slopes of the Central Negev and Sinai and the Transjordan plateau, reflect a movement away from Palestine. While something of the society of the northern agricultural heartland survived in patterns of transhumance during the centuries of drought, the spread of pastoral groups over the steppe must have fostered entirely new societies and political structures that had little to do with the agricultural heartland. When the drought finally ended in the twentieth century BCE, and sedentarization and intensive agriculture returned to the heartland, regional differences became more marked and the population of greater Palestine became fragmented as people settled down and tended their own valleys and lands.

Not all those who had turned to pastoralism returned to the agricultural fields. Some four centuries had intervened. At the height of the Middle Bronze prosperity (*c.* 1800 BCE), pastoral societies continued to exist throughout greater Palestine. They are clearly distinguishable from town-dominated, agricultural and sedentary peoples. They are likely to have come from many of the Early Bronze IV settlers of the steppe, who (when good weather returned, towns grew, and markets reopened) adjusted their lives to a greater specialization in pastoralism, in hopes of meeting the demands of new markets.

2 The early West Semites

With the return to a wetter and cooler climate, the second great drought came to an end. It was followed by a period of economic prosperity. In

Egypt the pharaohs of the twelfth dynasty reasserted Theban control over the Delta. Overland trade routes to southern Palestine brought prosperity and stability. Egypt's trade to Phoenicia went by sea. It dealt primarily in lumber and manufactured goods. The overland trade routes linked Egypt to its primary sources for olive oil, wine and wool. Olive orchards and vineyards became the nearly exclusive cash crops of southern Palestine. New olive and grape hybrids were developed to increase production.

Palestine was by no means a single region. Trade from central and northern Palestine (the central hills, the Jezreel, the lower Galilee, the Hazor region of the Upper Galilee, the northern Jordan Rift and northern Transjordan) led northwards to Phoenicia and to the cities of Syria and Mesopotamia. The north, which supported the greatest part of Palestine's population, began to develop an economy and culture that was distinct and much more prosperous and independent than that of the south. With an annual precipitation that was nearly three times that of southern Palestine, the northern regions had a greater potential in wine, olive oil and grains than their neighbours in the more arid south. They were also able to maintain a much longer period of economic stability.

Throughout Greater Palestine, settlement increased dramatically. Even in the regions of the southern Judean hills and the coastal plain that had been abandoned during the drought, a greater population than ever before was supported. Throughout Palestine, most of the major regional towns were fortified and took on the character of small burghs, which dominated neighbouring villages. Towns such as Byblos, Hazor, Beth Shan, Megiddo, Gezer, Ashqelon, Shechem, Jerusalem, Lachish and Gaza established dominant political control in their regions. They did so through land ownership, locally accumulated political power and through the control of markets. They asserted their influence over religion and local temples, and created tax systems for their patrons.

Although they are few, we can learn a great deal about Palestine of this period from written texts. We have three forms of very early direct evidence for arguing that the Semites had long settled and dominated this region in the Early Bronze Age. Almost all early geographic names in Palestine have a Semitic character. From inscriptions in the Ebla archives from Syria, written in Akkadian, almost all personal names that have been found associated with the southern region, are Semitic. Many show a West Semitic form. Also, the Egyptian language itself, which is written as early as 3000 BCE, shows strong influences from the West Semitic language. This is apparent both in some few aspects of the grammar as well as in several basic West Semitic nouns that are used in Egyptian, for which Egyptian itself has no equivalent. So, for example, the words for 'eye', 'hand' and 'death' are written in Old Kingdom Egyptian with the West Semitic words: 'yn, yd and mt.

We have three early groups of related texts that list the names of both towns and rulers of Palestine. They are usually referred to as the 'execration texts', for they seem to have been used by the Egyptians to curse the enemy towns and princes listed on them. The three groups of texts refer to Palestine over the course of at most 2 generations. They can now be dated between about 1810 and 1770 BCE, that is, to the height of the Middle Bronze period. Many names of Palestine's best-known towns appear for the first time: Byblos, Shechem, Ashqelon, Hazor, Beth Shemesh, Pella and Jerusalem. The towns are listed with the West Semitic names of their 'princes' or 'chiefs'. Some towns are presented with the name of a single ruler, others with two or more. Some are presented as divided between a northern and southern, upper or lower town, each with its individual 'prince'. Some towns, like Byblos, are simply listed as the 'peoples' of the town, without the name of a ruler.

The familiarity of so many of the town names is a striking confirmation of continuities in this region that will continue over the next millennium and a half. The variations in the naming of single and multiple rulers may also indicate that a patronage form of political structure is already firmly established. This form of political control, where a single town stands under the protection of a single patron or is governed by agreements between two or more patrons, dominates both Palestine and Syria in antiquity. As we will see below, it is well supported by archaeological evidence.

From the end of Egypt's Old Kingdom, West Semites and West Semitic groups are frequently met in Egyptian texts. Many are called by the general name *Amu*, which seems to be a term vaguely signifying 'Asiatics'. Others are called by another generic term, *Shutu*, which is a name referring to people living in the desert. These words are used interchangeably with 'highlanders': the *Hurru* and the *Medaw*. Egyptian scribes use these names without much discrimination. They signify little more than people from the regions of Asia, and are used to refer to groups who live in the eastern desert of Egypt and in the Delta, in Sinai, the Transjordan, Palestine and Syria. The name 'Egyptians', like the term 'people', is understood to refer to those native to the central Nile valley, and especially those under the political control of Thebes. Occupants of the Delta to the north, of the desert regions of the east and west, and of the upper Nile in Nubia to the south, are only 'Egyptians' when they have been integrated into Egyptian society and live under Theban rule.

3 Palestine conquers Egypt? c. 1730–1570 BCE

A consideration of Egypt's relationship with Syria and Palestine is helpful in dealing with the problems of writing ancient history, particularly in regard to the rule over central Egypt by the pharaohs of the Delta for a period of about one and a half centuries. It would be helpful in understanding the importance of reading biblical texts critically, rather than from the perspective of the naive realism common to much biblical archaeology, if we also look at similar problems in reading ancient Near Eastern texts. This period of Egyptian history is particularly helpful because we have both traditional and archaeological texts that relate to the history of this period. It is, moreover, a great favourite of Bible historians who have long tried to associate the patriarchs of Genesis with Egyptian political history.

We have ancient texts, including one from a participant in the civil wars that closed this period, that refer to the Delta's control of Thebes as an 'Asiatic' conquest and a foreign rule, which ended with expulsion. The earliest of these texts are to be attributed to the pharaoh Kamose, who ruled the central Nile Valley from Thebes just before the beginning of the eighteenth dynasty. Our texts are a pair of steles that were erected in the Temple of Karnak. Their style takes the form of monumental propaganda, written to celebrate Kamose's wars. He fought to unify Egypt after years of conflict between Egypt's three regions: the Delta of the north, Nubia of the south, and Thebes of the central Nile, thought of as Egypt proper by the writers of our texts. These monuments describe the onset of war against the 'Asiatics' of the Delta from the perspective of Thebes. The rulers of the Delta are called the 'Hyksos', a word that has been translated 'foreign princes'. Allegedly, they conquered 'Egypt' some 160 years earlier (1730 BCE). Kamose asserts that they had overthrown the dynasty of Thebes and had ruled Egypt illegitimately. The task fell to him to drive these 'foreigners' from Egyptian soil. They were finally defeated and expelled from the Egyptian homeland by Ahmose, the founder of the eighteenth dynasty.

In an early eighteenth-dynasty tomb inscription, an Egyptian commander of a ship recounts his experiences as a young man during the wars against the Delta capital of Avaris, in which he, fighting for the pharaoh Seqnen-Re, had killed two enemy soldiers and had been decorated for valour. He also recounts the fighting in the south in which he participated. He had taken an enemy as prisoner and had been decorated once again. Finally, he reports the sacking of Avaris and the siege of Sharuhen, from which he was awarded slaves as booty. He goes on to recount a series of campaigns in Nubia and later in Palestine.

We have a very brief royal inscription of a century after the conquest of Avaris. It is helpful to us, as it refers back to this period when the Delta ruled Egypt as a period of shame. One sees already the growing legend of interpretation that understands this former period of dominance by the Delta specifically as 'foreign' and 'anti-Egyptian'. The text implicitly redefines 'Egyptian' from the perspective of Thebes. Queen Hatshepshut, who ruled Thebes from 1486 to 1469 BCE, gives us one of our earliest examples of the widely used propaganda motif of 'king as restorer of the true past'. We will see a more systematic use of this same motif to justify wars of conquest by the kings of Assyria, Babylon and Persia. It is a literary tradition which describes past enemies as destructive of piety, peace and culture, and the new ruler as their restorer: 'I have rebuilt what had gone to pieces ever since the "Asiatics" were in their capital Avaris in the northland . . . I have got rid of those the gods hate, etc.'

Yet much later we find the 'Asiatic' ruler of the Delta, 'Prince Apophis', of the now distant past, as a leading character in a legendary schoolboy's wisdom story. In contrast to the propaganda of the Theban Hatshepshut, this use of the Hyksos in folklore gives the rulers of the Delta equal status with the king of Thebes. 'There was no Lord . . . or king of the time' but 'only King Seqnen-Re in Thebes and King Apophis who ruled over the town of the Asiatics in Avaris'. This folktale is drawn on the scale of such earlier descriptions of Egypt's divisions as we find, for instance, in a schoolboy's copy of the first of a pair of steles at Karnak:

> The mighty king in Thebes, Kamose . . . was the beneficent king. It was Re himself who had made him king and who had assigned him strength in truth. His majesty spoke in his palace to his nobles . . . 'Let me understand what this strength of mine is for! One prince is in Avaris, another is in Ethiopia, and here I sit associated with an Asiatic and a Nubian. Each man has his slice of this Egypt, dividing up the land with me. . . . My wish is to save Egypt and strike at the Asiatics.'

That we are dealing with an inter-regional conflict within Egypt and a civil war becomes particularly clear in the more cautious and less romantic response of Kamose's counsellors:

> The great men of the council spoke: 'Look, it is Asiatic water as far as Cusae.[1] They have hung out their tongues all trying to speak at the same time,[2] while we are comfortable in our Egypt. Elephantine is strong and the centre of the land is with us as far north as Cusae. Their richest fields are now being ploughed for our purposes, and our cattle are being pastured in the Delta and emmer is sent to us for our pigs. Our cattle have not been taken. . . . He holds the land of the Asiatics. We hold Egypt. Should someone come and attack us, then we will act against him.'

Kamose, however, did not listen to such counsel. Instead, he set out not only to make history, but also to make a history that understands Egypt – the entire Nile valley – as essentially Theban, and to define the rulers of the Delta as alien and foreign to the land he ruled.

This great effort of propaganda was successful. Its sway over modern

---

[1] About 25 miles south of Heliopolis at the southern apex of the Delta.
[2] Apparently a reference to competing groups in the Delta.

historians, however, is due to Josephus, the Jewish 'historian' of the Roman period. Many more than a thousand years later than our latest Egyptian texts, and well more than a millennium and a half after Kamose's sack of Avaris, we find a story of this conflict in Josephus, who claims as his source an earlier Egyptian historian, Manetho. According to his account, the Hyksos are identified as foreign rulers in Egypt for more than 500 years. Their rule had been the result of a mysterious, unopposed conquest from the east. They are referred to as 'shepherd kings'. Josephus' Manetho links them with the patriarch Joseph of Genesis and with the Israelites of the Exodus. Josephus demonstrates in his account his extraordinary ability to synthesize fragmented and confused knowledge about the past. He presents this mid-second-millennium regional struggle for control of the Delta as an expulsion of the Hyksos from Egypt, and links it with what was, in fact, the dominance of Palestine by the Assyrians eight centuries later! More, Josephus' Manetho describes a vast exodus of Asiatics from the Egyptian Delta to Palestine, and in citing him, Josephus explains the original settlement of Judea and the founding of Jerusalem.[1]

During the late nineteenth and twentieth century CE, many historians and Bible scholars have tried to harmonize these accounts, much as Josephus tried to do, by linking them with the Bible's stories of the patriarchs and the Israelite exodus from Egypt. All but a few modern scholars have accepted the conclusion uncritically that the Hyksos were originally Palestinians who conquered Egypt and, after nearly two centuries rule there, were expelled much as is recounted in the Egyptian texts cited above. Hardly any have chosen to question the historicity of Theban propaganda about the Hyksos' 'expulsion from Egypt'. Some have even argued that the biblical patriarchs Joseph and Jacob were Hyksos kings! Although none follow Josephus' efforts to link the expulsion of the 'Hyksos' with the founding of Judea and Jerusalem, or with the Assyrians, many have tried to associate these fictions closely to the story of Moses in the Book of Exodus.

Archaeological evidence of cultural ties between southern Palestine and the Egyptian Delta has been used to support belief in the soundness of Manetho's account, as well as to claim that this tradition provides an historical background to the Jacob and Joseph tales in Genesis. However, historical links between Egypt and Palestine are no more than what one must expect, given the very active trade between these two regions, and the continuum that existed between the cultures of Egypt and Asia. This is particularly clear when one considers the elements shared between the Delta and southern Palestine from very early periods. During the height of Palestine's Middle Bronze prosperity, the influence of Palestinian and Phoenician material culture in the Delta increased markedly.

Egyptian inscriptions show that the Delta pharaohs at Avaris were called

[1] Josephus' account can be found in *Contra Apionem* 1, 14.

'Hyksos' and were frequently referred to by the word *Amu*. This is normally and correctly translated 'Asiatics'. Egyptian texts, however, commonly referred to Semites generally by calling them 'Asiatics'. Asia, from the perspective of many in central Egypt, began at Heliopolis, or, as with Kamose's advisers, already at Cusae, south of the Delta region. This term *Amu* had been used since Old Kingdom times to refer to shepherds in the Delta, as well as to the indigenous population of Egypt's eastern desert. In the Middle Bronze Age, when regional struggles dominated Theban politics, many were thought Asiatic who nevertheless spoke Egyptian and who were culturally indistinguishable from Egyptians. They were 'Asiatics' simply because they came from or lived in the Delta. In a parallel political struggle of Thebes with the southern region of Egypt, Thebes called all southerners 'Nubians'. This marked the south's implicit independence from Thebes. The name 'Egyptian' is not properly a gentilic in the ancient world, nor do the terms 'Nubian' or 'Asiatic' refer to any kind of ethnicity. Within Egypt, the names 'Nubian', 'Egyptian' and 'Asiatic' refer to people who live within the three distinct geographical regions of Egypt; namely, the upper Nile, the lower Nile and the Delta. That 'Nubian' and 'Asiatic' might also be used for other peoples outside of Egypt merely exposes their potential political use in a struggle for hegemony. Physically, Egypt's indigenous population displayed an unbroken continuum from Negroid to Mediterranean types, as one might expect.

Early Egyptian references to the Hyksos, beginning already in the seventeenth dynasty, refer to rulers who were indigenous to the Delta. They did not come from Palestine. By the end of the eighteenth century, they extended their political hegemony to Thebes. By the sixteenth century, they are allied with the rulers of southern Egypt, and possibly may have had ambitions of dividing central Egypt with the 'Nubians'. The so-called 'expulsion of the Hyksos' was a political reassertion of traditional Theban patronage over the Delta's rulers. Neither political propaganda nor the language of racist exclusion are modern inventions. The famous inscription of Meri-Ka Re, dated to the late third millennium BCE, already raises the self-pitying complaint of the Egyptian, that is, Theban, aristocrat: 'Asiatics are becoming people everywhere!' Palestine never conquered Egypt.

Some few Palestinian sites that are mentioned in texts dealing with the war between Thebes and Avaris are easily understood as towns allied to and possibly in the control of the Delta pharaohs. They were never bases of Hyksos power. Once the war turned against the Delta, these Palestinian towns are likely to have become places of refuge. The war against Avaris was fought to free Thebes from its client status. The Delta pharaohs had never actually occupied the central Nile valley, nor had they ever ruled it directly. The issue initially at stake was not occupation, or even conquest, but patronage. Ahmose would rather collect tribute than pay it.

The war of words that was engaged by the use of the terms 'Egyptian' and 'Asiatic', and which has infected all of our texts from Kamose to Josephus, has in fact a three-thousand-year history. Already in the Narmer Palette – one of the very earliest readable Egyptian texts – the creation of the first dynasty of Egypt's Old Kingdom under the centralizing authority of Heliopolis was celebrated with an illustration of the pharaoh's conquest of people living in the marshlands of the eastern Delta. These marsh-dwellers are described with the pre-hieroglyphic picture-symbol for 'Asiatics'. Controlling the Semites of the Delta and of the eastern desert was a major preoccupation of Heliopolis' court propaganda. This policy created the well-known stereotype scene that has been found on so many Egyptian reliefs from the first three dynasties. The pharaoh is drawn striding into battle and clubbing to death a fallen, naked and bearded Semite. This motif became a ready symbol of Egyptian, and later Theban, military power.

The differences between Egypt of the Nile valley and Egypt of the Delta are profound ones, though they have little to do with race or language associations. The Delta, although dominated by the culture, language and economy of the much more populous region of the Nile, was able to maintain a broad mix of occupations. The economy was very different from the Nile valley's. Delta farming depended on canal systems, on irrigation and on controlled flooding. Fishing and fowling dominated the marshes, and sheep and goats the Delta steppe. These occupations were foreign to the Nile's floodplain. The Delta was heavily influenced by international trade, both overland and by sea. The Delta was Egypt's point of entry from both Asia and the whole of the Mediterranean. Its population was also considerably less dense than the Nile's. Politically, it developed small village and town patronage systems, much as one finds in Syria. The region may also have developed pyramidal alliances of independent patrons, much like the coalitions one finds in Palestine and Syria. These contrast sharply to the state bureaucratic structures of Thebes.

4 The Hyksos in Palestine?

The different perspectives of historiographies like Josephus' are easily overlooked, when one asks whether his synthetic reconstruction is believable in view of earlier Egyptian texts. If we decide to ignore Josephus' historically chaotic references to Assyrians and to the founding of Judea and Jerusalem, there are few inescapable contradictions between his account and one that could be drawn from one or other Egyptian scribe 1,400 years and more earlier. Josephus' account can even be supposed to supplement and support these texts in the form of a 'fuller' understanding of the past.

One of the worst aspects of our history-writing about ancient Egypt and Palestine, and especially our early histories about the Iron and Bronze Ages, is that we arbitrarily 'enhance' them with paraphrases of stories that were written centuries later. We are invited to do so by fictions like Josephus'. These narratives are cast as 'origin stories'. As such, they offer our histories a wholeness and a completeness that critical historical accounts cannot have. Although biblical scholarship is no longer writing the Bronze Age history of Palestine on the basis of traditional tales about the patriarchs of Genesis or the like, scholars writing Egyptian history still do use such uncritical paraphrases and harmonies, such as one finds in the classical origin stories of antiquity. Old-fashioned biblical archaeology is alive and well west of Suez. Raising this issue should not turn into a debate on whether Manetho or Josephus is a better historian than Moses. We need an alternative perspective for writing history, whenever our information is so partial and so fragmentary that coherence has to be created by our only surviving source.

In arguing that the Delta dominated Egyptian politics during this period, I am reading texts. Some, however, would argue that this neglects the archaeological evidence, from the excavations of Avaris to the tells of southern Palestine. The absence of any evidence for a known Palestinian base of the late eighteenth or early seventeenth century, from which an Asiatic invasion of Egypt might be launched, is well recognized. Nor do we have any reason to assume that the 'Hyksos' capital in the Delta, Avaris, dominated Palestine. The Avaris excavation cannot address the question of the *origin* of the Hyksos.

It is correct beyond question that there was a great deal of trade between Palestine's southern coastal plain and Egypt. We have already seen that such trade exists as early as the twentieth century BCE, and it continues to expand until at least the eleventh century. Similar trade existed between Palestine's Jezreel valley and the Phoenician coast, and between the town of Hazor and the North Mesopotamian city of Mari. In neither of these cases, however, would any scholar suggest that military conquest had been involved. Of course, in the ancient world, at least as much as today, commercial exchange is always closely tied to political involvement. Yet political influence and empire are two different historical realities. The progression from trade to influence to imperial conquest is neither an obvious nor a necessary one. One needs evidence. We know that the eighteenth- and nineteenth-dynasty pharaohs from Thutmosis III on were able to launch and maintain imperial armies in Asia. We also know that they controlled the territories they conquered at that time. There is nothing we know from the 'Hyksos' period that suggests that a centralized power ever existed on Palestinian soil, which could launch a successful army against Egypt. Western Palestine's distinct economic and cultural regions were incapable of creating a military system large enough and sufficiently well-disciplined and rewarded to control Palestine. The second-century Maccabee, John Hyrcanus, was the only ruler who came close to this, and he was able to do so only with Roman concurrence. That such a centralized government could control Palestine's endemic fragmentation and at the same time launch a military force capable of gaining political control over a population many more than ten times its size is historically unthinkable. Whatever Josephus may have wished to argue, such a picture of the Hyksos has Palestine against it.

The question of the Hyksos in Palestine requires that we have some understanding of the society of Palestine of the time: its population, transport and communications, its economy and especially its political structures. The always sound observation that armies move on their bellies should force historians to consider the enormous support structures necessary to field a major army, to maintain it in the field and to secure its loyalty. Scholars have traditionally talked about the political structures of Bronze Age Palestine as an 'interlocking system of city-states'. Such terminology is as harmful as it is undiscriminating. Palestine at this early period had no cities, aside from Hazor of the very distant north. It has only villages and small towns. The population of the largest was only a very few thousands at best. To speak of a 'system', interlocking Palestine's towns into some politically coherent and cooperative structure, is clearly distorted. To speak of 'state' structures among such towns confuses Bronze Age Palestine with Renaissance Italy!

Much of the archaeological interest in the Hyksos in Palestine has been based on a very specific type of massive fortification that was built around many of the larger towns in Syria, Palestine and the Delta. Apart from the fact that for a century now archaeologists have excavated these enormous structures and called them 'Hyksos fortifications', we have not learned that the peoples who lived within the protection of these different towns were ever related to each other. We have no historical warrant for calling them 'Hyksos fortifications', as if this were an ethnic or a political term. These impressive fortifications are engineering feats, and engineers travel. The identification of these burgh-towns with Josephus' biblically oriented understanding of the Hyksos has seduced us. Little effort has been made to understand their political function. We haven't asked why such structures were built, beyond the obvious issue of defence! Yet these fortifications raise further doubts about the existence of a centralized power in Palestine. I would think it very difficult for any alleged central government to raise an army or sufficient taxes in the hope of financing foreign adventures, when most significant towns under its administration boasted such impressive fortifications. How would the assumed central government force such towns to comply?

146 · *The Mythic Past*

The problems raised by the existence of such fortifications can be resolved if we look for a moment at Palestine's Late Bronze period. This was the period, after all, that gave most scholars an understanding of the region's city-states. During the Late Bronze period, small villages had been almost entirely abandoned and, apart from the coast, most of the population lived in towns. The towns, however, were for the most part unfortified. This absence of fortification worked because these towns were under the protection of an Egyptian imperial administration. It was the Egyptians who were most interested in preventing the building of fortifications during the Late Bronze Age, because these towns were in the hands of local chiefs and patrons, and could be used to support resistance to the interests of the Egyptian empire. Correspondence between these local patrons and Egypt shows that the towns were in constant competition with each other. At the same time, Egypt's imperial control was limited to areas around the towns. The countryside was unsafe, and could not support small, unprotected villages and hamlets. This picture of the Late Bronze Age under a highly centralized empire stands in stunning contrast to the picture of many of the same towns, heavily fortified during the 'Hyksos' period of the earlier Middle Bronze Age. A centralizing force would not, could not, and in fact in the Late Bronze Age *did not* tolerate major defence works around Palestine's towns. The existence of such so-called 'Hyksos fortifications' in the Middle Bronze Age is itself a major argument against supposing that there had been any centralized authority over these patently independent burghs in Palestine.

Moreover, while the lack of fortifications during the Late Bronze period reflects limited controls of Egypt's empire, and a kind of *pax aegyptia*, we should not be too hasty in drawing the conclusion that the presence of such fortifications implies the existence of external threats to Palestine's integrity. Nor should we think of the Middle Bronze Age as a period of ongoing conflict. The large number of small, unfortified villages witness against this. We have every reason to believe that the periods in which Palestine's towns were individually fortified – notably in the Early Bronze II, Middle Bronze II and the early Iron II periods – were all times of peace: periods in which prosperity reached new heights. These fortress towns should be understood as *small-region* defences. They are indicative of the defences of towns that are independent both of imperial forces outside Palestine and of any centralizing trans-regional state authorities within Palestine. They are assertions of local autonomous patrons. They are burghs.

We should not be distracted by the implicit denial of the historical pictures we have from the Bible's great Canaanite/Israelite and Israelite/Philistine conflicts which we used to think of as historical. Nor should we be distracted by stories about a centralized state like David's or Solomon's,

Ahab's or even Hezekiah's or Josiah's, which biblical archaeology has so long identified with the fortifications of the Iron II period. The coherence and correctness of such 'history' is no more secure than biblical archaeology's understanding of the Hyksos during the Bronze Age. Whether the fortress towns belong to the Middle Bronze Age or to Iron Age II, we need to ask about the function of fortifications.

There are many different types of walls, gates and building techniques in Palestine's fortifications. The methods of construction are quite different in each of three major periods in which peace and prosperity governed Palestine. The Early Bronze tells show a number of enormously wide stone boulder constructions. The Middle Bronze fortifications characteristically centred on large ramparts of dirt, often supported and strengthened by paved ramps, with mud brick inner and outer walls. In a few large sites, citadels were constructed. Functionally, the Iron Age casemate constructions are the most sophisticated, as they could be used alternatively for storage and for defence. All, however, reflect labour-saving techniques, and all require a minimum of engineering skills.

The boulder construction of the Early Bronze period engages massiveness as a principal strategy. The walls can hardly be knocked down, only breached through the slow process of dismantling. Such massive fortifications are also cheap to construct. They require neither skill nor a labour force beyond what a small town itself could supply. Their massiveness adds the psychological advantage of the appearance of invincibility, certainly giving pause to an inexperienced enemy, incapable of mounting a long siege, or untrained in military strategy. At the same time, the relatively weak defences allocated to these towns' water resources make such massive fortifications very vulnerable to a professional army. That they were, in fact, effective – and over a span of centuries – requires the conclusion that they were defences constructed with quite small and not terribly competent enemies in mind. Attacks, if they occurred, must have lasted for only very short periods. That is, the Early Bronze fortification walls were conceived as local defences against competitive patrons of neighbouring towns. They were not built to withstand attacks by the professional soldiers of an empire.

The great earth ramparts – the so-called 'Hyksos fortifications' – of the Middle Bronze II period are *functionally* similar to the Early Bronze burghs. They are structurally very different. They were superior in many ways. Their steeply pitched, paved ramps, separating the inner and outer walls of the fortification, could not be scaled except at the cost of casualties. They could not be easily dismantled, and the loose dirt-fills with which they were constructed prevented tunnelling. They were a near-perfect defence, effective against nearly all strategies except that of siege warfare, and against any army except a professional one. They were also much more labour-efficient than Early Bronze fortification walls, especially for towns situated in Palestine's valleys and plains.

The casemate construction of Iron II fortifications were also designed with labour efficiency in mind. They served two different functions. They provided towns with store rooms and living quarters in times of peace. These could be filled with rubble under threat of an attack, and quickly converted into an immensely frustrating fortification barrier. Water sources also received increased protection at this time, at the cost of considerable engineering skill and effort. These Iron Age water tunnels might well suggest efforts to deal with threats from professional and standing armies, which had the ability to mount sieges and undertake warfare over extended periods of time. That is to say, the Iron Age fortifications were also directed against armies from outside the region. In contrast to both the Early and Middle Bronze fortifications, Iron II defence technology implies differences in the societies and political structures that supported their construction. The engineering demands and the skills of stone-cutting and brick-making imply a greater organization and therefore a greater centralization, which might well have been beyond the abilities of every town's independence. Much more importantly, the double function of the casemate design implies the town's confidence in an early warning safeguard for its defence systems. Such defences require conversion time between a perceived threat and an actual attack on the town. This indicates that the defences were not built against a potential enemy immediately down the valley. They rather stood against the enemy from outside the region. Iron Age defences imply regional powers.

There also must have existed political coalitions and systems of mutual protection among such a fortified town and its neighbours within its own region. These burghs give us archaeological evidence for small regional, political structures, which were somewhat greater than the small locally independent patronage systems that had built the fortified towns in the Bronze Age to provide local protection to their clients. This conclusion is supported by the construction during Iron II of regionally defensive forts and chains of forts, which protected entire agricultural regions and controlled free movement through the steppe and border areas.

In all of these periods, the fortifications seem best suited to protect the agricultural population of small regions. One does not find these kind of structures associated with the subordinate towns of a great state or empire. These are characterized rather by garrison towns and fortresses con-structed for and by standing armies. Such began to appear in Palestine only under the Assyrian period's imperial control. The typical fortified town of Palestine protects itself and the people living within a discrete region. That is its most distinctive characteristic and function. Such burghs are marks of peace, political stability and prosperity. They do not indicate times of widespread violence. They give evidence of the autonomy of a region's villages and towns. Palestine, with its heartland of villages, divided as it is by and in its many regions, was defined in its most affluent periods by the independence and autonomy of small patrons. These burghs are products of local politics: of the influence and wealth of local families and their 'houses'. Such is the context in which they should be interpreted. They established the negotiating power of the local inhabitants and their patron. The political character of this form of society is reflected already in the 'Execration Texts'. Palestine, until the Assyrian period, was a land of stable, autonomous towns ruled by their 'princes' and chiefs.

If this revised view of the Middle Bronze II period has been helpful, we can ask our question again: Could any town or coalition of towns have engaged in the kind of political struggle, in the kind of financial and military build-up necessary to successfully field an army sufficient to threaten, conquer, occupy and govern an ancient Egypt, many times its size and population? The prospect is unlikely. The archaeological evidence for the military and political structures of Palestine's many towns and regions stands wholly against it. Throughout the history of the South Levant, until the raising of the Maccabaean rebellion against the Seleucid king Antiochus IV in the second century BCE, personal coalitions of small patronates and such limited regional states as Edom, Judah, Ammon, Moab, Israel, Tyre and Ashqelon seem to have been defensive coalitions. Inter-regional politics was neither centralized nor imperial in form, and wars seem to have been fought for very limited goals. Local armies, to the extent that they existed at all, were defensive. Standing professional forces, available to the ambitions of any given ruler, did not exist here. Explanations of the Hyksos myth as Theban propaganda concerning a permanent systemic and regionally defined conflict between Thebes and the Delta are immediately at hand. Such explanations accord well with the anti-Asiatic rhetoric of Kamose in his efforts to make his claims on the Delta's patronage sound legitimate.

The political system of patrons and clients fits the different regional economies typical of Palestine. This kind of politics and social organization stands in contrast to the great bureaucratic states of Egyptian and Assyrian imperial fame. It totally excludes a Palestine that could conquer Egypt. It also stands against historical ideas of a Solomonic empire. Historically, it is very difficult to speak of a Palestine during either the Bronze or Iron Ages. Palestine is a geographical idea that we have. It fits no historical reality. The stories of Solomon and David, and even the story of good king Josiah, must wait for a second-century John Hyrcanus before they can find an historical context that makes sense. Before the Hellenistic period, the political centres of southern Syria are many. Centralized governments are small, regionally bound, and economically competitive.

5 Armageddon and Egypt's adventures in Asia: c. 1468 and 1288 BCE

Critical to an understanding of the history of Palestine and to the relationship between the Bible and archaeology is the transition from the Late Bronze Age to the beginnings of the Iron Age. Because of the Bible's chronology, this period has been identified as particularly creative of Israelite identity. Yet when one investigates the history of Palestine independently of the biblical view of the past, this period betrays little evidence of biblical Israel's emergence.

The settlement of Palestine's fragile regions during the Middle Bronze Age had been possible because of the improved climate. Their stability was aided by new technologies related to irrigation and drainage, by improved tools – especially the development of harder bronzes – by the systematic use of fallowing, crop rotation and fertilization, and by the improvement and perfection of terracing and cistern development. In addition, new forms of olives and grapes thrived in the period's less arid climate. These, however, proved unable to withstand even short periods of drought.

Beginning around 1600 BCE, Palestine entered a prolonged period of recurrent dry spells. Highland agriculture, centred on olives and grapes, was devastated. For nearly a century and a half, the economic instability of these areas of Palestine led to the highlands being almost entirely abandoned. Only a few areas survived, such as the group of small villages in the valleys around Shechem, or those along the Ayyalon valley near Jerusalem. There is some indication that the countryside became unstable and dangerous in most regions. Small-village life disappeared as the population sought the protection of the larger and more stable towns.

As far as we know from excavations and archaeological surveys, the sedentary population now took different forms. There were those who carried on traditional farming in the larger towns. Others expanded pastoralism in a transhumant form of nomadism, living on the steppe through the winter and returning to the heartland to graze their flocks in the fields after the harvest. The number of displaced persons increased considerably at this period. Without protection or patron, they became outlaws and bandits. They lived off the trade caravans and border settlements, while taking refuge in the caves and woods of the hill country. The widespread instability of the countryside was centred on them. This was aggravated in regions that had been abandoned by settlements, as the towns were unable to police areas at any great distance from their homes. During the fourteenth and thirteenth centuries, the Palestinian highlands were plagued by such bands of bandits that ravaged and disrupted the trade routes. Occasionally these bandits hired themselves out to towns as mercenaries or labourers. Under circumstances of great duress, some sold themselves as slaves. These 'bandits' or 'outlaws' (which is the meaning of the term *apiru* used for them) were a recurrently disruptive force. This pejorative name with which they had been cursed survived them, showing up in biblical stories. The word 'Hebrew' is one of the names that are put in the mouths of foreigners, speaking of the early Israelites in the Exodus or Samson stories. It is also used of autonomous individuals like Abraham and David in Genesis and the books of Samuel.

The one stabilizing force in Palestine came from the Egyptians. They attempted to maintain the trade routes by bringing Palestine under the direct control of imperial troops. The Egyptian presence, from the middle of the fifteenth century, with its garrisons and imperial administration, allowed the largest of the towns to maintain prosperity in the face of a deteriorating international economy. In the first half of the fifteenth century the Egyptian pharaoh Thutmosis III set out to gain control of the overland trade routes. After an overnight march through the strategic Megiddo pass, controlling access to the Jezreel valley, he accepted the patronage of most of Palestine. According to Egyptian texts celebrating this conquest, his forces destroyed a coalition of Palestinian rulers on the edge of the swamps and marshlands near the ancient city of Megiddo. This victory introduced the Egyptian empire into Asia. Egyptian troops were maintained in the Jezreel valley and Palestine's southern coastal plain for the next four centuries. Their presence committed Egypt, at great cost to its treasury, to the support of Palestinian stability.

What began as a police action committed Egypt to a permanent interest in Palestine. Having destroyed all organized opposition to their control of the trade routes, the Egyptians also faced the much more formidable task of dealing with Palestine's deteriorating agricultural economy. After a futile half-century of attempting to pacify Palestine from a distance, dismantling fortifications around potentially recalcitrant towns, and resorting to expensive punitive expeditions every spring in order to collect taxes and reassert sovereignty, Egypt's problems with the insecurity of the trade routes and supply of resources remained unresolved.

Although it is uncertain whether its motivation was to discourage any ambitions the Hittites of Anatolia may have had, by the end of the fifteenth century Egypt had established a permanent military presence that effectively brought the bulk of the Palestinian lowlands under imperial patronage. It also encouraged other regions to recognize Egypt's dominance. Military garrisons were built at Gaza and at Beth Shan. This effective but expensive process was supplemented by a series of treaties with the various patrons of towns in the hills and lowland districts. Some of the more important of these were Byblos, Tyre, Acco, Hazor, Megiddo, Shechem, Jerusalem, Gezer, Lachish and Ashqelon. Patronage over Palestine's local rulers supported efforts to control the economic and political centres of the region. Their goal was to monopolize trade. Through them, and through them alone, goods and produce should enter the markets. The cooperation of local rulers with Egypt also pacified Palestine and maintained its prosperity during the fourteenth and thirteenth centuries.

The benefits to Egypt were sound enough. Both the 'Way of Horus' along the coast and the 'King's Highway' through the Transjordan linked Egypt with its interests in Syria and North Mesopotamia. These became vital pipelines to Egypt's economy. The sea routes to Acco, Tyre and Byblos were critical links in a chain of ports that included the cities of Ugarit, Alasiya, Troy and Mycenae. Such trade provided Egypt with needed timber and oil. While Egypt's natural resources included an abundance of grains, flax, cotton, beef, milk and cheese, it was dependent on foreign suppliers for other products and raw materials. Palestine was among its most important suppliers: timber from Phoenicia and the Galilee, but also from the central hills. Olive oil came to Egypt from the orchards of the Palestinian highlands. This oil was not only a staple and necessary food in the normally low-protein diet of the ancient world, but a fuel for lighting as well. Wine, a most precious luxury item, was a complement to the beer-drinking regions of Egypt, and the usual libation to Egypt's many gods. Wools, cheese and meat were supplied by steppeland herders. Phoenician craftsmen were employed to satisfy a growing taste in Egypt for luxury goods and for elaborate construction projects. Labour gangs were formed of workers from the impoverished steppelands and settled near the copper and turquoise mines of the southern Negev and the Sinai. Finally, prisoners of war, recruits and mercenaries answered the demands of Egypt's expanding imperial army.

Some of the long-term effects of Egypt's dominance were harmful to Palestine and to Palestine's future. Imperial control prevented local powers from controlling any of the region's resources and population. This created a political immaturity that was disastrous when the Egyptians finally began to withdraw at the height of the economic chaos brought on by the Mycenaean drought at the end of the thirteenth century BCE. Similarly, Egyptian hunger for timber and the overexpansion of the olive industry brought irreversible deforestation and erosion of soils in some of Palestine's most fragile regions.

Some of Egypt's interests in Palestine, related to the copper and turquoise deposits of the Sinai and Negev deserts, had begun already in the Chalcolithic and Early Bronze periods. It was then that copper had first made its impact on the ancient world as a material for tools and as a precious metal. While mining was organized both from Palestine and from Egypt, the labour force for the mines and smelting sites was drawn from the sedentary and nomadic pastoralists near the mines. This work supplemented their income from their flocks, while supporting and stabilizing their economies. They also profited from the Egyptian trade routes across the central Negev and along the North Sinai coast. During the Egyptian empire, these nomads and pastoralists were a significant and distinct element of Palestine's population. They played a major role in the eventual settlement and occupation of the highlands of Judah in the tenth and ninth centuries, and influenced the region both religiously and culturally.

Palestine's fate during the second half of the second millennium did not depend on regional events and affairs. It hung in the balance of geopolitical forces, on which the people of Palestine had little influence. Of central importance was the Hittite–Egyptian axis, which was both competitive and cooperative. While the Egyptians held Palestine, the Hittite empire, with its capital at Hattusas (modern Boghasköy in Turkey), controlled most of Anatolia and the northern rim of Syria. These two great powers shared a condominium in Phoenicia and coastal Syria. Their understanding and cooperation fostered an expansive and lucrative sea trade. In turn, the technological demands of shipbuilding and sailing formed a sound foundation for the development of large skilled labour forces.

When international trade struck hard times, and particularly the late fourteenth century saw very hard times, the two empires fell into competitive conflict. Each tried to keep its share intact in the depressed economy of international trade. The first quarter of the thirteenth century found the Hittites at war with Egypt. The economic and political stresses that had accumulated over centuries of recurrent recession in agriculture, caused by an extraordinarily hot and dry climate, affected all areas of the eastern Mediterranean basin. Anatolia had been severely affected and, long since centralized under the rulers of the Hittite empire, began to expand its borders and threaten the independence of rulers in Syria and North Mesopotamia. Already at the end of the fourteenth century, the control of Hittite expansion was a focus of Egypt's Asiatic policy. War came to a climax in a pitched battle at the Syrian city of Kadesh in 1288. Great losses were suffered on both sides. While the Egyptians were driven out of Kadesh, aggressive expansion by Hittite forces in Syria virtually ended. The significance of the slaughter at Kadesh, however, lies beyond the battle itself.

After this defeat, Ramses II's army was racked with revolts. It had borne the brunt of the cost of his expensive misadventure. Egypt lost its enthusiasm for an Asiatic empire. Support of the high-maintenance trade routes in the far north deteriorated. Civil unrest and religious opposition at home was doubly encouraged when closure of the timber trade disrupted both construction and funeral industries in Egypt. An increased military commitment to the stability of the central coastal plains and lowland valleys of Palestine brought ever-diminishing returns. A series of plots and intrigues by court factions bitter over the military failure at Kadesh effectively paralysed royal authority and its control of important groups within the army. Egypt was also unable to respond quickly and decisively to the influx of refugees from the Aegean and Anatolia. Their successful settlement in Egyptian territory undermined imperial authority dangerously.

The Hittite losses at Kadesh sorely stressed their military establishment at home. The gradual political disintegration of the Hittite central administration began. Although the Hittite forces gained control of Kadesh, they hardly won the war. They were all the less able to respond to the growing economic crisis caused by the deepening Mycenaean drought at the end of the thirteenth century. This eventually pushed the empire to collapse.

The growing weakness of the Hittite central administration had made it unable to respond to the early stages of the agricultural depression caused by the Mycenaean drought. A serious failure to ration food stores forced them to go begging to Egypt to survive. Finally, the empire disintegrated at the height of an influx of refugees from Mycenae. The financial depression was crippling. Deepened by the agricultural disruption that followed, the cities were unable to support the influx of refugees from the Aegean. They also lacked military strength to successfully repel them. With the closing of its ports, Ugarit, the greatest and most important coastal city of the eastern Mediterranean, no longer had the resources to rebuild when an earthquake split it in two. The devastating fire that followed finished the city. In an extraordinary episode that still needs explanation, Ugarit disappeared from the map, never to be seen again. The cumulative effect of a long succession of disasters that had begun at Kadesh brought Phoenicia and coastal Syria to the edge of total collapse.

A downturn in the volume of trade, created by the withdrawal of Egyptian- and Hittite-owned commercial interests, affected seaports such as Byblos, Tyre and Acco. This sped the collapse of sea trade throughout the eastern Mediterranean, and produced a domino effect on overland trade in Palestine, which now became entirely dependent on its Egyptian markets. The long process of the withdrawal of Egyptian interests, along with the spread of refugees in the wake of the Mycenaean drought, undercut the economy.

The collapse of overland trade from the north, undermined the trade-dependent agriculture of Palestine and created a major recession. The weakening of the Egyptian presence and the near-total withdrawal of their interest in the highlands exacerbated the inability of towns such as Jerusalem and Lachish to police the highland forests and wilderness. The social fabric of Palestine was already severely torn when the drought that had devastated Mycenae and the Aegean spread eastwards to Anatolia, Syria and Palestine. The highly productive but more drought-sensitive strains of olive trees, which had proved so profitable in the Middle Bronze Age, were wiped out when the drought intensified around 1200 BCE.

CHAPTER 7

Palestine's many peoples

1 The great Mycenaean drought: c. 1300–1050 BCE

Towards the end of the thirteenth century BCE, the long period of aridity that had marked the climate of the Late Bronze Age turned more severe. The great Mycenaean drought, named after the period of aridity that was involved in the collapse of ancient Mycenae, disrupted civilization throughout the northern and eastern part of the Mediterranean basin. It was followed by a collapse of international trade, and the haphazard destruction of many of this huge region's cities and towns. Drought alone hardly created the whole of this chain of disaster. However, it played a significant role. The empires of Hatti and Mycenae and the North Syrian state of Amurru collapsed. The drought was to last nearly two centuries. The only major Mediterranean power to survive intact was Egypt, where the flood agriculture of the Nile was not as vulnerable to drought as the rainfall-dependent Mediterranean economies of Greece, Anatolia and Syria-Palestine.

Beginning around 1250 BCE, the Mediterranean suffered a severe drop in sea levels. Average temperatures rose and rainfall decreased sharply. The height of the drought was reached around 1200 BCE, and it lasted until around 1050 BCE. The drought varied significantly from region to region. Its effects were most severe in the Aegean and along the Anatolian coast. With the collapse of Mycenae, large numbers of people became refugees.

The onset of famine and widespread starvation uprooted whole communities and forced people to leave their homes and farms. Many moved southward to Egypt, both by land and by sea. Other refugees were drawn to the Phoenician coastal plain and to Palestine. They settled their families where they could. Over the course of several generations, they integrated with the local populations all along the Mediterranean shore. With their transition, a new and distinctive culture arose that was marked by both Aegean and Levantine characteristics.

Although there is much evidence that the integration of these refugees had been gradual and peaceful, some undoubtedly took lands by force, and yet others were received with hostility. Many were repelled by the military, wherever it still had the power. The refugees added pressure to the local regional economies, already severely stressed by the drought. Once international trade began to break down, the social and political fabric that supported trade-oriented agriculture in scores of interdependent sub-regions also began to disintegrate. Towns were abandoned. Fighting broke out in some places, and a number of normally productive and populated small valleys reverted to wilderness. This tendency was most marked in the marginal areas of Palestine's highlands and throughout the south. Not a single major region of Greater Palestine was unaffected by the drought.

Palestine's economy had been severely weakened by the deep depression of sea trade that came as the result of the Egyptian withdrawal from Syria after the battle of Kadesh. Mycenae had also been active in seagoing trade in the eastern Mediterranean. Its collapse brought further depressive economic stress to all of the port cities on the Mediterranean coast. When the Hittite empire in Anatolia began to disintegrate, overland trade with Egypt was immediately affected. Palestine lost its markets to the north, and the safety of surviving caravan routes, previously protected by Egyptian–Hittite treaties, was no longer assured.

Farming in Palestine entered a period of crisis. Towns were abandoned in the late thirteenth and early twelfth centuries. Some were destroyed by earthquake and fire, others by military force and rebellion. All faced the threat of economic and political collapse. Some, like Hazor, were partially destroyed, but then resettled in impoverished conditions. Others, like the town of Taanach in the Jezreel valley, were abandoned completely. Still others, like neighbouring Megiddo, were able to maintain their occupation throughout this period of change and transition. The agricultural heartland of Palestine faced significant disintegration. The lowlands suffered a severe drop in total population, though many farmers were able to hang on by opening new lands in less productive areas. The population in these lowland valleys was scattered in smaller, more viable units, spread over increasingly larger areas. Many of the displaced lowlanders were encouraged by Egypt's continuing need for timber and olive oil, to move out of the lowlands and into the lower Galilee and the central highlands south of the Jezreel to cut timber and, after clearing new land, to create new terraces and orchards.

Egypt's response to the onset of the drought, the breakdown in international trade and the potentially chaotic impact of the refugee problem was complicated. The Egyptians were active in encouraging new areas of settlement and in maintaining order. Egypt attempted to shore up collapsing regions through direct grants of foreign aid from its granaries. In this way, wheat was sent from the Syrian city of Ugarit to support those hard hit by famine in the Hittite empire. Egypt also took pressure off some of the more severely affected regions by allowing immigration into the Delta and the Nile valley. Such refugees arrived both by sea and overland from the Aegean, Anatolia and the severely impoverished steppe and desert regions of Sinai and southern Palestine. The archaeological remains from Palestine, especially those from excavations at sites such as Dor, Tell Zeror, Ashdod, Ashqelon and Tell Qasile, show that many of the newcomers (called in Egyptian texts *Tjekker, Peleset* and *Denyen*) were quickly integrated with the indigenous populations of the coast. Others moved from Palestine and Cyprus southwestward into Egypt's Delta, where, in the reign of Ramses III (1182–1151), they met resistance. Egyptian records mention intensive fighting, including sea battles. In these inscriptions, the Egyptians claim a complete victory and the total destruction of the invaders. Yet obviously the success of the Egyptian army was hardly total. These same texts make it clear that the refugees did settle in the towns of the Delta with their families and their cattle. Still others were hired into the Egyptian army. Egypt's 'victory' was merely monumental.

In general, there is no doubt that the encounters with the refugees were hostile. After all, the local populations were hardly looking for more mouths to feed in a period of deepening drought. Many regions closed their borders and resorted to force to repel refugees who fought to stay. Many were killed and many starved. Crops were stolen and towns burnt. Nevertheless, by the second half of the twelfth century BCE, the archaeological evidence all along Palestine's coastal plain clearly shows that the immigrants from the Aegean had become thoroughly integrated into the populations where they had settled. They had adopted the Semitic languages and the Semitic gods of their hosts (especially Dagon and Ba'al Zebub), and they had deeply affected the culture of the region. Lowland Palestine, and especially the southern coast, adopted much from the immigrants. This is most obvious in the use of clay anthropoid sarcophagi (especially at Beth Shan) and zoomorphic clay vessels used in religious cult (especially at Tell Qasile). Such culture adoptions can also be seen in the wide dispersion of the decorative pottery known as 'Philistine Ware'. All of these objects reflect the assimilation of originally Aegean traditions of craftsmanship and pottery into the Palestinian economy. The new culture was a fully assimilated Palestinian one. How much these immigrants brought permanent changes to the folklore and crafts of other regions of Palestine can only be speculated on.

In support of Egypt's long-range goal to maintain overland trade with Palestine – which, with the collapse of trade with Lebanon, had become its primary source for timber and olive oil – the pharaohs of the nineteenth and twentieth dynasties committed more troops to Palestine. They were primarily interested in controlling the lowland highways. The coastal road from Gaza to Jaffa, and the great valleys of the Jezreel, Beth Shan and the northern Jordan rift, were all supported by the Egyptian presence. While Egyptian influence in the highlands and in the regions in the far north virtually ended, the imperial presence in the lowlands increased and the economy was stabilized. Egyptian commercial towns were built in the southern coastal plain. There they played a role in integrating the refugees from the Aegean with the indigenous population. Many towns in Palestine survived. However, the costs of the Egyptian investment were high, and returns very limited. By the eleventh century, the towns that the Egyptian presence had kept in existence through these worst of times slowly took the road to recovery, as the drought ended. The population began the slow process of rebuilding the economy and reviving their society.

2 Developing highland settlements

Before the drought, the bulk of Palestine's population lived in major towns in central valleys and on the coastal plain. Small-village life and most of highland agriculture had long since virtually disappeared. By the time the drought ended around 1050 BCE, however, the distribution of the population had altered considerably. Already in the thirteenth century, in an early response to the worsening climate, farmers began to move out of the larger towns. They cultivated more remote and isolated parts of the lowlands. This development was marked in the central coastal plain. From around 1200 BCE, villages multiplied throughout the Acco plain, the Jezreel, the Beth Shan and the northern Jordan valleys. As the numbers of refugees in the lowlands swelled, they began moving into the highlands, and especially into the central highlands north of Jerusalem.

When Egypt's trade with the Hittites, North Syria and Lebanon had first broken down, they lost most of their suppliers of timber and oil: two essential products that Egypt, with its flood agriculture and desert climate, could not produce itself. It had been largely to ensure such products that Egyptian armies first expanded the empire into Asia. The Mycenaean drought now forced the Egyptians into restructuring their interests. During the first half of the twelfth century BCE, after Ugarit and Hatti had fallen and Mediterranean shipping had ceased, Egypt intensified its presence in Palestine. It looked to this region to supply its markets. Egyptian garrisons were strengthened in the Jezreel alley, at Beth Shan and on the southern coastal plain. Egypt introduced Egyptian trading colonies for the first time and built garrisons for troops to protect them.

This increased imperial presence was a necessary element in stabilizing the economy of the lowlands. It provided a trade outlet to its agriculture, and encouraged resettlement in some of the abandoned areas of the lowlands. It moved refugees and homeless into the lower Galilee and into the highlands to cut timber and build villages. This relieved the towns of much of the pressure of displaced persons in the process of reconstructing their shattered lives. Through most of the drought, the political stability that Egypt's presence provided enabled the town culture of lowland Palestine to survive. This helped Palestine avoid much of the devastation that the Aegean and coastal Anatolia had suffered.

With the backing of the interests of Egyptian trade, willing to pay inflated prices for both timber and oil, entrepreneurs moved to open ever larger areas of the highlands to settlement by refugees and other displaced persons. Timber-cutting and terrace-building, expansion of herds and investments of heavy labour in vineyards and orchards led to permanent settlement. The Egyptians had long encouraged the expansion of Palestine's small timber industry. Although prime timber and easy accessibility to the coast encouraged rapid deforestation of the western slopes of the central hills, permanent settlement proceeded much more slowly than elsewhere in the highlands. In the course of the twelfth century, small settlements began the long and expensive investment of terracing the northern and western faces of the slopes, creating olive orchards and vineyards.

By the end of the drought, more than 200 small villages and hamlets dotted the highlands north of Jerusalem. They were supported by improved techniques in water and grain storage. Imperial interests led to the control of highland bandits and made the wilderness safe for new settlement. By the second half of the eleventh century, settlers numbered many thousands. The economy they developed was geographically mixed. Some areas supported grazing and grain production, others were suitable for farming only with the building of terraces. Grapes and olives, fruit and nut trees were planted. The basic core of the highland population centred itself on the central plateau and in intermontane valleys. These settlements provided stability, markets and a wide variety of field crops for the more specialized horticulture of the western slopes and the grazing of the eastern steppe.

This was far from a subsistence economy. The settlers were hardly independent. The different regions for herding and terracing all required cooperation. Opening the land to production involved not only land clearance, but also, in the case of terracing, a decade-long process of land development. The cash crops involved in herding and olive oil production – and these were the most important crops of these highland regions – require a substantial market economy for their survival. Herding economies do not exist on their own. Nor do olive oil industries. They are tied to barter, trade and interdependence. This was an economy ripe for expansion once the broadening recovery reopened trade routes.

The population of the central hills expanded during the course of Iron I. Along the steppelands and the desert fringe and in the central range, where herding was a dominant factor, the population doubled in size. Along the western slopes and in the foothills, where terracing and olives governed the economy, and where the total population had been considerably smaller, the population grew by a factor from 2.5 to 5. Both olive and fruit production required settlers to solve the ecological problems related to limited water resources. There were also problems of land clearance and terrace building. Once a core of settlement was established in each subregion (sometime around the end of Iron I), only ecological capacity seems to have limited the expansion of settlement growth. We find relatively little growth and increase along the desert fringe and in the marginal south-central regions. Large increases occurred in the populations of the agriculturally more viable north-central range and along the northern slopes. The settlement of the southwestern slopes and the foothills also show a dramatic increase, possibly reflecting the growing importance of oil and wine as cash crops, following the revival of international trade during the Iron II period.

Early settlement of the central hills focused on fertile interior valleys, where a mixed agriculture could be supported. Many of the later settlements expand the regional occupation beyond these valleys into areas where grains and herding are likely to form a proportionately greater part of the economy. A similar pattern of expansion emerges in the settlements of the northern slopes region. The foothills developed a higher proportion of grazing than any region outside the desert fringe zone. When the economy of the central hills as a whole is considered, both grain-producing and livestock-producing areas expand proportionately to the rise in population. Horticulture, on the other hand, shows a disproportionate increase. This is particularly strong in the later Iron II period. Greater stability and labour investment in terrace-based agriculture was obviously spurred by the revival of trade. These areas of orchards in the central hills are incapable of supporting mixed farming. They are oriented to cash crops, such as nuts and fruits, wine and oil. Because of this, their development requires regional trade. Their relatively rapid expansion during the Iron II period therefore suggests expansion into extra-regional trade. Efforts to gain access to markets would, in turn, encourage centralization.

The highlanders seem clearly to have come from people displaced from the lowlands. It is unlikely that large numbers of nomadic pastoralists would have entered this region. Prior to land clearance, natural grazing areas are quite limited here. These are found primarily on the eastern slopes. Some of the western slopes could have supported pastoralism in small intermontane valleys only after forest lands had been cleared. Pastoralists could have existed only in relatively small numbers. Once the sedentary agricultural population from the lowlands had stabilized the region, pastoralists would have been threatened by displacement and given limited tolerance in an agriculturally dominant economy. Political pressure on nomadic pastoral groups to sedentarize might be expected. References to such independent pastoral groups in various Egyptian texts at the end of the Late Bronze period give reason to accept that. The initial pressure of the drought would have encouraged shepherds to move away from the steppe and into the better-watered highlands. The return to a better climate around 1050 BCE, would likewise have supported a shift to agriculture.

During the drought, after the emergency stores of Palestine's lowland towns were depleted, people moved into the small agriculturally viable niches of the highlands. The most important area that attracted new settlement was the central region of Ephraim. Some settled in small hamlets in the grazing regions of the area. These have been found all along the eastern rim of the highlands, where sheep- and goat-herding could prosper. Even in drought periods, highland rains were sufficient to maintain some forms of dry agriculture.

The ecology of the central hills had previously provided barriers to widespread settlement that placed a cap on the capacity of the population to grow throughout most of the second millennium BCE. Over the four hundred years before the Mycenaean drought struck, most of the highlands had become covered with untamed forests. Small areas of settlement existed only in the larger valleys, which were blessed by abundant spring water. In most of the highlands, however, springs were scarce. The limestone subsoil was so fissured that water storage was difficult. Lacking the ability to store water, there had been little incentive to exploit the region, even where agricultural soils were rich and deep. The western slopes of the hills were so rugged and steep as to discourage ordinary agriculture. When new lands were finally opened to farming, the need for supplemental water, necessary for maintaining settlements through the normal summer dry seasons, was solved in a variety of ways that were new to Palestinian technology. The most important of these were the use of slaked-lime plaster for lining cisterns cut in the soft but permeable limestone, and the construction of large clay jar containers for both water and grain storage.

3 Judea's independent history: c. 1000–700 BCE

Other parts of the Palestinian highlands had a very different history. Both during the drought and in the period of recovery, the experiences and lifestyles of the populations of these other regions were as various as were the regions themselves. There is a wide diversity in both topography and ecology in Palestine's hill country: the Upper Galilee, the lower Galilee, the Carmel range, the hills of Samaria, the Jerusalem Saddle, the Shephelah, the Judean highlands and the Transjordan plateau. These many geographical differences find echoes in each region's strikingly different economy and history. Although scholars have tended to see the history of the Galilee, for example, as an extension of what developed in the central hills, in fact it had a very separate and unrelated history.

The Upper Galilee received more rainfall than any other region of Palestine. It is a rugged region, heavily wooded and difficult to settle. Its western escarpment had always been associated with Phoenician coastal towns, providing timber, hunting and some summer grazing. Like the central hills further south, this region had received an influx of refugees during the Mycenaean drought. They settled in small farming villages and hamlets, some of which developed olive and fruit orchards. The history of these settlements continued to be tied to Phoenicia. The eastern part of the Upper Galilee, on the other hand, was oriented to towns such as Hazor and Dan near the Sea of Galilee and the Hula basin. It developed areas for grazing and grain agriculture as well as olives and fruits. In the western Galilee, one notices an increase in the number of settlements beginning as soon as farming in the coastal plain had begun to disintegrate. Nevertheless, in these higher and more rugged hills, agriculture was much more difficult than it had been in the south. Villages were fewer and more widely scattered. Economic and cultural ties were not with the Palestinian lowlands, but with the coastal settlements.

As different as the Galilee was from the central hills, the contrast that needs to be drawn with the highlands of Judah in the south is yet greater. In Palestine we find both a Mediterranean climate, supporting a variety of types of dry agriculture, as well as a steppe climate, which supports, at best, drought-resistant grains and grazing. The border of aridity in Palestine, which marks the transition between these two zones, normally falls along the southern rim of the Judean highlands. During the Mycenaean drought, this border of aridity moved northwards and lay just south of Jerusalem. As a result, the Judean highlands were dominated throughout the drought by pastoral nomads. There was no sedentary population to speak of apart from a dozen or so scattered hamlets.

In the Bronze Age, Jerusalem had never been very closely tied to the Judean highlands. It had been a town of the Jerusalem saddle, which dominated the head of the Ayyalon valley. This valley descended from the highlands westward to the coastal plain. Although Jerusalem is not known to have existed in the earliest part of this period, the population of the region as a whole survives the onset of the drought, and continues through this period in severely stressed and diminished circumstances. Agricultural recovery followed a pattern similar to other regions in Palestine.

The Judean highlands lie south of Jerusalem. At the end of the Bronze Age, they were largely empty of settlement. These hills were occupied by pastoralists and dominated by the Shephelah town of Lachish to the southwest. With the support of the Egyptian trade network, Lachish dominated olive production in the southern Shephelah and functioned as a central market for the meat, cheese, butter and wool of the highland shepherds, linking them directly with the overland trade routes of the coastal plain.

When the drought ended and international trade came once again into its own, Palestine's olive industry boomed. Lachish, as the dominant city of the south, expanded its production into the Judean highlands, which once again fell within a Mediterranean climatic zone. New and expanding trade supported agricultural settlements and terrace-building where, earlier, only grazing had been possible. The nomads, whose grazing lands were converted to orchards, were the only barrier to the expansion. Lachish, now certainly with the support of Hebron and possibly Jerusalem, set up a system of watchtowers and small forts throughout the highlands. Similar police posts were established in the grazing lands of the Beersheva basin to the south. Their function was to control access to the highlands and the movement of nomads in and out of the area. These forts were also used to force the nomads into sedentarization. By the end of the ninth century, most of the Judean highlands had been cleared and terraced. The region had become one of the most important olive-growing regions in Palestine, and boasted a mixed population of terrace farmers and village pastoralists.

The general geographical disposition of the Judean highlands, with its eastern border in the Judaean desert and its southern in the expansive steppelands of the Beersheva basin and the southern coast, placed the settlements of the region in a natural relationship with the pastoralists on the steppeland of Palestine's southern rim. The fact that agriculture typically involved a commitment to herding as a way of reducing the impact of drought opens this territory to settlement whenever the climate encourages agriculture, as it did during the Iron II period.

Judea's openness and vulnerability to the larger steppelands that border it on three sides, the marginal nature of its agriculture, its ecological fragility, high risk of deforestation, and the dominance of sheep- and goat-herding, all suggest that the largest portion of its new population in the Iron II period had come from the shepherds of the steppe. It is also during this period, and especially in the ninth century, that the primary agricultural regions of Palestine had developed centralized, regional forms of government. Small states like Phoenicia, Philistia, Israel, Aram, Ammon, Moab and Edom were created. The development of Arab-controlled overland trade made a major impact on the economies of these emerging states. Judea attempted to control the freedom of its pastoralists to police this important new adjunct to the economy. The forts, which have been found in the steppe of both the Northern Negev, the Judean desert and in the Transjordan, give clear evidence. Judea's pastoralism of the Late Bronze and Iron I periods shifted to a Mediterranean form of sedentary agriculture, centred in the olive industry during Iron II. This shift was due to a forced sedentarization policy that could only have been carried out with the help of the political power of the region's towns.

The greatest expansion of settlement occurred in Judaea from about 900 to 700 BCE. An extension of Jerusalem's political influence to the south is not clearly supported either by excavations in Jerusalem or by the archaeological surveys of the Judean hills. Jerusalem's dominance over Judea is unlikely to have developed at any period earlier than the seventh century, and perhaps not before the middle of that century, when the population of Jerusalem explodes. Only after Lachish had been destroyed by the Assyrians in 701 does Jerusalem develop the political or economic structures and capacity of a city. Only then is the agriculture of the Shephelah oriented around new smaller towns, lying close to the Judean watershed and within easy access of a populous Jerusalem. The political development of Jerusalem lagged behind the consolidation of the central highlands further north. This conclusion cannot be avoided. Jerusalem is not known to have been occupied during the tenth century. The basis of power in Jerusalem, before the seventh century, was related to the city itself and to the Ayyalon valley, not to Judea. Jerusalem did not take on the role of capital for the regional state of Judah with control of the highlands, until after Lachish had been destroyed.

4 The states of Israel and Judah: c. 1000–600 BCE

The earliest part of this period in the hill country has been traditionally presented as the 'Golden Age' of an ancient Israel with its capital in Jerusalem. The era has been associated with a 'United Monarchy' wielding the political power of a Saul, a David and a Solomon and controlling a huge land-bridge from the Nile to the Euphrates, as well as with the concept of a temple built by Solomon as the centre of the worship of Yahweh. These images have no place in descriptions of the real historical past. We know them only as story, and what we know about such stories does not encourage us to treat them as if they were or were ever meant to be historical. There is no evidence of a United Monarchy, no evidence of a capital in Jerusalem or of any coherent, unified political force that dominated western Palestine, let alone an empire of the size the legends describe. We do not have evidence for the existence of kings named Saul, David or Solomon; nor do we have evidence for any temple at Jerusalem in this early period. What we do know of Israel and Judah of the tenth century does not allow us to interpret this lack of evidence as a *gap* in our knowledge and information about the past, a result merely of the accidental nature of archaeology. There is neither room nor context, no artifact or archive that points to such historical realities in Palestine's tenth century.

One cannot speak historically of a state without a population. Nor can one speak of a capital without a town. Stories are not enough.

An historical state of Israel came into existence and was sustained by the development of an olive industry built with a newly developed and expanded system of terracing in the course of the ninth century BCE. This small state was comparable to other states of Palestine such as Ammon, Moab and Edom. It was organized around the settlements in the hill country between Jerusalem and the Jezreel valley, from the watershed to the western slopes. The immediate origins of this population rested in the settlement of the displaced part of the population that had abandoned the lowlands in the wake of the Mycenaean drought discussed above.

When greater Palestine recovered from this drought, the lowlands led the revival and re-emergence of the larger economy with the help of the revival of international trade. As international trade increased in the course of the tenth century, Palestine's lowland towns entered a new cycle of expansion and prosperity in which the towns whose political and commercial structures had benefited most from Egypt's presence were destined to lead the way: Beth Shan and Megiddo in the Jezreel; Dor, Ashdod, Ashqelon and Gaza in the coastal plain; Gezer and Lachish in the Shephelah. With the revival of shipping by the Phoenician towns of the north, Palestine began to flourish as never before.

When we try to understand the development of the small state in Palestine's central hills that had come to be known as Israel, it is necessary to pay attention to the unique interdependence of the economies of the three regions that made up the bulk of the territory of these hills. This was not a subsistence economy of independent frontier farmers. It rather involved a complicated system of interrelated villages and hamlets. They were entirely dependent on trade and barter with each other for survival, and, at least in the western olive regions, for their establishment. Neither pastoralism nor horticulture are economies that can survive in isolation; that is, as subsistence farming. Neither can provide an adequate diet through its own produce alone, and both require several years of development without profit before they are able to yield a sustainable harvest. Rather than subsistence economies, both are based on what we might call 'cash crops'. These are crops that are grown primarily for markets. They require the existence of a complex society to work. Two of the social requirements that dominate this form of agriculture are the mutual cooperation of villages and the subordination of the economy to markets. As the population of the highlands grew, they required an intensification of their dependence on *external* markets. They could not exist, let alone prosper, apart from the greater world with which trade linked them.

The population of the central hill country responded to a growing market. Frontier farmers turned a wilderness, which had been the central hills, into the richest olive-producing area of Palestine. Clearing timber, they systematically introduced terracing on a large scale. From these terraces, the olive became Palestine's principal export. With the opening of international trade in the tenth and ninth centuries, marketing required both administration and centralization. Within a short time, other forms of statehood followed, including a dynastic kingship, comparable to those that had earlier existed in Shechem and the towns of the lowlands. There is little that we can say specifically about the earliest development of this 'state of Israel', which in the course of the ninth century centred on Samaria as its capital. Although the heart of this new highland state had been based on the economic cooperation of its farmers, the state, once established, took on a life of its own.

While the central hills north of Jerusalem have a settlement that reaches back more than three centuries before the region was organized under a state form, Jerusalem's history during this period remains impossible to write. Although the Egyptian Amarna letters, which give us correspondence between Palestine's petty princes and kings and the Egyptian pharaoh of the late fourteenth and early thirteenth centuries, tell us much about the town of *Urusalim* and about its patron and king, Abdi-Hepa, we know nothing about this town from archaeology. We are not even certain where it was located, though we have every reason to believe that it was Jerusalem. The Iron Age town of Jerusalem on Mount Ophel, which had been excavated by Kathleen Kenyon before the 1967 Israeli–Arab war, offered no significant remains from the Late Bronze Age: hardly potsherds. Moreover, there were no Iron Age structures earlier than the tenth century. From that period we find a massive retaining wall, but precious little else. To write history on the basis of ignorance, without evidence, is not permissible. We have no choice but to begin Jerusalem's history with the Iron II period. This is a history of a small provincial market town at the head of the Ayyalon valley. There is no reason to change this description until after the fall of Lachish in 701 BCE. From that time, Jerusalem's power and influence extends southward over the Judean highlands. By the mid-seventh century, the town greatly expanded and developed a population of perhaps as many as 25,000. At first, then, it has the character of a small city, capable of being the highland capital of the Assyrian client-state called Judah.

The hills of Judah, which extend southward from Bethlehem to Hebron, had been nearly empty of settlements during the earliest period of the Iron Age. In the southern steppe, land clearance and new settlement does not begin to expand until the tenth century. As international trade grew, demand for both timber and olive oil encouraged the building of terraces in the Judean highlands. The farmers of the Shephelah built vineyards and orchards there. Hardly before the middle of the ninth century does it become likely that the towns around the Judean highlands began to encourage, and then force, the sedentarization of the region's nomads. The economic incentives to develop olive and almond orchards on their grazing lands extended the use of terracing throughout the southern hills. Lachish is the town most likely to have established a system of fortified police posts in the highlands and the Northern Negev. These were presumably built as part of the effort to force the nomads to settle in villages. By the end of the ninth century, the Judean highlands had become a major producer of olives with its main markets in Hebron, Lachish and Jerusalem. As an olive-growing region, and at the same time a region on the edge of the steppe, the area developed a mixed population of terrace farmers and village pastoralists.

Assyria, a great imperial power at this time, developed a growing interest in the west, and especially in Syria and Palestine's trade with Egypt. By the early ninth century, the already cooperative producers of olives in the central hills began to establish greater control over their own markets through what might be best described as a cartel. The purpose was to control the production and harvest of olives, maintain price levels through developing of a single market that they could influence, and protect the interests of the producers. These interests, shared by most of the central highland's farmers, led to the establishment of a central administration, eventually housed by Samaria. Other forms of statehood, including a dynastic kingship comparable to those in Phoenicia, followed. The kingship developed from traditional forms of patronage and centred on the great families of the area. Judging from our earliest records that refer to this small state, one of the first families to control the highlands bore the name 'House of Omri'. The Bible has an origin story for this name. It tells a tale of Samaria's legendary founder, one Omri, purchasing a hill on which Israel's capital Samaria was then built. The true history of the shift of power and influence in the highlands between the long dominant region around Shechem to the new town of neighbouring Samaria remains unknown.

The early state of Israel had its origins in the olive industry's expanding demand for trade. Centralizing the hill country was a rational response. The international trade route crossed through the Jezreel valley just north of the highlands. This route also provided a field of competition on which the Assyrian and Egyptian economic interests could struggle for domi-nance. Solidarity at home among the producers of goods allowed many of the small regions to play their roles in this larger contest. However, while the heart of the new highland state had been originally centred on the economic cooperation of its farmers, the dependence of such economic cartels on Assyrian–Egyptian trade shaped their destiny as vassal states of empire and forced them into the hazard of ever supporting the strongest. While coalitions and some competition were possible among these secondary states, and shifts of allegiance from one great overlord to another occurred often enough, political or military roles of independence were not among the choices available. These were not sovereign states, nor anything similar to the great regional states of Europe, but houses of patronage with local clients. They were built as pyramids of largely autonomous personal commitments and contracts for protection and support.

5 The anatomy of the gods

Just as the population and economy of the historical states of Israel and Judah originated as developments of the indigenous population of Palestine, which distinguished itself in its separate regions by its commitment to a Mediterranean economy, so the beliefs and religious practices of the states of Israel and Judah reflected religious traditions common to Palestine and the South Levant.

The highlands of Judah and Israel during the Iron Age shared in the religious character of the other regions of southern Syria. Regionally recognized gods, both great and small, characterized religious observance and piety. The power of the state in religion was neither great nor dominant. States were very small affairs, and had little power to affect forms of worship outside the towns that functioned as capitals. Regional characteristics of religion developed over time, and, like language dialects, became fixed as a result of stability rather than political dominance. Changing political realities of empire and trade, however, influenced religious forms strongly. It is hardly surprising that many regions – Palestine's southern coast in particular – reflected the influence of Egyptian religious traditions, especially cults of the goddess Hathor. The cult of Seth took on a hybrid Semitic–Egyptian style, and lunar and solar elements entered the cult with trade from both Egypt and Mesopotamia. Phoenician and coastal Syrian influences had, of course, been dominant in Palestine for millennia. If one were to classify the kind of religion here, one would not hesitate in describing it as 'fringe Phoenician'. Temples were not as important as they were in Phoenicia. Palestine's society was not as literate, and a lot less public, but if one were to think of any of the artistic qualities of Palestinian religious forms – architecture, statuary forms and poetry – one could not help recognizing this child of Phoenicia. At the same time, a strong influence from the steppe and desert regions of the south is also obvious, particularly in the areas of Judah and Edom.

Typical of Syrian and Palestinian religions, is the markedly fluid nature of the relationships between gods of different places. The identities of gods were unstable – not just their names but also other characteristics. Chameleon changes occur from region to region and from one period to another. The complexity of religious expression found both in the highland states and in other regions of Greater Palestine does not differ in form or content from practices known throughout Syria. It cannot be claimed that the religion of either Israel or Judah was in a substantive way different from those of Ammon, Moab or Edom. Nor can it be claimed that the Bible reflects the religion of Palestine's Iron Age directly.

The invention of new ancestor gods was an Assyrian imperial policy that helped create religious ties between societies around regional and local deities. Its counterpart was to develop legends about the 'return' of 'old', long-neglected and forgotten gods. The promotion of imperial interests, and especially the growing practice of forcibly moving people from one region of the empire to another, tended more and more to explain different and distinct gods as expressions of a single concept, representing the divine. It is also from the Assyrians' perception of empire as a world-embracing political reality, and from their view of the king as the supreme servant of the gods, that we find an increasingly universal concept of divinity developing in Syria and Palestine in the course of the Iron Age. Early references to the 'Lord [*Ba'al*] of Heaven' encourage an understanding of transcendence. The more abstract and distant conception of the divine, which included all of the powers of the gods and all that was divine, seems to have been the first step towards a comprehensive view of the world of religion. It was a more philosophical rendering of the story motif of the 'divine council' or 'assembly of the gods'. Tracing what we know of the cult of Yahweh, one can recognize this imperial concept of the god of heaven, which lay at the roots of the Bible's later understanding of Yahweh as the old and traditional name of such a god. It was this transcendent and universal deity, however, who could be described as the God of gods, lord of lords, and finally as the one, true, and only God.

Recent interest in the history of intellectual views and concepts has brought us a long way towards understanding the development of such ideas in Palestine, and hence the assumptions reflected in many biblical narratives. What we did know about Palestine's religion during the Iron Age has long seemed an embarrassment to conservative scholarship. Evidence accumulating from excavations hardly supported a picture of Mosaic monotheism that one might expect if one read the Bible as history. Even the cult of Yahweh proved to be more typical of the ancient Near Eastern religious world than of biblical tradition. Many scholars have been inclined to offer complex reinterpretations of this evidence in order to bring it into line with their understanding of biblical monotheism. Some deny the existence of the historical and archaeological evidence for ancient Palestinian religion. Such misunderstanding, if not misrepresentation, has become commonplace in theology.

Throughout the ancient Near East, religion gave expression to a variety of relationships in society. The central and most important functions of nature, society, economics and politics – all those powers upon which one's existence depended – were expressed in the metaphors of personalities through story, song and ritual. By creating a narrative world of actions, plans and desires of gods and goddesses, civilization was able to give emotional expression to its ever more complex experiences. As functions within society grew increasingly more differentiated, this metaphorical religious world, in which the emotions of power and powerlessness could be expressed, also grew in complexity. Kings, merchants and commoners formed bonds of relationship, both with each other and the world they created with their language.

As the politics in Palestine were regionally localized and the economies limited to only a few interacting regions, the development and definition of its religions followed a pattern that mirrored people's lives. The religious world-view of Palestine shared many of the perspectives of Mesopotamia and Egypt. The divine was understood in the form of powers that controlled and governed the functions of natural and human orders. This divine world – especially the world of the 'high' gods reflected in the cult, in personal names and in legend and tradition – was expressed using a quite limited number of deities. Gods were unknown and unpredictable by definition. They were created to reflect unseen powers that determined the most fundamental aspects of survival. They personified the ineffable power of the state and the inscrutable truth of justice. They dramatized the weather and the sea. They focused attention on the anxieties and joy that surround the fertility of herd animals, crops and people themselves.

Already from the Bronze Age, El, the father of the gods and creator of heaven and earth, with his consort Asherah or Astarte, the 'Queen of Heaven', was the chief deity and head of the pantheon in both folktale and song. Ba'al (= 'lord', 'master') was his chief executive. Ba'al was often accompanied by the relatively generic female deity, Asherah, who was described as the 'mother of all living', and given a role in both fertility and mourning. Names given to the chief executive varied considerably in the several regions of Palestine. He embodied the true and ultimate king or patron of the state. The human king, accordingly, took on a representative role. He was not the patron himself, so much as his servant, the executor of divine patronage on earth. The functions of the patron deity follow a common pattern in Palestinian states. Such deities were rallying points of unity. They reflected a growing development of self-understanding as distinct states and 'peoples'.

Most of the regions of Palestine, which were geographically and politically integrated, usually had only one primary and distinctive god, apart from El. This patron deity was responsible for most divine functions. A female deity, usually named Asherah or Astarte, shared divine rule over the state's human clients as the god's consort. The functions of these female gods were considerable, and went well beyond the central roles of fertility- and life-giving. They frequently involve eroticism, warfare, wisdom, health and sickness. At times, the goddess was associated with cults belonging to special groups such as women, sailors and hunters. Because of the influence of men in politics and in the army, states were often distinguishable by the names of their male patron deity, while female deities tended to remain functional rather than personal. Among such male patron deities, we find Ba'al in Phoenicia, the Galilee and in the highlands of Israel. In Israel one also finds Yahweh. In the southern coastal plain, Dagon was the most distinctive patron god. Although both Ba'al and Yahweh are names that are used frequently in the Persian period, one finds indications of a cult of originally Egyptian deities on the coast and in the Shephelah: the goddess Hathor and the solar god Amon. Yahweh and Ba'al are both used in Judea, though Yahweh is dominant. In Edom, the patron deity is called both Qaus and Yahweh. In Moab and Ammon, the worship of Moloch and Chemosh was typical. These deities could be and were distinguished from each other just as the states for which they functioned as patrons were different. However, it is to be doubted that two clients *of the same state*, one of whom understood his divine patron as Yahweh and gave his children names using this divine name, while the other spoke of Qaus as his god, understood themselves as having different patrons. That is, apart from the distinction of their name and its state associations, one cannot conclude that we are dealing with clearly *different* gods. It would be more appropriate to understand them as different manifestations of the divine. Different people knew God by different names. What distinguished the gods and the states were the ruling houses to whom the client owed allegiance. The king, as head of his patronate, served as the servant of the deity, who was the true head of state. Comparably, when we find *different states* with patron deities bearing the same names, as with Ba'al or Yahweh, one is dealing with different and competing manifestations of a deity. The names by which a god was known were a human affair. They did not define the deity.

Syncretism, or the practice of using the name of one god to translate that of another deity of a related culture, is commonplace in greater Palestine. Distinctive executive gods are often identified with El. In a single text, the same eighth-century king of Hamat bears the name of both Yahweh and El in the variants of his name: Yaubidi and Elubidi. Executive gods are also consciously identified with each other. Yahweh can be understood as identical to both Ba'al and El. Forms of syncretism also occur in the lower order of local deities: with the gods of towns, mountains, springs and regions. Most commonly the names El or Ba'al are found in such forms, but Yahweh, or the name of one of the other high gods of the region, is also worshipped. The gods are given specifically descriptive titles and epithets: El Qonearz: 'El the creator of the earth'; Ba'al Shamem: 'Lord of the Heavens'; Yahweh Sebaoth: 'Yahweh of Heaven's Army', etc. These should be understood as distinct manifestations of the deity, much in the way that modern Catholic piety towards

Jesus is expressed in worship of the 'Sacred Heart' or the 'Infant of Prague'. On reflection, such deities are recognized as the same god. There is also evidence of a few minor deities such as Azazel in the scapegoat ritual of Leviticus 16 and Lilith, the goddess of the night and mother of Cain. Of course, in the world of stories and song – which are uncharted refractions of belief – there are many more. Not only are minor deities portrayed as persons, like Satan in Job, but monsters show up. Here we find Rahab, Behemoth and Leviathan. Finally, there are a variety of messengers and servants of the gods, both divine and human.

The West Semitic perception of gods in Palestine is markedly male-centred, which reflects the dominance of men in the creation of cultural and commercial products. Goddesses such as Asherah and Astarte do, however, play significant and indispensable roles, especially with regard to fertility. Female metaphors are favoured in the roles of nurturing, healing and sometimes warfare. Before we dismiss this ancient religion as just one more product of male dominance, we should try to understand it; we should remember that the most common sacred figurine found in Palestine has been that of a naked woman, and at times goddess, moulded in clay. Hardly demeaning, such motifs of eroticism and fertility are essentially religious celebrations of life. In the understanding of humanity implicit in the creation and garden stories of Genesis 1–3, and consistent with much of the Old Testament, three aspects of human experience are defined as sharing in the divine: life, knowledge and fertility. Portrayals of female sexuality are expressive of divine love, creative in its fertility (Gen. 4: 1). These figurines are not high art, nor are they much related to the cult of temples or state; most of them are objects of the household cult, the protective guardians of individuals and families. References to sexuality and fertility in Semitic texts are often elusive and euphemistic. As these practises are little reflected in accounts relating formal cults, they are among the most important evidence we have of popular religion.

In the public worship of gods, temples, open-air altars and shrines need to be mentioned. Both temples and altars supported a class of officials, priests and priestesses who performed the religious rites that were necessary for the public care of gods, especially those involving the sacrifice of animals and agricultural produce. In major temples, there were a variety of functionaries besides the priests who offered the sacrifices. These include choir directors and cantors, male and female. We know little about how sexual rites related to fertility were performed or about the roles variously played, other than that they were practised with both male and female sexual servants. Such was appropriate to a culture which found life as its central metaphor of the divine. Since a primary purpose of public worship of the gods was to safeguard the future and prosperity of the state, communication with the gods and knowledge of their will became a dominant preoccupation of state cults. This need developed a variety of visionaries, soothsayers and oracles. All played the role of mediator between the people or the king and the deity. They also functioned as advisers to the king.

Within the related cultures of those who spoke Semitic languages and dialects, this divine world was varied and stratified by functions. One might well speak of four distinct levels, or classes, of gods and goddesses:

a) *El, the creator of the world and father of the gods, with his spouse.* This divine couple is usually presented in stories and prayers as very distant monarchs without very complex personalities. El is seen as possessing all of the powers that belong to gods, who, as his children, carry out – or, as in some stories, do not carry out – his will. Imperially majestic, and placed at a far remove both from the other gods and from this world, he functions as an ultimate explanation and first cause of all that exists. In worship, El is commonly approached in a variety of manifestations. These different Els are those many different functions over which he has ultimate control. His consort, however, the queen of heaven, is more approachable. Accordingly, she is a more regular object of worship and prayer.

b) *Major administrative deities.* These are both gods and goddesses. They are found in the characters of a small number of high administrative deities who are responsible for most of the major forces in the ancient world: the state, the army, justice, death, fertility, love, the weather, the sea, etc. These gods are the ones who are seen to hold 'real' power. They become the principal characters in stories and song. They are honoured through dedications, monuments and temples, and portrayed in statues and symbols. They are fed and given gifts in ritual and festival. Their instruction is sought and their forgiveness is begged, because they are the ones who ultimately determine human destiny. These deities are by far the most interesting and instructive. They are the shakers of the world, and are understood as competitive powers over such central realities as weather and the sea, fertility and death. They also protect and use the army and determine the destiny of the state and city, even justice and morality. These are the primary religious gods reflected in public cult, prayer and tradition. They are portrayed with rich and complex personalities. In Syria and Palestine, they are limited in number. In isolated regions, a single divine pair perform all of these functions.

c) *Middle management.* These are mid-level administrative gods of families and clans, subordinate to the great or 'high' gods and related to specific places and smaller regions. They may be named in, and occasionally associated with, a story or song. More often, they are related to specific rituals or rites of passage of individuals. Deities who function as personal or family guardians also belong in this category. Even in the very small societies one finds in more isolated regions of Palestine and Syria, gods of this third class are abundant. In contrast to high gods such as Yahweh, Ba'al and Marduk, they are given limited personalities and functions in stories, as watchmen in I Enoch, messengers of Yahweh in Genesis and Exodus, sons of God in the divine assembly in Job, or as the doorkeepers Tammuz and Gizzida in Gilgamesh. They play very particular roles – gods of mountains, woods, the desert or the steppe, specific winds, crops and trades. They are family or guardian deities, or officials of the divine court.

d) *Impersonal gods*. One must also consider the variety of impersonal, or barely personal, powers: those magical forces of good and evil that support and terrify people. Included among these are demons of the desert, Liliths of the night, the forces of disease, aspects of fertility and eroticism, the guardians who give power to the evil eye, the shadows of past dead, whom one stumbles across, or the spirit of an ancestor that gives strength and protects. In this final class of deities belong a wide variety of forces, both personal and impersonal: demons, but also powers of good luck and charms.

The range of beliefs and gods that are involved in societies with religious complexity, such as the Egyptian, Babylonian, Phoenician and Greek, is very much greater than those we find in most of the West Semitic societies of Palestine. This striking difference between what scholarly tradition and jargon often likes to describe as 'polytheistic' and 'henotheistic' forms of religion describes only the surface of reality. It is both confusing and misleading. Such differences are rather strongly influenced by three different factors. The single most important is the involvement of the great cities of the ancient Near East, with inter-regional and international commerce and trade. Trade brings to these cities a multilingual and multi-ethnic orientation that contrasts with the relative isolation and homogeneity of most regions in Palestine. Cultures such as those of Phoenicia or of the later Nabateans, which themselves were built on trade, are also strongly influenced by such cosmopolitan and hence complex theological understandings of the world. Especially creative in the religious traditions of Egypt and Mesopotamia was the direct influence of imperial forms of government. Here, a highly centralized government has made long-standing efforts to integrate different regions and peoples. This stands in contrast to Palestine, where imperial administrations encouraged forms of home rule and largely avoided interference with local cultic life. These differences in the complexity of religion are direct reflections of the history of political, military and economic relationships. People share and take part in the beliefs and ideas of the people with whom they live and do business.

Nor are the terms polytheistic and monotheistic accurate descriptions of religion in antiquity. Within the ancient Near East, from early times, all religious thought shared some aspect of both polytheistic and monotheistic metaphors of the divine. Such was the nature of religious thought in this world. This world-view understood gods specifically as reflections of the functions of power as they were perceived within the human world.

Writers and artists, and political and religious functionaries in the ancient world, were perfectly aware that they were speaking a language of literature and metaphor. Creating the world of the divine implies a recognition of the spiritual dimension of human life. Intellectually, the existence of a world of the spirit in ancient ritual and literature implies far more than the existence of belief in gods. Creating and multiplying gods as expressive of an understanding and belief in a transcendent is the centre of this world of literature. Gods were well known as products of human culture. Divine functions were given coherence and unified in a world-view of the transcendent, refracting the ephemeral world of human experience. The growth of imperial influence on religious thought, already marked in the Assyrian period, became quite explicit in the Persian and Hellenistic worlds. The more universalist concepts of an imperial world encouraged a more explicitly monotheistic language of religion and philosophy.

It is possible that the earliest references to Yahweh occur in the Early Bronze Age. The earliest group of texts that may contain the name comes from the Syrian city of Ebla, where the element *yaw* included in some personal names could be an abbreviated form of the divine name Yahweh. There may also be early references to this deity in names found on tablets from the Late Bronze city of Ugarit on the Syrian coast. These names use the element *ya*, which like *yaw*, *yah* and *yahu* at times expresses the divine name. These elements are also found as part of similar names in the Hebrew Bible. Good examples of this pious practice are the names *Milkiya* or *Milkiyahu* ('my king is Yahweh') or *Natanya, Yonathan, Nathanyahu* and *Nathanyaw* ('gift of Yahweh'). Nevertheless, this element in the Ugaritic names could be read as merely a normal grammatical ending of a shortened name, without any reference at all to a deity. We have no clear evidence to help us be more definite, and little reason to expect the appearance of this deity so early or so far north.

Another candidate for the earliest reference to this deity suggests a very different context. New Kingdom Egyptian texts refer to the area of southern Edom on the western fringe of the Arabian peninsula. These texts are associated with groups of desert-dwellers referred to by Egyptians as *Shasu*. Some of these Shasu were referred to as the 'Shasu of Yahweh'. Here the name Yahweh is used as a place name. Some scholars have speculated that the 'full' name of this place in the desert must have been Beth Yahweh ('house', 'temple' or 'shrine of Yahweh'). Many find this appropriate because the much later Old Testament stories and songs also associate Yahweh's origins with the regions of Seir, Edom and the southern deserts. Moreover, texts of the first millennium about Yahweh have been found in the Sinai. They refer to him as Yahweh of Teman (a desert region to the south of Edom). That these Late Bronze Egyptian texts do in fact relate to the god Yahweh is still far more than we know. First of all, the name Yahweh in these inscriptions is used as a place name and not as a divine name. Moreover, the normal form of the divine name in inscriptions is *Yah, Yaw, Yahu, Yo* or *Yeho*. Only occasionally, as in the Bible or in other late texts, do we find the spelling *yhwh*. The name Yahweh occurs in the Bible with a very specific literary pun on the verb *'ehyeh*, which identifies Yahweh as 'God with Israel'. This we will discuss in another chapter. It is nevertheless possible that Egyptian texts do in fact refer to a Late Bronze deity Yahweh.

That the god Yahweh may have been known over such a large geographical area during the third and second millennium – from Ebla and Ugarit of Syria to the southern desert of Edom – and that it might appear as both a tribal deity of pastoralists as well as part of a rich multi-religious environment of cities such as Ebla and Ugarit, is not as unlikely as had been at first imagined. The Bible frequently recognizes that Yahweh was worshipped by others than Israel. It understands him as having come from Midian, Teman and Seir. We also have a number of first-millennium Assyrian and Persian period texts that demonstrate just such a geographical spread of the worship of Yahweh. There is clear historical evidence that the Bible's was not the only religious tradition that recognized Yahweh as God. It also must be expected that the specific origins of this name occurred long before the earliest texts we have.

While there are no *certain* references to the god Yahweh in the third and second millennia BCE, references from early first-millennium texts in both personal names and other inscriptions are common. They have an immense geographical range: from the Sinai to the city of Hama in Syria. Texts from Sinai and southern Palestine refer to Yahweh as the god of Samaria. They mention his wife Asherah. Undoubtedly, the divine couple were the dominant deities of Palestine's highlands. In the Persian period, Yahweh is worshipped along with his wife Asherah, together with Ba'al and other deities at the town of Ekron in the southern Palestinian coast and as far south as Elephantine in Egypt. Biblical texts identify Yahweh as the name of the traditional deity of the ancient state of Israel, for whom a temple was built in Jerusalem. This deity was understood as identifiable with the universal God of spirit *Elohe Shamayim*.

The second-century CE tradition of Philo of Byblos, which gives witness to the worship of the deity *Yaw* in Phoenicia, clearly shows that this deity continued to be worshipped in the eastern Mediterranean region until at least the end of the Graeco-Roman period. Although metaphors and symbols were used in art and literature that understood Yahweh in forms common to Hellenistic religions throughout the world, specific exclusive forms of monotheism began to develop as early as the Persian period. From the third to seventh century CE such exclusive forms of religion grew to dominate the ancient world.

For more than two millennia, beginning with the monumental codes of ancient Sumer and extending through the ten commandments of the

Bible's *torah* to the codification of Roman law, ideals of society and proper living were expressed in themes of song and story. They were written more formally and more directly – if less persuasively – in lists of instructions and wise sayings, in poetic speeches and prophetic oracles. A typical fashion of such lists was to present them as instructions of a former king or famous wise man of the past. We often find them rendered as the words of a seer or prophet, or within a story or description of a vision or dream, as a gift given directly from a god. Such forms are basic to folklore and to the tales of every region's tradition. The Hammurapi code, for example, was published by the royal court in Babylon as a monumental display of how the king, the obedient servant of the god Marduk, had established justice as God had demanded of him. Such texts formed an everyday part of school lessons for the education of scribes and officials.

In the Bible, we find such traditions presented as God-given laws and instructions, through which courts and human judges could bring justice to human conflict. We find them in some of the songs attributed to the great King David. We find them in the wisdom of Solomon, in the poems out of the whirlwind in the Book of Job, and in the instructions of the teacher in Ben Sira. Perhaps most importantly of all, we find such compositions in the form of long monologues on the past about justice, faithfulness and mercy that are frequently projected as oracles into the mouths of famous dead prophets, as in the books of Isaiah, Jeremiah and Ezekiel. The implied reflection is a very simple one, and metaphorically very true: precious human wisdom is hard-won, fragile and inspired. It is a gift from God. Error and injustice are human; justice and understanding, divine.

We have a nearly universal tradition in the ancient world, that law, justice and human destiny are all in God's hands: the human institutions related to them have been given to people by God. This is especially true of law codes, but may include the entire judicial system. The power of the king is rooted in divine appointment, and the king's central role is thought of, idealistically, as carrying out God's intentions. There is a divine plan, though we do not know it, and the gods have determined the fate and destiny of humanity.

There is another concept very closely related to this. Each state, people or independent city has its own god. As this deity is their personal patron, so are they uniquely that god's people. Usually this is portrayed in the language of a guardian deity. The god protects, guides and fights on behalf of his people: provides for them as a good patron does. But he also makes demands of them. Above all he requires loyalty and obedience. Defeat in war, plagues and famine are typically understood as punishments, brought on a people by their own god for having broken the familial form of relationship they should have with him. This dual perception of God as a god of justice and of patronage marks the Semitic religions not only with a very personal character, but with the virtue of loyalty. Religious perceptions such as these are both the context and the foundation of the understanding of God that we find in the Bible.

CHAPTER 8

Under the shadow of empires

1 The war for the Jezreel

The political and military history of the Iron II period that we are able to write today is radically different from the Bible's plot and purpose. The Bible's story is a theological one, which centres on the conflicts of Jerusalem and Samaria with the will of their god. It ends with Yahweh repenting that he has created Israel as his own. God's servants, Yahweh's messengers, the kings of Assyria and Babylon, destroy Samaria first and scatter its population. The goodness of the Judean kings, Hezekiah and Josiah, delays Yahweh's anger and Jerusalem's rejection. Yahweh's patience, however, ends. The 'day of wrath' brings the Babylonian army to Jerusalem, leaving the city and its temple devastated. Its king is removed to humiliating exile. Yahweh repents of his eternal promise to his son David.

The historical picture of these events is substantially different. Samaria, and especially Jerusalem, play much smaller roles in Palestinian politics than the authors of the Bible ever imagined. Real politics was determined by the ongoing negotiation between Mesopotamia's kings and the kings of the Nile. The importance of the historical politics of Palestine ever lay in agriculture, the trade routes and geography.

The Jezreel valley entered the new prosperity of the tenth century with political power fragmented among several competing towns, from Tell Keisan of the Haifa Bay coastal area to Tel Yoqneam, Megiddo, Tel Ta'anek, Tel Yin'am and Beth Shan at the descent to the Jordan. This well-watered, rich agricultural plain with its excellent, largely frost-free climate, was capable of supporting a large and stable population. Close local control of drainage systems and small-scale irrigation were essential to prevent the silting up of the River Qishon's sluggish waterways. Without them, salinization of soils increased. Marshlands and malarial swamps developed in the valley's centre. In the best of times, the Jezreel and the connecting Beth Shan and northern Jordan valleys, supported perhaps a majority of Palestine's total sedentary population. It was hardly accidental that the Egyptian empire of the Late Bronze Age chose Beth Shan for its primary military base in the north. Certainly, no power could control Palestine without controlling the Jezreel. When the Egyptians withdrew from Palestine in the course of the eleventh century, the central valleys fragmented into their traditional regionalism. Each of several dominant towns controlled the economy and small villages of its immediate neighbourhood. No single power controlled the whole of the region's wealth. The potentially rich north-south trade route passed through the heart of the Jezreel and connected the coastal plain to the upper Jordan valley. This route linked all of Palestine's important agricultural sub-regions. As agricultural prosperity gradually recovered, it was closely followed by an increase in the volume of international trade between Egypt and Assyria. Absent Egyptian hegemony, however, the lack of a controlling force in Palestine's northern regions, fostered instability at the area's economic centre. Beth Shan dominated the gateway to the Jordan, but it was a relatively small town, and had neither an army nor the ambition to expand into the Jezreel, there to challenge its larger neighbours. In fact, this was true of all of the towns in the central valleys: large and populous enough to dominate the patronage of the local agricultural economy, they were hardly yet capable of greater ambitions. It was left to Phoenicia, and especially the great city of Tyre, to compete with Damascus in an effort to fill the political vacuum left by the Egyptians. Throughout most of the recovery of the early Iron Age until the end of the tenth century, these two regionally dominant forces dominated the Galilee between them. The small mountain villages of the western Galilee were oriented toward the coast, while the eastern Galilee, with its rich agricultural lands around Hazor on the southern slopes of the Hulah Basin and near Tel Dan at the Jordan's source, fell within the Syrian sphere of influence.

With the growth of trade at the end of the tenth and in the early ninth centuries, Phoenicia and Syria turned to assert control over Palestine's north. With the consolidation of the central hills under Samaria in the early ninth century, a three-way struggle for dominance of the Jezreel developed. None of these efforts was entirely successful. Neither Damascus, Tyre nor Samaria was able to assert decisive control over the valley. Instead, the region was marked by failed treaties and a low level of intermittent warfare that went on for more than a century without resolution. That such long-term political and economic instability was allowed to continue in the region is a testimony to the weakened political and economic strength of the great states in Mesopotamia, Anatolia and Egypt. It is also evidence of their lack of interest in the affairs of Palestine. Trade had not yet grown attractive enough to Egypt to justify committing the troops and financial resources necessary to dominate and pacify the region. While the tenth-century pharaoh Sheshonk I may have entertained visions of a return to an empire's ambitions in the region, his actual campaigns, which may have reached both Megiddo in the Jezreel and Byblos on the Phoenician coast, seem to have been confined to a minor punitive expedition: a form of taxation through booty. On the other hand, any direct entrance into Palestinian affairs on Assyria's part ran the risk of confrontation with the very real military force of Egypt, in whose sphere of influence Palestine traditionally lay. It is unlikely that Assyria considered challenging this tradition before the second half of the ninth century.

The failure to develop a major centralized power in Palestine left the region fragmented among a large number of competing small states, the largest of which were Damascus, Amurru, Tyre of the Phoenician cities, Israel in the central hills, and the Transjordan states of Ammon and Moab. The entire southern region lacked centralization except for a few small autonomous towns. Among these were Jerusalem and Hebron of the hill country; Gezer and Lachish of the Shephelah; Ashdod, Ashkelon, Ekron and Gaza of the southern coastal plain; Beersheva and Arad of the northern Negev; and Bosra of the southern Transjordan. Regional political structures throughout Edom, Judea and the steppelands were undeveloped. These areas were dependent on the major market towns that controlled their economies. This endemic fragmentation into its many small regions left Palestine not only torn by recurrent regional conflicts, but extremely vulnerable to the armies of major powers from outside Palestine.

That the instability of the Jezreel was finally resolved was due to interference by the Assyrian empire late in the ninth century, which brought clear economic and political benefits to the greater region. Assyria had already long asserted its interests in the west. Tiglath Pileser I had sent a series of campaigns to pacify the regions of Amurru, Hatti and Lebanon. He claims to have fought against the Aramaeans along the Euphrates some twenty-eight times. Much later, in the first half of the ninth century, Ashurbanipal II, after successful campaigns to the west, claims rich tribute from the Hittite city of Carchemish, from Amurru and from the Phoenician cities, including Byblos, Tyre and Sidon. It was in the second half of the ninth century, however, in Shalmaneser III's war against the Syrians, that the Assyrians first asserted imperial ambitions in the west. In this campaign, the submission not only of Syria (i.e., Damascus) but also of Hatti, Amurru and Phoenicia were goals. Shalmaneser gives his own accounts of the campaign. After having offered sacrifice to the god Hadad in the temple of the Syrian city of Aleppo, which had surrendered to his forces, he marched against a Syrian coalition from the cities of Hamath, Qarqar and Damascus. This coalition included forces from Phoenician Arwad, and from Israel, Arabia and Ammon. He describes his victory as so great that the souls of the dead were spread across the valley in such piles that they could not go down into the netherworld. The plain was not large enough to bury them. 'With their corpses, I spanned the

Orontes before there was a bridge!' He claims decisive victories against further coalitions of a stock 'twelve' kings in the sixth, eleventh, twelfth and fourteenth years of his reign. In the eighteenth year, he lays siege to Damascus and receives tribute from Phoenicia and a king of Israel ('Jehu, son of Omri').

It was at the end of the ninth and the beginning of the eighth centuries, in the campaigns of Adad-Nirari III, that the Assyrians finally succeeded in occupying Damascus. They turned their interests towards Palestine, including Tyre and Sidon of Phoenicia, Israel and Edom. In the third quarter of the eighth century, Tiglath Pileser III moved Assyrian interests to reassert authority over Damascus, Byblos, Tyre, Samaria and the states of the north, and into southern Palestine as well. They fought against Ammon, Moab, Ashqelon, Judah, Edom and Gaza. The king reports deporting people from Israel and replacing its king, Peqah, with a king of his own choice, Hoshea. As an Assyrian vassal, Hoshea's Samaria is given control over the Jezreel. With the authority of Assyrian troops and under Assyrian patronage, Israel finally gains undisputed control over the Jezreel for the first time in 731 BCE. Such 'control' was to last less than a decade.

2 The historical Israel

The many different societies that had begun to develop in Palestine during the tenth and ninth centuries all had their own regional differences in economy, language, religion and culture. By the close of the ninth century, they were well on their way towards emergence as distinct regional states, each with a political identity closely associated with the primary geographical regions it controlled. When Assyria began expanding its interests into Palestine in the mid-ninth century, however, the growth of such regional identity was undermined. The first Assyrian policy was to subordinate these patronage states under the empire as subject vassal states. Once their army had stabilized the area, they systematically proceeded to integrate the component regions directly into the imperial system, as part of the provinces ruled by Assyria.

During the first century of Assyrian control, following the battle of Qarqar in 853 BCE, until the mid-eighth century, Assyria's influence on Palestine proper had been felt primarily in the direct and indirect costs of war. Further costs came with taxation as treaties subordinated the Palestinian states to the Assyrian king as vassals. The regional economies were integrated into the international trade of the empire. The sovereignty and autonomy of these regions were decisively curtailed. Even greater changes took place after Tiglath Pileser's accession to the throne in 745 BCE. In his western policies, Tiglath Pileser began a process of cumulative subordination of Syrian and Palestinian agriculture to Assyrian interests.

In 733/732, he conquered Damascus and annexed it as a province. The petty kings of Palestine, including those of Byblos and Tyre, Israel, Ammon, Moab, Edom, Ashqelon, Gaza and the Judaean territories, reconfirmed their allegiance as vassals of Assyria. With its takeover in Damascus, Assyria became a direct participant in the affairs of Palestine and especially of the Jezreel.

The Assyrian army introduced the policy of population transference, which involved the transportation and deportation of peoples across the empire. It then transformed what had begun as a military policy of provincial control, into a political weapon that was designed to control both the provinces and the populations of the great Assyrian cities. Rulers and states that were compliant with Assyrian interests were allowed to survive intact as clients of the empire. The social fabric of states that directly resisted the Assyrian armies faced systematic dismemberment. The goals of these deportation policies were extremely diverse and were not limited to punishment for resistance and insurrection. One objective was to eliminate local rivals to Assyrian power and any who developed the potential for resistance or rebellion. A further and major benefit was the control, through threat of deportation, of political and intellectual leaders in the territories conquered. The policy also served as a form of military conscription. The expanding empire required an ever greater supply of young men for its armies.

The Assyrians resettled a large proportion of the deportees in Assyrian cities as well as in other troubled spots of the empire. In this way, the imperial government established groups within the subject population who were entirely dependent on the authorities. They could be counted on to be loyal. It was in the economic interest of Assyrian cities to create monopolies of craftsmen and skilled labourers. Less skilled workers supplied the cities with labour gangs for building monuments and public buildings. They provided a work force for such large-scale projects as bridges and canals. Fortification walls and paramilitary border settlements were established along the empire's frontier.

Sometimes whole villages were deported from conquered territories and used to restore and rebuild cities. They repopulated abandoned or empty lands, and they undermined the 'ethnic' coherence of other subject regions. In all, many hundreds of thousands of people were transported across the extent of the Assyrian empire during this long period of Assyrian expansion. The Assyrian ideology of democratic equality within the provinces was touted as a benefit of empire. This was not only propaganda but also policy. It resulted most immediately in creating subjects of empire. Such 'citizenship' undermined local loyalties and the power of long-standing local patrons with their clients. It needs to be recognized that the Assyrian theology of 'right of conquest' gave the Assyrian king full rights of patronage over the lands and the peoples he conquered. It also gave him the responsibility of 'shepherding' and 'protecting' his 'servants'. The creation of empire involved an extensive displacement of goods and populations from the provinces into the sprawling urban centres of Assyria. Nevertheless, the greatest single cost of such large-scale transportation was the damage to and at times near total collapse of indigenous regional infrastructures in most territories that fell directly under Assyrian rule. Vassal states, on the other hand, were able to maintain their social infrastructures through submission to the Assyrian overlord.

When Tiglath Pileser's army stormed Damascus in 733, Damascus' competitor Israel, a relatively small state centred in Samaria, supported the Assyrians, hoping to gain its reward in the Jezreel. That hope was shattered, however, when Assyria annexed the Jezreel to its newly established Aramaean province. Hapless Israel, having fought 'successfully' against Damascus for the Jezreel, now found itself sitting on the southern rim of the empire itself. Politics was a dangerous game for little states to play. Victory over the fox in Damascus had brought a bear to Israel's doorstep. Tiglath Pileser's policy was bent on progressive and controlled annexation. Following a pretext for direct intervention, his successor Shalmaneser V laid siege to Samaria. The city capitulated to Sargon II. This brought an end to the highland state in the year 722. Sargon II deported part of Samaria's population as slaves and used others as a cavalry contingent in his army. He reorganized the town under the patronage of one of his own officers who acted as governor over what became a new Assyrian province.

The end of Israel's sovereignty led to the systematic destruction of any autonomous integrity it may have had. An unknown portion of the population of Samaria and people from some of its towns and villages were deported to Syria, to Elam and to the great cities of Assyria. Other groups of people were brought to Samaria from Elam, Syria and Arabia. They were settled in the highlands and in some of Israel's richest valleys. Some few areas of this fertile hill country seem to have been abandoned and to have reverted to wilderness. However, the archaeological chronology for such changes remains uncertain. It is a mistake to think of the people or its culture as having ceased to exist at the end of the eighth century. Not only did it survive, but it remained large and stable enough to integrate the newcomers in language, culture and religion. Politically restructured, it continued to exist as a small highland society subordinate to the empire. Its customs and traditions remained largely intact. The failure of historians to address the continued history of Samaria after the Assyrian takeover is due to their use of the Bible as if it were Palestine's primary history.

The Bible, however, uses the destruction of Israel as a state by the Assyrians as one of its classic examples of how 'old Israel', a faithless people, was destroyed and ceased to exist because it had not been faithful to its God. *For the Bible*, the false Israel no longer existed. This, of course, is a theological not an historical statement. The two should not be confused. The biblical narratives turn their attention, after Samaria's fall, to the story of Jerusalem and Judah's destruction. The Bible concentrates only on the closing scenes of the story of 'old Israel'. The northern tribes of Israel, after Samaria's fall, are no more. This is not history. It is theology using history as a metaphor, theology written from a much later Jerusalem's perspective.

When Sargon II accepted Samaria's capitulation and systematically dismantled its state structures, the town of Jerusalem, Israel's southern neighbour, supported Assyrian policy. The Assyrians accepted Jerusalem's allegiance for about twenty years. Once they had consolidated their power in central Palestine, the Assyrians finally risked a direct confrontation with Egypt. Impatient with the Egyptian policy of fomenting rebellion along its southern flank, the Assyrian army moved into the Egyptian sphere of influence in the southern coastal plain and the Shephelah. This formed part of a long-range preparation for a drive into Egypt itself. For the moment, the Assyrian forces were satisfied with positioning themselves for an assault. Sennacherib briefly placed Jerusalem under siege as he moved against the Shephelah and the southern coast. The city survived this time.

This short-lived success for Jerusalem gave birth to a story in Kings which, however fictional, is unquestionably one the Bible's most authentic war scenes. It is found in II Kings 18–19. The Assyrian general confronts Jerusalem's population. In the Bible's story world, the city was protected by its God. The speech of Rabshakeh captures imperial deportation policies perfectly. His peace terms are an offer one can not refuse, presented with exquisite irony in Rabshakeh's voice. The author waits for the very last words to fall from the general's mouth before exposing the threatened violence implicit in his offer:

> Hear the word of the great king, the king of Assyria! Thus says the king: Do not let Hezekiah [Jerusalem's king] deceive you for he will not be able to deliver you out of my hand. Do not let Hezekiah make you rely on Yahweh by saying, 'Yahweh will surely deliver us and this city will not be given into the hand of the king of Assyria.' Make your peace with me and come out to me; then every one of you will eat of his own vine, and every one of his own fig tree, and every one of you will drink the water of his own cistern; until I come and take you away to a land like your own land, a land of grain and wine, a land of bread and vineyards, a land of olive trees and honey, that you might live and not die. (II Kings 18: 28–32)

II Kings' narrative is a theological text. It extols the virtue of trust in divine providence. Rabshakeh's speech goes beyond the mere statement of Assyrian policy. It also prepares us for the story's dramatic reversal in

Jerusalem's unpromising fortunes. In his hubris and pride, not only does the Assyrian general taunt Jerusalem's good king, Hezekiah, but, in ignorance of the true God, he dares to mock Yahweh:

> Do not listen to Hezekiah when he misleads you by saying: 'Yahweh will deliver us.' Has any of the gods of the nations ever delivered his land out of the hands of the King of Assyria? Where are the gods of Hamath and Arpad? . . . Have they delivered Samaria out of my hand? Who among all the gods of the countries have delivered their countries out of my hand, that Yahweh should deliver Jerusalem out of my hand? (II Kings 18: 32–35)

Hezekiah's pious humility contrasts instructively with the blasphemy of the Assyrian general. Like David before him (II Sam. 15), good King Hezekiah turns in prayer to recognize Yahweh as his refuge – 'that you, Yahweh, are alone God' (II Kings 19: 19) – and, as in the David story, Yahweh saves the kingdom for his servant. Sennacherib's god, in contrast, is unable to save his king:

> That night the angel of Yahweh went out and killed 185,000 of the Assyrians, and when men arose early in the morning: there were all dead bodies! Sennacherib, king of Assyria left and went home and lived in Nineveh. And as he was worshipping in the temple of Nisroch his god, his sons killed him with the sword. (II Kings 19: 35–37)

That is the Assyrian campaign of biblical legend. In contemporary Assyrian accounts of the campaign, Sennacherib claims to have put Jerusalem under siege and to have attacked and then reorganized its territory of Judah. He subordinated some of its towns under the patronage of Padi, the king of the coastal town of Ekron. He claims that the siege of Jerusalem had been successful as he lists tribute that Jerusalem's king Hezekiah sent to Assyria. He closes the account with his recognition of Hezekiah as his client. The Assyrian text presents the account as a rebellion among client states, with the siege and reorganization as Assyria's response.

Historically, the Assyrians' campaign does not seem to be directed against Jerusalem. It is oriented rather towards putting down a rebellion in the coastal town of Ekron and in the Shephelah's town of Lachish. Lachish had been a key to olive production in the Judean highlands, and had apparently been the region's primary threat to Assyrian policies, which supported Jerusalem's control of Judea. When Lachish fell in 701, it was destroyed. Apparently, its entire population was deported. Large bas-reliefs celebrating this victory by illustrating the Assyrian army's destruction and burning of the city once decorated the walls of Sennacherib's palace at Nineveh. Today, these famous reliefs can be seen in the British Museum. Lachish was never rebuilt. Assyria proceeded to annex the coastal towns, including Ekron, and most of the Shephelah. This area was placed under direct Assyrian administration. The primary task of the campaign was to stabilize the region by reorganizing its olive industry. Jerusalem, as an Assyrian client state, was a willing collaborator, and played a major role in this reorganization. Once rid of the competition from Lachish, Jerusalem expanded its hold on the Judean highlands and extended its influence southward into the northern Negev. The integrity of the Judean mountain range lent itself to the funnelling of produce northwards along the watershed to Jerusalem. As the chief market town of a now much expanded region, Jerusalem grew some five-fold in the course of the next half-century.

Simultaneously with the reorganization of olive production through Jerusalem, the Assyrians built up coastal Ekron as their southern provincial producer of olive oil. They installed presses there, with huge storage vats to supply Assyria's overland markets. Like Jerusalem, Ekron saw a half-century period of extraordinary growth. Both Ekron on the coast and Jerusalem in the hills became the dominant economic centres of their regions. With support from Assyria, Jerusalem had finally become the regional capital of Judah. By the mid-seventh century it was a city with some 25,000 people. With its development as an economic and political centre, Jerusalem began to take on cultural and religious functions similar to what Samaria had carried out in the north. It is at least possible that the temple dates from this period. Evidence, however, is wanting. This development may not have occurred before the Persian period.

While the importance of the city of Jerusalem looms large in biblical stories, its actual historical importance in both the politics and the economy of the hill country regions was short-lived. Jerusalem, with a population of about 5,000 people from the mid-ninth to the end of the eighth century, had hardly been in a position to compete with the regionally far more powerful town of Lachish. Certainly, it was Lachish that had dominated the olive industry, which was the primary cash crop of the region. Only after the destruction of rebellious Lachish and the deportation of its population in 701 was Jerusalem allowed to expand and become the regional centre of trade.

The history of the development and importance of Jerusalem up to the time of its destruction early in the sixth century has little common ground with traditional reconstructions of the history of Israel that have been written to date. These have been based primarily on paraphrases of the much later, theologically oriented, biblical traditions. The poetic and literary theme of the success of the unpromising, seen for example in the David and Goliath story, or indeed the story of Jerusalem as a great city and capital of empire, is a motif that runs through the Bible's traditions. Such stories are always attractive. This is not only because audiences are always filled with little people, but also because in the 'real world' such successes are rare. Nevertheless, this dominant motif of the Bible does have historical reality behind it. That reality was harsh and brutal. Stories about the success of the unpromising belong to a form of literature that is the possession of the defeated and the oppressed. It is the unsuccessful who most need to be able to believe in the possibilities of the unpromising. They too dream of changing the world.

The real history behind the story of the loss of old Jerusalem's greatness has its creative centre in the Babylonian empire's expansion southward to confront Egypt, swallowing Jerusalem in half a bite on its way to the Nile. The prosperity of Jerusalem's olive merchants was short-lived. Already by the second half of the seventh century, Assyria's hold on Mesopotamia was destabilized. In 612 BCE, after forming a coalition with Babylon against the Assyrians, the Medes attacked and burnt the Assyrians' capital at Nineveh. While the imperial government survived yet a short while in Harran, Babylon consolidated its power in the east. Taking advantage of this impending transfer of empire, it quickly moved its army into Palestine and southern Syria.

Once the Babylonians, however, were successful in taking Harran, Nebuchadnezzar positioned the Babylonian forces to march against the Egyptians. This was to assert his claim as Assyria's successor. At the battle of Carchemish in the far north in 605 BCE, Nebuchadnezzar defeated Pharaoh Neco. With this victory, southern Syria and all of Palestine became his for the taking. The next few years were committed to the consolidation of the empire by moving against those who had allied themselves, willingly or unwillingly, with the Egyptians. They had gambled and lost. In 597 BCE, Jerusalem surrendered to the Babylonian army. The king and his court were deported, along with the upper strata and skilled craftsmen of the city and Judah's major villages.

The Egyptians did not go away. They continued to put pressure on the states of southern Palestine to resist the Babylonian takeover. In 588, the Babylonian army again marched against Jerusalem. This time the city resisted and was placed under siege. In 586 BCE, Jerusalem fell to the Babylonians. According to the biblical narrative, the city was burnt and its walls were levelled. Following earlier Assyrian policies, the Babylonians deported the population of Jerusalem and its king as well as many of the villages. Through this deportation and the punitive measures used to govern this impoverished and depopulated region over the next decade, the Babylonians destroyed both the state and the society that had been Judah. Like Israel in the eighth century, Judah ceased to exist as an autonomous political reality in Palestine.

That the city was entirely destroyed must be doubted. The parallels with Samaria alone require our reservations. Of the destructions of the three cities of Samaria, Jerusalem and Babylon that Jeremiah describes, for example, none are known to have been destroyed. Contrary to the story in II Kings, Samaria survived its destruction. Babylon was not destroyed at all. According to the legends recorded on Persian monuments, Cyrus entered the city unopposed. We only have stories from the Bible about Jerusalem's fate. The several different traditions relating Jerusalem's fall, its people's fate in exile and their eventual return are inconsistent with each other. The Book of I Esdras (4: 42–46) refers, for example, to the mainline story of Cyrus' promise to rebuild Jerusalem as a promise given by his successor Darius. This narrative similarly speaks of the Edomites as the ones who burned the temple rather than the Babylonians. Jeremiah gives an account of the entire population of Jerusalem going into exile . . . three times! II Kings' story of Jerusalem's total destruction and total deportation is a story that is required both theologically and by the dynamics of a greater story whose subject is the death of 'old Israel', Yahweh's rejection of his covenant, and his promises to David's descendants. The story of the exile to Babylon is a variant of the story of Israel in the wilderness. It tells of transition and change, of repentance and conversion. This is a time of preparation for resurrection and rebirth. It is a time of waiting for the new Jerusalem. The stories of Jerusalem's rebirth and the Bible's stories of the 'new Jerusalem' are best-known from the books of Chronicles and Ezra. They have a close variant in the Book of Nehemiah's story of the rebuilding of Jerusalem. These stories all require an Israel that repents for its sins in its exile in Babylon. They require an empty city when the exiles return. So Chronicles ends and Ezra begins with Cyrus' instructions for the new Jerusalem, and Nehemiah 1–4 finds us with a Jerusalem empty of people. But this very same role of Jerusalem as a wasteland can be played in the Book of Jeremiah's lamentations by a Jerusalem as a spiritual wilderness. Jerusalem becomes a city filled – like Sodom and Gomorrah – with evil people: those who do not know God. They too are in exile, waiting for the repentance that alone leads to conversion to the 'new Israel', and the 'new Jerusalem'.

The historical difficulty is precisely that we cannot get out of this theological context in which the Bible tells its story. We cannot speak of the tradition as historical at all. The Bible isn't interested in telling us anything about the past. It is using old traditions about the past as parables. The historical problems about Jerusalem's fall are not like those about David and Solomon, about Moses and Joshua, or about the patriarchs, where we find ourselves within an entirely fictional world. Rather, in these narratives of Kings, we are talking about real kingdoms and real kings. We are also talking about real war – if not always about real battles. Yet the narration is so unhistorical in both its interests and its goals that we have no way of distinguishing what is historical from the account itself. While reliable history needs confirmation and support from dependable sources, from inscriptions and from records, in this case we shall see that such sources are very hard to come by.

In writing about the historical developments of Palestine between 1250 and 586, all of the traditional answers given for the origins and development of 'Israel' have had to be discarded. The patriarchs of Genesis were not historical. The assertion that 'Israel' was already a people before entering Palestine whether in these stories or in those of Joshua has no historical foundation. No massive military campaign of invading nomadic 'Israelites' ever conquered Palestine. There never was an ethnically distinct 'Canaanite' population whom 'Israelites' displaced. There was no 'period of the Judges' in history. No empire ever ruled a 'united monarchy' from Jerusalem. No ethnically coherent 'Israelite' nation ever existed at all. No political, ethnic or historical bond existed between the state that was called Israel or 'the house of Omri' and the town of Jerusalem and the state of Judah. In history, neither Jerusalem nor Judah ever shared an identity with Israel before the rule of the Hasmoneans in the Hellenistic period.

In short, the only historical Israel to speak of is the people of the small highland state which, having lost its political autonomy in the last quarter of the eighth century, has been consistently ignored by historians and Bible scholars alike. This is the Israel whose people, understanding themselves as 'Israelites', return to the light of history as the same highland farmers they had been for millennia. They are referred to in the stories of Ezra 4 as enemies of Benjamin and Judah. Their offence: they wish to help in the building of a temple to 'the God of Israel' in Jerusalem. They are rejected in the story by Ezra's Jews and given a sectarian identity as 'Samaritans' by historians. This Israel is not the Israel that biblical scholars who write 'histories of Israel' have been interested in. It is not the Israel that we find in our biblical narratives. It is historical Israel.

3 Deportation and return

If such is our historical Israel, then where are we to look for the origins of the biblical 'Israel', the Israel that lies at the centre of biblical tradition? How are we to describe the origins of the presumably distinct people who stand behind this Bible? To answer these questions, we need to address the long-term effects of the imperial resettlement policies that had been introduced so systematically by the Assyrians. These policies began as early as the Assyrian period and continued under both the Babylonian and the Persian empires. They had a very complicated impact on the development of ethnic and national identities within the empire. They also played a decisive role in the growth of ideas about monotheism and about saving 'messiahs'. The metaphors of the restoration of Israel's God in

Jerusalem, the rebuilding of the temple and the return of a repentant remnant from 'exile' – all these images find their origin in such policies. All of these concepts play a vital role in the creation of a 'new Israel', a new 'people of God' centred in Jerusalem.

The success of the costly and complex political policy of population resettlement depended on the imperial administration's ability to develop and transform what had originally begun as a military strategy of regional pacification through social dislocation. It created the empire through relocation, resettlement and reconstruction. Taking rulers and upper classes captive and deporting them to regions in the heart of the empire was useful. It punished rebels and got rid of potential troublemakers. It enabled the governors of new territories to create terror through hostage-taking. It complicated any local successor's claim to legitimacy. At the same time, it put the administration of regions into the hands of local interests who were dependent on the empire for their survival and acceptance. Population resettlement did much more than handle the pacification of newly acquired territories. Undermining the local patrons basic to the political structures of the region, it recreated them as dependencies of Assyria's patronage.

This population resettlement programme was backed by extensive political propaganda. The conquerors of new territories couch surrender in terms of 'liberation', and 'salvation' from former oppressive rulers. Deportation is described as a 'reward' for populations who rebelled against their leaders (so the general's speech in the tale in II Kings 18–19). The people are always 'restored to their homelands'. Such returns involve the 'restoration' of 'lost' and 'forgotten' gods, following long periods of exile. The primary purpose of these policies was always transparent. In order to administer large territories newly conquered or taken over, the empire had to eliminate the possibility of armed resistance, and punish rebellions when they arose. The obvious tactic was to execute leaders and potential leaders of rebellions, but, as permanent as death seems, this was a temporary solution at best. Imperial administrators were fully aware that, at least in their opposition to empire, the local population – and especially the more prosperous who were vulnerable to taxation – supported their leaders. Execute a local king and you still had to deal with his successor, who was as much afraid of his 'subjects' as of the Assyrians, Babylonians or Persians. Taking the ruler captive was useful, as it complicated any successor's claim to legitimacy. It required, however, a willingness to take over the administration of regions whose local interests were hostile to those of the empire.

Except in cases of concerted and prolonged rebellion, mass executions were abhorrent to the self-understanding of the imperial ruler. He was 'shepherd and guardian of justice' for all of his imperial subjects. Large-scale deportation was far preferable, because by destroying the indigenous infrastructure it provided a final solution to rebellion and opposition. It was also preferable because such dislocated individuals and groups could be put to useful ends. As refugees, uprooted from any source of wealth or power except their own individual skills and abilities, they became wholly dependent on the good will and largesse of the empire. Resettled in the great cities of the empire, or in villages and towns of foreign territories, with their survival dependent on their future support of imperial goals, their allegiance to the state was assured. Grateful for the freedom and equality in their new homes, they served as a countervalent force against any local opposition the government faced in its great cities.

Far preferable to the costly use of troops to force compliance, was to gain the willing acceptance and support of those transported. The situation required persuasive interpretation. Here our texts, from as early as the mid-ninth century, are a great help in deciphering the goals and direction of imperial propaganda. In these texts, deportation is not presented as a punishment, so much as an act undertaken on behalf of the people. It promoted their interests and protected them. It saved them from their former rulers who had oppressed and enslaved them. Some early texts present the Assyrian king as the saviour of the people, who, after freeing them from enslavement forced upon them by their rulers, returned them and their gods to the homelands from which they had been exiled. Here, the dislocated peoples were encouraged to think of themselves in terms of restoration rather than punitive deportation: as saved from exile by the will of the king. They became returnees to their homelands, reunited with their lost and forgotten gods.

While the sophisticated reader might think of such propaganda as transparent lies, the propaganda was followed up by action. The deportees received land and a renewal of prosperity from the Assyrians upon resettlement, they were given support and protection against the indigenous population, who naturally viewed them as intruders and usurpers. Both the Babylonians and Persians, as successors to rather than as creators of empire, applied such propaganda to their population policies as a way of bolstering both acceptance and legitimation of their rules among the subject peoples. They could – with far greater likelihood of acceptance – lay claim to roles of liberator. The ultimate purpose was to wipe out regional and national distinctions and create an imperial citizenry that was faithful to the government, subject to and dependent on the empire. Propaganda moved away from the language of threat and terror, in favour of an effort to win support and loyalty. If this struggle for the minds and hearts of the people could be won, infrastructures could be rebuilt to enhance and support a new prosperity.

Two examples clarify these policies. The Babylonian king Nabonidus decided to rebuild the old Assyrian city of Harran and to establish there a temple to the god Sin as a state, imperial religion. He brought many different peoples from Babylon, Syria and Egypt, rebuilt Harran, and spoke of his project as a restoration of their homeland to citizens returned from exile. He renewed their forgotten traditions and brought all of their old gods back to their homes. The god Sin, a new god of a new population, is declared to be the true and original ancient god of the city. This last step was facilitated by identifying this traditional deity of the region with the 'God of Heaven'. The emperor was presented as the restorer of the gods and of the indigenous populations. Similarly, the Persian successor to Nabonidus continued such policies. He portrayed the earlier Babylonian king as the destroyer of religious integrity, responsible for the destruction of proper worship and piety everywhere. In reaction to such evil, Cyrus, himself, is presented as one personally chosen by the gods to restore temples and true religion, a benefactor who returned the scattered peoples to their homelands. This transportation of gods and peoples under the guise of restoration was presented as the primary function of empire. The policy was reiterated in deportation texts under Cyrus' successors, Xerxes, Darius II and Artaxerxes. Policies of systematic deportation had begun as early as the ninth century under the Assyrians. They were continued by the Babylonians and the Persians.

As could be expected, these changing political realities found expression in the religious concepts of the subject peoples affected. Such political propaganda, when successful, was also mirrored by changes in religious world-views, which became increasingly universalist and homogenous. These ideas were combined with the imperial practice of inventing ancestral gods to create religious ties between societies, around regionally localized deities. The deportation practice of 'restoring' long dead gods to their rightful lands easily lent itself to the imperial idea that distinctive regional deities were manifestations of a single transcendent reality. Such ideas came to dominate religious language and metaphor.

Religious concepts and practices were not abandoned. They were adjusted and reinterpreted. Over the centuries these long-standing practices proved successful because they preserved the traditional social and religious fabric of subject peoples, at the same time as providing an acceptable means to accommodate political realties. For resettled populations, regionally distinctive and localized religious beliefs were maintained by identifying gods of comparable functions in one region with those of another. Common elements were stressed and local distinctiveness diminished. Hadad of Syria became identifiable with Ba'al of Phoenicia or Chemosh of Ammon. Ishtar of Babylon was seen as Astarte of Syria–Palestine.

The language of political propaganda helped to change and determine the language of religious metaphor. It played a vital role in the development of ideas that become reflected in the Bible as monotheism, restoration, the self-understanding of having been a people, who had suffered exile, the restoration of a lost god to his temple, and the role of a messiah or saviour acting to carry out the will of their god. This was language intrinsic to empire.

Under the rule of the Persian kings, a number of groups and families were transferred from Mesopotamia and resettled in southern Palestine. A new colony was established in and around Jerusalem. Those resettled were accompanied by traditional political propaganda. The Bible's stories about a return from exile frequently centre on a royal decree from one or other of the Persian kings. Four times stories about a decree of Cyrus offer accounts of the decree itself. These can be found in Isaiah 44–45, II Chronicles 36, Ezra 1 and I Esdras 2. Isaiah's account is given in song celebrating Cyrus as Yahweh's messiah, and I Esdras offers Cyrus' decree in the form of a highly dramatic proclamation by the king inspired by Yahweh. Ezra and Chronicles offer a short paraphrase of I Esdras' narrative. This paraphrase is given as Cyrus' own words in Ezra 1: 2–3:

> Yahweh, the God of Heaven, has given me the kingdoms of the earth, and he has charged me to build him a house in Jerusalem, which is in Judah. Whoever is among you of all his people, may his god be with him, and let him go up to Jerusalem, which is in Judah, and rebuild the house of Yahweh, the God of Israel: he shall be the God who is in Jerusalem.

The content and purpose of the decree in these stories are entirely consistent with early deportation practices. They are also comparable to the historical practices of Cyrus and other Persian kings. The large number of variant stories of return and the attempt to integrate the accounts of carrying out the decree, as are found in Ezra and Nehemiah, have led a number of scholars to suggest that there had been as many as four distinct 'returns' from Babylon: under Cyrus (538), Darius I (521–485), Artaxerxes I (464–423) and Artaxerxes II (404–358). While this explanation of multiple returns is certainly a possible one, the assumption mixes story and history indiscriminately. There is no reason to limit ourselves to these specific periods of resettlement. There is also no reason to limit ourselves to the Persian period. Jerusalem had been subject to practices of population transference since the eighth century, and there is no reason to believe that its experiences were substantially different from those of its northern neighbour Samaria. Cyrus and the Persians play a particular role in the narrative reconstructions of later biblical tradition. As saviours, they brought the people back. They restored their God to them, just as the Assyrians and the Babylonians had played roles of destruction and deportation. But these are roles in story, not history.

Given the number of different and distinct variants of our traditions about the return, reconstruction of the history of this period is not possible. That the texts are moreover dominated by propaganda and by fictively created perspectives prevents us from accepting them as reports of historical events. Much like the traditions relating to the destruction of Jerusalem and the deportations of its population, the stories of return are far more useful for what they imply than for what they say. They imply a religious self-understanding and a self-perception based on a tradition of political propaganda that was created for very anti-historical purposes. What actually happened to the residents of Jerusalem and of Judah that had been resettled elsewhere in the empire by the Assyrians is not specifically known. The fate of the victims of Babylonian deportation policies is equally unknown. We can say that the names of West-Semitic peoples from Palestine and southern Syria appear in large numbers as residents of Assyrian cities. Military colonies with soldiers from Palestine were created in Egypt and elsewhere in the Assyrian period. We know that large 'Jewish' communities were established as far away as Babylon, Alexandria and Rome during the Hellenistic and Greco-Roman periods. That a significant population of deportees and their descendants from various regions formed part of most large cities in antiquity seems to be likely. That they had experienced such deportation as exile, however, is known not to have always been true. The metaphor of exile that we meet so often in the Bible is more a part of the stories of return than of destruction. It is in the return that Judah and Jerusalem become Israel. It is in the return that the 'God of Israel' – historically long established in Samaria – is given a home, a temple, in Jerusalem. It is in the return that the people of Judah came to understand themselves as 'the children of' Israel and as the 'new Israel'.

The history of the transference of peoples from Mesopotamia to Jerusalem and Judea escapes us. We find explicit narratives of the building of Jerusalem and of a temple in Ezra, Nehemiah, I Esdras and Josephus: without much agreement. A letter from Elephantine from the late fifth century refers to a high priest in Jerusalem, and, by implication, a temple. However, that the history of Jerusalem and of Judah from the sixth to the fourth century was dominated by the rebuilding of Jerusalem, and the establishment of a community centred on the temple dedicated to Yahweh, is neither known nor obvious. That is the understanding of the past promulgated by later writings that interpret the past under the perspective of the development of a unified people in relationship to their God. This people was first formed in the repentance and conversion of exile. They understood themselves as part of that people and identified themselves as coming out of exile. But the land and Jerusalem was not empty. Groups transferred to this region from Mesopotamia each and all took up the locally indigenous culture, language and religion. Most came to accept these traditions as their past.

The tradition was hardly monolithic; it had many variations. That of the Samaritans was self-consciously different, returning the people to Samaria.

Yet other traditions like the Damascus Covenant of the Cairo Geniza and the Dead Sea scrolls had quite other stories of return with which people identified, while yet others knew nothing of either exile or return.

4 Palestine under a shifting empire

When Alexander III succeeded to the throne of Macedon in 336 BCE, he began building an army to resist the Persian threat to the Aegean. In the two major battles of Siranicus (334) and Issus (333) in Asia Minor, he defeated the Persian troops under Darius. After consolidating his hold on the Anatolian peninsula, he marched through Syria and Palestine and reached Egypt in 331. He moved his army eastward through Mesopotamia and arrived in India in 326. There his army revolted and stopped him.

The Persian empire was now in the patronage of Greek generals. Expanding on the Assyrian experiment with Aramaic, Alexander consolidated the cities and commerce of the empire by introducing schools and the Greek language into the conquered territories. His purpose was to integrate the Persian empire and to support the development of the Greek form of city. Palestine and Syria were formed into a province, with Samaria as its capital. Palestine now, for the first time, began to develop true cities. Once Alexander's troops took Egypt, he built the city of Alexandria as the intellectual and political centre of his east Mediterranean territories. Continuing imperial policies of deportation, he transported a portion of Samaria's population to form the nucleus of what was later to become an important 'Jewish' centre of learning. To secure his provincial capital against rebellion, he resettled Macedonians in Samaria.

In the traditional histories about the period following Alexander the Great's conquest of the empire, one is used to seeing Judaism described as an already mature religion based on a centuries-long tradition of monotheism that reached back to the time of ancient Israel. Judaism's supposedly unique form of exclusive monotheism is placed on a collision course with a self-assertive polytheistic Hellenism. Such Judaism is also typically portrayed as ethnocentric, provincial and reactionary. It is seen as a cult-centred society that had fanatically resisted the universalism and humanism of the Greeks out of a narrow xenophobia.

It needs to be recognized that many of these modern accounts of early Judaism reflect a Christian apologetic that often saw pre-Christian Judaism as a religion that had lapsed from its former glory as a religiously creative and vibrant prophetic 'Old Testament' Israel, and had turned inward towards a legalistic formalism. Traditionalist and ancient Near Eastern Jewish reactionaries were contrasted with the revolutionary 'new' religion of Christianity, embraced by the universalism and humanism of Europe. In the version concocted by this anti-Jewish rhetoric, Judaism had rejected its own messiah and reverted to a chauvinistic nationalism, while Christianity had embraced Hellenism. Christianity turned Judaism itself into an 'old Israel' rejected by its God. The Judaism of history, however, was something other than that portrayed by such implicit anti-Semitism.

When Alexander's armies overran the Persian empire, and with it Palestine and Egypt, they brought with them teachers and schools as well as architects and craftsmen. As new territories were pacified, they were also transformed and centred in towns that were created in the image of the Greek city. The Greek language, philosophy and art were used to create citizens faithful to their new Greek patrons.

The town culture of Palestine was thoroughly Hellenized. Jews, rather than resisting the Greek world and its philosophy, were among the leaders in the intellectual life of Alexandria, Antioch and Babylon as well as Palestine. Some of the most provincial backwaters of greater Palestine were transformed by the new ideas, art and culture of the empire. This was especially true of the regions and the towns that were related to trade. Just as the Arabs of fabulous Petra created a Greek city and civilization out of the rock cliffs of the Edomite and Sinai deserts, so early Judaism was transformed in its enthusiasm for Hellenistic humanism. The centre of religious concerns shifted away from cult and temple and the formal practices of state-oriented religion, and focused instead on education and on the personal study of literature, philosophy and tradition. Far from entailing an intrinsic conflict between an indigenous and local Hebrew or 'Semitic' culture and a universal Hellenistic one, the Jewish culture that developed was an Asiatic form of Hellenism, a culture which ranged from Babylon to Rome and had developed from the imperial world-views of the Babylonian and Persian periods. Both Hebrew- and Greek-language collections of Jewish literature developed. Both were systematically structured along the classical imperial form of a universal chronology, ordering tradition in the form of universal history from the beginning of time to the present. The Jews also created school traditions that were centred in systems of commentary and discussion and whose copying and transmission were secured in a variant of a Hellenistic type. It achieved a moral and philosophical quality akin to the Greek traditions centred on Homer and Plato.

After Alexander died, Palestine reverted to its old role of land-bridge between Egypt and Asia. It became disputed territory between Alexander's successors: on one hand the Ptolemies of Egypt, centred in Alexandria, and on the other the Seleucids of Antioch and Babylon. The Ptolemies were able to assert control over Palestine for most of the third century. They integrated Palestine's towns and cities intellectually and culturally with Egypt. Jerusalem in particular leaned towards the Ptolemaic political sector, while the competitive Sebaste (= Samaria) developed alliances with the Seleucids in the north.

In the second century, the situation changed dramatically. After defeating the Ptolemies in 198 BCE, the Seleucids took over the governance of Palestine. In their efforts to include this newly conquered province under Antioch's central administration, the Seleucids systematically set out to destroy what remained of the Palestinian-Egyptian axis. Certainly relations turned bitter, and the Seleucids acquired a harsh reputation, however deserved, for their policies in governing the southern region of Palestine. But after the battle of Magnesia (190 BCE), where the Seleucids were defeated by the Romans, their hold on Palestine weakened considerably. Egypt took advantage of this and sought to reassert its interests in Jerusalem.

What began as a pro-Ptolemaic rebellion in Judea over control of the selection of the high priest has been seen as creating an anti-Seleucid and anti-Hellenistic nationalist movement. The Maccabean rebellion is credited with a significant development: the political independence of Jerusalem from the Seleucid empire. The Seleucids' anti-Egyptian policy apparently first came to a crisis when Antiochus IV insisted that Hellenistic Judaism in Palestine follow the Hellenistic model of Antioch rather than that of Alexandria. He is said to have sent a punitive expedition to Jerusalem to arrest its pro-Egyptian sympathizers. This threw Jerusalem into the arms of the Maccabees. For some years, they had been leading a pro-Egyptian rebellion which encouraged local religious cults and a less centralized form of Hellenism. Antiochus IV reacted to Jerusalem's resistance by banning all religious practices not in line with Antioch's. His actions were seen as suppressive of what were understood by the rebels as the particularly Jewish practices of circumcision and sabbath observance. The Maccabees went on to encourage a rebellion with nationalistically motivated, anti-Seleucid violence. This was presented in the tradition as an effort to save true custom and religion from the foreign and pagan, polytheistic Greeks. Revolt against the Seleucid empire was licensed as patriotic. Although likely to have been originally instigated independently by the Egyptians in Alexandria, the Maccabean revolt's most important and most faithful supporters were Egypt's Roman allies, who had been expanding their interests eastward to strengthen their hold on Mediterranean shipping after their defeat of the Phoenicians of Carthage. It was probably with Rome's most important geopolitical blessing that the Maccabees were able to turn Antiochus' punitive visit to Jerusalem into a cause that later tradition could identify as one of national liberation. The first indigenous state over this region was created in 165 BCE. However, it still lacked definition. It was not a nation. The Maccabees neither controlled Palestine, nor were they really independent of Rome's patronage.

Until war broke out between Antiochus IV and the rebels in 167, the Hellenistic empire, and Hellenism generally, had not been antagonistic to local regional traditions of religious piety and belief. Quite the contrary. The Macedonians, like their Persian predecessors in empire, shared the universalist concepts of humanity, and a basic belief in the ultimately spiritual reality of the divine. This world-view supported considerable tolerance for a wide variety of religious forms and expressions, perceiving them simply as particular regional and local forms of a common belief. This belief was universalist if not entirely monotheist.

An essentially political and geographically based competition for dominance over Palestine was given its religious and cultural dimensions by those who wrote as much as two centuries later. Josephus himself writes after Jerusalem had been destroyed by the Romans, at a time when the meaning of his religious tradition was under drastic revision. He drew on and strengthened those aspects of tradition and belief that saw the core of the tradition as unique and as antagonistic to foreign oppression. Here, certainly, Antiochus fell victim to propaganda. All that was Greek was easily identified with what was oppressive. The Maccabees were given a political identity that was defined in terms of loyalty to Palestine's local deity, Yahweh. This has galvanized and altered our understanding of Jewish monotheism as an exclusive worship of the one and only true God. Jerusalem is presented as claiming not only hegemony, but exclusivity. It was in this context of 'Talibanism', reflected in the formation of the traditions in the Books of Maccabees, that the major collections of the Hebrew Bible took their definitive shape.

CHAPTER 9

Historians create history

1 The historical David and the problem of eternity

The historical discussion today about the role and nature of the tenth
century in the history of Palestine is a close variant on the old question that
teachers of philosophy put to their students, about whether there is a
sound of trees falling in the woods when there is no one to hear it. Our
biggest problem with writing the history of the tenth century is that one
doesn't write history without evidence. This century of Palestine's history
is as silent about Jerusalem and monarchies as was Yahweh's voice when he
passed before the prophet Elijah at Horeb. Once we look quite clearly at
the completeness of our ignorance on such matters, we are all the better
prepared to state what we have evidence for and do know about Palestine's
early history.

This chapter will try to address the question of historicity directly. It
takes up two problems: that of the tenth century and the 'United
Monarchy' on one hand, and that of the exile and return on the other. For
the one we have too little evidence; for the other too much. We have
discussed both of these issues in our sketch of various pivotal periods of
Palestine's history. In this chapter, we will consider them by asking how
much we can use the biblical stories to help us write a history of Palestine.
To what extent do the biblical legends deal with an historical past? Do they
give us evidence that we can use in our own reconstructions of the past?

Unlike the problems of historicity of some of the traditions we have
already discussed, that of the United Monarchy and of the tenth century
(including the reigns of Saul, David and Solomon over a united Palestine)
is not directly tied to efforts to claim that the wonderful stories about these
kings and their rise to power were in fact histories. That claim has
frequently been made, of course, but it does not take a central place in the
discussion of historicity. The dominant literary beauty and strength of
these stories has always been recognized. That they reflected history has
been assumed as necessary, though never argued. It is thought necessary to

the establishment of Israel as a nation, embracing both the Iron Age highland states of Judah and Israel. It is also often thought to be implied in the existence of a Davidic dynasty, as well as in the stories of exile and return.

In fact, arguments for the history of other periods – from the time of the patriarchs to the period of the judges – have usually taken the period of the United Monarchy as the destination of their role as origin accounts. It has been as the origin of an Israel of the United Monarchy with its capital in Jerusalem that such origin stories were understood to have meaning. Even in very recent histories of Israel, the United Monarchy has served as a kind of historical watershed within the biblical account. What came before it is often described as prehistory and folklore. From Saul on, however, we are thought to be so close to historical realities that even critical historians have been quite satisfied to offer a paraphrase of the Bible's tale.

Certainly we are dealing with some of the Bible's and even the world's greatest stories, so vivid that their very clarity and brilliance have been interpreted as a mark of their closeness to the events they recount, to what scholars liked to think of as this very golden age's genius for history-writing. Already in the nineteenth century, much of the Bible's narrative tradition was thought to have been written during four different periods: the tenth–ninth centuries, the eighth century, the seventh century and the sixth–fifth centuries. The stories of David's rise to power and the succession narratives were placed among the earliest of such traditions. Following nineteenth-century principles of evidence, eye-witness or near-contemporary accounts were understood to possess greater value as evidence for historical events than secondary or derivative sources. These stories were often even described as having been written within the court of David himself. Once contemporaneity with the 'events' recounted could be claimed, and in fact was claimed, often and repeatedly, one needed only to see them as plausible to accept them as history.

Some arguments have not even aimed to be plausible. The association of the Bible with religious faith has often been understood by biblical scholars to give warrant to the emptiest of propositions. Only a few years ago, the author of some of the Pentateuch's earliest tales – a writer fabricated by the nineteenth century, and known to scholars as 'J' – was identified as a woman of David's immediate family. The novelty of this assertion was sufficient to win the approval of much of the popular press. Even some scholars accepted this fiction on the sheer merits of the beautiful and commanding rhetoric in which it was couched.

While such an argument had only its originality to recommend it, others, equally vacuous, have been put forward on the grounds of scholarly authority. In this manner, the legendary stories of Solomon's fabulous wealth have been claimed not to be so legendary after all. For at least some, the Bible's accounts become believable as history because the narratives describe a Croesus-like Solomon in a manner reminiscent of the way the kings of great states like Egypt, Assyria and Babylon liked to describe themselves. Among such accounts of great wealth is Esarhaddon's grandiose claim of having layered gold 'like plaster' on his palace walls. Flights of fantasy hardly ever make good history. Having been a plasterer, I find the Assyrian metaphor powerful, yet I might be left to doubt that even so great a king as Esarhaddon layered gold that way in history. There is no quibbling here: we need to keep the fantasy and the miracles in the stories! What we are dealing with is not evidence of 'ancient practices' at all, but only an example of an ancient literary motif that finds its way into tales from Homer to Scheherazade. That an Assyrian king should use such a motif to give himself heroic proportions is hardly a surprisingly new form of political advertisement. The Bible's stories of Solomon's great wealth are like the stories of his wisdom. Having composed three thousand proverbs, like his Arabian successor with her thousand and one stories, Solomon – outdoing David – 'sang songs, a thousand and five' (I Kings 4: 32).

Another, and far less foolish, claim for historicity was put forward a generation ago by archaeologists. The original argument was simple and its confirmation dramatic. I Kings 9: 15's brief description of Solomon building fortification walls for the towns of Jerusalem, Hazor, Megiddo and Gezer was linked to a gateway and fortification excavated at the ancient site of Hazor in the eastern Galilee. A near-contemporary gate had been excavated at Megiddo. This was not only built to a very similar architectural design, its huge stone blocks had been cut with the very same technique. While nothing of this period had been found in Jerusalem, the site of Gezer was excavated by the British early in the century. Half of a very similar gate with comparable measurements had been found at the site. It had, however, gone unnoticed because it had been connected by mistake with a building belonging to the Hellenistic period. In 1966, the excavators at Gezer decided to excavate the missing second half of Gezer's gate. The present author was a junior member of the archaeological team that found this structure at Gezer in the 'spring dig' of 1967. Although great effort was concentrated in finding this gate and identifying it with those at Megiddo and Hazor, it was already obvious before we broke ground, that this was a 'Solomonic gate' and contemporary with other 'Solomonic gates' at Megiddo and Hazor. The form and measurements of the gate confirmed this. The associated cities and stratigraphic chronologies of three major sites were quickly and disastrously adjusted on the basis of what were now considered 'historically confirmed' passages of the Bible. This supposed confirmation of the historicity of Solomon's building activities not only affected our understanding and dating of these sites, it also led many historians and archaeologists to affirm the cultural, material and political greatness of a 'United Monarchy'.

This fabrication began to come apart when Israeli teams uncovered yet other similar gates at the non-Israelite site of Ashdod and at the site of Lachish in the southern Shephelah. The excavators dated these a full century later, and attributed them to an entirely different archaeological period from the gates of Hazor, Megiddo and Gezer. In a few short years, the Solomonic gates became 'so-called Solomonic gates'. As more and more information accumulated, historians began the process of downgrading Saul, David and Solomon's kingdom and empire to a 'chieftainship'. While the issue of the dating of these gates, and of 'monumental' architecture attributed to tenth-century Palestine, or then again more likely to the ninth century, continues to be debated by field archaeologists, it has become clear that we are lacking any really usable chronology for the period.

In the summer of 1993, a fragment of a stele with an inscription was found at the site of Tel Dan in northern Palestine. Among other things, the text referred to a 'king of Israel'. It also bore the letters '. . . *k bytdwd*'. This was quickly read as *melek byt.dwd* and translated '[Kin]g of the House of David'. It was interpreted in the sense of 'king of the dynasty of David'. The inscription was dated to the early ninth century BCE. It was thought to recount a battle that was described in I Kings 15: 16–20, an 'event' dated to the year 883 BCE. Not only was this new inscription the earliest known reference to a king of Israel, however unnamed, it was also claimed to provide conclusive evidence that the biblical David had once existed and had been the founder of the ruling monarchy of Judah in Jerusalem. Scholarly journals as well as popular newspapers and magazines celebrated this discovery with great enthusiasm.

However, there were problems with the discovery – with the reading of the text, its dating and interpretation – and these problems have not yet been resolved. The difficulties were obvious to many as soon as a good photograph of the text was published. Some were typical of most new finds, especially those that are met with great fanfare and enthusiasm. Inconsistent descriptions appeared of how and where the text had been found, whereas to some the dating of the archaeological context seemed optimistically early; others suggested that the form of writing should be dated a century or more later than had originally been proposed, perhaps even to the late eighth or early seventh century. To read . . . *k* as *mlk* = 'king' was just guesswork, of course. Nothing in the inscription itself required that the word or name *bytdwd* be directly linked to Jerusalem and to Judah. It might well refer to a place much closer to Tel Dan.

As in many place names, the first part of this name, *byt*, can be translated as 'House', and reflects the patronate that rules the town. Also commonly – especially when *byt* has been joined to the name or epithet of a god or goddess – it can be translated 'temple'. This is found among place names in Palestine such as Bethel ('The Temple of El') and *beyt dagon* ('the temple of Dagon') of the Samson story.

The second part of the name in the Tel Dan inscription is *dwd*. This is certainly the way the name of the biblical hero David would be spelled in early Hebrew writing. However, 'David' is very unusual as a name. It is used as a personal name in the Bible only for our particular hero. It also occurs as the epithet for a deity (*dwd/dwdh*) in at least one other eighth-century inscription, the famous Mesha Stele from Transjordan. *Dwd* is not the name of a god, but it could be a divine title and be translated 'the Beloved', which has echoes in many biblical metaphors. In the Mesha Stele, it seems to be used as a divine title for Yahweh, the ancient deity of Palestine and the name of God in the Bible. This has led some to suggest that the name *bytdwd* of Tel Dan's inscription possibly referred to a place called 'Temple of Dwd', which might have been located somewhere near Tel Dan in northern Palestine. If we were to understand it in the sense of the 'dynasty of *dwd*', the inscription would give evidence of a 'House of David' that existed at the time of the inscription. It tells us nothing, as such, of a person David as the founder of that patronate in an earlier period.

However, even this gloss reads the text too much in the light of popular ideas about the Bible. When we look at the way the words 'House of David' are actually used in the Bible, understanding it as a reference to an historical David becomes very difficult. The Bible does not use the term 'House of David', in the way the British use a similar term, 'The House of Stuart' – that is, with the specific meaning of 'dynasty'. In the Bible, the terms 'House of Saul' and 'House of David', are often used to refer to the patronage of the hero himself while he is still alive (e.g., I Sam. 24–26). Moreover, we also find such terms as the 'House of Jonathan', though we have no story of Jonathan as the head of any state. The term 'House of David' in the Bible captures the narrative metaphor of patronage. It refers to all who belong to such and such a leader: what in Corsica and Sicily until modern times was spoken of as 'the family' and in ancient Israel as *byt 'b* ('patronate', literally: 'father's house'). This fictive language of family – 'brother', 'son', 'father', 'servant', 'cousin', etc. – uses terms borrowed from language reflecting personal commitment and trust. It is used to express various forms of commitment, agreement and allegiance. In this way, for instance, David is referred to in the biblical story as the 'son' of Saul, and as the 'brother' of Jonathan. Saul is described as David's 'father'. In the Bible's stories about the United Monarchy, the 'House of David' and the 'House [that is, 'Temple'] of Yahweh' are very closely linked. The real head and founder of the 'House of David', in fact, is Yahweh. The 'House of David' that is eternal is no dynasty of a person called David, but rather the temple of Yahweh in Jerusalem. That is, *byt.dwd*: the 'Temple of the beloved'. David is an eponymous hero. In the origin story of the temple's founding, the role of David gives expression to the confidence, and to the hopes and promises, that the people of a much later Jerusalem attached to their temple.

As further fragments of the inscription or of related inscriptions were published, confirmation of the original reading has become even more elusive. While I have become convinced that the published fragments in fact belong not to one but to two different, related inscriptions, other scholars have found indications that have led them to argue that the inscriptions are forgeries. At present this issue is unresolved and awaits an investigation of the Israel Department of Antiquities.

As long as we had no independent history of Palestine, there was precious little on which we could base a history of Israel except ignorance. For some, there has been an incentive to believe the stories of the United Monarchy as historical. Historical completeness and coherence needed them, after all. States of Israel and Judah certainly existed in ancient Palestine. The Bible's story of Saul, David and Solomon seemed to be a necessary story of their origin. This kind of argument concerning biblical characters has often been used, not only about David, but about Moses and about Adam and Eve as well. One might always argue that if they hadn't existed, we would have to invent them. The argument does not rest on logic – the patronates of the highlands, the religion implicit in the Bible and the human race must all have had founders! It rests rather on the romantic expectations we have of history. All great institutions need great origins. Unless, of course, we introduce the proverb that great oaks from little acorns grow. If ever there was an example of a story accepted as history because we needed it, the complex story of David provides it. If there had been no United Monarchy, there could not have been an historical Israel as the Bible understands it. The very idea of a history of Israel presupposes the United Monarchy's existence. But this is also to say that if there was no United Monarchy, then our understanding of the Bible has to change.

Perhaps we could critically revise our understanding of what Saul's reign was really like, or whether David was as great as the stories make him out to be. We might ask whether we should think of them as chieftains rather than as kings. Perhaps we might question whether Solomon really constructed his temple in Jerusalem. Perhaps he only remodelled it, or was otherwise associated with it. Perhaps it was not Jerusalem but another city whose temple was important in history. Many have made efforts to change our stories to tempt us to believe them all the more. To doubt that the Bible is talking about history, is to question the entire enterprise of biblical archaeology.

The question today is whether the Bible in its stories is talking about the past at all. The Bible does not exaggerate the exploits of David. The issue is not that Solomon was never as rich as the stories make him out to have been. We aren't dealing with issues of scepticism. In fact, scepticism has little place in the discussion, and is often misleading. The point to grasp is that the Bible's stories of Saul, David and Solomon aren't about history at all, and that to treat them as if they were history is to misunderstand them.

If one were to write a history of ancient Palestine for the period in which biblical scholars like to place Saul, David and Solomon, one would give an entirely different picture from that presented by the Bible. This is not because 'the Bible is wrong', but because the Bible is not history. To compare the Bible's stories about David with early Iron Age Palestine is like comparing the story of Gilgamesh with Bronze Age Uruk, Achilles with ancient Mycenae or Arthur with early medieval England. It is not only that one lacks evidence for understanding these stories as accurate accounts of the nation's past. Stories and history have always dealt with quite different kinds of worlds. That is as true of ancient stories as it is of modern ones. Whether we are dealing with Homer, the Bible or medieval epic, the quest for an historical heroic age must disappoint its hopes. Not only has such a period of romance always been cast in a time before history begins, but their characteristics of authenticity and appropriateness to a given (later) culture mark these traditions as fictional. Fiction is the clear creation of the bearers of tradition. It captures the hearts as well as the minds of its readers. It educates the emotions, and it creates its own world according to its own rules.

In the history of Palestine that we have presented in this book, I have argued that there is no room for an historical United Monarchy, or for such kings as those presented in the biblical stories of Saul, David and Solomon. The early period in which the traditions have set their narratives is an imaginary world of long ago. It never existed as such. In the real world of our chronology, only a few dozen very small scattered hamlets and villages supported farmers in all of the Judean highlands. Altogether, they numbered hardly more than two thousand persons. Timber, grazing lands and steppe were all marginal possibilities. There could not have been a kingdom for any Saul or David to be king of, simply because there were not enough people. Not only did a state of Judah not yet exist, we have no evidence of there having been any political force anywhere in Palestine that was large enough or developed enough to have been capable of unifying the many economies and regions of this land. At this time, Palestine was far less unified than it had been for more than a thousand years. Jerusalem of the tenth century can hardly be spoken of historically. If it existed at all – and years of excavation have found no trace of a tenth-century town – it was still centuries from having the capacity of challenging any of the dozens of more powerful autonomous towns of Palestine. It would have to compete politically and economically for control of the highland forests and pastures of Judah, which had larger and far better-located towns, especially Lachish in the southern foothills. Of the several, largely isolated hill country regions, only the central hills that lay between Jerusalem and the Jezreel valley formed a coherent unit. In the early Iron Age, this region had only been able to organize a pyramiding political structure of small highland patronates. These did not develop the complexity of a small-state structure, holding and controlling the best part of this region, for at least two and a half centuries later than the time to which David is wishfully dated.

Jerusalem had been a small market town that dominated the Ayyalon valley throughout most of the Bronze Age. Its relationship to Judah was marginal. It first took on the form and acquired the status of a city, capable of being understood as a state capital, some time in the middle of the seventh century. Following the fall of Lachish, Jerusalem was able to extend its financial interests into the southern highlands, and to imperially dominate most of Judah, as it took on the role of an Assyrian vassal state on the fringe of empire. In this role, its primary function was as a market for the Judean olive-growers. It funnelled this valuable produce to the Assyrian processing centres especially at Ekron on the Palestinian coast. This hardly provided Jerusalem with a position of anything that might be described as dominance in Palestine. Only Shechem and Hazor, located in highland plains of extraordinary fertility, were able to establish controlling centres in Palestine's hills. Dominance normally belonged to the towns of the lowlands and coastal plains: towns such as Gaza, Ashqelon, Jaffa, Akko, Megiddo, Taanach, Beth Shan, Dan, Arad, Beersheva and Jericho. Jerusalem was unable to maintain its expanded role – one in which its population increased to nearly 25,000 persons – for more than a half century. By the early sixth century, the city had already lost its autonomy. Its king had been deported and its population was being restructured by the Babylonians.

While it is difficult to estimate the degree of Jerusalem's destruction and recovery from this disaster, revival in the Persian period seems to have been slow, and prosperity modest at best. During the early Hellenistic period it was Samaria, not Jerusalem, among the highland centres, that received settlers from Macedonia. And it was Samaria that was the dominant town of the hill country at least until the second quarter of the second century BCE, when Jerusalem went over to the Maccabean rebels and supported their successful revolt against Antiochus IV. It is during this next century, prior to Pompey's conquest of the region for Rome, that Jerusalem was finally able to establish itself – for the first time in history – as both religious and political centre for nearly the whole of Palestine. Many have found both David and Josiah reflected in the image of John Hyrcanus, one of the Hasmonean kings of this period. Surely our philosopher king Solomon is a Hebrew-speaking Alexander.

The stories of the golden age of the United Monarchy reflect the fantasy and ambitions of Jerusalem of the Maccabees. The image of this single kingdom ruled from Jerusalem hardly goes back in history any earlier than this period when the drama of the eternal Davidic dynasty and its forty kings first had an audience to play to. There is no doubt that the stories of the United Monarchy offer us an origin myth of the ill-fated state of Israel past, which ended in destruction and deportation at the hands of the Assyrians and Babylonians. There is also little doubt that Palestine's early relationship with the Assyrian, Babylonian and Persian empires, as well as details of the regnal history of both Samaria and Jerusalem, have provided the framework for this politically and theologically motivated account of Samaria's and Jerusalem's fall from grace, which we find in the books of Samuel and Kings. It is the story in I Kings 11 – the story of Solomon's acceptance of the foreign gods of his 700 wives and 300 concubines – that offers an explanation as to why gods such as Astarte, Chemosh and Moloch were still worshipped in Palestine. It also gives us a clear theological foundation for the shift of II Kings' story plot from the golden age of David's glory and of divine protection, to a period of Jerusalem's diminished status and judgement.

The parallel story in II Chronicles 9–10 maintains an idyllic version of Solomon's reign, even to the point of arguing explicitly that Solomon's wife, the pharaoh's daughter, did not desecrate the temple (II Chronicles 8: 11). Rather, Solomon's empire, stretching from Egypt to the Euphrates (including the great Syrian trade centres of Hamath and Palmyra), was not only just as great and glorious as David's; it was this 'United Monarchy' as such that offered the ideal picture of the 'true Israel'. The 'fall from grace' in this variant of II Kings was the sole property of the northern kingdom for Chronicles. For the author of this variant collection of the tradition, it was this Israel that was a false Israel, and evil. Judah became the remnant of Israel's golden age, as the 'new Israel' becomes 'all Israel'. Divine judgement is described as coming upon the state according to the goodness of each of its kings. Also unlike II Kings, the Chronicles variant does not end with Jerusalem's destruction, nor with the exile of Jerusalem's people. Rather, this variant account ends by looking forward to the restoration of both temple and people under Cyrus. Unlike the story of II Kings, David and Solomon's temple is to be reborn in Chronicles. In this closure of Chronicles and in its linkage to Ezra, we see the whole of the story in terms of God restoring the lost glory of Israel.

It is also in this story – as in II Kings' portrayal of Jeroboam and Ahab as evil kings – that one finds the narrative's real historical referent: not in a far distant past, but in the author's immediate past and present. The north's abandonment of the house of David in Chronicles mirrors the Seleucids' rejection of the true successors of Alexander: Egypt's Ptolemies. It was Antiochus IV of Syria who was the Ahab of history. He brought false gods to Israel: he desecrated the people's true allegiance to Yahweh. Finally, it is in the rededication of Jerusalem's temple in 164 BCE that

Yahweh returns to 'dwell' in Israel. This is the turning-point reflected in the Chronicles' story, wherein the promise to the House of David finds its renewal in the actions of Yahweh's servant and messiah, the ancient Persian king of fame and legend: Cyrus. It is to just this larger political world of history and independence in the Hellenistic world of the second half of the second century BCE that the national epics of Samuel–Kings and Chronicles were addressed.

The relationship between traditional narratives, of the kind that we have in the Bible, and history is a very complicated one. Reasonableness or plausibility, or any argument that attempts to show that an event in a story was possible, does little to distinguish ancient stories from ancient fiction. Nor does it do to use the occurrence of miracles and divine acts as criteria of the obviously fictional. The wonder of divine action is, after all, the very reason that many of these narratives were written and preserved. Moreover, to the extent that history was understood in the ancient Near East, the world of the narrator has always been understood to have been something created by God – including the historical events that brought about the present. Finally, the understanding of event and time in the Bible's traditions is quite different from what we often assume about them. The interests of both writers of history and collectors of traditions past are centred in the time and events of the author's present. This can hardly be otherwise. These writers were trying to express what they understood about their world and what they understood to be the traditions from the past that were available to them. More than that, the writers of our Bible were hardly passing on a tradition that already existed as finished. They were transmitting, shaping and creating a tradition as they preserved it. They did this in the manner and in the style with which they were familiar and which made sense to them.

The stories, for instance, of the building of the temple by David or Solomon, Cyrus or Nehemiah (and the mirroring of these stories in the ark and tent of the wilderness wanderings and in the altars built by the patriarchs), were narratives that established a pattern of fitness and propriety surrounding the restoration of temple services in 164 BCE. Just as the great leaders of Israel's past had built a home for Yahweh so that he would live in Israel, so the writers of the tradition wished to understand the temple's rededication under the Hasmoneans as the means through which God was present to them. Similarly, the acts of 'desecration and blasphemy' of an Antiochus IV were understood to have been the same crime: whether committed by Solomon for his wives, by Aaron and the wilderness generation, by Jeroboam and the false shrines of Bethel and Dan, or by the much later and contemporary Samaritans. It is theme not event that was central to tradition-building. The tradition is not a linear series of events or periods associated through patterns of cause and effect, the way our school textbooks have taught us history ought to be. The traditions rather presented recurrent patterns of relationships, offering the reader instruction. The great themes of being Yahweh's people and of Yahweh being Israel's God, of understanding God as a God of mercy and forgiveness and of remembering that the true Israel, the true philosopher who seeks self-understanding, and the truly pious who sees his life's meaning in the study of the *torah*, is none other than one who listens to the lessons of tradition – these issues are what the Bible is about. It is not about the past.

Multiple revelations of the *torah*, whether by Ezra or Moses, and whether at the mountain of God, at Horeb and Sinai, at Kadesh or in a chance discovery in the temple, all reflect the many ways that God is with us. We have variant tales and motifs – common enough to folk-tale scholarship, but intolerable to historical reconstruction. We have three stories of Jerusalem's conquest, only the best of them being that under David's leadership. We have two giant-killers, responsible for Goliath's death. Even worse for historicism: we have different Sauls and different Davids and different Solomons. However, such variations enrich the tradition rather than embarrass it. Which ten commandments story can we dismiss without loss? Which of the flood stories, which crossing of the sea? Or is it Elijah and Elisha's, or Joshua's crossing of the Jordan that we can do without?

It is only as history that the Bible does not make sense. Although many traditions appear incompatible or unacceptable when these ancient narratives are mistaken for history, when they are understood as the stories they are, they awake echoes of each other. They create a thematic whole.

2 The exiles: historical sources

Apart from the traditions of Israel's origins, there are two great defining story periods that have influenced the Bible's perception of old Israel and formed its description of the past. The period of the 'United Monarchy' was a great golden age, comparable in many ways to Arthur's early England. It was centred in the figure of David, the heroic and eponymous ancestor and founder of Jerusalem's House of David. This, much like the House of Omri in Samaria, was the historical name of Jerusalem's patronate. This 'House of the Beloved' not only evoked the temple as the centre of old Israel's story, it found in the stories about David a fictional representation of Yahweh's eternal rule over his people from Zion, his holy mountain. This was the tradition of Israel past, of Israel lost.

The other tradition centres on the 'exile and return', which is a defining origin story of a 'new Israel'. This origin story is equally legendary. Following the legendary motifs of the phoenix, the exile carries us through the death of the old Israel to the resurrection of the new. It is through the motifs of dying and rebirth that the stories take on their substance in the Bible's vision of the past. Critical histories of this period have largely failed. Evidence for the history of this period – beginning with the fall of Jerusalem in 586 – is much like our evidence for the tenth century. Its historical trees have fallen unheeded, and we know little of them.

The common imperial policy in the ancient Near East of population transference was first of all a policy of 'pacification'. It was a military strategy that has been used by armies throughout history. Armies change and transform the societies of the regions they enter. Such changes are rarely if ever undone. While generals crush opposition and resistance to their occupying armies as a matter of course, there are considerable variations in the efficiency with which this is done. The variance is often not best explained by the simple brutality or compassion of those issuing orders. Other factors often play a more important role. Some of the factors that played a role in the policies of Assyria's generals were: the safety, morale and discipline of their troops; creating fear and terror within the conquered territories, wherever the army's hold on a region suffered resistance; destroying the integrity of the indigenous society and leadership that showed itself resistant or potentially resistant to Assyrian policy; reducing hatred of the occupying forces by presenting the army as agents of positive change; creating dependency and loyalty to the imperial administration; fulfilling short- and long-range plans to integrate the territory into the imperial administration: rebuilding the social fabric of the territories wherever destroyed, supplying the needs of other regions of the empire; supplying the expansive demands of the army itself for new troops; creating economic monopolies of skilled tradesmen in Assyria's cities; and finally maintaining support for war at home by satisfying needs of the cities for cheap labour and profits.

Important to a successful outcome of these truly complex policies was the behaviour and attitude of the people who came under the control of the army. The massive population transference involved in such policies of deportation was an ancient war crime, condemned and criticized long before the poems of the Book of Amos were written. This 'pacification' of the countryside had been a practice of armies since at least Egypt's Old Kingdom in the Early Bronze Age. Cyrus was hardly the first imperialist who learned that his purposes could be achieved even more effectively if he could change the understanding of those he conquered. Loyalties could be created through indoctrination: through propaganda. Arguments were developed to persuade people to accept what was being done to them. Whenever possible they should welcome it. Combining propaganda with terror proved doubly effective. The execution of 'past oppressors' and 'enemies of the people' was infinitely more productive than doing away with the leaders of the people and the enemies of Assyria. Policies were created to alienate people from their rulers. Combined with selective executions, as implicit warnings of the consequences of disobedience, such reinterpretation of reality was profoundly effective in creating loyalties. The frequent use of enslavement, the threat of starvation and the separation of families effectively silenced the voices of independent thought.

Ancient siege warfare lent itself readily to this kind of psychological war. Carrots could be offered: the promise of food and water, plans for reuniting families that had been separated, the prospect of land and hopes of a new life. These all created believers in a new past. The habitual self-presentation of the conquering army as an army of liberation, whose generals became near-cosmic saviours – hardly modern – is also a constant feature of imperial propaganda.

We saw how the Pharaoh Ahmose in the sixteenth century BCE had cast himself in this role of saviour, as he drove the 'hated' Hyksos from Egypt. He described them as foreigners who had shamelessly oppressed the people. Centuries later, an Assyrian general, conquering a village in the Lebanon (an area not previously visited by the Assyrian army), presented himself as the liberator of the village, when he destroyed the 'brutal thief' (that is, the former village chief) who had oppressed them for so long. This same general deported the entire population of another town, while telling the people that he was returning them to their 'original home', the 'original lands', from which long ago they had been uprooted by their oppressors. The Babylonians had rebuilt the formerly great Assyrian trading centre of Harran in northern Mesopotamia. We also saw the dedicatory inscription in which the Babylonian king explains to the people that Sin, the ancient god of Harran, had ordered him to restore the god to his house in Harran, and to return the people to their homes and to their true worship, which the (former) Assyrian administration had allowed to go to ruin. The people who are intended to understand themselves as 'returned' were in fact deportees from Arabia, Elam (i.e., Afghanistan) and Egypt. When in their turn the Babylonians were defeated, they were subject to the same propaganda at the hands of the Persians, when they were accused of having abandoned 'right religion' and of having allowed the gods and the temples to go to ruin. In fact, the anger among the gods which this neglect of religion had created is given as the reason for the Babylonians' defeat. The new Persian emperor, Cyrus, puts himself forward as the protector of traditional religion throughout the empire. He is the liberator of those who had been enslaved by the Babylonians. Even Babylon itself is described as having opened its gates to his army and having welcomed his arrival. Not only the Bible's Yahweh but other gods appeared to Cyrus to give him instructions concerning their peoples. They ordered him – who as conquering king of kings presents himself in the humble role of servant of the gods – to restore people to their homelands, rebuild the homes (temples) of the gods, and re-establish the societies that the Babylonians had left in ruins. This is the language of propaganda, the language of deportation and population transference. People were uprooted and, with all the goods they had in the world on their backs, they were forced to move thousands of miles to a land in which they had never been. These were the circumstances in which those who had 'returned' from exile to their ancient 'home' in Jerusalem came to understand themselves.

The Bible and related traditions associate Israel and Judah with imperial policies of massive population transference more than a dozen different times. Some of these transports have also been confirmed by extra-biblical records. The first three occurred at the hands of the Assyrians. In his campaign of 733–732, Tiglath Pileser deports people from several towns in northern Palestine in connection with his conquest of Damascus. These towns, including Hazor, are understood in the biblical narratives to belong to Israel, but also involve regions in the Galilee and Gilead. In 722, the Assyrians under Shalmaneser took Samaria. In transforming the region into a province, they transferred people from the region to Assyria: to 'Halah on the Habur, the valley of Gozan and to the cities of the Medes'. They also transferred peoples into the region, including populations from Hamath and Babylon (II Kings 17). The third population transference under the Assyrians occurs during the reign of Sennacherib. The Assyrian text mentions only the deportation of peoples from the region. It is said to have affected Jerusalem, Judah and the coastal plain in the campaign that destroyed the town of Lachish in 701. There are at least two (Jeremiah refers to three) other transferences of people away from the area under the Babylonians in 597, and then what is often described as a final destruction of Jerusalem and deportation under Nebuchadnezzar in 586. However, we must notice that II Kings' description of Jerusalem's fall includes two successive deportations in which *all the people* were carried off. This, however, still allowed enough for 'all the people small and great' to escape to Egypt after the assassination of the Assyrian puppet, Gedaliah (II Kings 25).[1] Four further transfers occur in the stories of Ezra and Nehemiah and are attributed to the Persian period. They are said to occur under Cyrus (538), Darius I (521–485), Artaxerxes I (464–423) and Artaxerxes II (404–358). These refer only to transfers of population to the territory from Mesopotamia. Traditions also refer to population transfers in the early Hellenistic period, from the city of Samaria (Sebaste) by Alexander to Egypt and to Samaria from Macedonia. The opening column of the Damascus Covenant, found in Cairo and among the Dead Sea scrolls, refers to an Ezra-like figure, the 'teacher of righteousness', who brought 'a remnant of Israel' back some 390 years after they had been deported by Nebuchadnezzar. The Jewish rebellions of 67–70 and 135 CE against the

---

[1] Much in the same way, the plague stories of Exodus are able to kill off all of the Egyptian cattle twice.

Romans each, in their turn, resulted in comparable policies of population transference. Finally, Samaritan traditions, known from later medieval texts, include a tradition of return from exile to Samaria as well as a return tradition of Jews to Jerusalem. These traditions are also reflected in the poems of Ezekiel 36 and Jeremiah 21.

Without arguing that each of these traditions is historically accurate – it is clear that they are not – there is enough evidence and confirmation from independent records to understand the biblical stories as reflecting imperial policies from the Assyrian through the Roman period. The traditions reflect what was a staple of imperial military policy for over a thousand years. No single tradition alone is enough to say that any specific event certainly occurred, yet such events, and their implications for social coherence and identity, were part of the fabric of the society of Palestine under imperial control.

We have no proven connection between any of the known deportations and a corresponding 'return', and we have much reason to assume that such connections are rather the results of interpretation and understanding. Similarly, we have reason to assume that deportations from Samaria and Jerusalem were hardly total. The literary motif of total deportation is hyperbolic, expressive of the totality of the disaster. This is true of the accounts of the deportations from Samaria in 722 and the 320s, from Jerusalem in 586 BCE and again from Jerusalem in 70 and 135 CE. We also have much reason to believe that such transfers were often multilateral, involving both several different destinations for any town's population and the deportation of populations from several regions. In the case of Samaria in 722, we have both biblical story and Assyrian record referring to several distinct peoples transferred to Israel, and the Assyrian representation of Lachish's fall and deportation in 701 shows that this Judean town was only one part of a widespread resettlement policy. The stability of regional economies alone demanded a minimum of reciprocity. Archaeological surveys for sixth-century Judah, and estimates of Jerusalem's population in the fifth century suggest that Jerusalem did not lose all its people in deportations of the early sixth century. A substantial social continuity can often be suggested by the history of settlement and by the lack of major disruption or change in the material culture. The indigenous material culture has continued to dominate after such disruptions. At the same time, disruption and radical transformation has been confirmed in the Judean hills at the end of the eighth century and in the Galilee at the beginning of the Persian period.

On the level of individuals and of local town societies, the trend of change over centuries from locally indigenous regional cultures to an imperial society is overwhelming. Those who had been imported into Palestine to replace deportees were part of a recurrent process of integration with the host region. As they integrated, they came to identify themselves with that group. At times, as in Samaria, this identification was through an understanding of themselves as people who had always lived in the region. At times, as in groups moved in large numbers to such a non-West Semitic area as Babylon, or those who maintained a role opposed to the local population, as in the military colonies of West Semitic soldiers established in Egypt, identity took the form of understanding oneself as living in a diaspora: away from one's homeland. At times, as in Jerusalem, identity came through the bulk of the population coming to understand themselves as exiles who had returned to their original homeland. At yet other times, completely new identities were created. At all times, however, such understanding began with the need of reinterpreting one's situation through a description of the past. Both politically and literarily, this was done quite independently from whatever that past might actually have been.

In every deportation and resettlement, rebuilding the infrastructures of a society involved problems of integrating the refugees or deportees into an already established society that had very little reason to welcome them. In the case of Samaria and Jerusalem, at least five major long-term effects resulted from such difficulties. 1) Aramaic, the official international language of the Assyrian, Babylonian and Persian empires, became a viable language in Palestine. It was perhaps the only language with which the linguistically very diverse groups in Palestine could communicate with each other and with imperial officials. 2) The process of unifying the people of Palestine, and especially the Persian province of Jehud in the south, through the development of common traditions of origins was largely successful. By the end of the early third or second century, this had already encouraged people in the province – whatever their historical origins – to accept as their own the ancestral tradition of having returned as Jews from Babylon. There were also many quite diverse people in Palestine and from Palestine who came to identify themselves around the quite distinct religious and traditional concept of being descendants of ancient Israel. Many frequently understood this in a sectarian way and found identification of themselves as a 'new' or 'true' Israel, rejecting others as 'old' and 'false'. 3) Some of the conflicts between some groups of returnees and more indigenous groups were never resolved. Ironically, the Jerusalem tradition reflected in the stories of Nehemiah, Ezra and Josephus understood some of these conflicts as due to the foreign roots that this tradition attributed to the whole of Samaria's population. 4) The separate and distinctive tradition of Samaria resisted integration into a trans-Palestinian identification of 'Judaism'. While Jerusalem accepted Samaria's Pentateuch and many other story traditions, each group maintained its own cultic centre. Once the different biblical traditions were developed during the Maccabean and early Roman periods, most other regionally identifiable groups both within Palestine and in the diaspora adopted one or other form of this Bible as their own origin tradition. 5) Finally, ideological differences between the self-identities of different, at times regionally defined groups led to competitive and irreconcilable claims by many groups in both Palestine and the diaspora to be the sole 'legitimate' heirs of Israel.[1] These conflicts confirmed the sectarian nature of most groups who were claiming this tradition as their own.

Contrary to expectations, a reading of the Bible as history does not become easier as we come closer to the time the texts were written, only more frustrating. Books such as Ezra and Nehemiah in the Bible, I and II Maccabees and I Esdras in the Apocrypha, the Dead Sea scrolls' Damascus Covenant and Josephus' *Antiquities of the Jews* possessed a great freedom in their writing. They told stories about the past whenever they had one to tell, recycling them as if they were true accounts. Many were made up in the hopes of weaving a continuous narrative. They answered questions that were related to their own world, and their authors were well rewarded for their cleverness and for the grace and power of their writing. Precious little is known about the past except for these stories, and most modern historical scholarship paraphrases one or other author of choice, usually for no other reason than that they are thought believable. That is, because they are good stories.

These works are not very different from the collections of texts and traditions about the apparently far more distant past. These we find in the Pentateuch, Jubilees, the books of Joshua to II Kings, and in I–II Chronicles and Daniel. The theme of origins, with its central functions of tradition collection and philosophical discussion, is oriented more towards techniques of balance and reiteration than to criticism and historical warrant. What is theologically and philosophically true takes precedence over whatever might have been known about the past. In II Kings, we find stories that formed the heart of its interest in the past. In a classic form of a folktale's ever-ironic claim to being historical, II Kings again and again delights in offering subtle footnote references to royal archives (such as the 'Chronicles of the Kings of Israel') for any who might be interested in what II Kings is not.

When the later writers of traditional histories, from I and II Maccabees to Josephus, follow in this vein with references to 'sources' – especially to sources we no longer have, and many of which may never have existed – we must remember that, whatever the truth of such claims, we have access to the worlds of II Maccabees and Josephus only from the perspectives they allow us. When II Maccabees 2, for example, opens the 'records' and the 'writing' of Jeremiah to talk about teaching the law of Moses to the people, or hiding the ark of the covenant on Moses' mountain until a time when 'God shows his mercy and gathers his people again', we can draw

---

[1] Our understanding of Israelite and 'Jewish' religious identity is vital here and must be dealt with in greater detail below.

one of two conclusions. The author is either creating, or he is transmitting, pious fictions in support of the claim that the Mosaic tradition lives on after the exile. In neither case do we learn anything about an historical Jeremiah – only about the Jeremiah of story and legend. Similarly, when Josephus tells us of a letter written centuries earlier by Aristeas, which recounts the origin of the Greek translation of Jewish traditions in Alexandria by seventy elders, we must not imagine that we are learning anything about the origins of the Greek Bible. We learn only what is implicit in Josephus' accounts: of the existence of the Greek Bible *in Josephus' time* and of an effort – whether Josephus' own or his source's – to offer an aetiology that marks this translation as authentic and divinely inspired. Josephus himself undermines trust in Aristeas' letter when he recounts the same legend in the form of a speech of Aristeas.

The problem of the fragmentation of our evidence, and of our enduring ignorance about nearly every aspect of the history of the Persian and Hellenistic periods, as about any of our so-called biblical periods, is serious. The lack of primary sources, together with a wealth of literary and theological discourse, render this second temple period nearly inaccessible to history. Our secondary sources, however, are many and varied and give us a wealth of story. It is not that we know nothing of the past. Rather, we lack a coherent narrative, either from the Bible or any other contemporary writer, that can offer a structure to our history of this period. We are left with a fragmented and a doubtful past.

3 The myth of exile

With the metaphor of exile in the Bible, the central problem has never been a lack of evidence showing whether an historical situation in fact once existed. Deportation texts alone, and the extensive imperial policies of population transference that were carried out over a period of more than a thousand years, provide a more than adequate background against which the Bible's literary metaphor of exile might find resonance in its audience. Many of these texts evoke emotional and intellectual perceptions of deportation as political and personal 'exile'. This same emotional resonance is already implicit in the historical propaganda of the Babylonian king Nabonidus or of the Persian Cyrus in their claims of returning people and their gods to their homes. Such passion is dramatically captured in II Kings' story of the Assyrian general at Jerusalem's walls, offering the people exile 'that they might live and not die'. No, the problem is not whether there was ever an historical exile; nor has it ever been that the Bible's stories about the exile are not believable. There was exile . . . often.

The historical problems arise with the question of continuity: the continuity of people, their culture and traditions. When we read the Bible's narratives, are we looking at the means by which a culture and a tradition created continuity and coherence because of and out of the discontinuities of the people's experiences? Are the emotions of exile evoked in the implied feelings of those who were uprooted and deported different or comparable to those implied perceptions of people of another generation, or even centuries later, who heard the messages of a saving Nabonidus and Cyrus? When Shalmaneser took Samaria, were the people he deported from Samaria to live in Halah in northern Mesopotamia 'returning' home? Or did they too live in exile, perhaps to 'return' to Jerusalem under Artaxerxes? Or did the people Shalmaneser brought *to* Samaria from the Syrian town of Hamath think of themselves as being forced to live in exile, while yet others 'returned'? And how did the people of Samaria see themselves three hundred years later? And Judah's exiles under Senna-cherib, did they return? Or did anyone return? Those who understood themselves as having returned, and whose traditions are celebrated in story a half-millennium later: were they in fact brought to Judah by Sennacherib or to Jerusalem by Nebuchadnezzar, rather than by the later Cyrus, Darius or Alexander? And how could the authors of I Esdras or II Isaiah know? What we have in the Bible's stories of deportation, exile and return are examples of how literature plays with the metaphors that experience has created for us. It is to this literary play, to the myth of exile, that we should now turn in asking about the quality of this biblical tradition that is so firmly and unquestionably anchored in history.

For all the importance of the remnant theology surrounding the stories of Judah's return from exile in Babylon as a metaphor of divine mercy, we must never forget that this metaphor's closest variant is that of Israel and Judah's total destruction. This formed a chain of tradition that survived just as vigorously as that of 'return'. This variant, with its associations with motifs of 'new life', finds its centre in the metaphor – already discussed – of a 'new Israel'. The well-known 'root of Jesse' motif in Isaiah is a metaphor that plays on the image of the dead stump of the Davidic dynasty that lies just as firmly within the heart of exile poetry as does the alternative theme of continuity and return. Central to the revival of this tree is the Old Testament hope in what is a theology of resurrection. It is only in an historical world that such contrasting metaphors as death and survival are marked as contradictory. In literature, the motifs of resurrection, rebirth and return are complementary variations of a tradition's coherent vigour. Hardly contradictory, they are functional equivalents.

A related problem for those interested in the history of an exile is the seeming lack of fixed substance in some of the literary perceptions of the exile: both in the idea of an exilic period and in the metaphor as such. We have, in fact, no narrative about the exile in the Bible. We do have alternative stories, such as the doublet-stories of Israel's enslavement in

Egypt, which leads to the Exodus story of return, and of Israel's forty years of being tested in the wilderness, which is followed by (re-)entry into the land of a new generation. We also have stories of going into exile and stories about coming out. But the history of the exile is a history written on blank pages. That we do not have an exilic narrative must at least raise for us the question of whether any such historical period of the past is in fact the subject of the traditions we do have. Why is it that this one indisputable period of the Bible's history is one that the Bible shows no interest in making part of its narrative?

The Book of Nehemiah opens when the Persian courtier Nehemiah hears of Jerusalem's disaster: that 'the walls had fallen and that the gates had been burned'. The news of Jerusalem's emptiness leads to a prayer of repentance in which Nehemiah plays the dramatic role of representing in his prayer 'all who would return to God with repentance and keep his commandments'. The God of heaven hears his prayers. When he repeats his lament to King Artaxerxes and asks permission to rebuild the city, it is granted. The theme of Jerusalem's total destruction: turned into a desert by the wrath of God, is a very important one theologically, and performs a double function. On one hand it marks Jerusalem's destruction as the result of the deity's exhausted patience in the chain of stories of ever-recurrent human rebellion that had begun in Genesis. This final destruction, complete and unforgiving, is the punishment, long threatened and delayed, that had been promised as far back as Exodus 23. In the wilderness, Yahweh had promised Moses: 'I send my angel before you to guard you and to bring you to the place I have prepared.' This guardian spirit, however, is hardly a beneficent creature, but takes on the role of a mafia-like enforcer: 'Listen to him and respond to his voice; do not rebel against him; for he will not forgive your crime. My name is in him.' So this long-distance prophecy of Jerusalem's destruction is recalled in the language of desolation and in the image of Jerusalem as wilderness. On the other hand, it is also this same wilderness metaphor that leads Nehemiah to repent on behalf of the people. This repentance leads to Jerusalem's renewal and rebirth, as Nehemiah takes on the role of Yahweh's angel who now leads this new 'Israel' to the place that God had prepared.

These same interlocking motifs of destruction, wilderness and return are found in the metaphor of Isaiah's song of return in Isaiah 40: 1–3 that so famously captures the suffering of Jerusalem's exile in his great poem of consolation:

> Give comfort, give comfort to my people, says your God. Speak tenderly to Jerusalem. Cry out to her that her slavery is over. Her crime is forgiven; for she has received at Yahweh's hand, double for her sins . . . A voice cries in the wilderness: prepare Yahweh's path; make straight the way of God through the desert.

In his book, it is Nehemiah's Isaiah-like voice that cries from Jerusalem's wilderness and goes to prepare the way. The Book of Lamentations also builds the same kind of theology from Jerusalem's loss. It visits not Babylon, but impoverished Jerusalem (1: 1ff.). Lamentations opens with the motif of the emptiness of Jerusalem: 'How lonely sits the city that was full of people! How like a widow she has become, she that was great among the nations . . .' That the text speaks of the exile as present is explicit in verse 3: 'Judah has gone into exile in affliction and hard labour. Now she dwells as one among the nations, but she finds no rest . . .' In chapter 2, we read of Jerusalem's destruction and of the deportation of its leaders: 'Her gates have fallen to the ground; he has ruined and broken her bars; her kings and princes are among the nations; the law is no more and her prophets obtain no vision from Yahweh.' The poems speak of great suffering, of death and of despair: 'In the dust of the streets lie the young and the old; maids and young men have fallen by the sword; in the day of your [i.e., God's] anger, you have killed them, slaughtering without mercy . . . On the day of Yahweh's anger, none escaped; none survived.' Jeremiah speaks for all of Jerusalem. 'I am one who has seen suffering; he has brought me darkness without light . . . He has forced me to live in darkness like the dead of long ago.' The image is of Jerusalem as a desert: 'How like a desert this city that was full of people.' Yet this empty Jerusalem is a theological Jerusalem, not an historical one.

Chapter 5 opens with a summation of Jerusalem's disgrace in the voice of its people: 'Our inheritance has been turned over to strangers, our homes to aliens. We have become orphans, fatherless; our mothers are like widows. We must pay for the water we drink; the wood we get must be bought. With a yoke on our neck we are hard driven . . .' The desert is not an empty but a moral wilderness. The city is filled with people . . . and crime:

> Women are raped in Zion; virgins in the villages of Judah; princes are hung up by their hands. No respect is shown elders; young men are forced to grind at the mill and boys stagger under loads of wood; the old have quit the city gate and the young their music. The joy of our hearts has ceased; our dancing has turned to mourning. Zion is a wilderness. Jackals prowl.

This exilic Jerusalem of the wilderness, this city in the hands of the godless, where women are raped and heroes hung, is the same Jerusalem that is visited by Jeremiah's scorn: 'Run back and forth through the streets of Jerusalem, look and take note! Search her squares to see if you can find a man; one who does justice and seeks truth; that I may pardon her.' (5: 1) The scene echoes Abraham's confrontation with Yahweh in Genesis 18: 24: 'Suppose there are fifty righteous; will you then destroy the place and not spare it for the sake of the fifty righteous?' At the debate's closure,

Yahweh declares that for the sake of ten – a blessed minyan, the number required for public prayer – he will not destroy it. Sodom, like Jerusalem, *is* destroyed.

Just as the story of Sodom and Gomorrah's destruction epitomizes Jerusalem of the exile, in Jeremiah's Lamentations the wilderness as godless chaos subject to Yahweh's destruction marks this same Jerusalem of the exile as a wilderness of the soul seeking repentance. This becomes very clear when we read a poem in Hosea 2 that is about Israel rather than Jerusalem. This interesting song, which we will return to below, has much in common with Lamentations 5. In Hosea's poem, Israel is portrayed as the prophet's wife, a prostitute, whose children are named 'my people' and 'she is granted pity'. The poem opens with Hosea playing the role of Yahweh speaking to the children (Hosea 2: 2–3):

Plead with your mother, plead – for she is not my wife, and I am not her husband – that she remove her whoring from her face; her adultery from her breasts: that I not strip her naked and make her as on the day of her birth; that I not make her a desert; turn her into a wilderness and kill her with thirst.

The poem presents a picture of Israel's destruction by Yahweh as a punishment for turning to the worship of Ba'al. In the closure of the poem, however, the theme of wilderness returns. The wilderness now reiterates the wilderness of the Exodus; it becomes a place of testing, of repentance and forgiveness: as a doorway of hope and return: a promise of Israel's rebirth (Hosea 2: 14–15):

Look, I will seduce her and bring her out to the wilderness; there I will speak tenderly to her: I will return to her vineyards and make the Achor Valley a doorway of hope. She will respond to me as she did when she was young; when she came up out of the land of Egypt.

Historiography and the past are abandoned in these verses as the song turns to the universals of the soul's relationship to its God. The theme of wilderness as the place of repentance and turning to Yahweh marks it indelibly with the eroticism of piety's joy and utopian hope. From wilderness springs creation and new life (Hosea 2: 21–23):

I will make a bond for you with the animals of the fields and the birds of the air and with those that creep on the ground. I ban the bow, sword and war from the land. You will lie down in safety. Our marriage will be for ever: a betrothal in righteousness and justice, in steadfast love and in mercy. I marry you in faithfulness and you will know Yahweh. On that day, says Yahweh, I will respond to the heavens, and they to the earth and the earth will respond to the grain, the wine and the oil; and they will speak to Jezreel. I will sow myself in the land. I will have pity on 'Not-pitied'. To 'Not-my-people' I will say 'You are my people'; and he will answer: 'You are my God.'

It is clearly a mistake to see in Lamentations a contradiction to an historical account of Nehemiah's empty city. Rather, the metaphor of Nehemiah's empty Jerusalem is reiterated in Lamentations. It is only our own historical expectations that see the image of Jerusalem as an empty and abandoned wilderness and Jerusalem as filled with violence as contradictions. For both Nehemiah and Lamentations, as for Hosea's Jezreel in Israel, it is because of sin that the desert is found. This is how Mount Zion is a wasteland. I would even suggest that it is very much Lamentations' understanding of Jerusalem that lies at the heart of the Old Testament metaphor of exile. Exile is Jerusalem as a wasteland; it is the emptiness of the soul; it is to be without God. This is not historiography at all, but a metaphor of pietism. It has its roots in diaspora Judaism's self-understanding as a 'new Israel'.

Jeremiah, in his Lamentations over Jerusalem in the exile, like Hosea in his poems about Israel as a prostitute-wife with her bastard children, have Nehemiah's return as their points of departure. It is in an Israel redivivus that punishment, destruction and the wilderness of exile all take on meaning within the tradition. It is the 'New Jerusalem' and the Chronicler's 'New Israel', that all hold as a central theme. Collecting origin traditions about the returning 'remnant' of Israel lost, Nehemiah as origin narrative centred in rebuilding and return *has no place* for a populated Jerusalem in his story, any more than the Book of Lamentations' poems, centred as they are in the motif of Jerusalem's repentance, has room for an Israel in Babylon. Unlike the old, lost Israel, this New Jerusalem is supersessionist. It is Israel saved: a new generation. If we might draw on the overlapping syntax for 'return', 'turn' and 'repent', only those who are among the remnant who have 'turned' (in Lamentations 'repentance' and, in Ezra/Nehemiah 'returned') belong. Only those whom Yahweh has changed in the wilderness, who have again become 'his people', can respond with Hosea's children: 'You are my God.' In such supersessionist logic, which is so close to the heart of the Bible's sectarian understanding of the true believer as one who has been chosen by God, the dark night of the soul (expressed biblically in the metaphor of exilic wilderness) as a time of testing and rebirth is both a central and an essential aspect of piety's self-understanding.

We have many variants of Nehemiah's 'New Jerusalem' and of Chronicles 'New Israel'. We have Ezra's renewal of the *torah* and its own cluster of variations. I Chronicles 9's story of David's establishment of the temple service, and II Chronicles' and Ezra's messianic Cyrus, who builds a home for the God of Israel in Jerusalem, close off the past and take a new departure for the future. We have the 'New Israels' of I and II Maccabees, the 'New Israel' of the Dead Sea scrolls' Damascus Covenant, as well as the post-70 CE generation of 'New Israels': Jamnia's[1] and Josephus', Mark's and Acts'. We also find New Israels implicit in each of our Old Israels: from Genesis' to Isaiah's and Jubilees': from those of the Psalter to the commentaries of the Dead Sea scrolls.

It is in texts such as Zechariah 8 that we come closest to the core of the tradition that gave rise to the concept of Israel, which structures most of the Old Testament's collections. The context is Zechariah's identification of Jerusalem as the city called 'Yahweh's holy mountain' (Zech. 8: 3). 'I will save my people from the East and from the West; I will bring them home that they might live in Jerusalem, and they will be my people and I will be their God to live in faith and righteousness' (Zech. 8: 7–8). This is an ideological vision of the Old Testament that includes the wildernesses of both Nehemiah and Exodus. It is a vision stamped with the hope of a diaspora's heavenly Jerusalem.

Israel's entry into bondage in Egypt and its return out of the desert have variants both in Moses' vision of the desert from which Yahweh carried Israel on eagle's wings, which we find in the Book of Deuteronomy (32: 10), and in Jeremiah's metaphor of the desert's nothingness. It is in chapter 4 that Jeremiah addresses the theme of return to a Jerusalem populated by the old Israel of destruction. 'If you return, O Israel; return to me says Yahweh. Remove your abominations from my face and do not hesitate.' Jeremiah addresses Judah and Jerusalem with the metaphor of fallow land, offering an implicit theological critique of old Israel's circumcision: 'Break up the fallow ground and sow not among thorns. Circumcise yourselves to Yahweh by removing the foreskins of your hearts.' The fallow land and the desert stand as metaphorical parallels: both demanding a righteous sower. The desert wind is a wind of judgement: 'A hot wind from the barren highlands: a wilderness for the daughter of my people: it is I who speak in judgement.' Now he turns to a moral translation of the metaphor interpreting true circumcision as that of a circumcised heart: 'Wash your heart from wickedness, that you may be saved.' The historiographic references to impending war and disaster demanding righteous hearts finds its summation as Jeremiah has Yahweh address Jerusalem in schoolmasterly disdain (Jer. 4: 22):

For my people are foolish; they know me not. They are stupid children; they have no understanding. They are clever at doing evil; how to do good, they know nothing of.

It is in the prophetic vision of verses 23–26, however, that Jeremiah finally captures Jerusalem of the exile in cosmic proportions:

[1] According to early Jewish legend, the first rabbinic council establishing Judaism of the Mishnah.

224 · *The Mythic Past*

I looked on the earth; it was formless and empty: to the sky; it had no light. I
looked at the mountains; they were quaking: all the hills moved back and forth.
I looked; there was no human: all the birds of the air had flown. I looked; the
fruitful land was a desert: its cities were laid in ruin. Before Yahweh: before his
fierce anger.

In these powerful, terrible verses, the poet portrays exilic Jerusalem –
this land of an ignorant people who do not know God – as an empty earth:
as the world before creation. It is an image much like that of Genesis 1: 1:
'When God set about to create the heavens and the earth, the earth was
formless and empty and darkness was on the surface of the deep.' So too
Jerusalem of the exile has returned in Jeremiah's vision of the desert's
formlessness before God's creative and life-giving breath moved over the
surface of the waters. Jerusalem is without God. It had no light; the
mountains were no longer held firmly on their pillars; there was no
humanity; no birds of the air. Instead of Genesis 1's divine spirit moving
with its creative force, God's fierce anger governs Jeremiah's poem. It is in
the face of such a wilderness Jerusalem that the poet in chapter 5
desperately searches Jerusalem's streets for a just man, that God might
pardon the city.

The metaphor of Israel's origins out of the desert of exile finds its
creative centre in the origin story of creation itself. The Genesis story
brings out of the nothingness of Jeremiah's *tohu wa-bohu* a wasteland that
must be traversed before one comes to a new world created by God's will.
This is the world of a new Jerusalem, which stands opposed to Genesis
11's old Babylon's Jerusalem: with its tower built by men's hands. Does
Jeremiah's metaphor evoke a new creation for his new Jerusalem? Or does
the story of Genesis' creation evoke Jeremiah's metaphor of primordial
chaos, and place Yahweh's forgiveness of his people at the creation? Is it in
the middle of such intertwining tropes that we shall ask after our historical
referent so that we might know what happened? Where lies our story's
referent: in the creation or in the exile?

The best that can be offered in answer to such a question lies outside the
explicit reference of our texts, outside of the past of the world of tradition
in which both our narratives play. It is in a world implicit to our texts and
to our tradition as a whole. Our best answer, I think, can be found in the
confident cadences of Psalm 1 and 2's joint introduction to the Psalter,
which will be discussed in more detail in chapter 10 below.

Happy is one who does not follow the counsel of evildoers or take the path on
which sinners walk, or sit among scoffers, but is one who has his joy in
Yahweh's *torah*; who loves Yahweh's *torah* and studies it day and night. He is
like a tree who is planted on the banks of a canal. It will bear fruit at the right

time and its leaves will not fall (Ps. 1: 1–3).' 'Happy are all who find refuge in Him (Ps. 2: 12).

This context in piety is the historical reality that gave rise to our literary traditions, not what they may or may not have known about the creation or about Ancient Israel or about Jerusalem. The myth of exile is their myth, not ours, and it is certainly not history's. Those who follow the way or the advice of the ungodly, they, like the lost generation, are given over to the desert and to death. It is this motif that is reiterated throughout the theological metaphors of the tradition: in the murmuring stories, in Saul's fall from grace, and in Samaria's, Jerusalem's and Babylon's destructions. All celebrate Yahweh's cosmic victory over the ungodly on the 'day of wrath'.

PART THREE

THE BIBLE'S PLACE IN HISTORY

Introduction to Part Three

The Bible often presents itself as an account of the past, yet its interests are not historical ones. It is rather concerned with the nature of God's integrity, his unity: how the divine can be both transcendent and present in the world; how God can be one and yet find many forms in which he is known. The Bible is not only taken up with divine mercy and justice, it is also baffled by God's hiddenness. It is interested in questions about the good life, the reflective life. It is passionately concerned about the meaning of life in the face of the patent cruelty and injustice of experience. We find some of the most beautiful poetry in the Bible. It can be pious, lyrical and erotic. It can also be some of the angriest. We have narratives of epic proportions, as well as brief aetiologies and folktales. They are at times stunningly profound and evocative. There are both romances and adventure stories. Some are moralistic and a few sentimental. There is patent racism and sexism in both theme and story, as well as some of the world's earliest condemnations of both.

When we separate the Bible from history we are not getting rid of the Bible. It is where it has always been: playing among its stories and legends. History is a modern interest that the Bible rarely shares. It does use occasional tidbits of history here and there. It often refers to places, great figures and even some of the things that occurred in the past, and it occasionally seems to understand something of these episodes.

The past century's efforts of Bible scholars to use the Bible for constructing a history of Israel have failed miserably. Much of the reason for this failure lies in a brand of scholarship that was more apologetic and theological than critical and historical. These scholars were trapped within the circular arguments of Western European assumptions about having roots in the ancient Hellenistic world and about an understanding of the Bible as a part of the European origin story through Christianity. This scholarship never escaped the traditions it thought it was critically examining. Its methods for recognizing the historical were its undoing.

For instance, the scrutiny of historicity can be a very useful tool for asking questions about the validity of historical sources. No historians nor reporters worth their salt would function long without it. However, this concern, which asks such questions as: Did she really say that? or Did that really happen?, is a question that is only decisively effective when it is answered in the negative. That is, the question of historicity is a tool that is used to cast doubt on one's sources, to test them. It protects the historian from obvious mistakes by eliminating potential, but misleading, sources of evidence. Our access to singular events or eye-witness accounts in the ancient world of the Bible is almost nil, but – given the thousands of years of transmission involved and our great ignorance of most of the ancient past – the only events and accounts that can be dismissed as implausible or impossible are those that are miraculous or otherwise demonstrably impossible.

But to dismiss accounts of such events simply because they are impossible isn't much help, as we can always imagine the story minus the miraculous. Would that make the less miraculous more historical? Two different accounts, one with a miracle and the other without, cannot be distinguished in their power to be evidence for history. We have already seen a perfect example of this from the Bible. We should take the case of Numbers 13, where we find the story of Moses sending Israelite spies into the Valley of Eshcol. They returned with a description of a land whose rivers flowed with milk and honey. Giants, they said, lived in the valley, and the Israelites had felt like grasshoppers in the face of these Anakim. As evidence for their report they brought back a single bunch of grapes that took two men to carry. Few would credit this story as history; and who would quarrel with them? Deuteronomy 2 and 9 tells much the same story. This time, however, more plausibly. Here the Anakim are powerful people and rather tall. It is their cities, not the people, whose towers reach up to the sky. Is that less miraculous variant any help to an historian?

Judgements that events are plausible, likely or even probable are hardly ever very good tools for an historian. History doesn't require the plausible. It requires evidence. What should happen rarely does. The most implausible of events, however, do happen – often! It is far more frequently good fiction that requires plausibility. For most of what we think of as history in the Bible, we have no evidence.

During the past century and more, what we have come to know as the 'history of Israel' has been much like Deuteronomy's variant of the story of the valley of the giants. The Bible's stories have been paraphrased. The extraordinary has been reduced and the long chain of legends and tales made coherent and continuous, a narrative extending from the times of Abraham and Moses, the conquest and the Judges, and the history of the united and divided monarchies, to the exile in Babylon, and from the return under the Persians and the rebuilding of the temple to the Maccabees of the Apocrypha and finally the Palestine of the gospels. Neither a critical history

– whether Israel's or Palestine's – nor an historical understanding of the social world of the past was ever really consulted as a context in which the Bible could be understood. It was rather the Bible that became both the context and the source for our understanding of the history and social world of Palestine's past.

Too much criticism has been addressed to the miracles and mythology in the Bible because of their implicit negation of the historical. The stories, however, are not believable as stories without them. To take the mythology or the miracles away does not make them either more understandable or more acceptable today. A modern reader understands stories and their function quite well. These issues have distracted scholars mostly because of their habits of looking at the Bible stories as if they were histories of the world that we live in. We forget that most people in the world in which the Bible was written, also lived in a world where miracles occurred only in stories. In that world too, they happened only to other people long ago. That is, like us, the writers of the Bible also lived in a world where God was silent. The long-standing effort to see the Bible as history has come from two quite different incentives. On one hand, there has been the effort of conservative theology, with its roots in fundamentalism and Christian apologetic. This has understood the Bible's truth primarily in terms of history. An historical Adam and Eve were long defended, and, to this day, books that present themselves as scholarly continue to debate the pros and cons of Noah's flood, the destruction of Sodom and Gomorrah, or the story of Israel crossing through the Red Sea on dry land. The contamination of scholarship by such concerns has been much greater than is usually recognized. Understanding the Old Testament as a history related to Christian origins has resulted in the theological orientation of the Bible being largely ignored. An understanding of prophecies about the messiah and promises of salvation fulfilled in the New Testament required a reading of these texts as both history and as predictive of the future. As such readings have become less and less tenable, because of our expanding understanding of the history of the ancient Near East and in particular of Palestine, nearly any aspect that can link the Bible with historical events has been invoked in defence of such naive realism.

On the other hand, quite aside from this effort to read the Bible as history, the developing fields of ancient Near Eastern studies and especially Palestinian archaeology have had a great need of the Bible. The Bible provided a language and a coherent picture of the past that archaeology lacked. To speak of the Bronze Age in Palestine in terms of a Canaanite culture was to give to the discipline a unity and significance it would otherwise lack. Similarly, to speak of the Iron Age in Palestine as an Israelite period allowed scholars to interrelate the different and various aspects of the region as if it were a functional whole. Indeed, the history of Israel was the first task of Palestinian archaeologists. Their efforts to reconstruct that history justified the great expense intrinsic to archaeological research at a time when tourism was not yet able to support such costs. The critical study of the history of Israel was first of all an archaeological project that proposed a critical alternative to an understanding of archaeology as biblical illustration. The existence and definition of an Israel that was identifiable with the entirety of the region's past, and could link that past with the broader history of the ancient Near East, was a necessary creation of this new academic field which was in search of both justification and funding. The quest for an historical patriarchal period, situated as many as fifteen hundred years earlier than the Bible's stories about it were written, was hardly independent of this effort. The self-understanding and funding of the discipline of Palestinian archaeology required that to create an historical Israel meant seeing it in the broader context of ancient Near Eastern studies as a whole. Similarly, the centrality of a biblical Israel with its vision of David's empire overshadowed and distorted every alternative history for both the Bronze and the Iron Ages. This archaeological project needed an Israelite ethnicity of biblical proportions. It is part of the growth of this discipline, however, that in recent years has called such requirements into question. The collapse of academic support within biblical studies for the fundamentalist project of Bible history, and the technical and critical development of Palestinian archaeology have now made it possible for archaeology to be understood as a discipline independent of its early fixation on the Bible's stories.

In order to try to read and understand the Bible – or any other ancient text – as its authors intended it to be understood, or as it was understood during its formative period, we need historical contexts. These will not tell us what the Bible is saying, and we will never have a *right* context that will *prove* finally that the Bible means one thing and not another. Rather, we have need for contexts that will help us understand the Bible in the same way that we understand any literature, whether ancient or modern. In the last chapters of this book, I outline three kinds of historical contexts that better support a critical and historical reading of the Bible. I also discuss, within these contexts, the biblical metaphor of God. This metaphor is at the centre of the Bible's theology. It is also fundamental to understanding the Bible's literature about a transcendent, monotheistic understanding of the divine in the personal terms of family. Especially important have been the relationships of a father to his child and of a husband to his wife. If we can better understand the Bible on its own terms, from within its own context in history, literature and intellectual life, this book will have reached its goal.

a) *The Bible's world in ancient history.* The context of early Judaism's social world relates to the Bible in several ways. A text – like anything else – is a product of its times. Understanding these times will in turn help us understand this literature, whether or not there are direct, or only indirect, references to the real world in that literature. Whether a text is historical in its referents, or whether it reflects some understanding about the historical past, literature always tells us, at least implicitly, about society. A knowledge of ancient society and history will also give us a context for understanding references authors make. In this chapter, we take up the issue of the development of self-identity that is so central to the Bible's theological purpose. This refraction of historical society is implicit to our texts. The self-understanding as children of a 'new Israel' is both a product and a defining point of departure for all of the traditions of Judaism.

b) *The Bible's literary world.* Authors live in a world of language and texts. The more we understand that, the better we can understand what the Bible is talking about. The context in which a small story or poem is found is important, and should not be ignored. Other literature of the Bible will make us familiar with styles and oddities, motifs and patterns, themes and prejudices. Palestine's literature, and the literature of the ancient world contemporary with the Bible, tells us much about what people were doing when they wrote things in the ancient world. They didn't always write for the reasons we do. We need to learn to distinguish this world of literature and art in which stories and poems and song are found – the world of motifs, metaphor and language – from that other world in which we all live, whether or not we understand and respond to it in speech.

c) *The Bible's intellectual world.* The focus of the Bible's intellectual world has been centred in the very particular literary development of a personal, yet monotheistic sense of the divine. An understanding of this theological world, which has its historical context in the writing of biblical texts, is necessary to any understanding of the Bible. This core of biblical theology will be addressed from the perspective of three interrelated metaphors, with which we can gain entry into its intellectual world. They are the theological motif of the divine as both personal and transcendent, the problem of the one and the many, which finds its biblical resolution in the understanding of God as 'father'; and the rich mythological literature about this father's sons. It is finally as 'sons of God' that the tradition captures its intended audience.

The intellectual world or world-view of the Bible shares much with our own. It is also often markedly different from it. The Bible's wisdom literature and philosophical writings give us our most immediate access to this world. Its direct makers are story-tellers, playwrights, poets, teachers, musicians and artists, whose theology and understanding of religious belief are very important. This is not because ancient society was significantly more religious, superstitious or gullible than our modern society is. It wasn't. Theology is just as important in understanding our own intellectual world, in its poverty and its richness. Religious beliefs are important because they tell us how people understand and value themselves, how they see humanity, and how they perceive the world as both real and unreal. Ironically, the intellectual world in which the Bible was formed doesn't tell us much at all about ancient deities, though it mentions them often. In fact, many of the movers and shakers of the late Persian and Hellenistic intellectual world were very sceptical about religion and about traditional views about the gods. Many – like their counterparts among the early Greek playwrights – rejected the gods outright, and made fun of them. Others – like the philosopher Aristotle and the Bible's own author of Ecclesiastes – were agnostic. Unwilling to attribute personal will and passion to the great power that created the world, they were deeply suspicious of the many traditional stories that made the gods too personal, with all the adventures and interests of people. The self-interest and narcissistic self-absorption of the human creators of such gods was all too obvious. It is not the modern world that discovered that gods had been created by intelligent men. This is a central issue of the Bible's formation. The Bible's often agnostic writers resorted to 'the way of unknowing' to speak of the divine. Like Job, they describe the divine as unfathomable, and they portray formal religious beliefs and ordinary piety as nonsense or worse. Quite typical, and I believe reflective of the central core of ancient understanding, was the assertion that ultimate reality and the truly divine was spiritual and transcendent. The reality of the divine was beyond human understanding and escaped our capacity to express it meaningfully. The Greek philosopher Plato and the Bible's writers of Isaiah 40–56 and Exodus are powerfully expressive of such awareness about human ignorance and the gods. So too are both Jonah and Ezekiel, each in their own very different way. Traditional religion, and even the traditional gods like Yahweh, are seen to be expressive of a transcendent spiritual reality that men do not know, but merely guess at. Traditional beliefs are recurrently understood as misleading: a trap to those who live an unreflective life. Life is humanity's share in the divine. Our hold on it, however, is transient. Its meaning escapes us . . . as does everything that people know. A better understanding of this intellectual world is a necessary requirement for reading the Bible.

CHAPTER 10

The Bible's social and historical worlds

1 Israel and Palestine's hidden peoples

Our perception of peoples and nations is a political view of human society. This is easily illustrated by an ironic anomaly of early Israelite history. In II Kings, the legendary founder of the northern kingdom of Israel, and builder of its capital, Samaria, was an Israelite general, Omri. Assyrian texts refer to ancient historical Israel as *Bit Humri*, the 'House of Omri'. Omri also shows up in the famous Mesha inscription as a personification of Israel's army, occupying Moab. The names given to this founding king and eponymous ancestor of historical Israel are obvious versions of the well-known Arabic name *Omar*. That this not only surprises us, but will be seen by many as unacceptable if not wrong, is reflective of our perception of both ethnicity and nation as fundamental and implicit aspects of ancient societies. The concept of ethnicity, however, is a fiction, created by writers. It is a product of literature, of history-writing. As it is commonly used today, it distorts the past far more than it informs.

Nevertheless, words such as *ethné* and *goyim*[1] clearly reflect an ancient perspective, if not an ancient historical reality. The early Greek collector of many of the stories of Asia, Herodotus, uses this term and even defines it for us. For Herodotus, the five elements of an ethnos are: a people united, a common language, a defining religion, a land of their own, and a common past and future goal. These same five elements form the essential themes that are developed in the biblical narrative. Quite clearly, the goal of the biblical narrative is to present Israel as a people. One could say that the story is ethnographic rather than historiographic in intention. That is to say, it is not writing a history, but rather *defining* a contemporary society as a people. It is creating a reality by creating a past for a society that identifies itself theologically with the 'new Israel'. The biblical narrative is not the origin story of a nation like other nations. That is denied over and

[1] 'Peoples', in Greek and Hebrew.

over again. It is an origin story of a people opposed to the nations of this world: a 'people of God'.

It is not enough, however, simply to correct our own historical understanding of the past, which affects the understanding of ancient Israel as a people. We must also consider the Bible's theology that is critical of the past Israel that it presents. The Bible understands old Israel as lost Israel. In this judgement, the Bible also questions the appropriateness of seeing that ancient Israel – and for that matter ancient Judah as well – as the 'people of God' that the Bible had created for heuristic purposes. The Bible is here emphatically not this ancient people's book.

The biblical origin stories centre themselves in the coherence of a people, comparable to that defined by Herodotus, in its land, with its own language, religion and history. Historians, however, have concentrated on asserting an originating unity for the same people, which they believe must have first bound an historical Israel together as a people. They have used, for the most part, a rationalized paraphrase of one or other of the biblical narratives of Genesis–II Kings regarding each of these five unities. This issue of ethnicity runs through the very heart of the current academic debate over the early history of the south Levant and biblical origins. The ethnic character of the discussion of Israel's origins, and indeed of the entire question of Israel's earliest history, has marked the academic discussion since the nineteenth century.

The region of Palestine as a whole is centred on the eastern Mediterranean shoreline. It is defined by the fertile Mediterranean climatic area of the southern Levant on both sides of the Jordan rift. It includes highlands, intersected by low-lying valleys. It also includes large areas of steppeland, found especially in the south and east where the region joins the Arabian and Sinai deserts. There is little coherence in the region as a whole. Geographically, it is best understood as the southern fringe of Syria. Among its many names in early records are Upper *Retenu* and *Kinahhi* ('Canaan') found in Egyptian texts. The region has been known as Palestine since the Assyrian period. This same name was used by the sixth-century Greek writer Herodotus, and is commonly used during the Roman period. In modern times, the name Palestine was used throughout the British mandate period. Since the creation of the state of Israel in 1948, and especially since Israel's military occupation of the West Bank in 1967, the names Israel and Land of Israel have competed with Palestine. In more recent times, both names, Israel and Palestine, have become viable from the perspective of different historical and political claims by modern Israelis and Palestinians. These are frequently used to refer to different parts of the larger region.

Both economically and geographically, the southern Levant is Herodotus' Palestine: Syria's southern fringe. It has neither an integrity nor a unity of its own. The region's Mediterranean economy, with its regionally determined primary specializations in grain agriculture, herding, horticulture and viniculture, fosters a differentiation and separation of the population into many small groups. These distinguish themselves both politically and in terms of sedentarization. The geographical fragmentation of the landscape, moreover, promotes local autonomies in small towns and local clusters of villages and encampments. Since the Bronze Age, this regional character supported a patronage form of society centred on small autonomous burghs. These fortress towns provided Palestine's many small enclaves with both markets and defence. Region-wide political domination, when it has existed at all in the south Levant, has ever been imperial and external.

The politicization of geography and history that is so apparent today, as different political goals dictate very specific understandings of the past, might help us to be sensitive to the relative nature of the histories we create. Neither the history of ancient Israel nor of ancient Judah that historians write today is or should be the Bible's history. Nor is the history of Israel the same as the history of the region of southern Syria that is called *Eretz Israel* in so many texts of the Bible. Israel's ancient history is only a very limited part of the history of this greater region. It involves the region of the central highlands north of Jerusalem and south of the Jezreel valley, during the ninth and eighth centuries. No one has yet written the history of this Israel for periods later than the Assyrian takeover of the region. This history is different from the many related, but nevertheless separate and distinct histories of Judah, the Jezreel, the Gilead, the Galilee, the Negev, the Shephelah, the Jordan valley, Phoenicia, Philistia, Ammon, Moab, Edom, and many others. Most of these histories have only recently begun to be written. All of them have long been overshadowed by the imaginary history of the Israel of theology.

These hidden histories have been bypassed by the common usage of our field. We usually do justice to the Stone Age, but the Bronze Age is often described in terms of an introduction to a history of 'earliest Israel'. The past twenty-five years, which have seen this biblically oriented history of Israel deconstructed step by step, have been a willing prisoner of what I think of as a 'watershed' mentality. We are perfectly ready to accept that the Bible's 'earliest' periods were not historical, and as evidence has accumulated we have reluctantly accepted that ever more recent periods were similarly unhistorical. The period before the flood was the very first to become unhistorical. Then came the patriarchs, the Mosaic period, the conquest and the period of the Judges. However, we have been loath to make such judgements. Period after period has been tenaciously retained as valid history until proven entirely impossible. As soon as we find anything at all that can be linked with historical evidence, we stop being critical. We have insisted that the biblical narrative be historical. While we can accept the most rigorous of methods for that part of our history that comes before the watershed, as soon as we cross over into the area we think of as a known past, we quickly resort to the fundamentalism of our childhood.

There is a problem with the question of historicity. I cannot imagine what a biblical text would look like that was judged to be 'historically reliable'. One of the problems with dealing with the traditional histories of the ancient world is that we can only identify the degrees of their unreliability. The razor's edge of a question like historicity identifies fiction, not history. In spite of being trained to use this tool critically, most historians who claim to talk about the 'history of Israel', are really offering us one or other paraphrase of an ancient story. To pay so much attention to biblical views of the past, or for that matter to views like those of Josephus, is a serious error. We all know that the world an author reflects is the one he knows. If we want to write sound and critical history, we need to concentrate on what is implied in a text about that world. Traditional histories are themselves remains of the past. As such, they are data, not evidence. If we see our goal as reconstructing the past, we are pursuing an impossible dream. The past does not and can no longer exist. Archaeological materials and texts – remnants of the past – do exist. When we write history today, we attempt to explain, understand and describe these fragments of the past. History is interpretation of data that exists now. This is why we cannot write history without evidence. It is also why what we write is so fragmented and partial. We are ignorant of most of the past. And that is the beginning of wisdom in history-writing.

The history we create will vary greatly from period to period depending on the data we have available. In the Late Bronze Age, for example, literary texts might easily dominate in our history and encourage us toward writing intellectual history. For this, we are grateful to the collections of poetry from the ancient town of Ugarit on Syria's coast. If we are interested in the developments of societies, and especially in cultural and economic history, then material remains from archaeology, and information drawn from geography, climate studies, soils research and the like, provide us with indispensable primary evidence for writing our history. If, on the other hand, we are dealing with the Hellenistic or Greco-Roman periods, biblical texts, intertestamental literature and the scrolls from the Dead Sea become paramount for understanding an ancient literary and intellectual world. These written materials will provide us with our primary sources.

2 The theology of the way: sectarian reflections on life and society

The central motifs of an 'old' and a 'new' Israel are linked together in the single dominant metaphor of biblical philosophy: the theology of the way. Old Israel walked in the way of the godless, but the new Israel fears God, trusts in Yahweh, loves the *torah*. This metaphor is most exciting in Isaiah's poetry and most systematically developed in the Book of Psalms.

The Book of Psalms is a large collection of poetic texts presented as 150 songs. It is not the only such collection. Among the Dead Sea scrolls we find a number of others, sometimes arranged by themes: wisdom songs, songs with which to exorcise demons, messianic psalms, etc. Our biblical collection, with its songs of praise, its songs of David and Asaph, its pilgrimage songs and laments, seems to have originally come from just such smaller collections. There is no great difference between the songs collected in the scrolls and those we find in the Bible. Nor is there any significant difference between the biblical and the non-biblical songs found at Qumran: neither in the way they were composed, and collected, nor in the way they were used and interpreted. In fact, it is quite clear that the process of song collection and writing, which created our biblical book, was not yet complete when the Dead Sea scrolls were written.

The biblical book has five parts to it, each dedicated to 'the eternal praise of Yahweh'. The collection closes appropriately with five songs of praise: Alleluia songs. More than two dozen other songs begin or close with such words of praise: 'Alleluia!' 'My life, praise Yahweh!' 'Yahweh be praised!' or the like. Clearly, not only is this book of songs collected with the theme of praising God defined as their purpose, but many of the psalms collected were written to express celebration. It is also interesting – and very important for understanding the Psalms – that the use of this motif of praise has the secondary function of drawing together diverse themes and discussions, and interpreting them collectively as a form of praising God. We have good reason to argue that the book as a whole as it now exists in the Bible was understood as a book of songs of praise. It is a psalm book of a group, a community, a society that finds itself identified as those who are addressed by the reiterated exhortation, 'Praise God!'

This intensive hortatory allows us to speak of a voice of these songs and of a coherent audience that is implicit in them. There is hardly a song in the Psalter that sings with a different voice or in a different context. This coherence in the voice of the Psalms is emphasized when we look at the implicit author's reflections on the past. This is not a voice from the cult of old Israel of the ninth or eighth centuries BCE, or of Judah's of the eighth or seventh century. It is also hardly the voice of a temple community that so many scholars once imagined to have existed in the fictional Jerusalem of Ezra or Nehemiah of the Persian period. This voice that calls on its audience to praise God calls forth images not of an older and earlier Israel, but specifically of the Israel we meet in the Bible. The songs don't refer to a past; they are sung within the context of tradition present. The community's self-understanding implicit in these songs is that of the descendants of Israel, the 'children of Israel'. They stand in the path of the 'true Israel', whose truth and reality is not conceived either historically or ethnically. Rather, it is rooted in theological and philosophical reflection on the tradition, which is understood increasingly metaphorically. The many references to the temple, to the king and to the acts of God in the past are not references within the community's memory, but to the community's tradition, which is literary. On the evidence provided by the Psalms themselves, their collective authors know no more about their 'past' as children of Israel than we do merely from reading the literature that has survived.

If we wish to define the community that is implicit in the creation of a book like the Bible's Psalter, it helps to turn again to the Dead Sea scrolls. Although we can not yet identify these scrolls with a particular settlement such as Qumran, or with a particular group such as the Essenes, the similarities of the unique psalms of these scrolls to biblical psalms strongly suggest that a community comparable to that implied by the Bible also developed these texts. A similar perspective is also implied in New Testament texts. This is not to say that the communities implied by the three groups of texts – the Psalter, the psalms of the Dead Sea scrolls and the New Testament – were identical, nor that there were any specific number of such historical communities. What is implied is a common sectarian theological perspective. And we have no reason to believe that the sectarian characteristics of these three different communities were originally competitive with each other. They all, however, stand against what might be called the community of the 'old testament', namely that faithless lost people of Israel's old covenant which Yahweh had long ago destroyed. This metaphorical 'old testament' is neither a text nor a people that ever existed. It is a negative theological concept: a literary metaphor.

The common sectarian language of the biblical Psalter, the Dead Sea scrolls and the New Testament, creates a polarity and contrast between the 'path of truth' and the 'way of fools'. There is neither compromise nor confusion between knowledge and ignorance. The whole of this literature is impregnated with such sectarianism and with its implicit rejection of old Israel's 'godless path'. Such sectarianism is implicit whenever and wherever the tradition gives expression to its piety. Nowhere is this clearer than in the wisdom poetry of Psalms 1 and 2, which together introduce the theological substance of the Psalter. The very opening verses of the Psalter are painted in the black and white of this sectarian pietism:

> Happy is the one who does not walk in the counsel of evildoers nor stand in the way of the godless, who does not sit in the seat of those who mock. He rejoices in Yahweh's *torah* and loves the tradition day and night. He is like a tree, planted close to the water's canal. It gives fruit on time and its leaves never fall. Everything he does, succeeds. (Ps 1: 1–3)

The stark sectarian contrast between the counsel of evil and the love of *torah* which identifies the singer of the Psalms is also taken up in the Book of Jeremiah. In Jeremiah 17: 5–8, a close variant of this same 'Lego-block' of tradition is used to describe ancient Judah headed for destruction and exile:

> Cursed be he who trusts in men and seeks strength among mortals, whose heart turns away from Yahweh. He is like a bush in the desert, blind to any happiness that comes. He will live in the hard desert, on the salt flats where none can live. Blessed is he that trusts in Yahweh and finds refuge in him. He is like a tree, planted close to the water's canal, which sends its roots into the stream. He has no need to fear the summer's heat when it comes. Its leaves are green. It has no fear of the year of drought and never ceases to bear fruit.

In both our texts, those who trust in the human are cursed; those who trust God are blessed. The tree living from the water is ever green, ever bearing. In Jeremiah it stands in contrast to the desert fate of a bush without water. This desert motif is particularly interesting as it echoes a motif of Genesis 1: 2's 'shapeless and empty nothingness' that existed before the creation. In Jeremiah 4: 23–26, this was interpreted as the desert of Israel's exile. The ever-bearing tree is echoed in the great passage of Job 14: 7–9. The fate of humans is compared to the hope of a tree. Job gives expression to the Bible's systematic contrast between the death-bringing 'acts of men', which lead to nothingness, and the creative 'acts of God', which create new life for a new Israel:

> For a tree there is hope. If it is chopped down, it can live again. It never stops setting new shoots even when its roots are old in the ground and the stump dies. It grows once more. As soon as it finds water, it sprouts branches like a new-planted tree.

The passage in Job continues with its psalm-like contrast: 'A person, however, dies and it is over for him . . . a human being lies down, and does not rise again', etc. The poetry of the philosophical traditions, that we find in the Psalms and Job, establish principles, while the prophets apply them to the story tradition. The discussion as a whole is surprisingly unified. The same contrast is established between the divine and the human. The creation story of Genesis 1 is the prime metaphor. Good is that which God alone does. That is true reality. Those who understand walk in God's ways. What mankind does, stands in stark contrast. The way of mankind is the way of fools and the godless. That path had led to ancient Israel's destruction and death. This contrast is set as a philosophical principle in Psalm 1's introduction.

The metaphor of contrasting ways of life, which sets this philosophical perspective, is hardly unique to the Bible. It is a firmly established principle in ancient Near Eastern wisdom literature, from at least the beginning of the second millennium BCE. In the Bible, we find a fixed and established contrast between a way of life that is evil and does not succeed, and a path that is good. This way is happy or blessed. The path of the godless is the way of flesh, the way of pain, of evil. It is the way of one's own thoughts, of mankind, of violence, of sinners, of fools and the like. The way of Yahweh is the path of the spirit, of joy, innocence, piety and wisdom, of righteousness, peace and goodness, truth, holiness, humility and life, the way of Zion. This is the way of David and of Solomon. Both of these contrasting clusters of motifs are firmly fixed. They do not cross over the metaphor's black and white division of good and evil. The path of evil implies the way of sinners, the godless and the way of mankind, just as God's way is precisely the way of the spirit and of philosophy. One can in fact say that 'the way of mankind' is never 'God's way', *as a philosophical principle*. Although the language varies considerably and many motifs are used, there is but a single perception of reality that all give voice to. Such perception constantly presents the adherent to such a philosophy with the exclusive choice of either/or. It is a sectarian, and implicitly fanatic, demand for decision and choice. One is either for or against God: for or against the tradition.

The recognition of this theological context of the Book of Psalms suggests that they are interpreted by their collectors within a context of education and pietism. Such intellectually oriented traditions as this theology of the way is clearly expressed in the Psalms' concentration on the place of the *torah:* the 'teaching' or the 'tradition'. One 'finds joy in Yahweh's *torah*; one loves the tradition day and night'. One commits oneself to *torah* study without limit. This too sets the tradition in contrast to old Israel and gives expression to the new. Joshua 1: 8 offers us a story variant of the psalmist's principle:

> Keep this book of *torah* always on your lips; love it day and night. Do carefully all that is written in it; it will be for your good and you will find success in it.

Matthew's gospel gives this theology of the way a place of honour in Jesus' teaching in the context of his sermon on the mount in Matthew 5: 3–12. 'Blessed are the poor in spirit, for the kingdom of heaven is theirs,' etc. Matthew lists eight positive ways of our early tradition, before closing with a threefold negative way as contrasting response:

> Blessed are the poor in spirit, for theirs is the kingdom of heaven. Blessed are those who mourn, for they shall be comforted. Blessed are the meek, for they shall inherit the earth. Blessed are those who hunger and thirst for righteousness, for they shall be satisfied. Blessed are the merciful, for they shall obtain mercy. Blessed are the pure in heart, for they shall see God. Blessed are the peacemakers, for they shall be called sons of God. Blessed are those who

are persecuted for righteousness, for theirs is the kingdom of heaven. Blessed are you when men scorn you, speak evil and lie about you for my sake. Rejoice, be happy, for your reward is great in heaven. This is the way they persecuted the prophets before you.

Luke's gospel (6: 20–26) offers yet another variant, with, however, a careful balance of four positive and four negative ways. A fragmented text from Qumran (4QBeatitudes) gives a similar eight-fold list, with contrasting positive and negative ways. One finds the love of *torah* likened to a man's love for his wife.

The New Testament is quite explicit about its participation in the Bible's theology of the way. This is clear from Matthew 11's story about John the Baptist, where Jesus, citing Isaiah, describes John as 'more than a prophet. He is the one about whom it is written: "I send my angel before you; he will prepare your path." ' Throughout the whole of Matthew's gospel, Jesus' way is God's way. The story had begun with John's question: 'Are you the one who is to come?' Matthew has Jesus answer by giving six signs of the theology of the way, and has him close with a warning hint of the negative: 'The blind see. The lame walk. Lepers are clean. The deaf hear. The dead rise and the good news is announced to the poor. May he be happy who is not offended by me.'

At the close of the story in 11: 16–17, Matthew offers a dramatic parable which, like Jeremiah, interprets this theology in terms of a theatrical presentation of Israel's fall. 'This generation', in Matthew's eyes, goes the way of old Israel:

With what should I compare this generation? Children, sitting in the square shouting to each other: we played the flute for you but you wouldn't dance; we sang a song of mourning, but you did not weep.

There are many nuances and variants to the 'way of truth and righteousness'. The most dominant are those that deal with the great and beloved teacher. The richness of this well-known figure encourages us to recognize its important pedagogical role. The Psalms offer the theology of the way in a context of pietism: in pious songs of praise and reflective prayer. Stories and legends about the beloved teacher mark this context as educational and scholarly. Such literary dramatizations present the either/or demands of the theology of the way in the form of philosophers or 'teachers of righteousness'. Such are Solomon in the Book of Ecclesiastes, Jesus Ben Sira in Sirach, or the anonymous 'teacher of righteousness' in the Dead Sea scrolls. We also have the teachers of the *torah:* Moses, Joshua, Ezra and Jesus, and teachers of the covenant renewed such as Josiah, Ezra and Jesus. All, in one form or another, teach the way of truth and *torah*.

Moses – whose *torah* is described as the teaching of God – is certainly the best example among these figures in the Bible in its expression of the theology of the way. This is precisely because his teaching is never his own. He plays a dumbling's role. He can't talk. He doesn't want to lead. He breaks the tablets of the Ten Commandments in his anger and he is disobedient. That is, he is *only* a human being. His teachings are God's. In a contrasting manner, Ezra, in the Book of Ezra 7–8, is portrayed as a learned scribe, a great teacher and judge who instructs the whole nation in 'the *torah* of the God of heaven'. Ezra is another Moses in the manner of Exodus 18: the idealistic representative of the oral *torah*. In contrast, Nehemiah 9's story of the new Israel receiving the *torah*, portrays an Ezra who reads the *torah* to the people. This is the written *torah*. In the paraphrase given of his reading it is clear that it is the Pentateuch as *torah* that is the object of the narrative. Such historicization or dramatization of the role of teacher, as we find in the Moses and Ezra traditions, has led to a story development that is quite comparable in its size and importance to the development of the stories of Samuel and Kings. These stories give the theology of the way both positive and negative illustration. King Saul, who was a good king in his own eyes, failed in one thing: doing the divine will. He is placed in contrast to the new messiah, David, who, praying on the Mount of Olives in II Samuel 15, represents the pious in his prayer that not his but God's will be done. Throughout the whole of Kings, the contrast between the path of Yahweh and the way of the ungodly dominates: Solomon and his wives, Ahab and Elijah. The entire fate of Israel is reduced to an illustration of the evil 'way of Jeroboam'.

The role of the beloved teacher easily gives way to a close variant: the teacher as founder of a community of the new Israel. Ezra and Jesus are certainly the Bible's best-known examples of such figures, but the pattern is already set by Moses with Israel at Sinai. It is found again in Joshua's role as the first teacher of the way of the *torah* in Joshua 1: 7–9. It belongs closely linked to the motifs of leaving the desert, returning from exile, coming to the promised land and entering 'God's kingdom'. Outside of the Bible, the Damascus Covenant's 'teacher of righteousness' is a figure who has saved the repentant remnant from destruction to found, like Ezra, a new Israel. He is the teacher who leads the people along 'the path of God's heart':

When he [i.e., God] remembered the covenant of the very first, he saved a remnant for Israel and did not deliver them up for destruction. And at the moment of wrath, three hundred and ninety years after having delivered them up into the hands of Nebuchadnezzar, king of Babylon, he visited and caused to sprout from Israel and from Aaron a shoot of the planting, in order to possess his land and to become fat with the good things of his soil. And they realized their sin and knew that they were guilty men; but they were like blind persons and like those who grope for the path over twenty years. And God appraised their deeds, because they sought him with a perfect heart and raised up for them a Teacher of Righteousness, in order to direct them in the path of his heart.[1]

The manner in which this figure of beloved teacher becomes romanticized and idealized follows a form of dramatizing narrative. Focus on the teacher as model becomes a form of hagiography and *imitatio*. One can walk in the path of righteousness and truth through listening to the teacher: through obedience and discipleship. This follows much the pattern of the Psalter's use of David. Such commentary brings us quickly from literary to historical contexts. Increasingly and rapidly, the societies that read and studied such traditions and that identified such pietism as their own model themselves on the literary images of the traditions themselves. This takes on the form of a way of life.

3 New life and resurrection

The love of the *torah* urged by Psalm 1, and its close variant in the opening of the Book of Joshua, support two distinct clusters of motifs around a metaphor of a tree planted by a canal. The tree is lovingly cultivated. It lives and bears fruit. The tree is well cared for. It stand in its Eden with Yahweh as its divine gardener. Echoes of the paradise story, with its tree of life in the centre of the garden, from which life-giving water springs and flows to the four rivers of the world, are heard throughout the Bible's variants on this metaphor.

Psalm 92: 12–14, clearly echoing the songs of the beloved's garden that we find in the Song of Songs, also shares in this literary cluster surrounding the tree of life. 'The righteous thrive like the palm tree, and grow great as the cedars of Lebanon. They are planted in Yahweh's temple; they thrive in the courtyard of our God. Even in old age,[2] they bear fruit and are fresh and green.' In Psalm 52: 8, the singer himself sings with the voice of this metaphorical tree: 'I am as the green olive tree in God's house; I trust in God's eternal steadfastness.'

That these are not isolated metaphors, but an intellectually coherent cluster of motifs, reflective of an implicit theological discussion, becomes very clear when we notice the various forms that illustrations of the *via negativa* take. We find ourself in a coherent world of contrasting images.

---

[1] The translation is the author's revision of F. Garcia–Martinez, *The Dead Sea Scrolls Translated* (Brill, Leiden, 1994), p.48.

[2] Here we have an echo of the Abraham story (see Gen. 18, especially vv. 11–14), marking the patriarchs as models for the theology of the way.

The barren desert is contrasted with the cultivated garden. The well-watered, fruitful tree is compared with the motifs of dried chaff and wilderness bush. The way of God and the way of men: all images of life and renewal of life are alternatives to death. We see this already in these same Psalms, 52 and 92. Just before the lines bearing the metaphors of the good tree are sung in both these psalms, we find their contrasting motifs. In spite of the fact that the stanza in Psalm 52: 2–4 speaks explicitly of people who talk about and plan evil, verse 5 makes it clear that the singer's implicit metaphor of the tree with its cultivated land/desert contrast is central: 'God will destroy you forever and drive you out of your tent; *he will pull you out from the living land by the roots.*' Similarly, Psalm 92: 6 complains of the lack of understanding of Yahweh's enemies. This intellectual image of the way of the godless nevertheless calls up an analogue of a plant that quickly sprouts and blooms, only to be destroyed forever (92: 7).

This form of theological reading of the tradition, while lending itself much to historicizing a sectarian understanding of the world in the stories of ancient Israel, also finds its expression in provocative discourse. It easily shows itself as a form of preaching, becoming a practical theology. The reading of the tradition calls the audience to a way of life to be lived out. New Testament examples of this are abundant, giving expression to the metaphor of the teacher as 'the way, the truth and the light'. This urges those who see themselves as his students to follow his example. The stories themselves rest on the already long-established function of so many of the older biblical variants in this discussion. Isaiah 6: 8–13 gives us an excellent example of such use of the tradition. It is the prophet's voice we hear when the scene opens:

> I heard the voice of my lord say: 'Whom should I send? Who will take the message for us?' I answered: 'Here am I; send me.' So he told me: 'Go and say to this people: "You shall hear and hear but not comprehend; you will see and see but not imagine." Cover this people's heart with fat, make their ears heavy and close their eyes, so that they cannot see with their eyes, hear with their ears or comprehend with their heart, that they repent that he might heal them.' I asked: 'How long, lord?' and he answered: 'Until the cities lie deserted, without inhabitants: houses without people, and the earth has become a desert. Yahweh will be rid of the people, and the land will be empty, abandoned. If a tenth part should remain; that too will be rooted out: as when a terebinth or an oak is felled, there remains but a stump. It is that stump that is holy seed.'

Notice the technique used in creating this prophetic scene. Implicit in the opening is a mythological context, as in the opening of Job's book. A divine assembly lies at a heavenly distance from the world of men, with the divine 'master', playing the role of anti-teacher, deliberating how he is to prevent his teachings being followed on earth. Here too Isaiah plays the role of anti-prophet. He is over-eager: not like the great Jeremiah or Moses, men whose fate is controlled by their God. Isaiah wants to bring the message. Here he is the mirror image of his opposite: Jonah, who fled to sea to escape being given just such an assignment to Nineveh. The same understanding of reality exists in both stories: God is in control; he establishes destiny. Jonah's role, however, was played out as the one successful prophet in the Bible: his preaching led to Nineveh's repentance. Isaiah plays a caricature of the prophets of the past. He will preach so that the people do not hear, see or understand; that they do not repent; that they are not saved. Isaiah's messianic 'lord' in this scene has total control, like Yahweh of the Exodus story hardening the heart of the pharaoh. The prophet becomes Jeremiah-like in his impatience for Israel's salvation. He asks, How long? As long as mankind's alienation from the earth in Genesis, an alienation that ends only in our death when we are reunited with it, for Isaiah's master responds: when they are all gone: when the land becomes a desert again. A repentant remnant? Even that image of hope is rejected. If a tenth should survive, that too will be destroyed. The tree's hope, which seemed so promising in Job, becomes a dead stump. It is in such blackness of Job-like despair that the poet finally allows the impossible irony of divine grace, a 'holy seed', to appear.

It is a difficult and certainly dark theology that is presented here. Old Israel – with its prophets – belongs to the way of human understanding. It comes to nothing and is without meaning. All reality is God's: what he wants, what he does. Isaiah's people – his Israel and his Jerusalem – are a lost people: marked for death. The text's perspective is rather that of a new Israel: that which has come out of the past's 'dead stump'. The scene is played from the vantage point of philosophy and its function is to understand the past. What the prophet does and what ancient Israel did, repentant and not repentant, is all much the same. The prophet's message prevents understanding. It was God's purpose to destroy this people, so that there might be a 'holy seed'. The motifs gathered here are important: destruction and deportation. There is no repentant remnant here. The image of the desert evokes the totality of Sodom's destruction. The hopeful metaphor of the tree is handled with a harsh irony. It is on the motif of hopelessness that the poem turns: a tree felled: Isaiah's dead stump.

Even though Isaiah 10: 18–21 will bring this motif of Israel's dead stump together with the metaphor of a repentant remnant leading to the new Israel,[1] the poet here in Isaiah 6 does not deal either with a motif of

---

[1] The metaphor of the new Israel as a repentant remnant is clearest in texts of implicit preaching as in Amos 5: 3–4: 'The town that sends out a thousand men, will bring only a hundred home; that which sends out a hundred will bring only ten back to Israel's house. Yahweh says this to the house of Israel: "Seek me and you will live!" '

survival or with a repentance leading to salvation. The dominant motifs are rather of destiny created, determined by God. They deal with renewal of life and resurrection. The denial of hope is emphatic and necessary. The life of the new Israel is a pure gift. The total destruction of old Israel is required of the metaphor: there is no remnant. Nevertheless, a stump remains. That such a worthless dead 'remnant' is declared 'holy seed' is intended to astonish. The metaphor functions much in the same way as Hosea 1: 8's child who is 'not my people'. It is that hopeless child that hears the words of Hosea 2: 23's, 'You are my people. It is this child that will respond "You are my God." ' The centre of interest in this theology of the way is not what happened or didn't happen to ancient Israel. Ancient Israel is nothing more than a source of powerful metaphors. It is the response to the divine that is the focus and goal of this theology of the way, not a judgement – either historical or theological – about events past. A 'dead stump' becomes 'holy seed' just as the desert's formlessness and emptiness led to creation in Genesis 1: 2. The theme is from death to life. Resurrection lies in the journey of the soul. The poet seeks such metaphorical contradiction with purpose. The metaphorical tree of death in the shadows of the garden story becomes the tree of life. Just so does the poet find his way back to the tree that had been long blocked by the cherubim's magic sword of Genesis 3. Isaiah is a discursive commentary on the tradition: the tree of death is Israel past. Hope's tree – the tree of life – has become its dead stump, a worthless remnant, a stump which in Job's despair of things human sends out shoots of new life: 'it never stops sending out new shoots' (Job 14: 7–9). Where is Job's tree's hope? Not in the tree. In Isaiah the tree has been chopped down by the Assyrians, in Jeremiah by the Babylonian army. But even so, hope springs new. The roots seek water and water brings life. In this pious metaphor of divine mercy, hope resides in adhering to the 'path of God'. No stump is dead. As soon as the water of divine grace reaches the roots, just so quickly does the tree become as a 'new-planted tree', which in Jeremiah certainly is the self-understanding of a new Israel.

The poem in Job 14: 7–15 works this same metaphor, and finds a comparable resolution. The harshness of human life is expressed in the figure of the suffering Job who attempts to plead his case before his silent God. Such a life is worse than death: 'Would that you would hide me in death's realm, that I might be safe until your anger passes. Set a limit and then remember me again!' Job remarks: 'There is hope for a tree.' But for a person? In just a few phrases Job's author creates a picture of the saving renewal of life, a resurrection on the basis of the ever-new hope that every tree's dead stump has. Like Jeremiah's Israel, he would hide until God's anger passes. Job will trust in a renewal of life. He asks his question clearly, unequivocally: 'Can one who is dead live again?' In this characterization, Job's character takes on new possibilities as pietism's model of patience: 'I will endure . . . till my redemption comes.' There is hope for one who holds to the path of Yahweh. Just such texts express the theology that forms the foundation of a variety of dramatic forms and historicizations.

Expressions and motifs used to describe the way of evil fill out and deepen the theme of new life and resurrection. In contrast to the qualities of life given by the tree standing by the water, Psalm 1's introduction to the Psalter offers us the image of chaff, which surfaces once again in the well-known metaphor of separating the wheat from the chaff. 'The godless are like chaff that the wind blows away.' Those who walk in the way of the *torah* stand fast; while those who walk in the path of the godless are blown away by the spirit.

A very interesting dramatic form of this motif can be found in Psalm 35: 4–6, which is presented as sung by David:

> Let those who seek my life be put to scorn and dishonour; let them who plan evil against me be set back and shamed. Let them be like chaff in the wind: with Yahweh's messenger driving them off. May their path be dark and slippery with the angel of Yahweh in pursuit!

As is so typical of the use of the figure of David in the Old Testament, pietism's image of the godless as chaff in the divine wind takes on mythological shape. Yahweh's messenger plays out a role of saving deliverer of the pious and of scourge of the impious. This is a role that we will see below taken up in Psalms 2 and 8 by a mythological David as messiah. Here, it is David's opening prayer in Psalm 35 that opens the poetic imagination to metaphorical battle: 'Fight, Yahweh against those who would fight against me; go to war with them who pursue me with war.' Yet, even here, the poem remains as a dramatization of a personal religious struggle: 'Tell my soul: "I am your salvation." '

While Psalm 35 has given the metaphor a context within the traditions of David's wars of both story and mythology, a variant form of dramatization of this same block of tradition is given in Jeremiah 23: 12. Here, it is the enemy that takes shape in the story of the fate Jeremiah declares for godless prophets and priests: 'May their path be slippery; may they stumble in the dark where they shall fall.'

We can also see a double variation of this same pietistic form of turning proverbs into story, and giving 'enemies' of God imaginative forms in the poem collected in Job 21: 17–26. In verse 18 the poet sings of the godless as 'straw before the wind; as chaff that the spirit drives away'. As chapter 14 had questioned the hope of resurrection, implied in the metaphor of a tree, Job 20–21 questions the truth of the theology of the way. This concerns the destiny of the godless. First, Zophar instructs Job in the wisdom of this theology. In doing so, the text reflects the rhetoric of both the prophets and the Psalms:

You know that it has always been so, since humanity was first placed on earth, that the celebration of the godless is short, and their happiness but for a moment . . . He will blow away like a dream, never to be found; he will fly like a vision of the night . . . Heaven will expose his guilt. The earth will rise against him. Rivers will sweep his 'house' away; taking it away on the day of wrath. This is the inheritance that God has dealt out for the godless. This is the fate that God has determined for him. (Job 20: 4–5, 8, 27–29)

The author has Job respond with his small question challenging the established pietism of his peers and their understanding of the divine:

Why are the godless allowed to live? Even when they grow old, they are strong and healthy . . . they are not struck down by the rod of God . . . they live out their days in happiness . . . How often does the lamp of the godless go out? . . . How often do they really become like straw before the wind, like chaff which the wind blows away? (Job 21: 7, 9, 13, 17, 18)

Job questions the theological establishment here. It is Zophar who gives voice to the typical use of this metaphor in the Bible. The Psalms describe the enemies of God, of David and of pietism. Jeremiah describes Israel and Jerusalem past as godless and doomed to destruction. In doing so, both offer the established truths of theology. Job, however, disputes such confidence, and his challenge to pietistic faith, in answer to his friend Zophar's reiteration of this theology, underlines the lie of his friend's dogmatism: 'How empty is the comfort you bring me; how false your answer.' (Job 21: 34) The Bible's theology is not a theology of truths. It is a way of critical reflection. It is learning and discourse. In the Book of Job, which opens with Yahweh betting with Satan about whether Job walks in the way of God or not, this discourse reaches a critical high point.

The use of biblical narrative to give dramatic form to this piety rarely allows the lure of story to blind the discussion to its real context in this larger philosophical discourse. This becomes particularly clear when we look at the way Hosea mixes his metaphors about the godless as ephemeral with the motifs both of morning dew and chaff in the wind. Hosea 13: 2–3 brings it into his description of old Israel's Ephraim:

They go on to sin more and more; they make images of gods for themselves, idols of silver: the work of clever men . . . They sacrifice humans, they kiss calves: therefore they will be like the morning dew, like the early, fleeting dew, which like chaff is blown from the threshing floor.

The dread implications of the threshing floor as expressive of divine wrath are unavoidable. This is the second time that Hosea takes up this cluster of motifs. In 6: 4–5. Hosea has used it to describe the basis for Yahweh's decisive rejection of the Israel and Judah of the past:

> What am I to do with you, Ephraim? What am I to do with you, Judah? Your loyalty is like the morning dew, like the early, fleeting dew. Therefore I will cut them down with the prophets: kill them with my own words. My judgement will be on them as light.

The intellectual implications of this commentary on Judah and Ephraim's promised destruction should not be missed. It is not a reference to nations of the past, but to current text and tradition. Not Assyrian and Babylonian swords, but the intellectual weapons of words punish such faithlessness. There is no deportation from the land threatened; nor is a foreign exile the people's fate. Ephraim and Judah are to be alienated from their destiny in history's light.

A large cluster of motifs is implicated here, as we are brought back to the positive metaphors of light and water, linked to life and resurrection. It is the contrasting despairing judgement on Ephraim and Judah that carries implications of a variation on Job's critique. This passage of Hosea is given as a response to the opening verses of chapter 6, offering us pietism's confident voice. Ephraim and Judah play the roles of Job's friends:

> Let us return to Yahweh. He has ripped us that he might heal us; he has struck us that he might heal us. He will give us life after two days; raise us up after three, that we might live in his presence. Let us know Yahweh; let us try to know him. He rises as surely as the morning dawn. He will come to us like the showers, like the rain that waters the earth. (Hosea 6: 1–3)

Shall Ephraim and Judah have their hope that Job, Jeremiah and the Psalms have promised in their metaphor of the tree, in the promise of Isaiah's holy seed? Where is the stream on whose bank Psalm 1's tree of life stands? With the Book of Job, Hosea stands on the critical side of this discussion. It rejects Ephraim's and Judah's hubris and confidence of living in God's presence. Hosea stands not only with Job here, but, with its motif of repentence, in agreement also with Jonah (2: 9–10), Psalm 71: 20 and I Samuel 2: 6. Salvation comes from Yahweh, and as he wishes it. Hosea returns us to the central biblical perception of the divine: that his will is everything. It is the prayer of David and of Jesus on the Mount of Olives; it is Jonah's prayer in the belly of the whale; it is Hannah's prayer. This is nothing to give one confidence. There is no security, no certainty here.

Certainly, the one text most playful and full of fantasy, among the many that deal with the theme of new life and resurrection, is the comic story of Ezekiel's macabre journey to the valley of death that we find in Ezekiel 37: 1–14. The hand of Yahweh takes Ezekiel to a valley that is full of bones.

He shows Ezekiel all around. All these huge number of bones are dried out, and so Yahweh puts Job's question to Ezekiel: 'Can these bones live?' Ezekiel answers, quite appropriately if also ironically, that only God can answer that question. Yahweh then orders Ezekiel to prophesy to these bones:

> 'You dried-up bones, hear Yahweh's word! So says Yahweh, my lord, to these bones: "I give you the breath of life. So, live. I put sinews on you. I cover you with flesh. I cover you with skin and give you life's breath, so that you will be alive. This I do that you might understand that I am Yahweh." ' I prophesied as I had been ordered, and while I prophesied, there was a rustling sound and the bones came together . . . (Ez. 37: 4–7)

After the bones come to life and stand there as a great army, Yahweh explains to Ezekiel that these bones had been the people of Israel who had said: 'Our bones are dried up; our hope is swallowed; it is all up with us.' (Ez. 37: 11) He then orders Ezekiel to prophesy again:

> 'So says Yahweh's God: "My people, I open your graves and lead you from them to bring you to the land of Israel. In this way, you will understand that I am Yahweh . . . I will give you my spirit and you will live, and I will let you live in the land . . ." ' (Ez. 37: 12–14)

This is the breath of Yahweh of the garden story which makes the clay figure of a human into a living creature (Gen. 2: 7). It is the divine spirit of Psalm 104: 29–30: 'When you take away *your* breath they die and become dust again; when you send your spirit, you create life and make the world new again.' When the author has Yahweh explain that he brings Israel, his people, from its grave, he is echoing the same motif of a more historicized variant of a return from exile from the previous chapter (36: 24): 'I will draw you from the nations and collect you from all the lands. I will bring you to your own country.' The bringing together of these two variants in Ezekiel clearly demonstrates the tradition's understanding of the return from exile as resurrection. In the same way, the renewal of life in the new Israel is expressed through the metaphor of a newborn child. Israel that was dead lives again.

This metaphor is put to pietism's purpose in terms of the theology of the way in Psalm 30, where resurrection becomes the leitmotif of the entire psalm. This is the explicit declaration of verse 3: 'You brought me from the realm of the dead; you let me live, that I not go down to the grave.' The psalm, offering some eighteen different variants of this motif, could well be called 'the resurrection psalm'.

I'd like to close our discussion of resurrection texts in the Old Testament with reference to the Book of Daniel 12: 1–3. This passage clarifies the metaphor by bringing a dehistoricized understanding of the exile together with the either/or demands of the theology of the way:

> At that time, Michael, the great prince will arise, who will stand by the people. It will be a time of trouble, such as there has not been since there had been a nation. At that time, your people will be saved: all who are inscribed in the book. Many of those who sleep in the ground, will waken, some till eternal life and some to shame and to eternal horror. The wise will shine with the brilliance of heaven's firmament and those who led many to righteousness [will shine] like stars forever and always.

The inclusion of the mythological prince Michael, the watcher over the people,[1] marks this variant as entirely unhistorical and metaphorical. This is also clear from the pedagogically interpretive verse 3, granting eternal life to those who teach others. The story's separation, however, of those who are to awaken to eternal life from those who face eternal horror and scorn presents Psalm 1's divisive choice. A total commitment to the *torah* stands opposed to the way of the ungodly as an ontological principle. Again and again, the biblical texts demonstrate the inescapable sectarian character of their language and imagery. In doing so, they tell us much of the social context of the Bible's composers and those that maintained it as their tradition. It seems appropriate now to address the concrete historical contexts for the development of such sectarian societies in ancient Palestine.

4 Prospects for the Bible and history

We have not one history of Palestine to write. There are a dozen or more histories along the southern fringe of greater Syria. In no period does this become more apparent than in the Late Bronze to Iron II transition period, from the late thirteenth to early ninth century BCE. The entire region suffers economic crisis, periodically intensified by droughts, collapse of trade and changes in imperial and political support systems. Some regions suffer major immigration, especially from the Aegean and from coastal Anatolia, and a long process of assimilation. Other regions become seriously depopulated and are threatened with demographic collapse as towns and villages are abandoned. Some areas undergo a shift towards more drought-resistant economies, and even desedentarization as large numbers seem to turn to pastoralism. Still other regions experience an influx of refugees who found new settlements. These bring with them

---

[1] Also see Dan. 10: 3–21 and Rev. 12: 7.

demands for land-clearing and terrace-building. While no region remains unchanged, each region has its own timetable and specific histories of stress, imperial support, collapse or recovery. Of the many geographically distinct regions of Palestine, it can be said that no two of them witnessed a common history of transition from the end of the Late Bronze Age until the Iron Age proper. Neighbouring regions affected only a sub-region's periphery. All of this suggests a small-region orientation of the people at the beginning of the Assyrian period. If one must speak of ethnicities at this early period – and I do not think we can – we must speak of some dozens of groups within western Palestine alone.

The intrusion of imperial politics into the region, however, and the establishment of Assyrian authority with its support of some of the larger forms of political patronage in Palestine in towns such as Gaza, Ashqelon, Lachish, Jerusalem, Gezer, Samaria, Akko, Beth Shan, Hazor, Dan and elsewhere, did not support population integration or the development of national autonomy. It rather worked actively against integration. The nature of competition between Palestine's many lesser patrons effectively prevented any single region from developing an indigenous threat to Assyrian interests. Tyre, Damascus and Samaria competed for the Jezreel; Tyre and Damascus for the Galilee; Ammon and Israel for the Gilead; Jerusalem and Lachish for Judea, etc.

The widely used Assyrian policies of deportation and population resettlement, inherited and used in turn by the Babylonians, Persians and Macedonians, systematically fragmented the Palestinian infrastructure. Such policies destroyed both the continuity and the coherence of regional associations. Even the propaganda of 'policies of return', had this effect, creating foreign colonies entirely dependent on imperial patronage for their legitimacy. Witness the destruction of the Jewish temple belonging to the military colony at Elephantine by the local population of 'Egyptians', as well as the biblical traditions of rejection and conflict between those identified as 'returnees' and groups identified as Samaritans or 'people of the land'.

The period in Palestine from the ninth to the fifth centuries BCE hardly promoted the development of any durable and regionally coherent population. Region-wide coherence was undermined severely by the traditional political structures of the Levant. Not only did imperial forms of despotism maintain a balance of competing regional powers, but local systems of patronage prevented the accumulation of power locally except in forms of coalitions among traditional competitors. Both loyalties and military potential were fragmented. This is apparent in the proliferation of fortifications around most of Palestine's small towns. In the Persian period we have the imperial province of Yehud, but that was no more reflective of a people than other Persian provinces. This is no less true of Samaria. Any constructs of ethnic or cultural unity must at least begin with evidence, and here, the texts from the Jewish colony of Elephantine may prove more important for Jerusalem's history in this period than anachronistic biblical ones.

Texts do not give direct evidence for the construction of a history of any world of the past asserted by their authors, but rather for the history and perspective of the authors' own world as implied in the texts' projections. This world is rather Greco-Roman than Hellenistic. We should be dating not traditions but the historical contexts of *texts*. These are first known from Qumran in the second century BCE, in contexts which clearly show that the formation of biblical books is still in process. No Bible as such existed in the Hellenistic period, only some very specific texts and collections of them. The analysis and interpretation of these texts is our primary historical source for understanding Hellenism in Asia. The intellectual worlds of the Old and New Testament text-traditions hold a common perception, distinguishable at most as older and younger contemporary witnesses of a common tradition.

5 Continuities and discontinuities in Palestine's history

The biblical tradition does not offer a representation of the past so much as it presents the understanding and meaning that the biblical authors' contemporaries attributed to the past. The history of Palestine, which we have traced from at least the late Neolithic period, reflects a continuity of the people of Palestine. Historically, if we are to ask where the people who wrote the Bible come from, we should first point to this Neolithic period when the early villagers and farmers of Palestine adopted and developed the Semitic language and established their own version of a Mediterranean economy. The social and cultural continuities of Palestine's population from that time are marked and unequivocal. We see them in the material remains and particularly in the styles of pottery from cooking pots and storage jars, as well as in the later developments of lamps and common ware. We find them in the structures of the economy, the political structures of patronage, the types of settlement, even the continuity of the trade routes. The establishment of the empire, first with the Assyrians, which was to continue until modern times, changed few of these structures. The development of religious beliefs was also progressive, involving as much a reinterpretation of the old as an introduction of the new. The foundations of biblical thought were centred in an inclusive monotheism, which was based on a reinterpretation of Palestine's religious past. The characteristic of the Bible as collected tradition confirms continuities it created. Judaism and Christianity, though themselves later than the writings taken up in the Bible, clearly understood themselves as heirs to this intellectual tradition. As Judaism gave way to the dominance of Christianity in the Byzantine period in the course of the fourth century CE, and when both Christianity and Judaism gave place to Islam in the seventh, changes took place in the religious thoughts of the population, but such changes were both developmental and incremental. Even the great displacements of the twentieth century, leading to the establishment of the state of Israel, have been understood in terms of return. They are spoken of in the language of continuity.

From such a perspective, one must say that Palestine's population has ever set a high price on its continuity. Even the disruptions of imperial population policies had been reinterpreted in favour of continuities. Indigency was given the immigrants as their birthright. Historical continuities were also in fact great. Although deportation and exile, and subsequent changes of identity and self-understanding, have been the fate of many during the history of this region, continuity has played a countervailing role. The state of Israel ceased to be in the year 722 BCE, but the people and many of the villages and towns of Israel continued and the historical continuities of this highland population with the medieval and modern Samaritan communities around Nablus can be confirmed through continuities of the agricultural population in the Shechem valley and elsewhere in the central highlands. Economic and cultural continuity can be traced back to the Early Bronze Age. One must not imagine the Assyrians creating a *tabula rasa* of the highlands in 722. They had a territory to administer and to draw taxes from. While the genetic mix of the population must have been substantially altered by these changes, many remained in the region and provided the language, culture, religion and way of life for the varied 'returnees' who were brought to the land from Arabia, Elam and Syria. Not all went into exile; nor did all go to Egypt. The archaeological continuities are marked, as are the continuities of language, culture, religion and way of life. 'Race' in the modern discriminatory sense is not an issue during this period. The year 586 BCE disrupted and changed political life in Jerusalem. That was politics. The lives of most people were picked up again and continued along old lines. The end of Palestine's regional states brought the population into an imperial context. National identity with the formation of ethnicity had failed.

The primary referent of the Bible's fictive, familial and ethnic unity is not reflected in the narratives of patriarchs, judges or kings. These are all stories about old Israel. The primary identification is found rather in the stories, songs and metaphors of 'exodus', of 'wilderness', of 'exile' and 'return'. These centre on the motif of the *benei Yisrael* as the 'people of God', as Yahweh's 'first-born' and as his 'inheritance'. These stories all are solidly rooted in the self-defining, grand epochal line of a God without a home or a people searching for a people without a home or a God. It is in this metaphor that we find the foundation and matrix for the ethnographic metaphor of all Israel. This metaphor gives voice to the 'new Israel' with its centre in Yahweh's temple of the 'new Jerusalem'. This is an identity that is formed from the perspective of the sectarian theology of the way.

In the biblical discourse about the presence of the divine, the multiplicity of divine names, epithets, art and symbol become transformed. The Bible offers an interpretation of the divine as a coherent reality of the heavens. It also interprets the diverse characteristics that are found reflected in human traditions as false and distorting. It is in this restructuring of tradition that the implied authorial voices of the Bible are most clearly debating the 'new Israel'. To apply this biblical view to the Iron Age is anachronistic. The Yahweh of history is as different from the Bible's Yahweh, as the Israel of history is different from the Bible's new Israel.

The question of Yahweh's historicity is quickly clarified with reference to the Yahweh of history, which we reviewed already in chapter 7 above. The earliest known references to Yahweh come up in the form of a toponym in Egyptian texts of the fourteenth to thirteenth century BCE and we have considerable historical evidence for a plurality of Yahwehs from the Iron Age. We know a Yahu or Yau of Nebo. We also know of the Yahwehs of Teman and of Samaria, and we possibly have pictures of them from Kuntillat Ajrud, a ruin in the northern Sinai. These references to Yahweh could well imply the existence of cult places or temples to the deity. We also have many personal names with a *Yah, Yau* or *Yahu* divine element in them. These have a considerable geographic spread in the West Semitic world. Such names include the royal names *Azriyau* and *Yau/Ilubidi* in far north Hamat in Syria. Such well-known evidence reflects a number of societies that variously identified such central divine functions as fertility and weather with a deity whose name was Yahweh. *Ba'al* and *Hadad* are better-known names for this same divine function among West Semites.

We find Yahweh also in later periods: from *Yahw* in Elephantine of the Persian period to the *Yao* mentioned in the writings of Philo of Byblos. Nor is the god *Ieuw* of northern Syria, mentioned by Eusebius, to be ignored. In the Persian period, we find coins with Yahweh's image and symbols. In this same and in the following Hellenistic periods, we find Yahweh temples at Elephantine, Jerusalem, Arad, Samaria (near Mount Gerizim), Leontopolis, Araq el-Amir and Cyrenaica. Temples known from excavations, such as the Iron Age altar at Arad and the Hellenistic reconstruction at Beersheva, are also claimed as Yahwist, but only on the strength of assumed similarities to a biblical Yahweh.

6 Many Judaisms

Our problem of historicity is not entirely resolved by a comparison of the Bible's theological reinterpretation of Yahweh with the historical Yahweh of Palestine. Just as the historicity of the Bible's literary perceptions of Yahweh is largely anachronistic, and is hardly confirmed by any Yahweh of history, early or late, so the literarily and traditionally derived perceptions of early Judaism have departed from any known historical reality. They too are anachronistic.

Although the name Judea is a geographical term occurring in Assyrian period texts, referring to the highlands south of Jerusalem, in the Persian period the name is political. It is the name of the Persian province. The Assyrians' name for the southern highlands, *Jaudáa*, and the Persians' imperial name, *Yehud*, were no more reflective of a people than were any of the other names for regions of the empire. Moreover, the geographical spread of people referred to as Yehudim is so great that it would be rash to assume that this name refers to their place of origin. Nor should we continue to understand this term as ethnographic, without evidence. By the beginning of the rabbinic period in the second century CE, the term *yehudim* is clearly religiously descriptive, and neither ethnic nor geographic. Folk-etiologically, the term *yehudim* has been associated with the divine name *Yahu*. It defines *Yehudim* as adherents of *Yahu*. It is this religious association that seems most constant in the spread of the use of the name *Yehudim* in the Roman empire.

Already in the Elephantine texts, the name *Yehud* seems to have been used for a definable group of people who were called 'Jews'. It is not understood in a geographical sense, but in the context of the religious affiliation of some of the people in this military colony in Egypt. The word *Yehudim* might be understood as a self-identification centred in a religious relationship with the god Yahweh. These 'Jews' are not residents of Judea. Nor is it likely that they originally came from Judea rather than some other region of the south Levant. They are members of a religious association of those who centre their lives in Yahweh. These texts are well worth looking at more closely.

Yedoniah, a priest of the military colony at Elephantine in Egypt, sent a letter, dated to 407 BCE, on behalf of his fellow priests and the 'Jews', the citizens of Elephantine, to the governor of Judea. He asked administrative permission to rebuild their temple, dedicated to the god *Yaho*, which had been destroyed by 'Egyptians'. Yedoniah also refers to an explanatory letter they had already sent to the sons of Sanballat, the governor of Samaria, and to an earlier – never answered – letter to the high priest in Jerusalem. Yedoniah accuses the priests of the temple of Khnub of conspiracy in the temple's destruction, which had been carried out by troops from the fortress of Syene.

Yedoniah claims that the temple and military colony of the Jews had been in Elephantine since pre-Persian times. He obviously claims religious ties between the Elephantine temple and the temple community and 'Jews' of Jerusalem. This sentiment is perhaps not reciprocated. Although some scholars have argued somewhat inconsequently that Elephantine's Jews must have come from Israel rather than Judah because of the non-observance of Josiah's reforms and cult-centralization in Jerusalem, they are correct in their assumption that the term 'Jews' here makes no implicit reference to a place of origin in *Yehud*. Reference to place of origin in the letters from Elephantine seems rather to be the function of the term 'Aramaean', which is used in contrast to 'Egyptian' in the texts. That the 'Jews' of Elephantine are likely originally from the south Levant may be judged from the dominance of West Semitic, and especially Yahwist-theophoric, personal names. There are also many Hebraisms in the Aramaic of these texts. The implied use of the Hebrew language, however, does not alone signify any specific ethnicity or ideology. Moreover, the other West Semitic deities supported by this Jewish garrison – Yaho, Ishumbethel and Anathbethel – reflect broader Syrian, and probably south Syrian origins.

Other deities – of international origin – are honoured by Elephantine's Jews. An oath is sworn to the goddess *Sati*; and greetings are given in the name of *Bel* and *Nabu*, *Shamash* and *Nergal*, *Yaho* and *Khnub*. The nexus of religion and family makes it difficult to conclude that the 'Jewish' religious associations of the Elephantine community, suggested by their names and that of their deity, are to be translated with any confidence in terms of ethnicity. Ethnicity is difficult enough to identify in the best of circumstances. Far from the relative homogeneity of a provincial home-land, émigrés are, ethnically speaking, notoriously promiscuous.

Mibtahiah, daughter of Mahseiah the son of Yedoniah (Yahwist names all), is a wonderful example for understanding Jewish associations in the diaspora. Her grandfather Yedoniah is described as an Aramaean, or Syrian of Syene. Her father, Mahseiah, in another text, is described as a 'Jew'. Obviously this is a term that does not exclude one also being an Aramaean. In a contract for Mibtahiah's third marriage, her father is described, like his father before him, as an Aramaean of Syene. Mibtahiah's first husband has a Yahwist name, Yezanaiah, as well as a Yahwist patronym: ben Uriah. Her second husband, however, bears an Egyptian name, Pi', with an Egyptian patronym: Phy, who was a builder in the fortress of Syene. Her third husband, also a builder, bears the Egyptian name Ashor, with the Egyptian patronym, Seho. He later adopts the common Hebrew name Nathan. Whether this was done for family or for religious reasons is a moot point.

In biblical traditions, Yehud is identified with Judea and variously constructed as the region controlled by a small temple society centred in

Jerusalem which lies just north of Judea. It is undoubtedly in this Persian period that Jerusalem first becomes identified as the city of the Jews, of the Yehudim, but it is not clear that this has any geographical significance in the biblical texts. The personal name *Yehudah* also occurs first during this period, and is found in the Bible both as the eponymous ancestor of the biblical tribe of *Yehudah*, and as a cue-name for the one who in Judges conquers the highlands of *Yehudah*. The self-understanding implied of a religious Judaism (as in the texts from Elephantine) is found in the authorial voice of biblical texts such as the Book of Psalms. These texts look back upon ancient Israel as lost. They create a 'new Israel', centred in the study of the *torah*, given to them by the long forgotten God of Israel past. Like Israel's troops in the story of Joshua 24, they reject the past to choose a new way, the way of Yahweh. This is also the perspective of the stories in Josephus about John Hyrcanus. He is seen as re-establishing a new Israel throughout the newly conquered lands of Palestine.

It is interesting that the concept of *Eretz Yisrael*, the 'land of Israel', in these stories is established not through ethnic identification, but through religious conversion. This is again the understanding of a 'true' – not an ethnic – Israel that is given to the founding figure in the Damascus Covenant: the 'teacher of righteousness'. We have seen that this language reflects a sectarian perspective. The true Israel is understood to refer to those who hold to the way of truth. In just such a context, Josephus presents the Pharisees as Jews for the 'new Israel'. In contrast, the Hasmonean-anchored Sadducees are presented as adhering to the old Israel and to the temple. However, the historically indistinguishable *sadiqim* ('the righteous') stand solidly in just such a sectarian-defined path of righteousness as the 'new Israel'. This is a profoundly theological, not an ethnic definition. It is, moreover, a perception and self-understanding that must force the historian to avoid speaking of Judaism and Israel as a historical people at all, except in this very religiously defining sense as a people of God. Jews, Idumeans, Galileans and Samaritans, as well as Essenes and Pharisees, the writers of the gospels as well as the early rabbis of the Talmud, all understood themselves with the self-defining term *benei Yisrael*. The gospels – with all of their seemingly anti-Semitic abuse of the term 'Jew' – are thoroughly 'Jewish' works that are centred in this same sectarian and biblical view of the 'new Israel'. They see Judaism, as do the rabbis, from a religious perspective.

7 The 'Jews' according to Josephus

In book 12 of his *Antiquities of the Jews*, Josephus recounts an aetiology of the Jews of Egypt from deportations under Ptolemy 'from the mountains of Judea and from the places about Jerusalem, Samaria and near Mount

Gerizim'. These he describes as 'two groups' – nevertheless Jews all – who dispute about whether they should send their tribute to Jerusalem or to Samaria (*Ant.* 12.1.1). The interesting issue is not that Josephus might know anything at all about these people in Egypt. His story presents the diaspora Jews as simultaneously of disparate origins and loyalties, and as nevertheless functioning as a single community. In the next chapter, in a context associated with his variant of the Letter of Aristeas, Josephus presents a tradition of Ptolemy Philadelphus having set free 120,000 people from Jerusalem. They had been enslaved and brought to Egypt (*Ant.* 12.2.1–3). Again, the interesting question is not one of historicity. The important question is rather whether Josephus' aetiological motif of a deportation 'from Jerusalem' is not based on his understanding of 'Jew'. The use of the term for these people in Egypt rests on their religious affiliations, rather than either geography or origins. This religious association may also be behind the Persian use of the name *Yehud* as a reference to the province of Jerusalem rather than to the highland region of Judea to the South.

Josephus' implicit association in these texts of Samaritans with his diaspora Jerusalemites is an important text to remember when we read some of his more polemical descriptions of Samaritans in an unrelated effort to define them as non-Jews. For example, in *Antiquities* 12.5.5, Josephus presents the Samaritans as (falsely) claiming that their observance of the sabbath and properly performed sacrifices on Gerizim derived from their 'forefathers'. Josephus tries to refute these Samaritan claims. He argues that not only were Samaritans in fact not Jews, they were Sidonians. They themselves, he asserts, had affirmed that they were 'alien from their nation and their [that is Judaism's] customs' and had even asked that the name of their temple be changed to the 'Temple of Jupiter Hellenius'. Such a statement, however, holds implicit a Samaritan self-understanding that 'their nation and their custom' can be seen as Jewish. Josephus further accuses them of perversely trying to obtain a remission of taxes by claims of descent from Joseph, Ephraim and Manasseh, and by claims of observing the Jubilee year. They assert, argues Josephus, 'that they were [really] Hebrews but [only] had the name Sidonians' (*Ant.* 11.8.6). Josephus presents them as liars, claiming to be Jews when it suits them and then claiming to be Medes and Persians, and – in the very same context (!) – as being 'Sidonians living in Shechem' (*Ant.* 12.5.5).

Josephus, of course, ignores his own explanation given in the speech of Aristeas in *Antiquities* 12.2.4f., that Yahweh was identical with Jupiter Hellenius, and that such a renaming of the Samaritan temple hardly involves apostasy. Also implicit in Josephus' slander of the Samaritans is that they understood themselves as Hebrews, observed the sabbath, the Jubilee year, proper sacrifice and maintained themselves as the *benei Yisrael*, whatever the truth of the claim that they were Sidonians, Medes or Persians might be. That they were not in fact alien to the tradition is also obvious. Josephus reports that people who had been accused in Jerusalem of breaking the sabbath or food taboos took refuge with the Samaritans. However, he describes them as having done so by pleading that they had been originally falsely accused. Implicitly, Josephus' witness here is evidence that the Samaritans upheld the tradition (*Ant* 11.8.7).

We find that Egyptians are Jews, Syrians are Jews, Samaritans are Jews. Josephus refers to 'Jews throughout the inhabitable earth, and those that worshipped God, even of Asia and Europe'. The specifics themselves are impressive: he refers to Jews as having been carried captive beyond the Euphrates. Citing Strabo, he speaks of a large portion of Alexandria taken up by Jews, of Jews living in many of the cities of Egypt, as well as in Cyrene and Cyprus. He describes Jews as controlling Cleopatra's army (*Ant*. 13.10.4 and 14.7.2). Their great power in Egypt he explains by their having been themselves originally Egyptian. He writes in connection with a revolt in Cyrene, of 'our people, of whom the habitable earth is full', and of Jews in every city. 'It is hard,' he writes, 'to find a place . . . that has not admitted this tribe of men and is not possessed by them'. He also speaks of the Jews of the diaspora much in the manner of Philo: model citizens of the empire. He tells of many nations, imitating the Jews and, having learned from them, supporting 'great bodies of these Jews', and becoming prosperous using their laws.[1] This picture of the 'Jews' of the diaspora is matched by his description of the 'Jewish' cities of Palestine at the time of Alexander, including the cities of the Transjordan, of Idumea, Phoenicia and even 'the principal cities of Syria'.

In these descriptions of Josephus, his understanding of 'Jews' in the diaspora is determined by his wish to describe Judaism as comprising *all* who believe in the almighty God. Even his more limited description of the followers of Jesus, among whom he includes both those he calls Jews and Gentiles, forms part of his comprehension of Judaism (*Ant* 18.3.3).

While Josephus has trouble in recognizing any among the growing adherents of monotheism as not having been Jews, Philo, in making uncompromising distinctions between Hellenists and orientalists, makes sharp and uncompromising rejections. For Philo, the Jew of Alexandria, it is 'we Greeks' who stand in the path of truth, over against the Barbarians. It is however 'we Jews', the descendants of the *Hebraioi* who stand over against the Egyptians. Jews stand against the godlessness of the *ethné*. Any argument against understanding early Judaism as an ethnic group or nation could hardly be stronger than Philo's own.

Philo's perception stands solidly within the context of the biblical theology of the way. He pits the way of the godly – those who are

---

[1] *Ant*. 14.7.2. One might also think of his references to Jews in Babylon (*Ant*. 15.2.2 and 18.9.1) and his description of the influence of thousands of Jews in Rome (*Ant*. 18.3.5).

committed to a life dedicated to the *torah* – against the way of the ungodly. He presents his perception of the Jew and of Judaism clearly within the context of the 'new Israel'. He historicizes the godlessness of the biblical tradition's 'old Israel' with reference to the uncivilized nations of the Orient of his own time. Philo's historicization of such ideological metaphors is fully comparable to what we have seen of Josephus' literary techniques. Chronicles gives Hezekiah's reform a rhetorical balance with the use of a three-fold Samaritan ancestry: Ephraim, Manasseh and Asher. With this same literary manner, Josephus presents the Samaritans (whom he identifies as being Sidonians as well as Persians and Medes) as claiming descent from the tribes of Joseph, Manasseh and Ephraim. Similarly, Josephus elsewhere identifies Judaism itself in terms of the three-fold literary division of Sadducees, Pharisees and Essenes. Such efforts to historicize essentially literary concepts and metaphors are commonplace throughout our literature of Judaism. Only a Weberian sociology would derive a description of ancient society from these literary fictions. Whether they are found in the New Testament, in Philo or in Josephus, they reflect a literary world not an historical one.

In ignoring the literary character of biblical stories and traditions, whether of the Old or of the New Testament, we have ignored the collector's world in which the traditions were first interpreted. We ignore the author's world, centred in the religious sectarianism of true faith over against a false faith of the past. This sectarianism is not a religion of reform, but one of transformation and reinterpretation. In closing the Book of Kings, the tradition rejected that past world of kings and men, and with it that Jerusalem of old Israel with its temple that had been built by men's hands. The New Israel comes out of the desert, out of exile. The land is the empty land of Nehemiah 1–4 and of Leviticus 26. It is Jeremiah 4: 23's *tohu wa bohu*. It is I Maccabees 1: 37's variant of *creatio ex nihilo*. The New Israel begins at the creation. It is a celebration not of an ancient nation but of new life. Ancient Israel – from the garden story of humanity's search for wisdom to the end of God's patience in II Kings – belongs not to the creation's acts of God, but rather to the acts and to the world of men, where Jerusalem with its walls and its tower was indeed Genesis 11's Babylon. This Babylon is the Jerusalem where the kings of David's house, Yahweh's messiahs all, had done what was right only in their own eyes.

If Judaism is to be defined, as is common in recent scholarship, as the people who established and formed a revival of religion in the context of the Yahweh temple community of Jerusalem, such as we find in the narrative traditions of Ezra and Nehemiah, we have a double problem historiographically. First, we must assert the scholarly definition of the exclusiveness of the Jerusalem temple's claim: an assertion that has no historical or literary warrant. Such an assertion would involve historians in an anachronistic defence of the Jerusalem cult's legitimacy and orthodoxy, against such literary constructs as the 'people of the land' and the Samaritans of Ezra and Nehemiah. Second, historians would need to ignore the historical communities who were associated with the many other Yahweh temples and cults. While this problem might be solved by a 'many Judaisms' approach, this approach does not solve the theological and historical problem that rabbinic Jerusalem of the post-temple period is hardly to be understood as heir to any such temple Judaism.

Judaism of the rabbis is only with great difficulty perceived as an historical and social reality of any period prior to the second century CE. It has no centre and it has no unity in any earlier period. On one hand, what is understood as 'Judaism' reaches out centrifugally, embracing the whole of the classical world's monotheistic inclusiveness. On the other hand, 'Judaism' refers to religious and philosophical traditions, all of which share the common structure and self-understanding of the theology of the way. Such an ideology, when called upon to supply the *modus vivendi* of a practical life – a lived way of a community – falls victim to its structural weakness. It ends by supporting a hermeneutic perversion of its own self-understanding: forcing the exclusion of all and everything that distracts one from the path of truth and from one's dedication to the *torah*.

If the Jewish temple had ever held the centre of Judaism – as, for example, has been frequently argued in reference to the Hasmoneans, to John Hyrcanus' Josianic efforts to force conversions to Judaism, and to various historicized New Testament versions of a Jerusalem of Jesus' time – that role came to it definitively only as a direct result of the destruction of the temple in 70 CE. It is at that time that the role of the temple, as expressing the divine presence on earth, was recast in the form of the metaphor of a future and heavenly Jerusalem. It was not the rabbis' *torah* Judaism, centring itself on the spiritual heart of the tradition, that fell heir to the temple tradition. Rabbinic Jerusalem is hardly well defined as a religion in any strict sense of the word, any more than are the Tanakh traditions from which it springs. It is hardly like other religions of the ancient world, centred as they were on cults and sacrifices and the service of the gods. All such traditions are – as in Philo – transposed and reinterpreted in philosophical terms.

The central issue at stake historically is best defined as that which the hypothesis of 'multiple Judaisms' attempts to solve. The argument is quite elegant. It also provides a seemingly secure halfway house for the collapsing scholarship that has focused on issues of the historicity of our written traditions. These many Judaisms living in this essentially metaphorical world are the Judaisms of Elephantine, as well as of the many variant historical forms of *benei Yisrael* Judaism that dotted the Palestinian landscape and the shores of the Mediterranean. They include the *Shomronim* of Samaria, as well as the Samaritans and Jews of Josephus and the Hellenist Jews of Philo in far-off Alexandria. Among such Judaisms surely belong the Zadokites and the Nazirites, the Essenes, the Sadducees and the Pharisees.

These multiples of Judaism, however, are all caught in the warp of modernist scholarship. One and all, they are essentially literary Judaisms, whose self-identities have been defined by tradition. We also find here the Judaisms that have been defined merely by scholars as Jewish: that is, those hypothetical groups of Jews living in various hypothetical societies and communities implied by the quite varied 'sectarians' of the Damascus Covenant, the Dead Sea scrolls, the Apocrypha, the Pseudepigrapha, and indeed of the many variable Old Testament traditions, such as Ezra, Nehemiah, Deuteronomy, Exodus and Ben Sira, as well as by the voice of the gospels and the letters of Paul.

The basis of this conception of many Judaisms, however, is literary rather than historical. These multiple Judaisms are fictive entities. They reflect varieties of ideologies, identifiable only in limited ways with any people who lived in the ancient world other than the authors who created them. They are multiple not on the basis of communities, or on the basis of regional differentiations or chronology, though they have certainly been influenced by such variables. They distinguish themselves from each other according to literary patterns of perceiving. They represent one or other variant of the defining motifs of the 'new Israel' and of the 'new Jerusalem', of the 'way of righteousness', and the 'way of the *torah*'.

Historically, however, we have a decidedly different taxonomy – one in which the terms Jewish and Judaism are hugely anachronistic, having merely a referential and accidental quality, not a defining one. In this taxonomy, no coherent unity pertains other than those shared intellectual features common to an interrelated geographical area. Here we find people living in Judaea, Idumaea, Shechem and Samaria and its region, the Galilee and the cities of Palestine, together with associated populations in the Transjordan, Phoenicia, Syria and Alexandria. Here we find the many West Semites of Egyptian military colonies such as that of Elephantine and Herontopolis. We have any number of religiously comparable groups, including the members of the synagogues of the great cities of the empire from Rome to Babylon. We have people belonging to assemblies that, rejecting the distinction of Jew and Gentile, saw themselves nevertheless in concepts of a 'new Israel'. In such an historical taxonomy we find not only priests and official cult functionaries of the various Yahweh temples, or even adherents and supporters of the temples as such, but members of a variety of associations, religious and philosophical. These are the people who wrote and who supported the writing of the literature. They wrote in Hebrew, Greek and Aramaic. They wrote books we today think of as Jewish: the many anonymous and often pseudonymous works of the Tanakh; the Apocrypha, Pseudepigrapha, the Dead Sea scrolls, the gospels and epistles, as well as the works of such authors as Josephus, Philo of

Alexandria and Philo of Byblos. For such people, the terms 'Jew', 'Jewish', and 'Judaism' are historically highly equivocal.

Rather than replacing the history of the south Levant during the Hellenistic period with a paraphrase of First or Second Maccabees, we need to write a history for the whole of this region. Our history should be more than a history of Judea and Samaria. We need to think more about Philistia, Phoenicia and the Decapolis. We also need to think about the towns of the lowlands and of the coast. We must especially think of Beth Shan and the towns of the Jezreel, and we mustn't forget the Galilee. If the Bible remains our focus, we can no longer neglect the great intellectual centres of Alexandria and Babylon as we have. We might also think of religious ideas and the writings of texts during the Greco-Roman period more as an intellectual and philosophical movement within Hellenism itself than as a reactionary religious movement of Palestine's least Hellenized 'Jews'. Were the temples of Jerusalem, Samaria, Elephantine, Leontopolis and Beersheva expressions of religious coherence? Or did they reflect some of the many factions, each with its own political and religious aspirations? If Judaism were a religion that had its central originative core in the temple cult of Jerusalem, it could not be Samaritan; and not only not Samaritan, it could not even be 'Judean', understood ethnically or geographically. Similarly, if kingship continued to be an epitomizing factor of patronage, what was the significant factor of Idumean power in Judea: especially regarding their Herodian patron's relationship to Jerusalem's temple? Certainly many early texts – such as the sectarian literature in the Dead Sea scrolls – do not see the temple as the core of their religion, though they recognize its political and cultic value. Similarly, Elephantine's texts indicate that the Jerusalem temple and the Samaritan temple are both important non-monopolistic centres of their understanding of 'Judaism'. And how do the groups of Galileans fit in? If Idumeans and Galileans can be understood as *Yehudim*, what of the people of the Transjordan from Philadelphia to Damascus?

Could all who adhered to such a religion understand themselves as 'Jews'? Or, like the Samaritans, as *benei Yisrael?* The early Greek translation of the Bible is associated with the 'Jews' of Alexandria. Were such Jews transported to Egypt from Alexander's Samaria? Or were they 'Jews' because of their biblical faith? And where did the Jews of the later Jerusalem Talmud come from: those 'Jews' centred in the schools and synagogues of Tiberias and Zevad? This is to say nothing about the Jews of Acco, of Byblos and of the diaspora throughout the Roman empire. What does it mean to be a Jew in Palestine – or indeed in the diaspora – under the Roman empire? Why is it that the rabbinic traditions of the Talmud – arguably reflecting traditions of the second to fourth centuries CE – know so little of the immense world of the Jewish diaspora: a Judaism that was so wholly Hellenized and Greek-speaking? And how was this international culture –

so well reflected in the Septuagint and in many of the pseudepigraphic traditions – eventually lost to the Jewish world? Lest we be distracted by such questions, what were the non-rabbinic components of the complex region of the Syrian fringe in the Greco-Roman period? Are they to be understood as non-Jewish, anachronistically identifying Judaism as a product of the later Mishnah? What hidden historical societies does the Bible give voice to? Is the Bible itself expressive of Judaism or is it an anonymous voice for an entire region's intellectual tradition?

If we are to have a critical history, we must deal with the anachronisms we have created. Are the biblical books themselves a product of ancient Judaism? Does the continuity between the Bible and Judaism reflect a chronologically linear development, or is it an aspect of rationalistic anachronism, ideologically motivated. Is such hypothetical continuity asserted? Does Judaism's claim to the Bible obey the same imperative as Christianity's claim to the New Testament and the Septuagint, namely, by theological necessity? Historically, the Bible, and the books that make it up are products of the whole south Levant's world-view. Those who identified with it as their own tradition were those who emerged in the course of the first or perhaps better early second century CE as Samaritans, Jews and Christians. They were both Greeks and Hebrews. They were both indigenous and people of the diaspora. While all would identify their own heritage with the land 'of the Jews', this was a religious assertion, not a statement of historical fact. Just such associations to Judaism were created in Egypt, in Babylon, and in all of the great cities of the Greco-Roman world.

After Jerusalem was destroyed by Roman troops in 70 CE people picked up their lives and continued, and they did so again after Bar Kochba's revolt in the second century. When the vast majority of Palestine became Christian during the Byzantine period, no large numbers were driven out. The Jewish presence in Jerusalem does not end with either 70 or 135, but rather what ended was Jerusalem's and its people's self-understanding as Jewish. Though in the fourth century Monophysites were driven eastward ideologically, the indigenous population continued with a transformed understanding of itself and its religion. Similarly, in the seventh century, when the vast majority in Palestine became Muslim, few were driven from the land. Though many churches became mosques, the indigenous population continued with a transformed understanding of itself and its religion.

Today, the Jewish/Christian dichotomy dominates much of our perspective on early Judaism. This is an anachronistic distortion from the second century CE, and deeply sectarian in its essence. The dichotomy rests on a structural flaw within the biblical traditions themselves. It manipulates and historicizes the theology of the way, from which Judaism and the Christianity of the second century have taken their departures. It corrupts and distorts the tradition.

CHAPTER 11

The Bible's literary world

1 On Literature

Literacy in the ancient world was mastered by a very small part of any given society. Small farmers and shepherds had no use for writing, nor did the local patrons and strong men who typically controlled the small patronates in Palestine through most of the Bronze Age. Imperial governments, however, did have a use for it, and it is during the Late Bronze Age that we find correspondence to and from the local kings of Palestine's ruling towns and their Egyptian overlord. In the great trading cities of Syria, writing and record-keeping is a preoccupation of business since the mid-third millennium. The most important collections of texts that have been found in this region from the Bronze Age include Ebla (*c*. 2400 BCE), Alalakh (eighteenth century), Mari (eighteenth to seventeenth century) and Ugarit (fourteenth to thirteenth century). Some few texts from the Bronze Age have been found in Palestine itself. Egyptian texts about Palestine have been found from the late nineteenth and eighteenth century BCE. Most important has been a large collection of letters from the fourteenth century between the pharaoh and his Palestinian clients, found at Tell el Amarna in Egypt.

Commonly, writing was a highly specialized tool of commerce and political administration. It was carried out by professional scribes. What have normally been found have been business records, cultic texts, lists of all sorts, letters, decrees, annals, treaties, contracts, inscribed seals and monumental inscriptions. Writing of a more literary character included songs, proverbs, traditional narratives and epic poems. Dictionaries and school texts have also been found.

With the invention of the alphabet in the course of the Late Bronze Age, and with the development of linear scripts, access to writing reached beyond the scribal classes. Under the Assyrians, writing became increasingly common and involved a larger portion of the population. The Assyrian efforts to establish schools across their empire, and the use of

Aramaic as a common language, helped to integrate a society that had been fragmented into many different cultural and language groups. With these changes, an international context and world-view was introduced into a region that had ever been provincial and village-oriented. As local traditions and folklore were brought into a literate context, collected and interpreted, they were redefined by the much more complex, learned stream of tradition that they came to share. Local customs and traditions were transformed into literature. They were taught by teachers to their students.

Libraries in the Assyrian period were part of the world of prestige. Kings and great men of wealth purchased texts, and sponsored scholars and teachers. When the Persians, in an attempt to win over the provinces to their administration, introduced forms of 'home rule', they further encouraged the collection and codification of local customs and law. Schools and scribes became the centre of this development. Philosophy, law, narrative and song informed the region's culture. They also created a context for the development of a trans-regional and, especially during the Hellenistic period, international culture. Much of this work of collecting was both creative and original. It was in the effort to formulate the contemporary beliefs and understandings that were expressive of Palestine's traditions, that many of the earliest coherent texts of the Bible began to develop. They accumulated in various forms of collections and discussions about traditions and learning from the past. The ideological theme of restoring the past and reviving the local religious coherence of the subject territories encouraged the formation and creation of such literatures. They were centred on the leaders and events of the past as they were known and thought to have been by the scribes and teachers who discussed and created them in written and oral forms. Collections of regional 'libraries' took on the task of interpreting the traditions, as a national treasure lost and restored. This work developed a new self-understanding of the people. Their place in the world was assimilated, collected and given fixed form.

The interest in national roots and regional ethnicity was not unique or peculiar to Palestine, but was part of a widespread and extremely varied movement that stretched from the Aegean to Babylon and beyond. It was centred in religious festivals and public entertainment, and was also located in the efforts of schools and philosophers that sought to understand the world as coherent and meaningful. The understanding of the present as expressing the will of the gods was discussed by writers through narratives about how the gods of tradition had determined actions of people and national events in the past. Such stories were thought predictive and normative for the future, and formed an integrated part of education.

A desire to endorce the authenticity and binding character of the 'traditions' taught encouraged many writers of the Hellenistic world to set the traditions collected in the distant past. Chains of events were created that traced the roots of any given society from the present or the recent past back to ever earlier times, until they reached completion at the very beginning of time and the creation of the world. In providing a sense of the wholeness of tradition, this made possible a comprehensive reflection of the divine will for the whole of the people past and present. It placed the society in the universal context of world politics, as it also provided a fulcrum for traditionists and ethnographers everywhere. Put simplistically, it was a universal system of cataloguing traditions. It created the library as an adequate place for the wisdom of the past.

A coherent scheme or chronology was required that illustrated the acts of the divine will in a closed chain of cause and effect. In the Bible, two kinds of systemization are dominant. One governs the collections of psalms, wisdom and the prophetic books, where collections are typologically assembled. They are catalogued by attributing them to a great king, prophet or teacher of antiquity. The other system is found in the collections of narratives within successive chronologies. This we find in the chains of narrative from Genesis to Kings, as well as in the books of Chronicles. Chronicles is particularly interesting as it had been updated with the variant traditions of the Book of Ezra and the Book of Nehemiah. In the Greek-language variant of the tradition, this chain was updated or expanded at least once again with the books of Maccabees.

In these large collections of traditions, three different kinds of chronologies are used. Since all of them are secondary to the basic traditions that they systematize and order, they often come in conflict with them. The narratives are ordered in a chain of periods or epochs: the aetiologies of the world, the stories of the patriarchs, of the formation of Israel as a people in the Exodus from Egypt, the wilderness wanderings, the conquest, the judges, united monarchy, and finally the period of Israel and Judah to the destruction of Jerusalem. To some extent, this periodization strongly affected the development of the successive books of this chain, especially of Genesis, Judges and Kings.

However, an even more influential scheme is the related order of stories in terms of a succession of heroes or persons. Here two systems may be involved. One governs the collection into books: most noticeably the books of Moses, of Joshua and of Samuel. The other is found in the succession of the stories themselves. This is of course clearest in the genealogies of Chronicles and Genesis, and in the collected stories of Judges and Kings. In this a claim of authenticity is being made. The tradition grows from father to son since the beginning of the world. In Genesis the succession is unbroken, in Chronicles the genealogical chains cluster thematically rather than linearly and chronologically. Links are made throughout the narration to ensure it. One of the clearest of these links is made by the appointment of Joshua as Moses' successor. The genealogical link of Abraham to the sons of Noah serves the same function. Such an effort at linkage is also found in the creation of a fictive office of 'judge' to achieve a systematic successive chain of the otherwise wholly unrelated hero stories we find in the Book of Judges. Perhaps the most deceptive of all such links for the modern reader is the use and harmonization of dynastic lists to link a succession of otherwise independent stories about religious heroes and antiheroes such as Joseph and Moses, Elijah and Elisha and Hezekiah and Josiah. It is the creation of this extensive chain, beginning with the garden story of Adam and Eve, which rests uneasily behind the modern view of the Bible as history, dominated by a chronological succession.

A third scheme that is prominent in the Bible attempts to give absolute dates to the episodes of story, and to place them into a world history, beginning with the creation in the year 1. This scheme seems to be a relatively late development. Quite distinct schemes are found in some of our earliest formal collections of the Bible: in the Samaritan Pentateuch, the Greek version of the Septuagint and the Masoretic tradition of the Hebrew Bible. This last is ordered, as we have seen, on a scheme of a 'great year' of 4,000 years (an idea popular among many Hellenistic historians), which runs from the beginning of time to the year in which the temple was rededicated in 164 BCE, when the Maccabees broke from Seleucid rule. Such schemes used the chronologies already given in the stories and supplemented them with events known to the collector.

With the help of such frameworks, the writers of the Bible were able to cast their writings and ethnographic collections in the form of a heritage from the past. In doing this, they did not offer an historical perspective; they created history as a form of intellectual discussion. What had been a massive and incoherently disorganized literary heritage, embodied as much as not in their own creations, took on the form of an elaborate demonstration that the universal God of heaven had intended to bring them to this present world just so. To understand the divine will, they might reflect on the traditions that had created them. It is important to recognize that in these presentations of Palestine's world of story, song and legend, pious sermons, pithy statements, erotic poetry, diatribes and the like, an historical perspective is found only in the connections that existed between the stories and traditions. The collections of similar types of literature are only artificially – sometimes for purely pedagogical reasons – classified and linked together. Fictions of prophetic speeches, evocations of a blind harpist or a dead king, once wise and understanding, are used to dramatize them. The narratives themselves were intended for reflection. They encouraged piety. They provided amusement and understanding. They were intended for all the different things that theatre, education and philosophy does.

2 Tradition and story variants

Origin stories dominate biblical narrative from Genesis to the books of Samuel. These books explain in one way or another how old Israel and its world, how Jerusalem and its kings, came to be. Genesis tells the story of Israel's origin in terms of its ancestors. Exodus, Numbers and Leviticus collect a large number of variations of traditions and stories that play on themes about Israel's origin as a nation, its being chosen by Yahweh. These also include aetiologies, such as the origin of the Passover, the commandments and the laws that were given by God to Moses as he went up and down either Mount Sinai or Mount Horeb. The stories collect origin tales about Israel's priestly cast, the legendary ark and its sanctuary, and about the contract that Israel's God once forged with Israel at and as its foundation. The fifth book of the Pentateuch, Deuteronomy, reiterates many of these same themes and tales once again, as it recounts Moses' farewell speech to the people in three variants.

Origin traditions do not stop with the Pentateuch. Joshua's and Judges' narratives of conquest and settlement are offered with such clarity that many scholars are single-mindedly attracted to these traditions as historical memories of the nation's earliest beginnings. In these stories, Israel's foundation as a nation in possession of its land is described. In the books of Samuel, we find the origin stories of David's kingdom with its understanding of Israel not as a nation like others, but as a nation under God. Hidden within this narrative is the origin story of old Jerusalem's destruction; for it is Jerusalem's and Samaria's fate that dominates the entire story of old Israel from Genesis to the close of Kings, and that served as a foundation for a new Israel and a new Jerusalem.

The most striking characteristic of this long and complex tradition, as well as of biblical narratives generally, is its tireless repetition. Hardly a story goes by that does not have its parallel, its double, or its variant in one way or another. In the first eleven chapters alone, which in Genesis cover hardly as many pages, we find two creation stories, two stories of the flood and two accounts of how the nations spread over the face of the earth.[1] Without its variants, our biblical narrative would hardly fill half its present size. Both the extent and the type of variation is instructive. We have variations of heroes and their roles. Noah has three sons: Shem, Ham and Japhet, and so Terah must have his three: Abram, Nahor and Harran. Similarly, we have not merely the necessary one ancestral patriarch, but three: Abraham, Isaac and Jacob. Each has his antagonist: Lot, Ishmael and Esau. As Abraham has his two sons (Isaac and Ishmael) and Lot his (Ammon and Moab), so also Isaac must have two sons (Jacob and Esau), as must Joseph (Ephraim and Manasseh). If the youngest son inherits, he does so three times: Isaac, Jacob and Ephraim. If one pair quarrel, many

---

[1] Genesis 1–3, 6–9 and 10: 1–11: 9 respectively.

do: Cain against Abel; Jacob against Esau and Jacob against Laban. Sarah quarrels with Hagar and Rachel with Leah. Not to be left out, Abraham's shepherds quarrel with Lot's and Jacob's with those of Abimelek. It is hardly a surprise to the reader that when Abraham lies to the pharaoh, telling him his wife Sarah is his sister, he will do the same to Gerar's king, Abimelek. Just so, will Isaac tell this same lie to this same king of Gerar. Nor is it anything extraordinary to find Abraham celebrating the birth of his first-born twice, or poor Hagar weeping a second time in the desert and finding Ishmael twice-blessed. After so much, who will quibble with Jacob on his deathbed being tricked just as he had tricked Isaac on his? After Joseph has two dreams, why shouldn't the pharaoh? Why not have two brothers concerned for Joseph's welfare and a twice-told confrontation of the brothers with their father, when Joseph comes into prison both as keeper and kept? One objects to Joseph being sold to Potiphar twice no more than one later objects to the redundancy of the cattle's deaths in Exodus' plagues.

We are hardly out of Genesis. Multiple story variants run throughout the tradition. We have three accounts of Saul's death, and three of Goliath's. Jerusalem and Lachish are thrice conquered towns. As the tales of Abraham, Isaac and Jacob epitomize the narratives of Israel's origins, the stories of Saul, David and Solomon epitomize the origins of Israel's kingship; as indeed also, the books of Isaiah, Jeremiah and Ezekiel epitomize prophecy. Just as the heroes of Genesis are paired, so Moses is given his Aaron in Exodus and his Joshua in Numbers. Saul has a Jonathan and David a Solomon. Elijah has his Elisha and John his Jesus. When we think of the patriarchs with their lies of wives as sisters, we should also think of Exodus 3's theophany at the burning bush and the same story, sans bush, in Exodus 6. We should think of Moses on Sinai receiving the Ten Commandments in Exodus 20 and then receiving these same ten once again at Horeb in Deuteronomy 5. We should think of the stone tablets written by the finger of God in Exodus 31 with their copies engraved by Moses more prosaically in chapter 34. We can think of David twice being hunted by Saul in I Samuel 24 and 26. In one story he hides in a cave, in the other he comes to Saul's camp at night. In both, he has the chance to kill Saul, Yahweh's messiah, and does not. Both stories end in the recognition of David as Saul's successor and 'son'.

Such tale variants can be close or distant. The story of Genesis 19's rape of Lot's daughters by the people of Sodom is clearly echoed in Judges 19's dark tale of the rape of the Levite's concubine by the tribe of Benjamin. So too Jeremiah 5's prophetic search through Jerusalem's streets to find a single person who does right and seeks the truth self-consciously echoes Abraham's debate with Yahweh in Genesis 18 in search of a righteous *minyan* in Sodom's streets. Such parallels we find in the paired stories of Jesus and John's births, in the songs of Hannah and Mary, and in the miracle stories of Elijah and Elisha. But we should also mark well less obvious parallels, as between Kings' stories of Hezekiah and Josiah's reforms and Josephus' tale of John Hyrcanus'. These are but a single story caught in biblical time's reiterative web. The reading of Moses' law by Ezra in Nehemiah 8 is echoed in its variant narrative of Ezra as learned teacher in Ezra 7. This, in turn, is echoed in the story of the 'teacher of righteousness' in the opening page of the Dead Sea scrolls' Damascus Covenant.

Yet other variants involve the structural building of themes. The folkloric three-fold introduction is a favourite beginning for extended chains of stories. So we find the Jacob–Esau story opening with three short episodes in Genesis 25, epitomizing Jacob as a man of conflict. This marks the Jacob chain as one about Israel's ancestor. As he has done, the people he becomes also wrestle with God. When Rebecca is pregnant with the twins, Esau and Jacob, 'two nations' struggle for dominance in her womb. Even as they are born, Jacob disputes Esau's rights as first-born and grabs hold of Esau's heel. When the boys are grown, Jacob takes advantage of Esau's starvation by selling him a bowl of lentils at the cost of his birthright. In a similar manner, Exodus opens for us with a trio of stories about 'the new king of Egypt who did not know Joseph'. He is threatened by Israel's strength and is in fear that its people will escape the land. He puts Israel into slavery, but the more he 'plagues' them the more numerous and greater Israel becomes. So the evil pharaoh decrees that the male babies of the Israelites are to be killed at birth. The midwives, however, deceive him, as Israel again becomes more numerous and great. Finally, the pharaoh orders that every boy that is born must be thrown into the Nile. It is then, in this third tale, that the pharaoh gets his 'come-uppance'. All his fears are fulfilled. The child Moses is put into the Nile for the pharaoh's own child to save. Intensifying the story's irony, the boy grows up in pharaoh's own house. This is Moses, who in Israel's greatness will lead Yahweh's people out of Egypt. Similarly, the opening of the Abraham chain of stories is structured around three variant episodes in which Abraham builds an altar and Yahweh appears to him to tell him about what will happen in the story's course.

Such introductions are not ignorant of their redundancy, but use their variants to set themes that are later developed within a yet greater story. The introductions can also come in pairs, as in the double opening of Joseph's stories in Genesis 37, where he has a pair of dreams to recount. The dreams point ahead to the later paired dreams of the butler and baker in Joseph's prison as well as to the pharaoh's twin dreams of plenty and famine. They are also used to predict the story's outcome, when Joseph's brothers will recognize his greatness. It is this kind of narrative variation that we find in the opening of Samuel. Eli is a great man and priest at Shiloh, but he is old and his sons evil. Samuel is chosen to take his place.

Similarly, Samuel is a great man, and when he grows old his sons too are evil. Saul is chosen to replace him. Such variants in the structuring of the Bible's narratives are commonplace. Certainly among the most striking examples of such patterned structures are the opening chapters of Matthew's and Luke's gospels. These give us the famous variants of the Christmas story.

Even more striking are the narrative closures that we find ending the stories of Moses' and David's lives. The first we find in Deuteronomy and the other in the books of Samuel. Deuteronomy 32 follows immediately after the close of the third of Moses' farewell addresses. It is a long song, epitomizing and interpreting the Book of Deuteronomy, and perhaps the Peutatench as a whole, as a book of Moses' teaching. This 'book of the *torah*' is declared in the song's opening words as a declaration of God's greatness: 'He is the rock whose work is perfect. His paths, all, are right. He is a God, trustworthy, without betrayal. He is righteous and just.' The poem goes on for some ten stanzas reiterating this commentary on Deuteronomy as a whole, as a way of praising God in the context of the Bible's theology of the way. Moses is then given instructions for his death. This is followed in chapter 33 by a closing poem: Moses' deathbed blessing to each of the tribes of Israel. This follows the pattern of the deathbed closures of each of the successive stories of the patriarchs of Genesis. Its closest variant is found in Genesis 49, where the story of Jacob's life closes with a blessing on his twelve sons.

The story of David follows this same pattern. II Samuel 22 uses a variant of Psalm 18, whose ten stanzas interpret the entire story of David's life as a journey of the soul. Here we do not meet the David of Israel's past. This is David as singer of the Psalms and as Yahweh's messiah. David becomes the representative of and model for the pious, the implied hearer of the song. As in Deuteronomy's song of Moses, this audience is enjoined to walk in God's path. This theological interpretation closes with yet another song represented as the last words of David. It is short, and follows much the theme of Deuteronomy 32's opening stanza. It interprets David's life as a praise of God, in the language of this same theology of the way, which is so familiar to us from the Book of Psalms. This God is 'Israel's rock', and David is 'one who brings righteousness to men and rules in the fear of God'.

3 Copenhagen Lego-blocks

In the formation of the Old Testament, we are not dealing with even more ancient traditions of early Israel. We are dealing with traditions that have been presented and are understood as ancient. Our traditions – the earliest we have are among the Dead Sea scrolls – come from the Hellenistic and

Greco-Roman periods. Anything earlier is only known as a past narrated or as a past transmitted. This rich variety of texts presents us with some very concrete examples of how such writings as we find in the Bible were created. With the Dead Sea scrolls, we have an entry into the actual world of text-making, tradition composition and transmission. The Dead Sea texts make it possible to understand our texts before the process of tradition was completed. They present us with sources, drafts and versions of what only at a much later date came to be recognized as biblical tradition. They give us many of the texts of the Bible before they were collected as the Bible.

We have a large number of texts from the caves near the Dead Sea that present very brief compositions formed from passages that are similar to many found in the Bible. A good example of this is *4QTestimonia*, a text that has been created by putting together several segments or units of only a verse or more. These are much like what we find scattered throughout the books of Exodus, Leviticus, Numbers and Deuteronomy. This composition has a clear theme, and presents itself as a series of related divine utterances and predictions, all with messiah-like overtones.

And [Yahweh] spoke to Moses saying: [Deut. 5: 28–29] 'You have heard the sound of the words of this people, what they said to you: all they have said is right. I (only) it were given to me (that) they had this heart to fear me and keep all my precepts all the days, so that it might go well with them and their sons forever!' [Deut. 18: 18–19] 'I would raise up for them a prophet from among their brothers, like you, and place my words in his mouth, and he would tell them all that I command them. And it will happen that the man who does not listen to my words, that the prophet will speak in my name, I shall require a reckoning from him.' . . . And he uttered his poem and said: [Num. 24: 15–17] 'Oracle of Balaam, son of Beor, and oracle of the man of penetrating eye, oracle of him who listens to the words of God and knows the knowledge of the Most High, of one who sees the vision of Shaddai, who falls and opens the eye. I see him, but not now, I espy him but not close up. A star has departed from Jacob, and a sceptre has arisen from Israel. He shall crush the temples of Moab, and cut to pieces all the sons of Seth.' And about Levi he says [Deut. 33: 8–11] 'Give to Levi your Thummim and your Urim, to your pious man, whom you tested at Massah, and with whom you quarrelled about the waters of Meribah, he who said to his father . . . and to his mother "I have not known you", and did not acknowledge his brothers, and his son did not know. For he observed your word and kept your covenant. They have made your judgements shine for Jacob, our law for Israel, they have placed incense before your face and a holocaust upon your altar. Bless [Yahweh] his courage and accept with pleasure the work of his hand! Crush the loins of his adversaries, and those, who hate him, may they not rise!' . . . At the moment when Joshua finished praising and giving thanks with his psalms, he said: [Jos. 6: 26] 'Cursed be the man who rebuilds this city! Upon his firstborn will he found it, and upon his Benjamin will he erect its gates!' And now an accursed man, one of Belial, has arisen to be a fowler's trap for the people and ruin for all his neighbours . . . will arise, to be the two instruments of violence. And they will rebuild [this city and erect] for it a rampart and towers, to make it into a fortress of wickedness [a great evil] in Israel, and a horror in Ephraim and Judah. . . . And they] will commit a profanation in the land and a great blasphemy among the sons of . . . And they will shed blo]od like water upon the ramparts of the daughter of Sion and in the precincts of Jerusalem.[1]

The first segment of this text resembles a passage we find in Deuteronomy 5: 28–29. In the Bible's text, however, the statement is an address of Moses to the people, in which he quotes Yahweh. In the Dead Sea scrolls composition, Yahweh addresses Moses directly. Both versions appear to function in a very similar way. They seem to come independently from what we might call a common stream of tradition.

The second segment is nearly identical to what we can read in Deuteronomy 18: 18–19, while the third segment has its own introductory clause and offers such a distant reflection of the wording of the first part of Numbers 24: 15 that it may well have had an independent source. The larger, fourth segment is identical to Deuteronomy 33: 8–11. The fifth segment of our text offers a surprise. It is very much like the passage we find in Joshua 6: 26 and in the Bible is bound up with the well-known story of the fall of Jericho. The Dead Sea scrolls text, however, has nothing at all to do with Jericho. We read 'this town', instead of Jericho. Jerusalem is clearly its reference! The Dead Sea scrolls text goes its own way in order to describe Jerusalem's destiny. This segment shows that the text as a whole has its own independent purpose.

4QTestimonia is not a fragment of a larger text. It is a complete, albeit damaged, composition in its own right. Though short, and consisting of segments of composition we find elsewhere, it is a whole composition. Its form is neither accidental nor arbitrary. There are many possible explanations regarding its origin. The author may have used biblical texts as a basis for writing his own. Perhaps, on the other hand, we should understand this text as a variant of biblical tradition which had failed to be included in one of the Bible's books. The possibility that the biblical texts, with all of their many variations, were built up from just such kinds of texts becomes attractive the more we recognize that many of the Bible's books had not yet been completed at the time the Dead Sea scrolls were written.

There are a large range of texts like this in the Dead Sea scrolls. One of them, *4Q158*, is particularly instructive. It resembles the brief story of

[1] Quotation is from F. García Martinez, *The Dead Sea Scrolls Translated* (Brill, Leiden, 1994), pp. 137–138.

Jacob wrestling with God in Genesis 32: 25–33. In the text of the Dead Sea scrolls we find a complete story, while the version in Genesis breaks off uncompleted between verses 29 and 30. Genesis, moreover, refers to a blessing, but fails to actually give it. Should we think of Genesis giving a shortened form or a paraphrase of just such a story as we find in this more 'complete' version? Certainly, the many examples in the Bible of truncated, abbreviated and fragmented stories give us encouragement to do so. Such text and text fragments as we find among the Dead Sea scrolls may well represent an earlier or 'better' witness to the tradition than many of those we have in the Bible. We should also consider that the Bible's texts may have been written much in the same way as these texts have been. Texts similar to the ones we have discussed here are common. For example, Isaiah 36–39, II Chronicles 29–32 and II Kings 18: 1–20: 21 present us with three variants of a single tradition. The narratives found in chapter 20 of II Kings and chapter 38 of Isaiah create further expansions of the tradition, quite independently of each other.

The title of this section, 'Copenhagen Lego-blocks', refers to what is in Denmark the nearly ubiquitous child's building block. From this simple, rectangular shape all Danish children gain the means of constructing every possible world of their fantasy. Words like 'motifs' and 'metaphors' are rather too abstract for the items I would like to define as the smallest units of the tradition of biblical literature that have the ability to persist and to be used in variable forms. Like the Lego-block, many of the smallest units of our early Bible are quite plastic and easily transferable. They are suitable for multiple purposes. They cluster meaningfully and variably with other tradition blocks. The kind of variations of traditions that we have referred to in so many different ways involve very similar and often verbatim variants of one segment or another of an already existent tradition. The variable use of such tradition segments crosses every boundary of literary type and genre. They affect both the smallest and the largest compositions that we find in the Bible.

One might argue the principle that all biblical genres can be described as segmented texts. They are complex units of tradition that are composed of multiple smaller segments of material. Larger tradition units are created through the joining and selecting of smaller units. This principle is well illustrated by the patriarchal narratives of Genesis. The story of Abraham is a single chain of narrative that takes us along on Abraham's journeys from his altar at Moreh in chapter 12 to his story of the sacrifice of Isaac on Moriah in Genesis 22. This narrative chain is also a story made up of many shorter stories, each with its own plot and its own Abraham. The Jacob tradition is composed in an elaborate envelope structure. The story of the conflict of Jacob and his brother Esau encloses the story of Jacob's conflict with Laban, which story itself encloses the conflict story of Rachel and Leah. The patriarchal stories as a whole form a greater narrative composed of successive genealogies as segments: the genealogy of Terah (the Abraham tradition), of Isaac (the Jacob tradition), and the genealogy of Jacob (the Joseph tradition). These extend the genealogy of Adam, begun in Genesis 5, and carry us forward to the next segment of the tradition in Exodus.

In biblical poetry, it is commonplace to recognize that any given segment of a poem can be moved and easily exchanged and take part in many psalms and songs without structural damage. They can appear in the wisdom poetry of Job, the prophecies of Isaiah or the psalms of David, without significant variance. No great range of time separated these compositions. Three examples might illustrate this, but nearly the whole of the Psalter and the prophets, and all songs in narratives are implicated:

a) The first examples involve the motif of king and messiah as 'son of God'. In Psalm 2: 7 Yahweh says to his messiah: 'You are my son; I have given birth to you today.' This same phrase is directly echoed in Psalm 89: 25–26, where we read: 'I will give him power over the sea, dominance over rivers. He will call to me: "You are my father, my God."' The second segment of this tradition finds a more developed form in II Samuel 7: 13–14 where Yahweh says of David: 'He will build a house for my name and I will establish his royal throne forever. I will be his father and he will be my son.' A nearly identical variant of this is found in I Chronicles 17: 12–13: 'He will build me a house and I will establish his throne forever. I will be his father and he will be my son.' A variant of the first part of these passages is also found in Psalm 89: 4: 'I will establish your line forever, and build your throne in every generation.'

b) A stock pattern of introducing an oracle is placed in David's mouth to cite his last words at his death in II Samuel 23: 1: 'So speaks David, Jesse's son; so speaks the man whom the most high has raised up.' This same formula is expanded in the introduction to Balaam's oracle in Numbers 24: 3–4: 'So speaks Balaam, Beor's son; so speaks the man whose eye is open; so speaks him who hears God's words and sees with the vision of the almighty.' In verses 15–16, this introduction is used yet again, but closes with a further, internal expansion: 'so speaks him who hears God's words; who knows the knowledge of the most high, and sees with the vision of the almighty.'

c) By far the clearest and yes, *greatest*, example of this composition technique can be found in Psalm 119. This example makes it unquestionably clear that we are dealing neither with occasional citation or accidental recasting of materials, nor with the borrowing of one text by another. This is rather a technique central to writing poetry. Psalm 119 is a remarkable piece of writing. It is not at all a psalm, much more a *tour de force*. It demonstrates the techniques of a psalm-writer. Perhaps it was once the prize entry in a contest, or the result of a poet's wager! What it does for us is demonstrate how ancient poets worked. In form, it is an alphabetical acrostic. Such psalms use each letter of the alphabet successively to begin a verse. Fine examples of similar alphabetical acrostics, although partially inconsistent, can be found in Psalms 9–10, 25 and 34. Psalm 119, however, takes this playful genre to its logical extreme. It offers entire stanzas of eight lines each, in tribute to the alphabet's letters. Every line of each stanza begins with the same letter. With the 22-letter Hebrew alphabet, the poem is the longest of the Psalter. The achievement is nearly athletic in its intensity, as each of these lines offers a variant on a single motif: praise of the *torah*. All 176 segments of verse are each wholly interchangeable with the others. It makes terrible and boring poetry, but it instructs us precisely in the technique of poetry-writing.

We find this same technique in the production of many of the songs that have been collected together as sayings or oracles of various prophets of the past. In Jeremiah, for example, we have a long song about the Moabites in chapter 48: 1–47. Here, it is presented without title as a saying of Yahweh in the context of a series of similar oracles directed against one or other king of Israel. A somewhat richer variant of this poem is also found in Isaiah 15 and 16, where it is given the title: 'An oracle against Moab'. We are told at the song's closure in Isaiah 16: 13 that this had been what Yahweh had earlier said against Moab. Why? Isaiah doesn't tell us. However, the variant in Jeremiah tells us: 'In the end I will restore the destiny of Moab.' Nevertheless, here too, it is not in this poem that we find an explanation. It is in the poem's variant in Isaiah 16: 4–5 that we understand why Jeremiah is optimistic about Moab's future: 'When the oppressor is no more, destruction has ceased, and marauders have vanished from the land, then a throne shall be established in steadfast love in the tent of David. On it shall sit in truth a ruler who seeks justice and who is swift to do what is right.' This Lego-block has been intentionally integrated as a saving grace. It counterbalances the murderous lions establishing Moab's destiny for the remnant of the land that had been declared in Isaiah 15: 9: 'a lion for those who survive in Moab, for the remnant of the land'. What is implied in these comments is that *the composers of Isaiah and Jeremiah are talking to each other!* They are involved in a theological discussion. Recurrently, throughout the prophets, such text segments echo this motif of saving grace as a thematic counterpoint to prophecies of doom elsewhere.

As in the Book of Psalms, one finds short blocks of text given variant contexts throughout the prophetic books. Such are the nearly verbatim variants of the famous oracle written within the context of the philosopher's 'theology of the way' that relates Yahweh's *torah* to the new Zion in Isaiah 2: 2–5 and Micah 4: 1–4. Isaiah reads:

At last it will happen that Yahweh's temple mount shall stand unshakably, high over the mountains, raised above the hills. All nations will stream to it, many will come and say, 'Come, let us go up to Yahweh's mountain, to the house of Jacob's God. He shall show us his way, and we will walk in his path.' Yahweh's *torah* will go out from Zion; Yahweh's word from Jerusalem. He will judge between the nations and establish the destiny of many peoples. They will beat their swords into plough-shares and their spears into pruning knives. No nation will take up the sword against another; and they will no longer be learned in war: Come house of Jacob, let us walk in Yahweh's light.

Only the context is different. The Isaiah version presents the tradition block rather oddly as a 'vision' of a proverb over Jerusalem *and Judah*. In Micah the verbal genre is more consistently tied to an oracle against Israel. Not only does Micah's text lack the final exhortation to the House of Jacob, Micah closes with the echoing theology of Ezra: 1: 3, that the saving grace of Israel's God will come from Jerusalem. The extensive series of sayings collected to make up the Book of Micah are implicitly independent oracles. They create a text collage much like what we find in the shorter *4QTestimonia*. Joel 3: 10 uses the polarity of plough-shares and swords in a brilliant reversal of this well-known motif of peace: 'Beat your plough-shares into swords and your pruning knives into spears, that even the weakling might say, "I am a warrior!" '

As might be expected, substantial structural variants also occur frequently in poetry. Some are thematic variants, such as the oracles about Yahweh as the 'lion of wrath' against Edom. This, we find in Obadiah 1: 1–9 and again, even more explicitly, in Jeremiah 49: 7–22. The closure of the Jeremiah version of the oracle (49: 19–21): 'Like a lion coming up from the Jordan's jungle, etc.') has a nearly verbatim variant in Jeremiah's very next chapter (50: 44–46), where the lion finds Babylon as its prey. This is not only a reiteration of an oracle whose numerous variants can, for example, be found in Jeremiah 2: 15, 4: 7–8, 5: 6, 25: 38 and elsewhere, where this angry lion is repeatedly identified with Yahweh's anger and his vengeful destruction in one or other dramatic projection of the day of wrath. We not only have a brilliant integration of a single saying used variably against both Edom and Babylon, we have the projection of a mythological *topos* that can be accessed whenever appropriate. This same metaphor of Yahweh's anger as that of a lion on an at times cosmic day of wrath, bringing divine destruction, is also brought forward in Nahum 1–2 against Nineveh, the capital city of Assyria. The stock metaphor of this 'lion of wrath' is particularly transparent in Nahum 1: 6 and 2: 12–14. Nahum's use of this stock poetic material is particularly instructive because of the commentary on the Book of Nahum which has been found among the Dead Sea scrolls. In this *Pesher Nahum*, the prophet's image of the lion of Yahweh's wrath that is to bring about Nineveh's destruction is interpreted by the scribe of the scrolls in the context of past military attacks on Jerusalem, apparently drawn from Hellenistic lore.

The techniques involved in the composition of poetry also resemble those used in writing proverbs. In the genre of wisdom couplets, we typically find the building blocks in the form of statements and pithy phrases. These travel and can be used in a variety of ways. For example, Proverbs 13: 19 reads: 'A wish fulfilled does the soul good; but to turn away from evil is a horror to the fool.' In principle, each half of this couplet can be used in separate contexts. Each can be paired with yet other tradition segments in just as satisfying a matching. Moreover, collections of such traditional couplets offer multiple contexts for the very same proverb. These variations in text and context can be both complex and rich. The couplets of Proverbs 22: 28 and 23: 10 present us with the opening segment: 'Do not remove the ancient marker.' The saying is completed with the help of variant closures playing on the verbal motif of father: 'which your fathers have set' and alternatively: 'or enter the fields of the fatherless'. The variations render radically different meanings. The opening segment is also found in Deuteronomy 19: 14 in a very close variant of the Proverbs 22 couplet. Now, however, the context influences the phrasing as it is presented as a law of Moses: 'Do not remove your neighbour's marker; which the men of old have set.' Again, in a poem of Hosea, a legal motif is referenced as a metaphor for lawless Judah: 'The princes of Judah have become like those who remove the marker' (Hosea 5: 10).

It is precisely economy of composition that creates the similarity in a lot of biblical traditions, both those presented as songs, and those offered as wisdom. In fact, one might say that psalm verses and proverbs, and indeed prophetic oracles as well, are not different kinds of literature at all. They differ from each other only because of the fictional contexts in which they are placed: as belonging to a song of David, a saying of Solomon or an oracle of Isaiah.

In both Job 7: 17 and Psalm 8: 4, we find the famous interrogatory sentence: 'What is a person?' Job expands the entry segment with 'that you make so much of one'. He then couples this with the variation: 'and that you pay attention to one?' Job's question is capable of a positive orientation. Job, however, adds a closure that fits, but was not written for, the specific context of his story: 'What is a man, that you visit him every morning and test him every moment?' The implied answer to what has been offered as a rhetorical question reflecting Job's own sufferings, is pessimistic. Psalm 8: 4 offers a variant query in the opening by pairing the segment in another direction: 'What is a man, that you are mindful of one?' It closes its use of the couplet with a matching segment: 'or what is the son of man that you care for him?' Rather than allowing the verse's implicitly negative overtones, the psalm expands the motif. It parallels this composition with the splendid: 'You have made him a little less than God, and have crowned him with glory and honour.'

We find these same tradition blocks – with an interrogatory expansion in the manner of Psalm 8: 4 – once again in Psalm 144: 3–4: 'O Yahweh, what is a person that you would know one, or the son of man that you would think of him?' The response also expands – and this we should mark well – with a Job-like pessimism, with echoes of Abel in the Cain story of Genesis 4: 'A person is like a breath, whose days are like a passing shadow.' Thematically, these variations are hardly isolated from each other by either centuries or authors. They are part of the same literary and intellectual discussion. In fact, we can well argue that these texts reflect a contemporary discussion in progress. These texts about what a human being is, belong together within a genre of scholarly discourse. This implied discussion is nearly as vigorous as the discussions we will find below, in chapters 14 and 15, dealing with the multiple variations of stories about the sons of God and the wives of Yahweh. The expansive variant that we find in Eliphaz' speech in Job 4: 17–21 draws out the quality of this implicit debate well:

> Can a human being be more righteous than God? Can a man be purer than his maker? God places no trust even in his servants; with even his angels he finds fault. How much more with those who live in houses of clay, whose foundations are dust; who can be crushed as easily as a moth; who are destroyed between morning and evening, and who perish forever, without anyone taking notice. It is as it were their tent-peg was pulled up that they die; and that without wisdom!

We find a briefer version of Eliphaz' argument in Job 15: 14: 'What is man that he can be clean, or one that is born of a woman that he can be righteous?' As we collect variants, what previously appeared distant makes its own unique contribution to the discussion. Such is the case with Job 15: 15–16: 'While God does not trust even his holy ones – even the heavens are impure in his eyes – how much less one ugly and evil, a man who can drink malice like water?' The issue is central to the Bible's theology. Very interesting variations on this discussion are found in the tradition blocks of Job 21: 14–16 and 22: 17–20, the first of which plays on the question, 'What is the Almighty?' Only a single half-sentence is given verbatim in both these variants to mark them as a pair: 'They say to God: let us alone!' In Job 21, this statement is expanded with: 'We do not want knowledge of your ways. What is the almighty that we should serve him and what is our profit in praying to him?' In contrast, in Job 22 the tradition segment is coupled with the rhetorical question, 'What can the almighty do to us?' to form a unique statement. Chapter 22 then expands by engaging the implied debate itself: 'the counsel of the wicked is far from me; the righteous see it and are glad, the innocent scorn them: our enemies are wiped out; what remains is destroyed by the fire.' We find presented in these passages of Job, texts which could well be found in either the psalms or the prophets. Their real context is in the implied discussions of those collecting the traditions.

This technique of creating texts in psalms, oracles and proverbs is also found throughout the collections of laws and cultic regulations in the books of the Pentateuch. The wide range of this kind of variation is well known. Most of the Dead Sea scrolls traditions, as have been found in the text of *4QTestimonia*, belong to this type. A final example drawn from these collections might close our discussion. The best-known of the tradition belongs to the clusters of such tradition segments that form variations on Yahweh's *torah*. This collection occurs in four different variations: Exodus 20: 1–17, Exodus 34, Leviticus 19 and Deuteronomy 5–6. Only Exodus 20 and Deuteronomy offer us the stories in the Ten Commandments form that Martin Luther made so popular in Christian catechetical traditions. Exodus 34's version of the Ten Commandments – described as the one that Moses carved on the two stone tablets – concentrates on the cult and feasts. Leviticus, on the other hand, is composed as a collection of six negative and six positive commandments. Each of these variants shares in the much larger discussion of the countless biblical traditions that have tried to epitomize what God expects of adherents to the tradition.

Already with the listing of the Ten Commandments in Deuteronomy 5, the collector attempts to epitomize them even more in a single great commandment in Deuteronomy 6: 4–5. This is largely a paraphrase and expansion on the first of the ten.

> Hear O Israel, Yahweh our God. Yahweh is one. Therefore, you shall love your God with your whole heart, and with your whole soul and with your whole strength.

As a dramatic illustration of this epitomizing commandment, Deuteronomy 10: 12–13 integrates it within the story of Moses' farewell speech, which closes the Pentateuch's tradition of divine law-giving. Philosophical language dominates this passage, bringing together the commandment's simplicity with the educated metaphors of the theology of the way:

> Now, Israel, what does Yahweh your God require of you than to fear Yahweh your God, walk in his paths and love him. Serve Yahweh your God with your whole heart and your whole soul; so that you keep his commandments and his *torah* which I have given to you today, for your best good.

It is a variant of this tradition that Joshua identifies in Joshua 22: 5, as the *torah* given to Israel by Moses when he sends the people to occupy their lands after the stories of conquest:

To love Yahweh, your God, walk in all of his paths, keep his commandments and be faithful to him, serving him with all your heart and soul.

The prize for brevity and simplicity certainly goes to Micah, for the effort he makes in answer to the implied teacher's question in Micah 6: 8. This passage too uses the same kind of language as Deuteronomy 10. It sees the moral task of the believer in the theological terms of the way.

What does Yahweh require of you? Act with justice and steadfast love. Walk with your God humbly.

Matthew's gospel presents just such a question as we find in Micah, to his teacher Jesus. The question is put in language of the 'greatest' of the laws. 'Which is the greatest commandment in the law?' Matthew answers the traditional question with a double, contrasting variation.

You should love the lord your God with your whole heart, your whole soul and your whole mind. This is the greatest and the first commandment. And the second is much like it. Love your neighbour as yourself. The whole of the law and the prophets derive from these two. (Matt. 22: 37–40)

Luke has Jesus ask the question: 'What is the law? What do you read there?' In answer, the teacher acts the good student striving for completeness, and makes an effort to put his answer in the form of a single commandment:

You should love the lord your God with your whole heart and your whole soul and your whole strength and your whole mind, and your neighbour as yourself. (Luke 10: 27)

Finally in Mark's gospel, a scribe asks Jesus, not about the greatest of the commandments, but about 'which was the first?' Like Matthew, Mark's draw on tradition fits the enthusiasm of the eager student. Mark has Jesus offer not one but two commandments in response. For the first, he quotes Deuteronomy 6: 4, but he has the same expansion as we find in Luke. His doubling of this commandment, moreover, clearly departs from Deuteronomy's effort to epitomize the Ten Commandments. Although Mark's second commandment also repeats the substance of Luke, his wording searches for simplicity and balance.

The first is 'Hear O Israel the lord our God. The lord is one. Love the lord your God with your whole heart, with your whole soul, your whole mind and with all your strength.' The second is this: 'love your neighbour as yourself.' There is no other commandment greater than these. (Mark 12: 29–31)

Although the wording of many of our passages is very similar, and one certainly would describe all of these variants as close, each of our texts offers an independent and interpretive voice to the tradition as a whole. Again, expansive commentary and discussion characterize the development of the tradition.

4 The Bible and its authors

We should never forget that the Bible is a very old book. It springs from an intellectual world quite different from our own. That world, the source of the Bible's implicit concepts and metaphors, is a world that stretches from the western Mediterranean to India and from at least the third century BCE to the end of the first century CE. It is, however, a literary world, which is only implicit in our texts. It no longer comes easily to the reader. Yet it is to this world that this literature is addressed, and it is on our perceptions of this world that our understanding of the Bible is dependent. The fictive world of old Israel that is created by the narratives and poetry of the Bible is closed to us. The characters – both gods and people – which fill that fictive world are inaccessible to the reader apart from this greater, yet implicit, literary context. No David or Moses meets us apart from this world that has been created for us by the writers of the Bible. For understanding our texts, this is far more important to us than any historical world of the ancient past can be. The world of song and story is hardly a projection of any real world independent of the songs and stories that project it. It is a world created by writers in conversation with each other. All reading depends on our ability to enter the world of such discussions.

To help make this issue clearer, let us pose a problem for our reading of the Bible. Though we have talked a lot about the Bible collecting traditions, it is not clear at all that the Bible collects actual ancient traditions that once had a life apart from the text of the Bible, which its authors created for us. Yet our texts often present themselves as doing just that. The Book of Proverbs begins: 'The proverbs of Solomon, son of David, king of Israel.' When we open the Book of Jeremiah we are told that we are reading 'the words of Jeremiah, the son of Hilkiah'. Even inside stories, we are told that what follows is a tradition collected: 'God spoke all these words saying': and what follows in Exodus 20 is the Ten Commandments. But are we reading the words of God, a Jeremiah or a Solomon, or are we reading something else? The issue is not at all one of belief or truth-telling. It is an issue of reading and of what is implied in texts.

When we read ancient texts, we should not be too quickly confident about what is obvious. This habit of giving collected works a fictional context, almost a constant of biblical writings, is also a characteristic practice throughout the ancient world. It reflects the ancient understanding of truth and knowledge as stable aspects of reality. When Solomon tell us in the Book of Ecclesiastes that 'there is nothing new under the sun', he does not surprise any of his readers. No one thinks him particularly pessimistic because of it. Knowledge is an aspect of the divine. As such, it was present at the creation! Knowledge and understanding is the product of generations. Truth is not discovered but handed on. It is revealed to those with the patience and training to see what is already there. True education and learning lies in the skills of discernment, and all wisdom is tradition. Tradition is what the Bible means by its *torah*, and 'the righteous' are those who love the *torah* – that is, who give themselves to the study of the tradition – day and night (Psalm 1: 2).

An author's personality is subordinate to the tradition; it is not he himself who writes, but the tradition that speaks through him, its servant. The great Babylonian poet, Kabti–Ilani–Marduk, who once wrote a beautiful song to the divine Erra, describes himself as the 'compiler of its tablets'. He goes on to tell how the poem was revealed to him by the gods in a dream during the night. This should not be misread. It is not a modern author overwhelmed by the beauty and originality of his own words. It is specifically the poem's originality that is denied here in this discounting of the poet's authorship. The poet is a faithful servant of the gods. When he recited the poem in the morning after waking, 'he did not leave out a single line; nor did he add one to it.' Such divine inspiration is listened to even by the gods with respect. Even they must praise such a song. Future singers who sing it will be blessed; 'they who sing it will not die in destruction.' The scribe who commits it to memory 'will be honoured in his own land'.[1] For the house in which the tablet is deposited, 'peace will be assured'. Kabti–Ilani–Marduk is the composer of this song, but he transmits what is remembered. Composition itself is a form of transmission. It is not that ancient authors do not understand their own roles in writing. Nor do they devalue the uniqueness of their contribution to the literary and intellectual world in which they take part. They could be every bit as ambitious for themselves as any modern writer. But their understanding of knowledge, of wisdom and of what was real and true found different expression. Their own role in the creation and transmission of tradition was tempered by their respect for the world of language and thought that inspired them. So too, their hubris was tempered by the awareness of their ignorance of things divine.

The perception of authorship that dominated writing encouraged the

---

[1] Conversely, we have the tradition that a prophet is not honoured in his own land, because there, where the individual is known, it is difficult to believe that what is spoken is from the gods.

self-understanding of text production in the form of traditions collected from the past. This is the classic pattern for the whole of antiquity. The elaborateness of this conceit is already well established when we first find it. Contemporary with some of our very earliest written literature, we find authors creating fictive contexts for their work: attributing their knowledge to sources old and honoured. Egyptian manuscripts written in the first half of the second millennium BCE present us with a text that claims an origin in the fifth dynasty (about 2450 BCE). Even as old as that might be, the text elaborates on this fiction of ancient tradition yet further. These proverbs are offered to the reader as the instructions of the vizier of Egypt, Ptah-Hotep. They are offered in the form of an account of what the vizier told his son and successor on his deathbed. What he tells his son, moreover, is not the wisdom of his experiences as an individual having lived a long life, but 'the words of them that listen and the ideas of the ancestors, of them that hearkened to the gods'. This is the same motif relating to the wisdom of the ancient sages that is cited in Deuteronomy 32: 7. Comparable use of such 'testimonies', as Ptah-hotep's, are found throughout ancient literature. Genesis 49, Deuteronomy 33 and II Samuel 23: 1–7, collect the 'last words' or 'deathbed blessings' of a Jacob, a Moses and a David. They are poems that enlist a traditional and fictive motif in order to offer further commentaries on the narratives they close. But the specific genre of the Ptah-Hotep text is also itself a very conservative form of literary context. Such a convention functioned for more than 2,000 years in introducing collections of philosophical proverbs throughout the ancient Near East.

While there are numerous biblical works that use this form, by far the best example is the book called 'The Wisdom of Jesus the Son of Sirach', or Ecclesiasticus in the Catholic Bible. The author presents this collection of traditional philosophy as the writings of his grandfather. The content of the book is attributed to his grandfather's reading of the *torah* and the prophets, as well as to other old books. Its purpose is to help others 'in living according to the *torah*'. Like the author of Erra's poem, this author attributes the book's understanding and wisdom not to himself but to God: 'All wisdom comes from Yahweh.'

Similarly, the *Dialogues*, written by the fourth-century teacher Plato, eclectically gather the author's reflections in the form of philosophical disputations on what is real and unreal in human perception. Plato places himself in the role of student to the great teacher Socrates, who is given the role of creative voice. Here, the implicit modesty of Plato and ancient wisdom literature surfaces. In these dialogues, Plato nearly disappears from sight – and certainly absents himself from the reader's imagination, which concentrates rather on the author's voice in Socrates' mouth, while Plato himself takes the role of dutiful student of a tradition's wisdom. Similarly, the scribal grandson of Ben-Sirach or a wholly anonymous author as with Deuteronomy presents his work as the product of a great teacher. In the author's absence, the tradition can speak, unhindered by any scepticism we might bring to a writer we know. It is not Plato, but, rather, Plato's saint and martyr, Socrates, who speaks. This is done so that what Plato says may be heard.

To stay for a moment within the world of Greek tradition's three great philosophers, perhaps the most interesting example of this entire pseudonymous genre is given us by Plato's student, Aristotle. It is not a specific text that is given an aetiology, but a specific learned understanding of reality. Much like the poet of Deuteronomy 32, who sends his audience into the past for his teaching, Aristotle creates a philosophical past to ground the fundamental elements of his philosophy. The four basic elements of creation are exemplified in Aristotle by the teachings of past great men. The first was Thales with his teaching about 'water'. Anaximander followed with his understanding of undifferentiated matter, or 'earth'. Once the pattern was established, Anaximenes' championing of the principle of 'air', and Heraklitus' of 'fire', are predictable.

Aristotle's classic description of the world's fundamental elements is placed within the idealistic context of a great debate: that between the thesis of Parmenides that nothing changes, and that of Heraklitus that everything does. The solution is to be discovered in the synthesis of a third: Empedocles. There are not one but four principles: earth, air, fire and water. With such economy, Aristotle can present his reader with both a history and a basic introduction to philosophy! School philosophers have followed him ever since.

While the New Testament's great teacher is Jesus, who shares the role with his predecessor John and his successor Paul, the Bible as a whole gives pride of place to Moses as the teacher of tradition. So many share this role, however, that continuities are best followed, in the manner of Aristotle's 'pre-Socratic philosophers', by associating our history of great teachers with the history of ideas. Such meaning-impaired texts, for example, as we saw in Exodus 3–6, may be easier to understand if we direct our attention not so much to the historical and socially specific beliefs and metaphors of a world that we have created, but rather to more text-specific concepts such as ideation: the process and creation of ideas. This will involve us in an analysis of formulae, motifs and secondary verbal formations, and especially how they shape and affect understanding for the recipients of the tradition. I think we need to trace the process of idea creation before we can hope to understand what anyone may have believed. This is important when we address such pivotal concepts as 'god', and its many synonyms, particularly when we deal with the more self-consciously human world of commentaries on our traditions which understand themselves as only reflecting divine reality. A brief look at the single concept of 'Davidic messiah' may illustrate this for us.

5 The function of commentary

Both theologically and referentially, most of the texts that were to become the Christian Bible's Old Testament belong to an intellectual world that holds the New Testament in common. I do not mean that the Old Testament is contemporary with the New Testament. It is certainly earlier. Nor am I suggesting that the Bible has a Christianized Old Testament. It does not. Most of the works that belong to these 'testaments' reflect a single biblical tradition that has its roots in what is widely understood as early Jewish intellectual history. They relate to each other as older and younger contemporaries within a common discourse. The discussions about tradition that we find in the New Testament are not reinterpretations of a closed past. They are part of an ongoing transmission common to the whole of biblical tradition.

For example, the interpretation of the complex, but pivotally important, Immanuel stories of Isaiah in Matthew's story of Jesus' birth is an expansion of a tradition about the Davidic messiah as Immanuel, which we will discuss yet once again in our closing chapter. This interpretation is already implicitly spelled out in Isaiah 7–9's comprehensive identification of the variant traditions of the Immanuel child born as the saving divine presence for the new Jerusalem. In Isaiah 9: 2–7's interpretive commentary, Immanuel does not represent the destructive force of the Assyrian king on the day of wrath as in Isaiah 7: 14. The interpretation of the child to be born as Immanuel in chapter 9 is of a child of hope, placed in contrast to chapter 7's child. The interpretation reiterates the prophetic significance of Isaiah's first son *She'ar-yashub* (Isa. 7: 3: 'the repentant remnant'). This child in Isaiah 9 is born of Yahweh's wife, who is the 'new Jerusalem'. The divine presence, born of its mother's labour, is named 'wonderful counsellor, mighty God, eternal father, the master of peace'. Matthew 1: 23's use of Jesus to illustrate this role of Immanuel does nothing more than reiterate this traditional teaching of God's saving presence. Matthew does not change our understanding of Isaiah. He simply reads the text of Isaiah 7–9 as a coherent whole, as it was, in fact, intended to be read.

The Book of Isaiah presents a picture of a new Jerusalem and a new Israel. It speaks from the self-understanding of Jerusalem as a 'remnant saved'. Already in chapter 1's harsh context, Jerusalem's salvation is implicit in its contrast to Sodom: 'If Yahweh of the armies had not left us a few survivors, we would have been like Sodom' (1: 9). Similarly, chapter 10: 22's decree of Yahweh against Israel presents a riddle, whose interpretation is the key to reading the Immanuel passages of Isaiah 7–9. As Yahweh determines Israel's fate, a note of hope and of Israel's repentence introduces Yahweh's judgement: 'In that day, the remnant of Israel ... will lean upon Yahweh, the holy one of Israel in truth ... A remnant will return, the remnant of Jacob, to the mighty God (Isaiah 10: 20–22).' And then the riddle is given: 'Destruction is decreed; it overflows with righteousness.' The saving remnant is the overflow, coming from the fullness of the beaker of suffering. The events that give birth to the child of Isaiah 7: 14, bringing Jerusalem's destruction at the hands of the Assyrian army, is interpreted here in 10: 22 as Jerusalem's labour pains giving birth to the Immanuel of a 'new Israel'. Rendering a Hebrew version of the legend of the phoenix, this implicit interpretation shows the fateful child of Isaiah 7: 14 as the harbinger of the royal, messianic, hope-filled child of chapter 9. Just so, is he son of God and Immanuel!

In his Letter to the Romans, Paul well understood this. He follows the older discussion, in technique as well as content, in chapter 9. Citing a variant of the tale of the prophet's child of Hosea 1–2 (Romans 9: 25–26), he interprets the story in light of Isaiah's 'repentant remnant' of Isaiah 7: 3. Paul is well aware of the variety of saving children stories in the tradition and engages that same discussion. 'No matter that the children of Israel be as numerous as the sand of the sea, it is only a remnant that will be saved.' So says Isaiah 10: 21–22. Paul, like Isaiah, is interested in the remnant. Isaiah 1: 9's survivors serve also as Paul's interpretive key. Paul's closing argument in Romans 9: 33 offers exactly this commentary. Isaiah 8's destruction-bringing Immanuel is read in the context of Isaiah 9's saving, messianic child, who is God. Paul emphasizes the negative prophecy of Isaiah 8: 14. The child will be 'a stone, that will make men stumble; a rock that will make them fall'. He interprets this, quite appropriately, in the context of the 'cornerstone' of Isaiah 28: 16's remnant theology: 'he who believes in him will not be put to shame.' Here is no new interpretation, but an epitomizing paraphrase. Paul is not changing anything; this is Isaiah's interpretation and nothing more.

Nor can it be said that Paul reinterprets Isaiah's and Hosea's traditions messianically so that they may better fit Paul's understanding of Jesus, as is claimed by many modern scholars. It is not Paul but Isaiah who introduces the metaphor of the child as a stone against which men will stumble. And in drawing this metaphor, an implicit illustration is made of Psalm 25: 3's proverb: 'No one that trusts in me will be put to shame; let them be shamed who are faithless without cause.' For Isaiah, that stone is God; that is, 'God for us'. Paul is merely joining the tradition's discussion.

Similarly when Matthew cites Psalm 8: 2 in Matthew 21: 16, and refers to the truth seen by children: 'from the mouth of children and babies', he reads his text as a riddle, and interprets it within the same complex of tradition that is referenced by the psalm. Both Psalm 8 and Matthew echo the tradition of Hosea 2: 23: the child will say, 'You are my God.' Matthew interprets the psalm, however, in terms of the other Immanuel variants, and especially the child of Isaiah 8. He accordingly reads it as a metaphor for the Davidic messiah. Yet such an interpretation is hardly at odds with the psalm's interpretation. The psalm sees the divine name, which is recognized by Hosea's child, as a barrier or shield against God's enemies, a role that very much belongs to discussions about messiahs as in Psalm 2.

The messianic metaphors of Psalms 2 and 8 are not evidence of beliefs or expectation that such a figure will some day come and save the people. That is an expectation and characteristic implicit only in later literature. It is possible that such millennial beliefs do not become typical of the tradition until some time after Jerusalem's destruction in the year 70 CE. In the Old Testament, and in most New Testament texts for that matter, we are dealing primarily with literary metaphors and motifs. The recurrent interplay of such song and story did create what we can well describe as a metaphorical reality: a myth, as an expression of the heavenly reality implied by our texts. Here the heavenly battle of Yahweh and his messiah against the powers of evil, which is echoed in the daily struggles of the followers of the theology of the way, seems to have been quite real to the bearers of this tradition. In their faithfulness to the way of the *torah*, they too fight in such a battle. The evidence for this is abundant throughout most of the tradition that deals with the messiah. It particularly marks the traditions that have presented David as the messiah.

The manner in which such intellectual realities are created can be clearly seen by looking at the interpretive headings that we have discussed, found in thirteen of the psalms in the Bible. These headings each identify a song in the Psalter as one that was sung when David was in one or other crisis that we find described in the David stories of I and II Samuel. Both David and his story are understood as part of tradition past. Yet these headings reflect a relatively early perspective on the David tradition. They refer to a tradition of the books of Samuel that was earlier than the one we now have. The stories are not only not quite identical to those we now have, offering many differences in detail, but at least one of the psalm's headings refers to a tale we no longer have. Moreover, a close variant of yet another of these thirteen psalms, Psalm 18, is found, along with its interpretive title, in II Samuel 22. Together with the song of 'David's last words', it is used to close the story of David's life, much in the same way that the songs of Deuteronomy 32 and 33 are used to close the story of Moses' life. The song is placed here in order to interpret the figure of David for Samuel's audience. When the story in the books of Samuel, the primary narrative for David, took its current shape, that story was being interpreted and read in the manner of Psalm 18 and the comparable headings we find in the Psalter. This is not the young warrior and earthly king, but the singer David of the Book of Psalms. It is the messiah David of heaven's mythology.

The interpretive discourse of these thirteen psalm titles is two-directional. On one hand, they dramatize and interpret the psalms. They give them a context within the adventures of David. Each interprets its psalm as one that had been originally sung by David at a very specific time in the past: 'when he was running from his son Absalom' (Psalm 3: 1), 'when he played the role of a madman before Abimelech; so that he drove him out and he went away' (Psalm 34: 1) or 'when he was in the cave' (Psalm 142: 1). The psalms become available for psychological transference: a method of interpretation that we also find in such Hellenistic commentators as Philo, since the listener to the tradition identifies with its heroes – as David seeks help and salvation so do I; for I can sing with David's voice. In this way the reader of the tradition shares in David's past victories.

On the other hand, just as this heading spells out the context of the psalm's 'origins', in terms of a life of David, the psalm itself interprets the life and adventures of David for its audience. In all of our psalms, such an interpretation is consistently theological and mythical. David is everyman. He represents before God the psalmist and his listener in their prayer in a time of desperate need. David's is the implicit voice of the singer's 'I' in crisis. This personal, representative role marks the psalms as messianic. This is both implied and explicit, found in a clustering of wisdom motifs that adhere to the metaphor of the son of God and Messiah in such psalms as 2, 8, 89 and 110, where David is interpreted as the messiah struggling against his enemies, the nations of the world, in Yahweh's cosmic struggle. He is the representative of the righteous in the cosmic struggle of Yahweh against the nations. Finally, and associated with this same cluster of motifs, as highlighted in Psalms 1 and 2, David becomes the philosopher struggling to remain on the path of righteousness. In his song, David epitomizes the one who seeks refuge in Yahweh (Psalm 2: 11).

It is quite clear, from these titles, giving David these psalms to sing, that David's significance in his historical role in ancient Israel's past is hardly entertained. He rather has his meaning within the piety of the implied author. The real David exists within a mythological struggle. Some of the psalms, like Psalm 18: 50, explicitly understand David himself as a cosmic and messianic presence. All use a cluster of motifs that identify David within the context of just such a cosmic messiah. Psalm 18: 1–3 and 46–48 make particular reference to Psalm 8's war against the nations. Verses 6 and 13 tie Jerusalem's temple to the messiah's heavenly throne. Verse 7 calls up an earthquake, while verse 28 evokes creation's contrast between light and darkness much in the manner of Genesis 1 and John 1. The historical context of this war is the well-known theology of the way of Jewish philosophical pietism (vv. 20–24). David is hardly a figure of the distant past. He is the saviour of all who hold to the *torah* (vv. 25–28). Psalm 18's David is much like Psalm 8's messiah. The implicit voice of the psalm is the pious man's representative. He is saved by Yahweh in his struggle against his moral enemies (vv. 31–42). It is this 'I' who Yahweh makes cosmic emperor over the nations in verses 43–45.

CHAPTER 12

The Bible's theological world I: how God began

1 What the Bible knows and doesn't know about God

We might see the construction of a temple in Jerusalem after the return from Babylon as a viable historical basis for the beginning of the Bible's formation. This argument, however, refers to specific metaphors and intellectual ideas in the Bible. It particularly refers to what they imply about the world that created them. The argument is not adequate for dating the traditions historically. At most it gives us an earliest possible date some time after a community had been formed around Jerusalem's temple. This community came to understand itself variously as having returned from exile, being the remnant of ancient Israel, or by understanding itself as the new Israel. This process could possibly have been as early as *c*. 450 BCE or as late as the Maccabean period. Neither the return from exile nor the construction of the second temple under Ezra and Nehemiah are periods or events known to us from evidence. Known to us from tradition, not history, they are not entirely viable as historical contexts.

In this question of the possible historical contexts of the Bible's formation, we are compelled to begin, not from theory, but from the foundation of what is historically known about the tradition. This begins with the contexts in which our traditions have come to us. Only from secure contexts, where we know that the biblical tradition certainly existed, can we enter tolerably into the more speculative earlier periods of its formation. The Septuagint version of the Old Testament, whose origins we can reasonably date to the second century BCE or later, is not entirely a translation of the Hebrew Bible we know. Some of the traditions in the Septuagint are not found in the Hebrew Bible. Some books, like the Books of Maccabees, never existed in Hebrew but had been originally written in Greek. Yet others, like the Greek version of Samuel, should be described as variants of the traditions we find in the Hebrew Bible.

In II Maccabees 4, we find an interesting reference to a collection of texts that had been saved by Judas Maccabee from the wars. Whether this is a plausible and accurate depiction of some known library is uncertain. It could just as well be a fictional reference to traditions known. It might be read as supporting II Maccabees' view of Jewish tradition and of the Maccabees' role in protecting the 'traditional' way of life in Hellenized Palestine. The additional mention in II Maccabees 4 of the legendary library of Nehemiah as having been lost some time in the distant past is perhaps only a reference to a tradition otherwise unknown among the Nehemiah legends. It implies that the author of II Maccabees knows of no stable collection of written tradition that had survived the Maccabean wars intact. In this chapter of II Maccabees, dedicated to a recounting of the survival of tradition past, neither the traditions of Ezra's law-giving nor that of Nehemiah's library are any longer accessible. Only Judas Maccabee's efforts preserved what is now seen as a fragmented past. In itself, this text offers us a serious argument against understanding the final formation of the Bible much earlier than the end of the second century BCE. This is the appropriate date for the original text that II Maccabees claims to epitomize. Perhaps, our Bible should not be dated before some time in the first century BCE, when II Maccabees itself seems to have been written. Its writer, at least, knows no such Bible.

The Hebrew Bible that we know underwent a considerable revision some time after the rededication of the Jerusalem temple in 164 BCE. We know this because the chronology it uses, beginning in Genesis, is based on a scheme of a great year of 4,000 years that reaches its fullness with this rededication. The legends of Ezra and Nehemiah are also centred in this national ideology of the temple in Jerusalem. This theology has its first secure context in the intellectually charged movement of nationalism that followed the Maccabean revolt, and that centred itself in the traditions around the temple at some time after this rededication. This gives us a reasonable earliest date for the beginning of a comprehensive collection of the tradition. It is also first in the historical context of the Hasmonean state, created by the Maccabees, that Palestine possesses the national coherence implied by the development of a library, and which is so marked by the language of self-conscious ethnicity. Unlike many earlier periods in Palestine, we know that the Hellenistic period was both creative and literate. The development of tradition, an aspect of intellectual history, requires no broad chronological spectrum. It is both synchronic and diachronic. It is also first in this period that we have found texts similar to what we find in the Bible. The texts that have been found in Qumran show that the biblical tradition is already well advanced by the late second century BCE, and they show that at least the Book of Isaiah has been completed in all its 66 chapters. These texts also give evidence that much of the biblical tradition is still in the process of completion.

When we turn to the tradition itself for an understanding of its formation, our earliest possible context for the onset of the process of tradition collection must be placed with the identification of the bearers of this tradition as 'Israel'. Greek influence in the collective tradition need not necessarily lock us into the Hellenistic period. This understanding of 'Greek' influence reflects an artificial contrast by early scholarship between Greek literature and that of the ancient Near East. Arguments of derivation, however, are fragile and tendentious. *Palestine*, on the Mediterranean fringe of the Persian world, comes into contact with the Aegean world at least from the onset of hostilities between the Greek city-states and *Persia*. What we like to define as Greek thought is better viewed as a specific regionalization of an intellectual understanding that reflected perceptions of reality found not only in Greece, but across the entire ancient world. What each region developed was its own geographically particular literature: in far-off India as in Egypt, in Babylon as in Syria-Palestine, in Old Persia and in Anatolia. Both Hebrew and Greek reflect a comparable world-view from at least the fifth century.

For purposes of clarity, I would suggest that we think of the earliest sources of the Bible as reflecting one of three categories:

a) *Surviving fragments of the past.* These are traditions and fragments of traditions that come from intellectual contexts that were both earlier and independent of the texts in which they have been collected. Some of the materials collected can be shown to preserve or reflect original contexts that can be recognized by us as belonging to very early periods. Some of these – such as a small number of sayings or prayers that have been collected in Leviticus, the Shem and Ham genealogies we find in Genesis, as well as the genealogy of Ishmael, the story in Numbers about the prophet Bileam, the dynastic list of Israel from Omri on, perhaps the dynastic name of a 'House of David' in Jerusalem, as well as aspects of the destruction account of Samaria – have known roots even as early as the Assyrian period. Many motifs found in the Psalms, such as in Psalm 89 – in fact, entire stanzas of song – demonstrate a clear continuity of song and poetry in the region dating back at least as early as the poetry found on the cuneiform tablets of ancient Ugarit of Late Bronze Syria. Perhaps the earliest elements of biblical stories can be found in the many collections of names – especially in the collections of Genesis 4 and 5 – some of which are otherwise only known from Bronze Age texts. Not only the flood story, but both the garden story and the creation account of Genesis 1 offer variants of motifs, themes and episodes closely tied to Late Babylonian traditions or to the Gilgamesh and Adapa stories of yet earlier times. There are also many structural and thematic similarities between the collections of narratives that we find from Joshua to II Kings and the ethnographic tales that had been collected by the fifth-century Greek writer Herodotus. There are many more such fragments of traditions collected in the Bible.

b) *The world-view of exclusive monotheism.* These are traditions and aspects of the tradition that reject forms of syncretism. They reflect an intolerance of alternative religious expression, and they favour a universalist and exclusive monotheism. It is as yet uncertain that this intolerance is entirely due to the adoption of the sectarianism implicit in the Bible's theology of the way. Already by the late second century BCE, however – to judge by many of the Dead Sea scrolls – intolerant forms of sectarianism seem to have begun to distinguish and define communities which had accepted the tradition as their own. From as early as the Persian empire's efforts under Xerxes to centralize the government's control over religious ideology by banning some religious associations, many more pluralist ideas were perceived as a threat to the dogma the empire supported. Such discriminating intolerance becomes commonplace in ancient texts. Perhaps the originally Greek concept of the essential spirituality and individuality of the human person found a platform in Asia in which the gods, perceived as individuals, became implicitly competitive. This could be seen as the dark side of the story of a God without a people seeking a people without a God.

More than one recent book of biblical scholarship has explored the possibilities of radical political parties forming around a Taliban-like fundamentalist core of religious bigots. This work is very promising. Slogan-like references to 'Yahweh Alone!' as a rallying cry for such groups echo through many of our texts, and might well reflect such socially destructive movements. The historical existence in the Persian province of Jehud of a discriminating, potentially intransigent, and intolerantly repressive movement against dissidents might be inferred from parts of Ezra. Certainly the tradition was quickly understood as reflecting a worldview of *exclusive* monotheism, intolerant of the beliefs of others. Josephus' accounts of John Hyrcanus' military conquests of Palestinian regions not only echo II Kings' stories about 'good King Josiah', they also underline the social and historical realities of forced conversions in a religiously politicized environment. When historicized, the world-view of exclusive monotheism could be well epitomized by the metaphors in the Psalms about Yahweh and his messiah at war with the nations and the powers of the ungodly. Such metaphors form a slippery slope, and end in a personification of both good and evil, as in today's commonplace demonization of the foreigner and Islam in both Europe and the Americas.

The Aegean world's deep-rooted merchant's penchant for syncretism, with its inevitable tendency to see a plurality of religious expression as essentially an ordinary issue of commerce, met a surprisingly bitter and reactionary resistance in Palestine. For many, Yahweh represented the sole signification of the heavenly spirit. In contrast to the Persian empire's common language of a universal 'God of heaven', the Seleucids' indifference to local Palestinian traditions of expression, and their general lack of discrimination in the world of divine metaphor, encouraged radical intolerance and the perception of the 'dangers' of syncretism as foreign. This became a rallying cry of traditionalists and nationalists against the empire. Hellenism could be demonized as an all-pervasive power that threatened Palestine's very existence. In this struggle, language, tradition and God were seen to be at risk. The ideology of such exclusive monotheism led historically to political independence behind the armies of the Maccabean insurrection. Their success marked many in Palestine with a sharply distinctive national consciousness for the first time.

Exclusive monotheism, logically a secondary and reactionary development in the intellectual history of ideas, lies close to the time of the formation of our traditions. The need to reject the dominance of the Seleucids defined itself as a need to affirm monotheism in *exclusive and anti-Hellenistic* terms. This created a large spectrum of political, religious and philosophical divisions within Palestine's population that were not to be played out for some three centuries.

c) *The world-view of inclusive monotheism.* This belongs to the traditions within the Bible, and in other large composites of collected traditions, that express a specifically transcendent and universal monotheism. In contrast to exclusive forms, this monotheism included many polytheistic traditions and metaphors for understanding the divine. Such traditions self-consciously understand themselves as limited human expressions of what ultimately reflects a transcendent divine. The traditions, once collected, contributed to the development of a pluralistic world-view.

Wisdom literature in the Bible relates to the collections of *torah* and prophets much as commentary does to tradition. The specific collections that we have, such as can be found in the books of Proverbs, Ecclesiastes, the Psalms and Job, have a self-understanding as works of teachers about tradition. They bring us directly into the intellectual visions of the *torah* and the prophets from a perspective that looks back on a metaphor of 'exile'. They centre us in a contrast between an old and a new Israel. It is through the inclusive monotheism of such unique texts as the poetic work of Isaiah 40–55, and especially through the central understanding of the divine as transcendent, that Israel's and Jerusalem's disastrous past was interpreted positively as an expression of imminent divine mercy in the world. Isaiah 40's words of comfort to Jerusalem in exile have formed the focus within which the uncompromising description of Israel as unfaithful and rejected so often reiterated in the diatribes of Isaiah 1–36 is interpreted. The compassion of chapters 40–55 is found echoed in the only seemingly-merciless irony of the Immanuel prophecies of Isaiah 7–10. They rather offer a dramatic interpretation of God's presence to contrast the narrative's story of disaster with the grace given to the 'repentent remnant' with which the audience identifies, while the Old Israel epitomizes the role of the ungodly. This coherent vision of divine righteousness as expressed in forgiveness and redemption creates the tradition as a meaningful whole. The prophecy of doom and punishment pronounced to King Ahaz holds implicit the song of comfort and Jerusalem's ultimate forgiveness.

In books like Job, Ecclesiastes and Isaiah, we find an intellectual boldness and excitement that is much like what occurred in the writings of Plato or Sophocles in Athens. The stock phrases of tradition and piety are confronted directly, and the small ambitions of men are openly ridiculed. Even the ambitions of the pious and the wise are open to ruthless caricature. Such a voice, critical of tradition and its gods, is centred in a growing contrast between the divinely transcendent and the traditional gods of ancient song and story.

The gods of tradition are drawn both from their stories and from their traditional roles in temples. Quite explicitly, they are portrayed as the gods that men have known. We glimpse this growing critical contrast already piecemeal in cuneiform literature of the sixth century BCE. This theology is implicit in the Neo–Babylonian dedication steles in the temple of Sin in Harran, and in the Persian propaganda of texts such as the Cyrus cylinder. In both of these texts, the king assigns himself the role of saviour of the gods. This is an 'official' theology that implicitly deconstructs the reality of the gods of tradition. Such a critical distance from gods is also implicit in some of the early Aramaic texts which refer to *Ba'al Shamem* and to the 'God of heaven'. Such texts are marked by a philosophical and theological perception that is wholly different from a commonplace understanding of gods in their personal roles as story heroes and religious patrons.

From at least the twilight of the Assyrian empire in the seventh century BCE, the ancient world's intellectual perception of reality was forced into a defining crisis. Such change found expression in a growing awareness of the patent irrelevance of tradition past. The crisis was resolved in different ways by different peoples, across the immense geographical distances of the ancient world. In the Aegean, the intelligentsia rejected the gods and the cosmology of a Homer and Hesiod as no longer tenable. This rejection of the stories of the gods is clearly stated by the early distinctions that separated collections of legends from history as research. In the fourth century, Plato portrayed the ideal philosopher as a servant of reflection. Wisdom, for him, began in self-knowledge. The Greek playwrights, with their hermeneutics of mockery, gave the popular fantasies about the gods a ruthless exposure.

This 'twilight of the gods' in Greek intellectual life is played out in different ways in the growth of classical literary traditions across Asia. All find their point of departure in such critical thought about the gods of tradition. These traditions come to us in the collected scriptures of Zoroastrianism, of Buddhism and of the Bible. Each also took its written form, some time between the third and the first centuries BCE. Critical thought was not a discovery confined to the West. Southwest Asia also had to confront gods with clay feet, and did so with varying degrees of agnosticism. In the biblical tradition, this intellectual crisis was resolved by making a clear and distinct affirmation of the reality of life and spirit. This was defined as the true abode of the divine. Through a transitory hold on life, a partial and fragmented understanding of knowledge, and a limited experience of light, our earthly existence shared in such divinity, if only in perceiving our own distance from the divine. This true world of spirit, transcendent and unknown, was contrasted with the known realities of the human world, including the gods of our making. Human experience was perceived, through the metaphor of a mirrored reality, as intrinsically partial and ultimately mistaken, reflective of the real world of spirit through misdirection. In the Semitic world, the crisis that had begun in an intellectual tradition that was no longer believable was resolved by contrasting the perceived and the contingent, as limited human perceptions of reality with an unperceived understanding of all that was beyond such limited possibilities of thought. Spirit was ineffable. Divine reality was not the gods that men created; it was beyond conception. Traditional understanding and religion were not so much false, as human.

For many, removing the mythology from traditional beliefs changed them. Traditional concepts of the divine were thrown into a polarized contrast with the limitations of human activity, including its prolific manufacturing of gods. This human tradition of god-making, was understood as fragile. It involved incomplete and often erroneous efforts to express realities that were intrinsically foreign to humans. The stories of tradition were not rejected, they were pitied. Metaphors of God as patron, one who determined the destinies of nations, even images of the heavenly court, could be understood as human stories about the divine realm which was at an infinite remove from humanity, with all its limited and personal religious preoccupations. It is just such an image of the divine that we find in the Book of Job, with its dramatization of traditional piety and its caricature of the gods of its story. It is not the bombastic creator-God, speaking from the whirlwind in chapters 40 and 41, who personates this philosopher's God. Much more devastating is the brief submissive response in chapter 42, in which Job admits his ignorance of the divine. This is the heart of the drama. After having won the audience to support his cause, the plaintiff abandons it. Job's understanding is much like the ironic declaration of Solomon, who, as philosopher king of Ecclesiastes, describes his lifelong search for the spirit as mere 'chasing the wind'.

The theological revolution of inclusive monotheism doesn't move from a world of polytheism and stories about the gods' adventures to a vision of Mosaic monotheism in the faith of an all-powerful creator. That is a misunderstanding of biblical fundamentalism. It confuses the literary product of Exodus' story-plot with the understanding implicit in its creation. We are confronted rather with a crisis of awareness, a shift from the too simplistic understanding of stories to a doubt in such a god's existence. Recognizing that the world of gods was a world created by us was a recognition of human understanding as limited. *Such awareness understands that we do not know God.* This theology is at the heart of the *torah*. This is the Psalms' 'fear of God' that is righteousness. This is the Bible's self-knowledge that is the beginning of wisdom. The God of the Old Testament is the unknown God, the silent voice of Elijah, the God that Job knew only by hearsay. This is the biblical tradition's God. This is why it is on the tradition itself, rather than on any of its particular metaphors about the divine, that the Bible's attention is focused.

Such ideas are very much alive in the middle of the Hellenistic period. They had yet centuries to run their course. In Palestine they had already had a long history. The military and administrative conception of the emperor as king of kings did not only correspond with Persian religious ideology of the transcendent God of spirit, Ahura Mazda. It also corresponded with the conquered peoples' perceptions of the 'God of heaven' as understood in the distinct regions of the empire, as Marduk of Babylon, *Sin* of Harran, *Ba'al Shamem* of greater Syria and its biblical form, *Elohe Shamayim*.

Differences in concepts, which were no longer so much gods as referents to the divine and to the reality of spirit, are issues of translation. The divine evoked by such titles is hardly specific, multiple or personal. The divine world is no longer a world of gods, however much many people continued to identify their gods with the divine. Yahweh became the name and reflection of the divine. He was God for Israel: Immanuel. Gods belonged now only to a human world. They were divided by languages and by nations. It was people that needed this defining quality of names.

Somewhat in contrast to the Greek historians, philosophers and playwrights, the intellectuals of Asia chose to affirm the traditions of the past. They accepted them as expressions of true reality, perceived in limited human terms. This defining concept of inclusive monotheism finds its home in ongoing efforts to interpret polytheistic conceptions in universal and transcendent terms.

In biblical tradition, such inclusive monotheism is clear in what most scholars recognize as Hellenistic texts. For example, in Ezra 1: 1–3's citation of the Cyrus decree, *Elohe Shamayim*, identified as Yahweh, the known God of Israel, charges Cyrus to re-establish his people by building a temple in Jerusalem of Judah. In this text, the author expresses an understanding of the people in the province of *Jehud* as the legitimate successors of neglected or forgotten Yahweh traditions from ancient Israel (that is, from Samaria). It also identifies these traditions of Yahweh as traditions about God: *Elohe Shamayim*. This is exactly the identification that is carried out in the Pentateuch in the story of the burning bush. The God of the Bible is 'God', and Yahweh is his name. He is identified as the

God of their fathers. Through such traditions, the name of the traditional deity of Palestine, Yahweh, is identified as old Israel's name for the truly divine. The understanding of this old traditional deity is thereby transformed from that of a hardly-longer understood regional god of Palestine to the role of mediator of the Most High. Yahweh is presented as the name of the Most High. He is the ineffable God as Israel – with its human limitations – misunderstood him. As Immanuel, Yahweh becomes the cryptic cipher for the presence of the Most High in this world, who is recognized only by those who hear and understand. This is no longer a god of any cult, story, or oracle. The old storm deity of Palestine no longer exists. He has been transformed and reinterpreted in a new understanding. Yahweh, as a god, belongs to the traditions of old Israel, not to the faith of the new. As the name of God, however, Yahweh functions as mediator between the human tradition and the divine. He represents how people used to think about God who is ever transcendent and unknowable. The tradition is preserved, but radically transformed.

This enabled the collectors of the tradition to express their understanding of a universal world order under the transcendent deity Elohim. At the same time, they were able to preserve the *personal* aspect of the divine that had been basic to the traditional folklore of Palestine. This solution might be described as a form of Platonism, ridding us of the world of the gods as such in favour of a concept of universal transcendence. It also shares in a much more synchronistic Hellenism, understanding the existence of the world's many competing gods as variable mistaken forms of the tradition's merely human understanding. The Bible's inclusive monotheism expanded understanding of the divine to include both the personal and the universal. This enabled the collectors of the Bible to pursue their primary goal of preserving a shattered and fragmented past through a reinterpretation that reflected their own world-view.

2 Yahweh as God in Genesis

Theologians in the past have often arrogantly referred to stories as 'mere stories'. To speak of the Bible's stories was seen to implicate the Bible in lies. Nevertheless, I want to emphasize that we have failed to realize the implications that in Genesis we have only stories. They are complicated stories, rich stories, profound and moving stories, but, none the less, stories alone. I do not begin to imply by this that some of the stories in Genesis are not religious or pious stories. They are – some of them. What I do mean to say is that even these pious and religious stories have their first purpose in fiction.

For example, the story in Genesis 22, the sacrifice of Isaac, is clearly hagiographic, a saint's story of the first rank. The story is didactic in intent throughout. Although the story may be read as a unit by itself, it fits its present context, within the larger Abraham chain of stories, exceedingly well. When Genesis 22 begins, the Abraham chain narrative is already essentially completed. The plot's central promise to Abraham has been fulfilled in the birth of Isaac. Genesis 21's final tying up of so many of the intertwining threads of plot heightens the shock of Yahweh's test of Abraham in its unexpectedness. After all this, in spite of Abraham and Sarah's doubts and laughter, in spite of the pretensions of Ishmael's mother, and in spite of the two-fold threat to Sarah's sexual integrity and to Abraham's life, God has finally fulfilled his promise to the patriarch in Abraham's hundredth year. It is just then that the real test comes. It is entirely on Abraham's trust in Yahweh, and on that trust alone – on Abraham's belief that 'God will provide' – that the entire narrative hangs. The test is to be one of perfect obedience. Isaac is not merely Abraham's only and beloved son. He is the fulfilment of God's pledge to Abraham. The demand made of Abraham is that he must, with Isaac, also sacrifice the promise that Yahweh has made to him. That is the very basis of God's special relationship to him.

It is extremely important for understanding the intention of the story to notice that *we* do not go on this journey of faith with Abraham. Abraham is alone. We watch the performance, but we are not participators in it. From the very start of the story, the audience is informed that Yahweh is only testing Abraham. This is a literary device. It is used with even greater effect in the Book of Job. There the audience is privy to the meeting of Yahweh's divine council and overhears Yahweh making his bet with Satan. The religious sensibilities of the audience are being protected throughout, by their being clearly informed that the test is only that: a test. This story is of the same type as the medieval legends of the saints or the early Church's stories about the martyrs. It is comparable to an *imitatio Christi*. It is a parable, ending with the implied: 'Go, do likewise.'

The story of Abraham in Genesis 22, and the story about Joseph being guided by divine providence as well, are not hagiographic. They do not encourage the audience directly to have similar faith and trust, as the stories' heroes had. It is true that we are led to admire and to focus on Abraham's great faith, but it is an admiration as for a hero in a saga. Abraham's faith is admirable in exactly the same way that Lot's hospitality to the two strangers at Sodom in Genesis 19 is. It isn't, of course, that Lot valued his daughters so little. Rather it is because he valued them so much, that they are offered to the townspeople for rape. The kind of admiration we, the audience, have in such stories is the awe and wonder of entertainment: an awe and a wonder that cannot survive if taken too seriously. It is in just such an unserious, unmoral but, nevertheless, reflective and theological way, that we admire – with horror but none the less with real admiration – Laban switching brides on Jacob, or Jacob's own duplicitous bankrupting of Laban. So too do we admire Rachel's quick wit and luck in feigning menstrual cramps, thereby limiting Laban's search, and succeeding in her theft. This list can easily be extended. If these stories do something so serious as teach, they teach the way that most stories teach: by educating the emotions in a safe place and in a safe way. It is rash and foolish to jump to the conclusion that the protagonists of the stories of Genesis are intended to be emulated, or even that they are in any special way praiseworthy. They do, however, have their high spots. Certainly Joseph is always to be admired, except when he 'narks on' his brothers, or when he enslaves the people of Egypt.

It is not a good idea to believe in a god when he is a character in a story! Don't think for a moment that the narrator of Genesis or his audience ever believed in or prayed to that kind of a god. This is the world that the teller has created for his representation of old Israel, where sometimes iron does float on water, and where sometimes God is awful. The understanding of God that the narrator implies can be likened to Joseph's consolation he gives, weeping when his brothers ask him for forgiveness. What humans see as evil, God means for the good: in the case of the Joseph story – as with the greater story of Israel's remnant – 'to change it to good, that many may live' (Gen. 50: 20).

I'd like to demonstrate this point about the characters of Genesis, whether gods or patriarchs, with some further examples. The issue becomes clearest to me when I think of the very positive character of Abraham in Genesis 14. In this story, Abraham has been called upon as a military saviour. He responds by routing the kings of the north in running battle. In winning this fight, he saves the kings of the Jordan plain, and rescues his nephew Lot in passing. Such is Abraham's success. We have all read about such heroes. Abraham's character is brought out in very few words in his conversation with the king of Sodom over the division of the booty, to which Abraham had full right, of course, as victor in the battle. After Abraham has given a tithe to Melchizedek, the priest-king of Salem, the king of Sodom addresses him: 'Give me back the people, but keep all the goods for yourself.' Abraham answers the king that 'he would not take a thread or a sandal thong, or anything that is yours, lest you should say: "I have made Abraham rich." I will take nothing but what the young men have eaten, and the share of the men who went with me; let Aner, Eshcol and Mamre take their share.'

A thematic parallel can be observed here between Abraham's open-handed generosity and the generosity he had shown his nephew Lot, when he allowed him to choose the best land in chapter 13. In fact, it is this thematic parallelism that is one of the reasons for Genesis 14 being placed after the Lot story in the developing chain narrative that forms the heart of the Bible's tradition about Abraham. However, the personality of Abraham as the hero of Genesis 14 is unique. This is not the fatherly generosity of the Abraham of Genesis 13, careful to avoid even the occasion for conflict, any more than Abraham is here the bunco artist of Genesis 12, who would sell his wife to get rich at the expense of the Egyptians. Nor is Abraham in Genesis 14 the holy prophet of Genesis 20, whose cowardice has to be excused by the narrator on the plea that Sara was, after all, his half-sister. Nor is Abraham in Genesis 14 the stoic, obedient servant of Genesis 22 – that horrifying saint – ready to kill his own son if his God should demand it. And Abraham of Genesis 14 is certainly not the doddering old man, waiting by the oaks of Mamre, whose heart was full of welcome for a stranger. It is very difficult to see him as identical to the husband of Genesis 21, so helplessly torn by the conflicts of his wives as to accept the abandonment of his first-born son – even if it was on his God's instructions. No, here in Genesis 14, we have a soldier hero, of the like of D'Artagnan or Robin Hood – ever careful of and generous for his friends and his men, but careless for himself. He could be likened to a Samson, or a David; even a Joshua on his better days. This is the stuff of which heroes are made. The potential for emulation is certainly there, but can we seriously think of these stories, or of stories such as that of Jacob using extortion against his starving brother, or deceiving his blind, dying father, as stories dedicated to simple moral teaching? That would both pervert them and destroy them as stories.

We would also do well to avoid seeing the God of Genesis or Yahweh, who plays a role in so many of these stories, as identical to the God or Yahweh of the theological tradition that uses these stories with purpose. In Genesis, Yahweh's roles are as varied as the stories he appears in, though his function is ever that of old Israel's god. I have a personal and quite horrific reaction, as well as a sense of resentment, toward a god like that in Genesis 22, if we must mix him up with belief in the God of the real world. Can this be? A God, who sees into men's hearts, and then, for a game, would so pitilessly toy with a father's deepest feelings? The story when read, not as an act of God but as a story, is wholly without objection. However, I ask those of you who are parents: If this were truly God, would you even want to forgive him if you were Abraham? And how would you feel, at the end of reading about Job's trials, with your replacement set of children? Such a God of story needs a theological understanding and interpretation to remain viable. Although Genesis often offers hints at the significant difference between the God of its stories and the understanding of the divine implied by their author's voice, a radical transformation of the explicit narration of the Pentateuch must wait for the theophanies of Exodus 3–6. Until then, we are dealing with the legends of old.

3 Yahweh as godfather

Gods are created, but the true God is unknown. This important maxim lies at the centre of the Bible's theology.

The historicism implicit in the biblical theology movement of half a century ago is more modern than it is biblical. What is often referred to as the Bible's history has, in fact, nothing to do with writing history in any modern sense. The biblical basis for the theological language of salvation history is not a history, but a tradition. It is interested neither in the past nor indeed in the future. Both are but reflections for reality, and, as such, other than reality. The most disorienting difficulty with such readings of the Bible, is that they attempt to transpose a perspective of reality underlying biblical traditions into peculiarly modern terms. They permit reflection on our reality, but not reflection on what was real for the writers of the Bible. It was once fashionable for theologians to demythologize the Bible's story world – as if there were available modern equivalencies immediately at hand, with which we might translate the Bible's *mythos* into our own way of thinking. This was closely linked to the Protestant ideal of making the Bible's faith our faith. Strong was the confidence that the God of the Bible – or indeed Jesus – could somehow be translated and become our God, without substantial loss or distortion. This fundamental assumption (and I would say arrogance) of biblical theology had at its core a belief in the inadequacy of the world-view of the ancients. At the same time, it maintained a blind faith that this same primitive world's religious perception could become a saving perception in our world.

History – an intellectual construct about events of the past and their meaning – has been, until very recently, an inescapable and fundamental part of our thinking and of our understanding of reality. It forms the crux of the distortions of neo-orthodox exegesis. Such a perception of reality, however, is far from the intellectual matrix of biblical tradition. Unlike events of history, events of tradition do not share in reality because of the uniqueness or singularity of their meaning. 'Reality' for the Bible lies quite far from both this world and its events. 'History', like all of the events of human affairs, is, for the ancient traditionist, illusory. It is like the whole of this material, accidental and refracted world in which we live. Events in time are seen as through a distorting glass. True reality is unknowable, transcending experience.

Tradition is important heuristically. It brings understanding. Its recitation evokes truth. It does not recount it. Reality is not part of this traditional world, which is rather a world of human creation. Not even the gods of the tradition are real in themselves. They are only manifestations of God. Yahweh is God for Israel. He is Immanuel: God with us, *only significant because of his referent*.

Rather than as history, the Bible's tradition might better be expressed as reiterative and typological aetiology. I use the word aetiology with purpose. It is a story of the past that seeks to echo – through metaphor – the truth of what is known. The biblical stories about the faithless and shattered Israel, about its relationship to and its betrayal of its forgotten God, are hardly history, as we understand the word. The word history does not even exist in Hebrew. In the Bible's many stories and collected songs, written to create a self-understanding among its readers as the saved remnant of Israel, the Bible does not address or try to understand an historical past. The so-called 'deuteronomistic history', for example, from Joshua to the end of Kings, is not driven by any effort to explain either Samaria's or Jerusalem's destruction by its story of a god protecting the nation whenever it is faithful to him and punishing it in turn whenever Israel or Judah abandoned Yahweh's worship for that of his competitor Ba'al, as has been commonly claimed. This is not even the purpose of Kings. Such an interpretation confuses narrative plot and motif with theme and function. It mixes up occasion with purpose and significance. However black and white the evil and good of Judges and Kings might be, the simple-mindedness implied by this caricature should never be confused with authorial intent.

However much Josiah's explicitly tragic opposition to Yahweh and his servant Pharaoh Neco might be associated with the sympathetic portrayal of the people mourning him in II Chronicles 35, neither Josiah's death nor the portrayal of his goodness in Kings are refractions of any saving grace. Nor is the loss of Josiah in Kings a tragic loss in any classical sense of the word. However much the Book of Lamentations over Jerusalem's destruction might be associated with Jeremiah's passionate story,[1] and with the people's exile from Jerusalem, the history does not have mourning for its closure. Yahweh once destroyed Israel. Now he has destroyed Judah and Jerusalem with its temple and its king. He has not destroyed these that he might bring good out of destruction. Nor has he acted even because Israel and Judah were evil, but rather, more simply, he has done this by his choice and by his anger. This is not 'salvation history'.

The 'biblical view' of this narrative does not understand Yahweh's providence in terms of good rewarded and evil punished. That is a caricature attributed to one or other of Job's friends. For Kings, Josiah was good King Josiah. All other kings were unfaithful to Yahweh. But Josiah was good. For him, one might expect divine grace. 'Before him there was no king like him, who had turned to Yahweh with all his heart, soul and strength, following the whole of Moses' Torah; nor did his like ever come again' (II Kings 23: 25). Josiah's goodness, however, nowhere determines the story's outcome. Even more important, this is not a problem in the story. The narrative is not unresolved with Josiah's death. Indeed, the

[1] Compare Jeremiah 44: 1–14 with II Kings 25: 22–24.

Josiah story epitomizes II Kings' perspective of Yahweh's role in human history. It is in the form of a prophetic oracle that the death of Josiah acquires its context: 'I will take Judah away from my sight as I did Israel; and I will also throw off this city that I have chosen: Jerusalem; and also this temple in which I had said my name would live' (II Kings 23: 27)! The stated reason for this? Yahweh's choice and anger. This also is not 'salvation history'.

Unlike its tradition variant in Chronicles, the Book of II Kings does not present Josiah in any way as opposing God by attacking the Egyptian forces. The account is lapidary: 'Pharaoh Neco, king of Egypt, went up to the King of Assyria to the River Euphrates. King Josiah went to meet him; and Pharaoh Neco killed him at Megiddo when he saw him' (II Kings 23: 29). This is neither 'salvation history' nor any ideologically directed meaningful history. It does, however, reflect a perspective that bears looking into.

Neither promise and fulfilment nor reward and punishment are the root metaphors driving these narrative variants. Unlike the Josiah of Chronicles, the great ruler of Kings is not a Greek hero such as Oedipus, caught between the realities of his own greatness and divine purpose, however much his life, and the loss thereof, has been determined by fate. Josiah's death in II Kings is not the death of classic tragedy. It reflects a uniquely biblical perspective: of human goodness destroyed, unmourned. Yahweh of Kings is not the God of Jeremiah's restoration whom we meet in Jeremiah 33: 1–26. Nor is this God Chronicles' transcendent deity, which has so much in common with the more positive, indeed polyannic, theology of Jeremiah. This God is not terribly far from Job's Yahweh – that awful God of the whirlwind, in contrast with whom even the most innocent of men is but a worm. This is the same God whom those great agnostics, the implied authors of Ecclesiastes and Jonah, could not and would not understand. This is the God of the Saul stories and the God of the flood stories of Genesis: one who decreed both salvation and destruction for Israel. This was done not through justice nor for justice's sake. In this author's world, the fate of a man is insignificant in the face of divine will.

The closure of Kings, with its reassertion of the divinely arbitrary, disrupts any sense of the morally ordered world of justice of the sort that we find in Jeremiah and Chronicles. Yahweh's moral disorder receives faint mockery in the narrative's comparison with the human Evil-merodach's contrasting mercy to the captive Jehoiachin.

In the traditions collected in the Book of Judges, we find a modest intensification of the murmuring theme of the wilderness stories. The leitmotif of Judges finds Israel less innocent than the wilderness chain does: 'The people of Israel did what was evil in Yahweh's eyes' (Judges 2: 11; 3: 7; 4: 1; 6: 1; 13: 1). The ideological shift, however, is slight. The reiterated leitmotif remains that of backsliding Israel under Yahweh's patronage. Again, the question of loyalty is paramount. It is not Israel's behaviour but Yahweh's response that is the one uncertainty that determines destiny, whether there be judgement or mercy. The pendulum of Judges 1–16 does not swing between the innocence and guilt of Israel, with Yahweh in a role of judge. Far from it. That is the theodicy problem as the character Job would wish to pose it. Both Judges and Job's implied authors, however, search to express a truth that does not depend on human perceptions, but on the divine, and therefore ineffable, perception of God. They need to close on the motif of unknowing.

It is a demanding task put forward in Judges, but I think largely successful. The primary cycle of tales is linked with the first Book of Samuel by the inclusion of two dark stories in Judges 17–21. These are the story of Micah and the theft of his Levite by the Danites, and the story of a Levite and the rape of his concubine by the Benjaminites. These paired stories are set thematically within the perspective of I–II Samuel. With the help of a reiterated leitmotif, these dark tales are contrasted with an implied ideal of the monarchy: 'In those days there was no king in Israel; every man did what was right in his own eyes' (Judges 17: 6; 18: 1; 19: 1). This allows the evil times of the Judges to lend introductory promise to the theme of kingship as the end of the anarchy of the Judges (Judges 21: 25). Contrast is drawn between these 'days of the judges', the everyman–roles at the centre of these three intentionally black narratives now closing the Book of Judges, and what is 'right' *in expectation* of the kingship narratives of the books of Samuel and Kings. The root metaphor of this tradition is specifically 'righteousness'. That, however, is neither justice, moral uprightness, *nor anything that man may know*. What is in accordance with 'righteousness' is what is right in God's eyes. The contrast is not between injustice and justice, but between a human and a divine perspective. This is the central theme of biblical tragedy, not morality.

The Book of Judges' closure finds its proper echo in the opening story of I Samuel. Following the traditional story pattern of the birth of a saviour, I Samuel 2: 12 introduces Eli's sons as men 'who do not know Yahweh'. The contrast of the boy Samuel with Eli's sons establishes the context for Samuel's role as saviour: one who 'grew up in Yahweh's presence' (I Sam. 2: 21). Eli admonishes his sons. The issue is not one of human justice: how his sons dealt with the people they served. It centres on the contempt Eli's sons have shown Yahweh (2: 17–25). The ideology of the tale is captured in verse 25, which refers to central themes of the Book of Job. The story is marked by its running discussion with wisdom literature. A proverb is set for the implied reader: the moral of the story and the principle, illustrated by Levi's sons but narratively establishing Saul's fate. If someone commits crimes against another man, there is hope that God will intervene, but if the crime be against God, nothing can help.

Eli's speech awaits its echo and its ironic reversal in the future David's words to Saul that we find in I Sam. 26: 18–20. If it is God that sends Saul against David, the problem can be dealt with by a sacrifice. If, however, men have turned Saul against David, they force David away from allegiance to Yahweh. These are issues of loyalty not justice. The ideology of both stories is constant: Yahweh's patronage is the absolute by which all human endeavours are judged. Eli's fault, however, is a human one – his sons. It cannot be dealt with by sacrifice.

The chain of stories opens gently in chapter 3. Eli is as Yahweh to Samuel. Samuel believing Eli calls to him in the night, replies as servant to master: 'Here I am.' Eli – in his humility, the story's epigone of the 'righteous' – recognizes that it is Yahweh who is calling to Samuel. In a wholly unembellished description of Yahweh, and in echoing contrast to Judges 17–21, Eli offers us a preview of David's prayer of II Samuel 15: 26, which is so central to this story. He gives voice to the central truth of the greater story's theology: 'He is Yahweh; may he do what is right in his own eyes (3: 18)!' Judges 17–21's 'days' were days of anarchy, when men lived as if they were Yahweh. Such a life is the opposite of the Bible's 'righteousness'. The time of the Judges was hardly ideal. That was a dark time, a time of evil, when Israel had no king, no messiah to carry out what Yahweh saw as good.

An autonomous patron, one who does what is right in his own eyes, is the meaning of kingship in the West Semitic world. The politics of this world is one of patronage, not monarchy. To be a king is 'to be one's own man'. An equal constant of the West Semitic world-view, rooted in their understanding of the transcendent, is of the king as servant of God, who alone is patron. To be kingless – as in the 'time of the Judges' – is anarchic and nihilistic. Righteousness is the affirmation of Yahweh's patronage. This the story sets as the true mark and significance of Israel's kingship. The tradition is not at all democratic or anti-monarchic. Both are misreadings of the tradition.

This view of Yahweh is common to the whole of biblical narrative. One need not search the obscure corners of the tradition to find the substance of this divine metaphor. The best and the most influential stories of the tradition have transmitted and created this understanding of the divine in our lives. In the episode of the Joseph story in Genesis 50 that we have already briefly discussed, the brothers of Joseph seek his forgiveness. They are afraid of his anger now that the restraining influence of their father can no longer protect them. Joseph's answer in this most pious of biblical stories should change the way we think of piety! The brothers' plea that Joseph forgive their sin is dismissed outright. It is irrelevant. What happened, Joseph tells his brothers, happened only because of God's will, because he chose to save many people. What the brothers did – even their crimes against Joseph himself – is judged unimportant in God's eyes.

Joseph is the hero of this story, not because he was innocent and virtuous – one can only describe him as such by ignoring several of this story's episodes – but because he consistently plays the role of Immanuel, through whom God carries out his will and is present in this world.

Again, in the story of the plagues of the Exodus tradition, one does not find a contest between a good Moses and an evil pharaoh, nor between an innocent Israel and demonized Egyptians. Like the prophets Isaiah and Jonah after him, Moses is feckless, and the Israelites ever backsliding and ungrateful. The Egyptians are faceless recipients of destruction, and the pharaoh, whose heart is hardened against his own judgement by Yahweh for the story's sake, hardly worse than a fool. He is a helpless tool of the ironic fate that Yahweh wishes to visit on him. The power of such a metaphor resides in Yahweh's freeing the oppressed and the enslaved. However, we should not pass silently over the hardly hidden motif that *Yahweh created these same oppressed and enslaved* for the sake of his contest with the pharaoh. Yahweh chose the oppressed and enslaved as his own, and therefore oppression and enslavement is their fate. The story hardly involves issues of social justice, and hardly demands independence and freedom for its audience. The proper words are rather loyalty and submission.

One of the great paradigmatic heroes of this understanding of the divine in biblical narrative is, of course, Abraham. Abraham is both Yahweh's companion and the heroic exemplar of faith and righteousness. Here, I am not referring to any original Abrahamic tale – far better reflected in the Quran and appropriate to Ishmael – but rather the one we have in its specifically Jewish variant. The epitomizing tale is the great test we saw in Genesis 22. The language of this narrative is sparse, and one does well to attend to it. The audience is not at risk in the narrative. This was done 'to test Abraham'. That is, as in the story of Job, we are dealing with a wisdom tale. While the story reaches its plot resolution with Yahweh's replacement sacrifice – the ram caught in the bushes – that is hardly the story's dramatic centre. As a story, the plot never seriously entertains Isaac/Israel's death, however much it plays with such a motif for heuristic purposes. Not the audience but the hero Abraham must deal with the dread of the beloved's death. Genesis 22 is a difficult, intellectual narrative. It barely touches upon the emotional and personal nuances of such a test. For that theme, one must read Kierkegaard[1] or Job. Abraham, in his story, epitomizes *sedaqah*. This is normally translated as 'righteousness', but has a semantic range that emphasizes 'understanding, reflection and philosophy'. This is the test. The audience's attention and sympathy are drawn to Abraham, who plays here the same role as the God of II Kings for Genesis' audience. This is his son, his only son, whom he will sacrifice for righteousness' sake.

---

[1] The reference is to Søren Kierkegaard's commentary on this story in *Purity of Heart*.

Walking up the mountain with his father, Abraham, Isaac asks his child's question: 'where is the lamb?' – inescapably marked by the tradition of children's questions from the aetiology of the Passover *seder in* Exodus 12: 26: 'why do we do this?' – not to draw the attention of the story to himself, nor to shatter the story with pathos for his innocence, but rather to mark with the simplicity of this exchange with his father the coherence and completeness of Abraham's understanding and philosophy: 'God will provide.' Such is a true servant of God. Such is a divine understanding. The form of the test is nothing; the loyalty expressed everything.

In this world of biblical narrative, God is a God of mercy and of wrath, not a God of justice. Yahweh determines destinies; he causes hearts to harden and he causes repentance: as in Jonah's Nineveh and in Moses' Egypt. People are not 'free' nor is this world 'democratic'. It is a world of *mishpahot* and *beytim*: that is a world of 'families' and 'houses', a world of belonging and loyalty. To be a Jew is to be, as one of the *benei Yisrael*, bound by an oath of allegiance to Yahweh as to one's patron. Such 'righteousness' is not justice, but understanding: philosophy. Fate as decreed by the gods is not opposed to responsibility. It is rather a fundamental motif common also to the tragic heroes of Greek tradition. Accepting one's destiny renders balance. This is equally expressed in the order rendered by the Egyptian goddess, *Ma'at*, and in the 'peace' and 'grace' implicit in the Bible's 'righteousness'. In each of these traditions, such experience is attributed to divine grace.

To understand this perspective, we need to resist the demythologizing with which medieval scholasticism has domesticated these concepts in its effort to adopt them as its own. This is not a divine 'justice'. An ethics of justice implies not only responsibility, but an assertion of an ability to determine one's own future. It implies a rule by law, not the personal subservience and obedience that is ever implicit in biblical tradition. The word *ebed*, 'servant', is the central term that is expressive of piety in the whole of the ancient Semitic world, where law, as we know it, never existed.

The absence of a legal tradition is hardly accidental. The patronage structure of Levantine society precluded the development of a bureaucracy. The bureaucracy that is implicit in legal justice systems undermines the kind of despotism that is characteristic of the ancient Semitic world. The early cuneiform codes, so well represented by the famous Hammurapi stele, are aspects of royal propaganda, not of rule by law. They illustrate the king's claim to be patron throughout the land. It is his will that establishes right order. That is what is meant by despotism, not rule by law. This well-known stele presents the king, Hammurapi, in his role as the servant of the god Shamash, to whose patronage and justice Babylon is ultimately indebted.

The traditions collected in the Bible's 'Book of the Covenant' (Exodus

21: 2–11) and in the so-called 'Holiness Code' of Leviticus 17–26, the miscellaneous collections of tradition that are found in Deuteronomy 12–26, as well as the many collections of 'commandments' as in Exodus 20: 2–17, Deuteronomy 5: 6–21 and elsewhere, certainly belong to a form of wisdom tradition, which pragmatically epitomizes divine ascendancy. These were never laws governing the decisions of any courts or judges. They do not express the will of any legislature or assembly of the governed. They are so far from law that they do not even deal with the interests of kings or of states. They belong wholly and entirely to a storied language of metaphor. They belong to the impractical realm of philosophy's ivory towers.

Nor does the *torah* ever pretend to be law. Such legalism belongs to the language of critics, even to early Judaism's self-criticism expressed by a Paul. The metaphorical function implicit in the biblical and ancient Near Eastern traditions of divine patronage marks the entire concept of justice with religious piety. Not equity but submission is its governing principle. The ideological basis for such language rests not on an idealistic and rationalistic balance of justice and mercy, but rather on the emotions of trust and faithfulness that govern commitments. It rests on behaviour-governing concepts of honour and on the need for personal acceptance. These are all aspects of patronage, arbitrary and wilful. They proceed from decisions both of people and of gods.

A very informative story refraction of such aspects of totality and permanence in commitment in this world, structured by patronage, is found in Genesis 27: 1–45, the tale of Isaac's deathbed blessing to his sons. Once Isaac has given his blessing to Jacob – however deceived he had been and however dishonest Jacob was in obtaining this 'declaration of destiny' – once given, it cannot be gainsaid. This is not a world of contracts governed by fairness, justice and mutuality. In the real world, one would speak of such personal and emotional values that are expressed in Isaac's speeches in the context of *omertà*, a value by which one is inescapably bound to one's word. In story, however, such motifs as fate and destiny come immediately to hand. The power of a story's romance is never to be underestimated. In a society bound by such commitments, any world of law, governed by principles of fairness and justice, is pale and impersonal in contrast. It is hardly evocative of truth or expressive of the personally divine.

The role of the king in bringing about justice for his subjects is a motif that is as old as the image of the king as shepherd of his people. It is also as comparably personal. From Hammurapi to Solomon, the image of the just king is that of the enlightened king, inspired with divine wisdom. As Hammurapi's laws were not his own, but came to Hammurapi as the gift of Shamash, so too, Solomon's celebrated role as just king takes the form of the inspired judge able to discern divine truth, as in the story of I Kings 3:

16–28. The brilliant, if brutal, humour of Solomon's decision to cut the disputed child in two epitomizes such royal justice as divine. We ignore its brutality and admire its brilliance: 'All Israel heard of the judgement which the king had given, and they wondered at him, perceiving that his was a divine wisdom: creating justice.' And this is the crux of the matter, justice. In the Bible, it remains in the realm of metaphor. It is an act of *hesed* (divine 'grace'). It comes from divine patronage. Justice is created.

As the aetiology of wisdom is Solomon's vehicle, and that of the Psalms is David's, law properly belongs to Moses. Exodus 18: 13–27 is a fine origin story for law in the tradition of biblical Israel. It should not go unnoticed that in this tale, Moses is hardly wise. If anything, Moses' role is the opposite of Solomon's. Moses plays the 'dumbling'. The task he takes on, mediating between God and all the people, is an impossible one. The plot's problem is the difficulty of delegating judgements that are divine. As a Moses story, it is bold, touching as it does the theme of Moses as the sole mediator of *torah* from within a post-Mosaic perspective. From the secure position of the implied reader, Jethro's solution has only the appearance of solution. It is an aetiology for human judges or court-appointed ministers. They shall handle everything that is unimportant. Moses and God will then be free to deal with what is crucial and intrinsic to the administration of divine justice. It is a wonderful example of double reflection. The story plot's problem is resolved, but that of the story's referent – that which had won the story its audience – stands ever the more unresolved and demanding as the larger tradition enters the quest of the absent *torah*. The crux of the problem is the same root metaphor that Exodus shares with I Kings 3's story of Solomon's request for wisdom. This is the metaphor of biblical Israel under Yahweh's patronage. Justice as a given and known factor of human experience is denied. Justice is the will of God . . . And God knows what that is!

It is a very demanding literary project that the Bible sets for itself. The despotic and patronage-dominant ideology of the Old Testament is unbending in this recurrent and reiterated motif of Yahweh as ultimate patron. I hope that my third example will make this clear. It is, for historicism, a most troubling motif: of the king as unjust. While the leitmotif of I Samuel's so-called bad King Saul has led otherwise critical historians to speculate about an historical king of ancient Israel as a way of explaining the transmission and preservation of the Saul tradition, the literary world to which I Samuel belongs functions quite apart from such an assumed historiography. In fact – as the story presents itself – Saul is not a bad king, and certainly not unjust, as people and kings go. Not even the author of Chronicles – that ancient literature's enemy of the fallen and champion of the successful – can be described as 'anti-Saul', whatever the commentaries may suggest. At the height of the tradition's contrast between the heroic David and the murderous Saul in I Samuel 24 and 26,

David does not kill Saul, because Saul is Yahweh's messiah. Saul, expressing himself with evocative compassion, is moved to recognize David as his 'son David' (I Sam. 24: 16 and I Sam. 26: 21, 25). The story plot does not entirely ignore David's concern about Saul's attempt to kill him. The rhetorical thrust of the story moves David to complain most adamantly of a quite different issue. David's problem is not that Saul sought to murder him, but rather that Saul was driving him away from his allegiance to Yahweh (I Sam. 26: 20). It is this argument that wins Saul over and leads to his repentance. It is this argument that is close to the heart of our implied author.

One of the most strikingly classical aspects of this story of Saul is that there is no interest in 'bad King Saul'. Neither his madness nor his murderous hatred lead to his rejection. Those are human passions we all are well aware of. In fact, throughout, the story line is as sympathetic to such dark passions as any Greek tragedy. As in classical tragedies, Saul's most horrible deeds, rather than determining his fate, come as a result of his fate. Fate overcomes him, with but the slightest connivance on his part. Saul has nearly as little control over the inexorable evil of his destiny as Moses of the Pentateuch had over his wilderness death. His responsibility is there, but the story is not interested in it. The story in Samuel is not about a good King David and a bad King Saul. The story is about Israel and kingship and Yahweh. It is not about the past; it is about who is the true king of Israel. There is but one true answer, and this answer is neither anti-Saul nor pro-David. They are but servants of God – his messiah. The true king of Israel is ever Yahweh in his temple.

The story begins with an echo of the wilderness' murmuring motif: Israel asks the Moses-like Samuel for a king to succeed him. As in the Moses tradition, these demands suggest a rejection, not of Samuel, but of Yahweh (I Sam. 8: 7–9). The motif of kingship is marked with the shadow of rebellion. The people implicitly deny Yahweh as their true king. Now they ask for a king. A storm of thunder and rain interrupts to show us how wicked this demand was. We must remember that Yahweh had already accepted this request. This marks Yahweh as a character in the story, not as its implied author. If Israel and their king fear and serve and listen to Yahweh, all will be well. However, if they do not listen, but turn against this word of Yahweh, Yahweh's hand will be against both them *and their fathers*. Here, Israel's future destiny *determines the fate of the tradition's past!* Kingship's destiny has already determined the fate of Saul in our story. Narrative time here is neither linear nor progressive, but reiterative and typological.

One is hardly surprised that in Saul's inaugural saving deed as king for Israel in I Samuel 13 he sets out to destroy the Philistines. The story's central plot resides in the contrast between Saul's innocent naiveté and chapter 12's demand that Israel and its king listen to Yahweh's command.

Saul is rejected before he has properly begun. Saul's great lesson is simply put: his kingdom shall not continue. Yahweh seeks rather a man who will do what seems right to Yahweh (I Sam. 13: 14).

The motif is reiterated in chapter 15's victory over the Amalekites, to which the closure of Saul's story refers (28: 15–19). However, in the story itself in I Samuel 15, Saul defeats the Amalekites and completely destroys 'everything that was worthless and despised' (15: 9). Saul is quite explicitly the good king, the good general. He spares Agag and the best of the sheep and cattle, the calves and lambs. Yahweh, however, is hardly pleased at such appropriate and reasonable behaviour. In this anger of Yahweh, the narrative sharply and harshly distinguishes between the dual royal roles of 'king of Israel' and 'servant of Yahweh'. In the closing scene of this episode, when poor, hapless, innocent Saul declares to Samuel: 'May you be blessed by Yahweh; I have accomplished this command of Yahweh' (15: 13), he was hardly aware that he was undone.

Samuel and the story is not kind to Saul's victory. Saul is stopped in mid-sentence as Samuel demands to know: 'Do you want to know what Yahweh told me?' (15: 16) This tragic story is not about any personal hubris of Saul. It is about the hubris of the way of humanity that Saul represents. Even yet, the humility and goodness of Saul's personal character does not allow him to recognize his fate. Even so, when Samuel tells Saul that he has disobeyed and has done what Yahweh understands as evil (v. 19), Saul does not understand it this way; for he has 'utterly destroyed the Amalekites', to the benefit of the people. Saul, in good conscience, sacrifices to Yahweh. Saul is again condemned, and the story turns to its horrific, three-fold humiliating closure. Saul begs forgiveness that he might worship Yahweh. The first two of these pleas are refused (vv. 25–29). The kingdom is to be torn from Saul: 'Yahweh is not a man that he should repent' (v. 30). Saul, however, is a man and does repent, admitting his sin. He abandons his request for forgiveness: only that he might worship Yahweh. So Samuel turns back that Saul may worship. The story closes inexorably: 'And Samuel hacked Agag into pieces before Yahweh in Gilgal.' Unquestionably, Saul is rejected not because of any wrong that he has done, nor even because of any personal failure. He is rejected because he has done what he understood to be right. Such understanding is evil in Yahweh's eyes! It is the very theme of these stories that what is good and what is evil stands apart from human perceptions of justice and the right. Loyalty and allegiance are fundamental to this concept of a personal God. Sin is epitomized by apostasy and betrayal. True belief is submission and unquestioning obedience to the divine will.

If biblical studies is capable of critically clarifying its theology, we must be willing to maintain its integrity with both the past and the text. This is not after all our theology but the Bible's. It is the theology of our tradition. It is foundational to our religious self-identity, and it has created our language and the character of our metaphors. While acknowledging the great value of the intimate qualities of this language that involves the divine as personal, it is no longer obviously true for us any more. It is our past. It plays, however, a substantially dysfunctional role in our theological language today. The twentieth century's disquieting experiences with just such personal and absolute religious values intrinsic to despotism, should make us all hesitate before affirming such a perception for our God. Such traditions as these have a dark and even monstrous potential, of which this century continues to give us too many examples.

It is more than passingly interesting that, in discussions about the theme of justice and the Old Testament, the Book of Job is a favourite text. This may not be an altogether fortunate choice, if one wishes to promote thoughts of justice. Job can be a very explosive text for theology. The text does ask, why do innocents suffer? For that alone, it becomes a very modern text. It also asks whether God himself is just. Nothing is more modern nor more necessary today than asking that question. In our world, however, a world that needs justice if we are to survive the totalitarian potentials of the modern state and its dehumanizing fictions of nationalism, Job answers questions about justice in a very unsatisfying way – at least if one reads the surface of the text.

The greatest line of this book that is filled with great lines is, I think, given to Job's wife. She is the one, perhaps the only, truly feminist heroine of the Bible. She has none of the arrogance or long-winded nonsense of Job's friends. Nor is she inclined toward her husband's intellectual fecklessness. She has neither wish nor intention to talk – indeed, how silly – to God about justice. From the standpoint of justice, Job has only one chance for integrity, and it is the one that *Satan* has bet on and that his wife recommends to him: 'Curse God and die!' (Job 2: 8) Justice has a stake in the right of the individual, while patronage supports the personal. In Job's story, Job, chooses not his own truth, but the truth of human selflessness. His virtue is specifically in not cursing God. For him, the righteousness of God is of greater value than justice. It is Yahweh who wins the bet, and Satan, having bet on Job's integrity as a person, loses. Job shows himself to be the perfect servant in his acceptance of whatever misery God sends him.

It is in the image of this, Job's virtue, that the story's die is cast. This is certainly one of the reasons that the miserable love this great poem. Not only does it help one submit to senseless suffering, but one gains permission in the poem's reading to give voice to all the resentment that suffering injustice brings, but that good breeding does not permit. All the lavish richness with which Job's seemingly endless stream of poetry is marked, however, does not hide a very unsatisfactory closure. *Job never gets the hearing in which Yahweh answers him.* When Yahweh does respond to the victim of his glorification, the volume of his rhetoric silences Job. Job is reduced to an abject state of humiliation: 'I had heard of you only by the hearing of the ear. Now, however, my eyes see you. And so, I despise myself and repent in dust and ashes.'

Job's justification, if we are to call it that – and no modern can – resides in his admission that he did not understand whom he was dealing with. With such a story surface, the modern reader might well wish to go back to the speech of Job's wife: 'Curse God and die'. Certainly, one might be forgiven the wish that Satan had won this wager. If justice were the stake, this particular Yahweh would hardly deserve this Job as his servant. The cost of reader identification with the suffering hero of the book casts a cloud of doubt and suspicion over the entire enterprise. It demands a reflection that is not entirely unintended in the book's formation. The Book of Job indulges in a deconstructive laughter that peeks between the lines everywhere that Job's great whirlwind of a God echoes the piety of Job's friends! Is this message – not of the story's surface but of the story's *sedaqah* – a true understanding of the divine in our world? What, then, is the whirlwind demon's message about the divine? Is it truth? Or caricature?

4 How Yahweh became God

The two theophanies of Exodus 3 and 6 can be described with much justice as the heart of the Pentateuch. They are at the heart of the tradition's effort to express the sense of the transcendent as present in this world, the one single theme that dominates the *torah*. These passages have also been at the centre of the historical-critical controversies over the composition of the Pentateuch for more than a century now. Unfortunately, our problems are not solved by dismissing the earlier critics. The final form of the text so central to more modern literary critics is nearly impenetrable as a story. One can hurry by the difficulties in some levelling translations and paraphrases, but in Hebrew we do not have a story at all here. The call of Moses from Exodus 3: 1–7: 1 has so little coherence and makes so little sense that the question whether narrative sense was ever intended in this text is patent. Why the text had been formed is a question that must take precedence over those related to narration.

The problems begin with the divine characters of our narrative. In Exodus 3, we find ourselves with Moses at the mountain of Elohim, where a messenger of Yahweh appears to him. In the very next verse, this divine character in our story is referred to both as Yahweh and as Elohim. Unfortunately, this is not an unusual situation in the biblical stories of the Pentateuch. It brings to mind immediately the 'messenger of God' in the form of a cloud that we find in Exodus 14, who next morning and five verses later (v. 24) seems to be identical to Yahweh in a pillar of fire and cloud. Less confusing is the passage in Exodus 23: 20–33. Closing the so-called covenant code, a deity speaking in the first person as 'Yahweh your God', promises to send his messenger to watch over Israel as a kind of heavenly enforcer, offering a godfather's protection. This future messenger is clearly identified with the divine speaker. This is helpful to us, since in Exodus 3 a similar identification seems to be taking place, where the 'messenger of Yahweh'/'messenger of God'/or Yahweh of the theophany's opening, explicitly identifies himself with the God of Moses' father, as well as with what possibly are the various gods of Abraham, Isaac and Jacob. Moreover, Exodus 23: 25's 'Yahweh, your God,' could be a very interesting variant of modes of having a deity of one's own, which also underlines our text's distinction between the noun Elohim and the name Yahweh.

The reference to the patriarchs Abraham, Isaac and Jacob in Exodus 3 forces us to concern ourselves with the patriarchal stories of Genesis 16 and 21, where we find that some of the same patterns of narrative pertain. In Genesis 16, the saving 'messenger of Yahweh' is synonymous with Yahweh, but also with a 'God of seeing' in the closing naming aetiology, who in turn is identified by Hagar as 'God'!

Whatever our understanding, and whatever solutions we might suggest to the variance and fluidity of the divine protagonists in these early Pentateuchal stories, the regularity and consistency in the patterns of usage discourage us from seeing these variations as either insignificant or as accidental. Nor is the problem easily resolved by assigning different divine characters to different story sources. What is striking about both the Genesis and the Exodus analogies to the theophany stories of Exodus 3 and 6 is that the story episodes in which the divine names are found are much more coherent in their plots than a jumbled complex of distinct sources would allow.

The inclusion of these other stories in Genesis and Exodus within the interpretive literary matrix of Exodus 3 and 6 can also be argued on thematic grounds. Not only is the pool of divine characters shared in common, not only are they dealt with in similar, seemingly disjunctive ways, but all of these stories present at the heart of their narration a common plot motif: that of naming and identifying one or other traditional deity with God. Whether this traditional deity is in fact a God of the real historical past of Palestine, like Yahweh, or whether it is only a God found in story, like *El Ro'i* and perhaps *El Shaddai*, is irrelevant. Our effort should be to understand the intentions of the formers of the tradition. The variant nuances of this identification are, nevertheless, very relevant. They mark each story with its unique and surprising perspective.

The central perception of the divine behind the interrelated composition of these texts is the inclusive monotheistic perception of the divine spirit. This is the *Elohe Shamayim* that we find in Isaiah, Ezra or even, less majestically, in letters of the Persian period from the military colony of Elephantine. The variety of gods, and names of gods, that exist in this world, and the variety of gods that exists in the tradition, seemingly distinct from each other and differentiated by geography, by usage, by language, and by the individuality intrinsic in all human experience, all can be understood. They all, each in its own way, refer to the one ineffable divine. This power of spirit, expressive of the experiences of life's transcendence, like the Yahweh of Job and Jonah, has an essence beyond human perception and a reality beyond human understanding. From the perspective of the late Persian or early Hellenistic world, our texts read very differently from the way we have been used to reading them.

Also important – but not so obvious – is the astonishingly complex and striking use of possessive pronouns, connecting the different protagonists of our stories in Exodus. The thematic and ideological purpose of this leitmotif is clear. The pronouns link the two variant theophanies of Exodus 3 and Exodus 6 into a common narration. The classic and clearest formulation of this motif occurs in the speech of *Elohim* in Exodus 6: 7, where it is neither complex nor intrusive but direct and integral. 'I will take you for *my people*, and I will be *your Elohim*.' This is the same Exodus episode in which *Elohim* has identified himself with the *El Shaddai of Abraham, Isaac and Jacob* of the implied audience's forgotten past. This passage closes with the confirmation that the land that had been promised these patriarchs would become *the property of the benei Yisrael*. Here, the possessiveness of the language is emphatic as the implied audience of early Judaism's new Israel joins the narrative.

The story of Exodus 3 implicitly takes part in an intellectual discourse with Exodus 6, about how the traditions warrant identifying old Israel's God, who had long ago been Abraham, Isaac and Jacob's deity, as manifestations, hypostases, of God himself. In this story, however, *Elohim* does not merely say that he was the same *El Shaddai* the patriarchs used to know. Rather, he is the God of Abraham, the God of Isaac and the God of Jacob. The first time that God identifies himself in the Moses story comes just before this verse. It is important to recognize that the theophany story has begun with a yet-to-be-identified Moses. He has been described as a shepherd of his father-in-law, a Midianite priest called Jethro. This Moses is not the same, but only a close variant of the Moses who had married the priest Reuel's daughter in chapter 2! When Moses turns aside to stare at the burning bush, the deity identifies himself as the God of Moses' father – whether Jethro, Reuel or Moses' own, unnamed father is a moot point. This self-identification of Moses' family deity as *the tradition's God* opens the plot-line about who the characters of the story are. This plot-line begins in Exodus 3: 11 with Moses' question: 'Who am I that I should . . . bring the *benei Yisrael* out of Egypt?' The question of identity continues to dominate considerable portions of chapters 4 and 5 as a leitmotif, and this question remains unanswered until Exodus 6: 14–26, when we are given genealogies for Moses and for Aaron.

The function of this metaphor and its play on the characters of the story's identities is three-fold. In the story plot-line, it legitimizes and identifies the deity manifest. In its intellectual referent, however, it legitimizes and identifies the gods of the patriarchal stories and the gods of Israel's ancestors as truly expressive of the transcendent divine. Finally, in bringing these elements together, the story accomplishes the emotional task of identifying the divine possessively. Their god – the god of their forgotten tradition – is God himself!

One is no longer surprised by verse 7, when Yahweh, picking up the motif of the people of Israel complaining of their slavery of chapter 2, refers to 'my people'. Moses' task is to bring Yahweh's people (Ex. 3: 10) out of Egypt. He is instructed to describe this saving deity as 'the God of your fathers' in verses 13 and 15 in the episode, where Moses asks God his name, and is given the sound pun on the name Yahweh. In this passage, the affirmation of the 'God of your fathers', which includes these traditional deities as one with God, is not to be understood as a referent to the gods of Abraham or of the other patriarchs of Genesis. Like that theologically very different text of Joshua 24, it refers to *other ancient ancestral deities of the greater tradition*. In Exodus, however, the traditions of these gods are affirmed, not rejected.

This specific story-line, involving such complex differentiated language about the divine, is what drives the text. This is no accident of sources. Immediately following the *Yahweh/Ehyeh* pun of verse 14 ('I am who I am'), where *Elohim* and Moses are the protagonists, Moses is instructed by *Elohim* in a variant of v. 14: 'Say this to the people of Israel: Yahweh, the *Elohim* of your fathers, the *Elohim* of Abraham, etc. has sent me.' The third variation of this motif of identity, found in verse 16, ties the scene once more backwards to the affliction of chapter 2. It also refers forward to the land of Israel's destiny predicated in chapter 23. It is Yahweh who is as their God for them. Once again, in verse 18, the complexity of this self-identity and association builds further. In the expansion of this motif, *Elohim* identifies himself in terms of Egyptian perceptions: 'Yahweh, the God of the Hebrews' is identified as 'our God'. This does not so much identify the Israelites as Hebrews, as it identifies 'our God' with a deity that the Egyptians will recognize.

Exodus 6, as already discussed, finds this theme of Israel's bond with the divine at centre stage. It is similarly dominant in the closure of Exodus 23, where the implications are drawn out in the contrast between the gods of the legendary enemies of Israel, referred to as 'their God' and Yahweh, who is referred to as 'your God'. The narrative as a whole closes in Exodus 24: 3–8, with the people freely accepting the commitment of this mutual adherence and the obedience it demands. The entire episode is closely linked with three successive and variant theophanies on the mountain: Exodus 19: 2–6 (where Moses goes up to God and where Israel is declared to be Yahweh's unique possession), Exodus 20: 1–17 (the Ten Commandments) and Exodus 20: 22–23: 19 (a long miscellaneous collection of wisdom sayings). These passages are tied together not only by the interplay of language and metaphors about the divine. They link the language of the sending of the messenger episode of Exodus 23: 20–33 with the closing lines of the wisdom collection. In this way, the story's 'You will serve Yahweh your *Elohim*' of verse 25 joins verse 19 in language: 'The first fruits of the ground you will bring into the temple of *Yahweh* your *Elohim*.

In the closing speech of this greater tradition, in Exodus 23: 20–33, God, who identifies himself in the story as Yahweh, Israel's God, promises to send his messenger to guide Israel. Further, echoing the greater tradition's understanding of the historical disasters that had overwhelmed the lost ancient states of Samaria and Judah, this God warns: 'Listen to him, and hearken to his voice. Do not betray him, for he will not pardon your crime. My name is in him.' The prophetic function of declaring unforgiving condemnation on Israel's future betrayal or rebellion is grounded in this story in the messenger's possession of God's name. What is God's name? Moses had asked that question in chapter 3 and had been given an answer with the striking sound pun of verse 14: '*ehyeh asher ehyeh* (I am who I am): Tell the people of Israel '*ehyeh* has sent me.' This echoes the folk aetiology of the pun of v. 12: *ehyeh imak*: 'I am with you', which, echoing Immanuel ('God with us'), is of singular importance in the understanding of *Elohim*'s name in the closure of chapter 23. Yahweh's messenger, in his role as Immanuel, will be with Israel. It is interesting that the story of chapter 3 does not need to interpret the pun. It is transparent to its intended audience. Verse 15 carries the plot forward by answering the question in a different way: 'Yahweh . . . This is my name forever, and so I am to be remembered from generation to generation.'

With this passage in verse 12, most of the problems of Exodus 1–23's organization fall into place and become readable. A third variant of this motif, in Exodus 7: 1, drives home the ideological issue that is at stake: 'Yahweh says to Moses: See, I make you as God to Pharaoh, and Aaron your brother will be your prophet.' Aaron is here Moses' prophet on the analogy of Yahweh as God's prophet! Yahweh can be the guardian messenger of Exodus 14's pillars. He can also be the prophetic messenger of Exodus 23, protecting and condemning Israel. He is so specifically as Yahweh, God's name.

The burden of Exodus 3 and 6 within the literary context of Exodus 1–23 is to portray the old deity of Palestine past, Yahweh, and the stories about him, as a representation and expression of the truly divine. The narrative finds the ancient ancestral gods of Palestine's history and tradition acceptable. They are both historically contingent and specific hypostases of the one true God, *elohe shamayim*, the 'God of heaven'. As *Ba'al* is god for the Phoenicians, so Yahweh is God as Israel knows him. This is what Exodus 6: 7: 'I will take you for my people, and I will be your God' signifies: 'As Yahweh, I am God for you.' Here again Exodus 19 may be allowed to carry the interpretive weight of our story as God speaks to Moses as Yahweh: 'You shall be my own possession among all peoples, because all of the earth is mine,' a passage that finds echoing clarification in a context as distant as Deuteronomy 32: 8, in Moses' song to the assembly of Israel: 'When the Most High gave the nations their inheritance and distinguished people, he fixed nations' borders according to the numbers of God's messengers. So Yahweh's part was his people: Jacob his determined destiny.' This traditional deity of Palestine's ancient past, Yahweh, is by means of the Pentateuchal tradition (Genesis 17; Exodus 3–6; Exodus 23: 20ff.; Deut. 32: 8) reinterpreted and revivified as the divine messenger and prophet of Israel. That is, Yahweh is Immanuel: *ehyeh imak*. He exists as the heavenly divine with Israel: through his name.

In this form of inclusive monotheism, there is but one God for Israel: the God of heaven. The gods of nations and the gods of tradition alike are only human traditions. They are representations, manifestations, prophetic voices. They name the one universal spirit, who lies at the centre of the universe, beyond understanding.

CHAPTER 13

The Bible's theological world II: the myths of the sons of God

1 The birth of a son of God as a traditional plot motif

A full discussion of the use of myth in the Bible would take a book of its own. Here, we want merely to look at one of a number of mythical characters that one finds in the Bible almost wherever one might wish to open it. Within this story world, one finds a series of interacting characters. Taken together, they form a broad spectrum of wonderful creatures. In fact, one can well describe the Bible – and especially the stories in that long chain of narrative extending from the opening pages of Genesis' creation account to the fall of Jerusalem at the end of II Kings – as a chain of such heroes. They display a wonderful variety of the semi-divine, the miraculous and the wondrous, with an ever-recurring theme of divine presence in the world of humans. All take their part in the tragic dissonance of the union of the human and the divine. This world of Bible history is throughout a mythological world.

We find eponymous heroes, founders and fathers of cities and states; inspired craftsmen, builders of beautiful things; wise men possessed of divine understanding and judgement; seers and prophets, those who know God's will and speak with his voice; judges, charismatic warriors and saviours of Israel against its enemies; anointed kings and messiahs, servants of God, carrying out his will on earth, representatives of the people before God's judgement; sons of God, sharers in the divine essence, heroic figures who bring God present to his people; angels, mythological divine messengers through whom the divine communicates with this world, and finally Yahweh himself, the ancient God of Palestine who is God's name and representative for old Israel, and the God in most of our stories. All of these characters are defined by the theme of destiny, and by the need of humans to accept this expression of divine will. God's action in the world is to establish human destiny and history. Accepted, this is a destiny of grace and mercy. The narratives turn on motifs of faithfulness and loyalty to the divine patron. The acceptance of one's fate is the definition of wisdom and righteousness. The reiterative play of biblical stories, where God establishes and humanity rejects its destiny, centres on a variable, shifting balance of human and divine intermediaries. The central characters of biblical stories play out a recurrent 'Immanuel' motif, illustrating how God is with us. The stories develop in the contrast of a distant, absent and uncaring God with an intimate, ever-present and loving God. The role of the divine in human affairs is an issue about which biblical tradition is most ambivalent. God is with Israel for good, but he is also there for evil. He is ever there for Israel's protection and salvation, and he is there for its destruction and condemnation.

In this chapter, I have chosen the motif of 'the birth of a son of God' because it plays such a central role in the Bible's theology, a role that is continued in later traditions. The role of this 'son(s) of God' motif develops a very clear and specific function in our stories. It is one that has a quite wide range of narrative type, but is surprisingly coherent through most of its appearances. This is partially due to the existence of a story world of the gods that seems relatively common throughout the Semitic world and is familiar to us in the Bible. The song of Moses in Deuteronomy 32, for instance, calls its hearers back to the old myths of the past to give its account.

> Think of the days of yore; consider the years: generation upon generation past. Ask your father; let him narrate it; let the old one recount it for you. When El, the Most High, divided the nations, when he separated the children of humanity from each other, and when he established the borders of peoples according to the number of the messengers of God, so Yahweh's part became his people; Jacob became his inheritance. (Deut. 32: 7–9)

Here we have a picture of God, called for antiquity's sake 'El the Most High', with his court of messengers, each of which is a god who is given one of the nations on earth for his own, for his 'inheritance'. The fact that Yahweh gets Israel creates an aetiology for Israel, identified as the people of Yahweh, which is so central to the theology of the Pentateuch. The original Hebrew of the phrase 'messengers of God' has not survived. I translate from the early Greek version of the Bible. This well fits the metaphors of the wilderness stories. Many scholars, however, prefer the translation, 'according to the number of the sons of God', because the scene called up is very similar to scenes of a divine court of God and his sons, which is found elsewhere in the Bible. The motif of the 'sons of God' appears frequently in the Psalter in close connection with the figure of the messiah.

In the story that frames the operatic arias of Job, for example, we have a picture of Yahweh's court (Job 1–2). In this story, Yahweh assembles all of the sons of God. When they meet, they talk and gossip about what is happening on earth. Some of the gods travel to and from heaven and earth, and talk to the others about their travels and experiences. Among the sons of God in the divine assembly is one who has the cue-name Satan. Satan in the Job stories takes his name's role as 'prosecutor' – a fitting role among the many courtroom metaphors of Job's songs. Satan plays the role of divine prosecutor, the 'devil's advocate' of the heavenly court.

Many songs and proverbs, especially in the Book of Psalms and Ezekiel, set a scene in a similar divine court or assembly of the gods. Psalm 2, for example, speaks of Yahweh as enthroned in his heavens mocking the mere kings of nations on earth. It also speaks of Yahweh's son, whom Yahweh has established as king 'on his holy mountain'. It is a clear reference to a mythological figure – Yahweh's messiah – who rules from a heavenly Jerusalem and judges the world. A very similar picture is found in Psalm 110, where this messianic son of Yahweh is described as the 'lord' and 'patron' of the singer, a heavenly David, whom Yahweh gives birth to as life-giving dew from the womb of the dawn. This divine messiah, priest and king, fights a cosmic battle against kings. He judges the nations from his heavenly throne. The cosmic role of this messianic war also appears in Psalm 8, but nowhere is the mythological colour richer than in the ancient Psalm 89. Such mythic imagery is found again in the opening chapters of Ezekiel, as well as in both the Apocalypse of John 19–20 and the apocryphal works of the Songs of Solomon and the First Book of Enoch. In these poetic explosions of metaphor, we find a rather complex understanding of the divine.

2 Humanity and the divine

It is in the context of such imagery in the Bible's story world that the brief episode about the sons of God who marry with 'daughters of Adam' in the beginning of chapter 6 of Genesis has its place. The theme of intermarriage between the divine and human is a classic of both Greek and ancient Near Eastern mythology. The Bible's entry in this tradition is brief and unadorned:

> And so it was that when humanity began to spread itself out over the world, daughters were born. The sons of God saw that the women were beautiful and they married them, every one that they desired. So Yahweh declared: 'My spirit will not reside in people forever. After all, they are only flesh and their life-span but 120 years.'

The text allows that these marriages were taking place everywhere and often. Also clearly implicit in this account of such romantic adventures of the gods is that human cooperation and complicity play no role: beautiful women are taken. This contrasts strikingly with the Book of Jubilees form of this same story. Jubilees understands this misalliance as sin. For Jubilees this sin is moral justification for the flood story, which unlike the story in Genesis is understood as justifiable divine punishment for this sexual adventure with the gods.

It is in Yahweh's declaration that Genesis' treatment of the sons of God episode takes on emphatically different direction from Jubilees'. The role Yahweh plays is not that of a judge, and certainly not that of the punishing God of the flood story. Unlike Genesis, Jubilees has integrated the flood story with this story of divine and human sexual intercourse. In Genesis, the story is placed before, but remains independent of, the flood story. Genesis seems aware of the tradition of association between the two tales, but instead of making the more instructive connection that Jubilees does, it seems satisfied with gathering tradition. Rather than the doom-saying judge of Jubilees, Yahweh is portrayed as a philosopher, an observing interpreter; he becomes the story's implied reader. He is not involved in the story, he analyses and evaluates it. The union of the human and divine is neither evil nor sinful. We read, rather, a remarkably neutral observation about the intrinsic difference between what is divine and what is only human. The brief speech of Yahweh is not part of the story. The story itself is obviously already known to the reader. Genesis hardly bothers to relate details. What is the result of this divine/human miscegenation? Has humanity become divine? The answer is a very interesting 'not quite'. Yahweh's breath – that wonderful gift of life – does not stay with us for ever. We live for only 120 years. Miscegenation, we are told, poses no threat to Yahweh. People remained unchanged in God's eyes. Because they are only human, they are gone so quickly that they are hardly seen as either bad or harmful. They are far worse: they are uninteresting.

Yahweh's words are those of a philosopher who has been asked to give his judgement about some unsavoury incident: this scandal resulting from unfettered divine lust for a woman's beauty. His words are reticent words of realistic acceptance of the inescapable nature of being human: 'After all, they are only flesh. My breath won't live with them forever, their days are but 120 years.' This opens an argument that the text takes up again in the flood story. In contrast to Jubilees' moralizing interpretation, Genesis presents us with an entirely unhistorical, metaphorical understanding. The philosopher Yahweh cites a proverb: 'Humanity is merely flesh . . .' This comment links humanity not with the gods but with the essence of animals, 'flesh'. God can afford to ignore these marriages. People don't live long enough to compete with gods. The underlying, philosophical argument of the implied discourse is found in Ecclesiastes 3: 19: 'The fate of humans and animals is the same. As one dies, so dies the other. They both have the same spirit, and a human is no more than an animal.'

One finds this same kind of thinking in Genesis 9: 11, where humans are included in the reference to 'all the living creatures', and 'all flesh', which the deity of the story repents of having destroyed by a flood. In this passage of the flood story, the story's God also plays the role of philosopher for the story-teller. The discussion turns on the close association of the two phrases: 'all living souls' and 'all flesh'. The flood story echoes both the language and plot-line of the garden story. It also expands on the garden story's theology. When humanity has been created in this tale, the narrator tells us: 'When Yahweh's God shaped the human out of the soil of the land and breathed into its nostrils the breath of life, the human became a living being' (Gen. 2: 7). When the woman of this story finally does win wisdom for people by eating from the tree of knowledge, the creator prevents them from becoming gods themselves (Gen. 3: 22). He puts them outside the garden, and places invincibly armed monsters, 'cherubim and a flaming sword, turning in all directions at once, guarding the way to the tree of life' (Gen. 3: 24). Why? To prevent people from getting back to 'the way of the tree of life'. If they could, they would eat from this tree, become gods, and live forever. The same theme had been expressed long before in the Old Babylonian Gilgamesh epic: 'When the gods created man, they kept life in their own hands.' This the barmaid tells Gilgamesh, trying to discourage him from his hopeless quest for immortality. It is a standard philosophical distinction of ancient philosophy between the human and the divine. In the Bible, such philosophical writings find a central focus in the irony of Ecclesiastes: 'He has put eternity into human thought so that it cannot find out what God has done from the beginning to the end' (3: 11).

In fact it is this issue that the garden story centres on, not that of sin. In the opening of the garden story, focus is placed on an 'everyman' figure called in Hebrew *ha-adam*. This is well translated as 'earthling', as it means 'human' in Hebrew, and is derived from the Hebrew word for 'earth': *adamah*. The story describes Yahweh, like a potter, making this humanity out of clay. It is only after woman is made from the human's rib – the scene is of a form of cloning, much as many plants are reproduced – that this human takes on the role of the male person of the story, namely Adam. A similar punning play on words is used when this lump of clay is made into a living being. As in so many languages the Hebrew word for 'breath', *ruach*, can also signify 'spirit' and 'wind'. This 'earthling', becomes a 'living being' because it is given the divine spirit as its breath. This polarity between the insignificance of humanity, 'mere flesh', 'earthlings' that we are, and the life and wisdom of the divine that we are not is the very heart of the story. When the woman of our story looks on the 'tree of knowledge', and desires its fruit 'to make her wise', the ancient reader knows from the very start that her quest will fail. The author is citing Solomon in Ecclesiastes for us. The role the woman plays is a perfect dramatization of a famous proverb. Wise King Solomon, having spent a lifetime of philosophical study, turns his critical irony upon himself, and confesses with a deconstructive double entendre: 'I spent my life seeking wisdom (seeking the spirit), only to discover that I was chasing the wind.' So too, Eve, in seeking to become wise, ended in 'chasing the wind'. Back in the garden story, it is also in the 'spirit of the day' that Yahweh comes to determine the fate of the conspirators. When the story closes with Yahweh's declaration of humanity's destiny (Gen. 3: 19) – that humanity is to return to the dust from which it was made – the story again turns to the Book of Ecclesiastes for its inspiration, where, at the close of his collection, the philosopher lists a string of euphemisms about human death (Eccles. 12: 5–7):

> When the human goes to his eternal home, and the mourners go about the streets, when the silver cord is snapped, the golden bowl is broken, or the pitcher at the fountain, when the wheel is broken at the cistern, and *the dust returns to the earth from which it was and the spirit to God from which it came.*

3 Humanity and murder

While the stories about old Israel are stories about the dark side of human nature, these narratives are recurrently punctuated by closures and responses about mercy and hope. Few stories are as dark as the garden story's mate, the tale of Cain, and few are touched more by a motif of divine grace. This story too is about 'humanity', and together with the garden story it forms a paired thematic introduction between humanity's creation and the opening of the book with its title in chapter 5: 1: 'This is the book of humanity's development.' The Cain story is a very important bridge, as it intensifies the already dominant narrative theme of differences between the gods and men.

In the story's opening, all of our characters bear cue-names. There is Adam 'the human' of the garden story (Gen. 2: 7) and Eve, his wife, whose name is interpreted: 'the mother of all living' (Gen. 3: 20). Adam has sex with his wife, who bears a child whom she names 'Cain' (Gen. 4: 1). Adam's involvement, as far as the story is concerned, is not terribly important. It provides only the occasion of Eve's pregnancy; human fertility is not his to give but God's. When she gives birth Eve tells the audience: 'I have made a man with Yahweh!' Eve creates her children with God! Eve, the great mother of all, makes men. Her child 'Cain', whose name puns with Eve's word *qaniti* ('to make'), has the name of 'creature'.

Human life is born of god and woman. The child who is born is the creature, divine and human: he is us.

Abel is also a cue-name. This name ('mist', 'dew') reflects the frailty of all human life as momentary, passing, merely a breath[1] – an intensely compassionate name to attach to the life of a murder victim. Both Cain and Abel are from their births, like their father Adam, everyman. When we watch them, we watch ourselves. Their experience is our experience, and their understanding our own. The two brothers of our story, however, do double duty in the roles they play. Cain plays also the Canaanites, whose sacrifices in the Elijah story of I Kings 18: 20–40 go unaccepted, as Abel plays the role of Israel as Canaan's brother, a fleeting role of a nation that god once chose.[2]

As the story opens, Cain does what is proper for a farmer. It is important to recognize that Cain does nothing wrong at this point. He offers his crops as sacrifice and pays respect to his god. It is Yahweh who does not recognize or accept Cain and his offering. This is the story's plot and problem. The plot opening can be compared to the story of Jonah, and especially to the scene in which Jonah's shade tree grows overnight to provide him comfort from the sun. Yahweh causes it just as quickly to wither. The reason that Jahweh does what he does is hidden from Jonah. Just so, the reason that Yahweh does not accept Cain and his sacrifice is unknown. Cain's behaviour and sacrifice is every bit as good as Abel's. The theme, like that in the Jonah story, emphasizes divine freedom: both our inability to know god's purposes and his freedom to do what we least expect. God chooses not to accept Cain and his offering. The story's crisis is in its essence an intellectual debate. On one hand, the theological demand, even definition, of divine freedom is that it be complete and untrammelled. On the other hand, religious traditions assume that we know something about the divine. We expect – perhaps demand – that God does certain things in certain ways. Our stories engage this debate on the side of divine freedom. Like Cain's, the expectations of all who offer worship to god are that he will accept them and accept their offerings. Why else worship? The story gives the lie to such expectation as but a human conceit. The story as told in Genesis is both sympathetic and compassionate in its presentation of Cain's reaction. The plot takes a well-travelled road in world literature. In Bizet's *Carmen*, for example, one of the central motifs is *hatred born of unrequited love*.

[1] Psalm 39: 12 uses the Hebrew word for Abel's name, *hebel*, to express just this transience of human life: 'For I am your *passing* guest, a migrant like all my fathers.' Psalm 94: 11 captures another nuance of this same human fragility that Abel's story mirrors: 'human thoughts, that are but a *breath*'.

[2] Seth, whose name echoes the Akkadian *shutu*, 'the wilderness', promises a new beginning to mankind at the close of our story. He plays the role of *Israel redivivus*.

In Genesis, it is Cain's love for god that goes unacknowledged and unaccepted. The tragedy of our story has nothing to do with a lack of piety in this our representative. The story is rather about our needing (and needing absolutely) freely conceived acceptance. And it is also about the nature of love as freely given. How can such a demand be met except gratuitously: by grace? And so our story is also about the graceful quality of acceptance and love.

Like Jonah, who is scolded for being angry and depressed at the loss of his shade tree, Cain is called upon to abandon his anger. 'Why should you be angry?' At this point of the exchange, Yahweh expresses a studied lack of sympathy for Cain's perspective. This brings Cain's frustration to the centre of the stage, and exposes it to ridicule in god's eyes for its human frailty! Of course, Yahweh, as pedant, is correct. Every philosopher knows this. If one 'does what is right', it is enough for self-respect. Yet the pedantry also opens to view the vulnerability and implicit ambivalence of our all-too-human virtue of self-respect. After all is said, this is not why humans do 'what is right'. We need ulterior motives for 'self-respect'. We need acknowledgement and recognition 'to hold our heads up high'. This we all know. This is what lies at the root of Cain's anger. It is this creature's bad faith that Yahweh's cold logic exposes.

At this point, Yahweh's script-writer complicates the story by seemingly forgetting the plot-line. Yahweh momentarily becomes not the debating pedant, but the absent-minded professor. He loses himself in a footnote's excursion into a complex variable of scholarly proverbs. He has just told Cain that 'if you do what is right, you can hold your head up high.' This obviously has brought to mind the alternative: 'if you *don't* do what is right', what then? This is the way a scholar's mind works, not a story! It is hardly an issue that involves a story's plot. It is an aside. Yet it causes another pedantic citation of the well-known variant of the first. 'If you *don't* do what is right, sin will crouch at your door, and it will want to have you. Yet you must master it!' All thoughts of sacrifice, even of unrequited love, are long gone. The professor is lost inside one of his many parentheses. We have not gone back into the story but are involved in a moral sermon of a wholly different context. Up to this point, we had been given good old-fashioned theology of grace. Divine acceptance is not something earned. We cannot expect it. Nor can we demand it. It is god's free gift. In practice, goes the implied lecture, people should behave as is proper, without reference to what they might gain from their good behaviour. The sermon story was clear to that point. But now, suddenly, we find ourselves well outside of the Cain/Abel sacrifice story and are wandering somewhere within chapters 11, 14 and 29 of the Book of Proverbs! We are now trying to find our way through some of the finer distinctions separating the 'path of righteousness' and the 'way of all mankind'. Even Cain is momentarily forgotten as we try to wrestle with our teacher's question about the perennial choice between wisdom and folly.

This momentary excursion into other worlds intimates some of the issues that our text has at stake in its progress. We find ourselves wrapped in three different metaphors simultaneously evoked by Yahweh's speech about *not* doing what is right: threat, temptation and conquest. The temptation is, indeed, to murder. This, our author has interpreted as 'desire'. In fact, the text has turned itself into a commentary on the coming narrative and the author has become an exegete. Conquest is tentatively interpreted as self-conquest, as the narration engages his effort to unlock the scholarly riddle that his own divine character sets for him.

However, just as we, the reader, intimate so much, our author takes his interpretation of the wisdom saying in still another direction, which pairs itself with the spurned sacrifice episode: if we as Cain cannot assume God's acceptance of our sacrifices, what is god for us? Cain must overcome not the temptation so much as its threat to himself. This is not a conquest over himself. Certainly it does not deal with any conquest of Cain over sin. That issue plays no role at all in Genesis' account of the story. The story focuses once again on Cain, on his anger and on his depression. Cain up and murders Abel! Not because of Yahweh's not accepting Cain, but rather because of Cain's – everyman's – *passion for murder*. No motives are involved, but sin, crouching like a lion at his door: murder endangers the murderer. Abel's death opens a new plot-line, announced by the last part of the proverb cited. Cain's murder of his brother is now the point of departure. What is to happen now that the choice has been made, the temptation followed? 'What if one does evil?' Well, it has been done. What now? Cain has killed Abel. What now? A teacher's direct challenge to his own proverb.

'And Yahweh asked Cain, "Where is your brother Abel?" and Cain answered, "I have no idea. Am I the watcher of my brother?"' The emphasis is placed not on Cain's answer and protest, but on the interrogative: Who is the watcher, the caretaker? Having placed this question in the forefront, the author then turns to a debate scene with Yahweh determining Cain's destiny. Cain, like Adam, is the first farmer, and so his fate is the farmer's hard lot. The ground itself shouts out its distaste of man's preference for blood-soaked earth. It is not Yahweh who curses Cain here. This is not the garden story. It is the earth's anger itself that curses Cain. Yahweh delivers the message and waits to play another role. As the story's opening dealt with the theme of divine freedom, its closure turns to the question of human responsibility. With the earth's curse on him, Cain is no longer the farmer standing in contrast to Abel's shepherd. Cain has become the fugitive from the land. He is without land and without protection, helpless and afraid. The story presses its pivotal question: not so much the direct question of who is Abel's brother, but who is *Cain's* caretaker? Cain is us: everyman. The story asks: who cares for us? Who is our patron, our godfather? Faced with this question, the narrator cannot play Yahweh in the same role that he played in the garden story. He cannot here be one to curse humanity with all of its tragic alienation. Yahweh must take up a different role to play.

Confronted with the earth's curse, Cain complains. His punishment is too much to bear. Cain's terror is palpable. He does not ask for forgiveness. He is beyond that. Cain has done evil in large measure. For him the issue is one of survival. Everyone in his eyes – even god himself – is against him. The story turns back to Cain's question about Abel. Now it is rephrased by events: Who cares about Cain? And if god's love and recognition is not to be measured – as Yahweh taught us at the story's opening – who now cares for us? For if there is now no one to care for Cain, for whom is there anyone to care? Can one now abandon Cain the murderer and still hold to the divine demand of freedom that the story set out with equal logic against an innocent Cain? The intellectual rigour of the story's question is inescapable. The story's answer is unflinching. Yahweh is mankind's keeper, he is our keeper, and he accepts his role as Cain's protector. The story is pacifist. The mark of Cain, the murderer, is the mark of guarantee of one who is protected by God: even he, even us.

It would hardly be surprising if anyone were to protest against this pacifist's reading of the story of Cain. We have already a tradition of what the story of Cain and Abel is about, and we already 'know' what the story says. What I have presented of Genesis' story is not that. One might have a similar reaction in reading the Hebrew bible's garden story and looking for paradise there. One would as well look for original sin there, or for the devil – all in vain. With the garden story, we are familiar with other traditions and other interpretations. With their help we have learned about our paradise story and about our story of temptation and fall, which tells us what Genesis is supposed to say. Ezekiel, Ben Sira and Jubilees all have had a part in developing our understanding. Most important have been Paul's Letter to the Romans and Augustine, especially in his song, *Te Deum*, which praises Adam's fall as a 'happy fault'. Without it, Christian salvation – and its joy – would be unnecessary. What forms our conviction of a right reading of the garden story's tradition is a complex issue. With the bible's tale of Cain, however, we need merely to point to the apocryphal Book of Jubilees. In its story of Cain we read the tale that long ago supplanted the less imposing and more subtle tale of Genesis.

In Jubilees' version of the story, the theme is historicized. The narration recounts an event as of the past. The murder by Cain is central, and Yahweh takes up his expected role as judge of the sinner. In this version of the story, the 'mark of Cain' is no mark of divine protection. It is synonymous with 'the curse of Cain'. It is a terrible branding, marking not only him but his descendants as cursed:

And in the third week in the second Jubilee, she bore Cain. And in the fourth, she bore Abel. And in the fifth she bore 'Awan his daughter. And at the beginning of the third jubilee, Cain killed Abel because the sacrifice of Abel was accepted but the offering of Cain was not accepted. And he killed him in the field, and his blood cried out from the earth to heaven, making accusation because he killed him. And Yahweh rebuked Cain on account of Abel because he killed him. And he made him a fugitive on the earth because of the blood of his brother. And he cursed him upon the earth. And therefore it is written in the heavenly tablets, 'Cursed be one who strikes his fellow with malice.' And all who have seen and heard shall say, 'So be it.' And the man who saw and did not report it, shall be cursed like him. Therefore when we come before Yahweh our God we will make known all of the sins which occur in heaven and earth and which are in the light or in the darkness or in any place.

It is particularly interesting that Jubilees, like Genesis, also cites texts, namely 'the heavenly tablets', in support of its interpretation. The text referred to by Jubilees, 'Cursed be one who strikes his fellow with malice,' is very close to one of the proverbs that has been collected in Deuteronomy 27: 24: 'Cursed be one who kills his enemy in secret.' Similar proverbs show up in Exodus 21: 12: 'Whoever strikes one that he dies, will be put to death,' and again in Leviticus 24: 17: 'He who kills a man will be put to death.' Very generally speaking, these proverbs are all variations of one of the Ten Commandments we find in Exodus 20: 13 and again in Deuteronomy 5: 17, namely, 'Thou shall not kill.'

Jubilees' interpretation of the Cain story is, I think, particularly strong in the Christian tradition because of its closeness to the discussion about these proverbs cited in Matthew 5: 21 'You have heard that it was said to the men of old: "You shall not kill, and whoever does kill will be liable to the court." ' The writer of Matthew, very much like both the authors of Genesis and Jubilees, while perfectly willing to cite authority, has no difficulty in standing by his own interpretation: 'But I tell you that anyone who is even angry with his brother should be liable to the court.' The use of the motif of a 'brother's' anger suggests that the story is implicitly aware of Cain's story. In fact, when we look at the way each of our texts deals with this subject, it becomes clear that they are involved in a literary discussion. They add comments to the story. They suggest corrections, they disagree and, they affirm other readings.

It is, however, in the small collection of texts centring on this discussion, which we find in Numbers 35: 9–34 dealing with the motifs of flight and places of refuge, that we really first see the context of our stories clearly. This could well be a text the Cain story in Genesis illustrates. Let us begin with a proverb that discusses the difference between murder and manslaughter: 'And if he struck him down with a stone . . .' etc. (Num. 35: 17). While we are presented here – as in Jubilees – with a stone as the murder weapon, Numbers also offers a variant murder weapon, an 'iron tool'. Numbers 35: 20–22 offers three further possible contexts and means that would lead to a judgement of murder: stabbing someone one hates, lying in wait and hurling something, and striking someone with one's hand out of hatred. Here, quite clearly, the principle of premeditation is at the forefront of the discussion. Clarifying the principles further, the text offers three comparable alternatives of killing that would not be judged to be murder: stabbing suddenly without hatred, throwing something but without the premeditation of an ambush, and innocently throwing a stone without seeing a man who happens to be killed by it. One finds yet other variants in other collections. In Exodus 20: 12 we find listed variables relating to seeking refuge from blood revenge. In verse 18 of the same chapter, the text takes up attempted murder. Verse 20 deals with the killing of a slave and verse 22 with the killing of a foetus. This chapter of Exodus is dealing with material relating to the same intellectual discussion with which both Jubilees and Genesis are involved. It is the world that the stories of the bible illustrate.

Yet not all texts present the arguments as obviously driven by logic or a particular perspective on the issues. Often the text seems to be driven by a collector's motives. Texts are linked together in a very free-floating association of words, images and ideas. Such freely compiled collages are often much influenced by associations with stories. For example, the scribe collecting the traditions of Genesis has brought together variant stories of the flood. In Genesis 9: 4–7, the text, which begins within the flood story where God is instructing Noah about what he can and cannot eat, turns to broader intellectual issues. The collector introduces a thesis concerning a food taboo against eating meat with its blood. He draws conclusions regarding blood revenge, citing both the Cain and the flood narratives in the process. The text brings together known proverbs from different sources and about different issues. In doing so, it strings together pieces of tradition related more by language than by logic. The citation of the proverb: 'You shall not eat flesh with its life; that is, with its blood,' leads to what seems to be a confluence of this citation regarding a food taboo with both an anti-murder proverb and an aetiology for animal sacrifice: 'For your lifeblood I will surely require a reckoning, of every beast I will require it, and of every man.' The citation of the proverb related to punishment required for killing is an implicit reference to the Cain story. It offers perhaps an alternative answer that is implicitly addressed to Cain's question about whether he was responsible for his brother. Certainly, it seems to support the blood revenge that Cain feared would be raised against him: 'Of every *man's brother* I will require the life of man.' The text goes on to cite yet another reference and yet another argument, with reference to the creation story. 'Whoever sheds the blood of man, by man will his blood be shed, for god made man in his own image.' This argument – apparently supporting capital punishment – directly disagrees with Genesis' pacifist rendering of the Cain story. It is much more in line with the story as told in Jubilees.

The text draws on the flood story and cites once again the blessing of the creation story: 'be fruitful and multiply'. This is the same quotation that has marked the closure of the flood story as a new creation and a new beginning. This citation echoes Genesis 9: 1's citation of the same blessing. Together the double rendering of this blessing marks off Genesis' use of proverbs about life and blood as a discussion in its own right. This brief collection of different perspectives and even different discussions referring to the motifs of life and blood has nothing to do with the plot of the flood story. The flood story rather has offered what the story's collector obviously understood as a good context for this collage of loosely related proverbs. As the blessing concerns life and fertility, the discourse explores the value of life. Having said this much, however, we then must conclude that the motivations for writing such texts are far distant from merely recounting any traditions about food taboos or the death penalty. They are even further from telling a story. Even the interests of an implied reader seem to be ignored in this assemblage of citations. The motives of the text are much closer to those of a teacher or librarian concerned about how different aspects of a tradition might be organized, understood and preserved.

It is very important for our discussion of history to notice that neither Genesis nor Jubilees is interested in recounting events. Nor are they engaged in telling stories that they themselves made up. Both take part in a common discussion about the Cain story. Each supports an understanding and an interpretation of the story. Perhaps it might be put better: each projects and reconstructs a story in support of an interpretation of specific moral values, arguments and principles. The tale is not used merely as anecdotal evidence. It is too freely manipulated and openly appropriated. The story serves as an illustrative example. Jubilees presents it as an etiology for capital punishment, while Genesis offers instead an etiology of a divine protection.

Jubilees' account of the Cain story is more helpful than the tale in Genesis for giving us some insight into the way a story can be used to illustrate the author's philosophical principles. In closing its account of the garden story, which asserts that the tree of wisdom has brought death to Adam, Jubilees argues how this death was appropriate. Then it also tries to show how Cain's death was governed by an equally appropriate fate:

> And at the end of the nineteenth Jubilee in the seventh week, in the sixth year, Adam died. And all of his children buried him in the land of his creation. And he was the first who was buried in the earth. And he lacked seventy years from one thousand years, for a thousand years are like one day in the testimony of

heaven and therefore it was written concerning the tree of knowledge, 'In the day you eat from it you will die,' therefore he did not complete the years of this day because he died in it.

At the end of that Jubilee Cain was killed one year after him. And his house fell upon him. And he died in the midst of his house. And he was killed by its stones because he killed Abel with a stone, and so with a stone was he killed by righteous judgement. Therefore it is ordained in the heavenly tablets: 'With the weapons with which a man kills his fellow he shall be killed. Just as he wounded him. Thus shall they do to him.'

It is highly significant that in Jubilees' own account of the story of Cain, Cain does not kill his brother with a stone, but rather with 'malice', with 'hatred'. We have already learned that both enmity and stones belong to the Bible's larger discussion about murder and capital punishment. Jubilees' argument then makes quite good sense as an argument built not so much on the tale alone but on the related discussion in the greater world of scholarship that its account implied. Jubilees seals its discussion with a poem. The point is to mark the text as fitting and traditional. Jubilees' rationalization proceeds on the basis of logic, authority and – most important of all – balance. Genesis does the same in its version. It gives the story; interprets the issues of the story with citation of proverbs of authority, and seals its story with a song, marking the whole with a sense of balance and propriety. Genesis closes its argument with the song we find in chapter 4: 23–24, just at the end of the aetiologies relating to Cain's sons:

Lamech said to his wives: Adah and Zillah, hear my voice; you wives of Lamech, hearken to what I say: I have slain a man for wounding me, a young man for striking me. If Cain is avenged seven-fold, truly Lamech seventy-seven-fold!

The argument in Genesis is oriented towards the collection of tradition. The presentation of Genesis' values is often designed to surprise the reader. In presenting as Genesis does a 'lost and forgotten' tradition, representing the divine foundations of the community, the collector takes as a cardinal principle the thesis that ordinary human understanding is both in error and undependable. Hence, truth, to be convincing, needs to be surprising.

When we compare Genesis with Jubilees as we have, it becomes clear that the murder story and the proverbs cited are a given of the narrative. They are what the two accounts have in common. The same story is used by both. Both cite proverbs as the central focus of their exegesis, and both use songs to close their arguments! The structure of this three-part technique is a common tool of both commentaries. The tales give the framework, the proverbs the interpretive focus, and the songs close and support conviction. The common ground between the composition of Jubilees and Genesis is impressive. We have a common ideological perspective in the narratives, the same mixture of genres: tale, proverb, and song. We have common techniques of both argument and presentation; and, just as importantly, the same expectation of rationalizing satisfaction! There are also other characteristics held in common. The stories and their plots are destroyed by both the narrators' erudition and by their strong grasp of the tradition. In both Jubilees and in Genesis, the story, as a story, does not hold the author's attention. Their interest lies elsewhere in the discourse, and in the scholarly commentary on tradition, not on the traditions themselves. Jubilees and Genesis must be seen as sharing a common intellectual world.

4 The birth of the son of God and the sending of a saviour

While the early chapters of Genesis centre on stories and discussions about the relationship between the human and the divine in general, and so talk about all of humanity in terms of the characters in the stories, the use of the motif of divine parentage, much like that of divine image and the different ways in which humans try to be like the divine, served its function as a means of dramatizing both the closeness and the distance of the human and the divine. Authority, life and knowledge are all seen as essentially divine values within the world we know and live in. This perception finds expression in the Bible's stories. Similarly, the stories reflect a conception that humans play the role of God in this world. All of these stories equally share a theme of loss and pessimism. The stories create a contrast that repeatedly comes to the fore: the similarity of humanity to the divine is the source of a conflict in which people are too much like gods to ignore. God created the world good; and then he created man. The Bible rarely avoids the irony of this perspective. While the stories are wholly comfortable with mythical characters such as gods, angels, monstrous cherubim, half-divine and divine-like humans and the like, these story characters reflect a recurrent theme of possibility lost. The implicit discussion is ever about how the human and the divine are fundamentally opposite and even contrary.

When we enter the patriarchal narrative both the number and type of stories multiply rapidly. The plots take on a greater importance. The characters are drawn more fully and more satisfyingly. In the use of the motif of a son of God, and particularly in the traditional birth episode of a son of God, the dominance of the theme about the interrelationship between men and the divine comes to the forefront of the story's presentation. The motif, in fact, takes on the fixed function of specifically exemplifying God's presence in the world. This develops into one of the main ways that the biblical stories develop to talk about divine immanence. The variety of these stories quite consciously explores the potentially startling implications of piety's belief in God's presence, as well as such ideas of popular religion as that the gods control events in this world. Examples will tell far more than I can paraphrase about some of the rich literary possibilities that this motif opens.

Stories that open with the birth of a son of God, or with a comparable 'birth of a saviour' episode, are what you might call epitomizing stories. This type of story is presented to interpret and foreshadow the kind of role that the child is to play in later life. In a story form, the birth acts much like a cue-name. It performs the same function that the naming aetiologies do. Certainly the ironic wit of the punning explanation given to Noah's name in Genesis 5: 29, is an appropriate preparation for the flood story's destruction of humanity: 'and he called his name Noah, for this one shall bring us relief [ye*nach*menu: a pun on the Hebrew name *Noach*) from our work, from the toil of our hands and from the ground that Yahweh has cursed.' Such useful puns help us understand how the text and the tradition understood the story or character represented. Another type of epitomizing episode in biblical stories is also a common feature of most legend-building. This is the pattern of telling a story of a character's childhood that captures something of importance in his or her later life. The theme can be straightforward, even historical, as in the account of Mozart's great successes as a concert pianist at an early age. They can also be ironic and apocryphal, as in the story of Einstein flunking his first algebra examination. Two short biblical legends stand out in this regard because they each epitomize their hero role in representing the divine presence in their life.

In Exodus 2: 11–15, we find a dramatic miniature that acts as a bridge between two groups of Moses tales: between the stories surrounding his birth and rescue and the more complex narrative about the sending of the saviour that begins with Moses going out into the wilderness in Exodus 2: 16. Exodus recounts but the bare bones of this tale. It would be nearly incomprehensible except for its striking, dramatic presentation in two scenes, each a contrast to the other in their polarity. First scene:

> Time passed, and Moses was grown up. Once he approached his brothers to observe their slave labour. He saw an Egyptian kill one of the Hebrews, his brothers. He looked about, and as there was no one there, he killed the Egyptian and buried him in the sand.

Note the stress to identify Moses as 'brother' of the enslaved Hebrews he avenges. Moses is portrayed as the revolutionary saviour: the scourge of the oppressors of his people. He stands in solidarity with the oppressed. Second scene:

The next day, Moses again went out. He saw two Hebrews fighting. 'Why are you hitting your comrade?' he asked the one who was to blame. But he retorted: 'Who has set you up to be master and judge over us? Perhaps you will kill me too, just as you killed the Egyptian?' And so Moses grew afraid, thinking: So, it has been found out after all! When pharaoh heard of it, he wanted to kill Moses. Moses fled from pharaoh and went to the land of Midian, stopping at a spring.

This story of Moses functions much like the story in Luke 2: 41–52 of Jesus in the temple as a twelve-year-old boy. Jesus is found among the learned teachers, listening to and questioning them. The brief tale epitomizes Jesus' growth 'in wisdom and years and he was well thought of by God and men.' Both these stories in the Bible are predictive of their heroes' later stature and epitomize their central role in the narrative. At the same time, both are used as a bridge between the hero's childhood and his role as an adult. In Exodus, Moses is cast in his later role of saviour of the Israelites. The narrative's polarizing contrast is between the saviour's role that Moses plays and the image of the Israelites as feckless and protesting grumblers. This marks the role of these two scenes as two interpretive poles of the Exodus and wilderness stories to come. One cannot miss the prophecy implicit in the sarcasm of the Hebrew bully in scene two: 'Who has set you up to be master and judge over us?' Indeed, the audience is invited to ask, who? The question throws us ironically forward into the narrative of Exodus 18, where it is Yahweh who makes Moses 'master and judge' over Israel. It also introduces us to the beginning of the story of Moses as saviour of Israel, a story that opens once Moses moves out to the wilderness: at the burning bush on the mountain of God. The Hebrew's question to Moses introduces the audience to one of the central leitmotifs of the stories about Israel's murmuring in the wilderness: 'Who are you?' It is not only a question asked of Moses by the Israelites. This is also Moses' question of Yahweh at the burning bush: 'Who are you?' The question about who God is dominates the heart of the Pentateuch. The function of the bridge narrative of the Moses murder scene builds up and creates a discussion between the many originally independent stories that are tied together here. The story of Israel's birth as a people, and its role as the chosen people of God, as Yahweh's first-born and heir, begins when Moses enters the wilderness. It continues through the Pentateuch until Moses addresses the people in the farewell speeches that create the Book of Deuteronomy. The bridge narrative of Moses as revolutionary saviour links this narrative chain with the epitomizing tales of Moses' birth and rescue. It presents us with one of the most popular roles of biblical legend.

We have stories about the birth of sons of God and of saviours already from early Sumerian and Akkadian texts, in the world's first epic stories of Gilgamesh and Enkidu. Such stories are still with us into Roman times.

The story of Alexander's birth was certainly the most popular of these in the Hellenistic period. The story told of Moses' birth is in the mould of the Oedipus story, which is certainly the fullest tale of this type. The Moses tale is probably closest to the tale of the birth of the king of Akkad, Sargon the Great. This legend is known in a number of variants from the early sixth century BCE:

Sargon, the mighty king, the king of Agade, am I. My mother was a high priestess. My father I knew not . . . My mother, the high priestess, conceived me; in secret she bore me. She set me in a basket of rushes; with bitumen she sealed my lid. She cast me into the river, which rose not over me. The river bore me up and took me to Akki, the drawer of water. Akki the drawer of water lifted me up as he dipped his ewer. Akki the drawer of water reared me as his son. Akki the drawer of water appointed me as his gardener. While I was a gardener, Ishtar granted me her love, and for four years I exercised kingship.

Much like Genesis' stories dealing with the mythical possibilities of blood, spirit, life and wisdom, legends about the birth of a son of God or of a saviour are remarkably common in the Bible. If one were to investigate the nature of biblical theology, this tale type offers an informative context for understanding the intellectual world that underlies it. To consider only the best-known of these stories, we find the pattern of this story already in Genesis 11: 29–30, when we are told that Sarah is barren. Although the divine promise to Abraham of many children – as many as the sands of the sea and the stars of the sky – stands at the very source of our plot-line, Sarah cannot have children. This motif of barrenness intensifies by chapter 18 when Abraham has reached ninety-nine years old. Then, in reward for hospitality, Yahweh, in the disguise of a traveller, promises the pious couple a child when he returns in the spring. The story takes full advantage of the humour of such a statement given by a stranger, as the narrator has Sarah pun predictively in her 'laughter'.[1] In chapter 21 we learn that the child is finally born when Abraham is a hundred years old. We read in verse 1: 'Yahweh visited Sarah as he said he would, and he did to her what he had promised and she became pregnant, and she bore Abraham a son in his old age.'

We need to ask: what is it about Isaac that is like God, through which God's presence is shown? Genesis 21: 6 gives a very nuanced rendition of the play on Isaac's name: 'laughter'. 'Sarah said: "God has created laughter for me; everyone who hears will laugh over me." ' Laughter is divine. Yet it is in the Book of Jubilees' story of Isaac's birth that his divine paternity is most convincing. In chapter 14, Yahweh appears to Abraham in a dream

---

[1] The Hebrew verb for 'she laughed' is *titzchaq*, a pun on the name Isaac (in Hebrew, *yitzchaq*).

and announces that he will have a child. Jubilees lays stress on Abraham's (not Sarah's) inability to have children with the purpose of emphasizing all the more Isaac's divine paternity. Similarly in Jubilees 16, when Sarah is waiting for the child, the first quickening of the child and the counting of the months are emphasized.

> And we told her the name of her son Isaac – just as his name was ordained and written in the heavenly tablets – and [that] when we returned to her at a specific time she would have conceived a son ... And in the middle of the sixth month the Lord visited Sarah and did for her as he had said. And she conceived and she bore a son in the third month in the middle of the month [precisely nine months later!] in the time when Yahweh told Abraham.

That Yahweh creates life and gives fertility to the patriarch's wives, that it is by Yahweh that the wives are impregnated, is also clear in the story of the Leah–Rachel conflicts of Genesis 29 and 30. In chapter 29: 31, as Jacob no longer wishes to make love to Leah (just prior to Leah's giving birth to four sons by Yahweh), we are told: 'When Yahweh saw that Leah was ignored, he opened her womb' – that is, impregnated her. When Reuben is born to her, Leah hopes that 'perhaps now my man will make love to me again.' And also, as the story closes (Gen. 30: 22), the narrator tells us: 'God didn't forget Rachel; he heard her and opened her womb, that she became pregnant ...'

5 Samson as son of God and Nazirite

A number of other theological roles related to the metaphor of the son of God intrude themselves strongly and create considerable variety and flexibility in these narratives. Particularly important are those of prophet, Nazirite and messiah. One story stands out for its strong exploitation of the humorous potential of the birth story's plot-line. In the story of Samson's birth that is found in Judges 13, the narrative takes full advantage of the massive human confusion that comes into play whenever gods impregnate women. We saw this comic motif already in the Abraham and Sarah story of Genesis 18: 12. Behind Sarah's laughter at the thought of her and her old man 'having fun again', lay the hidden prophecy of the divine stranger's promise.

Matthew's gospel takes up the theme briefly, but only in a serious manner: in order to present the husband Joseph in the favourable light of trusting piety.[1] Luke's episodes of the conceptions of John and Jesus both introduce this comic motif. Variants of Sarah's question are voiced by both Zechariah and Mary: 'How can I know this as I am an old man and my

---

[1] See Matthew 1: 18–19. Contrast Luke 1: 18–23.

wife an old woman, advanced in years?' and 'How can this be, since I have never been with a man?' The stock nature of the material becomes quite clear when Zechariah's question is rebuked as doubt in order to draw the moral that nothing is impossible for God. Mary's answer is used to offer the opportunity of describing Mary's impregnation by the divine spirit and to make the argument that 'therefore the child will be called the son of God.'

In the Samson story, the comic potential of this motif dominates. The story of Samson's birth begins with the introduction of Manoah's wife in the same manner that Genesis 11 had introduced Sarah: as a childless woman who was barren. 'The Messenger of Yahweh looked at the woman and said to her: "You are barren and do not bear a child; now you will be pregnant and bear a son." ' The divine messenger here is much like the same figure of Genesis 16, whom Hagar called 'the God who sees'.

The divine speech of Genesis is highly reminiscent of traditional story patterns. One can hardly miss the mildly erotic overtones implicit in Yahweh's messenger 'looking at' the woman. All women who get 'looked at' by gods in the Old Testament become pregnant. Notice also the emphasis of the angel's speech: the impossible becomes possible. She who cannot bear a child will bear a child. This is Sarah's miracle; it is Hannah's and it is Elizabeth's; it is Mary's. It is the mark of the divine in this world. For God, everything is possible; especially the impossible.

In the opening chapter of the Samson story, this kind of joke grows to dominate the whole of the narration about Samson as son of God. Samson is a giant, like those born of the sons of God in Genesis 6, and Samson has divine strength. The story is a comic adventure of this figure of folklore, vigorously drawing on the amusement that the husband's ignorance of divine intervention allows.

After Yahweh's messenger visited Manoah's wife, 'the woman went to her husband and said: a man of God came to me. He looked like a divine messenger: terribly frightful! I didn't ask him where he was from; nor did he tell me his name. He told me, "You are pregnant, and you will bear a son . . ." ' (Judges 13: 6–7). The scene needs to be imagined dramatically. In the interpretation of Manoah's wife here, she recounts the previous third-person narrative about her encounter with the divine visitor. At the same time, her interpretation casts the encounter itself in the light of her own perspective. 'I didn't ask him where he was from; nor did he tell me his name.' Told this way, the wonder story distances itself, as the audience hears of the meeting from her human perspective. The implications of the woman's ambiguous 'a man of God' are exposed through her contrasting doubts about a 'divine messenger'. What did the husband hear? A man who his wife thought 'was like a messenger of God' visited her, and from this meeting she is expecting a child. Only the fact that the narrator's audience was also at the scene protects Manoah from a cuckold's horns.

Theologically, the narrative is hardly pious. It plays dangerously with both people's understanding and their evocations of the divine. The woman's description of her visitor, 'divine and frightful' – is this a supplement to the narrative or her woman's commentary? Would our interpretation be different if it were one or the other? Does our narrator imply that the difference between cuckoldry and divine blessing is precisely interpretation?

The story lays stress on this perspective in the next scene, where Manoah prays to Yahweh to send the 'man of God' back once again. Manoah's absence is offered in evidence that his wife's impregnation was indeed divine. 'Therefore, God's Yahweh visited the woman once more, when she was in the field and her husband Manoah was not with her.' The woman is again portrayed as naive. 'She hurried hence to tell her husband of it.' What she says to her husband is important. 'The man who came to me the other day has visited me once again.' Her husband follows his wife to meet the man. Manoah, who never interprets anything in this story, now chooses his words carefully: 'Are you the man who talked to the woman?' His politeness is such that he does not even speak of her as his wife! This politeness and clarity sets the tone for what follows. When the man admits that he was the one, Manoah leaves all unnecessary elements out in his request for assurances. '*When your word comes, what will the boy's family be and what is to be his destiny?*'[1]

The next scene introduces the well-known motif of trying to learn a deity's name. Themselves already an implicit answer to his questions, Manoah's words bear literary allusions regarding the boy, which yield a surprisingly rich reward from Manoah's role as our story's dumbling. The euphemism of 'talking with the woman' now presents us with its implication in the 'word' that is to be made flesh in the child Samson. This motif, echoing Genesis 1: 3's creative word, is picked up by the prologue to John's gospel (John 1: 14), where it is applied within a comparable context to Jesus. Samson's family, of course, is known to John's audience. He is one of the sons of God. This question about the boy's family and therefore about his destiny is an important one within the plot of the greater story. It leads to the angel repeating the requirements of the Nazirite. It is upon obedience to these that Samson's destiny depends.

These are two quite different nuances in the story's opening. The divine engagement in the plot opens the story to the stock motifs of the larger tradition about sons of God. There is also the comic perspective of the implicit author. This is again clearly obvious when the divine messenger first gives the woman instructions concerning Samson's role as a Nazirite 'from his mother's womb': 'Take care to drink neither wine nor beer, and

---

[1] The normal translation of this in most English Bibles is obscure. Few translate this plain meaning of the Hebrew.

don't eat anything that is unclean, for you are pregnant and shall bear a son. A razor must never be used on his head; for the child shall be God's Nazirite from his mother's womb.' There is much in this divine speech that allows the story to play with nonsense. The sense of the instruction to the woman seems to be that she should comport herself like a Nazirite in her son's stead. He will be a Nazirite even before he is born: 'from his mother's womb'.[1] Only the traditional pattern in our narrative's motifs could bring the instruction about the razor and the woman's pregnancy together. Yet, given that these elements of the tradition do come together here, the compiler of our text doesn't hesitate to use their incongruence to comic effect.

When the woman tells her husband in verse 7 that the 'man of God' has told her that she is with child and shall bear a son, and again when the angel repeats the Nazirite instructions to Manoah, variations of the instructions are given. While Samson, as scourge of the Philistines, fills out the heroic role of saviour much as Saul and David do in their turn, he is something quite different from what one might normally understand as a Nazirite. No Samuel or John the Baptist this man! It is in the context of such a contrast with the expected that the story builds its playful motif of Samson's magic hair. The concentration on this 'hippy-motif' draws us away from the theophany. It brings us to concentrate on the central leitmotif of the Samson story: his hair. For all of the Samson story's comic relief, its theme is tragic. He is a Nazirite from his mother's womb to his death. He must not cut his hair! His hair is his Achilles' heel. Of course, the instruction concerning the razor could not be left out. This is the one divine commandment, the obedience or disobedience to which determines Samson's fate in the story. His magic hair, the narrative basis for seeing him as a Nazirite, gives him a share in the divine spirit. That is his strength. The function of the Nazirite is just as it is expressed with John in Luke's gospel. He is filled with the holy spirit from his mother's womb. Likewise in Judges, Samson's strength is a function of the divine spirit.

In chapter 14, at the Timnah vineyard, a lion attacks Samson. 'Yahweh's spirit took him and he ripped the lion in two with his bare hands as if it were a kid.' Of course, it is unnecessary to accept the bravado of the author's implicit assertion concerning how easy it might be to tear a kid in two. What is clear is that Yahweh's spirit lies behind Samson's heroic strength. Again, when the Philistines have extorted the answer to Samson's riddle about the lion and the honey by threatening his wife, 'Yahweh's

---

[1] This reading is confirmed by the variant episode in the story of Elizabeth's pregnancy in Luke 1: 14–15, where we find this motif of the Samson story cited as the angel's prediction that John (described as a Nazirite) will be filled with the Holy Spirit 'from his mother's womb'. This prophecy is dramatically fulfilled in the marvellous aetiology of a baby's first quickening, when Elizabeth goes to meet the pregnant Mary in Luke 1: 41.

spirit grabbed him and he went down to Ashqelon where he killed thirty men of the town.' This 'big bow-wow' motif comes up again in chapter 15, where in yet another battle with the Philistines, Yahweh's spirit grabs him and he kills a thousand with the jawbone of an ass. With the story's closure in chapter 16, the motifs of the Nazirite, of Samson's strength through Yahweh's spirit, and of his uncut hair all come together.

The story's understanding of Samson in the ascetic role of a Nazirite is very limited, and even amusing. Far from an ascetic, monk-like Nazirite, Samson is a lover of women and a brawler among men. Of all the biblical stories involving the figure of the Nazirite, it is Luke's John the Baptist who is the best-known of any who play this role, even though Luke does not use the title itself for John. In fact, it appears that few of our stories understand much about what a Nazirite was in history, though they obviously refer to it. According to the Book of Numbers a Nazirite's oath was a promise that could be made by both men and women, a pledge to withdraw from one's normal life for a limited time. This separation from ordinary society was marked by not cutting one's hair or drinking alcohol. The references to Nazirites in the Bible's stories, however, are full of fantasy and hardly refer to any social reality. One story does not even understand the Nazirite as an ascetic. In Matthew 2: 23 the motif is used as a minor joke. When Jesus' family returns from Egypt, they settle in the town of Nazareth because of the 'prophecy' that he should be called a Nazirite. Apart from the fact that no such prophecy is known, other biblical narratives are generally not much better at dealing with this role. It is apparently only known from literature. This is no more clear than in the story of Samuel, where the young Samuel fills out the role of the Nazirite. As in the Samson story, the child Samuel is given in an oath by his parents as a Nazirite to God. Accordingly, Samuel grows up in the temple, where he waits, like John in the desert, for Yahweh's call. However, as John the Baptist does not drink wine or beer because he is filled with the holy spirit 'from his mother's womb', so too it is Samuel's mother (I Samuel 1: 15) who declares to the priest Eli that she has not drunken wine or beer – and therefore is not drunk. Rather she is filled with the spirit (the implied pun belongs to the text!), and thus she becomes impregnated! Rather than a reference to social realities of ancient Palestine, the Nazirite motif is one of the Bible's many saviour motifs that is closely tied to the son of God motif.

6 *The classic forms of the tale type: Moses, Samuel, John and Jesus*

There is a much greater use of the son of God motif in the stories and songs of the Bible than we can discuss. There are also many more variants of it in which the divine is described as being present, and as affecting the world, than this one mythological figure. Yet the wide range of such stories makes it very useful to bring out the interests and purposes the stories have served. In this section, we look at four miraculous birth stories. Together they portray the basic motifs of the mythology. They portray metaphorically the presence of God in a role that is both positive and necessary.

a) *Exodus 1–2.* Unlike most of the narratives of our discussion, the Pentateuch's tale of Moses does not develop the role of son of God in favour of the very human figure of Moses. Only very briefly, in one of the many variants of this narrative that occur in the books of Exodus, Numbers and Deuteronomy, does Moses become God for Israel. Such a metaphor of the divine is attached to Moses only once, in a quite elegant aetiology of the role of the prophet. Moses is described as one who is unable to speak properly. He is told by Yahweh that Moses will be God for Aaron and that Aaron will be Moses' prophet (Exodus 4: 16). Moses plays a whole complex of roles: prophet, judge and saviour. It is in the story of the golden calf of Exodus 32, however, that this plot theme of Moses as God for Aaron is played out. The story has been put together from three quite distinct, variant responses to the golden calf. In Exodus 32: 1–14, Yahweh becomes angry over the making of the golden calf and decides to destroy the people. Moses plays the role of talking Yahweh out of his anger. The episode closes with the narrator's comment: 'And so, Yahweh regretted the evil which he had intended to do to his people.' The second part of this story immediately follows (32: 15–29). It is Moses who now plays the angry role. His anger is played out instead of Yahweh's, as Moses speaks the words of condemnation to kill those who 'do not stand in Yahweh's path'. In the story's third part, Moses goes up the mountain to Yahweh with the hope of obtaining *redemption* for the people's sin. Why this particular word 'redemption' is used is at first puzzling. It can be clarified if we pay attention to what Moses actually does. When he first speaks to Yahweh, he tells Yahweh what the people have done and asks Yahweh to 'forgive' them. But then Moses takes on himself the role of redeeming saviour for the people's sin: 'But if not, then erase me from the book you have made.' Yahweh refuses this role of redeemer to Moses. Citing a first principle of justice, Yahweh argues that those who have sinned against him will be the ones erased. Accordingly, the third variant closes with Yahweh sending a plague against the people.

Although Exodus has little hesitation in dealing with Moses in a divine role, there are, nevertheless, good reasons that the specific role of son of God is not given to Moses and does not play a role in the tale of his birth. In the narrative tradition of the Pentateuch as a whole, Yahweh plays this role, while Moses plays more the role of his prophet. It is with Yahweh of the Pentateuch that we find the closest integration of the metaphor of the son of God with its function expressing divine presence in the world. The essence and meaning of Yahweh in Exodus, and his function within the related stories, is as the representation or revelation of God to and for Israel. As we have seen in Exodus 3: 12, when Moses is asking the God of the burning bush who he is, God answers by making a sound pun on the name Yahweh: *ehyeh imak* which in English means 'I am with you'. Yahweh is the divine presence for Moses and for Israel. This distinction between God and Yahweh is consistent throughout these stories. Yahweh is God's name, God's presence on earth, not God himself. It is the perspective of the Old Testament that Yahweh was the means by which old Israel knew God. In the closure of the Pentateuch, at the end of Moses' life, when Moses looks back at the entirety of his narrative and epitomizes it with the song we find in Deuteronomy 32, it is as 'angel' or son of God, that is as representative of the divine for Israel, that Yahweh is described.

Perhaps of even greater importance in the plot development of the Moses story is that Israel as a people takes on the metaphor of divine son. Israel is Yahweh's 'first-born son' (Exodus 4: 22–23), and the murderous contest between Yahweh and the pharaoh that marks the plot of the plague and wonder narratives, is a struggle over Yahweh's and the pharaoh's first-born. Theologically, Israel's role as son of God is understood as the principal means by which God is immanent in the world.

Although the motif of son of God is not used, the birth of the saviour story chain of narrative, which opens the Moses story, marks the Book of Exodus' first two chapters as belonging to the same intellectual and literary context as other son of God birth stories. The story itself is tightly structured and highly traditional. As I have mentioned, comparable examples have been found throughout ancient Near Eastern and Hellenistic literature. The birth story comes within the context of Israel's enslavement. The Israelites have become more numerous than the Egyptians (Exodus 1: 9). To deal with the threat they pose to the Egyptians, the pharaoh recommends that 'we deal wisely with them to prevent them from growing yet greater'. This motif of 'dealing wisely' places the pharaoh in the ironic role of a would-be wise man. Everything he does therefore causes the Israelites to increase even so. He forces them into slave labour. But the more they are enslaved, the more they increase. He then instructs the midwives to kill all the male children born among the Hebrew. But the midwives 'fear God', and this leads to the Israelites becoming a yet greater people. Finally, the pharaoh makes his third attempt: 'Every boy child will be thrown into the Nile.' Moses, however, lives. This leads to the pharaoh's greatest fear: that the Israelites will escape from the land. When Moses is born, his mother hides him in a basket and sets it adrift on the Nile. He is found by the pharaoh's daughter and becomes her son. The story doesn't end here but extends itself ironically into two further scenes. After Moses is grown and kills the Egyptian who was beating a Hebrew, the pharaoh seeks to kill Moses, forcing him to flee Egypt. Later, among the variants of stories in which

Yahweh sends Moses back to Egypt to confront the pharaoh in a contest which is to end in the death of the pharaoh's own first-born son, one variant (Exodus 4: 19) has Yahweh tell Moses that 'all those who had sought to kill you are now dead.' Moses returns to demonstrate Yahweh's presence in Egypt.

b) *Matthew 1–2*. In the first chapters of Matthew's gospel we find a double story told about Jesus. This gospel offers a son of God birth story and then follows it up with a variant of this tale type. The miraculous birth story begins with the clarification that the child's mother was engaged to be married. However, 'before they had come together, she became pregnant by the holy spirit.' When the 'messenger of the lord' explains to Joseph why his bride is pregnant, he instructs Joseph: 'Give him the name Jesus, for he will save them for their sins.'[1] Here we have a good contrasting variant on the Moses story. Matthew cites the Greek form of Isaiah 7: 14 as if the announcement of a child to be born were in the future tense, obviously interpreting it as a prophecy. The motif of miraculous birth that belongs to this story type is emphasized in the choice of the word 'virgin': 'A virgin *will* become pregnant and give birth to a son and you will name him Immanuel, which means, "God with us".' Matthew is engaged in complicated interpretation and discussion of the tradition. With the 'translation' of the word Immanuel for his audience by reference to Yahweh's explanation of Exodus 3: 12's 'I am [God] with you,' Matthew links Exodus to the Isaiah passage and both to the aetiology of Jesus, as one who saves the people from their sins. The role of Jesus in this gospel will be that of an Immanuel who is not only God with us, but will represent God, in the manner of Moses and Joshua before him, as saving people: not from Egypt nor from the Canaanites, but this time from their sins. The scene closes with a doubling of the assurance that it was God who had impregnated the girl: 'He [Joseph] did not lie with her until she had given birth to her son.'

The continuation of the birth story in Matthew's second chapter presents a thematic variant of the Moses saviour story. In the context of the story of the three wise men who come to give honour to a new king, old King Herod plays the role of Moses' pharaoh and orders all the male babies to be killed. After being warned in a dream, Joseph escapes *to Egypt* with the child and his mother. After Herod dies, Joseph has another dream. They can return because – and here we have a near verbatim quotation from the Moses story – 'those who had sought the child's life are dead.' While there is no question that Matthew is well aware of the stories of 'sons of God' in the Old Testament, he is not offering a new interpretation of them. Although it is clear that Matthew knows and shares much of the tradition with Moses, he does not refer to it in any way as

[1] 'Jesus' is clearly a cue-name. It is the Greek form of the name Joshua, which translated, means 'saviour'.

belonging to his narrative's past. Nor does he offer a contrast between the Moses of old and the Jesus of the future. Rather, Moses and Jesus play the same metaphorical roles. They both give literary portrayals of divine salvation. The story in Matthew centres itself no more in a Jesus of the author's past than the Exodus story centred itself in a Moses of his past. Both present theologically motivated fictions, using a common birth-story structure and the Immanuel motif to evoke the traditional understanding of divine immanence.

c) *I Samuel 1–2.* The story of Samuel's birth begins with a motif common also to the Jacob story's contest between Leah and Rachel. Elkanah had two wives. Peninnah had many children, Hannah none. As Jacob had loved the childless Rachel, Elkanah loved the similarly barren Hannah. The story opens with Hannah's personal, internal conflict. Her rival mocks and humiliates her, and her husband is distressed that his love is not enough for her. In her distress she cries bitterly and prays to Yahweh at the annual feast in the temple at Shiloh. As she prays silently, her lips moving but her voice unheard, the priest Eli thinks her drunk, rebukes her, and orders her to put the wine away. She tells him that she has 'drunk neither wine nor strong drink', but has prayed out of distress. Eli prays that her petition will be heard, and she returns home. There, her husband has intercourse with her and 'Yahweh remembers her.' And so she becomes pregnant and in due time bears a son. After the child is weaned, she returns to the temple and dedicates the child to the temple, where the child is to grow up.

The story fits well into the miraculous birth stories we have seen. The story's vocabulary itself fits it to this context: her prayerful 'spirit' her Nazirite-like abstinence from wine and strong drink, her becoming pregnant because Yahweh has remembered her and the dedication of the child to God all mark the story strongly. With the story's emphasis on the virtuous parents and the piety of the childless wife, the tale reads well as one of virtue rewarded. The theme of selfless piety is all the stronger in the woman's return to the temple and in her decision to give her son back to Yahweh.

But far more than the details of the birth, the mythological song of fertility that Hannah sings as she dedicates her child to the temple epitomizes the birth of the child and interprets it as a story of the messiah. This song introduces the theme of Yahweh's messiah as the leitmotif of the books of Samuel. In these opening chapters, a chain of narrative begins that leads from Samuel to Saul to David. It centres on the choice of David as Yahweh's messiah. This is the one who will carry out Yahweh's will for Israel. He is also a mythological figure, who fights Yahweh's wars and establishes his power cosmically. It is to this purpose that Hannah's song is sung, recurrently echoing the messianic Psalm 132. Hannah's reinterpretation of Psalm 132, to fit the context of her story of natural barrenness and

God-given fertility, enhances the song's celebration of messianic potency. The theme of salvation, of the hungry being fed, the rich overturned, the poor made rich – these pious praises are ubiquitous themes of the Psalms, referring to the messiah. Theologically central is the praise of Yahweh's cosmic power that belongs to the figure of David. Hannah's song opens in a celebration of the joy of her own sexual fertility and closes with the royal celebration of potency and salvation in David's rise. Hannah paraphrases the erotic phallic imagery of Psalm 132 where Yahweh declaims: 'I will make a horn grow for David; prepare a light for my messiah; I will cover his enemies in shame, but his crown will glow.' Hannah's song begins: 'My heart rejoices in Yahweh; for Yahweh has raised my horn.' (*Sic*!) Here Hannah claims this potency on her son's behalf. It is Samuel's story that leads to David's rise as a metaphorical illustration of divine potency. 'Yahweh will judge the ends of the earth; he will give his king strength and raise his messiah's horn.'

d) *Luke 1–2*. The double story of the miraculous births of John and Jesus, which Luke's gospel recounts, is by far the most complex of this type of narrative in the Bible. The central story is found in chapter 1 and centres in John's birth and the expectation of Jesus'. This is followed by three lightly attached closing stories that deal with Jesus' birth, his dedication at the temple, and Jesus teaching there as a young boy. Only the first two stories need concern us here.

The story opens with a scene that belongs to the side of tradition, with stories like those of Isaac and Samuel's birth. There was the priest Zachariah and his wife Elizabeth. They were pious and without fault in living by the *torah*. But they were childless: Elizabeth was barren and both were very old. One day, an angel visits Zachariah in the temple. Zachariah is startled and frightened. The angel tells him not to be afraid, as his prayer has been heard. His wife will bear a son. The child's name is John. As in all of our stories where this motif of naming the child occurs, John's is a cue-name, identifying the child. John is the 'gift of God'. That the naming of the child presents John as a son of God, as in the tradition, is clear from the following instruction and prophecy. The child must not drink wine or beer – that is, he will fulfil the Nazirite role – and he will be filled with the divine spirit from his mother's womb. He will have the spirit of Elijah and create a people prepared. This predicts the scenes of chapter 3 where John is given the role of prophet preaching repentance. Zachariah then echoes Sarah's astonishment: 'How can I know this to be true: I am an old man and my wife is up in years?' In a classical folktale manoeuvre to delay the plot with a test, the angel hears only the doubt and takes offence. 'I am Gabriel, who stands before God's face!' And then he punishes Zachariah by making him dumb until the time all that he has said comes true. Zachariah's inability to talk or tell anyone of his vision plays a function in the plot. Zachariah and the story's audience understand, but no one else does. This is to emphasize the even greater wonder that is expressed through Elizabeth's understanding that the child is God's.

The next lines are filled with the son of God tradition: 'From that time, Elizabeth his wife was pregnant. For five months, she hid herself saying, "So has the lord done to me, when he looked at me in order to take away my reproach among men." ' This motif of Elizabeth's understanding of her child as God's son is capped at the child's birth. Zachariah is still unable to speak and has not yet communicated anything of his vision. Yet, when Elizabeth is asked what the child's name is to be, she names him John; that is, 'gift of God'. When Zachariah confirms this by writing John's name on a tablet, the angel's second prediction is confirmed and Zachariah regains his speech.

The first prediction is equally weighted by the tradition. When Elizabeth is in her sixth month of pregnancy, this same angel Gabriel visits her cousin in Nazareth. Her name is Mary and she is a virgin engaged to be married. The angel comes to her and says: 'The Lord is with you, you who have been given his grace.' The poor girl doesn't understand, thinking only that this is an odd greeting, so the angel explains what he means by declaring the child a son of God and messiah: 'Don't be afraid, for you have found grace with God. You will become pregnant and give birth to a son whom you will call Jesus.'[1] Like Yahweh of Deuteronomy 32, the child will be called the 'son of the most high'. The 'lord God will give him his father David's throne.' A second time the girl fails to understand: 'How can this happen; I have never been together with a man?' Now the angel gives his message for this third time with unmistakable and graphic clarity: 'The holy spirit will come over you and the power of the most high will cover you. For this reason, the child born will be called holy, a son of God.' The scene closes with Gabriel giving the girl proof that the impossible has been possible for God. Her barren cousin is now in her sixth month. This invites Mary to the story's next scene when she goes to visit Elizabeth. As soon as Elizabeth hears Mary's greeting, her baby jumps in her womb and she 'became full of the holy spirit'. The use of the same wording as for Mary's impregnation is important. It fulfils the angel's prediction to Zachariah that the child will be full of the holy spirit from his mother's womb. Again, Elizabeth, without having been told anything by either Zachariah or Mary, understands both that Mary is pregnant and the identity of the child she herself bears.

Mary now sings her song. In the very next scene, when Zachariah regains his voice at John's birth, he sings its matching pair. Together, these two songs recast the central themes of Hannah's song. They interpret that song within the traditional theme of messianic response to the poor, and make it the centre of the Jesus birth story.

---

[1] Here too, the name Jesus is a cue-name, signifying 'saviour'.

Luke's well-known scene of Jesus' birth is found in the second chapter. Dramatically, it is quite sentimental, but like the previous scenes it is carried off with considerable ability. A census calls Joseph and his family to Bethlehem to mark again that this son of God is David's successor. There Mary gives birth in an animal shed because there was no room for them at the inn. This is told very simply, without any motif of rejection or exclusion by the good people of Bethlehem. Luke's point here is not one of class. It is rather a romantic and pious celebration of poverty. This messiah will fulfil Luke's proverb of chapter 6: 20: 'Blessed are you who are poor; for God's kingdom is yours.' An angel announces the birth of a saviour in the city of David. He is messiah and lord. 'With the angel there came immediately a heavenly army singing praise to God and declaring peace to men.' These poor shepherds then become Luke's first witnesses.[1]

---

[1] The theme of eye-witness is an important theme of Luke's narration, with which he opens his gospel.

CHAPTER 14

The Bible's theological world III:
Israel as God's son

1 Divine presence and the son of God

While the son of God motif appears in so many legends and tales of the
Old Testament in the form of the quite commonplace ancient Near
Eastern tale type of a 'birth of the son of God', or – as in the Moses story –
the birth of a saviour, it everywhere is used to present the hero of these
stories as, in one way or the other, making God present to Israel. This
presence of God betrays a wide spectrum of theological thought. Often the
hero stands far from the good. Cain is a murderer. In some stories, the
divine presence does little more than express the heroic, supernatural,
strength or invincibility, as in the story of Samson, which is so reflective of
Homer's story of Achilles or even Gilgamesh's role as the son of a goddess.
As a theological motif, reflecting the divine presence, no role is more
central in the Bible than the role that Yahweh is given in the song of Moses
that is sung from Mount Nebo in Deuteronomy 32: 8. The poem
illustrates the understanding of God the Most High reiterated in the Book
of Daniel (for example 4: 22, 29). He creates the world and proportions its
rule to whom he wants. In Moses' song the Most High distributes the
nations among the sons of God. It is Yahweh who, as one of God's sons,
receives Israel as his inheritance. Not only does Yahweh himself take up
the role of son of God here, but in Exodus 3: 12, when Yahweh meets his
son Israel, to choose Israel for himself, he explains to Moses this role. He is
ehyeh imak, God for Israel. He is God's presence in Israel. He is God as
Israel knows him. It is this Immanuel role that is given to every
manifestation of the sons of God in the Bible. That angels of God and sons
of God are commonly interchangeable in the Bible's songs and stories is
based on the function of angels and messengers of the divine: they reflect
God's presence. So the messenger of Yahweh who is a watcher over Israel
in Exodus 23 can also take the form of a pillar of fire to mark God's

presence in the tent of meeting. He can be a cloud-pillar in the flight from Egypt to hide the escaping Israel from the Egyptians. God's messenger can be the arrow of plague that visits disaster on Israel or its enemies, or the king of Assyria or Babylon who carries out God's will against Israel.

It is this theme of divine presence in human affairs, and not something that describes the virtue of any of the children in the stories, that dominates all the son of God stories. The problematic character of this divine presence – for good or evil – lies just below the surface of the best of these stories. Especially in the prophets, as we will see, this motif turns truly ominous for Israel.

This is no less true of the parallel stories in the New Testament, whether of John the Baptist or of Jesus. In John 7: 40–43, there is a brief description of 'the people' as students and philosophers asking whether Jesus as the messiah could be the ruler of Israel who is mentioned in the prophecies of Micah (5: 1–3): 'With a rod they strike the cheek of the ruler of Israel. You, O Bethlehem, Ephrathah, who is the least of Judah's clans, from you will come one who will be ruler in Israel, one whose origin is from ancient times. He will abandon them [and here, Micah echoes Isaiah 7 and 8] until she who is in labour has given birth. Then the remnant of our brothers will return to the people of Israel.'

In the Jesus birth story in Matthew, the magi cite a close variant of this same discussion. This occurs after Matthew has quoted from the birth story of Isaiah 7. It is already clear that both Matthew's and Luke's birth stories offer significant contributions to the Bible's philosophical discussion about the interrelationship of the human and the divine. Certainly Matthew, with its interpretation of Isaiah's story through the more positive lenses of the mythological divine son of Isaiah 9, is in full agreement that such a figure is implied in Micah's ruler of Israel. Luke, on the other hand, has supported a much more wide-ranging discussion, which engages the larger theological context.

Whatever any specific tendency of each gospel might be, their understanding of the function of this cluster of motifs is so competent and clear that we are forced to doubt the assumption that these stories are presented in the gospels as apologetic arguments about Jesus as an historical person of the past who had a special and unique association with the divine that is different from other use of such themes and motifs in the Bible. Only an historicizing reading of the New Testament and a misinterpretation of the texts could allow such a conclusion. Matthew's and Luke's birth stories were not written as historical accounts; nor were they understood to have been so written. That much is clearly obvious from the great, well-known and fully accepted differences in the narrative plots of their stories. They never tried to tell anyone how an historical Jesus had been born. These New Testament stories are rather an intensified continuation of the Bible's discussion. They are to be understood from within the perspective of this same larger tradition.

Although Mark has no birth story, it makes a central and important contribution to the Bible's discussion of the son of God metaphor. The opening statement of Mark shows that such is the author's intention. It is the central theme of the gospel: 'The beginning of the gospel of Jesus Christ, son of God.' Mark understands his gospel as taking part in the Old Testament's discussion on the theme of divine presence. The very next verse justifies this strong opening with a quote from Exodus 23: 20: 'I send an angel before you. He shall protect you along the way and lead you.' In Exodus, this Yahweh's angel bore the meaning of Yahweh as 'God with' or 'for Israel' as in Exodus 3: 12. The Book of Malachi, which is a small collection of questions and answers about the tradition, cites this same line from Exodus 23 and expands it to answer the question: 'Where is the God of judgement?' The answer in Malachi 3: 1–5 is a deft interpretation of Exodus' two scenes. On one hand, it identifies the two metaphors of God's presence, as Yahweh and as his angel, and on the other it marks the contradiction central to the tradition of a longing for justice: this God of judgement, fully aware of the potential horror implicit in this human desire for perfection.

> I will send my angel before me to prepare my way, and Yahweh whom you are looking for will suddenly come to his temple. The angel of the covenant whom you delight in, he will come . . . but who can survive the day of his coming? Who can stand when he shows himself, like the fire of the refinery? and he will be present as a refiner and purifier of silver: and he will purify the sons of Levi, and purge them like gold and silver, that they might become an offering of righteousness to Yahweh. Then, the sacrifices of Judah and Jerusalem would be acceptable to Yahweh.

In uttering his metaphor about moral purity, Malachi draws heavily on an Isaiah-like irony about the human desire to seek the fulfilment of their desires in the divine, by asking for God's presence.

Mark enters this discussion about how God is with Israel in the same manner, bringing together the two theophanies of Exodus in his portrayal of Jesus and John. John echoes the role of Yahweh's angel. Also, other motifs are included. As in the opening chapters of Luke's gospel, Mark's John takes up many of the motifs associated with the son of God in the birth stories. He portrays a Nazirite, sketched with dramatic fantasy. John appears on stage in Mark's opening scene dressed in crude camel's-hair clothing tied with a leather strap. He lives off grasshoppers and wild honey, he brings salvation out of a desert's emptiness, he calls Israel to repentance and brings divine forgiveness. John's is Isaiah's lonely voice giving comfort in the desert of exile, as Mark places in his mouth a citation from one of the most serene of all the Bible's songs, and the one on which the entire book of Isaiah pivots: 'Comfort, be comforted my people, says your God; words to the heart, to Jerusalem; call out to her that the war is past, her sin forgiven.[1] Mark gives dramatic structure to Isaiah's song through his characterization of John: 'There is one who cries from the wilderness, prepare the way of the lord, make his way straight.' To Jesus, Mark gives Jahweh's role. John is the messenger preparing his way.

The strong image of the wild ascetic preacher from the desert, coupled with Mark's citation of Malachi and Isaiah, marks the desert as the proving ground for forgiveness. That Jesus immediately leaves John to go out to the desert to be tested by Satan and purified in the desert's fire allows this brief scene of Mark 1: 12–13 to function as a metaphorical journey of Jesus as everyman. It is the divine spirit that drives him out to the desert. There he lives like Israel in the temptations of Exodus' wilderness wandering, with God's angels caring for him. Mark is not everywhere committed to this role for Jesus. He also plays the roles of healer, of teacher of parables. He is master over demons, lord over storms and the sea, and he is the cosmic messiah of the end of time. Such roles are collected around Jesus from the poetic imagery of the psalms and the prophets. They illustrate the many hopes of the tradition that God's kingdom, like that of Isaiah's forgiven Jerusalem, might be realized out of a poet's evocations. It is the theme of purification as preparation for this 'kingdom' that is supported by Jesus' role as everyman's experience of 'purification' through suffering. Following Micah's lead, the Jesus of Mark's gospel plays a role interpreting Isaiah's son of God. Mark thereby identifies Isaiah's child with the suffering servant of the songs of Isaiah 42–53. Mark's story returns to this theme at the very end of Jesus' life when – to use the language of metaphor – Jesus makes final preparations to enter his kingdom.

The present closure of Mark's gospel calls up a scene from Psalm 110: 1, where the royal son of God who comes into his heavenly kingdom sits at Yahweh's right hand: 'Yahweh said to my lord, "sit down at my right hand and I will make your enemies into a footstool for your feet." ' The gospel presents the scene more sentimentally. Mark presents Jesus alone with God, and leaves out reference to the humiliation of the king's enemies. The scene as Mark 16: 19 presents it, gives us the triumph but lacks the motif of divine judgement that the opening of the gospel requires. This is all the more confusing, as Mark is not much given to excessive sentimentality. He usually treats his readers' feelings with considerable respect. One might also complain that the present closure of the gospel that we find in Mark 16: 9–20 is redundant. The gospel already knows this scene of Jesus' heavenly glory. It has been presented in the theophany

---

[1] Throughout, Mark, like Matthew, emphasizes Isaiah's theme of forgiveness of sin as the heart of the concept of salvation.

scene in chapter 9: 2–8, where Jesus was transformed into his 'true' and 'eternal' form as one who, together with Moses and Elijah, lives glorified in heaven. 'He changed before their eyes. His clothes shone white, whiter than anything on earth could bleach them. Elijah appeared together with Moses and they talked with Jesus . . .'

In this earlier scene Mark had opened a quite significant variant of the son of God theme. This is the old mythological motif about heroes who have come so close to the divine that they themselves become immortal. The motif goes back at least as early as the Gilgamesh story's heroes of the flood story: Utnapishtim and his wife. As a reward for their virtue, they become immortal and live undying in the 'land of far away'. In the much later Jewish tradition, there finally develops a tradition of at least ten such men of God, allowing heaven to have an eternal minyan for their prayers. In the Bible's stories we find Enoch, who in Genesis 5: 22 'walked with God' and so was no longer on earth. In II Kings 2, Elijah is taken up to heaven in a storm. In a work called the Testimony of Moses, an extra-biblical variant of the story of Moses in the Bible, Moses does not die but is taken up to heaven. This too is Jesus' destiny as foretold in Mark's transfiguration scene, which shows us this heavenly Jesus.

Scholars have long been convinced that the present closure of Mark's gospel has been added to the original work. We should better think of Mark 16: 8 (or perhaps 16: 9) as the original ending. Absent the sentimental scene of Jesus' enthronement, the closure of the gospel brings the death scene of Jesus on the cross to the centre of Mark's stage!

At the sixth hour, darkness fell over the whole of the earth until the ninth hour. At the ninth hour, Jesus called out with a loud shout: 'Eloi, Eloi, lama sabachtani' which means: 'My God, my God, why have you abandoned me?' Some of them, who stood there and heard this, said: 'Listen! He is calling Elijah.' Then one ran out and brought back a sponge with vinegar, and attached it to a stick to give him something to drink while saying: 'Let's see if Elijah comes to take him with him.' Jesus gave out a loud scream and let the spirit out. The temple's curtain tore in two, from top to bottom. When the centurion, who stood opposite him, saw that he died so, he said: 'Truly this man was a son of God!' (Mark 15: 33–39)

It is a powerful scene without any excess of commentary. In his despairing complaint at death, Jesus is presented by Mark as God's suffering servant. That Mark quotes the song of David from Psalm 22: 2–3 for Jesus' dying words calls up the similar scenes of David and Jesus in their despair on the Mount of Olives. The allusion seems intentional, as the larger context of the Psalm suggests and which Mark's Jesus echoes:

My God, my God, why have you abandoned me? You are so distant from my shout for help and from my scream. My God, I shout to you by day and you answer not; and I cry to you at night, but find no peace.

We should also recall to mind the songs of the suffering servant in Isaiah 42–53 and the story of King Ahaz of Isaiah 7. Both accept their destiny, refusing to question God. Also like David on the Mount of Olives, Jesus has not put God to the test. In his humility he has followed the path of righteousness. He has put his trust in God. He was scorned and despised by men. Mark recognizes well that Psalm 22 marks this childlike submission and dependency: 'It was you that helped me from my mother's womb and brought me safely to her breast. I was given over to you from my birth; you have been my God from my mother's womb.' In verse 12, and especially in verse 19, the psalm calls upon the theme of 'God with us'. 'But you Yahweh do not be absent; my strength, hurry to help; save my life from the sword . . .'

In Mark, those who misunderstand Jesus' cry of despair, thinking that his call to God: 'Eloi, Eloi . . .' had been in fact a call to Elijah, implicitly bring the transfiguration scene of Mark 9: 9–13 into play when Jesus meets Elijah and Moses in their shared roles of men who have overcome death. An implicit prophecy is hidden in their misunderstanding: the messiah is to be betrayed; he is to be abandoned even by God: a prelude to his heavenly role. This role of suffering servant is brought forward in the scene's citation from yet another song of David, Psalm 69: 22: 'They gave me poison to eat and vinegar to quench my thirst.' Another, similar echo, from Psalm 22: 1–2 is created with Jesus' scream at his death. Jesus, as humble servant of the tradition, calls on God to be with him. At this scream, the curtain of the temple that closes off the Holy of Holies, that separates God from man, tears in two, marking his death. God is with him!

This nearly bitter, mocking irony of Mark's gospel finds its climax in the understanding of the Roman centurion as he hears this cry of despair and death. 'Truly this man was a son of God.' This officer's commentary finds its counterpoint in the twice-repeated divine affirmation from Psalm 2: 7, 'This is my beloved son,'[1] which is quoted in the critical scenes of the gospel's opening and in the story of Jesus' transfiguration. Behind the centurion's remark lies the hidden, dark side of biblical tradition: God abandons his children. It is Jesus' cry of despair that brings conviction above all doubt. In Mark's gospel, Jesus plays out his role of son of God. Like Israel his first-born, like Samson, Samuel and Saul, like the prophets Elijah and Jonah, and like Job in his role in this tradition, this role

---

[1] That Mark adds the word 'beloved' may emphasize the association of Jesus' role with the Old Testament figure of David that can be seen in many places of this gospel, as the Hebrew name *dwd*, which lies at the origin of David's name, means 'beloved' and David is known as Yahweh's beloved.

mediates and gives voice to the common human ambivalence about the divine in our lives. One enters the kingdom only in death.

This theme of the ambivalence surrounding the presence of God in Israel dominates Mark's account of Jesus as a vehicle for this presence. Mark's usage self-consciously mirrors II Samuel's presentation of David in the role of Yahweh's Messiah – especially in II Samuel 15 in the story of David on the Mount of Olives, but also in the use of Psalm 18 in II Samuel 22 and throughout the Psalter, where David takes up the messianic role of warrior in Yahweh's cosmic war against the nations, as in Psalms 2, 8, 89 and 110. This role of David in the Psalms and books of Samuel is also the context for understanding how Mark uses his Jesus in the function of representative of the pious in prayer. Yet the dominant metaphor is not only far from any historicizing interests in an historical Jesus or David, it draws on the messianic mythology as well to focus on the theme of divine presence in Israel, and in the real lives of all who identify themselves as a new Israel. Israel's divine sonship is part of their self-understanding.

2 Israel as a son of God

In the first of the Bible's stories about a son of God, the Cain story at the beginning of Genesis, the plot hinges upon Cain's sacrificial offering which is unacceptable to Yahweh. 'Do what is right', Cain is told. 'That is sufficient to hold one's head high.' The story of Saul in I Samuel opens on a related, contrasting motif. We find Saul's tale in I Samuel 13. It is a story of a sacrifice forbidden. Saul offers it all the same, because he thinks it good to sacrifice to Yahweh before battle. For his disobedience, Saul is rebuked and rejected by Yahweh as his messiah. His kingship, which Yahweh had established eternally over Israel, is now revoked (I Samuel 13: 13–14)! Both Cain and Saul's story illustrates the *topos*: God wants obedience, not sacrifice.

In I Samuel 15, we find the story's mate, except that in this case the king is instructed to offer a sacrifice: the captured Amalekite king who had been 'dedicated to Yahweh'. Saul, however, plays out the role of a good soldier, and spares the king's life, the best of the cattle and all that was valuable (I Sam. 15: 9). He does what is good in his own eyes. Here too, the theme is that God will have obedience, and what Saul has done is evil in God's eyes. He regrets that he has made Saul king. Samuel, whose role in the story as son of God has been to be God's presence in Israel, himself sacrifices the Amalekite king to Yahweh. It is obedience, not sacrifice, that matters. The demand on Saul is the same: whether he sacrifices or does not sacrifice is not the issue: obedience, to do what *is good* in God's eyes, is what is demanded so that he, like Cain, may hold his head high. The philosophical principle that this brutal story illustrates is not one that a sensitive reader today can be comfortable with. It is governed by the tragic and ironic perspective of the creation story of Genesis 1: God created the world good in his own eyes. He then created humanity, which wishes the good as it sees it. What is good is good as God sees it. That is what makes it good. Saul's story is unrelenting biblical tragedy. In doing what he sees to be good, Saul does evil in God's eyes. The story ends with Saul's humiliation. When Samuel, the son of God, leaves him, the presence of God goes from Saul.

The theme of obedience and sacrifice is also central to the Abraham narrative chain. In Genesis 12–22, Abraham wanders from sacrifice to sacrifice, just as he wanders from story to story. Yahweh accepts his offerings. With each successive episode in which Abraham builds an altar and sacrifices to his God, Yahweh appears to him and promises this childless man a son. Immediately Abraham has his son, however, he is told by Yahweh that he will have his sacrifice. The story has the potential of being emotionally so objectionable that the audience is told at the outset that Yahweh is only testing Abraham (Gen. 22: 1). Abraham is told to sacrifice this 'only son, whom he loved' to test his obedience. As in the Saul story, the theme is that it is obedience, not sacrifice that matters. In this story's illustration, the contrast of Abraham with Cain and Saul could hardly be more marked. Abraham obeys. He does what is good in God's eyes, and holds his head high. In a sentimental though effective scene, Abraham's son asks on the way up Mount Moriah to the sacrifice: 'The fire and the wood is here, but where is the lamb for a burnt offering?' Abraham hesitates not a moment. He has the philosopher's confidence: 'God will provide' (Gen. 22: 8, 14). The story could as well be an illustration of the philosopher's goal in Psalm 24: 3–5: 'he who ascends the mountain of his God, who has clean hands and a pure heart . . . to him shall God provide his blessing; righteousness from the God of his salvation.' In Abraham's story, Yahweh redeems Isaac with a ram. On this mountain of God, God provides (22: 14)! That tradition places this as the site of Jerusalem's temple is itself a major commentary on the story's theme.

Genesis is held together in a narrative of a continuous chain of sons, beginning in chapter 5. Adam was made in God's image and likeness, male and female (5: 1–2). Adam becomes the father of a son and that same image passes to Seth, and so to the chain of humanity. This motif implicitly understands mankind within the son of God metaphor. As we are all made in our father's image, we are sons of God. This self-identifying chain of continuity, which embraces all humanity, is well understood by the gospel of Luke, which draws on this theology when it presents a genealogy for Jesus beginning with Joseph and tracing it back to the beginning: 'son of Enosh, son of Seth, son of Adam, son of God' (Luke 3: 38).

As Adam was the son of God, so are we all. This is implicit in the genealogical leitmotif of Genesis: a *toledoth* of God's sons. When

Abraham's younger son Isaac displaces the first-born Ishmael, to become Abraham's only son whom he loved, and again when Jacob takes the place of his older brother Esau, Israel fulfils Genesis' chain of narrative in the role of God's 'first-born'. Within the context of the pivotal story of Abraham's sacrifice in Genesis 22, this reiterated role of first-born awakens unsettling echoes of Israel's and the temple's future fate.

In Exodus, the role of Yahweh plays out a variant of Abraham's search for a son. This theme of Yahweh's search for a people and of Israel as first-born is first made explicit in the deadly contest between Yahweh and the pharaoh. It is, however, the pharaoh's first-born who dies as the angel of death 'passes-over' Yahweh's first-born.

These motifs of sacrifice and death of the first-born, as the motif of Israel as the son of God, present themselves in their greatest range of theological development in the prophets. This cluster of motifs recurs so often in the poetic narratives collected in the so-called prophetic books that it is well to speak of two further variants of this tale-type. In these stories, the role of the wives is used to illustrate Yahweh's relationship with Israel. In the first group of tales, the children do not function as sons of God, representing God's presence in a larger narrative. Their role as children of God itself directly expresses God's presence in Israel's destiny. In the second variation of this plot motif, not the sons but the wives and lovers themselves play out the primary role of illustrating Israel's destiny.

3 The role of Immanuel and the son of God

Through its irreverent mockery, the Samson story offers a deeply critical reflection on any over-zealous piety about the tradition's many stories of sons of God. Ironic humour is rarely far from any of our stories. Less humorous, and offering an even more trenchant critique of the pietism of divine immanence, are three dark and pessimistic closely related narrative blocks in Isaiah 7–9. They share the common motif of the birth of a child whose name is or is interpreted as Immanuel; that is as 'God with us'. Isaiah presents the stories as a challenge to popular piety's request that God be with Israel. 'Do you,' Isaiah implicitly asks, 'really want God with you?' Isaiah presents this small collection of variant poems and short tale segments, accompanied by interpretive comments and discussion, which play variations on the common theme of the prophet or God who has Israel for his wife. Reading these poems and stories today is much like listening to an intense discussion, with the participants all talking at the same time. Themes overlap. Points are made in variant contexts. Above all, implicit participants know more about what is going on than we do. In the structural centre of this collection of variants we have Isaiah's two children. Both children have cue-names, positive and negative. His first child, already born, is called *Shear-yashub* ('Repenting remnant': Isa. 7: 3). This is an obvious portent of promise. The song is sung about the new Jerusalem. Isaiah's second child is born to a prophetess. To this child Yahweh gives the unhappy name *Mahar-shalal-hash-baz* ('Quick-spoil-hurry-prey': Isa. 8: 1, 3). The narrative interprets this awful name for the reader: before the child is old enough to say 'mummy' and 'daddy', Damascus and Samaria will fall to Assyria. In three stories Isaiah offers us his variations on the biblical topos of Immanuel, which in the prophetic literature takes form in two kinds of parable: of the prophet and his children and of Yahweh and his wives. The Isaiah tradition generally follows the first type.

a) The ironic story that is found in Isaiah 7: 10–17 is both an instructive and important narrative among those that use the son of God metaphor. The story begins as Ahaz, king of Jerusalem, has been placed under strong military pressure by the kings of Damascus and Samaria. The story's opening shows him to be a virtuous king. He refuses to challenge Yahweh by asking for a sign, even as he is invited to do so by the deity, who tells him he might ask for any sign that he might wish. Implicit in Ahaz' refusal is the pious faith that seeking a sign implies a lack of faith in Yahweh.

In presenting Ahaz in this light, the narrative certainly evokes such moral proverbs as we find in Psalm 95: 8: 'Do not harden your heart as you did at Meribah, as when you were at Massah in the desert, when your fathers challenged me and put me to the test even though they had witnessed what I had done.' A contrasting text, however, found in Micah 3: 9–12 seems to be referred to directly, and offers a fitting context for Ahaz' virtue. The kings of Jerusalem are threatened here by Yahweh for testing his patience with their belief that as Yahweh was with them in Jerusalem, no harm could come to them. 'Because of you, Zion will be ploughed like a field; Jerusalem will become a heap of ruins.'

In spite of Ahaz' refusal to ask for a sign, Isaiah gives him one anyway. It is entirely negative and given with biting sarcasm:

> Here, House of David, isn't it enough that you try human patience? Do you have to try my God's patience as well? Yahweh will give you a sign! A girl is pregnant and will give birth to a son. She will name him Immanuel [i.e., 'God is with us']. He will live off yogurt and honey until he first understands how to avoid evil and choose good. For before the boy understands how to avoid evil and choose good the land, before whose two kings you now grovel, will be made into a desert. And over you and your people and over your father's house, Yahweh will send days that have not been seen since Ephraim broke away from Judah: the king of Assyria!

That we find here a story intimate with the son of God birth story traditions is clear from the language of the announcement of the child's birth, as well as from the clear reference to the Nazirite tradition. Even though the description of the impending birth does not tell us how the girl has become pregnant, the purposefulness of both of these strong elements in the account makes it impossible to read the text as if it were some historical account and such descriptions mere accidents of fact. These are classic markers of our tale-type. Finally, that the child is to be named Immanuel or 'God with us', with its unavoidable implication that the child also functions as this cue-name literarily requires, is convincing confirmation that the child functions as other sons of God do. They make God's presence manifest in the world. They are Immanuels. The closing commentary on the prophecy about both Samaria's and Damascus' destruction, and about the terrible times ahead for Jerusalem, is also hardly an external gloss. It points to the presence of God. It is this that the child's name declares present. The Assyrian king's destructive presence will be God for Jerusalem. This will occur before the child is grown. Such is Ahaz' unwonted sign.

That the reader is invited to interpret the story's parable in terms of Israel's future is explicit. Isaiah tells us: 'I and the children Yahweh has given me are signs and portents in Israel' (8: 18). Just so, the stories receive a series of interpretations and expansions, explaining just what these signs and portents mean. Dominant are the two variant Immanuel expansions that we find in chapter 7: 11–25 and 8: 5–10. Together, they nearly overwhelm the motif of contrasting children, with which the central narrative is structured. These interpretive expansions are both negative and brutally ironic. Each is centred in the metaphor of Immanuel, the sign that God will be with Israel. In the first, we are given a story of a child born. It is a variant of Isaiah's second child, for it too bears the same negative fate for Israel. This child is called Immanuel, 'God with us'. Before he is grown, his name warns, Israel will be destroyed. The opening prose part of the narrative closes in verse 17 with an intrusive comment or gloss on the narrative: 'the king of Assyria'. Immanuel is the Assyrian king! This gloss isn't part of the narrative; nor is it intended to be part of the story. It is a theological comment, an interpretation of the story by its collector, what is seen in the Dead Sea scrolls as a *pesher*. It identifies the story's cipher. It is not the child to be born who is the king of Assyria. The child is a sign of Immanuel. It is God's presence in Israel that is the king of Assyria. God's presence brings destruction. To this story, the editor adds a four-fold poem, each part beginning with 'on that day'. These expand and make explicit this divine presence as destruction at the hands of the Assyrians.

The days of Yahweh – when Yahweh will be with us – are days of destruction, days to be feared. The imagery calls up war and destruction as a response of divine wrath and judgement. The development of the metaphor of the 'day of Yahweh' as the day on which Yahweh will come and judge Israel draws its strength most directly from a view of the past that sees the destruction of Jerusalem and old Israel as well-deserved punishments sent by God. In this view the kings of Babylon and Assyria act as God's messengers and servants. The people of Israel have trusted too much that God will be with them in mercy. Now the day of Yahweh will be a *dies irae*. Only those lucky few, 'who do no evil and tell no lies, but trust in Yahweh, need not fear the day that Yahweh, Israel's God, is with us' (Zephaniah 3: 7–12).

b) The foregoing story and commentary is matched by a poetic gloss attached to Isaiah's second child (8: 5–10). In this commentary, we are presented with a quite clear variation on Ezekiel's two sisters, Israel and Samaria, as brides of Yahweh. The first child, Immanuel, was Samaria. Yahweh's presence in Israel brought its destruction. As it too shared the 'quick-destruction' motif of Isaiah's second child, now that second child, sharing the Immanuel motif, becomes a sign of Yahweh's presence once again: in Judah. Destruction at the hands of the Assyrians again emerges as the poem's referent (8: 8).

This double-barrelled commentary is linked to yet a further expansive commentary on the tradition. It too is rooted in the theme of Yahweh's contrasting children. Now, however, we return to the positive nuances belonging to Isaiah's first child. We are offered a variant on 'Repentant-remnant'. The contrast rests on one who curses his king and God (compare Job 2: 9). Chapters 7 and 8's Immanuel theme remains dominant, and the editor offers positive reinterpretation of the whole, as a sign of God's saving presence in Israel. This collector's commentary on the tradition links (and identifies) the first-born 'Repentant-remnant', with the saving child born for David's throne in chapter 9: 6. True to its interpretive function, the text itself tells us how to read these chapters: 'Bind the evidence together; put a seal on the instructions to the students.' The hidden message – hidden in the stories of these children as 'signs and portents' of Israel's fate – is one of hope. Here, from Isaiah 8: 16 on, the teacher's *pesher* or 'interpretation' is explicit. We are given poems of hope and promise. These, the commentator explains, belong to the birth story of Isaiah's first child, 'Repentant-remnant'!

The birth story episode in chapter 8 is more complete than in Isaiah 7. We find a new variant of the way in which God impregnates the woman. In Isaiah 8: 1, the prophet is instructed to write down a name 'in human words'. The form of the request is a mildly ironic play on the literary prophet's conceit of writing down his prophecies in divine words. Yahweh wants to be understood, so he uses our language. The name Isaiah writes is a cue-name, though it is not as elegant as those in the variant stories in Hosea 1–3: 'Quickly spoiling, hurriedly becoming prey'. This is hardly a name one would wish on a child. Leaving nothing to misinterpretation, Isaiah then takes two trustworthy witnesses with him, offering the legal equivalent of proof of this child's divine parentage. He has sex, moreover, with a prophetess, so that Yahweh plays in this story both the male and female forms of the divine parentage. Impregnated, she bears a son. The child is given his name, one that determines Israel's and Damascus' destiny. It is to come about even more quickly than in the story-doublet of Isaiah 7: before the child learns to speak (Isa. 8: 4). Also again, God's presence is Israel's destiny at the hands of the king of Assyria.

This child too is Immanuel: 'God is with us.' In the two short poems that follow the story in 8: 5–8 and 8: 9–10 we come to understand what Isaiah means with this central theological metaphor of divine presence. It is well to remember that in spite of their great variety of story form and description, all of the son of God stories deal with a common thread in a wide-ranging discussion. It is a theme central to the theology of the Bible: the shared life and substance, the comparisons and contrasts, the similarities, the collating, clustering and mingling of motifs and forms relating to the divine and the human. We are dealing with a literature that is quite conscious of the fact that its language about God is human language, fatally flawed and implicitly fraudulent. Here in Isaiah, and again and again in our texts, the narrator's voice asks bluntly what it means that 'God is with us'. What happens when the divine becomes involved with the human? Is it really such a good idea?

c) The prose segment we find in Isaiah 8: 16 to 9: 1 is an interpretive essay introducing the poem of Isaiah 9: 2–7 as a prophecy transforming the destructive destinies determined in the prophetic tales of Isaiah 7: 1–8: 15. It opens with a declaration of the prophet's own hope (8: 17) in contrast to the old Israel of the Immanuel stories, represented by those who consult mediums and wizards rather than God, those who, 'cursing their king and their God', are 'thrust into thick darkness' (8: 21–22). With Isaiah's hope, such darkness and gloom is transformed into a metaphor of a woman in anguish: she is no other than Isaiah's wife, the new Jerusalem in labour. Her darkness is not gloom, but a portent of transformation. The child, 'Repentant-remnant', once the Immanuel of destruction, now takes on the form of a new birth. In this striking exegetical passage, themes of destruction are radically transformed into themes of hope: 'The people who have walked in darkness have seen a great light; those who dwelt in a land of deep darkness. On them has light shined ... Every boot of the tramping warrior in battle tumult, every garment rolled in blood, will be burned as fuel for the fire.'

War is transformed to hope. Yahweh and his spouse, the new Jerusalem, give birth to a wonderful child: the new Israel. The clear patterns of the mythology surrounding the metaphors of son of God and of Yahweh's messiah are transparent throughout. The central metaphors of Israel as Yahweh's first-born, of Samaria and Jerusalem as Yahweh's spouse, and of the people of God as an ideal of a new Israel, are brought together here.

Chapters 7 and 8's prophecies of doom about old Israel are reinterpreted and transformed by chapter 9's hope for the repentant remnant. Isaiah interprets these child Immanuels, with all their complex mythical echoes of the son of God and messiah traditions, very simply as God acting in this world. He defines this God as a God of mercy, a saving God. That is what Immanuel means: 'God is with us'. The child of Isaiah 9: 2–7 is God himself. The matrix of the Old Testament's theology about God's presence is captured by this powerful poem. It is sung by Isaiah's wife in labour, giving birth to the new Israel, Repentant-remnant's destiny: the new Immanuel: God with us.

> To us a child is born; to us a son is given; governance will be on his shoulders. His name will be 'wonderful counsellor, mighty God, eternal father, the patron of peace'. (Isa. 9: 6)

Isaiah 9, in paraphrasing the mythological and cosmic foundation of both chapter 7 and 8's stories of a child born, powerfully conveys the seductive power of such a projection of the divine.

4 The prophets and the son of God motif

When the Book of Hosea is read without the bias of efforts to create an historical prophet as part of ancient Israel's history, it emerges as a striking composition with two parts. The first (chapters 1–3) is presented as autobiographical parable, in which the prophet's marriage with a prostitute appears as a parody of God's relationship to Israel. Israel's fate is determined through the names of Hosea's children. The second part of the book (chapters 4–14) is a series of implicitly interpretive poems that offer commentary on the prose narrative. The theme is a call to repentance: 'Turn, O Israel, to Yahweh your God; you have stumbled in your wrongs. Speak up; turn to Yahweh and say to him: "you who forgive all fault, accept what we offer" ' (Hos. 14: 2–3). The implied author, taking the role of divine teacher, addresses the audience with a riddle in closing this work: 'I am like the evergreen cypress. From me comes your fruit. Who is wise enough to understand this, so discerning that he might know it? The paths of Yahweh are straight.[1] The righteous walk in it, while wrongdoers stumble.' (Hos. 14: 9–10) The story does not address ancient Israel of any pre-exilic time. The audience, the intended reader, is the student of philosophy, the pious adherent of the theology of the way of the Book of Psalms, the same as addressed in Psalm 1: 3–6: '[The righteous], he is like a tree . . . that yields its fruit in season . . . Yahweh establishes the way of the righteous, but the way of the wicked perish.' Hosea is not a man of the

---

[1] A pun on the name Israel: in Hebrew, the word for 'straight'/'correct' is *yesharim*.

eighth century, scarred by a travesty of a marriage. In a tale filled with ironic undertone, he parodies God's role of faithful husband to a faithless people. It is a romance: a tale of long-suffering patience, ending in grace.

It is also a story, self-consciously structured on a collection of tale variants, whose interaction builds a single coherent theme. Three successive stories, variants of each other, are offered in the three opening chapters of the book. The names of the characters in these tales are all cue-names, strengthening their intrinsically symbolic functions. In the opening story, Yahweh tells 'Deliverance' – that is, Hosea – to take a prostitute for a wife and have children by her. The audience is not left in doubt for a moment about the interpretation of these instructions, as Yahweh explains to this saving prophet: 'The land' [that is, Israel] has prostituted itself by turning away from Yahweh.'

Hosea marries the prostitute, 'Destruction' – that is, Gomer – and she bears him a son. Yahweh names the son 'God-sows', *Jezreel*, which is also the name of the great valley between the highlands and the Galilee. The child's name is a dramatic commentary on Israel's destruction. Why is Israel to be destroyed, its kingdom to come to an end? It is to punish Jehu for the blood he shed in the Jezreel (Hosea 1: 4–5). At first, the reference seems to be to the story we find in II Kings 9 and 10. However, although the story-collector of Kings hardly approves of Jehu any more than Hosea does (so II Kings 10: 31), the story we now have in Kings is entirely positive. It is Ahab and Jezebel who are bad, while Jehu fights side by side with Yahweh's prophet Elisha. He is Yahweh's messiah in the story; he is the one who fights Yahweh's wars. He is ordered to kill the prophets of Ba'al in the Jezreel, and to destroy Ahab and his family. That he carries out Yahweh's will, is stressed in the story's closure. Yahweh tells him: 'Because you have done well in carrying out what is right in my eyes, and have done to the house of Ahab according to all that was in my heart, your sons to the fourth generation will sit on Israel's throne' (II Kings 10: 30).

This is certainly not the story or the Jehu that Hosea knows and refers to! That Jehu, rather than being Yahweh's faithful servant and the enemy of Ba'al, had turned Israel away from Yahweh, and for this reason had brought about the end of the kingdom. This implicit variation of the story in Kings clearly points to a theological orientation and evaluation of the Old Testament narratives. It implies a substantial indifference in both Kings and Hosea to events as historical.

While Hosea will briefly return to the story of this first child in chapter 3, the text moves on to a variation of the tale, and it is this that dominates the rest of the chapter. Gomer gives birth to two children. The first is a daughter named 'Does-not-find-mercy'. Israel will not find mercy or forgiveness. She then bears a son, who is called 'Not-my-people'. With an echoing denial of Exodus 3: 12's self-identification of Yahweh as God for Israel ('I am with you'), Yahweh addresses the child: 'You are not my people, and I will not be with you' (Hosea 1: 9). The message of the story is transparent: these two children's names reiterate each other, and together determine Israel's fate. Also implicit is an ongoing discussion that Hosea's implied author has with the tradition of Exodus.

This narrative is as quickly abandoned as the first. Our text turns abruptly to commentary. In three short verses (Hos 1: 10–2: 1), Hosea interprets his two tales coherently. He takes an historiographical perspective that is quite breathtaking. This Israel represented by the prostitute's children is an Israel past. To contrast this old Israel of rejection with a hope-filled present, Hosea echoes Genesis' promise to Abraham in Genesis 13: 16. This new Israel will be 'as numerous as the sands of the sea . . . Where once they were named "You-are-not-my-people", they will now be called "Children-of-the-living-God" '. Hosea reverses time once again. His new Israel reflects the image of the united kingdom. Yahweh's day of wrath and punishment becomes 'a great day of the Jezreel'. This is now the good Jehu against evil Ahab. Hosea's boy can now be called: 'You-are-my-people'. His sister becomes 'You-have-found-mercy'. In these few literary strokes, Hosea gives a picture of Yahweh as the divine master over history, reversing Israel's fate and making the past present. Quite clearly, the structure of our text, with the narrative of the first chapters given a commentary by the poetry of Hosea's second part, shows itself as discourse. It is a discussion and an analysis of Yahweh's love–hate relationship with Israel. This is no prophecy of doom. It emphasizes rather a divine mercy without restriction. God rejected old Israel. With equal freedom Israel is now accepted. His mercy is divine, by virtue of being undeserved.

The rest of chapter 2 consists of two further variant responses. The first of these, in 2: 2–15, sets the theme of a second commentary to the story of Hosea and his wife as Yahweh and his, with the resounding echo of divorce: 'Say to your mother, say: "She is not my wife and I am not her husband." ' The divine poet pleads with his wife to put away her prostitution. He threatens to strip her naked. The poem presents Yahweh in a lover's quarrel about his wife's affairs with Ba'al and the other gods. It had always been he, Yahweh, that was her husband (i.e., her *ba'al*), who had given her everything she had. Yet she neglected and forgot him. In the closing verses of this poetic commentary, Yahweh confesses his enduring yet unrequited love to the reader, 'I will seduce her; I will bring her out into the wilderness and talk to her heart.' The wilderness holds an implicit reference to Moses and Israel in the Pentateuch. Again the poet has turned the past into a future harbinger of return to Yahweh. Jezreel's valley becomes now the valley of Akor: a gateway to hope! By this literary allusion, the author echoes the story of judgement and condemnation in Joshua 7, where Akor was the 'valley of trouble'. The past, the history of Israel's condemnation and rejection, has been reversed. Hosea's implicit commentator draws a message of hope from the tale of Yahweh's marriage to his prostitute wife.

In Hosea 2: 16–23, a third commentary completes the discussion. Picking up the 'great day of the Jezreel' from Hosea 2: 2, this final interpretation offers three short poems expanding this leitmotif. 'On that day,' says Yahweh, 'you will call me "husband": no longer "my Ba'al".' (Hos. 2: 16–23) The poet again reaches back into the past for the promise of God's eternal covenant to Israel and brings it into the present. On that day, Yahweh establishes his covenant with Israel for ever. In the final 'on that day', the poem returns to Hosea's autobiographical tale: 'On that day, I will show mercy to Does-not-find-mercy and I will say to Not-my-people, "You are my people", *and he will answer, "You are my God."* '

This double story of Yahweh's three children, with its triple commentary, closes here as the child 'turns' (implicit in the Hebrew: 'repents') and responds to his divine father. It is not surprising, however, that yet another commentator adds yet another variant interpretation to our text by providing us, in a very short chapter 3, with a third tale about yet another unfaithful wife for Hosea. This story also offers us an ironic caricature of Israel. The comments, with all their brutal sexism, have considerable comic merit. The woman, like Israel, had another lover and is an adulteress, so the prophet buys her for half price. He then puts severe conditions on her. She can't have lovers any more. Nor will even her husband, Yahweh, have sex with her. The story closes with a brief commentary, giving us the story's meaning with reference to the saving motif of the exile's repentance. Israel will live for a long time without king or prince, without sacrifice or cult. They then 'will turn and seek Yahweh their God and David their king'. Here again, in this last commentary, the history of the past is cast in terms of the present hope of the text's composition.

This basic theological tale of the prophet and his wife as a lightly veiled parable of the relationship between Yahweh and Israel, with its interpretive commentaries and discussion, and its free play with the metaphors of history, is not confined to Hosea. It is basic to prophetic discourse and basic to our understanding of the books of the prophets. They are all collections of complex poetry, song and historiographical comment put together in the guise of one or other great prophet's oracles and visions of his God. The story shows itself twice in Ezekiel.

5 *The parable of Yahweh and his wives*

a) The tale in Ezekiel 16 has some of the harshness of Hosea's sexist imagery. It is, however, more openly erotic in its intimate description of Yahweh's care for his young bride. The story begins with Jerusalem as an abandoned child. Her father was an Amorite, her mother a Hittite. She was cast out in a field, her navel cord uncut. She was unwashed, unclothed. No compassion, only abhorrence, when she was born. When Yahweh found this foundling lying in her blood, he said to her, 'You will live. I will make you many like the plants of the field' (16: 7). The child grew up to be a woman. Yet, 'still naked and bare'.

With recurrent echoes of the Song of Songs, Ezekiel describes a love scene between Yahweh and his bride Jerusalem. When Yahweh passed a second time, Jerusalem, the young bride, was ready for love. And so Yahweh 'covered her' by taking her for his wife. He then gives her a bath, washing off her hymenal blood and pouring oil over her. The motifs of blood from the variant scenes of the baby newborn and the nubile and virginal young woman are blended together here as Yahweh takes Jerusalem as his bride. Yahweh dresses her and covers her with jewelry. Jerusalem becomes famous for the beauty and splendour which Yahweh gave her.

Then the scene shifts once again. The dramatic descriptions of the opening episodes are replaced with commentary and scolding judgement. The same patterns dominate as we find in the stories of Hosea. Jerusalem trusted in her own beauty and turned to prostitution. Inverting Genesis' account of the creation of man in God's image (Gen. 1: 26), Jerusalem takes her jewelry and makes gods in the image of men. It is with such gods that she prostitutes herself (Ezekiel 16: 17). In this, she forgets his care for her when she was young. Ezekiel goes quickly through a history of Jerusalem as a history of prostitution: with the Egyptians, the Philistines, the Assyrians and the Babylonians. Yahweh will strip her naked and leave her at the mercy of these 'lovers'. Yahweh compares Jerusalem to her 'sisters', Samaria and Sodom. Then, much like the stories of Hosea, Ezekiel has Yahweh abruptly change. Instead of condemnation, he speaks of restoration. He will restore Sodom and Samaria, and he will restore Jerusalem. Again, as in Hosea, Ezekiel closes the story with a contrast of temporary punishment with an eternal covenant. This last, he will give to Jerusalem when he forgives all that she has done.

A variant of this motif of Jerusalem's sisters is taken up in Ezekiel 23. In this story, the introduction is offered in rapid sketch. There are two sisters, Oholah and Oholibah. They were prostitutes in Egypt when they were young. Yahweh married them, and they bore him children. Oholah is Samaria and Oholibah, Jerusalem. Oholah was unfaithful, and had the Assyrians and their gods for her lovers. Because of this, Yahweh handed her over to her lovers, who killed her and took her children. This, of course, is a transparent reference to Samaria's destruction and to the deportation of its inhabitants. Oholibah saw her sister's punishment but ignored it. She too took the Assyrians and their gods for her lovers, and even 'prepared a lover's bed' for the Babylonians. Yahweh then declares that what was done to Samaria will be done to Jerusalem. Her children will be killed and her houses burnt. Finally, echoing Hosea 3, this ironic story tells us that Jerusalem might yet learn to 'recognize God'.

This dark story closes in condemnation and punishment. It is followed by two expansive commentaries. The first of these (Ezekiel 24: 1–14) develops the theme of Jerusalem's siege at the hands of the Babylonians. It mixes a metaphor for Jerusalem as cooking pot, in which Jerusalem's best are boiled, their bones used for fuel. The second commentary (24: 15–27), parallels the metaphor of Jerusalem as the prophet's wife in the person of the prostitute Oholibah. Ezekiel's wife is to die. Ezekiel, however, is instructed not to mourn her. This 'sign' draws the story in chapter 23 to its proper conclusion. Yahweh's temple, 'the delight of your eyes', will be destroyed. Jerusalem's population, Ezekiel's children, will be put to the sword. This is no cause for mourning, because it will lead to what is good in God's eyes. 'The one who escapes will return . . . and they will know that I am God.'

As in Hosea, this entire discussion that we find in Ezekiel is harsh and insensitive, even brutally so, to the past. As an evaluation of Jerusalem's past, or of the sufferings involved in any city's destruction, it is heartless. But neither Hosea nor Ezekiel is centred on the city of the past, with its sufferings at the hands of the Babylonians. That is rather obviously far in the past. Jerusalem's end, like Samaria's before it, is likened to the destruction of Sodom and Gomorrah. It is a warning, a time of testing. The implied contrast is with the Israel and the Jerusalem that now turns towards Yahweh and is understood as a new Israel and a new Jerusalem. This Jerusalem is not governed by harsh prophets of doom, but by hope.

b) The parable of Yahweh and his wives is also played out in Jeremiah 3–4, and its theme referenced frequently throughout this book. Jeremiah presents his metaphor in the voice of the aggrieved husband. His Jerusalem has become another man's wife. Should Yahweh take her back? He cannot. Jerusalem is pictured in the role of a whore (Jeremiah 3: 1–2). A third image: she stands on the roadside, waiting for her lovers (3: 2). Yahweh has sent drought in punishment. In 3: 6–11, a prose commentary interprets this opening with reference to II Kings' stories of Josiah. After Israel had played the prostitute, Yahweh had divorced her. Judah is given the role of Israel's sister. She too was shameless, false, and a whore, only pretending to return to Yahweh. Yahweh now regrets the mercy he showed Josiah.

An interesting variation of the divine mercy is used here. In contrast to his anger with the hypocritical wife Judah, Yahweh chooses to forgive Israel and asks her to return to him. And then, blending Israel and Judah, Yahweh speaks of both as his *children*: 'Return, faithless children; I am your husband.' It is a post-exilic remnant he addresses: 'I will accept you: one from out of a city, another chosen from an entire family; I will bring you up to Zion' (3: 14). Jeremiah enters the theme of return: a husband begging his faithless wife to change. He asks now, in the language of pietism, for a circumcision of the heart, a moral and spiritual commitment (4: 4). In 4: 22, Jeremiah returns to the theme of his children. Now, they are foolish and lost: 'My people are foolish; they do not know me; they are stupid children, without understanding. They are clever at evil and do not know the good.'

In closing this metaphor of Israel and Judah as God's wives and children, Jeremiah looks on the earth in the desert nothingness of the exile, the *tohu wa-bohu* of the creation story of Genesis 1. Jeremiah plays a variation on Isaiah 9. Yahweh hears the screams of his daughter Zion. She is in labour trying to give birth to a child, but – echoing the bride of the Song of Songs threatened by the watchmen – is surrounded by her lovers, who are trying to kill her. Much like overlooking Sodom with Abraham in Genesis 18, Yahweh tells his prophet to run through Jerusalem's streets to find a single person who walks in righteousness and seeks truth. Then he can pardon Jerusalem (5: 1). It is from this desert that Yahweh will bring the new creation of a new Jerusalem.

In chapters 30 and 31, Jeremiah will have Yahweh return to these lovers of his youth and change their destiny. He will bring them back from the north. Again, the metaphors mix. Yahweh declaims: 'I am Israel's father; Ephraim is my first-born' (31: 9). Like a loving father, Yahweh forgives their guilt and forgets their sin (31: 34).

6 Israel as God's beloved

The stock story of Yahweh and his wives as it is played out by Hosea, Ezekiel and Jeremiah is a rough and pointed parable, that deals with the divine presence in Samaria and Jerusalem. But such critique and judgement is only half the potential of this powerful metaphor in biblical literature. The Song of Songs and Isaiah take the parable in a quite different direction.

Isaiah first introduces the metaphor of Jerusalem as Yahweh's wife in a song in chapter 5: 1–7, in a way that follows the pattern of Ezekiel so closely that the main outlines of the parable are clearly marked. The song has two voices. At first, it is the voice of a psalmist who sings to Yahweh, addressing him with the epithet 'my beloved'. This divine epithet, *dwdy*, echoing the name of Jerusalem's legendary King David (*dwd*), is closely linked to the temple on Mount Zion. Associated with these metaphors is the image of Jerusalem as Yahweh's garden on earth. It is just such a metaphor that is drawn on here. The song is about Yahweh and his vineyard.

My beloved had a vineyard on a very fruitful hill. He fenced it, cleared it of stone, and he planted it with grapevines. He built a watchtower on it and carved out a press. He waited: expecting grapes from it, but it bore wild grapes.

In a reversal of the proverb of the sour grapes eaten by the father cited in Jeremiah 31: 29–30 and Ezekiel 18: 2, these grapes wait for the divine teeth to be set on edge. The metaphor is a variant of Yahweh with his prostitute and errant wife. This becomes explicit as the song in Isaiah 5 changes voice with Yahweh singing his complaint to the people of Jerusalem. With all the confusion of the hapless cuckold, he asks the audience to judge between him and his vineyard: 'What could have been done more to my vineyard, that I have not done?' Yahweh goes on to describe his vindictive anger, much in the manner of Hosea and Ezekiel: how he will remove the vineyard's protective wall and allow it to be destroyed. He will let weeds grow and forbid it to rain. In the parallel structures of verse 7, Yahweh interprets the song for us. The vineyard is the house of Israel; the grapevine the people of Judah. This song with its commentary is followed in verses 8, 11, 13, 20 and 26 by a number of other voices, each commenting on the story. The entry of these voices shows that our biblical narrative is built from and has its context in a discussion about tradition. Sometimes, as in verse 13, the interpretation sticks to the point of Jerusalem and its destruction. Other times, however, as in verse 11, the discussion wanders among barely related social evils of the city, such as the dangers of drink. Quite impressive are the 'woes' that have been added in verses 20–23 by one of the discussion's participants. These try to turn the commentary to one about universal ethics. The discussion never does get back to the vineyard or to its disappointed gardener.

The motif of Jerusalem as Yahweh's spouse, together with that of the temple as his garden, appears again in the Song of Songs. There, it is a clear variant of the texts we have seen. In the Song of Songs, however, this motif has every positive nuance. The love of God for Jerusalem is compared to the erotic love of Solomon for his mistress. It is in the opening song of chapter 6 that the garden shows itself. The song sings of lovely Jerusalem's fretful longing for its God. 'Where has your beloved gone, you most beautiful among women? Where has your beloved taken himself, that we might seek him with you?' As the voice of the song shifts with verse 2's response, the singer is Jerusalem and Yahweh is her 'beloved' (again, *dwd*, as in David). The response is filled with a rush of erotic innuendo: 'My beloved is gone down into his garden, to the beds of spices, to feed in the garden, and to gather lilies.' This is the garden of 4: 16 and 5: 1's sexuality, as Jerusalem sings to its beloved God: 'Arise, north wind, blow wind of the south, let your spirit into my garden that the balsam may flow. May my beloved enter his garden and feed on its delightful fruits.' Yahweh responds: 'I am come into my garden, my sister, my bride, I have gathered my myrrh and my balsam; I eat the honey cake with its honey; I drink wine with my milk. Eat friends, drink, be drunken you lovers.'

It is this explicit, erotically metaphorical play on the theme of God's presence in the new Jerusalem that offers a powerful counterpoint to the Bible's literary world about old Jerusalem and the stories of its apostasy and destruction. Unquestionably, Solomon's Song of Songs offers us the most intense of the Bible's many variants on the theme of Yahweh's marriages.

CHAPTER 15

The Bible's intellectual world

1 Whose history is it?

It is time that we take up the question of the ownership of history. Writing is an exercise of influence and persuasion. This is just as true of history as of any other form of writing. And so, one must read what is unwritten and only implied. History is not the same as the past. The past does not exist for us. History – perceptions of the past as variable as the people who write them – is our way of talking about that past: those experiences and events that once may have been, but are no longer. History itself is created by its writers. It is a product of literature. As such, history belongs to those who do the writing.

The capacity and vulnerability of a tradition for creative reinterpretation is not restricted much by a tradition's content, nor by how close it may be to the origins of the tradition in the past. It is almost entirely determined by the bearers of tradition. A text such as those we find in the Bible is at the mercy of those who claim the tradition as their own and interpret it. Far too little attention has been paid to this question, which lies so close to the heart of history writing. When we ask about those who have transmitted the stories and have brought them through the centuries as meaningful, we can hardly avoid the conclusion that the history of Israel is for the most part European. Whether Jewish or Christian, this history is a product of, and has been central to, Europe's self-understanding. Europe has written it – and written it for Europe's own purposes! It does not do simply to go back to Jerusalem, Alexandria or Babylon, to some select period of classical antiquity, and to imagine our history taking place or our Bible being formed. First we must ask about how this Bible and this history has come to us. We must acknowledge that its context within our own world affects our understanding of this history's significance. It is not just the Bible we read with jewelled glasses of interpretation; it is history as well.

A pre-emptive claim on the history of Palestine supports European intellectual and spiritual claims of continuity with the Bible, and with what is asserted as Europe's past. Europe's self-identity as Christian has its origin story in the Bible – a story that reaches back to creation. It is the function of origin stories to offer their readers a place to find themselves. European self-understanding is not restricted to any limited number of biblical myths of origin, whether this is seen in the form of the old Israel of Genesis or of some new Israel such as that of the Book of Ezra or of the prologue of John's gospel. The European origin story has also been influenced by the myth of history; namely, a belief in the quest for a history of the past as it actually happened. This belief system draws on the emotional wealth of self-discovery. The reformation and renaissance of post-medieval society transmitted a very specific and idealized perception of a far distant past as the foundation of its own identity. Europe's search for its sources through a rediscovery of its classical and biblical roots created a need for the history it explored to be in fact the real past: a past that gave legitimacy to revolutionary choices. It is in such a dislocated context of faith that history has been believed rather than known.

Hand in hand with Europe's claims on the Bible have been its claims on a cultural and intellectual heritage in classical Greece and Hellenism. In the systems of European education, this tradition has been reiterated as Europe again and again has located its spiritual roots in the Roman imperium. The barbarism of the early Middle Ages, before Averroes and Avicenna lent themselves to Europe's re-education, is a dark period of our history which only Scandinavians – with their Viking myths – can feed on today with nostalgia. Europe's pre-emptive, and historically hardly justified, assertion of classical roots has created an identity that touches every aspect of its cultural reflection. Europe and the West's historical claims to the intellectual and spiritual property of ancient Syria and Palestine begin already in fourth-century Western Christianity's rediscovery of its religious roots in the 'Holy Land'. This has been reflected, for example, by the nostalgic research into early biblical antiquities since St Helena and Jerome. Their travels gave us both Jerusalem's *Via Dolorosa* and the first Western Bible. The effect of the dislocations implied by such 'rediscovery', so obvious in the medieval religious focus on the relics of the true cross and on sacred places, is most instructive when we take up questions of biblical archaeology's capacity to understand the past it excavates.

European identification with the Bible also finds its origins in the reforming traditions of the Renaissance and the Enlightenment. The first was crowned by the Protestant revolt which asserted for the Bible a critical place both in the theological world of the university and in the moral and spiritual life of everyman. The latter was marked by the paradigm of history at the centre of a modern concept of reality. The past was made to speak directly to us through the living voice of its old world-creating God.

Europe controls that past world, and its God, with a firm hand on history's creative helm.

For example, Napoleon's troops marked the beginning of modern scholarship's interest in the Middle East. The nostalgia of historical and archaeological scholarship has led to a reassertion of Europe's rights over Palestine's past. Not only is it part of our own vision of our patrimony in a civilization seen as having developed progressively over 5,000 years, it is also a key element of a religious struggle by Christians for their intellectual interests in the education in the West. In both these efforts, the peculiar Westernized concept of ethnicity, which has hidden Palestine's past, has functioned to support a chain of historic succession. This succession proceeds from the ancient Near East, epitomized in the Hebrew Bible, through Alexander's Hellenistic unities and on to the New Testament and to early Christianity. The primary heuristic function of such chains as this central linkage in the West's self-understanding is, of course, stability. But nostalgia – that historiographic description of the past as it informs us about ourselves – also creates both amnesia and myopia in the need to reduce the past's otherness. We only rediscover what we are able to recognize. Accepting ourselves as the lords of history comes at a price: that of the past's identity. This self-absorbed perspective, which characterizes European historicism, is reflected today in the ideas of progressive evolution that have taken on such a central role in European scholarship's uncritical view of the past as a preparation for Christian Europe.

As archaeological and historical scholarship transformed the Bible's story into Palestine's history – from the Bronze Age to Jerusalem's destruction by the Babylonian army – it transformed both the Bronze Age and the Iron Age in the process. Biblical archaeology's Iron Age became a rationalized paraphrase of the Old Testament: a secular Bible if you will. Its Bronze Age served as introduction to the Bible: important not in itself but for what followed. These were the lucky periods. For most scholars until very recently, the history of ancient Palestine ended in the sixth century BCE. Seemingly overnight, it ceased to be a functional part of the ancient Near East once Jerusalem had fallen. The six centuries between Nebuchadnezzar and Jesus belonged to hidden history. This was to be expected within the anti-Semitism of the old paradigm, in which this period – given over to an Israelite deformation into Judaism – was understood as a dark age. The so-called post-exilic period was a period of religious obscurantism, a time of the Bible's betrayal by a legalistic and xenophobic nationalism of what became known as 'early Judaism'. The nadir of the Old Testament was marked here, as the Bible left the ethical heights of prophecy to develop a Protestant caricature of Roman Catholicism: a priest-ridden, cult-centred, religious bigotry, waiting for its reforming saviour.

This 'post-exilic' period was understood as a period of transition and preparation, a period that led to Christianity. 'Histories of Israel' were not part of Jewish history. Judaism was out of step with history's march, which followed rather Christianity's drummer. In such a salvation-driven history, nothing of interest lay between the testaments. Palestine's Roman period was saved for Jesus' sake. Jerusalem's fall in 70 BCE was even extended by many to the Bar Kochba revolts and the expulsion of Jews from Palestine in 135 CE, with its graphic prefigurement of Europe's own final solution. However tasteless this modern closure of past histories of Israel, its intrinsic racism has gone unnoticed in the distraction of Israel's role within Europe's origin story.

After the closure of the Jewish rebellions of 70 and 135, Western historical enthusiasm follows the cross westward. 'Oriental' Christianity, however central it may have been to Christianity, is left once Paul is taken as prisoner to Europe's Rome. This is in line with Europe's self-understanding. The late Roman period in Palestine – even Byzantium's three centuries of Christian rule – have offered little of intellectual interest to the West since the Crusaders' sack of Constantinople. Islam – the midwife of the European Renaissance – is ironically an entire world apart. The intellectual distances here, of course, are our own: not the past's. The closure of Palestine's history with the banning of Jews from Jerusalem is a direct reflection of the Church's identity as the New Jerusalem and the New Israel. Through history, the Western Church becomes the legitimate heir of biblical faith: by the legerdemain of its historians! This self-understanding of the Church – won through critical reflection – may or may not be a legitimate perspective of theology. It is one that a self-critical perspective must challenge.

This European origin tradition perceives western Europe as a synthesis of two contrasting intellectual streams: of Judeo-Christianity on one hand, and of its antithesis, the Greek and Hellenistic cultural traditions, on the other. The perception of the Bible as a product of an 'Old Testament' and a 'New Testament' reflects this dichotomy. The Old Testament is not the Greek tradition, often called the Septuagint, which formed the greatest part of the first Christian Bibles, such as we find in the fourth-century codices: Vaticanus and Sinaiticus.[1] Rather, it was the 'Old' Testament, and it was placed so that it might introduce a superceding 'New' Testament; just as the 'old Israel' – now somewhat cynically identified with Judaism – might be identified with a Christian 'new Israel'. The Old Testament has increasingly become in this Christian and European tradition a Jewish Bible. It was Hebrew; it was oriental; and it has been ancient Near Eastern. Its language and its understanding were imagined to be radically different from those of the New, which belonged in the brave new world of Hellenism. And Hellenism – although most of this empire stretched across

---

[1] These can be seen today in the Vatican Library and the British Museum, respectively.

Asia's southern flank – was understood as Greek, European and civilized. Greek letters have played a privileged role in the European historical imagination. Not only was Greece a latecomer to civilization, largely expanding on the vastly older literate cultures and intellectual worlds of coastal Anatolia, Phoenicia and Egypt, but Hellenism inherited an older imperial view of the world. Hellenism was the cumulative product of international culture over centuries. Beginning already in Assyria's dominance over the Levant in the ninth century BCE, the ancient Near East had long developed an interactive, international culture that lasted until the defeat of Turkish forces at the end of the First World War!

Nor should we forget that Hellenism was a culture whose centres were hardly European. Hellenism was at home in Asia and in Africa: in Babylon and in Alexandria. These were its intellectual centres. This is not to say that the culture was Asian or that it was African either. At the height of Assyrian power, the empire stretched from the Nile valley to Afghanistan. Under the Persians, imperial power extended into the Indus valley, and trade relations extended to China. When Macedonian-led armies finally defeated Persian forces, Mediterranean Europe joined the empire. Even as Macedonian generals ruled, the centre of power remained in the East. As the empire divided along its ancient fault-lines, Asia (including most of greater Syria and Phoenician Carthage) found its centre in Babylon. Africa, including Egypt and Nubia, centred in the essentially Mediterranean city of Alexandria.

Rome came first to empire only as a result of its competition with Phoenician trading for control of central Mediterranean ports. It moved eastwards by way of Egypt. It was Alexandria's historical role that Rome parlayed into a successful bid for imperial power. Only following this successful takeover of a traditional seat of empire were the Romans able to unseat the Babylonian, Seleucid and Hellenistic administration of Asia. This was not a Roman empire, any more than it had been a Greek–Macedonian one. The Romans learned Greek as the empire expanded westwards. Nor did the empire come to an end with the fall of Rome. It had no essential European roots. The administration moved to Constantinople, then to Damascus and Baghdad, finally returning to Istanbul. It has been our European orientation that perceived this political world in terms of successive personal aspirations. This perception is largely fictive.

The historical chain of external domination of Palestine is nearly unbroken from the Assyrian empire to modern times. Even the nominally independent Hasmoneans of the Maccabean interlude reflected the growing reach of Roman power. The concepts of self-identity and self-understanding that belong to the European nation states, demand too different a view of sovereignty to have a place in antiquity. It was not the centralized and absolute monarchs of Europe who ruled in the ancient world, but a servant of the divine. The metaphor of king in the ancient world, signifying 'autonomy', is important to understand, as it is no accident that the biblical world finds such a profusion of kings among Palestine's scrub farmers. If the seat of government mirrors the divine king of kings, then one has to people the world – as in Grimm's and Scheherazade's tales, with as many kings and princes as possible.

2 Theology as critical reflection

Our European origin tradition has given value to the contrast of belief and knowledge. This polarity which divides reality into worlds of faith and science is reflected in the opposition we are given by historians between the world of the ancient Near East – a world dominated by polytheism, belief and superstition (to which the Bible of the Old Testament belongs) – and the world of Hellenism – a world where logic, reason and the ethical world of the New Testament rule. Critical to the acceptance of such a world-view is the initial perception of the difference between faith and science.

It is these artificial dichotomies of our own that need to be challenged. Just as there is no great sea-change between the Assyrian and the Persian, or between the Persian and the Hellenistic empires, the difference between the intellectual worlds of the ancient Near East and Hellenism is largely a product of the observer. If one skips half a millennium, as many biblical scholars generally have, and contrasts Assyrians with the philosophers of Alexandria, one finds a radical difference and otherness. But not only is the world of Hellenism a direct descendant of the intellectual culture of the ancient Near East, from Babylon to Thebes, but that Hellenistic culture itself, with roots centuries old, is a product of a civilization that stretched from the western Mediterranean to the Indus valley and from the Anatolian plateau to the Sudan. There is no particularly Greek way of thinking, any more than there was a Hebrew or Semitic. There never was a pre-logical way of thinking to contrast with Greek philosophy. Aristotle formulated and systematized what had been well understood for centuries. Formal philosophical texts appear already with some of our earliest texts from ancient Sumer and Egypt.

The empire established by the Assyrians was not the first effort to assert political power over an area of many languages and cultures, but it was the most lasting. Its policies of provincial administration and population transference went far in promoting an awareness of an interrelated world of many peoples within a common political context. When Nineveh fell to the Babylonians in 605 BCE, no empire fell. The old empire's administration moved to Babylon. When the Persian army entered Babylon in 539, the administration shifted from that of the Babylonian King Nabonidus and his court, to that of Cyrus and his Persians. The 'world' continued to be administered from Babylon. The new administration did not so much conquer the empire anew, as establish the legitimacy of its succession to empire. The Persians expanded the administrative use of the West-Semitic Aramaic language that had been introduced by the Assyrians. This helped unite the empire intellectually as well as politically. By the late fourth century, when the Macedonians marched through Asia under Alexander, they not only brought their Greek language to the empire in Asia and Africa, they effectively brought the Mediterranean regions of Europe for the first time into the cultural world of imperial thought.

The empire brought with it many changes, not the least of which were intellectual – changes in how people understood themselves as well as the world they lived in. One of the most profound is reflected in ideas about the divine, and particularly the contrasts between what is thought of as polytheism and monotheism. 'Belief' in God – whether of one or of many – was not so much a product of faith in tradition as it was a way of understanding and expressing the reality of the world that was experienced. In antiquity, discussions about the divine reflect aspects of reality consciously perceived as unknown. Such theology in which the Bible, both Old and New Testaments, shared, reflects a world-view whose *centre* lay in an awareness of human ignorance and of the deceptiveness of sensory perception, associated with a nearly universal recognition of ineffable and transcendent qualities in life, fertility and wisdom.

This theology was an aspect of ancient philosophy and science. It was not so specifically Hellenistic as it was a product of the unified intellectual culture that had been created by the empire as early as the Assyrian period. It is a knowledge that is specifically set in contrast and in opposition to the old story-worlds of gods. From the early historian Hecateus to Plato and the Greek playwrights, and from the Babylonian Nabonidus to Isaiah and the author of Exodus, polytheism and monotheism were hardly ever opposed to each other. They rather reflected different aspects of a common spectrum of intellectual development. There was continuity between polytheism and monotheism as well as a process of changing interpretation. Hardly sudden or revolutionary, the changes of world-view were the result of more than a millennium of cultural integration. Crisis in such change was associated first of all with the understanding of divine transcendence, and with ideas regarding the truth, function and legitimacy of the personal gods of story. The struggle over beliefs about the unity of the divine came late and always had an explicitly political focus.

From at least early in the Assyrian period of the empire, in what are often thought of as the polytheistic worlds of Egypt, Syria and Mesopotamia, reflective people had well understood a clear difference between the gods themselves and the statues and images that were used to represent them. They also understood the difference between the forces of nature and the divine powers that had created them. This can be seen in some of the descriptions of the high gods, such as the Babylonian god

Marduk. In the creation story, he is given fifty names of the gods. This metaphor allows him to take on the attribute of omnipotence. Marduk can create by word alone. He is seen as possessing, in his names, all the many powers one might attribute to the divine. Other stories about the origins of the gods frequently describe them as having come from a single parent or from an original divine couple. Such story motifs reflect an understanding of unity and coherence in a divine world that is very much like the opening narratives of Genesis. All such metaphors reflect an understanding of humanity as essentially one.

In dealing with the gods of other people, military victories encouraged the creation of descriptions loyally boasting of the gods of the enemy being carried off into captivity – even slavery. The patronage and hierarchy that was understood to exist among the many different regional deities clearly also reflects the political dominance of particular periods. At the same time, the deities of allied states, or of those with whom trade treaties were made, are presented in a way that identifies them with Marduk. The name of the god Sin, the patron deity of the Assyrian city of Harran, for example, is one of the names of Marduk. In an imperial world, where the king was also king of kings, there was also an imperial god, whose servant that king was. This did not merely place Marduk at the head of a pantheon. Just as all the powers of all the kings of the imperial world reflected but one king's power, the power of the other gods reflected the power of but one deity.

In the simpler West Semitic world these tendencies were much more clearly marked. In the world of trade and shipping, where contact among many cultures and languages was commonplace, Syrian and Phoenician merchants readily identified specific gods of one region with the gods of similar function of another region. In this way, Astarte could be identified with Ishtar in the east and with Venus in the far west. Yam could be identified with Poseidon, and Ba'al with Hadad and Yahweh. Such syncretism was encouraged by the fact that many of the names of West Semitic deities directly reflected a given deity's function. The name El translates simply as 'God' and is easily identified with the Aegean world's Zeus. Ba'al translates as 'master' or 'husband', Mot as 'death', Yam as 'sea', and the like. At times they distributed the functions differently, so that for instance Ba'al could be identified with both Hadad and El, or Yahweh with both Ba'al and Elohim. It is only a very small step to recognize that implicit in such gods were functions of a single divine world. As different peoples gave these functions different names, the recognition came quickly that the gods themselves differed from each other because of distinctions given to them by humans. The specific gods that people knew were the gods they themselves had made to express the divine world.

One of the most frequent ways that West Semitic story, poetry and prayer particularized gods for very specific functions was to take the name of a high god – usually El, but Ba'al, Hadad and Yahweh were used as well – and add a descriptive epithet. In this way, El developed many different faces. He was 'the most high', 'the merciful', 'the god of the storm'. Also places or names of specific towns or regions made these nearly universal deities more particular. So we find 'Yahweh of Samaria' and 'Yahweh of Teman'. We have Ba'al and *his* Asherah, as well as Yahweh and *his*, without confusion. The divine name came to reflect a very particular local deity. At the same time, a default understanding of universalism is implicit.

Intellectuals well understood the difference between stories and songs about the actions and behaviour of gods and goddesses, and the actual behaviour of the divine in the world. Such distinctions were made then, even as they are today, at the same time that the mass of people thought of the gods themselves in the temples, in the rain and in stories. The metaphors of language both imply and evoke their referents. There is a vast difference between the creation of the story-world of the gods and the reception of that story-world.

Finally, the awareness of the human role in creating the specific world of gods, as related to their functions and as reflected in stories, rituals and prayer, developed the need to speak of the divine as such, apart from what men had created as gods. Critical thought is not only modern. Circumlocutions were developed in West Semitic literature. A variety of expressions, such as 'the God of spirit' and 'the God of heaven' became most common expressions to describe the divine as transcendent. The abstract quality of such metaphors was a positive advance on the fifty names of Marduk. In the Bible, such a Marduk is expressed simply with the plural of the Hebrew word for 'God', *Elohim*. Plurality, in the sense of the power of all things divine, is implicit in the Bible's understanding. The earliest references we find appear in eighth-century Aramaic texts which mention *Ba'al Shamem*, 'the lord of heaven'. By the Persian period, one could argue that this view of the divine was the norm for Syria and Palestine. The world in which gods had many faces and many names was a world of human thought. It was well understood that the gods were human expressions about the divine. The truly divine was spiritual, and unknown. Unlike material things, which were both individual and constantly undergoing change, the God of heaven was spirit, one and eternal.

The development of such an understanding of monotheism was hardly antagonistic to the worship of a variety of gods. Quite the contrary, this variety of gods, of individuals and of gods who changed, was a necessary aspect of human relationships to the transcendent. Both the gods of tradition and the forms of worship became subject to such critical thought. Gods, as human reflections, could be false, just as their worship could be empty and corrupt. By the late fifth century BCE, one or other form of this transcendent monotheism is known in many different regions. In Greece, it can best be seen in the writings of Plato about the One, True, Good and Beautiful. In Babylon the god Sin is spoken of in some texts in the same way as *Ba'al Shamem* is in Syria. In Persia, Ahura Mazda is frequently so understood. In the Bible itself, many of the references to 'God' (*Elohim*), the 'God of heaven', 'God the most high', and 'God' in such expressions as 'God's Yahweh' should be understood in this way.

Well before the Bible was written, the understanding of the divine had grown to such an extent that no thinking person could really believe in all the stories about the old gods, as if they were stories about the divine. Better, we should say that people well recognized that stories about gods were stories, and not really about gods. Many – like the Greek playwrights and the philosopher Socrates of Plato's story – dismissed such stories as foolish myths. In Babylon and Persia too, gods could be spoken of as having 'clay feet'. The gods had been made by clever men. In the bustling, cosmopolitan world of empire, beliefs were being broken like so many old pots. One could dismiss the gods of stories and legend. One could also find a way of thinking of them with integrity. It is this kind of task that exercised many ancient writers of the late Persian and early Hellenistic periods. The early writers of the Bible were among them.

The first story in the Bible in which God meets Moses, the story of the burning bush in Exodus 3–6, illustrates well how a revision of a tradition's stories can revive and modernize old world-views and outmoded traditions by understanding them in new ways. Traditional beliefs in the old gods of Palestine are saved in Exodus by having Yahweh, the long-forgotten god of ancient Israel, understood not as God himself, but as the name, the representative of the true God – the way that ancient Israel knew the divine. Yahweh recurrently plays a role in the Bible's narratives as mediator between the Most High and Israel, sharing this role with his messiah, with his son, with the king and the prophets. Yahweh is the primary means by which the Old Testament represents the divine acting in this world. As one of the burdens of biblical narratives from Genesis to II Kings is to explain how it is that Israel had misunderstood what the truly divine was, this concept of God as expressed by the Yahweh tradition also plays the role of the philosopher's stumbling block, as it does so forcefully throughout the Book of Job. On the other hand, Yahweh is equally freely identified with the true God, when addressed directly in prayer and song, and plays that role in some narratives. The story of the theophany in the burning bush in Exodus 3–6 also explains how the divine had been hidden in the worship of the even more ancient gods of Palestine: the lost gods of the patriarchs. These included even an *El Shaddai* who was no longer either worshipped or remembered. The 'true meaning' of the many, now fragmented stories of patriarchs and heroes is gathered together to be remembered and preserved in a way that the past had not grasped or properly understood. More than that, the writers of the Bible were free to create all their great stories about Yahweh, that they might reflect how old Israel had understood – and had misunderstood – the divine.

3 The Bible and the theologians

Before we go further in the discussion about the understanding of the divine that is implicit in the Bible, we need to acknowledge an increasingly polarized dispute in which biblical and theological studies are engaged in the university. As biblical studies has become a modern and a secular field – with a broad and untheological audience – it has developed an increasingly strained relationship with theology. In particular, the branch of biblical studies devoted to the Old Testament can be found today building more compatible ties with the disciplines of ancient history, Near Eastern studies and the history of religions on one hand and with sociology, anthropology and literature on the other. There is no doubt that the rapid changes that have come about within our understanding of the Old Testament during the past generation have originated in such interdisciplinary associations. This has also had a negative side, clearly reflected in the weakening ties between theology and the academic study of the Bible, especially the Old Testament.

The role that the Bible has long played in theology as an origin tradition of Christianity created the fiction of an Old Testament as defining a part of the Bible. Whether one thinks of this as the Hebrew Bible or as the Septuagint, as reflective of early Greek language traditions, such biblical traditions function within theology in contrast to a New Testament. This New Testament is equally a creation of later theological tradition, rather than a perception of our texts themselves. This supersessionist contrast, which sees the New Testament as the (legitimate) successor of the Old, has had profound effects on how this literature has been read. It has not only devalued great parts of biblical literature in the lives of Christians. It has also removed the New Testament from its literary and intellectual context. The implicit anti-Semitism of evolutionary schemes of salvation history, culminating in the stories of Jesus, is a well recognized distortion of recent European theology. The transformation of the Old Testament into an historical world, however, has given such an Old Testament the function of a rather harmless introduction to the New Testament. This distortion has robbed the tradition of its soul. Such misuse carries its own falsification of the New Testament as well. The distortions are all the more apparent when historians of religion mimic their theological colleagues, perversely reading our displaced Old Testament literature as an origin story of Judaism.

The misappropriation of ancient texts for purposes contrary to the tradition's intentions, which two generations of theological use of the Bible have now encouraged, is one of those common abuses of intellect that Salman Rushdie has described in his book *Haroun and the Sea of Stories* as contributing to the pollution of the ocean of our language. That this poisoning occurs in deep waters, close to the wellspring of the traditions that render us human, makes this a particularly virulent and dangerous form of pollution. Theologians and officially appointed interpreters of the tradition have an obligation to society that in the Rushdie metaphor is comparable to that of his floating gardeners. Rather than adding to the pollution to promote their own interests, they should tear at the weeds that strangle the language of our tradition, and that lead to empty silence.

That the Old Testament is no longer believable as history offers really no difficulty to theology. It is after all very old. Myth and story is, again as Rushdie tells us, 'No Problem'. Traditions certainly need to be understood, purified, clarified and defended. But they have their own power: all that language has. Beyond the Bible, that we call here the Old Testament, and beyond the Christianity the older ones among us have known, there is the life of our language that is at stake. It is not that we ourselves can find the purest springs of truth itself, but the intellectual life which our language produces and preserves must be protected. It is the transposition of tradition, the manipulating and pre-empting of another's truth, the lies, the Khomeini-like, theologically motivated, interpretations and qualifications, that pollute. A theology without mythology is like a Judaism without *torah*, a Christianity without resurrection: a tradition without substance. It is the demythologizing of what is at its very core mythological that is *Khattam Shud*. It is finished. Without Grace. The End.

It is not necessary either to deny the tradition or to baptize it. It is only important not to lie about our past. Theology is not – or at least should not be – confined to blind searches for a truth that doesn't and never did exist. It is also our language. The gods have not made it easy to be a human being. All we have to fight them with is our language – our words, our texts and our traditions. There are different streams of language and metaphor, communicable expressions about human experience, each – in its survival – offering a living spring. Theology does not exist apart from metaphor. Nor does a Bible exist apart from its stories. *What did we mean by them?* and *What do we mean because of them?* are the two central questions that both justify and require that the Bible be understood as theology in its own right.

If, however, our understanding of the Bible is that it provides us with a reflection of the religious beliefs and practices of early Judaism, it needs to be appropriated not by theology but by the discipline of the history of religions. Such an option has several difficulties that I think are insurmountable. The Old Testament does not reflect any particular period or stage of Palestine's religion directly, whether of the Iron Age or of the Persian and Hellenistic periods. The understanding of Palestine's religious life conveyed by archaeological and written texts differs substantively from the interpretations of the biblical traditions. While this happens partly because the biblical traditions are much later than anything we might describe as 'Israelite' religion, it also derives from the fact that the biblical texts are not, for the most part, religious texts themselves. They are rather philosophical critiques of religious tradition and practice. The real Israel of the Old Testament is a theological, not a social reality. It cannot be identified with any historical Israel, even a Jewish one. This is not simply a question of chronology or material culture. It is a question of perception. Finally, the modern scholarly creation of a prophetic religion of monotheistic Yahwism, flies in the face of the specifically literary functions of our prophetic texts. It substantially distorts Old Testament monotheism within a false context of conflict with polytheism.

If we reject the 'history of religions' model, as we must, we might rephrase our question in a theological direction and in terms of the history of ideas. Not only has the Bible been formed of a collation of early West Semitic monotheistic traditions, it has itself served as a constituting tradition for both Judaism and Christianity. The Bible in its essence is a collection of traditions past. They are traditions lost, destroyed, betrayed and shattered, but nevertheless remnants of an Israel of which the bearers understood themselves as the remnant saved. Such texts are not reflections of any religion that once existed. They are rather interpretations of known tradition presented as that of the lost past. Such reinterpretive reflection marks them as critical texts and as commentaries. Their emphasis on listening and reading, on preserving, and on distinguishing thought and understanding, hardly implies an affirmation or commitment to cult and religion. It distinguishes the Bible as a philosophical document. It seeks enlightenment. After a long absence from the genre, the Bible shows itself as a work of theology.

Yet, the Bible's theology – the critical and historical theology that belongs to the text – is a very old theology. It is past and ultimately unrecoverable. We have evidence of it, and we can still read many of our texts profoundly and clearly. However, when we speak of a legitimate biblical theology we must not forget what we have learned. We are gardeners. We don't interpret texts, creating our own, so much as we create contexts in which texts might be read rather than misread. If we are to be faithful to our texts, we must listen to them and read them. Only then can our efforts have integrity. The world-view of the Old Testament belongs to a different age from ours. We are not, cannot be and should hardly look to become – even in imagination – Hellenistic Jews, that the text might speak to us. The text doesn't speak to us, nor was it addressed to us. To pretend that it does and was, is among theology's least critical and most self-serving lies. This book, the Bible, is written in a dead language, which had its competence and its signification within a culture that is long since forgotten. It was never written for us, and can hold false – when not falsified – messages for us. A contemporary theology that would see itself based on the themes, metaphors and motifs of Old Testament stories and poems is a highly artificial, and one must also say a highly arbitrary, exercise. Such exercises are best pursued for antiquarian and nostalgic reasons. For such laudable reasons, for example, our bishops carry shepherds' staffs, and we eat lamb at Easter! At their worst, however, such exercises easily become remarkably manipulative efforts to sell a modern reading as *the truth of scripture*.

Biblical texts are important because they have formed our consciousness and our language. They are the foundational remnants of an intellectual tradition common to the Western world. This language has provided us with a tradition of integrity, of criticism and of reform. Historically, the Bible has provided us with metaphors of the divine, of people and of the world. These metaphors, in later periods and in different contexts, provided a central impetus to the intellectual and political movements we now know as Christianity, Judaism and Islam. The Old Testament also provides us with a substantial bridge between the polymorphic intellectual and literary worlds of the ancient Near East and the international humanism of Hellenism. It provides us with avenues of approach to such central Western concepts as the personally divine. It also opens us to the critical development of a philosophy of religion. This is one of the central functions of our texts: reinterpreting no longer viable personal deities of Palestine's past in terms of a critical perception of both transcendent and ineffable truth. The current intellectual climate, painfully aware as it is of the increasingly obvious irrelevance of our religious traditions, offers a comparable crisis.

4 The prophets and history

Traditional historical criticism of the Bible has followed an assumption that the biblical texts reflect historical changes of attitude over centuries. They appear, as it were, emotions captured in ink. I prefer that we consider *recurrent emotions that we experience* every time we encounter a text, much as when we go to the opera. We are dealing with emotions of metaphor, not history. Who does not experience terror in Isaiah's prophecies of doom, false illusory hopes in the mercy granted Hezekiah, and despair in Jerusalem's destruction? How else could we be up to the lyricism of Isaiah 40 celebrating the ineffable quality of the compassion and mercy of the universal God?

This is a quite ordinary argument for textual coherence. In such wild swings of emotion as the Book of Isaiah displays, one does not find evidence demonstrating a history of changes in the tradition. These texts do not reflect distinctiveness of perspective and world-views at all. They display coherence, unity and contemporaneity throughout. The text as a whole expresses the ineffability of divine mercy through the forgiveness of the unforgivable. The unspectacular deduction that since the existence of so-called II Isaiah (Isaiah 40–55) is assumed by I Isaiah (Isaiah 1–36) it must be the earlier text begins to expose some of the distortions of how past theological scholarship has engaged history.

Traditions need someone to transmit them. The prophecies of Isaiah 1–36 were not preserved because they came true. That motivation would have ensured their being long forgotten. One does not save unhappy messages as precious documents of tradition. Nor does one honour bold truths of national dishonour and ruin. One gets rid of the messenger. Nor can we imagine that a somehow truer prophecy of a mitigated divine wrath would make a very compelling story. Black and white are the functional moral protagonists of story. A presentation expressive of divine mercy is, after all, a theological assertion. In theology, as in other fiction, only a forgiveness that forgives the unforgivable will do. Divine mercy needs a story that establishes the object of mercy as worthy of damnation. How else is mercy divine? It is merely human to forgive what is forgivable! This is fundamental to any theology of forgiveness. It is truly odd that theologians today would have their descriptions of the divine so ordinary and so human. As the Bible's God, however, is ineffable, I Isaiah must be dependent on II Isaiah, and therefore must come later, both thematically and functionally. This also implies that Isaiah's prose text reflects a fictional setting, not an historiographical excursion. Notice what this reassertion of Isaiah's God into his story implies for the genre of such collections of tradition. They begin to look a lot more like the books of Jonah and Job. They immediately fall into the genre of wisdom: philosophical reflection, sermons.

The difficulty of historicizing interpretations of the prophets can be seen in Exodus 23. Here, the guardian given by Yahweh to be with Israel as they enter the land is described as a messenger. He is introduced by Yahweh to Moses as a kind of mafia enforcer or secret service agent. He is drawn much in the manner of the 'watchers' of the First Enoch and Jubilees traditions. He will watch over Israel in its journey into the promised land and protect its people as long as they remain faithful to their divine patron, Yahweh. He will punish Israel with an unforgiving wrath if it is disobedient. Such moralities of loyalty and patronage are recurrent in the Pentateuch. As other nations will be treated by Yahweh in accord with the way they treat Abraham in Genesis, just so, Israel in the wilderness tradition is to be judged in accord with the way it either obeys or rebels against Yahweh's prophet Moses. Such prophetic roles are pervasive in Bible stories whose heroic protagonists are variously called judges, kings and prophets. As old Israel obeyed those who spoke for God, or as it rebelled against them, the nation was judged.

In considering the messenger of Yahweh in Exodus 23, it soon becomes clear that this speech points to a future outside the wilderness cycle of narratives. As the people of Israel prepare to enter the promised land in Exodus 23, they are warned that if they should disobey this divine prophet they will not be forgiven. Such disobedience will be unforgivable. We have all read the rest of the story. We know that, in fact, the traditions hardly ever tell us stories about obedience to prophets. Jonah is the only Old Testament prophet to whom anyone listened. And they were Ninevites who obeyed him! The one thing that is predictable about prophecy is that it will not be obeyed. We also have many stories of divine anger and punishment. Yet such punishment never comes with the unforgiving wrath that Exodus 23 – or indeed Isaiah 1–36 – promises and creates expectation of. It is not accidental that most of what scholars like to call 'pre-exilic prophets' speak very much like Exodus 23's enforcer. This could be called the motif of Yahweh as overbearing parent! Punishment threatened is total. This is essential to the definition of a 'prophet-of-doom'. In literature, the foreshadowing of doom is an implicit prerequisite of the classical tale motif, 'the success of the unpromising': the single most common plot element in the Bible. We are not dealing with 'big bow-wow' literature like Gilgamesh or the Iliad. The audience is filled with students of philosophy, not soldiers. Why must the Bible's threatened punishment be doom? Because Israel must be worthy of total destruction. In literature – and that is what we are dealing with in the Bible – such motifs presage not destruction and exile, but grace: not events at all, but the psychic phenomena of mercy, salvation and self-definition.

What we have commonly assumed to be the historical referent of Exodus 23 is impossible to identify. What was the coming destruction that the narrative so clearly refers to? The fall of Samaria in the eighth century? or of Jerusalem in the sixth? It isn't by accident that we have no way to answer the question, even though our choices stand more than a century apart. In biblical literature, such referents have become generic through the use of stock motifs. As references to future destructions within the tradition's story-world, they exist entirely in the realm of literary metaphor, repeating themselves for the benefit of human enlightenment. The real referent lies in a moral precept. The narration encourages and reflects commitment: not historically or chronologically to a past or to a present, but to a preferred mode of being. The leitmotif of the forgiveness of the unforgivable reflects a function of traditional early Palestinian narrative that encourages commitment to obedience and divine mercy, and abhors disobedience and divine wrath.

In regard to Isaiah, the critical questions of referent and context can be put succinctly: Is the world in which the prophet finds his interpretive context through the prose of such passages as Isaiah 36–39 (and 1: 1 as well) an external real world or an internal literary one: an historical world of event or a textual world of significance? That the Book of Isaiah does not know an Isaiah of the past so much as the Isaiah who is a prophet in the stories of II Kings, encourages us to see the prophetic book's Isaiah as a character of story.

We need a larger canvas. It is interesting that the story Jonah – even though the gospels have Jesus refer to its hero – is widely recognized by scholars as fictive, but the prophet Jonah of II Kings, strangely, is not. This Jonah, like the Gilgamesh of the Babylonian King list, is thought historical simply for lack of a whale! Yet, more than the whale has been involved in our pious distinctions among legends. Comparable miracles are an everyday affair in the lives of a Moses or a Joshua, without there being a consensus among scholars about their fictional genre. Why is it that the same moralistic tone and philosophical theme regarding God's ineffable mercy can mark the Book of Jonah in all clarity as a work of pious fiction, but not that of comparable literature in the so-called deuteronomistic history or in the other prophetic books? I think the answer is a simple one, and it has nothing to do with questions of genre: the Book of Jonah, like Genesis' garden story, no longer forms part of biblical scholarship's need for a closed hermeneutical circle of consensus that finds the so-called 'truth' of the Bible primarily in its history. Today, this hermeneutical circle is breaking.

How much longer can we assert that the Jonah of his tale is any more fictional than the Isaiah of his story, or, indeed the Hosea of that fantastic metaphor? How are Jeremiah's prose sections more historical than Job's? And we must not forget either the Elijah or the Elisha of Kings. Does the author of Jeremiah really use Kings in an historicizing effort, or does this text exploit a literary referent for literary purposes, expanding on it freely?

As books, the books of the prophets – much like Exodus, Leviticus and Deuteronomy – are all presented as prose narratives containing literature of other genres. It is important to identify what these other genres in fact are. They are hardly oracles! They do not look like oracles. They rather resemble poetic diatribes, wisdom sayings or sermons. Many of them are hardly distinguishable from psalms or the songs one finds in the operatic narrative of Job or in the Book of Psalms. I would encourage seeing the books of the prophets as expansive collections of pedagogically useful songs and metaphors. They have been given, much like the same kind of poetry we find in the book of Job, a story context *pro forma*. When we think of the so-called minor prophets, we must doubt that we have independent works. What we read is a comprehensive and coherent collection of rather miscellaneous materials, cast within the fictive form of twelve books about twelve great seers of the past. As a collection, it matches the twelve narrative books of the Genesis–Kings tradition.

5 *The meaning of texts*

Texts need to be read in their contexts. These contexts are historical. One aspect of this historical context is the text's place within the intellectual world of letters in which they were written. The other relates to the intellectual world in which they are read. In attempting to define a critical theology of the Bible, let me use three examples of central biblical themes to illustrate two questions: What do we mean by the text? and What do we mean because of the text? The first relates to the ordinary world of historical scholarship, not only of the text but also of our relationship to an ancient text. The second question attempts critical reflection on a text that has developed a tradition affecting our perceptions of the very text we read. This is a text whose reading affects our perceptions of ourselves. The three examples reflect variations of the historical dislocations that our texts have suffered. One deals with the implications of different world-views. Another implies the importance of being critical about religious perceptions. The last deals merely with pollution control.

a) *The garden story.* Would this story really work if the human had somehow the possibility of eluding the cherubim and walking in the way of the tree of life, that impossible task piety sets itself? Of course not. The essence of the story would be destroyed. We do die; and we fail – even in our piety. We do return to the earth. We are mortal. We have not yet found our way back to the tree of life. Within the world-view of the author and of the audience of this narrative, the story has an echo and resonance that enables one to come to terms with that most defining character of human life: our deaths.

Nevertheless, the garden story, understood as an aetiological reflection on mortality, captured the theological significance of the lives and deaths of its audience with great power. However, it also had an audience for whom it had never been written. To this audience it had equal import within the very different – now Christian – world of Augustine. Within this early medieval world, could the garden story's aetiology of mortality resonate with truth to its new audience? Just as assuredly, not! The reason for this is clear and obvious. Within the world-view that Augustine shared with his medieval Christian contemporaries, human beings were not mortal. Surely better, their mortality was being anxiously denied and transposed. They possessed immortal souls. Not merely their bodies, but their deaths, were hidden from them as illusory. And so, accordingly, the story came to resonate with a radically interpreted theme. It had become the story of original sin: an introductory tale to the history of salvation, looking forward to the new Adam. What I find interesting about this is that it was not the text of the story that changed, but its context, and the perception with which it was viewed.

Now – and this is a contemporary theological question that a reading of the Bible today poses – why is it that this old Hebrew story, resonant with human mortality as it is, rings true to so many today in a way that was not possible for centuries after Augustine? Has third- and fourth-century interpretation and theology, centred in its understanding of Jesus, really not resolved the problem of human mortality for our world? What is it about ourselves and our world-view, about our understanding of death today, that allows the garden story to become once again ours? How does it reach, not only across centuries, but into the quite different world of our perception? Just as the task of exegesis today is to read texts, so that what they once said may be heard again, we have the task of expressing what it is that has been heard in our world. For all that, the Bible's story is more helpful than Augustine's interpretation.

b) *Yahweh as Immanuel.* Yahweh, the god of ancient Palestine, is not the God of the Old Testament. The God of the Old Testament is the transcendent God of heaven. Exodus 3–6, we have seen, offers us a comprehensive reinterpretation of the ancient God of Palestine, Yahweh, as a way of expressing how the divine was present to ancient Israel. With this concept, early Judaism was able to understand itself as the saved remnant of or as the new Israel. Through this tradition, Israel is understood as a people who had *once* known God. Indeed, the Yahweh of these old forgotten stories created Israel, guided it, tested it in the fire of defeat and exile, and returned this people to their once promised destiny. This Yahweh of the tradition was variously identified as the messenger of God, a prophet and God for Israel. From the perspective of the world created by our texts, this once ancient and historical God of Palestine takes on a role as the God of the prophets. He is addressed, by David and others, in the Book of Psalms. He is Samaria and Jerusalem's spouse and lover in the prophets. He is identified with the gods of the patriarchs and with other deities of Israel's legendary past. Exodus 3: 12 interprets the meaning of Yahweh as 'God with you'. This is the heart of the Bible's understanding of the divine, the centre of biblical theology. Yahweh is an exploration of the way the transcendent is immanent. He is, for Israel, Immanuel. He is the means by which the ineffable God of the universe, the one true spirit, is known.

Many of these same motifs are used as metaphors for David, for Moses and, in the New Testament, for Jesus. They are motifs shared by nearly every central interpretive figure in the tradition, whether as saviour, king, priest, messiah, lord, messenger, prophet or Immanuel. All reflect the one same literary function: the one through whom God is present to Israel. They possess his name. Through these interlocking common motifs, one can see a harmonious metaphorical referent that, for some two and a half centuries, pointed to an understanding apart from the stories about either Jesus or Yahweh. The issue of divine presence is one that is the common property of both Old and New Testaments. It is essential as well to the

Dead Sea scrolls, to the Apocrypha and to the Pseudepigrapha. Ultimately, it stands apart from historical perceptions of Yahweh and Jesus, of a Moses or a David. Rather, and much more significantly, this single metaphor reflects the abiding importance of maintaining and understanding divine transcendence within the limitations of human perception and ignorance.

The resonance of such texts, however, with their traditional metaphors for the divine, radically changed as they were taken up within the mutually exclusive ideologies of early Judaism and Christianity. These competing understandings of Judaism and Christianity transformed common traditional metaphors for the divine into competing and excluding ideologies. At the centre of our stream of theological language, there exists a pollution that has corrupted our traditions of story. Within Christianity, at least, it has encouraged a competitive concept of the divine and of religious faith which is untenable, humanly speaking. A substantial core of Christian theology has preferred literalism and historicism to metaphor, and stands opposed to its biblical substance.

c) *'I know that you are a gracious God and merciful, slow to anger and overflowing in steadfast love and turning away from evil*; therefore, Yahweh, please take my life, for I would rather die than live' (Jonah 4: 2–3). The gracious god is revelation of the divine. This is contrasted to Jonah's epitome of human expectation that God will punish our enemies. However, God will not. He turns away from evil. With such a God – this gracious God of mercy, Jonah, living out the role of an Elijah-like prophet of doom, thirsting for the blood of God's enemies, finds himself unemployed! This tradition contrasting the ways of God and the way of mankind also has a metaphorical twin: Israel is intrinsically corrupt, backsliding, faithless. It is deserving of God's wrath and total rejection. It has committed unforgivable crimes. Therefore, God has chosen mercy and salvation for his faithful remnant.

This perception of divine mercy contrasting to the lack of understanding that men have of that, is the single most dominant theme in the Bible. Hardly any text entirely escapes it. It presents itself as the central theological perspective of text after text, whether we are dealing with prose narrative, with song or poetry, or with philosophical discourse.

It also has developed some of the Bible's most interesting metaphors for the divine. As our texts have played with the many variations on this theme, they have recurrently turned to one particular polarity. This is expressed in a variety of scenarios: a person, humanity, other nations, the king, Israel, its leader or leaders, even its priests, prophets and philosophers or the deity himself, have committed bloody, unspeakable crimes, or have been faithless, or have hypocritically betrayed the essence of their calling. Logic and truth require that justice and unblinking adherence to the laws, covenant or will of God enforce unforgiving retribution. At this pole of the tradition, prophets of wrath and doom abound. Adherents of other religions are slaughtered and commanded to be slaughtered. One has holy war. Mankind is destroyed by flood. Sodom is burnt from the face of the earth. Samaria is undone. Jerusalem is placed under siege. The black and white of fairy tales are our only colours. To mourn among such texts is inappropriate. The child in us knows that evil is what has been destroyed. Whether they are idol-worshippers or foreign neighbours, babies condemned under the ban, the Egyptians or the Assyrians under the wrath of Yahweh's plagues, or a seemingly endless list of individuals from Onan to Haman, evil is destroyed. Only when we get close to the narrative matrix: Jerusalem's destruction and exile, can weeping be seriously entertained.[1] In the mainstream of the tradition, the Babylonian captain of the guard of Jeremiah 40: 2–3 speaks clearly and succinctly for the creators of tradition: 'Yahweh . . . threatened this place with disaster . . . and now he has brought it about.' Literarily and structurally, such ruthlessness is necessary to preserve the impact of the contrasting polarity.

The book of Jeremiah's Lamentations, lying at the centre of our spectrum, comprises the beautiful Catholic songs of guilt, despair and repentance. The songs reflect on the loss of Jerusalem. They create, through their tears, the emotional transition to the new Jerusalem. Much of these songs echoes Job and Ecclesiastes. God is absent and silent.

Forced to be selective in the choice of illustrations, I find the contrast of Jonah and Elijah again very helpful. Of course, Jonah isn't really a prophet. The Book of Jonah deals with mercy as God's truth, while the prophet Jonah wishes himself to be a punishing prophet. Jonah becomes the anti-prophet. Through its irony, the story offers us in the comic Jonah the ever-elusive quality of truth that belongs properly only to divine perception.

I Kings 19: 1–18's story about Elijah establishes the prophetic template of our anti-hero. Just such a prophet Jonah would be, if only his God were a bit more old-fashioned. He would be horror itself, relentless in his destruction. Unsatisfied with just committing bloody murder, Elijah's wrath of Yahweh (don't miss how the fantasy of Yahweh's power can fracture even mountains!) piles up bodies for yet another generation of prophecy readers. Especially, the final scene of Jonah 4 draws on a variety of motifs from the Elijah story with devastating ironic effect. Both prophets are deconstructed by their authors, each under his own tree. There is an almost verbal identity in their begging Yahweh to take their lives. The assumption of both prophets – exposed by the motif of the suicide wish they share in common – is that it is their prophecies that save and destroy. This implied irony of the Elijah story is explicit in the re-use

---

[1] Apart from such secondary commentaries on the traditions as II Chron. 35: 25's reference to mourning for Josiah.

of this motif in Jonah. The irony is emphatically stressed in the contrast between the relentless devastation that the prophet Elijah had brought to Yahweh's enemies, and the peace and repentance that Jonah, the anti-prophet, brings. The Elijah story carries the key to the wicked exposure of piety's ruthless brutality that we find in Jonah's tale. The expectations of the 'true believer' are contrasted with the implications of the God Jonah professes to believe in. In Jonah this contrast is cast between the violent and warlike language of piety against 'godless' Nineveh, and the compassion of the merciful God of Nineveh. In Kings, the contrast is between the God of resounding glory and wrath that Elijah and the prophets represent, and the God of silence we have. The defining scene of Elijah in the wilderness in I Kings 19: 11–12 stands as implicit commentary on the prophet and on his narrative, which it closes:

> Yahweh is about to pass by . . . a great wind . . . splitting mountains . . . but Yahweh was not in the wind. After the wind, an earthquake, but Yahweh was not in the earthquake; and after the earthquake, fire, but Yahweh was not in the fire, and after the fire, the sound of a silent voice . . .

The Book of Jonah takes this commentary on the truth of our expectations about God a small step further by offering a caricature of the expectations of the prophets themselves. Such potent deconstruction of the God of the prophets is hardly as unusual in the Bible as biblical scholarship's tradition of hagiography on the prophets implies. The Book of Job not only mocks traditional piety – and along with it the so-called God of history – it mocks Job (personifying the piety of wisdom). The bombastic Yahweh of the whirlwind of this book stands as a comic figure that is cast in sharpest contrast to the absent, silent deity of Job's complaint and of the audience's reality. We all can understand that Ecclesiastes speaks of this unknown and unknowable God quite plainly. We also need to recognize that not knowing the divine is a central theme of the Pentateuch and a consistently recurrent theme of the tradition as a whole.

Imagining that the theology of biblical traditions is somehow a history of salvation is an exercise that is as perverse as it is futile, however much we try 'to see things through God's eyes'. This foundation explicitly explores a failed and betrayed covenant, a God of wrath and rejection, a glorious history past and shattered, promises broken, repeated condemnation and bloody reprisal. Recitations of the evil that God has done against Israel and the destruction of dreams and hopes that this Yahweh brought down inexorably on Israel's head is hardly a saving history! The so-called historical prophets (that is, the prophets of story and legend) who present us with such theological metaphor fit Jonah's caricature! The image of God they present is not a whit more intelligent than that given by Job's friends. Certainly the ability to preach on the basis of Old Testament texts has diminished in almost inverse ratio with the growth of influence of such naive realism. We have taken literary characters, the prophets, and we have read our texts as if these prophets wrote and spoke what was put into their mouths by God, and not by poets. Wholly uncritically, we have refused to use the simplest tools of reading to understand the perspective from which these great poems speak. It is hardly surprising that the so-called prophetic theology that has resulted from this abuse of scholarship and language has been both historically meaningless and theologically abhorrent.

When we turn in closing to address the question of what we have become because of our tradition, the traditional understanding of the prophetic texts must bring with them great discomfort. Again and again, they awaken murderous Elijahs and Jonahs for God's sake. In this awakening, they distort an entire tradition of quiet reflection about the transcendent and deafen us to Elijah's divine silence and to the Book of Jonah's divine mercy. The prophetic literature as a whole has no conflict with Jonah. It shares his voice. It plays variations on Jonah's themes. The story God of the prophets and narratives of the Bible is one who has turned away from the evil he intended against Israel. He is like the God of Genesis' flood stories. He has repented. He is the Book of Jonah's gracious God of mercy: slow to anger and abounding in steadfast love. The very keepers of the tradition have distorted it and prevent our access to it. The floating gardeners of scholarship, working in the deepest streams of our tradition, stand in the way of its recovery. They keep us from hearing the stories within streams unpolluted.

EARLY SEMITES

ATLANTIC
OCEAN

MACE

GREECE

MYCEN

● Gibraltar

BERBER LANDS

M E D I T

Cyren

M E D I T

N

S A H A

0   1000 km

0   620 miles

C H A D

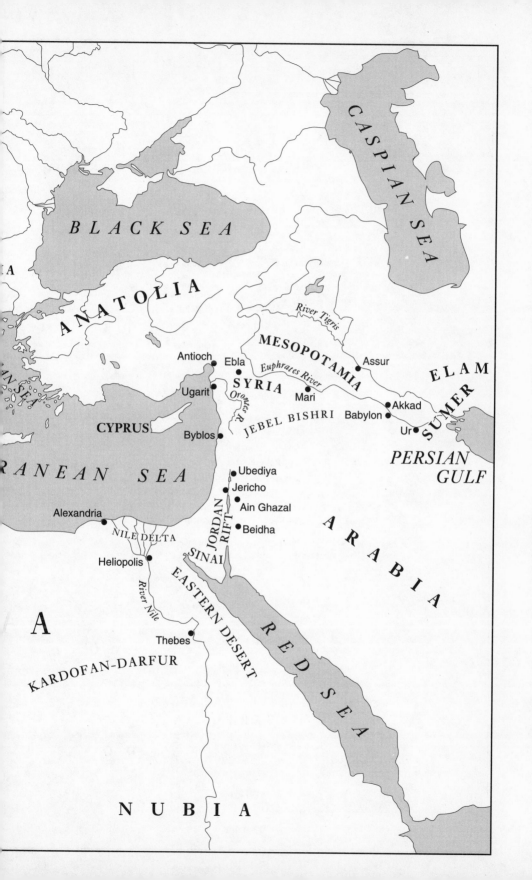

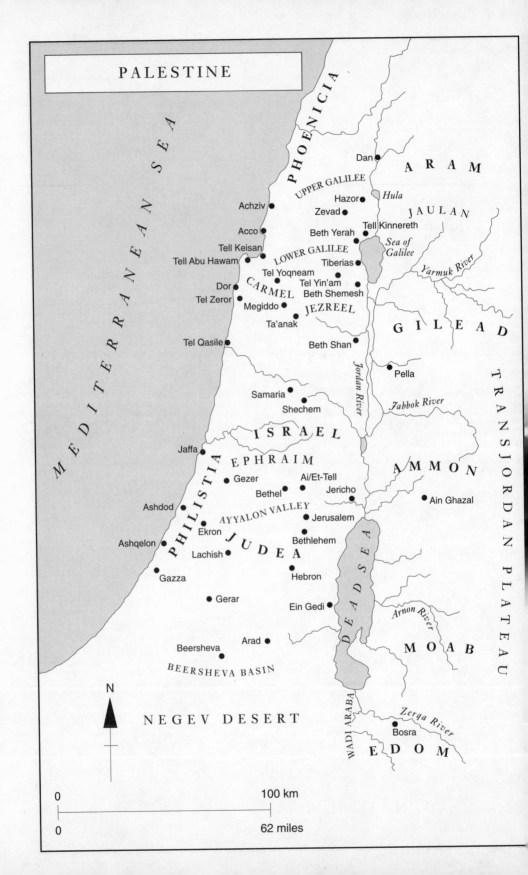

ANCIENT NEAR EAST

BLACK SEA

CASPIAN SEA

MEDITERRANEAN SEA

ANATOLIA

HATTI

Hattusas

PERSIA

Carchemish
Haran
River Tigris
Nineveh

MESOPOTAMIA

ASSYRIA

Aleppo
ARAM
Assur

Antioch
Ebla
Euphrates

Alalakh
Hamat
SYRIA
Mari
BABYLONIA

Ugarit
Orontes R.
Palmyra
GREAT SYRIAN STEPPE
Akkad

Alasiya
JEBEL BISHRI
Uruk

CYPRUS
Byblos
Kadesh
Babylon
Ur
SUMER

Beirut
Sidon
Damascus
PERSIAN GULF

Tyre

Samaria

Jerusalem

Alexandria
WADI ARABA

ARABIA

Kadesh
Barnea
Petra

NILE DELTA
Timna

Avaris
SINAI

SAHARA
Heliopolis

EGYPT
EASTERN DESERT

NILE VALLEY

Amarna

N

Thebes
Karnak
RED SEA

Elephantine
River Nile

0   1000 km

0   620 miles

PERIOD	PALESTINIAN ARCHAEOLOGY	AFRICA/EGYPT
1,400,000 BCE	Early/Middle Acheulian	
10,000 BCE	Natufian/ Mesolithic	←-----Wild grains/nuts-------------
8000 BCE	Pre-pottery Neolithic	←-----Agriculture and herding----------
		'Green Sahara'
6000 BCE	Pottery Neolithic	←----------------------------
		Closing of Sahara
	'Chalcolithic'	
4000 BCE		←----------------------------
3500 BCE	Early Bronze	Old Kingdom Pyramids
2400 BCE		
2300 BCE	Early Bronze IV	1st Intermediate Period
1900 BCE	Middle Bronze	Middle Kingdom
		'Hyksos' 1730–1570 (= 2nd Intermediate Period)
1600/1550 BCE	Late Bronze	New Kingdom Empire
		Amarna 1400–1350
		Ramses II 1270–1213 Merenptah 1213–1203

PALESTINE	SYRIA/MESOPOTAMIA	TEXTS AND BIBLE
	Homo erectus in Asia	
– – – – – – – – – Small villages – – – – – – – – – →		
– – – – – – – Villages and towns – – – – – – – →		
– – – – Drought – – – – – – – – – – – – – – – – →		
– – – – Sub-pluvial – – – – – – – – – – – – – – →		
Mediterranean economy Paronates/small burghs	Early Dynastic Sumerian city-states	
	Ebla/Akkad	
Drought Shift from agriculture to pastoralism	Ur III	'Execration texts' 1810–1770
Mediterranean economy Regional patronates/ burghs	Mari/Old Assyrian/ Old Babylonian periods Hammurapi 1792–1750	
Village and highland regions abandoned Battle of Megiddo 1468 Egyption rule	Hittite Empire	Nuzi texts Amarna letters Ugaritic texts Yahweh place-name in Sinai
	Kadesh 1288	
		Israel and Canaan as family eponyms on Merenptah stele

PERIOD	PALESTINIAN ARCHAEOLOGY	AFRICA/EGYPT
1300 BCE	Late Bronze/ Early Iron transition	← - - - - - - - - - - - - - - - - - -
		Migration of 'sea peoples'
		20th Dynasty
950 BCE	Iron Age	Shishaq 935–914
		Neko 610–595
539 BCE	Persian Period	
336–323 BCE		← - - - - - - - - - - - - - - - - - -
300 BCE	Hellenistic Period	Ptolemy I 305–282 Alexandria
		← - - - - - - - - - - - - - - - - - -

PALESTINE	SYRIA/MESOPOTAMIA	TEXTS AND BIBLE
– – – – Great Mycenean drought – – – – – – – – – – – – →		
Central and northern highland settlements Herding in Judean hills 'Sea people' settle coast	Ugarit falls 1180 Tiglath Pileser I	
Regional patronates of Tyre, Aram, Israel, Moab, Ammon, Edom and Judah under Assyrian domination Samaria falls 722 Lachish falls 01	Tiglath Pileser III 744–727 Sargon II 722–705	Mesha stele *bytdwd* inscription Kuntillat Ajrud
Jerusalem falls 586	Niniveh falls 612 Nebuchadnezar 605–562 Nabonidus 555–539	Deportation texts Lachish relief
	Cyrus the Great 559 Babylon falls539 Darius 522–486 Artaxerxes 465–424	Elephantine texts Early beginnings of biblical traditions
– – – – – Alexander's armies take over Persian empire – – – – →		
Ptolemaic dominance 312–198 Sebaste/Samaria Seleucid dominance 198–165	Seleucus I 304–281	Pentateuch versions and earliest biblical scrolls
– – – – Antiochus IV 175–164 – – – – – – – – – – – – – →		Massoretic Bible's chronology Other early biblical works, Apocrypha, Greek translations
Maccabees take Jerusalem 164 Greco-Roman period		
Hasmonean rule John Hyrcanus 135–105		Dead Sea scrolls Pseudepigrapha

PERIOD	PALESTINIAN ARCHAEOLOGY	AFRICA/EGYPT
63 BCE	Roman Period	←-----------------------
		Cleopatra VII 69–30
		←-----------------------
		←-----------------------
		←-----------------------
325 CE	Byzantine Period	←-----------------------
630 CE	Islamic Period	←-----------------------

PALESTINE	SYRIA/MESOPOTAMIA	TEXTS AND BIBLE
– – – – Roman rule – – – – – – – – – – – – – – – – – →		
Herod the Great 37 BCE–4 CE		
– – – – Augustus Caesar 29 BCE–14 CE – – – – – – – – – – →		
– – – – Vespasian 69–79 CE – – – – – – – – – – – – – – →		
Jewish rebellion 66–74 CE Jerusalem temple destroyed 70 CE		'New Testament' texts
– – – – Hadrian 117–138 CE – – – – – – – – – – – – – – →		
Bar Kochba's rebellion 132–135 CE		Mishnaic and Talmudic traditions
– – – – Constantinople – – – – – – – – – – – – – – – – – →		Earliest complete Greek bibles extant: Codices Vaticanus and Sinaiticus
– – – – Mamluk (Damascus) and Abbasid (Baghdad) rule – – →		Earliest Hebrew bibles extant: Aleppo Codex (10th century), Leningrad Codex (1008/1009) and Samaritan Pentateuch (1149)

Index of texts cited